International Handbook of Personal Construct Psychology

International Handbook of Personal Construct Psychology

Edited by

Fay Fransella
Centre for Personal Construct Psychology
and *University of Hertfordshire, UK*

JOHN WILEY & SONS, LTD

Other Wiley Editorial Offices

John Wiley & Sons Inc., 111 River Street, Hoboken, NJ 07030, USA

Jossey-Bass, 989 Market Street, San Francisco, CA 94103-1741, USA

Wiley-VCH Verlag GmbH, Boschstr. 12, D-69469 Weinheim, Germany

John Wiley & Sons Australia Ltd, 33 Park Road, Milton, Queensland 4064, Australia

John Wiley & Sons (Asia) Pte Ltd, 2 Clementi Loop #02-01, Jin Xing Distripark, Singapore 129809

John Wiley & Sons Canada Ltd, 22 Worcester Road, Etobicoke, Ontario, Canada M9W 1L1

Wiley also publishes its books in a variety of electronic formats. Some content that appears in print
may not be available in electronic books.

Library of Congress Cataloging-in-Publication Data
International handbook of personal construct psychology / edited by Fay Fransella.
     p. cm.
Includes bibliographical references and index.
   ISBN 0-470-84727-1 (alk. paper)
  1. Personal construct theory. I. Fransella, Fay.
   BF698.9.P47P47 2003
   150.19′8—dc21

                               2002154458

British Library Cataloguing in Publication Data
A catalogue record for this book is available from the British Library

ISBN 0-470-84727-1

Typeset in 10/12pt Times by SNP Best-set Typesetter Ltd., Hong Kong
Printed and bound in Great Britain by Antony Rowe Ltd, Chippenham, Wiltshire
This book is printed on acid-free paper responsibly manufactured from sustainable forestry in which
at least two trees are planted for each one used for paper production.

Contents

About the Editor

Fay Fransella is Founder and Director of the Centre for Personal Construct Psychology, Emeritus Reader in Clinical Psychology, University of London and Visiting Professor in Personal Construct Psychology at the University of Hertfordshire, UK. She has written eleven books, eight of them specifically relating to personal construct psychology and published over one hundred and fifty journal papers and chapters.

She trained and worked as an Occupational Therapist for ten years before taking a degree in psychology and a postgraduate diploma in clinical psychology in 1962. It was during her first job as a lecturer at the Institute of Psychiatry, London that she was introduced to George Kelly's personal construct psychology. It was a revolutionary alternative to the dominant behaviourism of the time. She found the view that we are all free agents responsible for what we make of the events which continually confront us particularly liberating. Since that time she has carried out research, mainly into problems of stuttering and weight problems, together with teaching and writing within the framework of Kelly's ideas.

International Advisory Panel

List of Contributors

Professor Jack Adams-Webber, *Department of Psychology, Brock University, St Catharines, Ontario, Canada L2S 3A1. E-mail: jadams@spartan.ac.brocku.ca*

Scott A. Baldwin, *Department of Psychology, University of Memphis, Memphis, TN 38152, USA*

Don Bannister, *Deceased*

Associate Professor Richard C. Bell, *Department of Psychology, University of Melbourne, Victoria 3010, Australia. E-mail: rcb@unimelb.edu.au*

Dr Sean Brophy, *Rainsford, 59 Beaumont Road, Dublin 9, Ireland. E-mail: seanbrophy@eircom.net*

Dr Trevor Butt, *School of Human & Health Sciences, University of Huddersfield, Queensgate, Huddersfield, West Yorkshire HD1 3DH, UK. E-mail: t.butt@hud.ac.uk*

Professor Gabriele Chiari, *Centro Studi in Psicoterapia Cognitiva, Via Cavour 64, 50129 Firenze, Italy. E-mail: g.chiari@cesipc.it*

Dr Nelarine Cornelius, *Brunel School of Business and Management, Brunel University, Uxbridge Campus, Uxbridge, Middlesex UB8 3PH, UK. E-mail: nelarine. cornelius@brunel.ac.uk*

Ms Jacqui Costigan, *Late of La Trobe University, Bendigo, Australia.*

Professor Rue L. Cromwell, *1104 Prescott Drive, Lawrence, Kansas, 66049, USA. E-mail: cromwell@ku.edu*

Dr Malcolm C. Cross, *Department of Psychology, City University, Northampton Square, London EC1V 0HB, UK. E-mail: m.c.cross@city.ac.uk*

Dr Peter Cummins, *Consultant Clinical Psychologist, Head of Adult Psychological Services, Coventry Healthcare NHS Trust, Gulson Hospital, Gulson Road, Coventry CV1 2HR, UK. E-mail: petercummins@dial.pipex.com*

Dr Pam Denicolo, *Institute of Education, Faculty of Economic and Social Sciences, Bulmershe Court, University of Reading, Earley, Reading RG6 1HY, UK. E-mail: p.m.denicolo@reading.ac.uk*

Dr Julie M. Ellis, *Head of School, School of Health and Environment, La Trobe University, Bendigo, PO Box 199, Bendigo 3552, Australia. E-mail: J.Ellis@bendigo.latrobe.edu.au*

Professor Franz R. Epting, *Department of Psychology, University of Florida, PO Box 112250, Gainesville, FL 32611-2250, USA. E-mail: epting@ufl.edu*

Fay Fransella, *Professor of Personal Construct Psychology, University of Hertfordshire, c/o The Sail Loft, Mulberry Quay, Falmouth TR11 3HD, UK. E-mail: Ffransella@aol.com*

Professor Martin Fromm, *Lehrstuhl für Pädagogik, Universität Stuttgart, Dillmannstrasse 15, 70193 Stuttgart, Germany. E-mail: martin.fromm@po. unistuttgart.de*

Dr Brian R. Gaines, *Centre for Person–Computer Studies, 3635 Ocean View, Cobble Hill, British Columbia, Canada V0R 1L1. E-mail: brian@repgrid.com*

Marco Gemignani, *Department of Psychology, University of Florida, PO Box 112250, Gainesville, FL 32611-2250, USA*

Dr James Horley, *Department of Psychology, Augustana University College, Camrose, Alberta, Canada T4V 2R3. E-mail: horleyj@augustana.ca*

Professor Devi Jankowicz, *Graduate Business School, University of Luton, Putteridge Bury, Hitchin Road, Luton, Bedfordshire LU2 8LE, UK. E-mail: animus@ntlworld.com*

Dr Devorah Kalekin-Fishman, *Faculty of Education, University of Haifa, Israel 31905. E-mail: dkalekin@construct.haifa.ac.il*

George A. Kelly, *Deceased*

Professor Larry Leitner, *Department of Psychology, Miami University Oxford, Ohio 45056, USA. E-mail: leitnelm@muohio.edu*

Professor Miller Mair, *Kinharvie, 49 Dowan Hill Street, Glasgow G11 5HB, UK. E-mail: kinharvie@aol.com*

Professor James C. Mancuso, *15 Oakwood Place, Delmar, New York 12054, USA. E-mail: mancusoj@capital.net*

Professor Spencer A. McWilliams, *Dean of the College of Arts and Science, California State University, San Marcos, CA 92096, USA. E-mail: smcwilli@csusm.edu*

Professor Robert A. Neimeyer, *Department of Psychology, University of Memphis, Memphis TN 38152, USA. E-mail: neimeyer@cc.memphis.edu*

Dr Maria Laura Nuzzo, *Centro di Psicologia e Psicoterapia Costruttivista, Via G Pisanelli 2, 00196 Roma, Italy. E-mail: ml.nuzzo@cppc.it*

Professor Maureen Pope, *Institute of Education, Faculty of Economic and Social Sciences, University of Reading, Bulmershe Court, Earley, Reading RG6 1HY, UK. E-mail: m.l.pope@reading.ac.uk*

John Porter, *Interactions Ltd, Foxglove, Blackberry Lane, Delgany, Co. Wicklow, Ireland. E-mail: john@interactions.ie*

Dr Harry Procter, *Child & Family Therapeutic Services, Petrel House, Broadway Park, Barclay Street, Bridgwater, Somerset TA6 5YA, UK. E-mail: harry@procterh.freeserve.co.uk*

Dr Tom Ravenette, *Meadway House, 20 Meadway, Epsom, Surrey KT19 8JZ, UK*

Nick Reed, *74 Kingsway, Petts Wood, Kent BR5 1PT, UK. E-mail: grid@ndirect.co.uk*

Adrian Robertson, *Programme Director, Cabinet Office Centre for Management and Policy Studies, Sunningdale Park, Larch Avenue, Ascot, Berkshire SL5 0QE, UK. E-mail: adrian.robertson@cabinet-office.x.gsi.gov.uk*

Dorothy Rowe, *Professor of Personal Construct Psychology, Middlesex University, c/o The Garden Flat, 40 Highbury Grove, London N5 2AG, UK. E-mail: Drowe70@aol.com*

Dr Phillida Salmon, *162 Preston Lane, Tadworth, Surrey KT20 5HG. E-mail: p.salmon@ioe.ac.uk*

Dr David Savage, *Director of Applied Psychology, Physical Education & Sports science Department, University College of Chester, Parkgate Road, Chester CH1 4BJ, UK. E-mail: D.Savage@chester.ac.uk*

Professor Jörn W. Scheer, *Abt. für Medizinische Psychologie, Zentrum für Psycho-somatische Medizin, University of Giessen, Friedrichstr. 36, 35392 Giessen, Germany. E-mail: joern.scheer@joern-scheer.de*

Professor Kenneth W. Sewell, *Department of Psychology, Box 311280, University of North Texas, Denton TX 76203, USA. E-mail: sewellk@unt.edu*

Dr Mildred L.G. Shaw, *Centre for Person–Computer Studies, 3635 Ocean View, Cobble Hill, British Columbia, Canada V0R 1L1. E-mail: mildred@repgrid.com*

Associate Professor Dusan Stojnov, *Psychology Department, Faculty of Philosophy, University of Belgrade, Cika Ljubina 18-20, 11000 Belgrade, Serbia and Montene-gro. E-mail: dstojnov@f.bg.ac.yu*

Ms Jill Thomas, *Department of Psychology, Miami University Oxford, Ohio 45056, USA. E-mail: Thomasj7@muohio.edu*

Associate Professor Beverly M. Walker, *Psychology Department, University of Wollongong, Northfields Avenue, Wollongong, NSW 2500, Australia. E-mail: beverly_walker@uow.edu.au*

Associate Professor Bill Warren, *Faculty of Education and Arts, University of Newcastle, Callaghan, NSW 2308, Australia. E-mail: william.warren@cc.newcastle.edu.au*

Julie Watkinson, *School of Nursing & Midwifery, Flinders University, GPO box 2100, Adelaide, Australia 5001. E-mail: Julie.watkinson@flinders.edu.au*

Professor David Winter, *Department of Psychology, University of Hertfordshire, Hatfield Campus, College Lane, Hatfield, Hertfordshire AL10 9AB and Barnet, Enfield and Haringey Mental Health Trust, UK. E-mail: d.winter@herts.ac.uk*

Introduction

George Kelly launched his revolutionary ideas about the nature of being human nearly fifty years ago upon a world ill-prepared to receive them. This book is evidence that the value of those ideas has not only been seen by those who are primarily academics but also by those who are primarily practitioners. And not only by psychologists, but by those in many other walks of life.

So widespread has the interest in personal construct psychology become, that this book does not and cannot provide a complete coverage of personal construct work or of areas in which such work is relevant. To give as wide a coverage as possible, Section X consists of two chapters, in one of which five authors give 'tasters' of their own area of expertise. It was Kelly's view that the validity of any theory was shown by its usefulness. If that is so, then this book is evidence of the validity of personal construct theory.

Naturally, Kelly's ideas permeate the book. But it was also felt that it might be interesting to have each chapter begin with a quotation from some of his work that was pertinent for that chapter. Even today, some of his ideas are still novel. One major aim of the book is to show that Kelly's ideas are not being regarded as a creed but that people are all the time extending them and using them in ways not thought of in 1955.

THE STRUCTURE OF THE BOOK

To give the book some coherence, it has been divided into ten sections. They are by no means discrete topic areas, because that would be impossible. Personal construct psychology is about a person who cannot be divided up into bits—such as learning, emotion, perception and so forth. However, that does not mean there should not be sections on such categories at all. For instance, Section II is entitled 'Beliefs and feelings'. It is there because of the constant comment that Kelly's theory is a 'cognitive' one. That point is addressed in several chapters, but it seemed important to make it clear, once and for all, that thinking and feeling within each one of us are seen as inseparable.

Other sections are more easily recognizable, covering theory, practice and both of those in specific work areas. It needs to be emphasized that George Kelly's ideas are the core of this volume and that the text relates to the whole person. So although the same theoretical concepts may appear in different chapters, they are always from another perspective.

Throughout the book there are examples of how certain approaches and ideas may be put into practice. Personal construct psychology is designed to be used; it is not for armchair theorizing.

ITS CONTENT

Apart from the Kelly quotations at the start of each chapter—some long and some very short—the book also contains an edited version of Kelly's previously published chapter entitled 'A brief introduction to personal construct theory', plus two talks from previously unpublished manuscripts.

Probably the best-known writer about personal construct psychology, and certainly the person who more than anyone made psychologists first aware of its existence, was Don Bannister. Because of his depth of understanding of the theory and practice, two of his previously published chapters are included, plus one previously unpublished talk.

The key to the book is Section I, where the basic theory together with its underlying philosophy are outlined and commented upon. That section ends with details of some of the research that has been conducted on the theory. Anyone who has a limited previous knowledge of the theory and its philosophy would be well advised to at least browse through this section before moving to sections that are of particular personal interest. Those who are well-acquainted with Kelly's ideas may yet find it useful to take a 'revision course' and look at his 'brief introduction'. You may even find new ways of looking at old problems in the other chapters in Section I.

No book on personal construct psychology would be complete without mention of the tool for which George Kelly is probably best known—the repertory grid. Section III is about that and other methods and tools available. Skills needed by all personal construct practitioners are also covered. This book is not intended to be a how-to-do-it manual; however, there are examples of how to construct a ratings and a dependency grid, how to elicit personal constructs by 'laddering', how to create 'bowties', 'snakes and rivers' and much more. As far as possible, the book is as much concerned with ways of putting personal construct psychology into practice as it is about exploring the ideas contained within it.

THE LANGUAGE

There are two aspects to the question of language. The first is about the use of jargon. It has always seemed to me that jargon has its uses as a shorthand for communicating within groups of like-minded people. Mathematics would be the extreme example here. But when communicating with those interested in a subject but without detailed knowledge, then jargon is the enemy of communication. George Kelly says that he sometimes chose to create a new word for a new idea and sometimes used an old word with a new definition. All authors in this book have been encouraged to use the minimum of jargon, but if a jargon word is essential, they have been asked to explain that word briefly. If physicists can explain the complexities of their subject with great clarity to the non-physicist, then personal construct psychologists are obviously able to do the same.

The other issue of language here is about 'sexism'. George Kelly started writing in the 1940s when the use of the masculine pronoun was accepted as the general word to describe all of us. It will therefore be of no surprise to you to find that he makes no attempt to include the female version of such words. There were two ways to deal with this issue. Authors could have been asked to put 'she' or 'her' in brackets when using direct quotations from his works. Or, his quotations could be left as they are in the belief that anyone reading this book would realize that times have changed since George Kelly was writing. I sampled a number of opinions and came out in favour of the latter. Some comments were quite extreme, such as, 'If the reader does not understand that you can't *make* writers in the past speak in modern language, then they should not be reading this book!' Anyone reading his works will know that he was a man who would readily have changed his style of writing if he were still alive today.

SMALL POINTS

George Kelly's two volumes have had three publishers. First was Basic Books, then Norton Publications and then Routledge. When the Norton version went out of print, there was a period when the volumes were not available. Several people tried to find an American publisher, but the volumes are not big sellers and no publisher was prepared to take the risk. I was then lucky enough to know David Stonestreet, then psychology editor at Routledge. After several discussions and lunches, he was persuaded that he wanted 'to be the man who published Kelly'. However, there was a sting in the tail. I would have to get the two volumes typed onto disk! No mean task. But I found enough typists who were students at the Centre for Personal Construct Psychology in London who were prepared to share that task. It is for that reason that the volumes contain the words 'In association with the Centre for Personal Construct Psychology, London'. All that preamble is the run-up to the reason why the Routledge version, in 1991, is a problem. The printers decided to give it a different lay-out and so the page numbering is different. Not only that, whereas the Norton version had pages numbered from the start of Volume 1 to the end of Volume 2, the Routledge version starts Volume 2 again at page 1! Those who want to get the book from libraries will usually be given the Norton version. Those who have been buying the volumes in the past ten years will have the Routledge version. That is a long description of why, after each quotation, there is the lengthy: (Kelly, 1955/1991, p. 'Norton'/p. 'Routledge').

THEMES

Editing a book of this size gives the editor an opportunity to get an unusually broad overview of the subject matter. Apart from the realization of the breadth of interest in Kelly's ideas, there are themes that occur to me. Of course, another personal construct psychologist might well have come up with entirely different ones, but my themes are these.

A major theme arising from very many contributions is that personal construct psychology is crucially about asking questions. I should not really have been surprised at that revelation because the title of the book I wrote with Don Bannister in 1971 was *Inquiring Man*. That title I took from an interview I had with George Kelly in which he talked about the various roles people have played in society over the years. When he came to more recent times he suggested that the person seen from the perspective of his theory was ' "empathic man", or "inquiring man" ' (Kelly, 1966b).

A second theme is the discomfort that many authors feel about the still prevalent idea that the 'mind' and the 'body' are separate entities. Perhaps the chapters in Section II, as well as concerns expressed in various other chapters, will go some way to dispel this deeply embedded idea.

A final theme that comes out to me is the sense of excitement and involvement authors feel about their work and ideas. It seems to give many a sense of freedom, of being explorers travelling into new fields and seeing the theory as something to be worked with and not a sacrosanct creed. That is certainly how I feel myself.

Acknowledgements

It is difficult to know where to begin. So many people have done so much to help to get this book completed. But actually it is not so hard because there is one person at the forefront of my mind. Owing to her untimely death, Jacqui Costigan was unable to complete her role as an Adviser to the Volume and the piece she was writing on nursing. As an Adviser she was nearly always the first to respond to any issues that concerned me, and her comments were always very useful. She will not only be greatly missed by all those who knew her, but also by the personal construct psychology community itself. Her qualities at an organizational, academic and personal level are not easily replaced.

I now want to express my gratitude to all the other Advisers for their continuous personal support as well as most valuable 'advice'. Carrying out a task of this magnitude makes one feel that every problem needs to be dealt with at once, and one tends to become very person-centred. Not only Jacqui but many others were very quick to respond to the cries emerging from my mounds of paper, and I thank them all sincerely.

As to Wiley, both Vivien Ward, publisher in psychology and architecture, and Ruth Graham, senior production editor, have been unstinting in their assistance whenever it was called for. Even before the contract was signed there was help. That came from Peter Herriot who went far beyond the requirements of an assessor to give what proved to be invaluable advice on editing a book of this kind. Whether he will think I have followed his advice closely enough, time will tell.

Nothing is carried out in a vacuum. This volume was compiled in my home. The many hours at the computer, on e-mail or just shifting about mounds of paper was tolerated with great goodwill by my husband, Roy Hodson. He took on many duties that I usually undertake as 'woman's work' and only expressed concern when he thought I should take some exercise or get some rest. But I thank him also for being a great help in acting as 'copy editor' as the draft chapters came in. He is, after all, a very experienced editor in his own right.

Lastly, I must express my deepest gratitude to all the authors who have made this book into what it is. They have been unstinting in their patience as I tried to get some uniformity in the writing but at the same time allow room for individuality. There would be no volume without you.

The publishers wish to thank Joseph Kelly for granting permission for use of the previously unpublished material by George Kelly.

The Psychology of Personal Constructs and its Philosophy

INTRODUCTION

What better way to begin this guide along the highways and byways of personal construct theory than to hear from George Kelly himself (Chapter 1)? His 'brief introduction' to the subject, taken from a 1966 essay, says much, and implies much more again. Indeed, it may be sufficient to take some readers as far as they ever want to go in their study of the subject. But we must hope that it will merely whet the appetite of the vast majority of readers for more knowledge. For, as he says, much of his theory has been left out, since his chapter is an introduction and not a condensation. They should go on to savour countless further challenges to come from the biggest assembly of personal construct experts ever gathered together between the covers of a single volume.

Kelly is cheering up the reluctant newcomer to the subject even before the first page is finished. The psychology, he asserts, 'Does broadly suggest that even the most obvious occurrences of everyday life might appear utterly transformed if we were inventive enough to construe them differently'. There is a basic message of hope and deliverance here which would not be out of place in religious teaching.

You will find Kelly concise and witty as he describes the Fundamental Postulate of personal construct theory together with tightly drawn explanations of some of the corollaries.

While the reader still has some of the pure Kellyism fresh in the mind's forefront, Fay Fransella and Bob Neimeyer tell of Kelly, the man himself, from their extensive theoretical, practical and personal knowledge. They place the theory in the context of the academic climate at the time of its introduction. They consider aspects of the theory with which some people have found problems. Emphasizing that Kelly's ideas should never become a sacred text, they outline developments that have resulted from his ideas.

A previously unpublished talk by the late Don Bannister (who worked with Kelly for a few terms at Ohio State University) then follows. It points out those aspects of the theory that he considered to be most important. He particularly focuses on its reflexive nature, and reminds us vividly how revolutionary those views were in the mid-1950s.

In the next chapter Gabrielle Chiari and Maria Laura Nuzzo outline the philosophy of constructive alternativism that runs through everything in the psychology of personal constructs, and show its importance in the movement of constructivism. They also dwell on the still vexed issue of whether Kelly's theory is a 'cognitive' theory or a theory of human experiencing.

Jack Adams-Webber then summarizes much of the research that has been carried out in relation to personal construct theory. He cites Pervin and John as saying that: 'almost every aspect of Kelly's theory has received at least some study' (2001, p. 426).

CHAPTER 1

A Brief Introduction to Personal Construct Theory*

George A. Kelly

Who can say what nature is? Is it what now exists about us, including all the tiny hidden things that wait so patiently to be discovered? Or is it the vista of all that is destined to occur, whether tomorrow or in some distant eon of time? Or is nature infinitely more varied than this, the myriad trains of events that might ensue if we were to be so bold, ingenious, and irreverent as to take a hand in its management?

Personal construct theory is a notion about how man may launch out from a position of admitted ignorance, and how he may aspire from one day to the next to transcend his own dogmatisms. It is, then, a theory of man's personal inquiry—a psychology of human quest. It does not say what has been or will be found, but proposes rather how we might go about looking for it.

PHILOSOPHICAL POSITION

Like other theories, the psychology of personal constructs is the implementation of a philosophical assumption. In this case the assumption is that whatever nature may be, or howsoever the quest for truth will turn out in the end, the events we face today are subject to as great a variety of construction as our wits will enable us to contrive. This is not to say that one construction is as good as any other, nor is it to deny that at some infinite point in time human vision will behold reality out to the utmost reaches of existence.

But it does remind us that all our present perceptions are open to question and reconsideration, and it does broadly suggest that even the most obvious occurrences of everyday life might appear utterly transformed if we were inventive enough to construe them differently.

---

*This is an edited version of an essay written in 1966 to introduce a projected book on research in personal construct theory. It was then published in D. Bannister (Ed.) 1970 *Perspectives in Personal Construct Theory*. London: Academic Press.

International Handbook of Personal Construct Psychology. Edited by F. Fransella.

This philosophical position we have called *constructive alternativism*, and its implications, keep cropping up in the psychology of personal constructs. It can be contrasted with the prevalent epistemological assumption of *accumulative fragmentalism*, which is that truth is collected piece by piece.

While constructive alternativism does not argue against the collection of information, neither does it measure truth by the size of the collection. Indeed it leads one to regard a large accumulation of facts as an open invitation to some far-reaching reconstruction which will reduce them to a mass of trivialities.

A person who spends a great deal of his time hoarding facts is not likely to be happy at the prospect of seeing them converted into rubbish. He is more likely to want them bound and preserved, a memorial to his personal achievement. A scientist, for example, who thinks this way, and especially a psychologist who does so, depends upon his facts to furnish the ultimate proof of his propositions. With these shining nuggets of truth in his grasp it seems unnecessary for him to take responsibility for the conclusions he claims they thrust upon him. To suggest to him at this point that further human reconstruction can completely alter the appearance of the precious fragments he has accumulated, as well as the direction of their arguments, is to threaten his scientific conclusions, his philosophical position, and even his moral security. No wonder, then, that in the eyes of such a conservatively minded person our assumption that all facts are subject—are wholly subject—to alternative constructions looms up as culpably subjective and dangerously subversive to the scientific establishment.

Facts and Conclusions

But wherein does responsibility lie? Can we ever make facts, even facts that turn out as predicted, responsible for conclusions? I think not. Whatever the world may be, man can come to grips with it only by placing his own interpretations upon what he sees. While his ingenuity in devising suitable constructions may be limited, and many misfortunes therefore come to pass, still it is he, not facts, who holds the key to the ultimate future. This, it seems to me, makes him responsible, and suggests that it is quite inappropriate for him ever to claim that his conclusions have been dictated by any nature other than his own.

The Meaning of Events

Constructive alternativism stresses the importance of events. But it looks to man to propose what the character of their import shall be. The meaning of an event—that is to say, the meaning we ascribe to it—is anchored in its antecedents and its consequents. Thus meaning displays itself to us mainly in the dimension of time. This is much more than saying that meanings are rehearsals of outcomes, a proposition implicit in behaviouristic theory, or that the ends justify the means—the ethical statement of the same proposition.

Besides including anticipated outcomes, meaning includes also the means by which events are anticipated. This is to suggest that different meanings are involved when identical events are correctly anticipated by different sets of inferences. It suggests also the implication of quite different meanings when the basic assumptions are different, even when the chains of inference are otherwise more or less similar.

In all of this we look to events to confirm our predictions and to encourage our venturesome constructions. Yet the same events may confirm different constructions and different, or even incompatible, events may appear to validate the same construction. So, for each of us, meaning assumes the shape of the arguments which lead him to his predictions, and the only outside check on his personal constructions are the events which confirm or disconfirm his expectations. This is a long way from saying that meaning is revealed by what happens, or that meaning is something to be discovered in the natural course of events, or that events shape men and ideas. Thus in constructive alternativism events are crucial, but only man can devise a meaning for them to challenge.

When we place a construction of our own upon a situation, and then pursue its implications to the point of expecting something to happen, we issue a little invitation to nature to intervene in our personal experience. If what we expect does happen, or appears to happen, our expectation is confirmed and we are likely to think that we must have had a pretty good slant on the trend of affairs, else we would have lost our bet. But if we think the matter over carefully we may begin to have doubts. Perhaps a totally different interpretation would have led to an equally successful prediction; and it may, besides, have been more straightforward or more consistent with our conscience. Or perhaps our vivid expectations overlaid our perception of what actually happened.

So, on second thoughts, even when events are reconciled with a construction, we cannot be sure that they have proved it true. There are always other constructions, and there is the lurking likelihood that some of them will turn out to be better. The best we can ever do is project our anticipations with frank uncertainty and observe the outcomes in terms in which we have a bit more confidence. But neither anticipation nor outcome is ever a matter of absolute certainty from the dark in which we mortals crouch. This is what we mean by constructive alternativism.

The Conduct of Inquiry

One of the most exciting aspects of constructive alternativism is its bearing upon the conduct of human inquiry. According to the canons of logic, a statement, if meaningful, is either true or not true. Indeed, the logical positivists have reversed the logic and argued that the criterion for meaningfulness is whether or not a statement can be proved true or not true. This seems to mean that we should not ask a question until we have answered it. But constructive alternativism suggests that the canon itself is not fruitful, or at least that it tends to stultify fruitful endeavour. Besides, I note that most of the members of the famous Vienna Circle abandoned their extreme position—bursting with unanswerable questions, no doubt.

Since ultimate truth is such a long way off, it seems as inappropriate to try to capture it by, say, five o'clock on Tuesday as it is to claim that we already have it in our grasp. Thus any proposition we contrive must be regarded as a crude formulation of a question which, at best, can serve only as an invitation to further inquiry, and one that can be answered only through personal experience and in terms of the *ad interim* criterion of anticipated events. Indeed, the answer we get is not likely to be exactly an answer to our question at all, but an answer to some other question we have not yet thought to ask.

To this way of thinking the verbs in all significant statements a man makes are implicitly cast in an 'invitational mood' rather than in the indicative mood, or in one of the other moods recognized by English grammar. 'What', he says, 'would happen if . . . ?' We suspect, furthermore, that this is psychologically characteristic of man whenever he is not in a defensive posture, and that it characterizes his unspoken impulses as well as his articulate sentences. 'Please', he means to say, 'join me in pursuing the implications of this pose I have assumed.'

GENERATING PSYCHOLOGICAL THEORY

Since we are already on the threshold of psychological theorizing, we might as well get on with it, even though there is much more that could be said about the philosophical position of constructive alternativism. So let us talk about personal construct theory and we can return to philosophy later if necessary.

The question of just how a theory is generated is about as complicated as the whole of human psychology. Since theories—so far, at least—are devised by men, it seems unreasonable to claim that they are shaped by any process other than a psychological one. Yet for a long time we have been saying that one moves from old propositions to new ones by the logical procedures of induction or deduction, as if this could happen independently of the personal disposition of man. Indeed, I have come to doubt that the notions of induction and deduction tell us very much about what goes on. In the one case I suppose it means we listen to ourselves making a clutter of assertions only to end up trying to say them all in one mouthful. In the other we let loose with a high-sounding remark and then, like a four-year-old child trying to 'read' his own 'writing', struggle to figure out what we meant by it.

In formulating the theory I have called the psychology of personal constructs, I cannot say that I actually launched out deductively from the assumption of constructive alternativism as I have phrased it here, though now I can see how, with the help of a certain amount of idiosyncratic bias along the way, one could start with constructive alternativism and end up with personal construct theory. And I believe I can see how the clutter of events I experienced was important. Now that I think of it, I can remember a lot of relevant things that happened over the years. But not for one moment would I claim that these events converged to shape my theory. They seemed only to keep challenging it—and not always to be very constructive about it either. It may even be that I can remember these incidents now only because, on hindsight, they seem to confirm what my present formulation would forecast. And I am sure that I found myself perplexed and aggravated by many circumstances I have long since forgotten, and that what I came to think as a psychologist was what, over the years, I had jury-rigged as a man to cope with what was going on.

So let us not be hasty. Perhaps constructive alternativism was my basic assumption all along. I may only have delayed putting it into words. I recall that I have often felt that personal construct theory was as much an account of what had long been running through my noggin as it was the outcome of my laboured thinking after I told myself to go ahead and dare to write a theory.

All of this is to suggest that the psychological postures, mine included, that we accent with words, or dignify in philosophical terms, may be quite personal and may considerably antedate our verbal statements about them. There is even reason to dread bringing such nascent constructions to light lest they betray us as foolish or even crazy. And I must say, at some risk to myself I suppose, that to propose a statement of such sweeping proportions as constructive alternativism is to flirt with grandiosity—a symptom more often associated with psychosis than with genius. But just as good cannot be accomplished without risking evil, so enlightenment cannot be sought wholeheartedly without approaching the brink of what may turn out to be insanity. There is no such thing as adventure with safety guaranteed in advance, not even when sitting alone with a typewriter. Not that I have ever lost any sleep over that matter!

PERSONAL CONSTRUCT THEORY

Basic Postulate

A person's processes are psychologically channelized by the ways in which he anticipates events. This is what we have proposed as a fundamental postulate for the psychology of personal constructs. The assumptions of constructive alternativism are embedded in this statement, although it may not be apparent until later in our exposition of the theme just how it is that they are.

We start with *a person*. Organisms, lower animals, and societies can wait. We are talking about someone we know, or would like to know—such as you, or me. More particularly, we are talking about that person as an event—the processes that express his personality. And, since we enter the system we are about to elaborate at the point of a process—or life—rather than at the point of a body or a material substance, we should not have to invoke any special notions, such as dynamics, drives, motivation, or force to explain why our object does not remain inert. As far as the theory is concerned, it never was inert. As we pursue the theoretical line emerging from this postulate, I think it becomes clear also why we do not need such notions to account for the direction of movement, any more than we need them to explain the movement itself.

This is a *psychological* theory. Mostly this is a way of announcing in the basic postulate that we make no commitment to the terms of other disciplines, such as physiology or chemistry. Our philosophical position permits us to see those other disciplines as based on man-made constructions, rather than as disclosures of raw realities, and hence there is no need for the psychologist to accept them as final, or to limit his proposals to statements consistent with them.

In addition, I think the theory sounds more or less like the other theories that are known as psychological. This gives me an inclusive, as well as an exclusive, reason for calling it a psychological theory, although this is more or less a matter of taste rather than of definition. Certainly I have no intention of trying to define psychology; there are just too many things called psychological that I do not care to take responsibility for.

Some have suggested that personal construct theory not be called a psychological theory at all, but a metatheory. That is all right with me. It suggests that it is a theory about theories, and that is pretty much what I have in mind. But I hope that it is clear that it is not limited to being a metatheory of formal theories, or even of articulate ones.

There is also the question of whether or not it is a cognitive theory. Some have said that it was; others have classed it as existential. Quite an accomplishment; not many theories have been accused of being both cognitive and existential! But this, too, is all right with me. As a matter of fact, I am delighted. There are categorical systems in which I think the greater amount of ambiguity I stir up, the better. Cognition, for example, strikes me as a particularly misleading category, and, since it is one designed to distinguish itself from affect and conation, those terms, too, might well be discarded as inappropriately restrictive.

Personal construct theory has also been categorized by responsible scholars as an emotional theory, a learning theory, a psychoanalytic theory (Freudian, Adlerian and Jungian—all three), a typically American theory, a Marxist theory, a Thomistic theory, a behaviouristic theory, an Apollonian theory, a pragmatistic theory, a reflective theory, and no theory at all. It has also been classified as nonsense, which indeed, by its own admission, it will likely some day turn out to be. In each case there were some convincing arguments offered for the categorization, but I have forgotten what most of them were.

The fourth term in the postulate—*channelized*—was chosen as one less likely than others to imply dynamics. This is because there is no wish to suggest that we are dealing with anything not already in motion. What is to be explained is the direction of the processes, not the transformation of states into processes. We see states only as an *ad interim* device to get time to stand still long enough for us to see what is going on. In specifying ways of *anticipating events* as the directive referent for human processes, we cut ourselves free of the stimulus–response version of nineteenth-century scientific determinism.

In our present undertaking the psychological initiative always remains a property of the person—never the property of anything else. What is more, neither past nor future events are themselves ever regarded as basic determinants of the course of human action—not even the events of childhood. But one's way of anticipating them—whether in the short range or in the long view—is the basic theme in the human process of living. Moreover, it is that events are anticipated, not merely that man gravitates towards more and more comfortable organic states. Confirmation and disconfirmation of one's predictions are accorded greater psychological significance than rewards, punishments or the drive reduction that reinforcements produce.

There are, of course, some predictions we would like to see disconfirmed, as well as some we hope will indeed materialize. We should not make the mistake of translating personal construct theory back into stimulus–response theory and say to ourselves that confirmation is the same as a positive reinforcement, and that disconfirmation nullifies the meaning of an experience. Disconfirmation, even in those cases where it is disconcerting, provides grounds for reconstruction—or of repentance, in the proper sense of that term—and it may be used to improve the accuracy and significance of further anticipations. Thus we envision the nature of life in its outreach for the future, and not in its perpetuation of its prior conditions or in its incessant reverberation of past events.

Personal construct theory is elaborated by a string of eleven corollaries which may be loosely inferred from its basic postulate. Beyond these are certain notions of more limited applicability which fall in line with personal construct thinking— notions about such matters as anxiety, guilt, hostility, decision making, creativity, the strategy of psychological research, and other typical concerns of professional psychologists. These latter notions need not be considered part of the formal structure of the theory, although our theoretical efforts may not come to life in the mind of the reader until he has seen their applicability to the daily problems he faces.

Construction Corollary

A person anticipates events by construing their replications. Since events never repeat themselves, else they would lose their identity, one can look forward to them only by devising some construction which permits him to perceive two of them in a similar manner. His construction must also permit him to be selective about which two are to be perceived similarly. Thus the same construction that serves to infer their similarity must serve also to differentiate them from others. Under a system that provides only for the identification of similarities the world dissolves into homogeneity; under one that provides only for differentiation it is shattered into hopelessly unrelated fragments.

Individuality Corollary

Persons differ from each other in their constructions of events. Having assumed that construction is a personal affair, it seems unlikely that any two persons would ever happen to concoct identical systems. I would go further now than when I originally proposed this corollary and suggest that even particular constructions are never identical events. And I would extend it the other way too, and say that I doubt that two persons ever put their construction systems together in terms of the same logical relationships. For myself, I find this a most encouraging line of speculation, for it seems to open the door to more advanced systems of thinking and inference yet to be devised by man. Certainly it suggests that scientific research can rely more heavily on individual imagination than it usually dares.

Organization Corollary

Each person characteristically evolves, for his convenience in anticipating events, a construction system embracing ordinal relationships between constructs. If a person is to live actively within his construction system, it must provide him with some clear avenues of inference and movement. There must be ways for him to resolve the more crucial contradictions and conflicts that inevitably arise. This is not to say that all inconsistencies must be resolved at once. Some private paradoxes can be allowed to stand indefinitely, and, in the face of them, one can remain indecisive or can vacillate between alternative expectations of what the future holds in store for him.

Dichotomy Corollary

A person's construction system is composed of a finite number of dichotomous constructs. Experience has shown me that this is the point where many of my readers first encounter difficulty in agreeing with me. What I am saying is that a construct is a 'black and white' affair, never a matter of shadings or of 'greys'. On the face of it, this sounds bad, for it seems to imply categorical or absolutistic thinking rather than any acceptance of relativism or conditionalism. Yet I would insist that there is nothing categorical about a construct.

Neither our constructs nor our construing systems come to us from nature, except, of course, from our own nature. It must be noted that this philosophical position of constructive alternativism has much more powerful epistemological implications than one might at first suppose. We cannot say that constructs are essences distilled by the mind out of available reality. They are imposed upon events, not abstracted from them. There is only one place they come from; that is, from the person who is to use them. He devises them. Moreover, they do not stand for anything or represent anything, as a symbol, for example, is supposed to do.

So what are they? They are reference axes upon which one may project events in an effort to make some sense out of what is going on.

A construct is the basic contrast between two groups. When it is imposed it serves both to distinguish between its elements and to group them. Thus the construct refers to the nature of the distinction one attempts to make between events, not to the array in which his events appear to stand when he gets through applying the distinction between each of them and all the others.

But, while constructs do not represent or symbolize events, they do enable us to cope with events, which is a statement of quite a different order. They also enable us to put events into arrays or scales, if we wish.

One thing more has to be said. In order to make the point, I have had to talk about constructs in such an explicit manner that I have probably given the impression that a construct is as highly articulate and cognitive as my discussion has had to be. If I had been able to say what I have said in metaphor or hyperbole I might have left the impression that a construct had something to do with feeling or with formless urges too fluid to be pinned down by labels. But personal construct theory is no more a cognitive theory than it is an affective or a conative one. There are grounds for distinction that operate in one's life that seem to elude verbal expression. We see them in infants, as well as in our own spontaneous aversions and infatuations. These discriminative bases are no less constructs than those the reader may have been imagining during the reading of the preceding paragraphs. Certainly it is important not to consider a construct as another term for a concept, else a major sector of the arena in which constructs function will be obscured from view.

Choice Corollary

A person chooses for himself that alternative in a dichotomized construct through which he anticipates the greater possibility for the elaboration of his system. It seems to me to follow that if a person makes so much use of his constructs, and is so dependent upon them, he will make choices which promise to develop their usefulness. Developing the usefulness of a construction system involves, as far as I can see, two things: defining it and extending it. One defines his system, by extension at least, by making it clear how its construct components are applied to objects or are linked with each other. He amplifies his system by using it to reach out for new fields of application. In the one case he consolidates his position and in the other he extends it.

Note that the choice is between alternatives expressed in the construct, not, as one might expect, between objects divided by means of the construct. There is a subtle point here. Personal construct theory is a psychological theory and therefore has to do with the behaviour of man, not with the intrinsic nature of objects. A construct governs what the man does, not what the object does. In a strict sense, therefore, man makes decisions which initially affect himself, and which affect other objects only subsequently—and then only if he manages to take some effective action. Making a choice, then, has to do with involving oneself, and cannot be defined in terms of the external object chosen. Besides, one does not always get the object he chooses to gain. But his anticipation does have to do with his own processes, as I tried to say in formulating the basic postulate.

So when a man makes a choice what he does is align himself in terms of his constructs. He does not necessarily succeed, poor fellow, in doing anything to the objects he seeks to approach or avoid. Men change things by changing themselves first, and they accomplish their objectives, if at all, only by paying the price of altering themselves—as some have found to their sorrow and others to their salvation. The choices that men make are choices of their own acts, and the alternatives are distinguished by their own constructs. The results of the choices, however, may range all the way from nothing to catastrophe, on the one hand, or to consummation, on the other.

Range Corollary

A construct is convenient for the anticipation of a finite range of events only. A personal construct system can hardly be said to have universal utility. Not everything that happens in the world can be projected upon all the dichotomies that make up a person's outlook. Indeed I doubt that anyone has ever devised a construct that could cover the entire range of events of which he was aware. There are patches of clouds in every man's sky. This is to say that the geometry of the mind is never a complete system. The lines of reference here and there become lost in irrelevancies and make it practically impossible to write formulas that are universally applicable.

A construct has its focus of convenience—a set of objects with which it works especially well. Over a somewhat larger range it may work only reasonably well; that is, its range of convenience. But beyond that it fades into uselessness and we can say the outer array of objects simply lies beyond that range of convenience.

Experience Corollary

A person's construction system varies as he successively construes the replications of events. Keeping in mind that events do not actually repeat themselves and that the replication we talk about is a replication of ascribed aspects only, it begins to be clear that the succession we call experience is based on the constructions we place on what goes on. If those constructions are never altered, all that happens during a man's years is a sequence of parallel events having no psychological impact on his life. But if he invests himself—the most intimate event of all—in the enterprise, the outcome, to the extent that it differs from his expectation or enlarges upon it, dislodges the man's construction of himself. In recognizing the inconsistency between his anticipation and the outcome, he concedes a discrepancy between what he was and what he is. A succession of such investments and dislodgements constitutes the human experience.

A subtle point comes to light at this juncture. Confirmation may lead to reconstruing quite as much as disconfirmation—perhaps even more. A confirmation gives one an anchorage in some area of his life, leaving him free to set afoot adventuresome explorations nearby, as, for example, in the case of a child whose security at home emboldens him to be the first to explore what lies in the neighbour's yard.

The unit of experience is, therefore, a cycle embracing five phases: anticipation, investment, encounter, confirmation or disconformation, and constructive revision. This is followed, of course, by new anticipations, as the first phase of a subsequent experiential cycle gets underway. Certainly in personal construct theory's line of reasoning experience is not composed of encounters alone.

Stated simply, the amount of a man's experience is not measured by the number of events with which he collides, but by the investments he has made in his anticipations and the revisions of his constructions that have followed upon his facing up to consequences. A man whose only wager in life is upon reaching heaven by immunizing himself against the miseries of his neighbours, or upon following a bloody party-line straight to utopia, is prepared to gain little experience until he arrives— either here, or somewhere else clearly recognized as not the place he was looking for. Then, if he is not too distracted by finding that his architectural specifications have been blatantly disregarded, or that the wrong kind of people have started moving in, I suppose he may begin to think of some other investments he might better have been making in the meantime. Of course, a little hell along the way, if taken more to heart than most heaven-bound people seem to take it, may have given him a better idea of what to expect, before it was too late to get a bit of worthwhile experience and make something out of himself.

Modulation Corollary

The variation in a person's construction system is limited by the permeability of the constructs within whose ranges of convenience the variants lie. While the Experience Corollary suggests that a man can revise his constructions on the basis of events and his invested anticipations of them, there are limitations that must be taken into account. He must have a construct system which is sufficiently open to novel events to let him know when he has encountered them, else the experience cycle will fail to function in its terminal phases. He must have a system which also will admit the revised construct that emerges at the end of the cycle. If the revised construct is left to stand as an isolated axis of reference, it will be difficult for him to chart any coordinated course of action that takes account of it; he therefore can do little with respect to it except vacillate.

Perhaps it is clear from these remarks that what is meant by permeability is not a construct's plasticity, or its amenability to change within itself, but its capacity to be used as a referent for novel events and to accept new subordinate constructions within its range of convenience. A notion of God, for example, which includes an unabridged dictionary of all things holy, is likely to be impermeable. Anything new that turns up—such as an unbiblical event or idea—is likely to be excluded from the construct's realm of concern. Unless the novelty can fit elsewhere into some more permeable part of the construct system, it is likely to be ignored.

Fragmentation Corollary

A person may successively employ a variety of construction subsystems which are inferentially incompatible with each other. We must be careful not to interpret the Modulation Corollary to mean that a construct system has to be logically intact. Perhaps in any proximate transition in the human process there is an inferential relationship between antecedent and consequent at some constructive level in the person's system. But persons move from *a* to *b*, and on to *c* without always taking into account the fact that their overview of *c* cannot be inferred from their overview of *a*. A man may move from an act of love to an act of jealousy, and from there to an act of hate, even though hate is not something that would be inferred from love, even in his peculiar system. This is the kind of psychological fact to which the Fragmentation Corollary calls particular attention.

Perhaps I should add that I do not see this kind of 'irrationality' as necessarily a bad thing. For man, logic and inference can be as much an obstacle to his ontological ventures as a guide to them. Often it is the uninferred fragment of a man's construction system that makes him great, whereas if he were an integrated whole—taking into account all that the whole would have to embrace—the poor fellow would be no better than his 'natural self'.

Commonality Corollary

To the extent that one person employs a construction of experience which is similar to that employed by another, his processes are psychologically similar to those of the other person.[1] On the face of it, this corollary appears to assert pretty much what personal construct theory seems to stand for: The notion that behaviour is governed

---

[1] To my mild dismay I have only now realized that the word 'psychological' was misplaced in my original phrasing of this corollary. Instead of modifying 'processes', as I originally had it, the term should modify 'similar', as constructive alternativism would suggest. Sorry about that!

by constructs. But there is more to it than what such a simplified statement might be taken to imply.

If we do as most behaviouristically influenced psychologists do, and use behaviour as a synonym for all human process, we then might, I suppose, substitute the term 'behaviours' for 'processes' in stating this corollary. But what thoughtful behaviourists have in mind when they make behaviour the focus of their concern is the logical positivist position that anything that cannot be identified as behaviour is untestable and therefore a scientific distraction. If we were to take this stand—as I would prefer not—we would be concerned only with that phase of the experiential cycle I have called 'personal investment'. Personal construct theory would lead us, I think, to be concerned with the whole experiential cycle and the process which it represents, rather than with the behavioural phase only.

This corollary makes it possible to say that two persons who have confronted quite different events, and who might have gone through experiential cycles which actually seem to us to be quite different, might nevertheless end up with similar constructions of their experiences, and, because of that, thereafter pursue psychologically similar processes of further inquiry. Thus personal construct theory further releases psychology from assumptions about the identity of events and man's dependence on them. It leaves us free to envision man coping with 'familiar' events in new ways and cooperating with other men to produce novelties which make their world a different place to live in. Neither behaviourism nor phenomenology, as I see them, provides a psychological basis for this kind of forward movement in man.

Sociality Corollary

To the extent that one person construes the construction processes of another, he may play a role in a social process involving the other person. The implications of this corollary are probably the most far-reaching of any I have yet attempted to propound. It establishes grounds for understanding role as a psychological term, and for envisioning thereupon a truly psychological basis for society. As far as I can see, the term has only extrapsychological meaning elsewhere. This view offers, moreover, an approach to certain puzzling aspects of psychopathy, and it permits one to understand guilt in far more intimate terms than are possible within more conventional 'personality' theories, or within current theological doctrines. It leads us also to a position from which we can distinguish personality theories from others.

Let me start by trying to differentiate two levels at which I may try to understand another person—say, my reader. It is not hard for me to imagine him—you, I mean—at this moment a figure bending over a book. It—the figure—is skimming the paragraphs with the right forefinger in a position to turn to the pages that follow. The eye movements zig-zag down the page and quickly the next leaf is flipped, or perhaps a whole section—a chapter or more, is lifted with the left thumb and drawn horizontally aside.

What I am envisioning is a moving object, and whether or not I am correctly describing the movements that are taking place can be reasonably well confirmed—

or disconfirmed—by an observer who has been watching you for the past few moments, or if he saw a motion picture film of what has been taking place. This is to say, I have couched my picture of you in the terms of 'objective' psychology. I have offered a hypothesized description of a 'behaving organism'.

Ordinarily, if I wanted to play the game by the rules of objectivity, I would not stoop to ask you outright whether or not my description of your actions was correct; the noises you might make in reply could be taken in so many different ways I can be sure of being a 'scientist' only if I stick to what can be confirmed. Being a 'scientist' may be so important to me that I dare not risk sullying myself with your delusions. I shall therefore play my part and retain my membership in Sigma Xi by referring to your reply as a 'vocal response' of a 'behaving organism'. Hello there, Behaving Organism!

But now let me say it quite another way. There you are, my reader, wondering, I fear, what on earth I am trying so hard to say, and smiling to yourself as the thought crosses your mind that it all might be put in a familiar phrase or two—as indeed it may. You are hunched uncomfortably over the book, impatiently scanning the paragraphs for a cogent expression or a poignant sentence that may make the experience worth the time you are stealing from more urgent duties. The right forefinger is restlessly poised to lift the page and go on to discover if perhaps anything more sensible follows.

Let me confess that I feel at this moment like urging you not to try so hard. While it has taken me hours to write some of these paragraphs—the four preceding ones, for example—and I would like to think the outcome has been worth some of your time too; they were not meant to be hammered into your consciousness. They are intended, instead, to set off trains of thought. And, in following them, I earnestly hope we shall find ourselves walking along the same paths.

There now, isn't that the way it really is? It isn't? Then, tell me, what are you doing? And while we are at it, tell me also how my efforts strike you—I mean, what do you think I am trying to do, not merely whether I am making sense or not. Only please do not tell me that all I am really doing is pounding a typewriter in an effort to keep my wife awake; I have other psychoanalytically oriented friends who are only too happy to offer me that kind of 'interpretation'.

Although these two descriptions of my view of the reader both represent a wide departure from accepted literary style, I hope they will make clear the contrast between construing the construction processes of another person and construing his behaviour merely. In the first instance, I construed only your behaviour. There is nothing wrong with that, as far as it goes. In the second case I went further and placed a construction upon the way in which I imagined you might be thinking. The chances are that I was more or less mistaken in both instances, particularly in the second. But the point I want to make lies in the difference in my mode of construing you. In both formulations I was indeed concerned with your behaviour, but only in the second did I strive for some notion of the construction which might be giving your behaviour its form, or your future behaviour its form. If immediate accuracy is what I must preserve at all costs, then I had better stick to the first level of construction. But if I am to anticipate you, I must take some chances and try to sense what you are up to.

One does not have to be a psychologist to treat another person as an automaton, though training in 'experimental psychology' may help. Conversely, treating him that way does not make one into a scientist—though some of my colleagues may wish to dispute this. It is easy enough to treat persons we have never met as behaving organisms only, and many of us think that is the sophisticated way to go about secondary human relations. We may even treat our neighbours that way, especially if there are more of them than we care to know. I have even observed parents who go so far as to treat their children so, and they sometimes come to me for psychological advice on how to do it. I sometimes suspect it is because they have more children than they care to know. To be very frank about it, my construction of you, while writing some of these passages, has often lapsed into no more than that. And, if you are like me in this respect, there must have been moments when you regarded me as a disembodied typewriter, or as an Irish name on the title page of a book, or as a kind of animated sentence ejector.

Points about Roles to be Emphasized

I know from past experience in attempting to explain this notion of role that two things need especially to be made clear, particularly if I am trying to explain it to a thoroughly trained fellow psychologist. First, my construing of your construction processes need not be accurate in order for me to play a role in a social process that involves you. I have seen a person play a role, and do it most effectively—even in a manner quite acceptable to his colleagues—when he grossly misperceived their outlooks, and they knew it. But because he did what he did on the basis of what he thought they understood, not merely on the basis of their overt acts, he was able to play a collaborative role in a social process whose experiential cycle led them all somewhere. Experiential cycles which are based on automaton-like constructions do not, I think, generate social processes, though they may lead to revisions of the manipulative devices by which men try to control each other's actions.

The second point that experience has led me to stress is that my construction of your outlook does not make me a compliant companion, nor does it keep us from working at cross purposes. I may even use my construction of your view as a basis for trying to undo your efforts. But there is something interesting about this; there is still a good chance of a social process emerging out of our conflict, and we will both end up a good way from where we started—in my case, because the experiential cycle will reflect back upon my construction of your outlook, not of your behaviour only, and, in your case, because you would find that something beyond your overt behaviour was being taken into account, and you might revise your investments accordingly.

There is a third point that sometimes needs mentioning. What I have proposed is a psychological definition of role, and therefore it does not lean upon sociological assumptions about the nature of society or economic assumptions about the coordination of human labour. Being psychological, it attempts to derive its terms from the experience of the individual, though, once the derivations have been made, there are no necessary restrictions on pursuing implications on out into the world of the sociologist, or even into that of the mathematician.

Role and Experience

If I fail to invest in a role, and relate myself to you only mechanically, then the only thing that disconfirmation can teach me is that the organism I presume you to be is not wired up to produce the behaviours I thought it would, just as my typewriter does not always behave in the way I expect it to. When my typewriter behaves unpredictably I look to see if there isn't a screw loose, or if something hasn't gotten into the works. Sometimes I find I have struck the wrong key; I'll strike a different one next time.

And if I insist on construing you as I do my typewriter, I shall probably take my predictive failures as an indication only that I should look to see if there isn't 'a screw loose somewhere' in you. Or perhaps I shall wonder if I haven't 'struck the wrong key', or if something hasn't 'gotten into your works', like a 'motive' or a 'need', for example. I may even conclude that you are a brand of 'typewriter' that has been badly put together. Certainly if this is the way I go about concluding my experiential cycle, I can scarcely claim that I have engaged myself in a social process. Mine might be the kind of experience that gets the commonwealth's work done, but it would not be the sort that builds viable societies.

GUILT

It is in the context of the Sociality Corollary that one can begin to develop a truly psychological definition of guilt. This is not to say that such a definition has to be at odds with ecclesiastical or legal definitions, though it may indeed suggest quite different courses of human action where misdemeanour is involved. We shall be speaking, of course, about the experience of guilt and what it is like, psychologically.

Most psychological theories, both 'mechanistic' ones and 'dynamic' ones, regard the experience of guilt as a derivative of punishment. One feels guilty because he thinks he has made himself eligible for punishment. But suppose one does not see punishment as the appropriate treatment of wrong-doing, only as revenge by injured persons serving simply to make clear that they have been hurt. Or suppose one does not see wrong-doing as something for which he has been systematically punished. Can he still feel guilty? I think he can. I think Jesus thought so too, though very few ecclesiastics appear to agree with either of us on this point. Even the term 'repentance', which I think might better be taken to mean rethinking or reconstruing, as its etymology suggests, has come to stand for undertaking something irrelevantly unpleasant or punitive in compensation for disobedience, rather than doing something which will throw light on past mistakes.

As far as I can see, both from what I have observed and what I have figured out for myself, a person who chronically resorts to this kind of penitence to bring his guilt feelings back into comfortable equilibrium, or to write off his wrong-doing, ends up as a well-balanced sanctimonious psychopath. His only possible virtue is obedience and the society he perpetuates has no purpose except to uphold its own laws. I suspect, furthermore, that this is the net effect of any stimulus–response –reinforcement kind of theory, whether in psychology, religion or politics. And I have been moved to say, on occasion, that a psychopath is a stimulus–response psychologist who takes it seriously—a remark I find does not endear me to all my colleagues.

From the standpoint of personal construct theory, guilt is the sense of having lost one's core role structure. A core structure is any one that is maintained as a basic referent of life itself. Without it a person has no guidelines for staying alive. To the extent that one's core structure embodies his role also, as we have defined role, he is vulnerable to the experience of guilt. He has only to perceive himself dislodged from such a role to suffer the inner torment most of us know so well.

To feel guilty is to sense that one has lost his grasp on the outlook of his fellow man, or has unwittingly played his part in a manner irrelevant to that outlook by following invalid guidelines. If the role is based on one's construction of God's outlook, or the Party's, he has only to fail to play it or to find that in playing it he has grossly misinterpreted its principal dimensions, to experience a religious sense of guilt. With this goes a feeling of alienation from God, or man, or from both. It is not a pleasant experience and, if the perception of excommunication is extensive or the core role deeply disrupted, it may be impossible for life to continue. Indeed, among primitive people, life may be extinguished within a few days, and, among more civilized ones, it may be abandoned by suicide.

HOSTILITY

At this point let us turn back to the Experience Corollary and examine its contribution to our understanding of another puzzling matter—hostility. The Experience Cycle described in that section included a terminal phase embodying an assessment of the construction in terms of which the initial anticipation had been cast and the behavioural commitment had been made. If outcomes emerging successively from ventures based on the same construction continue to leave a trail of disconfirmations behind, it becomes increasingly clear, even to the most dim-witted adventurer, that something is wrong with his reference axes.

Of course, all he has to do when this happens is to start revising his constructs. But, if he procrastinates too long or if his core constructs are involved, this may prove to be a major undertaking. Constructs which are in the process of revision are likely to be pretty shaky, and if he has a great deal of importance resting on one of them, with no others nearby to take up the load, he may find himself on the verge of confusion, or even guilt.

Ordinarily one can loosen his constructs by falling back on more permeable constructions, as suggested by the Modulation Corollary. But if his superordinate constructs are impermeable he will find himself unable to range any new constructions under them. He will then be confronted with a far more extensive revision of his system than he would if he had more open-ended constructions to fall back upon. The upshot of all this may be that he will find himself precariously poised between the minor chaos that his recent disconfirmations have disclosed, and the major chaos that might engulf him if he attempted to make the needed repairs in his reference axes. In this predicament he may look for some way to avoid both.

One way to avoid the immediate chaos is to tinker with the validational evidence which has recently been giving trouble. There are several ways of doing this. One is to stop short of completing one's experiments. Graduate students are quick to catch on to this one. Another is to loosen up one's construction of outcomes, though this is likely to invite charges of being unrealistic. Still another is to claim rewards as valid substitutes for confirmations, the way doting parents and reinforcement theorists do. One does this by exploiting his dependency on people who are over-eager to be helpful.

But there is still another way. That is to force the circumstances to confirm one's prediction of them. A parent who finds that his child does not like him as much as he expected may extort tokens of affection from the helpless youngster. A nation whose political philosophy has broken down in practice may precipitate a war to draft support for its outlook. A meek and trembly spinster, confronted at last by the fact that it is her impregnable posture that renders her unmarriageable, may 'prove' the validity of her stand by enticing one of the male brutes to victimize her. Each of these illustrates an instance of hostility. What personal construct theory has to offer in this matter differs radically from what conventional psychological theory implies. As with other topics with which it deals, personal construct theory attempts to define psychological constructs in terms of the personal experience of the individual to which they are to be applied. Thus, in defining hostility, we do not say that it is essentially an impulse to destroy—even though that may be its consequence— for that sounds more like a complaint of the victim than a prime effort of the hostile person. Instead, hostility is defined as the continued effort to extort validational evidence in favour of a type of social prediction which has already proved itself a failure.

FURTHER IMPLICATIONS OF PERSONAL CONSTRUCT THEORY

Since this presentation is intended to be a brief introduction to personal construct theory, rather than a condensation of it, much has had to be omitted. The important decision cycles and creativity cycles which the theory envisions remain unmentioned until this moment, as does a radically different view of dependency. There are strictly psychological definitions of threat, impulsivity, anxiety, transference, pre-emption, constellatoriness and propositionality. There is a linguistic system called the language of hypothesis, an ontology exemplified in orchestrated approaches to psychotherapy, and a methodology of psychological research. The notions of motivation, needs and psychodynamics vanish under the light of the Basic Postulate which accepts man as alive to begin with, and the principle of the elaborative choice which takes care of the directionality of man's moves without invoking special motivational agents to account for each of them.

The concept of learning evaporates. The boundary between cognition and affect is obliterated, rendering both terms meaningless. Fixed role therapy illustrates one of a variety of psychotherapeutic approaches which, at first glance, appear to violate most accepted canons of mental treatment by recognizing man as his own scientist. A new view of schizophrenia emerges, as well as fresh interpretations of 'the unconscious', depression, and aggression.

But this is enough to mention now. All it has been possible to accomplish in these pages is to state the basic propositions from which hypotheses may be drawn, to illustrate a few of the lines of inference that may be pursued, and to encourage the more impatient readers to seek out the theory's most exciting implications for themselves.

CHAPTER 2

George Alexander Kelly:
The Man and his Theory

Fay Fransella
University of Hertfordshire, UK

and

Robert A. Neimeyer
University of Memphis, USA

> . . . thinking of the scientist and the thinking of the human subject should be considered to be governed by the same general laws. If the aim of science is usefully construed as prediction, why not try operating on the assumption that the aim of all human effort is prediction and see where this line of psychologizing leads us?
>
> (Kelly, 1955/1991, p. 605/Vol. 2, p. 35)

In 1955, two heavy volumes containing 1218 pages of *The Psychology of Personal Constructs* landed on the desks of psychologists. Kelly's 'brief introduction' in the previous chapter is, in relation to the two volumes, indeed brief. The reception of this revolutionary work was mixed. Jerome Bruner, among the most prestigious of the many reviewers, said:

> These excellent, original, and infuriatingly prolix two volumes easily nominate themselves for the distinction of being the single greatest contribution of the past decade to the theory of personality functioning. Professor Kelly has written a major work. (Bruner, 1956, p. 355)

We discuss some of the difficulties experienced by reviewers and subsequent readers later in this chapter. But, first, a word about the man who created this work.

International Handbook of Personal Construct Psychology. Edited by F. Fransella.
© 2003 John Wiley & Sons, Ltd.

GEORGE A. KELLY, THE MAN

His Education

George Kelly was born on 28 April 1905 on a farm near Perth, Kansas, to Theodore Vincent Kelly and Elfleda Merriam Kelly. He died on 6 March 1967, when he was Professor of Behavioral Science at Brandeis University, Boston, USA. His father was a Presbyterian Minister who gave up his ministry to take up 'hard scrabble' farming in a time and place that imposed both poverty and rural isolation on the hard-working family. Kelly says of his mother that she was the daughter of a Nova Scotian captain of a sailing ship who was driven off the North Atlantic Trade routes by the arrival of steamships. He had then gone into the Caribbean trade, making his headquarters in Barbados where his mother had been born. It is interesting that the 'spirit of adventure' symbolized by this maternal grandfather, seems to have seeped into the spirit of Kelly's later psychological theorizing.

Kelly also tells how his father set off in 1909 in a covered wagon to take up a claim in eastern Colorado, becoming one of the last homesteaders on the American frontier. But there was little water there to grow crops or raise livestock, so they returned to the Kansas farm in 1913 after four hard years of struggle. During that time Kelly did not attend any school and was educated by his parents. In fact, as far as one can tell, George Kelly's formal education was virtually nil during the first dozen years of his life. The first substantial period of formal education he had was from late 1918 to 1921 in Wichita. At 16 he then went to the Friends' University academy in Wichita where he took college and academy courses. He often told people that he had never graduated from high school—something that clearly pleased him. He then completed his baccalaureate studies in 1926, majoring in physics and mathematics. It is at Friends' University that we find the first evidence of George Kelly the thinker, the writer, a person with social concerns. He was awarded first place in the Peace Oratorical Contest held at the University in 1924 for *The Sincere Motive*—on the subject of war (Kelly, 1924).

Kelly gave up the idea of a career in engineering to study for a masters degree in educational sociology at the University of Kansas. In 1927, with his masters thesis not completed, he went to Minneapolis and supported himself by teaching various classes for labour organizers, the American Bankers Association, and prospective American citizens. He then enrolled at the University of Minnesota in sociology and biometrics, but soon had to leave because it was discovered that he could not pay the fees. In the winter of 1927, he found a job teaching psychology and speech at Sheldon Junior College in Iowa. There he also coached drama, laying the groundwork for his novel use of enactment in psychotherapy, and there met his future wife, Gladys Thompson.

Kelly's moves around academe were not yet finished. He received an exchange fellowship to go to Edinburgh University in Scotland to study for a Bachelor of Education Degree, which he completed in 1930. There was one last task—to get a doctorate degree—which he finally accomplished at the University of Iowa under Carl Seashore in the Department of Psychology. His PhD, on the common factors in reading and speech disabilities, was awarded in 1931. In that year he married Gladys Thompson and began seeking his first real position. America was in the midst of the Great Depression, which was decimating the economy, making it hardly an auspicious moment to launch a promising career.

His Professional Years

After what can only be described as an unusual educational history, George Kelly's first employment was in 1931 at the Fort Hays Kansas State College, where he served for 12 years. Faced with a sea of human suffering aggravated by bank fore-closures and economic hardship, Kelly found little use for the physiological psy-chology that had initially fascinated him, and soon turned his attention to what he saw as being needed—the psychological evaluation of school-aged children and adults. It was here he started to make his distinctive contribution to psychology. He was instrumental in setting up a pioneering travelling clinic that toured western Kansas and offered a psychological diagnostic and remedial service to children of that area. It was staffed solely by George Kelly and his undergraduate and post-graduate students, eventually being funded directly by the financially strapped state legislature (Neimeyer & Jackson, 1997).

While at Fort Hays Kelly started to develop his thinking about psychological change, leading eventually to the psychology of personal constructs, his philosophy of constructive alternativism, and the basics of fixed role therapy (see Chapter 23, pp. 237–245). Informing all of these developments was the view that persons have created themselves and therefore can re-create themselves if they have the courage and imagination to do so. Finding himself largely alone in his efforts to help trou-bled students, he turned to Freud's ideas for inspiration. Although Kelly developed a respect for Freud's bold attempt to 'listen to the language of distress', he ultimately rejected the idea that offering correct therapist 'interpretations' of client experi-ences was the key to change. Instead, he began to realize that it was what the *clients* did with his interpretations that really mattered, and the only criterion for a useful therapist-offered conceptualization was that it should be relevant to the client's problem and carry novel implications for a possible solution (Kelly, 1969l).

It was early on in his time at Fort Hays that Kelly wrote his textbook *Under-standable Psychology* (unpublished and dated 1932). There is also a draft manu-script of a book with W.G. Warnock entitled *Inductive Trigonometry* (1935). Both his interests in comprehensive theorizing and mathematics are to be found in the unique structure of *The Psychology of Personal Constructs*.

In the late 1930s Kelly was put in charge of a flight-training programme at Fort Hays College and in 1943 was commissioned in the US Naval Reserve, where he conducted research on instrument panel design and other problems of applied and clinical psychology. Shortly after the end of World War II, Kelly was appointed Pro-fessor and Director of Clinical Psychology at Ohio State University. During his nine-teen years there he formalized his theory of personal constructs and its assessment tool, the repertory grid. Apart from his two massive volumes, he published little, but played a leading role in defining the emerging field of clinical psychology through leadership positions in the American Psychological Association. Kelly also extended his influence internationally, speaking at a number of universities around the world, and cultivating enduring contacts with such young European psychologists as Don

Bannister in the UK and Han Bonarius in the Netherlands. In 1965, the American Psychological Association bestowed on him its Award for Distinguished Contribution to the Science and Profession of Clinical Psychology.

Kelly left Ohio State University in 1965 to take up the Riklis Chair of Behavioral Science at Brandeis University, Boston, at the invitation of Abraham Maslow, the prominent humanistic psychologist.

He was a remarkable man. Not only did he become a distinguished academic in spite of a very unpromising education, but he also influenced the nature of psychology itself in ways we shall describe later. But first we offer a few words about the nature of this author of an unorthodox, grand vision of how each individual person gives personal meaning to life, others, and the world in general.

The Man Himself

To take a look at Kelly the man we can use an essential feature of his own theory—its reflexivity. Personal construct theory emphasizes that, in all our interactions, the same explanatory framework is equally applicable to both parties—to scientist and subject, therapist and client, husband and wife, and parent and child. Kelly did not emphasize this important feather in his theoretical cap in his 'Brief introduction' (see Chapter 1), but it is mentioned by many authors in this volume, especially in the following chapter by Don Bannister (pp. 33–39). To try to find out something about the author of personal construct theory, we can be reflexive and look at him through the eyes of his own theory.

It is clear that Kelly viewed his work with some ambivalence. On the one hand, Al Landfield, a student of Kelly, claimed, 'I knew beyond a shadow of a doubt that Kelly's hopes for the theory went way beyond ordinary ambition. His hopes went beyond himself, I believe' (Fransella, 1995). On the other hand, Kelly (1966b) said that only one of the five books he had written had been published and that might have been a mistake. This radical shifting of views can be related to the theoretical bipolarity of all construing. As he says in Chapter 1 of this volume, all construing is bipolar—all personal constructs have opposites. It was as if Kelly felt the pull of those opposites in his own life, to the point of both boldly announcing and then questioning his own life work.

One major pull for Kelly was his great breadth of vision coupled with his equally great attention to detail. One can relate that also to the theory's *Creativity Cycle*. To create new ideas and new ways of relating to the world one cultivates a loose, wide-ranging view of events until a thought or feeling emerges that enables one to tighten, focus down upon that thought or feeling to see whether it really is a good idea or not. Kelly's own tendency to shift from breadth of vision to attention to detail gave many problems to those who knew him—particularly his students. Al Landfield claimed:

> Kelly was a revolutionary in the guise of a very formal man. No students would be called by their first name until they had been awarded their doctorate. He was bound by many such rules. Then the revolutionary would take over and he would become the warm, excited, involved, creator of ideas. (Fransella, 1995)

Could it be that this ability or tendency to shift from the tight to the loose construer in any way was related to his possibly conflicting religious experiences? He received his early life and education largely from his Presbyterian Minister father and lived for some time in the Bible-belt of America. He then was exposed to the much looser religious culture in his adolescence and early adult life at a Quaker College and then at a Quaker university.

GEORGE KELLY: INFLUENCES ON HIS THEORY AND PHILOSOPHY

Influences from Psychology

Many of the influences on Kelly's thinking are discussed in other chapters in this book. The obvious negative influences he saw at the time he developed his theory were behaviourism and the psychodynamic approaches, although the former seemed to be especially objectionable to him. He saw both of these as denying us any right to make decisions and be in charge of our own lives. The behaviourism of Kelly's day made the person a passive respondent to environmental events—in Bannister's (1966b) ironic words, 'a ping pong ball with a memory'. On the other hand, early psychodynamic theorists made the person a passive respondent to internal unconscious forces. For Kelly, we are forms of motion and we propel ourselves—no one or no thing does it 'to' us. Thus, Kelly seemed to be invested in being the 'loyal opposition' to the dominant psychologies of his day, challenging them while maintaining a commitment to developing a more humane alternative.

Influences from Philosophy

In contrast to Kelly's rejection of most of established psychology, he drew more eagerly on cutting edge developments in the philosophy of his day. He frequently cited the pragmatist and religious thinker John Dewey as one of the main philosophers to influence him, a connection Bill Warren analyses in Chapter 39 (pp. 387–394). Trevor Butt considers how Kelly's thinking may also have been influenced to some degree by phenomenology in Chapter 38 (pp. 379–386). Beyond these two sources of philosophic inspiration, it is clear that Kelly drew on the linguistic philosophy of Alfred Korzybski in his ideas that 'constructs' are interpretations that say at least as much about their human users as they do about the 'realities' they purport to describe. Likewise, Kelly acknowledged the influence of Hans Vaihinger's philosophy of 'as if' in his formulation of constructive alternativism, and the psychodrama of Jakob Moreno in shaping the make-believe, role-playing strategies that occupied an important place in personal construct therapy. Thus, although he was highly original, Kelly was situated within a broader set of intellectual developments in the early twentieth century, importing and systematizing these themes in the construction of a unique approach to psychology (Neimeyer & Stewart, 2000).

Influences from Physics and Mathematics

It has been suggested that Kelly's degree in physics and mathematics may have played a major role in the development of his theory and his method of measurement—the repertory grid (Fransella, 1983, 2000). Most strikingly, Kelly asked us to look at individuals 'as if' each of us were a scientist, each having a theory about what is currently happening to us, each making a prediction based on that theory and then each testing out that prediction by behaving. That is the basis of construing, and, in that model, behaviour becomes the experiment rather than an end result. Personal construct theory takes the quantum mechanics view that none of us has neutral access to reality. Einstein's relativity theory, among other things, sees the world as an undivided whole in which all parts merge into one another. Kelly says: 'The universe . . . is integral. By that we mean it functions as a single unit with all its imaginable parts having an exact relationship to each other' (1955/1991, p. 7/Vol. 1, p. 5). Al Landfield tells how a physicist commented at one of his personal construct seminars that 'Kelly's theory can be seen as a good theory of physics' (Fransella, 1995).

As to mathematics, there is a branch called *mathematical constructivism*. These minority party mathematicians stand against the majority who take the *Platonic* stance which says that mathematical statements are there to be discovered, having an independent reality apart from the human mind. Mathematical constructivists on the other hand argue, along with Kelly (1954), that such 'ideas are not discovered, they are invented'. In addition to this general philosophic compatibility with developments in mathematical theory, Kelly commonly drew on his love of mathematical concepts and methods to conjure and measure some of the complexity of psychological space. He is reported by Hinkle as saying: 'Johann Herbart's work on education and particularly mathematical psychology influenced me. I think mathematics is the pure instance of construct functioning—the model of human behaviour' (1970, p. 91).

Other Influences

Because of its great scope and richness, personal construct psychology can be viewed as situated in a vast web of reciprocal influences with other important developments in twentieth-century thought, and indeed, with broader traditions of human understanding that span millennia. For example, Mair (1985) has argued persuasively that Kelly's theory represents a counterpoint to the religious ideology of his conservative Christian parents, in which he emphasizes the human potential to live boldly and unconventionally, by audacious experimentation rather than blind faith in authority (see also Chapter 39 on personal construct theory and religion, pp. 387–394). Could that counterpoint be related to his later exposure to the Quaker religion during the latter part of his education? Existential themes of choice and agency clearly pervade the theory, as well as an ethic of advocating construing the outlooks of others as a precondition for meaningful role relationships on personal or cultural levels (see also Chapter 14, pp. 153–161). Deeper currents in Euro-American thought no doubt also shaped Kelly's thinking, such as his evident belief in human progress, and his fundamental individualism. But in a sense, Kelly's genius resided in the way he integrated these many streams of thought into a comprehensive, coherent, practical, and generative theory, one that is still being actively elaborated by psychologists and social theorists around the world. It is this final topic, the reception of Kelly's theory, to which we now turn.

DEVELOPMENT OF PERSONAL CONSTRUCT THEORY SINCE 1955

A consideration of the development of personal construct theory as a field since 1955 could yield a book in itself—indeed, it has done just that. Neimeyer (1985c) has drawn on models and methods devised in the sociology of science to depict the theory's social and intellectual emergence from the 'normal science' of its day. It first represented a radical departure in psychological theory, then moved through the evolution of small 'clusters' and larger 'networks' of like-minded researchers, to become the established and diversified 'specialty' that it is today. At each stage of its development, the theory has encountered important challenges, such as the premature death of its founder, the need to develop international cohesiveness in the pre-internet era, the establishment of training centres inside and outside academia, and the creation of respected publication outlets for the work of group members. That such challenges were met successfully is evident in the range and vitality of chapters that make up this volume.

Here, however, we would like to focus on four particular issues: the abstract, 'value free', orientation of the theory; the ambivalent relationship between personal construct theory and cognitive perspectives; the difficulty grasping the developmental implications of the theory; and the distinctive nature of its major methodologies.

FOUR ISSUES ARISING FROM PERSONAL CONSTRUCT THEORY

Its 'Value Free' Orientation

One of the remarkable features of personal construct theory—and one that no doubt contributes to the flexibility with which it has been applied to people and problems of all sorts—is its abstract, content-free orientation. Unlike many psychological theorists, Kelly did not propose a detailed list of human needs, motives, conflicts or ideals that presumably hold for all people, but instead focused on the general *processes* by which people made sense of, and navigated, the social world. This abstractness makes personal construct theory about as 'value free' as a theory of personality could aspire to be, and helps the clinician, psychological scientist and general observer of human events to 'step inside' the outlooks of those persons they seek to understand. Kelly enshrined a respect for individual and cultural differences in his basic theory, and advocated a *credulous*, rather than critical approach as the more enlightened way to either study human beings or attempt to promote their development across a range of settings. As Kelly (1955/1991, p. 608/Vol. 2, p. 37) noted:

> In the broadest sense we are restating here the philosophy of constructive alter-nativism. In a narrower sense we are describing the value system of the clinician [or psychologist more generally] as a kind of liberalism without paternalism. The clinician is not only tolerant of varying points of view . . . , but he is [also] willing to devote himself to the defence and facilitation of widely differing patterns of life. Diversity and multiple experimentation are to be encouraged.

Thus, decades before respect for diversity became the watchword in psychology and related disciplines, Kelly strove to draft a genuinely respectful psychology in which the active appreciation of alternative perspectives and ways of life was at the core.

Still, some have argued that personal construct theory is not truly value free; even celebrating and exploring diversity is, after all, a value. Clearly, Kelly did have his values, which he enshrined in his theory: risk-taking, adventure, creativity, and an unwillingness to settle for conventional answers to life's probing questions (Mair, 1985; Walker, 1992). In fact, it would not be too much to say that personal construct theory and like-minded constructivist perspectives even carry with them an ethical mandate, to 'try on for size' the initially alien or threatening perspectives of others, according them the same level of potential validity as one's own (Neimeyer, 2002b). Ultimately, then, personal construct theory enjoins us to deal with the question of values by both recognizing the values implicit in our own core constructs, and attempting, insofar as possible, to accord equal legitimacy to the value perspectives of those persons we seek to comprehend.

Personal Construct Theory and Cognition

One prominent psychologist who hailed George Kelly as the creator of the theoretical model of cognitive or thought processes was one of his students, Walter Mischel. In a personal tribute to Kelly, Mischel (1980, p. 85) said:

> That George Kelly was a very deep, original, refreshing voice was always evident to all who knew him well. What has surprised me was not the brilliance with which he first spoke but the accuracy with which he anticipated the directions into which psychology would move two decades later.

A little later, Mischel (1980, p. 86) continues: 'Long before "cognitive psychology" existed, Kelly created a truly cognitive theory of personality, a theory in which how people construe is at the core.'

Although Mischel's tribute appropriately acknowledges the role of Kelly's thinking in foreshadowing the enthusiasm for cognitive science and cognitive therapy that was so apparent in the second half of the twentieth century, many contemporary personal construct theorists take exception to their theory being closely aligned with cognitive perspectives. Certainly, Kelly took great pains to emphasize that his theory was at least as concerned with human passion and action as with thought, and at a fundamental level, he attempted to integrate all of these features of human functioning in his definition of the construct. In Chapter 6 (pp. 61–74), entitled 'The logic of passion', Don Bannister discusses the thought–feeling dichotomy.

The common tendency to assimilate personal construct theory into a cognitive framework ignores much in the theory—such as its novel treatment of emotions as signals of a sometimes threatening transition in our construing. In turn that reflects the priority of an ingrained cultural construct that contrasts thinking with feeling, as well as the role of historical accidents, such as the publication of the first three chapters of Kelly's basic theory as a convenient and widely read paperback, while the 'emotional' and 'action-oriented' parts of the theory were relegated to Kelly's two-volume *magnum opus* encountered by relatively few readers. The resulting selective reading of the theory has given it more of a cognitive cast than it deserves, with many of its radical implications for understanding human behaviour remaining to be developed. Gabriele Chiari and Maria Laura Nuzzo discuss the philosophical differences between cognitive and personal construct psychologies in Chapter 4 (pp. 41–49).

Levels of Awareness

One aspect of Kelly's theory that has not been emphasized, and which he recognizes in the penultimate paragraph of his 'Brief introduction' in the previous chapter, is that his theory includes 'fresh interpretations of "the unconscious", depression, and aggression'. Freud argued that some psychological energy had to be present to explain why people did what they did. He called it 'psychic energy'. Kelly said there is no need to create an energy system for human beings similar to that in physics. Human beings are not inert substances that need energy to move them. They are living matter and one crucial property of living matter is that it moves.

Having that as his starting point, he then agreed with Freud that much of human construing takes place outside of consciousness. Instead of 'the unconscious' as the reservoir of psychic energy, he suggested the notion that there are *levels of awareness* with 'conscious' construing being at the highest level of awareness. At the lowest level is 'preverbal' construing. That consists of discriminations a baby and young child create to make sense of their experiences but they have no verbal labels attached to them. These preverbal constructs can account for much of our seemingly irrational reactions to events. As we develop over the years, we find verbal labels to attach to many of them and so are able to look at them in the cold light of day to see if they are still useful ways of looking at events. Much of counselling and psychotherapy is concerned with exactly that—finding verbal labels to attach to our preverbal construings. Thus, those who call personal construct theory a traditional 'cognitive' theory—meaning that it deals with only verbally or intellectually accessible thought processes—are taking no account of the majority of what Kelly calls construing. It is interesting to note that in this respect Kelly foreshadowed more contemporary cognitive theories, which now routinely recognize the limits of consciousness in grasping the 'metacognitive' basis of much of human functioning. Clearly, people 'know' much more than they can tell, in the sense that some of the bases on which we construe events in our lives can only be inferred, rather than directly reported. Much more will be said about the role of non-verbal construing, particularly relating to core parts of our systems of meaning, in the chapters that follow.

Human Development

A recurrent complaint is that Kelly did not talk about development—that is, from birth to adulthood. It has been argued (Fransella, 1995) that the omission was deliberate, in the sense that the whole theory of personal constructs is about development—human beings are seen as forms of motion, no matter what our age. There is a second reason for the omission. The theory rejects all attempts to put people into categories or boxes. It follows that Kelly was sceptical of the prescriptive age-and-stage models that characterized the developmental theories of his day, even those of theorists like Piaget who shared some of his constructivist leanings.

A close inspection of Kelly's work shows that he was hardly lacking in experience with children. He spent several years at Fort Hays working extensively with children, and used frequent examples of children to illustrate theoretical issues in his two volumes. Instead, Kelly, like Werner and more recent developmental theorists, preferred to view human 'becoming' as a highly individualized process of psychological development, in which both children and adults constantly extend, revise and reorganize the system of meaning/emotion/action schemes that they construct (Mascolo et al., 1997). However, his rather abstract approach to developmental issues could have contributed to the relative neglect of this aspect of his theory, leaving its application to the world of childhood in need of further development. What we do know about the psychological development of children can be seen in the chapters of Jack Adams-Webber on research (Chapter 5, pp. 51–58), Jim Mancuso on how children develop psychologically and in particular their sense of self (Chapter 27, pp. 275–282) and Tom Ravenette on working with children and teachers when children are seen as having problems (Chapter 28, pp. 283–294).

Scientific Research

Kelly's influence here is profound. Although it is not claimed that he, alone, started the change in research methods, it can certainly be claimed that his thinking has played a part. He suggested that his philosophy of *constructive alternativism* was an approach to science that was an alternative to the scientific method favoured by psychology, for which he coined the term *accumulative fragmentalism*. Details of the differences are given in Chapter 4 (pp. 41–49).

Qualitative as Well as Quantitative Methods

Kelly's repertory grid technique represented a creative and flexible set of methods—much expanded by subsequent construct theorists—that allow qualitative data to be quantified. As described specifically by Richard Bell in Chapter 9 (pp. 95–103), the grid technique addresses a central goal in personal construct theory, namely, bringing to light the distinctive ways that individual human beings or groups organize and interpret some aspect of their experience. Kelly's unique contribution was to show how these data can be given arithmetical equivalents by placing them within a repertory grid matrix consisting of rows of personal constructs and columns of items to be construed by those constructs. Although grid methods have proved useful in even rather informal paper and pencil forms, countless researchers and practitioners have made use of the burgeoning number of sophisticated computer programs for eliciting, analysing and interpreting grid data.

Less widely recognized, but equally novel, were Kelly's contributions to qualitative assessment of personal construct systems. Indeed, methods like self-characterization, in which a person is invited to write a free-form description of him- or herself from a sympathetic third-person perspective, anticipated the present surge of interest in narrative concepts and methods in psychology. Kelly's characteristically detailed recommendations for analysing and using such material in psychotherapy are congruent with the current expansion of hermeneutic, constructivist and interpretive methods in the social sciences, recognizing the contribution of both words and numbers to psychology as a human science (see Chapters 12 (pp. 133–139) and 38 (pp. 379–386)). Many different ways of eliciting and making sense of personal constructs have been created since 1955. Some of these are described in Chapters 10 (pp. 105–121) and 11 (pp. 123–131). Greg Neimeyer also gives a useful account of many such measures (1993).

CODA

We have tried to provide some historical context for the chapters that follow, both in terms of Kelly's distinctive biography, and in terms of the subsequent development of his theory. Doing so is in keeping with Kelly's emphasis on reflexivity, which places the theorist firmly within the purview of his theory, as well as his focus on anticipation, on how construct systems evolve as they stretch to embrace the future. Personal construct theory has clearly evolved since its origins in Kelly's work, while nonetheless retaining its distinctive core commitments. As such, the theory represents not only a reflexive distillation of the themes of Kelly's life, but also a highly original anticipation of its extensions over the half-century that followed.

The next chapter, by Don Bannister, focuses on the profound differences between Kelly's ideas and those underlying behaviourism—the dominant psychology when Kelly created his theoretical perspective. In particular, he focuses on the central feature underpinning personal construct theory—that of reflexivity.

CHAPTER 3

Kelly Versus
Clockwork Psychology*

Don Bannister

> . . . if people find it of personal use, particularly if they find it extends their picture
> of their own possibilities, then that is the best test of personal construct theory,
> the most significant credit it could have.

George Kelly was fond of asserting that he had never met a psychologist who had just one theory about the nature of man. He argued that psychologists always had two. They had first a theory that describes how scientists have theories from which they derive hypotheses, which they subject to experimental tests and, in terms of careful observation of outcome, they reformulate or modify the theories, generate more hypotheses, subject them to experimental test, and so the cycle goes. Granted, that is a description of scientific methods, but it is also a description of human behaviour. Psychologists then have a second theory which (while the first one accounts for the behaviour of scientists and psychologists) accounts for the behaviour of all the rest of us who are not scientists or psychologists. This second theory may be of any kind; it may be about how you are swimming around in the ghastly swamps of your *id* or how you are bouncing from stimulus to response like a maniacal table tennis ball, or whatever. What is clear is that creatures of this second kind are highly underprivileged compared to creatures of the first kind.

Kelly went on to argue that it was uneconomical and discriminatory to have two theories. That leaves us with two ways of unifying our view of humankind.

Firstly, we could take in all the scientists and psychologists under one of the second theories and explain their behaviour accordingly. So, for instance, if I were appearing as a Freudian, I would have to explain that, tonight, I am not rationally presenting a theory, but simply sublimating my sex instinct, or if I were a learning theorist I might explain that I was suffering from a build-up of reactive inhibition, and so on and so forth. The other possibility is to take the first theory, the one about

---

*Unpublished talk for the Centre for Personal Construct Psychology in 1982.

International Handbook of Personal Construct Psychology. Edited by F. Fransella.

the theorizing experimenting scientist, and apply that to everybody, which is precisely what George Kelly did.

MAN THE SCIENTIST

So he came up with his model of 'man the scientist'. Obviously, in saying that all men and women are scientists he did not mean that all men and women wear white coats, have PhDs or are interminably dull in their discourse. He meant that we all have theories, sometimes confused or contradictory perhaps, but theories about our own nature, the nature of other people, the nature of the universe. If you are not in the Science Club, it will not be dignified by calling it your 'theory'. It will be variously referred to as your central nervous system, or your personality, your reinforcement history or your attitudes or whatever, but nevertheless, they are your philosophical metatheories. Because you have a theory you will derive hypotheses from it. Again, if you are not in the Science Club, these are not termed hypotheses, they are designated your expectations, your anticipations, habitual set or what have you. You will act on the basis of your hypotheses/expectations. That is to say, you will test them out. You will experiment, but again, seen as the object of scientific study rather than as a scientist in your own right, you will be said to be 'behaving'. Your experiments/behaviour will cast various lights on your hypotheses/expectations—sometimes you will be right, sometimes you will be wrong and sometimes you will find the outcome of your ventures totally irrelevant to the terms in which you frame them. Then you will modify, change, reformulate your theory/notions of what you are like, and what other people are like, and what the world is like.

So for Kelly the central question for psychology becomes how do people develop, share, and use their personal theories? Perhaps the most direct way of interrogating George Kelly's argument is to consider precisely what he meant by the term *personal construct system*.

He used the word *personal* in a very particular sense. He was using it to refer to the fact that there is a sense in which each of us lives in a unique world. Our worlds are different, not simply because we have experienced or are experiencing different events but because we interpret differently the events we do experience. What one person thinks is important another thinks is trivial; what one feels is exciting another feels is dull; ugly to one is beautiful to another. This central idea offers its own explanation for the mysterious but everyday fact that people respond to the same situation in very different ways. Joan and Jane are introduced to Peter, and Joan says 'Yummy' and Jane says 'Ugh'; Peter and Paul are in the same job and one thinks it's marvellous and the other thinks it's hell on wheels. Clearly there is no mystery if we accept that these people are not in the *same* situation. The situation is only the same seen from the point of view of some third person who is looking at it from the outside. Within the situation the two people are looking through their goggles, their personal construct systems, their philosophy, their viewpoint and seeing it personally and thereby differently.

Secondly, we have to consider Kelly's central construct, that of a *construct*. Kelly was irritatingly generous about definition and at different times defined a construct as 'a way of avoiding the obvious', or 'a way in which two things are alike and thereby different from a third', or a construct as a 'bipolar discrimination'. But we can recognize constructs in terms of these definitions more easily because we have labels for many of them: north–south, cheap–expensive, coming–going, lost–found, hopeless–hopeful, plus–minus and so on. There is the danger inherent in having so many labels for our constructs that we may come to see the construct as the same as the label and forget that the construct is the discrimination itself, not the label attached to the discrimination. Nor must we forget that there are many constructs for which we have no labels. We can spend hours listening to music and in a reasonable sense be said to be construing the music but not necessarily labelling it at all, words may have very little to do with it. Constructs may be preverbal in the sense of being discriminations developed before the infant had access to a language or non-verbal in the sense of having been elaborated without labelling.

Thirdly, Kelly referred to a personal construct *system*. Here Kelly is arguing that our constructs are ordered, arranged and linked; they are not lying about like dominoes in a bucket. There is something paradoxical about trying to prove by argument that constructs are linked, since argument itself is a process of demonstrating linkages for particular constructs. A dictionary is a catalogue of the modal links between constructs.

Thus Kelly presented this picture of each individual as unique. He was not thereby saying that we are enclosed individuals. We trade our construct systems, we communicate them, we dispute with them, we build them into bibles, novels, philosophies and scientific theories, we interact with one another in terms of them. Thereby our construct systems have a great deal in common, but at no point is it likely that your construct system is a carbon copy of anyone else's.

REFLEXIVITY

If we refer to Kelly's original assertion that all persons are scientists then (as he presented the argument) reverse logic is permissible and we can argue that all scientists are persons. This points to the reflexive quality of personal construct theory and I think it is the theory's reflexivity which distinguishes it most sharply from traditional psychological viewpoints. Interestingly, it is the feature of construct theory which has received the least attention, perhaps because the very idea of reflexivity is an embarrassment in conventional psychological discourse. Reflexivity demands that a theory account for its own construction. Psychologizing in all its forms, inventing personal construct theory or proposing any other psychological theory is a human act, a piece of human behaviour.

Therefore, if you are going to account for human behaviour you can reasonably expect it to account for that as well. In fact there is a long history of psychology not only ignoring this issue of reflexivity but producing bizarre paradoxes by ignoring it. In the 1970s, Milgram built himself a considerable and in some ways a deserved reputation for a series of very adventurous experiments on the subject of what he referred to as 'obedience to authority'. The design of his experiment was basically simple. He hired people, ordinary men and women, and told them that they were being asked to assist in a scientific experiment. These experiments concerned various things, but they hinged around the question of the effect of pain on human performance of various kinds. The setup was such that the innocent person participated believing that he or she was part of a scientific experiment assisting the main experimenter, Milgram. He or she was given control of an electrical apparatus which was wired up to the subject who was trying to do something like mental arithmetic and by pulling a lever he or she could administer more and more painful electric shocks. Milgram was interested in how much pain people would administer when instructed to do so under various conditions, and sadly found that they would administer a great deal. When these innocents began to administer 'pain' the subjects (actually Milgram's assistants) enacted pain, they screamed, pleaded, begged, wept, thrashed about on the floor, in order to see how long the innocent—the ordinary man or woman—would continue increasing the pain. The reaction to these experiments was intriguing. Many psychologists challenged Milgram on moral grounds. Though Milgram did debrief his subjects at the end of the experiment and explained to them that they hadn't actually administered any pain, that is probably not much comfort if it has been proved to you that you in fact seriously torment human beings, including taking the needle past the dangerous mark on the dial. To force such a conclusion on a person is hardly a kindly act. Milgram's defence was that he was doing it in the name of science and that this was the moral basis on which he stood. What does not seem to have been widely commented on is that this was precisely the basis on which his subjects were administering pain, the moral basis on which they stood. They thought they were assisting in a scientific experiment designed to increase our knowledge of humankind.

Reflexively, Milgram was proving his own point by the very act of carrying out the experiment and proving it far more effectively than did the data that he was assembling. But he does not seem to have been very clearly aware that he was envisaging two species—people and psychologists—with psychologizing being strictly limited in its area of application to 'people'.

Another tale of reflexivity concerns a Skinnerian token economy programme that was launched in a west coast American psychiatric hospital. It was the conventional type of behaviour modification programme in which the nurses had plastic tokens which they issued to any patient who was doing 'good things'.

Good things would be buttoning up your flies, turning up for meals on time, talking to other patients, or whatever. These tokens could be exchanged for goodies such as cigarettes, parole, and so forth. Tokens were not issued to patients who did not do 'good things'. The programme administrators were puzzled because none of the patients seemed to respond to the programme or be very worried about earning tokens. There was one exception, a keen patient who earned himself a great many tokens, but he was isolated; the general run of patients did not seem to care.

The programme administrators were puzzled because, whatever the long-term effects of such programmes, they do tend to have noticeable short-term effects. A commission of inquiry set to work to investigate the failure of the programme and discovered that the one patient who had earned all the tokens was an interesting man with a strong entrepreneurial instinct. He had his own private contract with his fellow patients, whereby when any of them smashed a window or took the teeth out of a ward orderly he generously rewarded them with tokens. The two token economy programmes nicely cancelled each other out. Incidentally, I once told this story to B.F. Skinner and it failed to enthuse him, even though I pointed out that it showed how widespread his ideas were becoming. However, it does raise a very intriguing point, which again I think is central to the issue of reflexivity. If a psychological theory is tested—that is, we try to find out if it will explain, predict and control human behaviour—then will the theory predict, control and explain the behaviour of someone who knows the theory as well as the theoretician, or even someone who has a better theory? This is an interesting puzzle for psychologists that seems to have no immediate parallel in the natural sciences. The biologist studying earthworms may well be able to lean heavily on the assumption that the earthworm is neither greatly interested in nor very skilled at critically reconceptualizing the theories of the biologist, but all human beings are in the psychologizing business. People are in a very real sense the equal of psychologists and the psychologist's possession of degrees, institutional backing and a socially approved position can in no way extract him or her from interdependent interaction with people—the psychologist–subject distinction is a social convention, which is to say that it is a scientific myth.

Reflexivity, then, is a bedrock assumption of personal construct theory. If you try to use the language, terms and assertions of construct theory you must accept that they are as applicable to you as they are to your subjects, your patients, and the world in general. If I as a psychotherapist am going to talk about the hostility of my client, or my client's failure to develop his superordinate construction, then it is also true that I must recognize the possibility of my own hostility towards the patient, of my own failure to develop my own superordinate construction, and so on. There are not two languages, two psychologies, one for them and one for me; there is one psychology for all of us.

The explanation may be that what you, as a therapist, are seeing as moving from bad to good, the client is experiencing as moving from the known to the unknown, or moving from some kind of structure and clarity to some kind of chaos. Again I think that the virtues of this kind of definition lie in its reference to experience. It is part of Kelly's central effort to construct a psychology not simply or even primarily of behaviour, but a psychology of experience.

FIXED ROLE THERAPY

This involves writing a new self-characterization based on one already provided by the client (described in Chapter 11, pp. 123–131). These are always written in the third person, beginning perhaps 'Joe Bloggs is . . .' and it is to be written as if by a sympathetic friend. Confronted with this self-character sketch, the therapist then writes a fixed role sketch—a character portrait—of an imaginary person. If the fixed role sketch is of Harry Hawkes, then Joe Bloggs becomes Harry Hawkes for a set period—say, three weeks. What might be gained by such a venture? To begin with he may find that people behave slightly differently towards him in his secret enactment of the fixed role, so that he acquires new evidence as to the possible responses and relationships of people around him.

I want to argue that fixed role therapy is worth a very detailed examination not simply because it is a useful tool in therapy but because it embodies within itself the moral argument of personal construct theory. This argument can be presented in the form of a question. Is it possible that your personality is an invention? Is it possible that laboriously through your life, step by step, you have been building a personality? Is it possible that you did not inherit your personality from your parents, that it is not fixed in you genetically or constitutionally or simply taught to you by your environment? The experience of playing an invented personality has these subterranean questions within it. Clearly the answer to these questions signifies much. If you reach the conclusion that what you are is to a significant extent your own invention, then this opens up the possibilities of reinvention and this is central to the personal construct theory argument about the possibilities of change—the possibilities of what Kelly refers to as elaboration.

CURIOUSER AND CURIOUSER

As a final way of distinguishing between Kelly's work and what I have referred to in my title as clockwork psychology, I want to refer to a traditional theme in orthodox psychology, a theme embodied in the notion of instinct or drive. My student days date back far enough to have contained quite solemn lectures on McDougall's fourteen instincts and since then the theme has continued even though fashion has dictated that it be talked about in terms of drives or needs or arousal level or what have you. Typical of the kind of classical arguments along these lines were experiments which accounted for animal (and by implication human) behaviour, in terms of, say, maternal drive, thirst drive, hunger drive and so on. What has always intrigued me about classic experiments in this field is that whatever was left over by way of behaviour that made no sense at all in terms of set drive categories, was put down to 'curiosity'. This served as a kind of handy waste basket for dealing with any variance left over at the end of the experiment. Perhaps one way of seeing Kelly's ideas is to examine the possibilities that he took this psychological waste basket of 'curiosity' and made it the central issue. Thus the inexplicable rat who, instead of following drives, sits chewing his whiskers, pondering the situation, becomes not the animal to be thrown out of the experiment but the prototypical construer.

A related experience in my early teaching days concerned the expounding of standard theories in psychology, Freudian theory, learning theory, information theory and so on. I duly learned that there were set constructs in terms of which it was legitimate to evaluate these theories, such as: Are they testable? What is the experimental evidence in their favour? How are the concepts within them defined? I fell into the habit of adding questions based on other constructs; for example, I would ask students if they thought any particular theory was a charitable theory or an insulting theory. I found that this was a kind of show-stopping question which was invariably followed by a long silence. It seemed that psychological theories, for my students, were outside the range of convenience of the construct *charitable-insulting* and they could see no point to the question. It still seems to me that such a question can reasonably be asked, indeed it might be worth while asking many related questions. Is this or that psychological theory liberating or is it imprisoning? Does it work personally for people who use it as a window to the world? Does it open up possibilities for them or does it close down possibilities? In asking such questions my intent was not to silence students but to draw their attention to the human right which I am certain Kelly accorded to all of us. This is the right to accept or reject a theory essentially because it does or does not make sense in terms of life as you have experienced it. The very notion of personal construing suggests that you should not finally value a theory in terms of how many books have been written about it, how many professors have espoused it, how many journal papers it has given rise to, how many experiments have been conducted in terms of it, and so forth. If a psychological theory makes no sense to you—that is, there is no way you can see how it relates to life as you have experienced it, or people and relationships as you have understood them, and if none of these concepts is illuminated by the theory—then you are entitled to reject the theory.

I think these are the grounds on which Kelly would ultimately want personal construct theory to be judged. If personal construct theory, in spite of its contradiction of many of the assumptions of orthodox psychology, becomes academically influential then that is cause for rejoicing. But, more importantly, if people find it of personal use, particularly if they find that it extends their picture of their own possibilities, then that is the best test of personal construct theory and the most significant credit it could have.

CHAPTER 4

Kelly's Philosophy of Constructive Alternativism

Gabriele Chiari

Centro Studi in Psicoterapia Cognitiva, Firenze, Italy

and

Maria Laura Nuzzo

Centro di Psicologia e Psicoterapia Costruttivista, Roma, Italy

> We assume that all of our present interpretations of the universe are subject to revision or replacement.
>
> Kelly, 1955/1991, p. 15/Vol. 1, p. 11

A REVOLUTIONARY ALTERNATIVE

Many psychologists prefer to regard psychology as a science that has become once and for all separated from philosophy, its ancestral roots. Science, they think, uses the scientific method, that is, a method that allows its followers to gain access to the ultimate reality, while the speculations of philosophers have no validity as to the knowledge of reality and the verification of truth. These psychologists fail to consider that the dependence of their inquiries, and of the very scientific method they hold so dear, are based on a definite set of assumptions—usually unspoken—whose questioning and analysis are exactly the prerogative of philosophy.

Kelly was aware that philosophical speculation is inescapable for any scientific investigation. In fact, he chose to state his underlying assumptions right at the beginning, thus uncovering the philosophical roots of his theoretical position.

He did that by coining two expressions that, consistent with his theoretical formulation, are shaped like the contrasting poles of a discrimination, a construct: *accumulative fragmentalism* versus *constructive alternativism*. Without entering the arena of the debate in the specialized field of the philosophy of science, Kelly suggested a revolutionary alternative to the prevailing notions about the nature of scientific knowledge, and pursued its implications at the levels of theory construction and of

International Handbook of Personal Construct Psychology. Edited by F. Fransella.
© 2003 John Wiley & Sons, Ltd.

its clinical and psychotherapeutic application. On the other hand, his theoretical approach can be, and has been, applied to all the areas subjected to psychological inquiry. What he did in the 1950s was so much ahead of its time that his work is only now at the cutting edge of contemporary psychology and psychotherapy (Chiari & Nuzzo, 1996a).

We refer to the first chapter of this volume, 'A brief introduction to personal construct theory', for an account of these theoretical assumptions about the nature of knowledge in Kelly's own words. We would like instead to comment on the position of constructive alternativism within the context of modern philosophy and contemporary psychology.

FACTS AND THEORIES: A CONTROVERSIAL RELATIONSHIP

Personal construct psychology, as well as many contemporary psychologies, reject observation as being the foundation of any scientific inquiry. Rather, they assume that some theory inevitably steers any observation and experimentation. They share the shift from observing in order to know, to knowing (theorizing, hypothesizing) in order to observe. In more technical terms, they reject the method of so-called 'logical positivism', espoused, for instance, by a certain behaviourism. According to that: (a) science starts from a correct and unbiased observation of facts; (b) such observation forms the basis from which to derive, inductively, laws and theories; (c) laws and theories form the scientific knowledge. That whole process describes exactly what Kelly called 'accumulative fragmentalism', the notion that knowledge derives from the accumulation of fragmented facts. On the contrary, in the modern debate on the nature of knowledge, the idea that all facts are theory-laden is increasingly widely held, thanks in particular to Popper's (1959) and Kuhn's (1962) criticisms of that inductive view. There has been a swing away from induction towards deduction, which gives priority to theories over facts. This is in parallel with a different view of the validity of scientific statements, that is, the way of deciding whether they are true or false. The main point, as suggested by Popper, is that the hypothesis is formulated so that it can be proved as false. If it is falsifiable, then it can be subject to severe empirical tests. As long as it passes the tests, it is not legitimate to say that it is true, but only that it is the best at our disposal for the time being. If the hypothesis does not pass the test, it can be replaced by a new conjecture. Science proceeds by way of conjectures and refutations: any person, as a scientist, does the same, according to Kelly.

PERSONAL CONSTRUCTIVISM AND COGNITIVISM

The above shift from empirical verification to falsification has contributed to personal feelings being seen as legitimate areas of the scientific inquiry, thus saving psychology's ambition to be a natural science. Maybe for this reason many commentators see personal construct theory as being one of the most important contributions to a cognitive theory of personality and psychotherapy. They do this although the original formulation of the theory precedes the official birth of cognitive psychology (Neisser, 1967) by more than ten years, and by about twenty years the most significant contribution to the development of cognitive approaches to psychotherapy (Beck, 1976). Yet, Kelly repeatedly rejected the label of 'cognitive' and stated clearly that his theory was about a great deal more than just 'thinking' or 'cognitive processes'. In fact, cognitive and personal construct psychology differ from each other about the very notion of knowledge.

The philosophical assumption of personal construct theory—as well as its theoretical implications described by the fundamental postulate and the corollaries—place Kellyian work outside the mainstream cognitive universe. Rather, they allow it to be numbered within the more recent constructivist approaches and alongside the social constructionist movement. On the other hand, many cognitive psychologists make reference to psychological constructivism as a philosophical assumption that even they share. Therefore, a clarification of the meanings that the term 'constructivism' has acquired in recent years becomes necessary in order to clarify the difference.

CONSTRUCTIVISM WITHIN CONTEMPORARY HUMAN SCIENCES

Many distinctions have been drawn by scholars pointing out relevant differences under the umbrella of terms like 'psychological constructivism' or 'social constructionism'. In fact, their spreading has proceeded at the same rate as the loosening of their meaning (Chiari & Nuzzo, 1996b).

Originally, the term 'constructive' was meant to specify theories of personality centred on the notion of 'construction of structures' which human beings— actively involved in what comes about—use to transform their world. It is no accident that Rychlak's (1973) handbook of personality and psychotherapy has a chapter specifically devoted to 'Two kinds of constructive theories: Jean Piaget and George A. Kelly'. There is, in Piaget as well as in Kelly, an understanding of the organism–environment relationship as characterized by reciprocity and complementarity. It means that the two interacting members cannot be considered independently of each other: both are necessary. This implies the rejection of a naïve, realist view of knowledge and the attempt at transcending the knowledge– reality opposition and its philosophical contrasting expressions: realism and idealism. Realism holds the view that material objects exist externally to us and independently of our sense experience. Idealism holds that no such material objects or external realities exist apart from our knowledge or consciousness of them, the whole universe thus being in some sense mental. The attempt to transcend such opposition is a distinctive feature of constructivism.

All the same, in more recent years 'constructive' has been progressively equated to 'active', so that psychological constructivism was defined as 'a family of theories that share the assertion that human knowledge and experience entail the (pro)active participation of the individual' (Mahoney, 1988). Given that many psychologies share a view of human beings as intrinsically active and therefore, in some sense, constructive, the above definition is not at all helpful in making specifically clear what constructivism is and what it is not. Indeed, in Kelly's assumption of constructive alternativism there is much more than a generic dimension of activity. We shall try to show this by locating personal construct theory within the variegated panorama of contemporary psychological constructivism.

Implications for Theory and Practice

Kelly's 'personal constructivism' can be regarded as the leading member of the 'constructivist family' (Chiari, 2000). Its topicality can be better understood just with reference to constructive alternativism. What kind of knowledge (and relation between knowledge and reality) is implied by it? What are its implications for theory and practice?

Certainly, according to Kelly, knowledge is not at all a mirroring, a *reflection* of an external, fixed reality 'out there', like in the naïve realist perspectives. Nor is knowledge an *invention*, a product of mind, as in the contrasting idealist speculations. On the other hand, Kelly did not share the view of knowledge—destined to become the view of the mainstream cognitive alternative—as a symbolic *representation* of reality. Representation, according to cognitive psychologists, allows us to grasp some aspects of the real world: there is a relationship between knowledge and reality in terms of a greater or less symmetry between the representation of an object and the object itself. Rather, for Kelly representation has to be understood in terms of *interpretation*: that is the word he uses in defining constructive alternativism as well as in explaining the notion of 'construing'.

The cognitive approach cannot be regarded as actually overcoming the realism/idealism opposition. The activity attributed to the person in the process of representing reality is limited to operations of collection and processing of inputs coming from 'out there'. It is the type of constructivism that von Glasersfeld names 'trivial constructivism' as opposed to the 'radical constructivist' perspective that he sees as the foundation of Piaget's theory.

> Radical constructivism [. . .] is *radical* because it breaks with convention and develops a theory of knowledge in which knowledge does not reflect an 'objective' ontological reality, but exclusively an ordering and organization of a world constituted by our experience. (von Glasersfeld, 1984, p. 24)

The radical constructivism that von Glasersfeld recognizes in Piaget can be easily attributed to Kelly.

According to radical constructivism, knowledge is a *construction* of 'realities'. The plural (realities) implies the possibility (or better, the inevitableness) of forming as many worlds as the personal constructions chosen to give meaning to events. The construing process is a recursive one—that is, a process that operates on the product of its own operation. In fact, it is founded on an individual's previous knowledge and therefore simultaneously constrained by it: '. . . no form of knowledge, not even perceptual knowledge, constitutes a simple copy of reality, because it always includes a process of assimilation to previous structures' (Piaget, 1971, p. 4). Following this process of integration, previous structures can remain unchanged or undergo a more or less deep modification, but without discontinuity with the previous state; that is, without being destroyed, but adapting themselves to the new situation. In von Glasersfeld's (1982) rephrasing, 'the environment is no more and no less than the sum of constraints within which the organism can operate. The organism's activities and operations are successful when they are not impeded or foiled by constraints, that is, when they are *viable*' (p. 615).

It is easy to find a similar view of knowledge in personal construct theory. It is enough to mention the recursion implied by the Experience and the Modulation Corollaries. According to the former, a person's construction system varies as he or she successively construes the repetitions of events. This progressive variation, according to the Modulation Corollary, must itself take place within a system, that is, it must be construed by the person. In simpler words, any new experience can acquire a sense only in the light of preceding experiences.

Given that the radical constructivist perspective stresses the possibility of interpreting the world in many, equally legitimate ways, we have called it *epistemological constructivism* (Chiari & Nuzzo, 1996b).

PERSONAL CONSTRUCT SYSTEMS AND AUTOPOIETIC SYSTEMS

Even if radical constructivism represents a revolutionary way of looking at personal knowledge compared with the more traditional views, an even more radical attempt at transcending the realism/idealism opposition can be recognized in two other contemporary developments: Maturana and Varela's theory of autopoiesis, and the social constructionist movement. In fact, according to their followers, there is no reality at all independently from an observer, that is, a living system able to draw distinctions in language. To give up the idea of a reality 'out there' implies the giving up of the idea of representation as a cognitive mediator between subject and object. Cognition and reality emerge from interaction between the person and the environment, and an immediate experience of the world comes before any explanation and distinction, before any construction of that experience. A similar understanding of the knowledge/reality relation can be found in the speculations of phenomenological and hermeneutic philosophers such as Heidegger, Husserl, Gadamer, Merleau-Ponty, Foucault, Habermas—and Maturana and Varela, as well as the social constructionists, make frequent references to their work (see also Chapter 38, pp. 379–386). The common premise is represented in the final analysis by the rejection of both an objectivist and a subjectivist position in favour of a consideration of the subject/object interdependence, of a mutual specification between knower and known. For this reason, we have called this type of constructivism *hermeneutic constructivism* (Chiari & Nuzzo, 1996b).

The Maturana and Varela (1980, 1987) reality is a domain specified by the operations of the observer; but they arrive at this theory about the nature of reality (called 'ontology of the observer') starting from a biological conceptualization of living systems as autonomous systems, that is, systems which specify their own laws, what is proper to them. The structure of the system realizes the organization of the living—the autopoietic organization—and specifies its domains as what can interact with it. As long as a living system finds an adaptation with the environment,

environment and living system act as mutual sources of perturbation, triggering structural changes: that is, there is a *structural coupling* between them. When a human organism enters into structural coupling with other human organisms, it is possible that their interactions acquire a recurrent nature. Within that consensual domain, linguistic behaviours and human consciousness can emerge as products of sequential coordinations of actions.

Cognition is thus a phenomenon that emerges as a kind of realization of the autopoietic organization, and is a constituent part of their being. In the strict sense, living systems are cognitive systems, and to live is to know.

If the range of convenience of personal construct theory is represented by what is traditionally meant by personality and psychotherapy, Maturana and Varela's comprehensive theoretical construction can be applied to living systems ranging from the cell to social systems. But more than that, it can invite personal construct theorists to a more careful consideration of the possibility (a) of giving up the idea of the existence of an ontological reality without falling into idealism; (b) of looking at personal knowledge as constitutive of the person: in other words, a person does not *have* a construct system, but *is* a construct system or, as Kelly says, a construing process; (c) of considering personal development as occurring necessarily in social interactions: the individual and the social dimensions are inextricably intertwined. Kelly's theory is imbued with the above issues, but they have not been adequately elaborated by his followers. Furthermore, a consideration of cognition as a biologically rooted phenomenon within a strictly constructivist framework can offer another advantage: it can help to make clear the relation between events pertaining to the domains of psychology and physiology as a consequence of their being construed by means of different systems specifying different realms. In other words, it can help to make clear the relation between core constructs and maintenance processes within a personal construct system, thus allowing an extension of personal construct theory's range of convenience to the otherwise hybrid domains of psychophysiology and psychosomatics (Bannister, 1968). It also relates to Kelly's alternative fundamental postulate (see Chapter 44, pp. 447–454).

PERSONAL CONSTRUCTIVISM AND SOCIAL CONSTRUCTIONISM

The recognition of the role played by language in the discourses about the world is also at the basis of the social constructionist movement (Gergen, 1985; Gergen & Davis, 1985). Within this movement, in fact, references to the theses of von Glasersfeld, von Foerster, Maturana and Varela are commonplace, so much so that the term *constructivism* is also used in referring to it. The term *social constructionism*, however, is preferred by the authors who want to emphasize the linkage with Berger and Luckmann's (1966) seminal volume on reality as a social construction, and to stress the presumed differences between constructionist and constructivist perspectives. Essentially, the social constructionist movement emphasizes the generation of meanings by people as they collectively generate descriptions and explanations in language.

That is the reason why social constructionism represents a conceptual point of reference for the social psychologists and psychotherapists who have adopted a hermeneutic perspective (that is, who regard the person as a meaning-generating being) and make use of the notion of narration.

LANGUAGE AND CONVERSATIONS

In fact, although it is possible to trace the origins of the narrative trend in the psychoanalytic field (Schafer, 1980; Spence, 1982), its most recent developments are located within the hermeneutic constructivist (in particular, the social constructionist) psychologies and psychotherapies.

To frame the narrative approach it can be useful to make reference to Bruner's (1986, 1990) distinction between two modes of thought, two different ways of construing reality, irreducible to one another (though complementary): the paradigmatic and the narrative. Whereas the paradigmatic mode (the logical-scientific, explanatory language) is deductive, demonstrative (aimed at demonstrating a truth) and quantitative, the narrative one (the literary language) is inductive, hermeneutic (interpretative) and qualitative. This distinction resounds with the philosophical distinction suggested by Dilthey (1924) between sciences of nature and sciences of mind, in terms of a distinction between different ways of coming to a knowledge: explanation and understanding, respectively. Bruner's purpose is exactly that of reorienting the course of psychology from a paradigmatic science—a science of explaining, like it prevalently still is—to a science of meaning, of understanding, like the constructivist and constructionist perspectives see it.

Personal construct psychology can easily become part of a narrative approach, as the contributions of Mair (1988, 1989a, 1989b) have shown. Mair paraphrases in a narrative key Kelly's original formulation, and suggests a story-telling psychology as discipline of discourse rather than as natural or social science. The utilization of personal construct theory in a narrative mode presents the advantage of turning the attention to a comprehensive, molar understanding of the persons in terms of their personal stories or, better, of the stories they are, thus grasping all the richness and deepness of their structures of meaning. According to Mair (1988), 'stories can be in many forms: fiction, fantasy, allegory, poetry, travel, science and science fiction, factual, instructive, entertaining. These many modes of story are available to us' (p. 134). And, since 'we live in and through stories' (p. 127), and 'different story-worlds offer different kinds of facts' (p. 131), his is an invitation to imagination, to the creation of alternative realities, to be multiple rather than singular selves, to replace a psychology dominated by theory—allowing only a single voice—with a narrative psychology in which many voices can converse and help others to converse, that is to live (see also Chapter 24 on narrative psychotherapy, pp. 247–255).

All the above is implied by the assumption of constructive alternativism. Moreover, Kelly's instrument of self-characterization is perfectly in line with the narrative approach and a qualitative analysis of personal experience (see Chapter 11, pp. 123–131). The self-characterization precedes by decades the present bloom of content and text analyses. In a period in which psychologists were eagerly looking for 'objective' methods of assessment, Kelly invited his clients to identify themselves in personally relevant ways, at the same time inviting psychologists to follow his 'first principle': 'If you want to know what is wrong with someone, ask them: they may tell you.'

PERSONAL CONSTRUCTIVISM AND POSTMODERN PSYCHOLOGY

Qualitative analysis was born and developed within postmodern thought. The postmodern thought is characterized exactly by a trend to substitute the concept of one reality independent from the observer with that of a social construction of realities by means of language. Moreover, it promotes a criticism of the search for foundations and denies the belief in a linear progress made possible by increasing knowledge by an 'accumulation of fragmented facts'. Nowadays postmodern thought is recognizable in philosophy (Lyotard, Foucault, Derrida, Rorty), sociology (Berger and Luckmann), anthropology (Geertz), psychology (Gergen, Shotter), literature (Borges, Eco), and even in architecture and law.

In psychology, the research process consists no longer of the representation of an objective social reality, but rather implies a co-constitution of the investigated objects by means of processes of negotiation and interaction with them. This is why the predominant approaches are narrative, hermeneutic, interpretive, deconstructive; and this is why the validation of results is on the basis of criteria of plausibility, consensuality, practical utility, rather than in terms of a correspondence to reality.

In the modernist context, narratives are substantially structures of language and, when they are generated within a scientific domain, can act as vehicles of objective knowledge. In the psychotherapeutic field, the modernist approach starts from an *a priori* narration of the therapist, and the clients' narrations are destroyed or incorporated, or in any case replaced, by the therapist's formulation. In the postmodernist context, having given up the idea of an outer world to reflect, scientific narratives do not lose their importance, but their meaning changes: they turn to constitutive frames of reality, and therefore gain their significance in terms of the forms of life which they invite, rationalize, or justify. 'They are not so much reflections of life already lived as they are the progenitors of the future' (Gergen & Kaye, 1992, p. 173).

Following on from George Kelly's thinking, psychotherapy, in the postmodernist approach, is seen as a reconstruing process, as client and therapist search for a new narrative. In the assumption according to which 'there is nothing in the world which is not subject to some form of reconstruction' resides 'the hope that *constructive alternativism* holds out to every man [. . . and] the hope that a psychotherapist holds out to his client' (Kelly, 1955/1991, p. 937/Vol. 2, p. 265).

CONCLUSIONS

What represents a hope for people fixed in a disordered or simply unsatisfying perception of themselves and the world can be regarded as a reason of dejection by the scientists striving to reach the ultimate truth. But constructive alternativism does not hinder science. Rather, it makes science a constructive venture instead of an attempt to reproduce reality. It invites scientists to transcend the obvious rather than to discover what is already given. It brings science nearer to art, in a way that only recently has appeared in the philosophy of science (see, for example, Feyerabend, 1984). For certain, such a science no longer implies a progress step by step from the known to the unknown; in fact, 'what we think we know is anchored only in our own assumptions, not in the bed rock of truth itself, and that world we seek to understand remains always on the horizons of our thoughts' (Kelly, 1977, p. 6).

CHAPTER 5

Research in Personal Construct Psychology

Jack Adams-Webber

Brock University, Canada

Nature can be regarded as open to an infinite variety of alternative constructions—some of them better than others, to be sure—and with most of the best ones yet to be concocted. In such a system the function of an answer is not to make further questioning unnecessary but to hold things together until a round of better questions has been thought up.

(Kelly, 1969k, p. 116)

The scope of research in George Kelly's personal construct psychology has been increasing steadily since its first publication in 1955. Its evolution is reflected in a rapidly growing literature addressing a continually expanding range of psychological issues (Benjafield, 1996). As Pervin and John (2001, p. 426) note, 'almost every aspect of Kelly's theory has received at least some study'. This chapter will focus specifically on several firmly established strands of ongoing research with clearly developed implications in terms of basic theoretical principles of personal construct psychology (see Chapter 1, pp. 3–20).

INDIVIDUALITY COROLLARY

The Individuality Corollary asserts that 'persons differ from each other in their constructions of events' (see Chapter 1, p. 9).

This implies that each individual relies on a unique repertory of bipolar 'personal constructs' (for example, *generous–stingy*) to interpret and anticipate his or her experience. A substantial body of empirical evidence, reviewed by Adams-Webber (1998), provides support for this assumption. For example, it has been shown repeatedly that individuals manifest highly stable personal preferences for using particular constructs to interpret events (for example, Higgins et al., 1982). Moreover, people typically evaluate themselves and others more definitely in terms of personal constructs elicited from themselves than in terms of 'supplied' constructs, which can

International Handbook of Personal Construct Psychology. Edited by F. Fransella.
© 2003 John Wiley & Sons, Ltd.

be presumed to be less personally meaningful to them (for example, Bonarius, 1977). Such idiosyncratic construct preferences also influence our degree of confidence in our own self-evaluations, as well as the extent to which we differentiate among other persons (Adams-Webber, 2001a). Not surprisingly, it is significantly easier to predict an individual's self-evaluations on the basis of his or her own personal constructs (Adams-Webber, 1998).

Not only do we prefer to use our own constructs to interpret our experience, but also each of our constructs is embedded in a personal context of meaning defined in part by its relationships of implication with other constructs (Hinkle, 1965; Fransella, 1972; Fransella & Bannister, 1977). This is illustrated by the finding that people draw relatively more inferences from information that is presented to them in terms of their previously elicited personal constructs (Delia et al., 1971). Indeed, the higher they rank a particular personal construct with respect to its relative 'usefulness for understanding people', the greater its 'implication potential' defined as the number of predictive inferences made about a hypothetical person from information encoded in terms of that construct (McDonagh, 1987).

COMMONALITY COROLLARY

The Commonality Corollary stipulates that 'to that extent that one person employs a construction of experience which is similar to that employed by another, his processes are psychologically similar to those of the other person' (see Chapter 1, pp. 13–14).

A variety of findings show how similarities in construing between persons facilitate interpersonal communication and mutual understanding in social situations. Such similarity also plays an important role in the formation, development and maintenance of role relationships. For example, a series of studies by Duck (1973) has demonstrated convincingly that friends typically show more similarity in terms of elicited personal constructs than pairs of individuals who are not friends. We are also able to identify accurately specific similarities between ourselves and particular friends with respect to shared personal constructs. Duck and Spencer (1972) showed further that this form of commonality between persons tends to be a precursor of friendship formation and not merely its product. In fact, similarity with respect to personal constructs has proved to be a significantly better predictor of friendship choices than is similarity in terms of responses to standard psychological questionnaires such as the California Psychological Inventory. Duck's research also reveals gradual changes in the nature of commonality between friends as their relationship develops. For example, once a friendship has become firmly established, similarity in terms of psychological constructs is more important than is similarity in terms of other types of constructs (Duck, 1973). Interestingly, Landfield (1971) reports that clients who drop out of psychotherapy early manifest less similarity with their therapists in terms of personal constructs than do clients who do not terminate psychotherapy prematurely.

Not only do people frequently use different constructs to interpret the same events, as is implied by the individuality corollary, but also it is unlikely that any two people develop personal construct systems with exactly the same pattern of implicative relationships between constructs. For example, consider the construct *frugal* versus *open-handed*. For some individuals frugality implies stinginess and is evaluated negatively, while open-handedness implies generosity and is evaluated positively. For others, frugality implies prudence and is evaluated positively, whereas open-handedness implies irresponsibility, and is evaluated negatively (Adams-Webber, 1997b).

On the other hand, there does seem to be considerable consensus within the general population concerning patterns of relationships among many constructs. For example, Bannister (1962) found that when people rated photographs of strangers on the basis of the same psychological constructs, there was significant agreement concerning the overall pattern of interrelationship among these constructs, despite the fact that there was very little agreement in terms of how particular photographs were rated. Applebee (1975) also showed that consensus among children about relationships between specific constructs increases gradually with age. As did Bannister, Applebee found more agreement among individuals concerning interrelationships between constructs than about the ratings they assigned to particular elements. Moreover, there seems to be significantly more agreement concerning the pattern of interrelationships among the positive poles of constructs such as *happy* than among their negative opposites such as *sad*, suggesting that normal usage of the former tends to conform more closely to their standard lexical definitions (Adams-Webber, 1979).

COGNITIVE COMPLEXITY

The Range Corollary specifies that 'a construct is convenient for the anticipation of a finite range of events only' (see Chapter 1, p. 11).

It follows that each personal construct has a limited range of convenience which, by definition, comprises 'all those things to which the user would find its application useful'. Thus, the more differentiated any system of constructs is in terms of the degree of functional independence among constructs, the greater will be its overall predictive capacity (range of convenience) in terms of the variety of events that can be anticipated within its framework (Adams-Webber, 1996b).

Bieri (1955) referred to the level of differentiation among an individual's personal constructs as *cognitive complexity*. He hypothesized that 'the greater the degree of differentiation among constructs, the greater will be the predictive power of the individual' (Bieri, 1955, p. 263). Using the repertory grid (see Chapter 9, pp. 95–103) to assess the extent to which individuals used different constructs independently of one another in characterizing the same persons, he found that this variable correlated with their accuracy in predicting specific differences between themselves and acquaintances. His measure of cognitive complexity also relates significantly to the degree of confidence expressed by individuals concerning their own self-evaluations on the same constructs, which may reflect their prior success in predicting behaviour ('validation') with those particular constructs (Adams-Webber, in press).

An alternative method of assessing individual differences in cognitive complexity is based on the assumption that 'the number of constructs in a person's system would reflect its degree of complexity' (Crockett, 1982, p. 73). In Crockett's Role Category Questionnaire (RCQ), respondents first nominate a list of acquaintances on the basis of a predetermined set of role categories, such as 'a person of the opposite gender whom you like', and then describe each of them as fully as possible within a three-minute time limit. The cognitive complexity score of each respondent represents the number of different personal constructs she or he used across all descriptions. Crockett (1982, p. 73) reasons that 'if such samples are obtained in a standard manner for a set of people, then the differences in the number of constructs those people employ may be assumed to reflect differences in the total number of constructs that are available to them'.

Several investigators have compared scores on Crockett's RCQ with various repertory grid indices of differentiation, including Bieri's, without finding any significant relationships (Applegate, 1990). Nor have RCQ scores been found to relate significantly to either IQ or independent measures of verbal facility (Burleson et al., 1991). In a review of research on cognitive complexity, Adams-Webber (1996b) notes that there is considerable support for Crockett's (1982) general hypothesis that our personal constructs, relative to others with whom we interact frequently and intimately, should be more complex than our constructs relevant to categories of persons with whom we interact less frequently. For example, men and women apply significantly more personal constructs to people of their own gender, and they use relatively more personal constructs in characterizing acquaintances whom they like than those whom they dislike (Crockett, 1982). Presumably, most people spend more time with liked acquaintances than with disliked acquaintances and, on average, they probably interact relatively more frequently with people of their own gender. Furthermore, the more often people interact with specific individuals, the more constructs they use to describe them (Zalot, 1977).

It has been found also that relatively cognitively complex individuals make more accurate inferences about the personal constructs of others in social situations (Adams-Webber, 1969); however, it is more difficult for another person to anticipate their self-evaluations in terms of their own personal constructs (Adams-Webber, 1998; Neimeyer et al., 1983). Such individual differences with respect to cognitive complexity can play an important role in the development of interpersonal relationships.

SOCIALITY COROLLARY

The Sociality Corollary specifies that 'to the extent that one person construes the construction processes of another, he may play a role in a social process involving the other person' (see also Chapter 1, pp. 14–17).

The Sociality Corollary implies that effective interpersonal communication and understanding require our making accurate inferences about how other individuals use their personal constructs to interpret their own experience. Thus, similarities (commonality) and differences (individuality) in both the content and structure of personal construct systems should play an important part in the development and maintenance of role relationships (sociality). For instance, we can hypothesize that the more cognitively complex individuals are in terms of the number of personal constructs that they use to interpret their own experience, the more constructs their potential partners in role relationships will need in order to effectively construe their construction processes (sociality).

Neimeyer and Hudson (1985, p. 129) conjecture that 'partners encourage each other's development by validating and extending their systems of understanding'. This suggests that a sustained role relationship between two individuals, at least one of whom is relatively cognitively complex, could facilitate the development of more cognitive complexity on the part of the other. Thus, we might expect to find a positive relation between the degree of cognitive complexity of one member of an established couple and that of her or his partner. In support of this hypothesis, Adams-Webber (2001b) found a significant correlation between the Crockett's RCQ scores of marital partners.

Whether similarity between marital partners in terms of cognitive complexity can be attributed entirely to their participation in continuing role relationships is not yet clear. Another possibility is that it could also be a precursor of their attraction to one another in the first place. Nonetheless, Neimeyer and Mitchell (1988, p. 137) hypothesize that structural similarities 'should be associated with attraction only after considerable information about the partner has become available'. Winter (1992, p. 63) cites specific evidence that, although 'similarity in attitudes predicts attraction at the beginning of a relationship, similarity at the level of structure of the construct system is more relevant at its later stages' (for example, Neimeyer & Neimeyer, 1983). Thus, as Neimeyer and colleagues (1996, p. 138) suggest, 'social comparison at the level of structural similarity may be possible only at later stages of relationship development'.

Another relevant variable is the degree of role relationship satisfaction experienced by partners. Harter and colleagues (1989, p. 140) point out that both sociality and commonality can contribute to relationship satisfaction. For example, Neimeyer and Hudson (1985) found that 'satisfied partners understand one another more accurately than do dissatisfied partners'. Neimeyer (1984) also has shown that marital partners with higher levels of structural similarity, as indexed by differentiation among their personal constructs, reported greater relationship satisfaction than did those with less structurally similar construct systems. A relevant question for further research would be whether similarity between partners in terms of the number of different personal constructs which they use to interpret experience also predicts their degree of satisfaction with their relationship.

As Neimeyer and Hudson (1985, p. 133) point out, 'the sociality corollary stipulates that genuine role relationships are limited by the interactants' degree of understanding; that is, by their ability to subsume one another's constructions'. Given previous findings that the more differentiated an individual's personal construct system, the less accurately other people can infer his or her self-constructions (for example, Adams-Webber, 1998), we might expect further that a couple could experience considerable difficulty in establishing and sustaining a mutually satisfying level of sociality if one partner were markedly more cognitively complex than the other. This hypothesis, if supported in future longitudinal research, would seem to provide at least one possible reason for 'dissimilarity between partners in their levels of cognitive complexity being associated with dissatisfaction' (Winter, 1992, pp. 142–143).

CONSTRUING SELF AND OTHERS

Kelly submits that '... the *self* is, when considered in the appropriate context, a proper concept or construct. It refers to a group of events that are alike in a certain way and, in that same way, necessarily different from other events. The way in which the events are alike is the self. That also makes the self an individual, differentiated from other individuals' (1955/1991, p. 131/Vol. 1, p. 91).

This argument implies that each individual's 'core role' identity involves a relatively stable pattern of perceived similarities and differences between self and other persons. As Bannister and Agnew (1977, p. 99) have put it, 'the ways in which we elaborate the construing of self must be essentially those ways in which we elaborate our construing of others for we have not a concept of self but a bipolar construct of self-not self'. Conversely, Lemon and Warren (1974, p. 123) infer that a person's judgements of others 'automatically involve a kind of self-comparison process ... (in which) the self-construct will act as an anchoring point to produce the effects of assimilation and contrast familiar in psychophysics'. Thus, as Gara (1982, p. 58) suggests, the self-construct seems to be a 'likely candidate for a universally used personal prototype', that is, it provides a standard against which an individual can compare and evaluate impressions of other persons. In Kelly's own words, 'his social life is controlled by comparisons he has come to see between himself and others' (1955/1991, p. 131/Vol. 1, p. 91).

The development of individual self-constructs has emerged as an important focus of research in personal construct psychology. For example, the extent to which children and adolescents differentiate between themselves and others has been found to increase progressively with age. Carr and Townes (1975) reported increases in the degree of differentiation between self and others during late adolescence. Adams-Webber (1985) subsequently found a significant relationship between age and self-differentiation in a large sample of 526 boys and 579 girls ranging from 8 to 19 years old. Specifically, the proportion of their different-from-self evaluations continued to increase gradually from 8 years of age until it eventually stabilized in late adolescence.

A logically related variable is an individual's level of identification with each of his or her parents. As Winter (1992) notes, an issue that has received considerable attention is the extent to which identification with the parent of the same sex is greater than that with the opposite-sex parent. Although an early study (Giles & Rychlak, 1965) suggested that adolescents characterize themselves as more similar to parents of the same gender, Ryle and Lunghi (1972) found that this difference obtained only for females. As Landfield and Epting (1987, p. 132) note, we also should take into consideration 'whether mother is differentiated from father'. Ryle and Lunghi (1972, p. 158) hypothesize specifically that 'perceived resemblance (of self) to parents is related to a perception of the parents as being similar to each other'.

Neff (1996) addressed all of these issues in a single study based on a relatively large sample comprising 192 girls and 173 boys ranging in age from 8 to 18. Firstly, there was a significant relationship between age and the degree to which children and adolescents differentiated between themselves and their parents of both genders, as hypothesized by Strachan and Jones (1982). Secondly, the extent to which they differentiated between their parents correlated not only with age, but also with the degree of differentiation of self from each parent separately, as hypothesized by Ryle and Lunghi (1972). Thirdly, across all age groups, both boys and girls differentiated themselves more from parents of the opposite gender, which is consistent with the earlier results of Giles and Rychlak (1965). Finally, as suggested by Ryle and Lunghi (1972), girls and boys differentiated themselves from their mothers to about the same extent; however, girls differentiated themselves from their fathers significantly more than did boys.

The well-documented tendency to assign a majority of other people to the positive poles of our constructs (for example, Lewicka et al., 1992) seems to be specific to those constructs in terms of which self is assigned to the positive poles. That is, when people evaluate themselves negatively on any bipolar construct, approximately half of their acquaintances also are evaluated negatively on that particular construct (Adams-Webber, 1992). This relationship could help to explain why depressed patients, compared to patients with various other psychiatric diagnoses, including schizophrenia, as well as people with no psychiatric problems, assign both self and others to the negative poles of more constructs, while paradoxically, characterizing others as less similar to self (for example, Space & Cromwell, 1980). On the basis of this finding, Space and Cromwell (1980, p. 156) suggested that 'low identification with others should be included along with other features of depression'.

In an experimental test of their hypothesis, Adams-Webber and Rodney (1983) instructed 'normal' adults to role-play a negative mood following imagined experiences involving intense disappointment. As predicted, they showed a significant increase in different-from-self evaluations from a previous baseline. Moreover, when the same participants enacted euphoric moods associated with imagined successes, their similar-to-self judgements increased significantly. These findings were replicated by Lefebvre and colleagues (1986). As Pierce et al. (1992, pp. 171–172) point out, 'it is remarkable that simulated mood states and pathological depression could yield such similar results'.

CONCLUSION

It seems clear that the pattern of development of research within the context of Kelly's theory since its inception has been influenced heavily by his 'idiographic' emphasis on individual differences in both the content and structure of the personal construct systems which we use to interpret and anticipate our own experience. His Individuality, Commonality and Sociality Corollaries have provided the conceptual foundation for the evolution of a new model of role relationships. Testing the predictive implications of this model has become a major area of investigation within Kellyian psychology. The extent to which we differentiate between ourselves and other persons, including our parents, has emerged as a central focus of research concerned with the structure of individual self-constructs and the elaboration of 'core roles'. Another salient strand of inquiry, which probably will continue to flourish, is represented by the already extensive body of literature on 'cognitive complexity' which stemmed originally from Kelly's Range Corollary.

The steadily expanding range of convenience of research in personal construct psychology over almost fifty years has demonstrated convincingly its fertility as a source of new hypotheses. Nonetheless, Kelly himself showed relatively little interest in the gradual accumulation of discrete findings which support his theory. For example, he did not spell out the implications of his fundamental postulate and related corollaries in terms of specific testable predictions. Instead, he advocated exploiting their heuristic value as an abstract framework for re-evaluating the significance of existing knowledge and launching innovative experiments in which the participants serve as our collaborators in the ongoing adventure of exploring yet unknown human potentials.

Beliefs, Feelings and Awareness

INTRODUCTION

Central to the chapters in this section is a theme from the previous section, that Kelly's theory can deal with feelings and emotions equally as well as it deals with thoughts or 'cognitions'.

Many are still of the opinion that the theory does not cover the former properly. Much of the problem stems from the fact that Kelly sees construing taking place at all levels of awareness, from the preverbal through to the conscious level that can rightly be called 'cognitive'. For Kelly, feelings can and do take place at a non-conscious level of construing.

Don Bannister's chapter on 'The logic of passion' is printed in full because it focuses totally upon that perceived dichotomy. In his view, 'a psychological theory cannot be a simple representation of a state of affairs. It must be a challenge, a liberating vision, a way of reaching out. If it is not, these things then it will be a justification for a personal and social *status quo*, a form of retreat, a prison.' He first argues that the problem arises from the thinking of our culture; that mind and body, feelings and thoughts are separate entities. He then puts Kelly's case suggesting that it need not be so; indeed, that there are many advantages to our being able to see that our thoughts and our feelings are all part of the same process. Personal construct theory is a theory of the total experience of being a person.

Spencer McWilliams extends the thinking–emotion theme to look at the nature of our emotional relationship with our strongly held beliefs. He says: 'In science and life we must find ways of dealing effectively with our passionate commitment to our beliefs on the one hand and the realization that we must hold these beliefs tentatively and revise or replace them when circumstances warrant. Unfortunately, we do not always behave as ideal scientists.' He describes our attachment to beliefs and ways to gain greater awareness of this tendency. Metaphors of anarchy and idolatry help us to understand why we may not act as 'good' scientists. We can apply Kelly's suggestion to use an invitational mood to language—instead of saying 'the floor *is* hard', we might say 'suppose we regard the floor *as if* it were hard' by using a technique called E-prime in which all forms of the verb 'to be' are excluded. Finally, he discusses meditation as a vehicle for enhancing awareness of our attachment to belief.

Peter Cummins concentrates on just one emotion: anger. He describes how he has used a personal construct definition of it to develop a programme designed to understand and so help men in trouble over their violent behaviour.

CHAPTER 6

The Logic of Passion*

Don Bannister

> If my 'anger' is rejected because I have no good 'reasons' or my 'argument'
> is dismissed because I lack 'feeling' then I accept that others experience me as
> segmented. I do not have to experience myself thus.

Psychologists strive for novelty while repeating the patterns of their culture. Thus, they have, in large measure, followed the lay tradition that man is to be viewed psychologically as a collection of poorly related parts. Psychology has been structured around concepts such as learning, motivation, memory, perception, sensation, personality and so forth, all of which clearly derive from common-sense language and each has been given autonomy as an *area of study*. Psychologists have invented little and contented themselves largely with refining notions which have a long and tangled intellectual history.

Perhaps the most unbreakable grip exercised by traditional thought over the formal discipline of psychology is manifest in the historic division of man into *thought and feeling*. The effect of this dichotomy has been to deny psychology any unity and produce what are essentially two psychologies: on the one hand, cognitive psychology with sub-psychologies such as memory, perception, thinking and reasoning; and, on the other hand, a psychology of emotion, ranging around such concepts as drive, motivation and libido.

So deeply ingrained in our culture is this division of man into his thinking and feeling aspects that it would have been surprising if psychology had, to any great extent, escaped it. It is grieving that it has barely thought to question it. We can observe this segmentation of man, both in terms of the way we analyse our personal experience and the ways in which our literature records it. As children we grow rapidly to accept the idea that we are, each of us, two persons—a thinker and a feeler. We learn to speak of our ideas as something distinct from our emotions, and we learn to speak of the two as often contrasted and competing.

So deep and continuous has this distinction been in our language, folklore and

---

*This work has been published previously in *New Perspectives in Personal Construct Theory* (1977) by Academic Press.

International Handbook of Personal Construct Psychology. Edited by F. Fransella.
© 2003 John Wiley & Sons, Ltd.

philosophy, that literary comments on it achieve the status of platitudinous but inescapable truths. Such 'truths' often espouse the rival and crusading causes of thought and feeling. Thus the thought/feeling distinction can be seen, in Kelly's terminology, as a superordinate bipolar construct.

Treasured comments can be found which praise thinking and condemn feeling. 'All violent feelings . . . produce in us a falseness in all our impressions of external things, which I would generally characterise as the "pathetic fallacy"' (Ruskin). Then again there is the kind of pronouncement which, while favouring reason, seems sadly convinced that passion will conquer:

> The ruling passion, be it what it will,
> The ruling passion conquers reason still. (Pope)

Then there are those comments which are contemptuous of the thought aspect of the dichotomy:

> And thus the native hue of resolution
> Is sicklied o'er with the pale cast of thought. (Shakespeare)

or Keats' cry:

> Oh for a life of sensation rather than of thoughts.

The contrapuntal relationship between the concepts of feeling and thought are further explored in those treasured platitudes which counterpose the two: Pascal's

> The heart has its reasons, which reason knows nothing of.

or Walpole's

> This world is a comedy to those that think, a tragedy to those that feel.

Our language is replete with expressions of the dichotomy: rationality versus emotion, reason versus passion, feeling versus thinking, the brain versus the heart, cognition versus affection, faith versus argument, mind versus flesh. Whole subcultures, periods and groups have swung the pendulum to those credos that worship the rational man, he who fights the forces of blind instinct, prejudice, chaotic emotion and bestial passion. Conversely the pendulum has swung oft-times the other way, to the Romantic and the apotheosis of emotion as the authentic, sincere and soaring expression of the true nature of man, as opposed to the mercenary practices of intellectualizing cleverness and bloodless logic.

THE USES OF THE DICHOTOMY

If the construct thinking versus feeling has enjoyed such a long history and played so major a role in our ways of delineating ourselves and others, then clearly it must serve many purposes and serve them well. It must reflect and express aspects of experience which we need to express and reflect. Even a cursory consideration brings to light some of the purposes the distinction may serve.

- If I am willing to negotiate my position and entertain yours, then I may say 'I think that . . .' and proceed to a verbal accounting. If I am unwilling to negotiate my position and do not wish you to challenge it, then I may say 'I feel that . . .'.
- If I want to notify myself or you of some, *as yet*, publically unsupported suspicion I may say that 'I know that the evidence is in favour of the view (thought) that . . . nevertheless I have this feeling that . . .'.
- If I want to picture and represent to myself or to you *conflicts* I am experiencing I can say that 'while I *know* (think) that I ought to do that, I *feel* that I ought to do this . . .'.
- If I want to make some kind of sense out of, excuse, respond to the inexplicable behaviour of myself, my neighbour, lover, friend, I can believe that the puzzling actions are not for this or that *reason* but are caused by mood, passion, over-whelming fear, rage, desire.

Historically, each pole of the thinking versus feeling dichotomy has had its impli-cations extensively developed so that we have arrived at an elaborate language of feeling and an elaborate language of thinking. We can make myriad subtle distinc-tions which stem from and support the basic idea of two occasionally interacting *personae* within each of us—a thinking man and a feeling man. Thus reason takes unto itself the subsets of memory, logic, the accurate and systematic observation of events: we can assess our thoughts as fulfilling the principles of the syllogism, the rules of linguistic definition, the fair weighing of evidence. Feeling has become feel-ings and we can work with the distinctions between sadness, resentment, exhilara-tion, tension, grief, triumph, anxiety—the pallet of passion enables us to portray the world and ourselves in many hues. Thus these developed subsystems concerning thinking and feeling are guides to action and movement so that we can *assemble arguments to influence* or *arouse feelings to attack*. Logicians can teach us strategies of thought while encounter group leaders broaden our resources for feeling. Lawyers can weigh evidence and poets evoke emotions (though be it noted that successful lawyers often plead poetically while great poets emote cogently).

THE LIMITATIONS OF THE CONSTRUCT

Kelly repeatedly made the point that a bipolar construct both liberates and restricts: it brings events within our grasp in one set of terms, while blinding us to other aspects of the same configuration of events.

Thus, in both the informal psychology of our culture and in formal academic psy-chology, the distinction between thought and feeling has often proved disintegra-tive and hindering. It is significant that it is precisely in those areas in which the distinction makes least sense that psychologists have spoken to least purpose. *Inven-tion, humour, art, religion, meaning, infancy, love:* all seem areas of particular mystery to psychologists and it may be that they puzzle us because it makes no sense to see them as clearly 'cognitive' or clearly 'affective'. Nor does calling to the rescue that holy ghost of the psychological trinity 'conation' seem to help matters.

The separation of feeling from thought seems to have driven psychologists into a barren physiologizing in a vain attempt to give substance to the dichotomy. Thus there is a long tradition in psychology which seeks to deal with 'emotion' by translating it into a physiological language and redefining it so that it even has a geography (*vide* the 'pleasure' centre) or a transporting fluid (*vide* endocrine secretion). Psychologists never seem to have broken entirely free from the kind of concretism, of which even a man as sensitive as William James was guilty, in arguments such as the following (1884):

> And yet it is even now certain that of two things concerning the emotions, one must be true. Either separate special centres, affected to them alone, are their brain-seat, or else they correspond to processes occurring in the motor and sensory senses, already assigned, or in others like them but not yet mapped out.

Equally in their ponderings on the issue of 'thought', psychologists have been driven to that ultimate in hardening of the categories, the notion of the 'engram'—the notion that a thought is somehow more real if you think of it as the permanently altered state of living tissue.

The central limit set to our understanding by our adherence to the bipolarity of thought and feeling has been that it has prevented us from adequately elaborating the notion of a *person*. Psychologists came close to beginning their study of a person with the concept of 'personality' but again they failed because this was turned into a segment, a chapter heading, a branch of psychology. Either personality is psychology or it is not worth the study. Thus a person is not emotions or thoughts, not cognition or drive. To speak of a person is to invent a concept which points to the integrity and uniqueness of your experience and my experience and to the wholeness of your experience of me and my experience of you. The distinctions that such a construct encourages us to make are those of time, the past and the future person and the continuity between them; the distinction between person and object; the distinction between the ways in which the person is free and the ways in which he is determined. None of these distinctions gains, and all are obscured by the traditional dichotomy of thought and feeling. Consider the distinction between free with respect to and determined with respect to. The very notion of feeling has developed in such a way as to entail the idea of determinism. Thus we are *overwhelmed* by rage, *seized* by anger, *moved* by joy, *sunk* in grief. It is interesting to note here our failure to develop the idea of feeling in its active sense as meaning exploration, grasp, understanding, as in feeling the surface of a material, feeling our way towards (Mair, 1972). Equally, psychologists have followed that intellectual tradition which makes rational thought almost something which is a determining external reality. We must *follow* logic, we are not credited with *inventing* logic. Had we pondered the person rather than the two homunculi of thought and feeling we would have seen man as an active agent rather than the passive object of the environment or his own uncontrollable innards.

WHATEVER HAPPENED TO EMOTIONS?

It is a platitude in personal construct theory, but a very powerful platitude, that to elaborate one's own understanding of oneself and the world it is necessary not only to develop new constructs but to escape from some old constructs. Yet to abandon a construct is to abandon a part of oneself and this is a task not lightly undertaken. However, George Kelly addressed himself formally to just such a task. He lists at one point the constructs that do not appear in personal construct theory although they are hallowed by respect and use in traditional psychology.

> For example, the term learning so honourably embedded in most psychological tests, scarcely appears at all. That is wholly intentional; for we are throwing it overboard altogether. There is no ego, no emotion, no motivation, no reinforcement, no drive, no unconscious, no need.

Clearly, in constructing his theory, George Kelly had a right *not* to use the constructs of other theories, just as each of us has an inalienable right not to use the constructs of another person. However, when this is done, both professions and persons tend to accuse the doer of failing to deal with *the facts*. If I do not deign to categorize people in terms of their 'intelligence' then others may respond that I am ignoring the *fact* of intelligence (and thereby being *stupid*). In psychology this strategy most frequently takes the form of transmuting a concept into a 'variable' and then arguing that it is something that *must* be taken into account.

There can be no onus on any theory to duplicate the constructs of another. To do so would have the effect of making alternative theories simply co-equivalent sets of different jargons. If my public theory or my private construct system lacks certain constructions, then you may legitimately ask me with what constructions I intend to deal with the kinds of problems that you handle by using the constructions that I have abandoned. But if you do so it must be a serious enquiry designed to find out how I am handling aspects of my world, what meaning I am giving to them, what usefulness I find in the constructs I am using. It must not be simply an attempt to prove that there are culpable gaps in my system because it does not exactly duplicate yours. To make such an enquiry seriously is no easy undertaking for we all tend to long for familiarity, even in what is new. This is presumably the reason why some vegetarians strangely refer to some forms of vegetable as 'nut meat rissole'.

Kelly left the great traditional dichotomy of emotion versus thought out of construct theory and proposed an alternative way of dealing with the kinds of *issue* that are classically dealt with by the emotion versus feeling dichotomy.

Inevitably it was assumed that he had somehow retained the dichotomy but failed to elaborate one end of it, one pole of the construct. In this case the accusation was generally that he had failed to deal with 'emotion'. Thus, when the two volumes presenting the theory first appeared in 1955, Bruner (1956) reviewed them favourably. But inevitably he saw the theory as a 'cognitive' theory—i.e. one which does not deal with 'emotion'. He commented on what he saw as its limitations as a 'mentalistic' theory which failed to deal with issues of emotion. Carl Rogers (1956) went even farther by not only pointing to the same 'deficiency' but waxing much more angry and much more concerned about what he saw as a failure to deal with the passions of mankind.

For two decades construct theory has been expounded, discussed and used. One might imagine that by now psychologists would have stopped construing construct theory pre-emptively as 'nothing but a cognitive theory'. One might hope that they would recognize the novel and adventurous attempt to elaborate a theory of man which did not dichotomize him into a reasoning man and a feeling man. One might hope that, even if they felt that this integrative venture had failed, they would recognize the *deliberate* nature of the venture and understand that it was not simply that Kelly had failed to consider 'emotion'. But, for the most part, psychologists are not, in philosophical terms, Kellyian constructive alternativists—they are naïve realists and emotion is apparently a *real thing*, not a construct about the nature of man. Two decades after the presentation of the theory we have exactly equivalent condemnations offered to those propounded by Bruner and Rogers. Mackay (1975, p. 128) opens his critical appraisal of personal construct theory as follows.

> PCT has been widely criticised on the grounds that it is too mentalistic. The ideal rational man, as depicted by Kelly and Bannister, seems more like a counter-programmed robot than a human being who is capable of intense emotional experience.

Peck and Whitlow (1975, p. 92) comment similarly:

> Kelly's approach to emotion is deliberately psychological but in order to achieve this position he is forced to ignore a wealth of knowledge from the field of physiology; furthermore some of the definitions seem to fly in the face of common sense. Bannister and Mair (1968, p. 33) state that 'Within this scheme, "emotions" lose much of their mystery'; it can be argued that they also lose most of their meaning.

Virtually every textbook over the past two decades that has dealt with personal construct theory has unquestioningly classified it as a 'cognitive' theory. Kelly was, in many ways, a man of real patience but even he chafed at the persistent attempt to allot him to constructs whose range of convenience did not span his work.

He used to plan/fantasize a new book which he might write to re-present construct theory. Essentially the content and force of the theory and the nature of its argument would remain the same but it would be stylistically re-presented as 'personal construct theory—a theory of the human passions'. His dream was to complete the volume and let the people who saw construct theory as a cognitive theory wrestle with the new presentation. Had he completed such a work it seems likely that he would have been open to academic attack for failing entirely to understand the rational aspects of man, the nature of thinking and the degree to which behaviour is a function of cognitive processes. In summary, then, psychologists have failed to take seriously Kelly's attempt to dispense with the thinking–feeling dichotomy. He stated it as explicitly as may be. Thus (Kelly 1969a, p. 140):

> The reader may have noted that in talking about experience I have been careful not to use either of the terms, 'emotional' or 'affective'. I have been equally careful not to invoke the notion of 'cognition'. The classic distinction which separates these two constructs has, in the manner of most classic distinctions that once were useful, become a barrier to sensitive psychological inquiry. When one so divides the experience of man, it becomes difficult to make the most of the holistic aspirations that may infuse the science of psychology with new life, and

may replace the classicism now implicit even in the most 'behaviouristic' research.

ALTERNATIVE CONSTRUING

Kelly attempted to deal with the kind of issue normally handled under the rubric of 'emotion' by offering constructs which relate to *transition*. The underlying argument is that while a person's interpretation of himself and his world is probably constantly changing to some degree, there are times when his experience of varying validational fortunes make change or resistance to change a matter of major concern. At such times we try to nail down our psychological furniture to avoid change or we try to lunge forward in answer to some challenge or revelation by forcefully elaborating our experience. Or we may be tumbled into chaos because of over-rapid change or move into areas where we cannot fully make sense of our situation and its implications and our system must either change or the experience will become increasingly meaningless. It is at such times that our conventional language most often makes reference to feeling.

Kelly strove to maintain construct theory as an integrated overview of the nature of the person; to deal with all aspects of our experience within the same broad terms. Whether he succeeded or failed, the theory is thus essentially grandiose in that it attempts to deal with all aspects of human experience. Thereby it is in contrast with most psychological theories which are essentially theories of something. Conventionally, even broadly structured theoretical frameworks such as learning theory specifically acknowledge that there are areas of human experience and behaviour which are outside their range of convenience—learning theory is a theory of learning. Other theories are much more explicit and limited, being theories of memory, or theories of perception or theories of sensation, and so forth. Most relevant to this argument is that they may be theories of cognition or theories of emotion.

CONSTRUCTS RELATING TO TRANSITION

In naming his constructs relating to transition, Kelly adopted a curious strategy. He chose terms such as guilt, hostility, aggression, anxiety, all of which have a traditional lay and formal psychological meanings and then redefined them in construct theory terms. In each case the new definition is cousin to the traditional definition but the differences are such as to cause some confusion on first inspection. Kelly was never explicit as to why he adopted this strategy rather than create entirely new names for these constructs. However, one suspects that he did little without malice aforethought, and one possibility is that he was trying to draw attention to the *difference* between his preferred definition and the standard one, by using the same term. The suspicion is strengthened when we examine the nature of the difference. In every case it seems that what Kelly is pointing to is the meaning of the situation for *the person* to whom the adjective is applied, as contrasted with the meaning of the situation for those of us who are confronted *by the person* to whom we apply the adjective. Thus standard ways of using terms such as *hostile* are such that the emnity, attack and hatred of the person is seen as directed towards us, almost as if they were traits of the person, almost as if they were unreasoning hatreds. True, we may enquire for what reason a particular person is hostile, but the term hostile itself does not carry with it any kind of causal explanation. In construct theory *hostility* is defined as 'the continued effort to extort validational evidence in favour of a type of social prediction which has already been recognised as a failure'. Essentially Kelly is pointing, in this definition, to the situation as it exists *for the person* who is being hostile. For such a person some part of his theoretical structure for making sense out of the world is threatened, some central belief is wavering and, because he cannot face imminent chaos, he attempts to bully the evidence in such a way that it will 'substantiate' the threatened theory. Similarly, the traditional definitions of *aggression* give it a meaning very much like the meaning we attach to the term hostility, whereas Kelly defines it as the polar opposite of hostility thereby seeking to draw our attention to the nature of aggression from the aggressor's point of view as distinct from its discomfort for those of us who confront it. Thus, *aggression*, as defined in construct theory terms is 'the active elaboration of one's perceptual field'. Aggression is the hallmark of a person who is being adventurous and experimental, who is beginning to make more and more sense out of a wider and wider range of experience and who is leaping into further experience to capitalize on the sense he is making. Truly it can be very unpleasant for us to face aggression of this sort because we may not always wish to be part of the other person's experiment, to be the means whereby he enlarges his understanding.

Kelly's definitions try to make us recognize that we can only understand the persons from within, in terms of the 'why' from their point of view. This places construct theory in sharp contrast to trait psychology which sees the person as *caused* from within or stimulus response psychology which sees him *as caused* from without. Kelly (1969m, p. 273) makes this point in the following words:

> If we are to have a psychology of man's experiences, we must anchor our basic concepts in that personal experience, not in the experiences he causes others to have or which he appears to seek to cause others to have. Thus if we wish to use a concept of hostility at all, we have to ask, what is the experiential nature of hostility from the standpoint of the person who has it. Only by answering this question in some sensible way will we arrive at a concept which makes pure psychological sense, rather than sociological or moral sense, merely.

A few of Kelly's constructs relating to transition are briefly examined in order to give some impression of the way in which the theory handles the issue of 'feeling'.

ANXIETY

Kelly defines anxiety as 'the awareness that the events with which one is confronted lie mostly outside the range of convenience of one's construct system'. Thus, anxiety is not seen as a kind of psychological ginger pop fizzing around in the system or physiologized into a chemical process or left vague as referring to an uncertain general state of the person. It is given a specific meaning in construct theory terms—it directs our attention to the range of convenience of a person's construct system in relation to the situation which he confronts. Anxiety is our awareness that something has gone bump in the night. The 'bump' is within the range of convenience of our construct system in that we can identify it as a 'bump' but the implications of the bump lie mostly outside the range of convenience of our construct system. What do things that go bump in the night do next? What can be done about them? A common objection to this definition of anxiety arises from the fact the people often claim to be very familiar with precisely those things which make them anxious. Thus students honestly claim to be familiar with examinations yet feel extremely anxious about them. But here we have to look at the exact meaning of the phrase 'lie *mostly* outside the range of convenience of one's construct system'. Certainly, as far as examinations are concerned, aspects of them are well within the range of convenience of the student's construct system. He is familiar with the whole business of answering two from section A and not more than one from section B, he is at home with problems of time allotment between questions, he is familiar with all those standard demands to 'compare and contrast', 'discuss', 'write brief notes on'. He may be a positive authority on strategies for revising, guessing likely questions, marking systems and so forth. Yet it is likely that there will be a whole series of questions relating to an examination, the answers to which lie in very misty areas. What will I think of myself if I fail this examination? What will other people think of me if I fail this examination? What will the long-term effect be if I fail this examination? It may be these, and a whole range of related questions, which run beyond the range of convenience of the construction system of a particular person facing a particular examination.

Not only is the definition cogent but, since it is part of a systematic theory, it relates in turn to yet further constructs within the theory. Thus, if we consider ways in which we handle our anxieties, we can observe at least two kinds of strategy which are defineable within the construct theory. We may handle our anxieties by becoming aggressive—that is, we actively explore the area that is confronting us to the point at which we can bring it within the range of convenience of our construct system. In Kelly's terms this would involve *dilation*—this occurs when a person broadens his perceptual field and seeks to reorganize it on a more comprehensive level. In contrast we can withdraw from the area altogether. This involves *constriction*—a narrowing of the perceptual field.

HOSTILITY

Kelly's definition of hostility, that it is 'the continued effort to extort validational evidence in favour of a type of social prediction which has already been recognized as a failure', can be exemplified by referring back to Kelly's root metaphor, his invitation to consider the proposition that 'all men are scientists'. We can recognize the plight of the scientist who has made a considerable personal and professional investment in his theory, but who is faced by mounting piles of contradictory evidence. He may well recognize the failure of his *predictions* in an immediate sense, i.e. that what he has predicted in a particular experiment has not happened. What he may be unable to recognize and accept is the overall implication that a series of such mis-predictions negates his total theory. His investment may be too great, his lack of an *alternative* theory too oppressive and he may proceed to cook the books, torment his experimental subjects and bully his co-scientists in a desperate attempt to maintain a dying theory. All of us have experienced this situation personally. Clearly hostility is not simply 'a bad thing'. Sometimes we cannot afford readily to abandon a belief. If the belief is central to our way of viewing ourselves and others and if we have no alternative interpretation available to us, then it may be better to maintain that belief, for a while, by extorting validational evidence, rather than abandon the belief and plunge into chaos. At crucial times the alternative to hostility may be psychosis.

This kind of definition has practical implications for the ways in which we can make change possible. It suggests that we must facilitate change not by assaulting each other's central beliefs but by helping each other to construct alternatives, beginning with areas of peripheral contradiction. Thus, we may gradually replace a central belief without the need for hostility.

We can recognize hostility readily when we witness someone destroying his relationship with someone else in order to 'prove' that he is independent. We see it in the teacher who has growing doubts of his own cleverness and therefore begins to bully his students into stupidity so that his superiority as a teacher is demonstrated. It can manifest itself with most brutal clarity in the behaviour of the person who has to physically beat his psychological opponent to his knees in order to prove that he is 'best'.

The whole conception of the nature of change and resistance to change implied in the idea of hostility recalls the traditional philosopher's model which compares the problem of life to the problem of rebuilding a ship while at sea. If we have to rebuild our ship while sailing it we obviously do not begin by stripping out the keel. We use the strategy of removing one plank at a time and rapidly replacing it so that, given good fortune, we may eventually sail in an entirely new ship. This kind of conception is particularly important in areas of deliberately undertaken change, such as psychotherapy, education, religious and political conversion. We must remember that those whom we seek to change—and it may be ourselves that we seek to change—must *maintain* their lives while change continues.

AGGRESSION

As has already been noted, Kelly defines aggression as 'the active of elaboration of one's perceptual field'. Thus, aggression is perhaps the centrally triumphant experience for a person. The aggressive poet is one who sees ways of transmuting more of his experience into verse, the aggressive peasant is the one who is grasping ways of making his fields grow more. Aggression is our willingness to risk in order to find out, our passion for truth given embodiment in action. Aggression is the flourishing love affair, the child learning to walk, the conjurer with a new trick.

Again, each construct within the theory links into the total structure. Linked to the idea of aggression is Kelly's notion of 'commitment'. Morris (1975) makes the point that commitment in construct theory terms, is not a static posture, a clinging to the security of a set position. It means the converse: commitment is to the *frontiers* of one's construct system, a willingness to risk elaboration into what is, at the moment of risk, the unknown.

Kelly discusses at length the nature of the strategies whereby we give force to our aggression and particularly the idea of tightening and loosening. When a construct is used tightly, it leads to unvarying predictions, its relationship to other constructs is fixed: when a construct is used loosely it leads to varying predictions while retaining its identity, its relationships to other constructs is tentative. Loosening is that phase in our inventive cycle when we step back to gain a wider perspective, when we take liberties with the logic of our construct system in such a way that we can examine new possibilities. Loosening is whimsy, humour, creativity, dreaming, a bold extension of argument. Yet to *remain* loose is to deny oneself the opportunity of testing reality, of embodying one's dreams in informative and informed action. Loosening must run into tightening, into operational definition, into concrete forms. When we tighten we give our ideas a form definite enough to yield up the yeas and nays of actual events so that armed with new evidence we can begin again to loosen and re-examine the meaning of what we have concretely found. In relation to the traditional thinking–feeling dichotomy, we can raise here two questions. If you consider your own experience of moving from tight to loose and back again to tight, do you regard this experience as best designated by the notion of 'feeling' or best designated by the notion of 'thinking' or is it not adequately designated by the construct at all? Equally, it is significant that if we look at the nature of areas such as 'problem solving' in Kellyian terms, then we are immediately enmeshed in precisely those constructs related to transition, such as tightening and loosening, which Kelly offered as his way into 'emotion'. We are not safely in the area of 'cognitive' psychology as presented in standard textbooks.

GUILT

Guilt is a significant concept, both in theoretical psychology and in social argument, because, at best, it fits awkwardly into the boxes of 'feeling' and 'thinking'. Thus, we often speak of guilt as a tremendously intense and disturbing feeling. At the same time we '*find* ourselves guilty', we argue for or against our guilt, our guilt is presented as a cognitive conclusion.

Kelly defines guilt as 'the awareness of dislodgement of self from one's core role structure'. Core constructs are those which govern a person's maintenance processes, they are those constructs in terms of which identity is established, the self is pictured and understood. Your core role structure is what you understand yourself to be. For Kelly, self is an element which must be construed as must any other element. Equally, therefore, its unfolding must be anticipated like any other element. You may find yourself doing things that you would not have expected to find yourself doing had you been the sort of person you thought you were. Indeed you are fortunate if this is not part of your experience. If you find yourself, in terms of those constructs/themes around which your behaviour is centred, behaving as 'not yourself', then you will experience guilt. The guilt is experienced not because one has defied and upset social taboos but because you have misread yourself.

Again, this is a construct about transition. Unbeknown to yourself you have changed and guilt comes when you experience your own behaviour as reflecting the change and thereby contradicting that 'self' which is now part of history and no longer valid as a contemporary guide.

WORDS AND CONSTRUCTS

The foregoing sketch was designed merely to indicate the directions which Kelly took in proposing an alternative to the superordinate construct of 'thinking–feeling'.

The question remains: Why has construct theory been so persistently seen as 'cognitive'? The answer may lie partly in an unrecognized tenet of the theory and partly in the way in which the theory has been received.

A central contention of construct theory is that constructs are not verbal labels. A construct is the actual discrimination a person makes within the elements of his experience. For a given person a particular discrimination may or may not have a verbal label, it may be partly or obscurely labelled with only one pole indicated or it may have been a discrimination which was evolved in infancy before verbal labels became part of operating strategies. Perhaps, because in *discussing* our own and other peoples constructions we have, by the nature of our act, to label them, we too often forget this definitive assertion within construct theory. Thus constructs are most often regarded as verbal labels and thereby denied 'emotional' meaning. For it has been a prime characteristic of the way in which the concept of emotion has developed that it should denote those aspects of our experience which are well nigh impossible to verbalize. *Ergo*, by a kind of chop logic, construct theory has been seen as 'not dealing with' emotions because it is seen as dealing with words.

Construct theory has been received rather than used. It has been given a modest place in textbooks but it has had only a limited experimental and applied career and this largely in the form of expansions in the use of repertory grid technique. It may be that our failure to argue about *experience* using construct theory has impoverished the theory (for theories live and grow by use) in what it has to say about those aspects about experience conventionally dealt with under the rubric of 'emotion'. If this is true, then it is only when we seriously undertake explorations of our own and other people's experience and behaviour in terms of constructs like guilt, aggression, anxiety, hostility, that we will begin to understand their meaning and their content. Until then, construct theory will appear impoverished by contrast with the richness of lay language as a way of talking about 'emotional' aspects of experience or the evolved usefulness of, say, psychoanalytic language as a way of delineating interpersonal drama.

THE NOTION OF PERSONAL TEST

The crucial and continuing test of any psychological theory is that it should challenge and illuminate the life of the individual from the individual's viewpoint. Traditionally, psychologists have used the construct *objective–subjective* to deny the validity of personal evaluation of psychological theories. It is not only admissible but most appropriate that psychological theories should be examined in the light of personal experience. The reflexivity argument—the notion that psychological theories should account, among other things, for their own construction—has two sides to it. The *nature* of an argument should not, of itself, deny its truth. An argument should be valid for the person by whom it is proposed.

The first demand is rarely made by audiences of and for psychologists. Granted, if a speaker were to say, 'I have proved beyond any possibility of doubt, by carefully controlled experiment, that in no circumstances can a human being utter a sentence of more than four words', we might sense some intrinsic invalidity. Yet we listen solemnly and frequently to psychologists who give us *reasons* for believing that man's behaviour is entirely a matter of *causes* and we rarely protest.

The corollary of the contention that the statement must fit the speaker, is the speaker's demand that the statement must fit him. Personal validity is a necessary basis for consensual validity. Otherwise the speaker is lying.

In terms of personal test, I experienced the need for Kelly's integration/abandonment of the feeling/thinking dichotomy long before he presented the personal construct theory or I read of it.

As an adolescent I accepted the distinction and duly thought of myself as a container for two homuncoli—a feeling man and a thinking man. Yet even while I accepted the distinction as reflecting inescapable reality, I found that it served me poorly. The legend seemed to have it that two *personae* were at war within me. If it were not for the harsh discipline of my intellect then, so it seemed, I could have enjoyed a much more intense freedom for and through my feelings. If it were not for the distorting and prejudicial effect of my emotions, then my thoughts would have been so much clearer, more finely formed and truthful. Given this kind of bipolarity I was to choose and re-choose between the demands of reason and the dictates of passion and whichever choice I made seemed somehow to diminish me. I was to be a more miserable lover because I was a better logician, a more muddled philosopher because I was a more sensitive man. In one area after another I was to be intellectual Roundhead or libidinous Cavalier. The choice seemed inescapable.

My then solution for this dilemma was either to alternate or to seek some middle position which made me a compromised representative of both. This seemed less damaging than to take up everlasting residence at one pole or other of the dichotomy but at best I felt/thought it to be a mean and confusing compromise.

Kelly, by offering notions such as tightening and loosening and above all by proposing the notion of constructs in transition solved for me an ancient problem. I could, in the vision of personal change and resistance to change, account for the intensity of my experience while accepting that the 'me' that changed or resisted change was a whole person and not a pair of warring dwarfs. And the 'me' that commented on myself I could see as reflexive and superordinate but still entailed in all levels of me.

I no longer see myself as the victim of my 'emotion'. My 'emotions' may torment me but I accept them as an integral part of me, as entailed in all that I have 'thought'. I now accept that in my 'emotions' lie the beginnings, endings and forms of my 'thoughts' and it is to what I have 'thought' that I 'feelingly' respond.

Nor can others so easily use the schism to confuse and condemn me. If my 'anger' is rejected because I have no good 'reasons', or my 'argument' is dismissed because I lack 'feeling', then I accept that others experience me as segmented. I do not have to experience myself thus.

CONCLUSION

The idea of thought and feeling as the two great modes of human experience relates to and bedevils a number of superordinate debates.

A popular vision of Art versus Science is because it aligns them along this dimension, thus denying the enormous complexity of structure which underlies poetry or music or painting and the intensely personal commitment which informs scientific endeavour. Equally, such a contrasting leads us away from an exploration of the nature of *invention* which is at the heart of both. The blinkering effect of such a contrasting of Art and Science manifests itself through our cultural inheritance and produces a myopia in our educational system so that 'artists' are kept ignorant of the creative possibilities of hypothesis while 'scientists' are encouraged to see themselves as routine clerks to nature.

The male versus female roles which are the root *personae* of society, pivot most often on some version of the belief that man is 'by nature' rational and woman emotional. There is no way of calculating how many lives have been constrained, if not crippled, by the attempt to live to such specifications but we can observe the liberating effect of a refusal to bow to the doctrine of the insensitive man and the fearful woman. In work, in relationships, in the very legal arrangements we live by, the thought–feeling dichotomy has been pedestal to man–woman, beginning with the tearful but charming little girl and the tough, capable little boy and elaborating into the adult who cannot find ways of sexually differentiating himself/herself that are not bounded by the poles of this construct.

Even the time line along which we live has been dominated by the exclusivity of thought and feeling so that we seem condemned to move from the enthusiasm and passion of *youth* to the wisdom and calmness of *age*. The range of our choice of style, cause, engagement is arbitrarily limited by what we are socially taught is appropriate to young and old respectively, and what we are taught derives much of its content from what are seen as the irreconcilable claims of passion and reason. A psychological theory cannot be simply a specification of what humanity is. Because it is self-reflecting it must be a tool that people use in going about the business of being persons.

A psychological theory cannot be a simple representation of a state of affairs— it must be a challenge, a liberating vision, a way of reaching out. If it is not these things then it will be a justification for a personal and social status quo, a form of retreat, a prison.

Most psychological theories have not sought to challenge the picture of people as segmented into thought and feeling. Indeed they have not even seen it *as a picture*, they have taken it as 'real' and worked within the boundaries thereby set. Kelly was truly adventurous in abandoning the construct and offering alternative ways of interpreting experience. The alternative he offered, the construct of 'change', is open to criticism, it is an invitation which we are free to refuse. The least sensible or gracious response to his invitation is not to see that it was being made, and to categorize Kelly as a man who did not understand 'emotion' and who thereby constructed a merely 'cognitive' theory.

CHAPTER 7

Belief, Attachment and Awareness

Spencer A. McWilliams

California State University, San Marcos, USA

A conclusion supported by the facts is likely to be a good one at the time it is drawn. But, because facts themselves are open to reconstruction, such a theory soon becomes a dogmatism that may serve only to blind us to new perceptions of the facts.

(Kelly, 1969b, p. 67).

As you will know from previous chapters in this book, George Kelly proposed that each person constructs a unique interpretation of the world and uses it to anticipate future events. As Kelly stated, a person 'copes with the world by erecting constructs or guidelines—verbal ones or reflexive ones—in terms of which he can fathom it and gain some sense of where he and it are going' (1969c, p. 178). More importantly, Kelly's philosophical assumption, *constructive alternativism*, proposed that we consider our present interpretation of events as 'subject to revision or replacement'. Kelly asked that we remember that the universe has no allegiance to any one personal interpretation of it. He suggested that we should regard knowledge as successive approximations rather than final and absolute and that we should not consider any interpretation as the truth or directly corresponding to reality. We use our present understanding to make predictions about the future but we should appreciate the actual experience of events that we encounter in our daily lives as they occur and remain open to revising our understanding and ideas accordingly. Kelly believed that to the extent that we do not hold strong attachments to belief in any particular construction we have more opportunity to entertain alternative ways of construing events, enabling us to live more effective and fulfilling lives.

Kelly used the 'personal scientist' metaphor as another way of characterizing this effective balance in human understanding, suggesting that our model of the ideal scientist can also apply to human life in general. The ideal scientist develops ideas about the world and invents experiments as ways of acting on and testing out those ideas. Scientists operate from deep personal commitments to their ideas, and these commitments serve as a driving force that impels testing the ideas to determine their

International Handbook of Personal Construct Psychology. Edited by F. Fransella.
© 2003 John Wiley & Sons, Ltd.

validity. That process requires a balance between this passionate commitment, on the one hand, and awareness of the interim nature of ideas, on the other. Maintaining the balance helps the scientist to perceive the results of experiments accurately and without emotional bias. The philosopher of science, Michael Polanyi (1958), noted an inherent hazard in a commitment to a belief that we view as corresponding to 'reality'. A belief that our ideas reflect a real world, and thus could possibly represent truth, rests on a belief that the world exists independently of our ideas about it. If so, then our ideas could be wrong, and reality may reveal itself to us far differently from what we thought.

In science and in life we must find ways of dealing effectively with our passionate commitment to our beliefs and to the realization that we must hold these beliefs tentatively and revise or replace them when circumstances warrant. Unfortunately, we do not always behave as ideal scientists. We often strongly believe in the validity of our ideas about the universe, particularly the images that we hold of ourselves. We identify with the verbalized symbols of our personal construing—ideas, beliefs or opinions—and such strongly held identification can sometimes interfere with openness to actual events and creating new ways of interpreting events. We see this process most strongly when it involves core constructs, our structure for understanding and predicting ourselves.

Core construing helps us to anticipate our own behaviour, particularly how we relate to others and how we survive in the world. Understandably, we hold tightly to the products of our core construing and the possibility of change in our self-image tends to arouse emotions such as threat, fear, guilt, shame, anxiety and hostility, as defined by Kelly and discussed by Bannister in the previous chapter. Such feelings often make us respond ineffectively. We may understand the world through the lens of our core constructs with little conscious awareness. We start to develop core constructs before we learn language, so they may well not always have clear verbal labels, in Kelly's terms. Core constructs can also show themselves directly in physical forms, demonstrating that construing includes both 'mind' and 'body', and enabling us to view some physical problems as preverbal core construing at work. Strongly held beliefs in our own personal constructs, particularly our self-image—the ways that we believe we must behave, and have others behave toward us, in order to feel safe—can run our lives rather than serve our lives.

To the extent that we invest our beliefs strongly in a particular construction of events, and particularly when we develop such strong attachment to these beliefs that we refuse to revise them, we may have emotional reactions to potentially invalidating events and fail to interpret events accurately and effectively. This chapter addresses the issue of our tendency to develop strong attachment to our belief in the products of our personal construing, particularly core construing, and ways that we might reduce the deleterious effects of this tendency by developing greater awareness of the process.

ANARCHY AND INSURRECTION

We can increase our awareness of the tendency to treat constructs as objective truth by understanding how we can make an 'institution' of our beliefs. The philosophy of anarchism, as applied to political processes, provides a useful analogy for exploring this personal process (McWilliams, 1988). Anarchist philosophy emphasizes the role of freedom and equality in facilitating human progress. Through social interaction people develop a natural sense of how to conduct themselves and live effectively and cooperatively. Collectively, we create social structures and processes based on this knowledge. We intend for these structures to serve human needs, but over time codification of the natural processes into legal, political and religious organizations may come to interfere with the human interests and needs that they originally served. Once established, the survival of the institution may assume greater importance than serving its original purpose. When that occurs, an institution may actually interfere with the very human need that it originally served. Anarchist philosophy distinguishes between revolution and insurrection: revolution refers to replacing one structure with another while insurrection seeks to weaken all structure so that a new natural order can prevail. The forms that evolve to serve human needs should not be allowed to develop into an institution and insurrection acts to throw off institutionalized forms so that the natural laws can re-establish themselves.

Application of that philosophy to our personal construing, by analogy, may help us to understand our tendency to 'institutionalize' our personal interpretations and beliefs and how that process may impede our ability to respond effectively to the ever-changing environment. We may come to see the labels and symbols of our core construing, which we identify as our self, as an institution by imagining a future and a role that we will personally play in that future. Kelly understood the self, or core structure, used for anticipating our personal maintenance, as a portion of the person's processes but not the totality, and requiring personal awareness of the self as the subject who has the experience. Without a sense of self, we would have difficulty transcending immediate needs and anticipating distant future. Thus, this sense of self serves us well. However, exclusive identification with this idea of self may impede our ability to continue to develop and evolve. We may treat the self, originally designed to serve personal maintenance, as an 'institution'.

The 'institutionalized' self-image may consist of rules that we follow rigidly regardless of whether they enable us to evolve our understanding effectively. The self-structure, a necessary component of personal evolution, may hinder evolution to more sophisticated or mature forms. The personal anarchist, analogous to Kelly's personal scientist, might follow 'personal insurrection', weakening strong identification with the way that we have symbolized our core structure and actively applying Kelly's assumption of the need to revise and replace our understanding, not by destroying our ability to deal effectively with the world but to stay open to current reality, as we construe it, without relying on rigid rules.

IDOLATRY AND ICONOCLASM

The concept of idolatry, borrowed from religion, provides another metaphor for exploring and articulating the human tendency to believe that our understanding directly depicts reality. We can liken our tendency to reify our construing, treating beliefs as existing independently of our creation of them, to 'idolatry' (McWilliams,

1993). Because we desire certainty we tend to certify our constructions as objective representations of the universe, forgetting that we have invented them. Kelly presumed the existence of a real universe and believed that we move towards knowing it, but he also assumed that the correspondence between our constructions and reality would occur at some infinitely distant time in the future. He warned that current truths may appear meaningless in the light of new reconstruction. The quest for knowledge and understanding requires awareness of the incomplete, ad interim, nature of our constructions and acknowledgement that final understanding always eludes us. Although these principles clearly suggest that we apply our beliefs humbly, we have the tendency to behave as though our ideas truly do correspond to the universal truth.

Idolatry exists when we treat a fictional image as real and 'worship' it as ultimately true. Religions construe idolatrous acts as sinful because they presume to know ultimate truth. Western and Eastern spiritual perspectives warn not to accept any image as ultimate—emphasizing the ineffability of truth—and advise not to think that current beliefs represent ultimate reality. Bakan (1966) applied the concept of idolatry to science and psychology, proposing that both express a human impulse to appreciate the nature of existence and the possibility of transcending any specific expression of it. That impulse presupposes that the manifest only represents a hint of a deeper reality that remains unmanifest. Human audacity reaches out to make contact with the unmanifest, which contains the more important, eternal, and universal reality. Bakan emphasized the importance of movement towards the unmanifest rather than reaching a final objective. However, in our desire for fulfilment we tend to accept a particular expression of the impulse as ultimate, committing the sin of idolatry by confusing the process of seeking fulfilment, or one of its products, with the fulfilment itself. When we do that we lose the sense that the unmanifest continues to exist and we forget that the search for it will never end.

Barfield (1988), using the concept of idolatry to explore how we view knowledge, called human perceptions 'representations', and suggested that reality consists of a system of collectively shared representations. The universe, the unrepresented, exists independently of human construction, a notion similar to Kelly's (1977) notion of the 'unknown'. As we apply representations, we tend to objectify them and perceive them as being 'out there', rather than as our own invention. Idolatry occurs when we forget that what we see as things derives from our construction processes. Any thing exists only as an artefact of human experience. Only the unmanifest, the unnamed, the unknown, the unrepresented, exists independently of human consciousness.

We can revise our beliefs more easily if we remain aware of the indeterminacy of knowledge, particularly when events in the universe fail to conform to our anticipation, as they ultimately shall. Within Kelly's model, we expect to revise our interpretations during the process of articulation and ultimately replace them as better understandings evolve. This humility reduces the tendency towards an idolatrous position on any particular construction. Kelly also suggested that we need not necessarily disprove one interpretation of an event in order to entertain an alternative. If we treat interpretations as personally invented propositions we do not assume that the universe holds any allegiance to them and we can more easily entertain a range of alternate possibilities.

We can transcend idolatry through deliberate awareness that we create our representations. Active, creative, imaginative and responsible participation in the evolution of human knowledge can occur to the extent that we attend to idolatrous use of construing and assume a more conscious stance towards our active, creative role in construing. Rather than worshipping images, 'personal iconoclasts' can 'destroy' the images to embrace revised understanding and new interpretations.

SPEAKING IN THE INVITATIONAL MOOD

We may find it useful to develop disciplined approaches to observing construing, articulating assumptions, and making the constructed nature of beliefs conscious. Barfield suggested that we might gain deeper participation in construing by using language metaphorically, where we consciously and intentionally indicate that an 'appearance' refers to something else. With intentional awareness we indicate that something we describe in manifest terms actually means something unmanifest. We find it difficult, however, to apply this metaphorical understanding to everyday speaking. Kelly (1969d) described how the normal indicative mood of the English language uses 'to be' verbs that attribute qualities to the universe. He proposed an alternative, the invitational mood, in which a speaker takes responsibility for attributing qualities to events and invites the listener to consider an interpretation of the event without precluding alternative interpretations. Casting a proposition in an invitational mood suggests that the subject remains open to a range of possibilities.

If we wish to use the invitational mood we need a practical way to speak in a manner that recognizes the hypothetical nature of interpretations and helps to avoid attributing permanent qualities to events that continually change (McWilliams, 1996). A technique from General Semantics may provide such a method. General semanticists have long raised concern about use of the verb *to be*, which attributes a fixed nature to a person or event and views qualities as inherent characteristics. Korzybski (1933), the founder of General Semantics, discussed problems with the verb *to be*. Kelly read Korzybski's work and found General Semantics in accordance with his view of how we invest meaning in the names we use and how that leads to a constant sense of the fixed identity of events.

A General Semantics technique called E-prime (Bourland & Johnston, 1991) attempts to apply these issues by excluding all forms of the verb *to be* (*is, are, was, were, am, be, been, being*) from English usage. Use of E-prime can serve as an application of the invitational mood by sensitizing us to our overuse of the indicative mood of *to be* and helping us gain greater awareness of our tendency to project our constructions onto the environment and then to objectify them. Use of E-prime helps to avoid unconscious pre-emptive construing, restricts use of the passive voice, which enables us to avoid personal responsibility for construing, and tends to prevent us from making permanent qualities out of the experience of a particular moment. By using E-prime, we accept responsibility for making attributions. We see more clearly that a human constructed the attributes in a process for interpreting recurrent patterns among events. E-prime removes some troublesome questions from consideration. For example, we could no longer ask questions such as, 'What *is* the meaning of life?', '*Is* this work of art beautiful?', or *Is* the President a liberal or a conservative?'. Instead we would have to say, for example, 'How can I find meaning in my life?', 'How do you experience this work of art?', or 'The President spoke like a moderate'. E-prime helps us to focus speech and understanding on direct personal experience and leads to speaking more propositionally in a way that leaves other possibilities open. We can also learn to translate the speech of others into E-prime and then respond to the E-prime version as a way to clarify the construing of others and reduce arguments. For example, if someone said, 'James *is* hostile', rather than replying 'He is *not!*' we might instead ask, 'What about James makes you say that?'

Of course, we would not wish to treat E-prime as an 'institution' or an 'idol'. Dogmatic use of E-prime will not automatically lead to propositional thinking and invitational communication, and we can find many ways to avoid responsibility by using ambiguous or evasive words like 'perhaps', 'seems', 'data indicate', and so forth. To benefit from E-prime, we must adopt a sustained acceptance of the value of questioning use of the indicative mood and our tendency to project fixedness onto the stream of events. Attempts to use E-prime may increase awareness of our tendency to project personal constructions onto events and help to express attributions or interpretations more propositionally.

MEDITATION AND THE ORDINARY MIND

Zen meditation practice provides an additional approach to understanding attachment to core construing. The Ordinary Mind School of Zen (Beck, 1993) focuses on core beliefs, comparable to core constructs, and emphasizes awareness of our response to daily experience, disciplining our mind, and reducing ineffective emotional reactions (McWilliams, 2000). The Ordinary Mind approach rests on a foundation of classic Zen teachings which describe construing and its relationship to awareness of the present moment by articulating our experience of events. As an event occurs it stands out as 'figure' from the 'background'. Through the five senses we gain awareness of that event, and then we interpret the event and label it. Finally, we judge the event as good or bad. Each of these components lacks permanent fixed identity. We tend to see the world as real and we mistake the form in which events appear to us as ultimate nature. But form does not have fixed substance and does not exist independently of our perception. Our mental activities (sensations, perceptions and choices) also have no permanent nature. We respond to form, which only manifests itself when a human apprehends it. Mind (construing) and form depend on each other. The phenomenal world thus has no permanent self-nature. If we can fully comprehend that construing has no permanent self-nature we can calm our mental processes, respond openly to new events, and reduce suffering.

Because we construe the world through our self-centred desires, we hold to ideas about what must happen to maintain our core identity. Since the universe holds no allegiance to our construing, events do not always correspond to our desires, and if we hold to our expectations we suffer dissatisfaction. More importantly, we do not experience the events clearly, and we thus fail to learn from experience. From the Ordinary Mind Zen perspective, we create dissatisfaction, unhappiness and suffering by separating ourselves from direct experience and viewing the world through our self-created, self-centred perspective. To the extent that we embrace life as it is, the here-and-now events, regardless of whether they fit with our anticipation or desire, we can perceive events more clearly, learn from experience, and behave more effectively.

Ordinary Mind Zen meditation practice focuses on regular daily sitting meditation, continuing perpetually for a lifetime, as the foundation for developing willingness to experience life 'as it is' independently of whether it corresponds to our expectations, convenience, or desires. Sitting meditation helps to develop an awareness of present bodily sensations and mental process and thoughts, the two basic elements of life experience, by witnessing the experience of the moment by observation and attention.

The practice includes three fundamental techniques: (1) focusing or concentrating, (2) labelling thoughts and experiencing bodily sensations and (3) attending to emotional reactions. Focusing provides a foundation for practice by helping to quiet the mind. Concentration may shut out life experience so while serving as an important stage in practice this technique alone has limitations. As sitting settles, we observe thoughts as they arise and fall and attend to physical sensations without 'doing something' about them. We may label the type of thoughts, which helps to see recurrent themes. Over time thoughts seem less important or urgent and we may lose interest in many of our cherished opinions and beliefs. As our interest in thought decreases we may experience growing awareness of bodily sensations, particularly tension. As Leitner (1999c) pointed out, 'our original constructs, those that serve as the basis of the entire construct system, have been created in tight relationship to our bodies. Through the years, these sensed bodily confirmations become more entrenched as we develop a meaning system based upon them' (p. 9). Full experiencing of core constructs requires awareness of these bodily sensations, which may lead to change in the quality of the sensations and the tension. The third component involves attending to how we react emotionally to experiences and events, and experiencing how thoughts create emotional reactions. We come to see an emotion–thought spiral, where emotional physical sensations lead to thoughts and the thoughts lead to more physical tension. By attending to the relationship between emotions and thoughts, and by observing how they come from holding on to beliefs, we can see the core beliefs or core constructs and the methods that we use to avoid awareness of them. By developing greater awareness of construing, by learning about belief and attachment to core constructs, and by entertaining a more detached perspective towards them, we can improve our effectiveness in relating to the world.

CONCLUSION

Developing greater understanding of our tendency to attach to beliefs and self-images through 'institutionalizing' or 'idolizing' them can help us to apply constructive alternativism actively in our lives. We can gain greater awareness of the way we speak, and can develop a more intimate experience of our core construing. These activities may transform the way that we experience the universe and ourselves by reducing our exclusive identification with our current beliefs and self-structure. We may experience such change as threatening because it requires modification of our core constructions. Due to our desire for consistency and predictability, we resist change, and we often attempt to incorporate new understanding into our existing framework. Our idolatrous tendencies may encourage us, for example, to translate the propositions raised in this chapter into terms consistent with our current 'institutionalized' construct system. Recognition of the metaphorical nature of construing may help us to resist this hazard. If we accept the invitation to explore our tendencies to objectify our beliefs and to gain greater awareness of our active role in creating our understanding, we may more effectively maintain contact with the eternal existence of the unknown and approach each new moment with greater freshness.

CHAPTER 8

Working with Anger

Peter Cummins

Coventry Primary Care Trust, UK

> ... if we apply the scientist paradigm to man, we someday are going to catch ourselves saying, in the midst of a heated family discussion, that our child's temper tantrum is best understood as a form of scientific inquiry.
>
> (Kelly, 1969e, p. 293)

A DEFINITION OF ANGER

There is relatively little within the personal construct literature written about anger. Two key sources are McCoy's paper 'Reconstruction of Emotion' (1977) and Viney's book *Images of Illness* (1983). There are also relevant papers by Davidson and Reser (1996) and Kirsch and Jordan (2000).

In her paper, McCoy takes up the challenge of emotion within personal construct psychology. In a sense this seminal paper can be taken as a challenge to all personal construct practitioners. McCoy has staked out territory which is immediately recognizable to any practitioner and said 'Here is my version of the definition of these emotions—what do you think!'. She suggests defining anger as 'an awareness of the invalidation which leads to hostile behaviour'. It is an attempt to force events to conform so that the prediction will not be construed as a failure, and the construction will not have been invalidated.

What McCoy is suggesting is that when we are invalidated we have a choice. We can either become anxious (in the Kellyian sense)—the resolution to which may involve radical and difficult core role reconstrual—*or* we may decide that it would be easier to become hostile. McCoy is proposing that anger is the awareness of invalidation and that this invalidation precipitates hostility (1977, p. 119).

McCoy's definition is both puzzling and provoking, and requires some redefinition. The particular difficulty is her insistence that anger and hostility are inseparably entwined. There is no problem in accepting that anger *may* be linked to the awareness of hostility. But is it always so linked? Can a person be angry in a way that is not hostile? It is possible to be angry as a result of invalidation and become anxious; for example, she thinks that she can fight anyone ... she gets beaten up, invalidated . . . angry . . . she may become hostile . . . she had a bad day . . . could have won . . . or she may become anxious . . . and refuse to leave the house at night in case she meets people who she cannot be sure of fighting.

If hostility is not essentially linked to anger perhaps a definition of anger could be used which simply says 'anger is *an* emotional experience of invalidation'. I emphasize the 'an' as anger is only one of a range of possible responses to invalidation. From this it would follow that the level of anger would depend on the level of invalidation. If we can understand what has been invalidated then we can begin to understand the anger. In other words, if we understand anger as an indication of a particular form of construing, then understanding the construing will begin to alter the anger construing process.

An obvious place to start is to find out why the person has developed his anger constructs. Working with people referred with anger problems, I have become more and more aware of the developmental process of developing anger constructs. There is, for instance, a specific developmental sequence which can be summarized as the absence of a parent (usually father) between the age of 8 and 10 or a very abusive parental relationship at about this time. When taking an assessment history from new patients again and again I discovered a familiar tale. For example, John who was abandoned by both parents, taken in reluctantly by an aunt, always told he was an imposition and treated differently from his cousins; Jack who was abandoned by his father aged 8 and was left with a mother who told him that he now had to be the man of the house; Jane who discovered at the age of 10 that she was adopted and that her real mother was in fact her 'older sister'.

Leitner and colleagues (2000) offer a very useful structure which allowed me to understand the developmental process of developing anger constructs. The central theme of Leitner's work is his idea that 'when exposed to trauma the process of meaning making itself can "freeze" around the issues surrounding the trauma'. He goes on to point out that as childhood construing is more simple and concrete one may:

> . . . be less able to tolerate the implications of events that threaten the very nature of one's relationships with parents and other people who can literally hold one's lives in their hands . . . this process of freezing meaning making is more likely to occur around issues of childhood traumas rather than ones that occur later in life. (Leitner et al., 2000, p. 179)

Of particular interest is his development of the idea of self–other constancy: 'without constancy one cannot integrate new experiences of the self and other into a coherent sense of identity'. Leitner goes on to point out that without this constancy I can see you as loving at one point and, when you are angry with me, I see you as evil and hating me. This is a very clear stage in children's development. I chastize a child for his behaviour and the response is an immediate 'you do not love me'. It is critically important to make the distinction 'yes I do love you, it is your behaviour in this situation that I do not like'. As children develop self–other constancy they become able to make this distinction. Without this development, as Leitner and colleagues point out, 'how intimate can a relationship be if when one is sad, angry, bitter or bored, the other's experience of their connection is destroyed?' (Leitner et al., 2000, p. 182).

FAMILY HISTORIES

As will be described later in this chapter, the most effective way to reconstrue anger is within a group setting. For most group members, a family genogram produced within the group revealed that anger had played a large role in their family of origin or, in some cases, of adoption. 'Each family necessarily evolves a unique construct system that structures the family members' perception of their lives and provides a rationale for their actions. It governs their interactions' (Procter, 1996, p. 163).

As described already, there appears to be a constant theme within our clients of early family rejections. That pattern in adults can usefully be construed using Procter's (1985b) idea of family construct systems. Procter shows how systemic bow ties can be used to explore people's interactive construing (see also Procter's example in Chapter 43.2, pp. 431–434).

Joan	John
Construct: *He does not listen to me*	Construct: *She ignores me*
Action: Stop talking to him	Action: Make her listen

As Procter goes on to show, this framework demonstrates how each action validates, more or less, the other's constructs. Procter suggests that 'we are connected together by a web of invisible loyalties which permeate our choices and actions' (1985b, p. 332). By exploring the generations of a family we usually reveal interesting patterns of similarity and contrast. As Procter (1985b) concludes in his paper: 'We should keep the shared social reality in mind and understand how it works, even if we decide to intervene through only one person' (p. 350).

ANGER AND GENDER

Following on from family interaction comes the question of gender. A recent analysis of the theoretical perspectives regarding the female and male experience of anger concluded that anger as a function of gender has not been adequately tested. It is therefore not clear how women and men differ, if at all, in their experience and expression of anger (Sharkins, 1993).

On a personal note, when I first started working with people referred due to anger problems, the people referred were all male with a history of violence both domestic and in social settings, mainly linked to alcohol. I then began to receive referrals of women who had lost their temper with their children. As child protection issues are often central we may, with permission of the client, provide Social Services with a report about how someone has responded to the group. It is for Social Services to decide if the group treatment has had sufficient effect to allay their fears concerning the safety of the children. We later accepted women who have a history of violent relationships, who often seem to demonstrate Sharkins' comment regarding the lack of difference in the experience of anger between the sexes. However, it is true that the majority of our referrals are male and the majority of referrals for deliberate self-harm are female.

ANGER AND CULTURE

The importance of family construing in the development of anger expression has already been mentioned. It also seems to be true that anger, and often violence, may be culturally construed. In a recent talk on violence, Professor Anthony Clare quoted an experiment looking at the contribution of testosterone to the expression of violence. Five monkeys were allowed to develop a social 'pecking order'. Then number 3 was given a large dose of testosterone. That did indeed make him more aggressive, but only to numbers 4 and 5; he did not try to challenge numbers 1 and 2. Many of our patients express the realization that as they alter their anger pattern 'I will have to change my friends as all our relationships include the expression of anger/violence'. As the person changes it is necessary to see him with his partner as the relationship often struggles to accommodate change. This is, of course, often the case where radical changes in construing are required.

WORKING WITH ANGER GROUPS

Because of the importance of gender, family, the perspective of others and cultural influences, it becomes clear that it is far better to run a therapy group than try to deal with people on an individual basis. The purpose of such groups is nicely summarized by Llewelyn and Dunnett (1987, p. 251):

> The group provides an opportunity for participants, including the leaders, to explore the implications of their particular construct systems, to examine the implications of specific pre-emptive or constellatory constructions, and to bring to the group results of experiments taking place both inside and outside the group setting.

As I had expressed my difficulties with the phrase *Anger Management* because I did not want my anger 'managed', I call the group the 'Working with Anger Group'. There is no better summary of the aims of 'working with anger groups' than that by Don Bannister (see Chapter 6, pp. 61–74):

> . . . we must facilitate change not by assaulting each other's central beliefs but by helping each other to construct alternatives, beginning with areas of peripheral contradiction. *Thus we may gradually replace a central belief without the need for hostility.* (My italics)

To encourage the construction of alternatives as far as possible, we have run our 'working with anger group' as a mixed group. While at times this has led to tensions—'you are the sort of bastard who beat me up'—it has also forced group members to begin to appreciate the other perspective. In personal construct terms, they are encouraged to develop their capacity to construe from the other's standpoint. When the group has been exclusively male it has been difficult not to have group members stick to a very limited understanding of a female perspective: 'all women are unreasonable and out to get all they can from you'—constellatory construing in personal construct terms.

KEY THEORETICAL CONCEPTS OF CHANGE

The two key personal construct concepts are those of Regnancy and Sociality.

Regnancy and Anger

Kelly defines regnancy as 'a kind of superordinate construct which assigns each of its elements to a category on an all-or-none basis'. For Kelly, 'therapy is concerned with setting up regnant personal constructs to give new freedom and new control to the client who has been caught in the vice-like grip of obsolescent constructs' (1955/1991, p. 204/Vol. 1, p. 241).

Epting (1984) gives the very helpful clarification that 'the regnant construct might be thought of as an express train that runs directly from the superordinate (value-like constructs) down to the constructs that are concerned with everyday activity'. He goes on to point out that 'following this flow of constructs reveals how one's values influence one's behavior' (p. 45). I use the example of travel in this context: 'You can travel from Coventry to Aberdeen by train without stopping or you can stop at every station.' Given that people's construing systems are hierarchically organized, that means that if you irritate me my first reaction may be to get annoyed; that is, I stop at the first station. However, another person's reaction to being irritated may be to knock the other person out. The individual skips all the early stations and proceeds immediately to an extreme solution. That pattern is often seen within the group. For instance, Jim came down the stairs one morning, saw that the table was dusty and reacted by hitting his partner. He presented this behaviour as being incapable of explanation. Anger just came over him; it happened for no reason and he was unable to control it. His ladder is shown in Figure 8.1.

Jim jumps directly from a dusty table to the meaninglessness of life. As Kelly comments, 'this kind of simplified thinking, stemming as it does from ancient logical forms, accounts for a lot of woodenheaded conflict in the world both between persons and within persons' (1955/1991, p. 482/Vol. 1, 356).

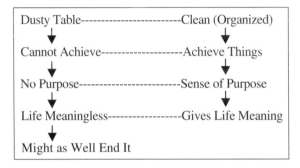

Figure 8.1 Jim's personal construct ladder

HOW MY PARTNER SEES ME	
Her Description of Me	*My Response*
Pig headed Stubborn Want too much Demanding Jealous of my mum	Aren't we all?—We all have opinions I'm standing my ground I'd like to be first It's the situation I'm not jealous, I'm annoyed
MY OVERALL RESPONSE TO MY PARTNER I say that you have not seen my change	

Figure 8.2   How my partner sees me and how I respond

Sociality and Anger

A key task of our approach is to find ways of getting participants to understand the other's perspective. Without exception, participants have been unable to see things as others see them. Male participants have a particular problem construing women. In a group's fourth session we explore this by getting them (a) to describe how their partners would construe them and (b) to produce their own responses to their part-ners' constructs. Figure 8.2 gives an example of what can be produced.

That exercise was completed with considerable hesitation due to the presence in the group of a female assistant psychologist. There were frequent references to 'nothing personal' with looks at her; they were not attacking her, this was just the way these men thought women are. At the end of the session the group members made such comments as:

'I feel really understood, I will sleep better tonight.'
'I had never seen it from her point of view before.'

THE THERAPY GROUP

The people referred to as the 'Working with Anger Group' are all living within the local community although commonly have a history of prison sentences. The strength of the common themes in the referrals is striking. These include the damage caused to these people's lives (and those of others close to them), a sense that the problem is getting out of control, and the eagerness of the referral agencies to assure me that these clients are highly motivated and worth taking on for treatment.

A real problem in running outpatient groups has been the rate of drop-out. Start-ing with eight members and ending up with four half-way through the life of the group is a common experience. I was therefore particularly interested in seeing whether I could run such a group in a semi-open format; that is, allowing new people to join the group as and when space became available.

The question that faced me was: 'Can the group members (who have been

THE IMPLICATIONS OF ANGER	
Undesired state Angry	*Desired state* Level-headed, stoned, chilled out, passive, happy, calm, normal
Disadvantages Upsetting people Stress Ill health Guilt Relationship problems	*Advantages* In control Organized Happier Content Better relationships
Advantages Not organized Being powerful One step ahead Able to go some Feel really good Control fear	*Disadvantages* Get nothing done Might be seen as soft More gullible Let things slide Sap Trumpet player for the Salvation Army

Figure 8.3   Example of an ABC inquiry of a group of participants

referred because of a perception/experience of them that their "angry" emotions were out of control), be enabled to reconstrue their anger?' *Or:* 'Can the group work with the idea that anger may be something that the person is unwilling to reconstrue despite the apparent mess it makes of his life?'

That idea seems validated by the second session of the group, which we described as 'looking at the pros and cons'. Within that session the group participants were asked to complete an ABC (Tschudi, 1977) on anger (see also Chapter 10, pp. 105–121). What they produced is shown in Figure 8.3.

As ever in my experience, when this exercise works it is immensely powerful. I really had to laugh at the description of the disadvantages of getting rid of anger. I do not know how well the Salvation Army is known outside Britain. Their bands are a relatively common sight, particularly at Christmas. It is such a powerful image, that without anger you become a trumpet player in a Christian army band! This exercise is one which usually has a major impact on group members.

At this moment it seems clear that the group members see anger as offering the greater possibilities. It protects them from the risk of threat, and as long as they stay angry no change is necessary. At one level of awareness, being an angry person works. It involves having a set of very pre-emptive constructs: either you are angry or you are not.

Anger appears to give people their chief means of anticipation: 'As long as I am angry I can cope with whatever happens to me.' However, as the group progresses the situational dilemmas faced by people with this construing strategy also become clearer.

A member of the group was clear that he got angry because of the unreasonable expectations of his wife. She laid down what he called ground rules; for instance, 'do not bring your friends into my kitchen, take your shoes off before entering the house', and for eighteen years he had resented these rules, complied intermittently with them and suppressed his anger. He was referred to the group with a 'nine-year history of low mood problems with aggression and anger control'. He seems to highlight the 'choice' dilemma:

> Anger as awareness of being put into the position of such a painful choice you have forced me to see that either I am a totally unreasonable man who does not value your opinion or I have to stay having mood problems and nightmares.

This particular client had tried to explain the situation by attributing the problems to his wife's premenstrual tension. I pointed out that it could be that *or* it could be that she tolerated him the other three weeks but was unable to tolerate him the fourth week. As often happens, this simple observation seems to have been a catalyst in getting him to contemplate the development of improved sociality with his partner. Up to this point he seems to have been using what McCoy describes as 'loving hostility':

> Loving hostility is that form of control with a relationship which keeps another individual from maturing. For example, a husband who treats his wife as an incompetent child.

Within the 'working with anger group' we thus decipher each person's construing system, understand that within the family context and go on to understand how the person uses these constructs to survive. From this each group member then begins to work out ways of reconstruing that allow the person to relate to people within their lives without being invalidated.

CONCLUSION

This chapter began from my clinical work and the ideas about anger provoked by McCoy's seminal paper. McCoy points out that anxiety need not culminate in hostility; rather, 'it can impel extension of the system so that construction can be a closer, improved approximation of "raw reality" than at present'. It was not clear to me why that cannot also be true of anger. That is, there is no necessary culmination in hostility as a result of the experience of anger.

My proposed definition of anger as 'an emotional experience of invalidation' falls within this. What I think we see within the group is the replacement of the belief that anger is the only way to keep control, be powerful, control fear, and so forth. A critical part of this is the development of a better attempt to see the world as others see it. This process starts within the group. It facilitates its members in developing the capacity to be aggressive in a Kellyian sense and, in doing so, to replace the central belief about anger. The most important experience within the group has been the clarification of the role that the experience of anger plays for each group member. As Aristotle put it: 'The middle state is praiseworthy—that in virtue of which we are angry with the right people, at the right things, in the right way and so on.' That nicely sums up the experience of working constructively with anger in group settings.

Evaluation

Due to real literacy problems, the best evaluation has been verbal. The group has given the following feedback:

- I couldn't believe that there were other people out there who were as angry as I am.
- It is always difficult to understand your anger. I am really surprised that I'm not the only weirdo with a bad temper.
- People with different backgrounds have angry outbursts.
- The group provides a great release of mental tension.
- The first thing I learned was to watch my physical state; if I am tired then I might snap.
- I listen to what you say and then try it out during the week.
- Sometimes the group only stays with me for a few days and then I say f*** it.
- It does last longer as the group goes on and you stay coming to it.
- We learn to step up to the fence and not bite, we are here to learn how to argue and not to lose our temper.
- The best thing I have learned is not to make others pay for my anger.
- Coming to the group has meant that I do not lash out when I get angry; I have learned to get angry but not violent.

From Theory to Practice

INTRODUCTION

This is the point in the *Handbook* where we move away from theory and into practice. And about time too, more restless readers may well think.

The repertory grid is probably better known than personal construct theory itself. Richard Bell offers a scholarly overview of the research that has been carried out into many aspects of the repertory grid technique. He also points to some of the questions that have yet to be answered.

Fay Fransella describes some of the skills required and tools used by personal construct practitioners. There should really be two chapters, but it became apparent that most of the skills described by Kelly were needed to use several of the tools. After describing some skill requirements for therapists, counsellors and other practitioners, she starts the 'tools' part by giving a blow-by-blow account of how a ratings grid can be created. She also pays particular attention to the way in which she uses the 'laddering' procedure.

Pam Denicolo gives examples of more ways of eliciting personal constructs, often based on non-verbal methods such as drawings, and pays particular attention to the selection of methods to fit specific contexts. She also includes a description of Kelly's other method of assessment, the self-characterization.

Mildred Shaw and Brian Gaines then explain their use of personal construct ideas in the development of 'expert systems'. Although this is a highly specialized, computer-based approach, they write in such a clear manner that readers will be able to see exactly what they are doing. For those who are knowledgeable, they provide details of websites where further information is available.

CHAPTER 9

The Repertory Grid Technique

Richard C. Bell

University of Melbourne, Australia

> . . . But we can look beyond words. We can study contexts. For example, does the client use the word 'affectionate' only when talking about persons of the opposite sex? . . . The answers to such questions . . . may give us an understanding of the interweaving of the client's terminology and provide us with an understanding of his outlook which no dictionary could offer.
>
> (Kelly, 1955/1991, p. 267/Vol. 1, p. 189)

WHAT IS A REPERTORY GRID?

The repertory grid is probably the most widely known aspect of the work of George Kelly. Originally called the 'role construct repertory test' it soon became known as the 'repertory grid'. The repertory grid is not simply a technique that is independent of personal construct theory (Bell, 1988). Kelly's Fundamental Postulate says that *a person's processes are psychologically channelized by the ways in which he anticipates events*. That underpins the repertory grid. The *ways* are the constructs of a repertory grid, and the *events* are the elements. The technique of the repertory grid thus involves defining a set of elements, eliciting a set of constructs that distinguish among these elements, and relating elements to constructs.

SOME HISTORY

Following Kelly's original publication of the technique in 1955, the repertory grid attracted only limited and sporadic attention in the following decade (see Bonarius, 1965, for a review of research up to that time). The turning point came with research by Don Bannister into the thought processes of schizophrenics in Britain in the early 1960s (see Chapter 20, pp. 211–222). The grid test of schizophrenic thought disorder, subsequently published with Fay Fransella (1966), drew

---

International Handbook of Personal Construct Psychology. Edited by F. Fransella.
© 2003 John Wiley & Sons, Ltd.

attention to the technique. Although this variant did not eventually succeed as a practical clinical tool, the general use of the grid *per se* became more widely known in Britain due to the availability of a 'scoring service' provided by Patrick Slater at the Institute of Psychiatry. Slater (1976) reports that by 1973 the service was processing 10 000 grids per year. The grid was less generally adopted in North America.

In the next decade, the grid was seen as dominating published research in personal construct theory (Neimeyer, 1985c). However, a recent count of references to 'Repertory Grid' or 'Rep Test' in the database, PsycINFO, shows that publication peaked in the late 1980s and has subsequently declined.

REPERTORY GRID DATA

A repertory grid may contain both qualitative and quantitative data. The identity of the elements and the nature of the constructs may provide qualitative information while the relationships between the constructs and elements may be interpreted as quantitative data. However, the information in a grid clearly depends on only the elements and constructs that have been included.

Choosing Elements

In standard grid elicitation procedures, elements are determined first, and constructs elicited from distinctions made among these elements. Therefore the choice of elements is crucial, yet oddly enough has been little studied. Most studies have followed the Kellyian process of defining the sample of elements by giving the respondent 'role titles' (such as 'rejected teacher' or 'ethical person') as a basis for choosing elements. The effect of this has only been empirically studied in a limited fashion. Mitsos (1958) compared 'acquaintances' as elements elicited by role title with those simply selected from a list, finding the role title approach showed greater consistency over time. Williams (1971) and McFayden and Foulds (1972) both varied the Bannister and Fransella (1966) grid test of schizophrenic thought disorder by comparing the standard supplied photograph form with an 'elicited persons' form, and both found that when familiar persons were used as elements, greater intensity and consistency indices were found. Adams-Webber (1997a) used both real and 'nonsense' elements in one of his many studies into the ratio of assignment to positive or negatively valued poles, finding differences in the ratios of assignment to poles. These studies thus confirmed that the choice of elements does, indeed, affect the nature of grid data.

Supporting evidence comes from Bell et al. (2002) who examined the sources of variation (in an *analysis of variance* sense) in grid data collected in a variety of ways and found that elements usually accounted for about four times as much variance as did constructs. Clearly the 'element choice' aspect of the grid is important and needs further research work.

Two process-oriented variants have been proposed. Keen and Bell (1981) described a procedure where constructs and elements were elicited alternately. Bell (1990a, p. 28) reported a small study where the Keen and Bell procedure did not produce any advantages (from a construct perspective) over traditional triadic construct elicitation. Shaw and Thomas (1978) described an interactive process, where the respondent was invited to supply a new element that would distinguish between constructs that were similar (in terms of having a high matching score). While the impact of these different procedures has not been closely examined, they perhaps point to an opportunity for more process-oriented research with the technique.

Eliciting Constructs

Perhaps the most basic concern for the use of *personal* constructs in a repertory grid is the issue of whether they should be elicited from the respondent or supplied by the person administering the grid. From a purely Kellyian perspective, the technique would seem to demand that the constructs be elicited from the person, since they are *personal* constructs. However, much research (and, as indicated above, research is a major user of repertory grids) demands aggregated data, and data cannot be aggregated without commonality. The theory provides for this in the Commonality Corollary that states: *to the extent that one person employs a construction of experience which is similar to that employed by another, his processes are psychologically similar to those of the other person.* This is an issue of some practical importance since the use of grids in organizational research is often concerned with the construing of groups rather than individuals, as shown for example by Fransella (1988; see also Chapter 33, pp. 329–338).

A tradition of research has focused on whether supplied and elicited constructs produce similar results. Adams-Webber (1970) reviewed studies such as this and concluded that although people preferred to use their own constructs, it made no difference when summary measures of grids were calculated. More recently the same author (Adams-Webber, 1998) found that when a person had to make inferences about another, those based on constructs elicited from the other were significantly more accurate than were those based on supplied ones. The issue of supplied versus elicited constructs would thus seem to depend on the context in which the grid is being used.

If, however, we adopt the elicitation perspective, we are confronted by a further set of issues. Kelly originally listed six triadic methods, the most influential being what he termed the 'minimum context' form. In that form the respondent is presented with sets of three elements (triads) and for each set is asked to specify some important way in which two of the elements are alike (the emergent pole of the construct) and thereby different (the contrast pole of the construct) from the third. This bipolar elicitation of constructs accorded with Kelly's Dichotomy Corollary. Some of Kelly's original variants on this involve use of a constant element (the self) or the sequential changing of the triad, an element at a time. Other approaches include pairs (two-element) elicitation of constructs, sometimes referred to as dyadic elicitation (for example, Caputi & Reddy, 1999; Epting, et al., 1993), although that terminology can be confused with the use of dyads as elements (for example, Ryle & Lunghi, 1970; Butt et al., 1997b). Comparisons by Caputi and Reddy (1999) and Hagans and colleagues (2000) suggest that different results are obtained under different construct elicitation procedures. Another technique for eliciting superordinate constructs was devised by Hinkle (1965) and is popularly known as 'laddering' (see Chapter 10, pp. 105–121).

Another important concern is whether the elements chosen ensure that the respondent's universe of constructs is appropriately sampled. Unlike the element situation where stratified sampling can be used through role titles, construct elicitation can use no such stratification (since the stratifying characteristic would be an imposed or supplied superordinate construct). The only way to ensure a representative sampling is through an appropriate sampling design. Bell (1990a, p. 27–28) has outlined the difficulties in achieving this when the grid contains more than seven elements. For example, in Kelly's original grid with 32 constructs elicited from 24 elements, almost 70% of possible pairs of elements were not considered. A recent example of the use of an appropriate design can be found in the grids of Leach and colleagues (2001).

Relating Elements to Constructs

In a number of practical situations, the focus of the technique is on the nature of the constructs elicited and these are used as qualitative data, sometimes as the starting point for other investigations such as 'laddering'. However, in other settings (for example, most research settings) there is an interest in relating elements to constructs. There are two related aspects to this: how the data are collected, and the scaling of the relationship. A choice exists on how data are collected for relating elements to constructs. Do we take each construct in turn and relate all the elements to it, or do we take each element in turn and consider its relationships to the set of constructs? Does it make a difference?

The issue of how elements are related to constructs has received more attention. Kelly's original grid allowed for three dispositions of elements with respect to a construct. The element could be set at one pole, or the other pole, or could be designated as not being related to the construct (theoretically, lying outside the 'range of convenience' of the construct). This last option, while theoretically attractive, posed problems for some subsequent analyses of grid data, and has consequently not been widely used. One of the earliest alternatives to the original method was to rank elements on each construct. This is discussed in some detail by Fransella and Bannister (1977, pp. 30–39) as, prior to the wide availability of computers, manual or calculator-based analysis of grid data was required, and ranks provide some simplicity in this. Of course, ranks impose a distribution of elements along a construct and restrict the free allocation of elements. Rankings were more popular in Great Britain while 13-point ratings were promulgated by Landfield (1971, 1977) in North America. This variant used a +6 to 0 to –6 rating basis. Recent research elsewhere (Krosnick, 1999, p. 544) has shown that the signing of numbers as positive or negative can influence construing. Simple ratings (such as 1 to 7) have been more generally used with the advent of computers. Computer programs (and websites) that can be used for the elicitation of repertory grids are listed in Appendix 3 in this volume.

ANALYSING THE DATA OF REPERTORY GRIDS

The compact appearance of a tabular representation of a completed repertory grid can be misleading with respect to the amount of data contained. For instance, if elements and more particularly constructs, have been elicited then these provide information to the enquirer. Landfield (1971) devised a coding system for the content of constructs of North Americans, which has not perhaps received the attention it deserves, while recently another such system has been proposed by Feixas and colleagues (2002) based on the constructs of Spanish subjects.

Attention has rather focused on the quantitative data in the grid, which can also be substantial. Sixteen elements rated on 16 constructs requires 256 judgements of a respondent, more than many personality inventories. Grid data can be analysed at the univariate, bivariate and multivariate levels to answer different kinds of questions about the psychological processes represented in the grid. An example of this kind of comprehensive evaluation can be found in Bell (2000d).

Indices

Where a ratings form of the grid is used, simple statistics can provide information about constructs and elements. Standard deviations will show how elements are distributed between the construct poles, while skewness measures will show lopsidedness (termed maldistribution by Fransella and Bannister (1977, pp. 83–84)). Landfield and Cannell (1988) developed a similar (but idiosyncratic) measure of the tendency to use extreme ratings (that is, locating elements at one pole or the other) in a grid called 'New Ord'. Interestingly, it was assumed by Landfield (1977) to be a measure of superordinacy of a construct. Chiari and colleagues (1990) have similarly argued, from a theoretical perspective, that superordinate constructs will be lopsided.

The basic building block for examining the structure of a grid is the relationship between pairs of constructs. Such relationships between constructs are usually measured by correlations or other measures of association, such as city-block distances (see Shaw, 1980, pp. 158–160). For relationships between elements, distances should be used (Mackay, 1992). As previously mentioned, in some computer interactive elicitation these indices are computed during the elicitation to provide the respondent with an opportunity of adding an element to increase the distinction between constructs or a construct to increase the discrimination between elements.

There has been a long tradition of summarizing indices of association, particularly among constructs, where it is known as 'cognitive simplicity-complexity' (Chapter 5, pp. 51–58). Bieri's (1955) original index was a simple sum of matchings of element allocation to constructs, consequently the values the index could take depended on the size of the grid and the kind of rating adopted. Other measures include Fransella and Bannister's (1977) 'intensity' (the sum of squared rank correlations multiplied by 100), Landfield and Schmittdiel's (1983) functionally-independent-construct 'FIC' index, the percentage of variance accounted for by the first principal component of construct intercorrelations (suggested by several authors) and Bell and Keen's (1981) use of intraclass correlations. While these measures tend to agree with one another (see Epting et al., 1992; Feixas et al., 1992), Bieri's index has attracted some criticism (e.g. Applegate et al., 1991), as has Landfield's FIC index (Soldz & Soldz, 1989).

Element indices have been less widely investigated and confined to grids where the 'self' appears as an element. One of the most robust indices is that attached to the allocation of self and other figures to positive and negative poles of constructs. Adams-Webber (1990) summarizes much of this work, although it has continued since, which produces some striking constants with respect to the proportions of total positive construals, positive construals of self, and like-self judgements. Of course, since these are constants they are of little use in considering relationships with other variables, but they have been used as the basis for conjectures about the possible mental models for such judgements (see Adams-Webber, 1990, for an outline of the possibilities).

The other kind of index associated with elements has been the notion of discrepancy between them. First noted by Jones (1961), with respect to 'self' figures as elements (such as 'me now', 'me in six months', 'actual self', 'ideal self'), the notion was used in clinical research by Makhlouf-Norris & others (for example, Makhlouf-Norris & Jones, 1971). These are usually calculated as distances. However the possible distances that can be calculated will depend on the rating scale used in the grid. Norris and Makhlouf-Norris (1976) wished to identify abnormally close or distant figures, so used random data in grids to provide a 'baseline' reference. Slater (1977) devised an expected distance which could be used to rescale individual distances so that they were comparable. Hartmann (1992) showed that Slater's correction did not take into account the number of constructs considered, and suggested a correction. A subsequent empirical evaluation (Schoeneich & Klapp, 1998) supported this change.

Representations

Summary indices such as those above play a large role in the use of the repertory grid in research. In individual contexts, such as professional settings, the demands can be different and a more 'qualitative' picture of the relationships among constructs and elements is often desirable. Such a picture can be obtained through quantitative modelling. The two traditional approaches to representing these relationships have been principal component analysis and cluster analysis. The former is the older tradition. Kelly, himself, outlined an approximate method of representing relationships among constructs, while Levy and Dugan (1956) showed how conventional principal component analysis could be used to show the structure of relationships among constructs.

The major advance was provided by Patrick Slater (1964), who showed that a related technique (singular-value-decomposition) could be used to provide an analysis that gave a simultaneous representation of constructs and elements. Slater referred to this as 'principal components', which led to confusion among those familiar with the traditional principal component approaches to factor analysis. More recently, correspondence analysis, or the similar technique, biplot (both also related to singular-value-decomposition) have also been used to provide joint construct-element spatial representations of repertory grid data. Multidimensional unfolding (a variant of multidimensional scaling) can also be used to provide a joint construct-element spatial representation of repertory grid. Leach and colleagues (2001) provide examples of representations of a repertory grid with these different approaches. Yet another approach which represents hierarchical structures among constructs (in line with Kelly's Organization Corollary) has been demonstrated by Sewell and colleagues (1996).

Cluster analysis has been popular, particularly in the United Kingdom, since Shaw and Thomas (1978) introduced the program 'Focus' that ran on early Apple computers. Most clustering that is relevant to repertory grid data is hierarchical clustering. Such clustering differs from principal components in that there are many criteria for the formation of a cluster (while there are only minor ·differences in principal component algorithms), and cluster analysis solutions can look very different from one another. Another difference is that, apart from one exception (Leach, 1981), cluster analysis is carried out separately on elements and constructs, although they might be visually represented by a computer program simultaneously as clusterings on the rows and columns of the grid matrix.

How well our representation of constructs or elements corresponds to the original grid data cannot always be determined. For example, while we can estimate the construct correlations from the construct factor solution and compare these with the original construct correlations, we cannot reconstruct the element data from such an analysis (it has been 'lost' in the calculation of construct correlations) and thus we cannot compare our construct factor analysis with the original grid data. In some kinds of analyses, such as correspondence analysis or singular-value-decomposition analysis (for example, Slater's INGRID) we can, however, measure the discrepancy between the grid generated from our representation and the original grid. Curiously this seems to be rarely done.

Most of the above representations of repertory grid data are based on association or distances. However the theory does not consider this kind of relationship between constructs, rather, through the Organization Corollary, hierarchical or super- and subordinate relationships are posited between constructs (see Bell, 1988). Such relationships are essentially asymmetric (unlike distances or correlations) and need to be modelled in different ways. Shaw and Gaines (1981) introduced such an approach using conditional probability as an asymmetric measure of association.

Computer software for analysing repertory grid software is listed in Appendix 3 to this volume, although standard statistical packages can also be used. Bell (1994) has produced a document showing how SPSS can be used to carry out a wide range of analyses, while Leach and colleagues (2001) have shown how SYSTAT might similarly be used.

MULTIPLE REPERTORY GRIDS

As indicated above, research often involves the use of repertory grids collected over a number of respondents and/or a number of occasions. Where each of these multiple grids is unique with respect to both elements and constructs, the only way in which the data can be aggregated across the grids is via the summary indices reviewed above. However, these summary indices have the disadvantage of suppressing the detail of the repertory grids. The alternative is to restrict either elements or constructs (or both) to be common across grids. Commonality of elements can be less of a problem when the elements are some common external event (such as types of tea, or aspects of lectures) but may be more of a problem when elements are less defined (a close friend). This issue has not been studied in detail. Commonality of constructs is possible (the theory has a corollary defining this) and Bell (2000a) has suggested a way in which the degree of commonality may be assessed.

If there is commonality of an aspect of multiple grids, then this may enter into the design of the study, either as a repeated-measures variable for significance testing or as a facet to be represented in spatial representation. Examples of such spatial representations (through individual differences multidimensional scaling or unfolding) has been described by Leach and colleagues (2001). If both elements and constructs are common, then the further possibility of three-mode factor analysis as a way of representing the data becomes possible. Kroonenberg (1985) provides an example of this.

Analysis of multiple repertory grids can usually be carried out through the standard statistical packages referred to above. At present there are few grid-specific programs for multiple grid data (see Appendix 3).

OTHER TYPES OF GRID

Repertory grids are not the only kind of grid associated with personal construct theory. Another kind of grid which is based on constructs is the implication grid devised by Hinkle (1965). A modification of that was used by Fransella (1972) in a study of people who stutter (see Chapter 20, pp. 211–222). Caputi and colleagues (1990) reviewed the methods of analysing Hinkle's data and presented a relational model that was advantageous in allowing the fit of the model to be assessed and a simultaneous estimation of all hierarchical relationships in the data. Kelly also devised a situation–resource grid (now often called a dependency grid) in which 'elements' are resources and 'constructs' are situations (see Chapter 16, pp. 171–180). While these grids can be analysed as ordinary grid data there is often an additional concern for the ways in which resources are allocated to situations. Walker and colleagues (1988), and Bell (2001), have devised indices (available in GRIDSTAT; Bell, 1998) which indicate the extent to which resources may be dispersed across situations and vice versa.

PSYCHOMETRIC ISSUES

The variety of ways of carrying out the repertory grid technique preclude an overarching conclusion about the reliability or validity of the technique. As an example, Neimeyer and Hagans (2002) varied four aspects of the repertory grid technique and found up to three-way interactions (between number of elements used in elicitation, wording of elicitation and rating direction) affecting Landfield's index of functionally independent constructs. Further, not all aspects of traditional test theory have the same meaning for repertory grid data (Bell, 1990b). Nevertheless some reviewers have adopted a traditional perspective (Jackson & Paunonen, 1981, p. 519; Neimeyer, 1985c, p. 153) and have suggested that the technique is faulty in psychometric terms. Such reviews have tended to ignore the evidence to the contrary. In a work that has often been overlooked, Bannister and Mair (1968) reviewed a substantial amount of research which show test–retest correlations of around 0.80 for construct choice, element choice and grid rating. Subsequent studies have confirmed these conclusions. For example, Lohaus (1986) found average test–retest reliabilities of 0.88 when subjects could choose their own rating schemes, and both Feixas and colleagues (1992) and Caputi and Keynes (2001) found substantial retest reliability (up to 0.90) for a number of grid measures.

Validity issues have been less commonly addressed in a measurement context although more widely carried out with respect to the theory of personal constructs (for example, Fransella & Bannister, 1967). However in a grid-measurement context, Dempsey and Neimeyer (1995) found convergence of repertory grids and implications grids with respect to the assessment of construct structure. In a more specific examination of grid indices, Applegate and colleagues (1991) reported a lack of convergent validity for Bieri's index of cognitive complexity, while Walker and colleagues (1988) demonstrated the validity of an index of dispersion of dependency derived from dependency grids. There are many more indices, however, for which evidence of validity or reliability is not available. Research with the technique continues, much of which is now reported in the *Journal of Constructivist Psychology*. For example, a special issue (April–June 2002) is centred on the work of Greg Neimeyer (2002).

CONCLUSIONS

The repertory grid technique has been the most widely known and widely used aspect of George Kelly's personal construct theory. Why is this? There are many reasons: it is a measurement device that has a solid conceptual basis for its structure; it provides a succinct representation of the way a person construes his world or some aspect of it; it is flexible in allowing for both individualized and normative kinds of assessment; it can be applied in an almost limitless range of contexts; and it can be used to provide many different kinds of information. While there have been concerns about a preoccupation with this technique (for example, Neimeyer, 1985c) and, as indicated in this chapter, some issues that need further examination, there is no other technique as general and as flexible as the repertory grid.

CHAPTER 10

Some Skills and Tools For Personal Construct Practitioners

Fay Fransella

University of Hertfordshire, UK

> It would, in my opinion, be a serious mistake for psychologists who hope to raise man from the position of an unwitting subject in an experiment to a posture of greater dignity, to abandon technology. The spirit of man is not enlarged by withholding his tools. . . . A man without instruments may look dignified enough to those who do not stand in his shoes, but he most certainly will be incapable of making the most of his potentialities.
>
> (Kelly, 1969a, p. 143)

This chapter has two main sections. There are skills that all personal construct practitioners need to acquire in order to carry out any intervention with a client, be it in psychotherapy and counselling or in coming to understand a child having trouble at school. There are also many tools that are available to personal construct practitioners to assist them in eliciting information about how a client construes his or her personal world. Skills and some tools are combined into one chapter because they overlap considerably—the skills are nearly all required by those who want to use the tools.

SOME NECESSARY SKILLS

The Ability to Subsume Another's Construing

An essential skill required of the personal construct practitioner is the ability to subsume the construing system of the client. That is basically the ability to see the world through the client's eyes. Kelly talks about this mainly in relation to psychotherapy and counselling. In that context the practitioner needs to subsume the

---

International Handbook of Personal Construct Psychology. Edited by F. Fransella.

client's construing under Kelly's *professional constructs*. These are such things as *tight* versus *loose* construing and these are outlined in David Winter's chapter on problems of construing (Chapter 19, pp. 201–209). Kelly puts it like this: 'since all clients have their own personal systems my system should be *a system of approach* by means of which I can quickly come to understand and subsume the widely varying systems which my clients can be expected to present' (Kelly, 1955/1991, p. 595/Vol. 2, p. 28).

Apart from the therapy and counselling situation, the ability to subsume the client's construing system is essential for anyone who is a personal construct practitioner. Subsuming is a basic part of Kelly's idea of role relationships expressed in the Sociality Corollary. He makes the point that subsuming another's ways of looking at things need not be reciprocal:

> ... while one person may play a role in a social process involving the other person, through subsuming a version of that other person's way of seeing things, the understanding need not be reciprocated. (Kelly, 1955/1991, p. 98/Vol. 1, p. 69)

It is useful to note that subsuming a person's construing is not the same as 'empathizing'. Empathy usually implies not only entering the other person's world but experiencing how the other person is feeling about that world. Subsuming involves seeing the world through another's eyes—and even experiencing some of the feelings involved—but also maintaining a sense of oneself as being separate from the other. Only in that way can one gain a personal understanding of that person and play a role in relation to that person.

Suspending Personal Values

There is a second component involved in understanding the construing of another. In actual fact, Kelly does not discuss suspension in relation to subsuming, but sees it in relation to memory and forgetting. Over the years of discovering the value of subsuming a client's construing, it became very apparent that the personal construct interviewer has to suspend his or her own values. If one does not, the other's construing is filtered through the interviewer's values. The only way to see the world as someone else sees it is to have no values through which it is filtered. The skill of suspending one's own values in order to truly listen to another is not an easy one to acquire, as many students of personal construct psychology have found.

Listening Credulously

The idea of listening credulously is mentioned many times in this volume as being one of the requirements of a skilled personal construct practitioner. It is sometimes believed that it applies to any and all work that a personal construct practitioner undertakes with another person. But that is to misunderstand what Kelly meant. He describes it like this:

... the personal-construct psychologist observes a person's own abstractions of behaviour. ... He starts by taking what he sees and hears at face value. He even takes at face value what he sees and hears about his subject's constructs. In psychotherapy this is commonly called 'acceptance' of the client. ... Our term ... is *the credulous attitude*. (Kelly, 1955/1991, p. 174/Vol. 1, p. 121)

What Kelly was proposing is that the personal construct practitioner is always trying to subsume the client's construing and this does not mean 'going along with how the client sees things'. 'Acceptance does not mean seeking mere commonality of ideas between clinician and client, it means seeking a way of *subsuming* the construct system of the client. One must retain his integrity in order to be of help to the client' (Kelly, 1955/1991, p. 374/Vol. 1, p. 277).

Once some understanding of a person's construing has been achieved, any programme to help the person reconstrue may well involve the practitioner in acting so as to invalidate some construing of the client. But that is always done in the context of attempting to 'hear' and 'see' how the client is construing that invalidation. The trap that needs to be avoided is to think that 'acceptance' is the end of the process. It is only the beginning. While even obvious lies are accepted at being meaningful and important to the client, at some later stage those lies may become the focus of the counselling if it is thought that would help the client reconstrue themselves and life.

Reflexivity

One final skill that is essential for anyone wanting to apply personal construct psychology in a professional capacity—or in daily life if they wish—is *reflexivity*. Kelly does not mention this in Chapter 1 of this volume, but Don Bannister discusses it at some length in Chapter 3 (pp. 33–39) and shows how reflexivity is central to all Kelly's thinking. To emphasize its importance, below is a description that Don Bannister gave to a group of American psychologists of how the ability to be reflexive discourages psychologists from diminishing their concepts of themselves and those they study. He said:

> ... At a joke level psychologists may argue that a particular psychoanalyst is writing a particular paper in order to sublimate his sex instinct, or we may toy with the notion that a book by some learning theorist is evidence that the said learning theorist was suffering from a build-up of reactive inhibition. But in our more solemn moments we seem to prefer the paradoxical view that psychologists are explainers, predictors, and experimenters, whereas the organism, God bless him, is a very different kettle of fish. ... The delight and instruction which many of us find in George Kelly's Personal Construct Theory derives in no small measure from the fact that it is an explicitly reflexive theory. There may be no onus on the chemist when he writes his papers on the nature of acids and alkalis to account in terms of his acid–alkali distinction for his behaviour in writing a journal paper. But psychologists are in no such fortunate position.
>
> Turning this issue of reflexivity the other way around, I am reminded of a recurrent theme in certain types of science fiction story. The master-chemist has finally produced a bubbling green slime in his test tubes, the potential of which is great but the properties of which are mysterious. He sits alone in his

> laboratory, test tube in hand, brooding about what to do with the bubbling green slime. Then in slowly dawns on him that the bubbling green slime is sitting alone in the test tube brooding about what to do with him. This special nightmare of the chemist is the permanent work-a-day world of the psychologist—the bubbling green slime is always wondering what to do with you.
>
> (Bannister, 1966, pp. 21–22)

Personal Characteristics of Psychotherapists and Counsellors

Four vital skills that a personal construct practitioner has to acquire have already been mentioned. These are being able to subsume a client's construing of the world (as far as that is humanly possible), suspending his or her own values, being able to listen credulously, and being able to apply the theory to one's own construing processes.

Apart from those, Kelly suggests that psychotherapists and counsellors should have four other skills.

Creativity

Kelly argues that every client will present new challenges which will mean that the therapist has to devise methods and construe in ways not used before.

> Creativity implies that one can construe elements as being alike and different in ways which are not logically deduced or, as yet, literally defined. Creation is therefore an act of daring, an act of daring through which the creator abandons those literal defenses behind which he might hide if his act is questioned or its results proven invalid. The psychotherapist who dares not try anything he cannot verbally defend is likely to be sterile in a psychotherapeutic relationship.
>
> (Kelly, 1955/1991, pp. 600–601/Vol. 2, p. 32)

Skill in Observation

In order to be alert and sensitive to a wide range of client responses, clinicians need to have a well-elaborated construing system of their own coupled with a variety of experiences. For instance, it is necessary to be able to decide when it is important to ask for a medical opinion about a client—perhaps the client's current confusion is the result of a developing brain tumour.

Clear Construction of the Psychotherapeutic/Counselling Role

In the reflexive manner that permeates personal construct psychology, the clinician has to be able to recognize when he or she is threatening or making the client anxious. In subsuming the client's construing system, the therapist and counsellor are able to maintain enough distance from the distresses of the client not to be overwhelmed by them. They have to be able to cease that role when they return home.

Verbal Skill

Kelly also says the therapist and counsellor need to be verbally skilled. That is not so much about vocabulary but about being able to get to the meaning that often lies behind the words.

SOME 'TOOLS OF THE TRADE'

Kelly created two 'tools of the trade', one being the repertory grid (see Chapter 9, pp. 95–103) and the other the self-characterization (see Chapter 11, pp. 123–132). Here we are concerned with 'how do you do it?' Richard Bell gives an extensive overview of many aspects of repertory grid methodology, so the following is an example for those who want to explore the methodology by designing a ratings grid themselves.

Repertory Grids

First of all, a grid is nothing more than a blank matrix. The job of the designer is to fill it in with 'element' labels at the top of each column, 'construct labels' on either side of each row and ratings in each of the cells showing how the person construed each element in relation to each construct.

Richard Bell, in Chapter 9, describes ways in which the elements can be chosen and constructs elicited. As he says, the choice of elements is crucial and relates totally to the purpose of the grid. Choice of elements is centrally determined by asking the question 'What am I trying to find out by using this grid?' Having decided on the purpose—for example, why people choose specific makes of toothpaste—the elements must then cover the broad spectrum of toothpaste available. They must also be within the range of convenience of the constructs being used. It is no use, having elicited constructs from different toothpastes, adding an element 'my favourite jewel', as that is unlikely to be within the range of convenience of such constructs as *has a peppermint taste*. One of the best examples of a range of convenience problem comes from Brown's review of the *Semantic Differential* when he asked 'is a boulder sweet or sour?' (1958).

Most grids are designed to find out how a person construes people or events in their lives. If you wanted to find out whether people taking part in a course you are running have the same views about their organization, then the elements would be about their work and their organization, such as:

'my manager', 'my job now', 'my organization', 'the best manager I can think of', 'how my organization will be in 3 years' time', 'how customers see my organization', 'how I would like my job to be', and 'my organization 3 years ago'.

These elements include the essential 'ideal' element. That element acts as an anchor against which all other elements and constructs can be compared. If that ideal does not have mostly very positive ratings, then something is going wrong from the client's point of view—perhaps he or she just does not want to complete the

	My manager	My job now	My organization	Best manager I know	My organization in 3 years	As customers see my organization	How would like job to be	My organization 3 years ago	
Constructive	5	3	7	1	5	7	1	7	Mundane
Disorganized	6	2	2	6	4	1	6	1	Organized
Listens	4	6	5	1	6	6	1	2	Doesn't hear
No clear view	4	5	4	6	4	3	7	5	Takes strategic view

Figure 10.1   Ratings grid

grid and is answering randomly. Those elements enable one to see how the organization is perceived in the present as compared with the past and the future, how immediate authority is perceived and how the recipients of the service or product provided are perceived. The constructs elicited were:

> *Constructive* vs. *mundane; disorganized* vs. *organized; doesn't hear* vs. *listens; has no clear view* vs. *takes a strategic view; easy-going* vs. *rigid; in tune with things* vs. *discordant; communicates well* vs. *communicates badly.*

A grid form into which ratings can be inserted is shown in Figure 10.1.

Ratings can be elicited from your client by having each element written on a small card and spread out on the table in front of the client. It is sometimes useful to have the scale range indicated. If you use a 7-point scale—which is most common—then it would be shown as '1 . . . 7'. That applies whether or not the evaluatively more positive pole of the construct is on the left- or right-hand side of the card. In fact, it is important to have some positive poles on the left-hand side of the grid and some on the right. Most computer programs will sort out the constructs so that all the positive poles are on the same side (see Appendix 3 for details of some programs).

To elicit the ratings, the client is asked to look at the first element and then at the first construct and decide, first of all, whether 'my manager' is best described as being *constructive* (ratings 1, 2 or 3), or as being more *mundane* (ratings 5, 6 or 7). In the example, the person said 'my manager' was slightly on the *mundane* side, giving that cell a '5'. The client then gives ratings for all the elements on construct 1, *constructive* versus *mundane*.

Different Types of Grids

Many grids have been created along these lines. For instance, Ryle and Lunghi (1970) found it useful to have constructs elicited in terms of relationships. The *dyad grid* uses elements such as 'you in relation to your priest' and 'your priest in relation to you'; 'you in relation to your mother' and 'your mother in relation to you'.

The task for the client is something like 'are there any ways in which your relationship with your priest is similar to or differs from your mother's relationship with you?'

Then there is Bob Neimeyer's *biographical grid*. For this, the client identifies significant events or stages in his or her life (Neimeyer, 1985b). The client can then be asked to construe these events indicating, as usual, how any two of them may be alike and thereby different from the third, or simply being asked to describe the events.

The *exchange grid* (Mendoza, 1985) has been used in many contexts, especially where team building is involved. Members of a group or couple complete their own personal grids, A's, then one or others complete the A grids 'as if' they were the other person and produce the B grid. Comparisons of the A with the relevant B grid can be very informative. Like most procedures in a personal construct context, these grids need to be carefully handled because the comparisons may well cause people to feel personally threatened or to become anxious.

One type of grid has been found useful in relation to decision-making issues. Shaw and McKnight (1981) suggest that once a grid on, say, the construing of cars, has been completed with a 1 to 5 rating scale, with 5 being the most favourable rating, constructs in the grid are changed so that all favourable poles of constructs are on the left-hand side of the grid. Naturally, in a grid about cars, the elements are different types of car. The ratings are simply added down each column to give an overall rating for each car. One step further measures the relative importance of each car. Each construct is assigned a number from 1 to 10, with 10 being given to the most important construct. The rating for each element on each construct is multiplied by the assigned number indicating construct importance. Those numbers are then added up to show precisely the relative importance of each car.

Dunn and his colleagues (1986) describe the 'policy grid' they designed to study 'frames of reference towards criminal justice information policies in a large urban municipality'. In fact, as Richard Bell says, it is the very versatility of this type of repertory grid that is both its attraction and its challenge.

Such grids are basically determined by their elements. If one uses situations for a person to construe—such as someone who stutters—then one has a 'situations' grid. If different countries serve as elements, then one has perhaps a 'cultures' grid. Sometimes a particular grid is developed so as to become an assessment tool in its own right. Such a grid is the one developed by Bob Neimeyer on the construing of death.

The Death Threat Index

Bob Neimeyer describes his long and fruitful line of research deriving from personal construct theory. It examines the degree to which people are aware of imminent, comprehensive change in their core role structure when asked to reflect on their own mortality. The original, repertory grid-based measure of this concept, the Threat Index (Krieger et al., 1974), required eliciting a sample of death-relevant constructs (for example, *painful* versus *painless, meaningful* versus *meaningless*) from the respondent through a comparison of situations involving death, such as 'a tornado kills three children in an elementary school', 'your grandmother dies in her sleep'. The person then rated the elements 'self', 'preferred self' and (personal) 'death' on these constructs. The number of *splits* in which both self-elements were aligned with one construct pole, and death with its contrast, served as the index of the subjective threat that would be entailed in construing the death of self as a personal reality. The Threat Index was streamlined into a standardized measure using frequently occurring constructs and its validity and reliability documented in dozens of studies, making it the best established measure in the entire literature on death attitudes (Neimeyer, 1994).

The availability of a solid measure of death threat made possible numerous applications to such topics as the death threat experienced by suicide intervention workers (Neimeyer & Dingemans, 1980), the link between death anxiety and the completion of one's existential goals (Neimeyer & Chapman, 1980), and the personal anxieties about death experienced by gay and bisexual men living in the shadow of the AIDS epidemic (Bivens et al., 1994). Later research has expanded this focus to include the threat and discomfort of counsellors working with clients presenting with either death-related problems, such as grief or AIDS, or with non-death-related problems, such as marital discord or physical handicap (Kirchberg et al., 1998). As hypothesized, counsellors reported greater discomfort in responding to the death than non-death situations—a response that proved to be mediated by the personal death fears of the counsellor. Moreover, the least empathic responses were provided by counsellors who construed death in fatalistic terms on the Threat Index, suggesting that working with death and loss can prove especially challenging for those counsellors whose personal constructions of death leave them vulnerable to such work.

Further details of repertory grid theory and methods can be found in the forthcoming second edition of the *Manual for Repertory Grid Technique* (Fransella, Bell & Bannister, in press).

Laddering

It is difficult to decide whether laddering is a skill or a tool. It is really both. A very complex skill to learn and one of the most useful tools to have come from personal construct psychology. It is primarily used to elicit superordinate, more value-laden constructs from individuals. It is sometimes very useful to put one or two of these into a person's grid. When Denny Hinkle first described this procedure (1965), he did not call it laddering. It seems likely that Bannister and Mair (1968) coined that name.

Hinkle called it 'the hierarchical technique for eliciting the superordinate constructs of the preferred self hierarchy'. His theory of construct implications is described in Chapter 20 (pp. 211–222). Here the focus is on the method.

Ever since Hinkle described the procedure, people have argued about how it should be carried out, its usefulness and its validity—does it 'really' elicit superordinate personal constructs? The method he described is clear enough. You ask the person to say which pole of a construct he would prefer to describe himself and then ask why he prefers that pole rather than the other. 'What are the advantages of this side in contrast to the disadvantages of that side, as you see it?' One of Hinkle's people preferred to be *reserved* rather than *emotional*, because being *reserved* implied being *relaxed* while *emotional* implied being *nervous*. Thus, *relaxed* versus *nervous* is the first laddered superordinate construct. Hinkle then says that you ask the question 'why does the person prefer to be *relaxed* rather than *nervous*?' That is repeated until the person can produce no more constructs. These instructions are very general when one starts to try to ladder someone, so it is not surprising that there are differences of opinion about how one should do that.

Since I was one of the first to use the technique in research and therapy (Fransella, 1970), and have taught it to many hundreds of people over more than 35 years, I shall here write in the first person and present the way I use it.

To me, laddering is a complex skill and not a simple interviewing technique. The snag is that it looks simple. But it first of all requires the use of the three skills already mentioned—the ability to be a credulous listener, to suspend one's own value system and, thereby, to be able to subsume the client's construing. It is in the process of laddering that one gets nearest to that experience of being almost a part of the other person. Larry Leitner talks of this as 'distance' between two people (Chapter 25, pp. 257–264). That can happen because one of the most important aspects of laddering is to be able to concentrate 100% on what the client is trying to say. Very often clients find it increasingly difficult to put their more superordinate constructs into words and it is important to glimpse what it is they are struggling to convey. Not, I hasten to add, so that one should help with the words, but rather to gain an understanding of the meaning that lies behind the words.

I think it useful to see laddering as a structured interview. It is structured in that one needs to ensure that the person does not stray away from the current ladder. If the person appears to be straying, one can simply ask 'is that the same thing we have been talking about before on this ladder?' It is structured also in the sense that the interviewer is definitely in charge and the client is not free to roam at will. It is definitely, in my view, not some free association exercise. I also think it very important to keep the person self-focused. 'Why is it important *for you* to be . . . ?' Otherwise one can just get generalizations.

The first decision to be made is which construct to start the ladder on. A client may have provided perhaps ten personal constructs from one of the elicitation procedures (many of these are described in Chapter 9 (pp. 95–103) as well as in Chapter 11 (pp. 123–131). If you are doing research, then you will have worked out a formula, such as choosing the first, third and fifth elicited personal construct. If it is in the context of helping a person reconstrue, then I use three criteria: the two or at the most three constructs to be laddered should be relatively subordinate, should look different from each other, and look as if they are likely to develop my understanding of the client's construed world. The relative subordinacy of constructs is, of course, a very evaluative choice. What is subordinate to me may well be superordinate to my client. But I will have learned a fair bit about the client from conversations and from the elicitation procedure. So, I do not go for such constructs as *respected, helpful* or *likeable* as they are fairly superordinate to me already, but I might choose instead constructs such as *studious, talkative* or *easy-going*.

An example of a ladder comes from my work with those who stutter. We were starting to ladder from constructs elicited for this person's 'non-stutterer' grid and

I selected the construct *nice personality* versus *disinterested in other people*. His preference was for being a *nice personality*.

Q. What are the advantages for you of being a nice personality?
A. People enjoy being with you.
Q. Whereas those who are *disinterested in other people*?
A. Are not enjoyable to be with.
Q. Why is it important, for you, that people enjoy being with you?
A. They are likely to open up to you—you get to understand them.
Q. Whereas? (*Here one can indicate by gesture that you are looking for the opposite.*)
A. They remain a closed book.
Q. That is very interesting. I'm just wondering why you like people to open up to you?
A. Because it shows people are relaxed with you and trust you and respect you.
Q. Whereas, if they remain a closed book?
A. You never get to know them—people rarely open up to stutterers.

So, we ended up on the non-preferred pole, where the person actually lives. That example raises one of the questions most often asked. *'How do you know when to stop?'* I stopped there for two reasons. One was that I think it is not always useful to go beyond superordinates to do with trust and respect. The other was that he had come out with an idea that he had never thought of before. His stutter was indeed very bad and he could see just what he was missing by being as he was. There could be little doubt that this revelation was disturbing to him and any further exploration would have been counter-productive for him.

Another common question is *'Do you always ask for an opposite?'* My answer here is 'it depends'. It depends on how the interview is going. If it is running smoothly and the client clearly understands what he is supposed to be doing, I may only ask for an opposite at every second or third rung. If the process is rather laboured, I find it good to ask for opposites more often. As in this case, it is not necessary to use words to elicit the opposites; a hand movement with the word 'whereas . . . ?' will suffice.

One of my personal rules when teaching laddering is that one should never ladder on the non-preferred pole of a construct. That pole nearly always has negative connotations and I feel I have little idea where it might ladder to. It is also likely to be a very depressing experience. People quite often give their replies in relation to the non-preferred pole, as in the example. There is no problem with that. But if the laddering is to continue, I think one should return to the preferred side of the construct.

Another question concerns *'What does one do if a person replies with more than one construct?'* In the example, the client gave three constructs at the end, so that did not matter. If that happened on a ladder that was to be continued, I would ask the person which best described the importance or the advantages of *people opening up to you*. One last point about the example, more words were spoken than appear in that text. But not a great many more. For me, conversation to do with the construing interferes with concentration and can easily turn into part of a therapy or counselling session. Of course, there is nothing wrong in using laddering in that way, but if it is being used as a short-cut to getting as much insight into the world of the client as possible in the shortest space of time, then general conversation should be kept to a minimum.

This second, shorter example comes from teaching laddering to a group of people. I think it serves a useful theoretical purpose if one starts at a very subordinate level. If one can get a ladder to 'work' from, say, shoes, one can point out that, indeed, construing takes place at different levels as stated in the *Organization Corollary*. How people construe shoes may do well as the starting point of a ladder, but I recommend that you do not choose to ladder constructs to do with hair. Both men and women have a great deal invested in how they wear their hair and—once tried, never again!

If students are sitting around a table, I have found it useful to have coloured folders on the table from which they can choose when they arrive. For the laddering they can be asked if anyone went for a particular colour. You ask for a volunteer from those who made a definite choice and then try to ladder the colour construct.

Q. You chose the green folder. What is the opposite, for you, of green?
A. Well, there are some I definitely would not choose—let me say *grey*.
Q. OK. So you prefer a green folder to a grey one. Why is that? What is special about the green one?
A. The green one is *bright*.
Q. Whereas the grey one is . . . ?
A. It's dull.
Q. Would it be right to say you prefer *bright* things in general to dull things? (*An attempt has to be made at some point to move it away from the specific starting point.*)
A. Oh, yes!
Q. So, in general, what is it about *bright* things that make you prefer them to *dull* things?
A. They make me feel good.
Q. Yes, I can see that. But what is it about *bright* things that makes you feel good?
A. Well, that's not easy. It's something to do with sparkling. It's like a bright star that beckons you. It reminds you that the world is full of wonderful things to be discovered.
Q. Whereas *dull* things . . . ?
A. Make you feel enclosed, trapped, what you have is all you'll get.
Q. So, I think I understand about the bright star, but just to be certain, can you say what it is that is so good about the bright star and everything?
A. You know you are alive.

When people talk about *being alive*, or say *that is what one is on earth for* or *one must do what one can for others*, I am prepared to say that is the top of the ladder. The other point I would make about that example is my not accepting the answer 'it makes me feel good'. People often respond with that or such things as 'makes me happy' and these are, of course, personal constructs. However, they are not helpful on most occasions. Most of us want to feel alive and to be happy. I like to ask the additional question to find out what the ingredient is that leads to one feeling alive or happy. That usually gets the ladder on the move again.

One final common issue concerns what is seen as the client giving an answer that looks very much more subordinate than superordinate. The ladder seems to have stopped going up and to have started coming down again. The most usual reason is that the client cannot find an answer that goes to a more abstract level of construing and, since an answer is required, they give an answer that is familiar to them.

But that is not always the case. For instance, Butt (1995) talks of snakes and ladders and gives an account of his client going from *relaxed—tense* to *able to be myself with others—put up a front*, then to *assert myself—give in to others* the preference to being about to assert herself was that she could *deal with my mother* and the reason why she preferred that was because *mother makes me feel so guilty*. One point to make is that Butt says the construct *able to be myself with others* versus *put up a front* clearly has a wider range of convenience than *deal with my mother*. It may well have a wider range of convenience, but Hinkle was talking about networks of implications. These are not necessarily the same. What is implied by *deal with my mother*? The fact that it is linked to feelings of guilt means she is aware that she is constantly being dislodged from her core role. That may suggest some quite superordinate construing involved in not being able/willing to deal with her mother. Could it not be that, for the present, the whole world for this lady centres around her mother and the guilt she is made to feel about her? Its range of convenience is narrow, but range of implication is vast. Being able to be herself with others is much less important, has many fewer implications, compared with dealing with mother.

Whether or not that is a valid point to make in the specific case of Butt's client, there is no doubt that sometimes clients do give a reply that sounds like something that has gone before or to be more subordinate. If that seems to be happening, it is important to check, repeat the question and to indicate you would like the client to think about the answer again. If the same response is given, then it is clear that the client either does not want to continue the exercise or has really reached the 'top' of her ladder. Perhaps she is not used to the intellectual exercise of trying to find words for some feelings or ideas that she has never put into words before. In the end, the client must always have the last word. Perhaps, as is often the case, the construct with which the laddering has started is, itself, at an already very superordinate level. So the person really struggles to provide answers but just cannot do so because there is nothing higher up the ladder—she must come down again or feel she has failed in the task.

Costigan and colleagues (2000) discuss their use of laddering in relation to how psychiatric nurses construe their changing role, and provide a very useful commentary on its general use. They also emphasize the care that must be taken with laddering. When teaching people about laddering, I never fail to say that it is not a party game. It can, indeed, be quite psychologically damaging to some people who become faced with an aspect of their own construing that they did not know was there. They now 'see' a previously unknown aspect of their construing and find that knowledge most disturbing. It is therefore always important to keep a keen eye on the person you are laddering and to stop at the first sign of unease. If the laddering is taking place in a counselling context, then it will be up to the counsellor to decide whether it is useful to continue with the process or not.

Bob Neimeyer (1993) has described a useful variation of Hinkle's laddering which he calls *dialectical laddering*. It is of use when a client finds it impossible to say which pole of a personal construct is preferred. Both poles have negative implications. In his example Suzy said she had difficulty trusting anyone, but both *trusting* and *distrusting* had disadvantages. He then asked 'What would be the implication for you of being *trusting*?' She replied *burdening others* with its opposite *being controlled*. That then led to *not relaxed* and *relax control completely*. All other constructs were similarly undesirable at both poles. He then went back to *controlled* versus *burdening others* and asked her to try and find some way of bringing them together— an alternative that would create a synthesis. She came up with *realistic trust*. That questioning was repeated for *not relaxed* versus *relax control completely* and the synthesis was *relax control to some extent*. And so the process continued until all the constructs had been dealt with in this way. Neimeyer says that, of course, this cognitive exercise is not a 'cure' in itself, but that Suzy found the process genuinely therapeutic and they continued to explore the implications of this major reconstruction of her world.

Support for Hinkle's Ideas

As a direct test of Hinkle's work, I checked to see whether the laddered constructs for my group of stutterers (Fransella, 1972) had more implications than the previously elicited constructs. They consistently did. Eric Button (1980) also found that superordinate, laddered constructs had more implications than subordinate ones with a group of anorexic women.

Neimeyer and colleagues (2001) carried out a validity study of Hinkle's hypothesis that laddered constructs are more important than non-laddered constructs, and so the procedure provides a measure of hierarchical structure. The authors interviewed 103 university students and carried out laddering with each one. Their findings supported Hinkle's hypothesis that laddered constructs are more important than subordinate ones. In addition, their results confirmed what most practitioners know, and Hinkle also found—that laddered constructs take more time to put into words than do more subordinate constructs. One other measure Neimeyer and his colleagues took was the 'meaning' of the constructs. They found that significantly more superordinate constructs fell into the *Existential* category than subordinate ones and that more subordinate constructs than superordinate ones fell into the *Specific Interests* and *Relational* categories. Thus, as one would expect, superordinate constructs were found to be more value-laden than the more subordinate ones.

Summary on Laddering

Several people have provided lists of do's and don't's for laddering. For instance, advice is given on the Internet at http://www.EnquireWithin.co.nz/busChap3.htm, but my own view is that the only way to learn laddering is by practising it. I have given indications above of what I find useful, but it is such a personal skill that each person who masters it will have developed his or her own style and will have a personal list of things to do and not to do.

Pyramiding

Al Landfield described a way of moving downwards to more concrete or subordinate constructs which he called *pyramiding* (1971). Most practitioners and clients find this considerably easier to work with than laddering.

The client is asked to think of a person they know and to select one characteristic of that person and then proceed along these lines: 'He is kindly.' 'How would you describe a person who is not kindly?' 'He is unkind.' 'What sort of person is a kindly person?' 'He would take care of someone if they were in trouble.' 'What sort of person is an unkindly person?' 'He walks on the other side of the street.' The procedure continues in this way asking about one pole of the construct and then its opposite.

Once that pyramid has been created, Landfield suggests that further questioning might be along the lines of asking how the client would know, say, that a person was kindly. The client might reply, 'He has a kindly smile.' Once one gets to that level, one is into behaviours. That can be extremely useful when designing behavioural experiments that a client might conduct between therapy sessions. Or, sometimes it is useful to know more precisely what a particular superordinate construct actually means. Then one can start directly with the 'how do you know that someone is (for example) *trustworthy*'?

The ABC Model

In 1977, Finn Tschudi, in collaboration with Sigrid Sandsburg, wrote a chapter on 'Loaded and honest questions' in which he described the ABC Model. He suggested that Kelly's definition of 'disorder' as representing 'any structure which appears to fail to accomplish its purpose' was too flexible. The authors preferred to use 'symptom' and 'symptomatic behaviour'. Thus, symptomatic behaviour becomes any behaviour 'which obliquely gets at the issues which are important for the person'.

A typical form of construct network consisting of three constructs—which they label A, B and C—helps to locate the important issues that are obliquely related to the symptom. A central feature of this model is the question: 'What keeps the person from moving?' There must be some advantage to remaining as, say, a smoker, when the person explicitly says she wants to give up smoking.

The method goes like this. The person says she wants to change from, for example, being a smoker to being a non-smoker. That forms the first step in the method. The second step is to ask the person to state the advantages of being a non-smoker and the disadvantages of being a smoker. Now, the C level looks for the double-bind or 'implicative dilemma', as described by Hinkle (1965). Such implicative dilemmas result in preventing the person from moving from the undesired position to the desired position. For example, it might go like this:

A. The statement of desire to change

A1: Being a smoker   A2: Being a non-smoker

B. The disadvantages of A1 and the advantages of A2

B1: 1. It makes a lot of dirt   B2: 1. Everything is much cleaner

  2. It ruins your health   2. It is much healthier

C. The disadvantages of the desired state A2 and the advantages of the present state A1

C2: 1. It gives me something to do   C1: 1. Feel ill at ease in company
     with my hands

  2. You are more popular   2. People who don't smoke
                                          are not popular

That procedure is useful in many contexts other than the clinical one. In the work context as 'I want to be more assertive'. In the marital context as 'I want to listen to my husband more'.

Nick Reed and I have modified the ABC Model so that it can be used for decision making, calling it 'Quandary Resolution'. By just putting forward two possible ways of moving forward, looking at the disadvantages and disadvantages of both as above, the desirability of one over the other often emerges very quickly.

As with laddering, the ABC Model needs to come with a health warning. It can show to clients the advantages of remaining as they are before they are psychologically ready to deal with that revelation. Again, it should not be viewed as a party game.

The Core Process Interview

In this interview, described by Helen Jones (1993), clients have the opportunity to look at how their lives have progressed and at the choices they have made that have affected their lives. It focuses on the good rather than the bad experiences. She describes it as consisting of the following seven parts.

1. *My life till now*: The client is asked to think back over his or her life and to divide it into four natural divisions of time in relation to age—and then to say what those age 'chunks' are. These might be '0–11', '11–16', and so on.
2. *Reminiscences*: The client is now asked to think of two occasions in each period when he or she felt really wonderful about life. As far as possible, the replies are written down verbatim.
3. *Unique qualities*: What were the special qualities about that time?
4. *Other happy times*: The client is now asked to describe seven other occasions in which his or her life felt really good. That is followed by a request that the client think of another occasion when he or she felt as good or happy as that time. There is then a request for two memories from each of the other time 'chunks'.
5. *Review*: The client is then passed the notes that have been made and asked to highlight passages that seem particularly important in terms of fulfilment.

Looking at these highlights, the client is asked to 'highlight the phrases that best complete the sentence "For me to be fulfilled . . ."'. A statement is sought from the highlighted passages.

6. *Fulfilment*: That is the statement that has emerged from the previous stage.
7. *Simple truths*: Jones says: 'It is always a lovely feeling to write down these simple things; they always ring true for the individual concerned. It is a powerful experience' (Jones, 1993, p. 20).

Jones uses this procedure after completing a resistance to change grid (see Chapter 20, pp. 211–222) and finds that the fulfilment statement closely reflects the relative importance of the values that emerge from the grid.

Viney Content Analysis Scales

These are standardized scales designed to tap into a variety of psychological states, especially positive and negative emotions. Computer-supported versions of all of these Australian scales have been developed. These scales include: the Cognitive Anxiety Scale, the Origin and Pawn Scales, the Sociality Scales, the Positive Affect Scale and the Content Analysis Scales of Psychosocial Maturity. Their psychometric qualities are impressive. Linda Viney and her colleagues have provided a scoring manual for the *Content Analysis Scales of Psychosocial Maturity (CASPM)* (1995c), and one of a number of chapters describing these scales is Viney (1993). Some of these scales are also discussed in Chapter 26, pp. 265–272.

The Self-image Profile

This is a standardized tool (Butler, 2001) that compares how children rate themselves on a 6-point scale compared with their rating of how they would like to be. The discrepancy between the two is seen as a way of assessing children's self-esteem. The 25 items in the Self-Image Profile were selected from the 12 most frequently elicited positive self-descriptions and the 12 most frequently elicited negative descriptions provided by large groups who were asked to describe three ways in which they think about themselves. The self-description scales contain only one pole of each construct.

The Profile can be changed to contain a child's own personal constructs. It then, of course, becomes a form of repertory grid. Some examples of the uses of the Self-Image Profile can be found in Butler and Green (1998).

SUMMARY

The skills described are requirements for any personal construct practitioner. Some are quite straightforward and others, such as suspending one's values, require considerable experience to achieve. The same applies to many of the so-called 'tools'.

Many of the 'tools' ask the clients to explore their construing that has, up until that point, not been available to them consciously. The construing is present, but words have to be found to explain their meaning to someone else.

The grid, discussed here and in Richard Bell's contribution (Chapter 9, pp. 95–103) together with the self-characterization are Kelly's 'methods of assessment'. Pam Denicolo, in the next chapter, discusses the latter together with the elicitation of meaning by non-verbal means. She particularly emphasizes the importance of the context in which the 'tools' can be used.

CHAPTER 11

Elicitation Methods to Fit Different Purposes

Pam Denicolo

University of Reading, UK

> I am suggesting that the avoidance of subjectivity is not the way to get down to hard realities. Subjective thinking is, rather, an essential step in the process the scientist must follow in grasping the nature of the universe . . . science tends to make its progress by entertaining propositions which appear initially to be preposterous.
>
> (Kelly, 1969d, p. 150)

This handbook is replete with examples of how the key instrument of personal construct psychology, the repertory grid, has been used in its traditional form, and in imaginative variations of it, to explore personal construing (see Chapter 9, pp. 95–103). Indeed, the repertory grid is probably the most frequently encountered technique used to serve this purpose, and is often the first one met by novices to the field, so much so that personal construct psychology and the repertory grid are sometimes viewed as synonymous. However, there are other techniques that have been used by personal construct psychologists to good effect.

While these techniques are based on the kind of questioning that underpins repertory grid elicitation, they each have a benefit to offer to particular client groups or to suit different situations experienced by practitioners and researchers. Despite Kelly's suggestion in relation to the self-characterization that if you want to know something about a person, then ask him and he may tell you, the mode of asking using any technique certainly has an effect on the answers received. Establishing rapport and a common purpose, with agreement about how far and with whom the information will be shared, are fundamental to all personal construct dialogues. The actual technique used should then be selected from the plethora designed to suit different clients and contexts.

Some examples are provided in this chapter to demonstrate the range available as alternatives, or additions, to grids to illuminate the uniqueness and complexity of the perceived world of the person. As a prelude, though, some theoretical considerations underpinning the development of these techniques are reviewed.

International Handbook of Personal Construct Psychology. Edited by F. Fransella.
© 2003 John Wiley & Sons, Ltd.

LOOSENING PERCEIVED CONSTRAINTS

Kelly was critical of over-reliance on psychometric methods. He emphasized that knowing that there was a correlational link between two variables did not help him to decide what approach should be taken with an individual client. He also questioned the utility of research that used approaches that did not lead to emancipation for the participants. He suggested that there should be more emphasis in psychology on studying the individual; hence his creation of, first, the Repertory Test for eliciting personal constructs, and then the repertory grid with its method of statistical analysis for those who wanted to 'get beyond the words'. That basic stance is also a fundamental tenet adopted by qualitative/interpretative researchers today.

In the process of encouraging participants or clients to reveal personal meaning, to articulate tacit knowledge, personal construct psychologists have used a variety of techniques in an attempt to embody the spirit of Kelly's writing and the challenge it presents to its users. He encouraged us to look at his theory and suggestions for practice *as if* they might be useful ways of looking at things, discarding aspects that do not prove useful. Thus we are specifically invited to engage in theoretical extension, elaboration and reformation to inform our practice by extending our horizons.

Practitioners using personal construct psychology are no less prone to perceiving artificial constraints on their horizons than are their clients. Those for whom an allegiance to 'qualitative' practice is an important construct may eschew without further consideration methods that are highly numerical or require statistical manipulation of the data since they are perceived as fitting a 'quantitative' approach. As previously described by Pope and Denicolo (1986) at the height of the qualitative/quantitative debate, novice researchers have found some comfort in the traditional formulation of ratings grids because they appear to pose less threat within the, then prevailing, quantitative tradition in psychology. This was perhaps a sensible resolution to their paradigm dilemma at a time when short papers were favoured for publication in journals since 'a grid is worth a thousand words'.

In such cases the difficulty inherent in the use of the terms 'qualitative' and 'quantitative' to describe *approaches* to research becomes apparent. Those terms are more appropriately used to describe *data*. Thus, those subscribing to an interpretativist/constructivist approach, with a focus on meaning exploration, may use tools and techniques that produce either qualitative or quantitative data. Indeed, they may use a range of such techniques, some more structured and numerical than others, in order to build a mosaic of meaning, each technique contributing a small tile or 'tessera' to the picture. As Kelly demonstrated, numbers need not be anathema to constructivists, nor yet should they become an obsession.

Bannister recognized that the grid had encouraged many psychologists to value the central tenets of personal construct theory. Nevertheless he raised a caveat about unwarranted concern with the statistical analysis of the resulting data, saying that the:

> grid method is a Frankenstein's monster which has rushed away on a statistical and experimental rampage of its own, leaving construct theory neglected, stranded high and dry, far behind. (Bannister, 1985, p. xii)

In this he was urging a greater emphasis on understanding meaning through construct elicitation and the raw grid data than on the statistical analysis *per se*.

Rather than neglect the essentially idiographic nature of constructivist data collection, practitioners should consider the purpose of the activity engaged in, their own skills and the inclinations of the clients to express their meaning in a preferred form, if they are to be responsive to situations they encounter. The techniques described below are useful for different purposes and provide some possibilities from which to select a form most conducive to the aptitudes of the joint explorers of meaning systems. They all produce a mass of rich but unstructured data that requires skill in making it manageable by the identification of key themes, categories and patterns that are meaningful to all engaged in the task. Nevertheless, although insightful interpretation of such complex verbal data is demanding, it can be rewarding if the elicitation process has been one that the client/participant finds helpful in the articulation of their embedded meanings.

ALTERNATIVE TECHNIQUES

It is fitting to begin with Kelly's qualitative method of assessment, ground-breaking in its time, and to follow this with techniques selected from a range devised subsequently.

Self-characterization Sketches

Because of shyness, or concern for implications, some requests for information about self produce rather self-conscious, sanitized responses. Kelly's original version of the self-characterization sketch has much to commend it for occasions when the goal is inducing self-understanding as a prelude to considering change. The procedure involves asking the person to write a character sketch of himself or herself, as if a principal character in a play, from the perspective of a friend who knows the person very *intimately* and who is *sympathetic*. It should be written in the third person, beginning something like: 'name (e.g. Joe/Joanne) is . . .'. The phrasing of this request:

- permits people some latitude to use their own constructions of self;
- emphasizes that it is structure rather than detail that is important;
- allows them to make themselves plausible from an outsider's perspective;
- indicates that something more than a superficial description of appearance is required;
- frees them from feeling threatened into providing either an incriminating description or a litany of what they 'ought' to be like.

Such sketches are replete with constructs, the emergent poles at least, not only about how people view themselves but how they perceive the worlds that they inhabit. While these can then be explored further, perhaps using laddering, pyramiding or ABC techniques (see Chapter 10, pp. 105–121), analysis of the sequence and linking of ideas, the organization of them, shifts in emphasis, the emergence of themes and the repetition of them, all provide evidence of personal viewpoints. Kelly suggests that the first sentence may be productively viewed as if it were a key statement about the person's view of self. Similarly, he suggests that the last sentence is a good indicator of where the person considers he or she is going. What is excluded is also relevant. In characterizing oneself, it is likely that important features will be included that distinguish self from others. Thus, if mode of dress has little significance to a person, then it is unlikely to be mentioned. Trevor Butt (Chapter 38, pp. 379–386) writes further about the 'credulous approach' advocated for the analysis of such sketches and their value at the beginning of a phenomenological inquiry (see also Chapter 10, pp. 105–121).

The self-characterization has been productively used with novice professionals describing themselves in the professional role. For example, 'Josh as a nurse is primarily concerned with helping patients...'. Such a sketch enables the practice supervisor or mentor to appreciate areas of concern or confidence, while the novice is alerted to current priorities, and sometimes to those being ignored—sketches can act as springboards to considering alternative self-constructions. When self-characterization sketches are elicited at intervals and compared, development can be demonstrated, as with Fransella's (1981) client who used the self-characterization as a means of helping himself to reconstrue over time.

Bow-ties

Procter has had extensive experience in both personal construct psychology and family therapy work which has resulted in innovative assessment and intervention techniques. One of these involves the 'bow-tie' principle (Procter, 1987, see also his discussion of family therapy, Chapter 43.2, pp. 431–434), named from the pattern formed when constructs and resultant behaviour are elicited from each member of a couple or larger group. The behaviour of the individuals in relation to the perceived constructs of the other may serve to reinforce the actual constructs of the other, leading to the continuance of their own behaviour. A form of 'zigzagging' questioning of the individuals about how they construe themselves, what they think the other thinks of them and how they consequently behave in response, demonstrates the pervasive and pernicious feedback loops in operation as each person tests out his own hypotheses about the other and has them apparently confirmed.

For instance, a manager may perceive herself as a democratic leader, delegating tasks and encouraging her employee to make decisions about them. She is disappointed in her employee. She perceives him as lazy, unable to take responsibility, so she refuses to continue to give guidance. She produces more tasks for him that require self-organizing behaviour and independent decision-making. In contrast, the employee perceives himself as hard-working, his job as responding to the manager's needs. He is frustrated by 'unclear' tasks. He spends time on strategies to explore actual requirements before starting on the task. The vicious cycle continues, sometimes exacerbated by other members of the team. Some colleagues reinforce the manager's view by complaining about the employee's continuous questions and his apparent inability to get on with the task. Others reinforce the employee's viewpoint by commenting informally on the vagueness of the manager's direction.

It is only by uncovering and recognizing these self-fulfilling prophecies that construing can be challenged and reconsidered to end this destructive cycle.

The Lying Game

Bright (1985) considered the general philosophy of lying as a human activity and how it might be used within a personal construct framework to help people to shift away from the constraints of troubled construing towards recognition of potential change. Acknowledging Kelly's principle that you cannot fully understand what people are saying until you gain some notion of what, for them, is the opposite, Bright devised a game based on lying—a game because there is no real intention to deceive.

The technique is particularly useful when people, perhaps enmeshed in describing how they feel, have difficulty in expressing the contrast poles of constructs. These lies can be especially informative when explored further for their implications, heightening awareness of 'truth'.

Respondents are asked to write down lies about themselves within a chosen parameter, for example, myself as a worker or a parent. When an individual is unable to produce any more relevant lies, two columns are added to the side of the page in which to insert the respondent's replies (Y or N) to these questions:

1. Would you like this lie to be true?
2. Would you like other people to believe this lie?

This produces the following potential patterns of response for each lie: NN, YY, YN, NY

- An NN response indicates complete rejection of the lie, with no wish for change.
- A YY response indicates a wish for change at a high level of awareness—a good start.
- A YN response indicates a wish for the lie to be true but not for others to believe it—perhaps a wish for change that would be unpopular with significant others.
- An NY response indicates a concern for image presentation rather than a desire for change—a potent source for skilled exploration.

The game format is relaxing so that people can more readily produce lies about themselves, the fun element ameliorating the sense of being tested sometimes experienced with grids. The next methods use other means to achieve a similar aim.

Illuminative Incident Analysis

Cortazzi and Roote (1975) developed this technique as a means of investigating the thoughts and feelings of members of teams. Though team development can be encouraged by a frank interchange of ideas and feelings about incidents that have happened while the team have been working together, the emotion connected with

Figure 11.1   Tightrope walker—an example of a drawing used for illuminative analysis

certain incidents often blocks verbal discourse. Words can also hide reality whereas feelings, as every art therapist knows, are more accurately portrayed in drawings. The drawings encourage all team members to confront their own feelings about the incident and allow, by comparisons between drawings, each one to come to an understanding of the other's perspective. Thus drawings are a conduit from the non-verbal to the verbal. A new member of a research team produced the drawing shown in Figure 11.1. He portrays himself as blindfolded, setting out across a tightrope. Though it is firmly tied to his previous experience, the end-point is shrouded in mist while the rope itself is fraught with obstacles. He clings to a trusty pole—current knowledge—to keep himself steady.

The researcher was relieved to find that he was not alone in experiencing trepidation, and that more experienced colleagues would be willing to lead the way.

Analysis of such drawings requires the combined efforts of the listener and the producer of the drawing to interpret the nuances encapsulated in the lines, to tease out their full significance. In other words, the drawing in its production provides the first step in expressing ideas and feelings and then acts as a catalyst to the verbal commentary.

No artistic prowess is required because it is the simple, unrefined nature of the line drawing that allows it to capture the essence of meaning. The illuminative value of simple drawings is further demonstrated by Tom Ravenette who uses drawing to elicit the meanings of specific situations with children (see Chapter 28, pp. 283–294). The use of illuminative incident analysis is demonstrated further in the next technique.

Interview about Instances

Osborne and Gilbert (1980) used this technique to explore students' views of the world in relation to scientific concepts. They generated a series of cards, each showing a stick figure (for example, a golfer) engaged in an activity (hitting a ball with a club) that represents the scientific concept being explored (in this case, both force and energy). The cards were used as a stimulus to conversation about the concept. From analysis of the conversation the alternative, but coherent, understandings that students have about the concepts were demonstrated. These frequently diverged from scientists' views. Awareness of such alternative frameworks by a teacher is important in helping the students to move from a layperson's understanding towards that of experts in the field. See Chapters 29 to 32 (pp. 295 to 326) for coverage of the role of pupils', students' and teachers' construing in the learning process.

Such uncomplicated drawings encourage a focus on the action depicted, so this method can be readily adapted for use in a variety of situations in which understanding process is the focus. Similarly the next technique uses a simple drawing technique to explore the influence of the past on the present.

Snakes and Rivers

Contradictory as it may seem, the anticipatory power of constructs lies in the past. In order to come to an understanding of the present we need to compare and contrast it with experiences we have had previously and use these to predict the future. The success of our predictions will depend on our selecting appropriate and relevant constructs and being willing to contemplate adapting them to fit current circumstance or amending a network of constructs to meet new situations.

Thus biography has an important influence on the constructs we bring to bear on any situation in which we find ourselves. The ones that predominate are likely to be those that have served us well in what appear to have been similar circumstances in the past. Since much of life is hectic, encouraging action rather than reflection, we are often unaware of the constructs guiding that action and from whence, in our pasts, these are derived. This means that, although well established, some of our personal constructs may now be redundant or even counter-productive. However, unless we become consciously aware of them and attach words to them, they cannot be challenged, and they remain influential in how we relate to events.

Denicolo and Pope (2001) devised 'career snakes' for exploring the useful and redundant constructs held by professionals about their development in their roles, and later used them to research commonly held productive and limiting constructs within professions. Similar to the Salmon Line (see Chapter 31, pp. 311–318), the rationale for the technique drew on a recognition that constructs evolve over time and are particularly influenced by formative experiences. Only by reflecting on their origins can the opportunity be provided for contemplating alternatives and breaking free from biography.

Participants draw up in private a representation of their working lives in the form of a winding snake, each turn of its body depicting a personal experience that influenced the direction that their career took. These turns are annotated briefly (Figure 11.2), forming the bases for later discussion and elaboration with the researcher, about their significance as formative experiences both for career decisions and for their personal style as practitioners.

The subsequent discussion generally requires little input from the researcher,

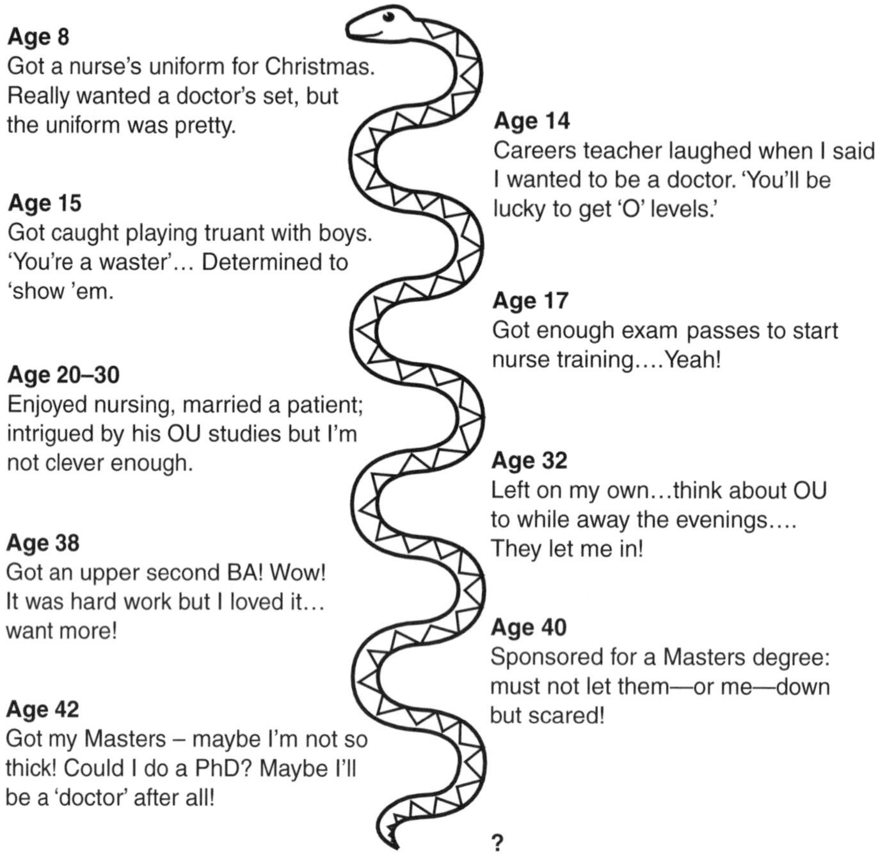

Age 8
Got a nurse's uniform for Christmas. Really wanted a doctor's set, but the uniform was pretty.

Age 14
Careers teacher laughed when I said I wanted to be a doctor. 'You'll be lucky to get 'O' levels.'

Age 15
Got caught playing truant with boys. 'You're a waster'... Determined to 'show 'em.

Age 17
Got enough exam passes to start nurse training....Yeah!

Age 20–30
Enjoyed nursing, married a patient; intrigued by his OU studies but I'm not clever enough.

Age 32
Left on my own...think about OU to while away the evenings.... They let me in!

Age 38
Got an upper second BA! Wow! It was hard work but I loved it... want more!

Age 40
Sponsored for a Masters degree: must not let them—or me—down but scared!

Age 42
Got my Masters – maybe I'm not so thick! Could I do a PhD? Maybe I'll be a 'doctor' after all!

?

Figure 11.2   A career snake

other than interest, as participants interrogate themselves about reasons for isolating a particular incident, how it was influential and perhaps still is. They often report feeling empowered by the experience. Many researchers now using the technique to explore the influence of previous experience on current practice prefer the title 'rivers of experience' in deference to those who dislike snakes! The 'river maps' encourage participants to discuss other topographical features of their lives, high points, rapids and calm sections, demonstrating yet again the power of metaphor (Mair, 1988) in eliciting and elucidating constructs.

Metaphors are often found in everyday speech to provide the connecting threads between constructs and their personal meaning, as well as being graphically evocative.

Metaphors and Artefacts

Some writers contend that all language is metaphorical. Lakoff and Johnson (1980) illustrated how metaphors pervade our lives not only as descriptors of people, events and objects but also in governing and orientating action. A salient example provided is the terms in which argument is described in Western languages—to be won, using ammunition and counter-attack, for instance. Examining documents and records of people's descriptions of their worlds for the *metaphors they live by* can be a rich resource for understanding the meaning they attribute to them.

Similarly, asking people to provide a metaphor to describe themselves, or a situation, can provide a conduit to their pervasive constructs. For those who are less adept at using figurative language forms, or reticent about personal disclosure, a less invasive alternative is to ask them to identify an artefact that represents something they think or feel about themselves or their role. The artefact may be a picture, photograph or an object such as a treasured ornament or favourite tool.

CONCLUSION

The examples of techniques described above represent only a selection of those available. Several can be used together, or in conjunction with grids, to explore meaning more fully. These innovative techniques reinforce Kelly's point that we are only restricted in developing our construing by the limits of our imagination.

CHAPTER 12

Expert Systems

Mildred L.G. Shaw

Centre for Person–Computer Studies, BC, Canada

and

Brian R. Gaines

Centre for Person–Computer Studies, BC, Canada

> There once was a passionate dame
> Who wanted some things made plain,
> So she punched up the cards,
> Filled tape by the yards,
> But—somehow—*it just wasn't the same!*
>
> (Kelly, 1963, p. 229)

The role of personal construct psychology in computer research and applications concerned with the development of 'expert systems' and their beginnings in 'artificial intelligence' and 'cognitive science' are covered in this chapter. Research on expert systems led to the identification of the 'knowledge acquisition bottleneck', that it was generally extremely difficult to make overt the presumed knowledge of human experts in order to program it for computers.

The history and reasons for the adoption of repertory grid methodologies and tools to overcome the knowledge acquisition bottleneck are described. Then a more fundamental analysis is made of why expert systems to date have had only limited success, and the merits of a personal construct approach to emulating human expertise in greater depth than has been achieved with existing cognitive science models are presented.

RESEARCH ON PROGRAMMING COMPUTERS TO THINK

The arrival of the first commercial digital computers in the 1950s led to widespread interest in the potential applications of computing. The use of the term 'giant brains' became common in the press although it was clear that the precise, logical operations of computers had little in common with the human brain. However, interest in simulating human thought processes was common among the early computer

International Handbook of Personal Construct Psychology. Edited by F. Fransella.
© 2003 John Wiley & Sons, Ltd.

pioneers. Alan Turing, a brilliant Cambridge logician who had helped to develop computers to break enemy message encryption during World War II, wrote a paper on 'Computing machinery and intelligence' for the journal *Mind* in which he considers the question 'Can machines think?' (Turing, 1950). He answers it in behavioural terms, proposing what has come to be known as the 'Turing test', that if a person communicating with the computer and with another person through the same medium (such as communicating teleprinters) cannot distinguish them correctly, then the machine, for all practical purposes, can be said to think.

Research on programming computers to think became widespread. McCarthy and colleagues (1955) proposed to the Rockefeller Foundation that it fund a study of *artificial intelligence* (see also Jack Adams-Webber on this topic in Chapter 43.5, pp. 443–445) to be carried out during the summer of 1956 at Dartmouth College, Hanover in the USA. The year of this proposal also saw the publication of Kelly's seminal work on personal construct psychology but, as discussed in the following section, the pioneers of artificial intelligence and cognitive science never became aware of this work. The next decade was also the era of the development of 'computer science' as a new field of study when computers were very expensive, and university and funding agency budgets were hard-pressed to supply the demand for computer facilities. In Britain the competition between those wishing to undertake research in computer science and in artificial intelligence was so intense that the UK Science Research Council commissioned Sir James Lighthill to report on the state of the art in 'machine intelligence'. His report (Lighthill, 1973) was damning about both the achievements and the prospects for such research and had a strong negative influence worldwide on funding for research to program computers to think (Fleck, 1982).

Embattled AI researchers focused on specific goals to develop programs that emulated human expert performance in fields of obvious practical value such as mineral exploration and medical diagnosis, and in the mid-1970s announced a number of breakthroughs in what came to be called 'expert systems' (Michie, 1979). The first successful expert systems were DENDRAL (Feigenbaum et al., 1971) for reconstructing molecular structures from mass spectrometer data and MYCIN (Shortliffe, 1976) for diagnosing microbial infections from medical data. The systems were programmed as collections of 'production rules' that expressed a relationship between a premise and a conclusion such that if the conditions of the premise were satisfied then those of the conclusion could be drawn. For example, a rule from MYCIN is:

If: (1) the infection is primary-bacteremia, and
      (2) the site of the culture is one of the sterile sites, and
      (3) the suspected portal of entry of the organism is the gastro-intestinal tract,
then: there is suggestive evidence (0.7) that the identity of the organism is bacteroides.

Such rules are obtained from specialists in microbial infections and their application to particular data is fairly simple data processing. The rules are validated through their application to many cases and revised when they fail to give the correct diagnosis. MYCIN was designed to interact with a clinician in order to make a diagnosis and suggest therapy for a particular patient with a suspected microbial infection. It first gathers data about the patient and then uses this to make inferences about the infections and their treatment.

The success of the early expert systems attracted industrial and research attention, and a major industry developed in the early 1980s. The research objectives were then defined by one of the commercial AI pioneers, Hayes-Roth (1984), in a workshop on 'AI Applications for Business' in May 1983. He enumerated some situations appropriate to expert systems, such as: the organization requires more skilled people than it can recruit or retain; job excellence requires a scope of knowledge exceeding reasonable demands on human training and continuing education.

As a modern example of the success of expert systems technology, the April and July 2000 issues of *InTech Magazine* published by the Instrumentation, Systems and Automation Society have a two-part paper from Eli Lilly on the use of an expert system in its fermentation plant (Alford et al., 2000). The evaluation in 2000 corresponds well to Hayes-Roth's predictions in 1983. Within a few weeks, the expert was satisfied that the expert system reliably came to the same conclusions he would have by looking at the same data. The expert system then took over this part of the expert's job, freeing up 40 hours a month of his time for other work.

THE KNOWLEDGE ACQUISITION BOTTLENECK

Expert systems appeared at first to be a major validation of the possibility of digital computers being able to emulate human thinking, and there is continuing evidence of some successful applications. However, the industry has not grown to the extent predicted, largely because programming such systems has been very much more difficult than expected. Feigenbaum (1980), one of the pioneers of expert systems, termed this the 'knowledge acquisition bottleneck'. Hayes-Roth and co-workers (1983) in their book *Building Expert Systems* noted that, since the programmer has far less knowledge of the domain than the expert, communication problems impede the process of transferring expertise into a computer program. The vocabulary initially used by the expert to talk about the domain with a novice is often inadequate for problem-solving; so that the programmer and the expert must work together to extend and refine it. One of the most difficult aspects of the programmer's task is helping the expert to structure the specialist knowledge, to identify and formalize the expert's concepts.

From a personal construct perspective, the task of the expert system programmer is to reconstruct the conceptual and operational framework that an expert in a domain uses to solve problems in that domain, noting that the terminology used may be highly idiosyncratic, that is, personal to the expert. However, the expert is, by definition, someone who is effective at problem-solving in the domain and, hence, her or his knowledge is valid in some practical sense. The expert's knowledge has been acquired by some mix of processes, such as trial and error, mimicking others, reflection on personal experience, reading text written by other experts, conversations with others, and so on. That corresponds to Kelly's notion of an individual as a *personal scientist* (Shaw, 1980) about which he asks:

> Might not the individual man, each in his own personal way, assume more of the
> stature of a scientist, ever seeking to predict and control the course of events
> with which he is involved? Would he not have his theories, test his hypotheses,
> and weigh his experimental evidence? (Kelly, 1955/1991, p. 5/Vol. 1, pp. 4–5)

Kelly merges the notions of prediction and control into the unitary notion of *anticipation* and hence his Fundamental Postulate: 'a person's processes are psychologically channelized by the ways in which he anticipates events'.

Thus, from a personal construct perspective, the task of the expert system programmer is to model the personal construct system of the expert in operational form as a computer program such that the program is able to anticipate events in the same way as the expert. It was suggested in the early years of expert systems (Gaines & Shaw, 1980) that new methods for rule extraction made Kelly's repertory grid a suitable tool for eliciting knowledge from experts. Existing computer programs for interactive elicitation of repertory grids were rapidly modified to support knowledge acquisition for expert systems (Shaw & Gaines, 1983; Boose, 1984). The approach proved successful in industrial applications (Boose, 1986), and a framework based on personal construct psychology became accepted as the foundation for developing knowledge acquisition techniques and tools (Ford et al., 1993; Gaines & Shaw, 1993).

A PERSONAL CONSTRUCT ALTERNATIVE TO RULE-BASED COGNITIVE MODELS

While repertory grids were widely used as knowledge acquisition tools in the 1980s and 1990s, expert systems themselves failed to achieve as much as had been expected, and a large-scale artificial intelligence industry did not materialize. Various writers have speculated on the reasons for that failure, the deepest analysis being that of Dreyfus and Dreyfus (1986). They see the problem as a manifestation of Wittgenstein's (1953) argument that the notion of human behaviour following a rule is paradoxical because, as he showed, by a suitable interpretation every course of action could be made to accord with the rule.

The pioneers of cognitive science had modelled the human mind as a repository of so-called 'production rules' (Anderson, 1983) and the designers of expert systems had followed this model in their 'knowledge representation' schemes. Dreyfus and Dreyfus argue that such representation is a major weakness and that systems based on it could never fully emulate human expert behaviour. In the AI literature, Clancey (1989) has criticized approaches to expert system development based on the assumption that expertise can be captured in overt knowledge, and has noted that all processes of behaving, including speech, problem-solving and physical skills, are generated on the spot, not by mechanical application of scripts or rules previously stored in the brain. He argues that knowledge is a capacity to behave adaptively within an environment; it cannot be reduced to representations of behaviour or the environment.

Repertory grid-based knowledge acquisition tools had of necessity delivered knowledge in the form of rules so that it could be utilized by existing expert system knowledge representation tools. However, the analysis leading to the rules is not part of the construction process and may be regarded as an artefact of the need to use rule-based expert systems technology. Kelly developed personal construct psychology from a perspective that was consistent with that of Wittgenstein, and did not introduce rules in his psychological model. For him construing was all that was necessary to account for human behaviour, and anticipation was a by-product of construction. That is, construction intrinsically supported anticipatory processes without the storage of anticipatory 'rules' but, at a particular stage in the construction of experience, these anticipations might have a regularity that an observer could ascribe to 'rules of behaviour'. This corresponds to anticipations being 'supervenient' on constructions, to use a technical term from the philosophy of mind (Kim, 1993). However, as the person construed more experience, then the anticipations might change and the observer could construe this in terms of the person 'learning new rules'. Kelly also emphasized time and again that personal construct psychology does not need a notion of 'learning' on the part of the person or personal scientist. Construction alone was sufficient to account for the person's mental processes and behaviour, and it could also account for the models being produced by observers or psychologists. The Wittgenstein paradox presents no problems to personal construct psychologists because there is no assumption that human behaviour is rule-governed.

It is unfortunate that the development of cognitive science in the mid-1950s became dominated by those whose background was in mathematical logic. Kelly published his major work on personal construct psychology in 1955, and it could easily have become adopted as the foundation for what became called 'cognitive science' and provided foundations for artificial intelligence and expert systems. In the few years until his death in 1967 he made a number of presentations to wider audiences that might have triggered recognition of the far-ranging implications of his work. In April 1961 he presented personal construct psychology to Luria and other members of the Moscow Psychological Society in Moscow as 'a mathematical approach to psychology' (Kelly, 1969f) paralleling the development of mathematical psychology in the USA by Miller, Mosteller and others (Hirst, 1988). In June 1962 he was an invited commentator at a conference on 'the computer simulation of personality' held at Princeton University and stated:

> In this connection I would like to make a plug for the psychology of personal constructs. Not only is it a system built upon the notion that scientists and human beings, alike, approach truth by erecting simulation devices—called constructs—but is a theory deliberately formulated in a language system which is based on binary elements and which does not accept the so-called subject–predicate error of the Indo-European language system. (Kelly, 1963, p. 228)

However, Kelly's work was not recognized in the 1950s by computer and cognitive scientists.

PERSONAL CONSTRUCT PSYCHOLOGY AS A FOUNDATION FOR MODELLING HUMAN EXPERTISE

The models of human thought processes derived from personal construct psychology and from mathematical logic can be contrasted through a simple example. Suppose a child has three constellations of experience:

child is well-behaved; mother is attentive; mother smiles;
child is naughty; mother is attentive; mother frowns;
child is passive; mother is inattentive.

A machine-learning program might derive the rules:

child is well-behaved **implies** mother smiles;
child is naughty **implies** mother frowns;
child is passive **implies** mother is inattentive;
child is well-behaved or naughty **implies** mother is attentive.

So that a child who is well-behaved might infer that her mother will smile, but how does the child know when she is well-behaved?

A personal construct model would be that the child construes her three sets of experience in terms of the constructs: *well-behaved* versus *naughty*, *attentive* versus *inattentive* and *smiles* versus *frowns*. Supervenient on the construing of the three constellations of experience are *all* the compatible anticipations, that is, those above plus:

mother smiles **implies** child is well-behaved;
mother frowns **implies** child is naughty;
plus others.

These reverse implications will be used to give meaning to the construct *well-behaved–naughty* in novel situations. To act to make the mother smile the child will choose situations where the child is well-behaved and the mother smiles. If the child wants the mother's attention then the child may choose situations where the child is naughty, the mother frowns but also pays attention to the child. There are no 'rules of behaviour' but there is the choice of situations in a rather more flexible way than would be entailed through sets of rules. In addition there is an increasing repertoire of behaviour as the child construes new situations in terms of her behaviour and the mother's smile or frown. One might say the child is 'learning' but there is no specific mechanism for learning, only for construction. One might say that the mother's smile 'reinforces' good behaviour but there is no reinforcement, only construction and choice. Kelly's view is that construction provides a complete account of human behaviour and can also model the constructs of different schools of psychology.

Now apply that model to human expertise. It models the expert as a construing agent not as a 'knowledge base' of rules. The model automatically updates as more experience is construed, that is, as the expert system attempts to solve more problems. The experience can be used in a variety of ways to solve problems and to give meaning to new situations, for example, the availability of a new drug or treatment. 'Knowledge acquisition' is intrinsic to personal construct-based expert systems and does not need to be treated as a separate phase. Expert knowledge can be transferred to the system not only through exemplary problem-solving but also by commenting on the system's problem-solving and by choosing problems for the system which are at the limits of the system's current capabilities. That is, experts can make

their behaviour available to be mimicked and can also act as coaches commenting on performance and setting tasks, all major strategies in supporting human
development.

An example of repertory grid-based expert system development and application tool is WebGrid, which is freely available on the World Wide Web
(http://repgrid.com/WebGrid/). To use WebGrid an expert enters exemplary situations and, once some have been entered, can enter test cases to see how the system
performs (Gaines & Shaw, 1997). If the system is incorrect, the expert can change
the result and enter the corrected test case as an additional example until the system
is generally correct. The system retains only the repertory grid of constructions as
its knowledge base. WebGrid can produce sets of rules at any stage that characterize and explain its model of expertise at that stage, but these are not stored, just
produced on request, and are truly supervenient on the expert's construction.

CONCLUSIONS

Expert systems were recognized as a breakthrough in artificial intelligence, in programming computers to emulate human thinking. However, they were based on a
form of cognitive science that took mathematical logic as its foundations and was
not well suited to modelling the full richness of human behaviour. Personal construct psychology developed over the same time period but was not recognized by
those working on artificial intelligence and cognitive science as a complete psychological system providing more effective foundations for cognitive science and expert
systems. Repertory grid elicitation *was* recognized as a valuable knowledge acquisition technique with which to develop rules for expert systems, but the knowledge
transferred in the form of rules was static and brittle, and did not lead to the systems
being open to experience. It would be timely to adopt personal construct psychology as the foundations of cognitive science and use it to build expert systems that
fully emulated the capabilities of human experts, not only to solve problems but also
to be effective in dealing with new problems as they arise.

ACKNOWLEDGEMENTS

Financial assistance for this work has been made available by the Natural Sciences and
Engineering Research Council of Canada.

URLs

WebGrid can be accessed at *http://repgrid.com/WebGrid/*
Related papers on WebGrid can be accessed through *http://repgrid.com/reports/*

Individuals in Relation to Society

INTRODUCTION

Apart from the general comment that Kelly failed to deal adequately with feelings and emotions, another criticism is that he talked only about individuals and not about groups of individuals and society at large. It may therefore be somewhat surprising to find one of the largest sections in this book to be about individuals in relation to other people, in relation to groups of people and to society generally.

The first two chapters look at the individual as a member of a society or culture. Devorah Kalekin-Fishman explains her thinking about social relations. She explores the idea that sociology has something to offer personal construct psychology and personal construct psychology has something to offer sociology. Jörn Scheer looks at the larger social scene, this time in relation to cross-cultural construing. He describes the various problems involved and suggests ways in which these might be overcome.

The smaller social scene is the theme of the next two chapters. Jim Horley is a forensic psychologist who has worked for many years trying to understand and help those who fall foul of the law. He limits himself here to a discussion of 'sexual offenders' such as child molesters and rapists. So great is the amount of personal construct work being carried out with 'offenders', that Jim Horley has edited a book on the subject. Beverly Walker looks at what personal construct theory has to offer in relation to the dependency of an individual upon other individuals. She describes the form of grid Kelly created—now called a 'Dependency Grid'—and gives examples from her own work on dependency.

Two chapters then discuss personal construct psychology in relation to politics. A previously unpublished talk by Don Bannister relates how politics may be construed and discusses the political implications of personal construct psychology. Dusan Stojnov then talks from personal experience as one who lives in what is now Serbia and Montenegro. He looks at the different ways in which 'rational' and 'irrational' behaviour is construed as well as the nature of choice and how psychological transitions may relate to politics. He uses his own research to illustrate his view that a personal construct approach to politics has much to offer to increase our understanding of it. It might even, he suggests, help politicians to reach conclusions on how the public may understand—or misunderstand—their policies.

CHAPTER 13

Social Relations in the Modern World

Devorah Kalekin-Fishman

University of Haifa, Israel

> You can have no such thing as an individual unless you have a group.
>
> (Kelly, 1932)

The Fundamental Postulate and the Corollaries of personal construct theory articulate the relationship between the individual and society and are in accord with different schools of sociology. The venture has the practical consequence of providing a broader base than is customary for delving into how the social infuses the shaping of the individual than is customary. Moreover, by exploring the potential of interaction between personal construct theory and theories of social structure and process, a radical road for the future of personal construct psychology suggests itself.

Developments in the theorizing and application of personal construct psychology have led to an interest in explaining how people function as part of society. There are, furthermore, vital points of contact between concerns of researchers in psychology, who increasingly find it necessary to account for the effects of the social on the individual, and those of theoreticians in sociology, who are attempting to establish how comprehensive social structures and processes are linked to human experience. Different components of Kelly's theory solve conceptual problems that impair the applicability of sociological theories, and alternative constructions of social structure and social process enhance our understanding of how society impacts the person.

DEVELOPMENTS IN PERSONAL CONSTRUCT PSYCHOLOGY

It is generally accepted that constructive alternativism is the philosophical basis of the theory, yet practice may fall prey to conventional orthodoxies. Although most counsellors who use Kelly's theory acknowledge wide-ranging sociocultural influences on the person, problems may arise because the nature of the process is likely

International Handbook of Personal Construct Psychology. Edited by F. Fransella.
© 2003 John Wiley & Sons, Ltd.

to be taken for granted. Kelly understood the difficulty. Defining culture as 'a validational system of events', Kelly (1955/1991, p. 693/Vol. 2, p. 96) goes on to point out that:

> The clinician, although he is aware of cultural homogeneities, is unaware of their heterogeneities. He assumes that his client goes swimming along in a smooth stream of cultural and neighborhood expectancies... [looking] for validators rather than implausible causes.

To the extent that this tendency is prevalent, counsellors may misconstrue how others perceive social realities. If and when this happens, the counsellor or therapist relegates constructive alternativism to the level of a rule of thumb.

That is understandable because of the tendency to rely on the Commonality and Sociality Corollaries as the prime means of access to clients' bonds with society. Indeed, these Corollaries have been shown to explain how individuals construe and experiment with face-to-face relations in organizations, in families, with friends, and in creating culture (Kalekin-Fishman & Walker, 1996; Scheer, 2000). That focus, however, leads to a narrow view of the nature of society and of its potential for affecting members. Taking into consideration diverse scientific views of how society operates, the range of convenience of the Fundamental Postulate and of all the Corollaries can be extended to include alternative constructions of the social and its effects, many of which are unexpected.

Complementary developments in contemporary sociology support the view that it is important to find the connections between sociological theory and psychology.

A SOCIOLOGICAL DILEMMA: ESTABLISHING LINKAGES BETWEEN THE PERSON AND SOCIETY

Sociology is often called a multi-paradigm science because there is to date no theoretical school that describes the how's and why's of social order and disorder exhaustively (Ritzer, 2001). Ruling schools of thought offer diverse approaches to understanding society. Yet, the challenge to resolve tensions between sociological conceptualizations of how society can be understood and the perception of how people get on in everyday life (bridging the macro–micro gap), poses a reality test that none of the paradigms passes adequately. None provides for an image of the individual that is 'true to life'. Because social structure is central to sociological thinking, the individual is often viewed as a consequence of macro-societal processes and structures, or even as a rather troublesome appendage (Durkheim, 1964/1895).

Thus, prominent schools of sociological theory, which focus on interpretations of how society as a whole works (theories of consensus and conflict theories alike), fall short of resolving the issue of how the macro and the micro are mutually produced and reproduced. True, some theoretical paradigms (such as exchange theory and phenomenological sociology) base research on an examination of individual action and feeling. But apart from the rather simplistic image of the individual that each of these schools proposes, they also imply a crude additive construction of macro-processes in society. The 'cultural turn' (Bauman, 1973; Jameson, 1991) in the social sciences renews attempts to describe and explain the encounter between society and the person by linking personal identity with culture. This orientation does not, however, fully account for the dynamic dialectical relationship between what individuals do and the actions for which responsibility can be assigned to society as a whole. In the literature, it is customary therefore to resort to common-sense generalizations about human beings as individuals.

In sum, despite the limitations found in the theoretical frameworks developed to date, sociologists and psychologists rarely enter into a productive dialogue. If we rely on Kelly's explication of personal construct theory, however, it becomes possible to trace specific connections between macro-frameworks conceived in different ways, and the sundry types of individuals that make up any society. What is proposed is a reconstrual of the Fundamental Postulate and significant Corollaries so as to construct a viable bridge between the domains of sociologists and the enclaves of the psychologist. For the community of sociologists, this is a bid to deepen analyses of society by providing a complex understanding of how individuals maintain social structure. For the community of psychologists, the sociological paradigms can enrich the ways in which it is possible to interpret how individuals construe the reality in which they live. If this approach is accepted, the openness to alternative constructions of the social can add to the perspectives that inform exciting research as well as boost the capacity of counsellors and others to proffer assistance that is relevant in differently construed contexts.

It is important to emphasize that the attribution of one or another kind of interpretation of the nature of society need not be held to be a revelation of certainty. Each of the paradigms is an invitation to broaden one's framing of the social. For even in a single community, people may adopt constructions of the social, which, although unconventional or outside the ken of the psychologist, are theoretically justified on sociological grounds. The prospect of different interpretations of the nature of society and its modes of functioning provide the psychologist with tools for understanding the social implications of various kinds of construals and variously structured systems of constructs. Thus, alternative hypotheses about what constitutes a viable construction of reality (if only for the time being) can enrich the repertoire of perceptions about how individuals may fit in and how they can be helped to do so.

COMBINING THE SOCIAL AND THE PERSONAL

To illustrate the possibilities for combining the personal and the social the following refers to the affinity between personal construct psychology and aspects of four theoretical approaches in sociology: Bourdieu's (1977) reflexive sociology, Parsons' (1949/1937, 1966) structural functionalism, Garfinkel's (1967) ethnomethodology, and critical theory that derives from Marx and Engels (1970/1845–6).

Bourdieu's 'Habitus' and the Fundamental Postulate

Stating that '*a person's processes are psychologically channelized by the ways in which he anticipates events*', Kelly's Fundamental Postulate explains the acquisition of a central concept in contemporary sociology, 'habitus'. As elaborated by Bourdieu, 'habitus' refers to the cluster of dispositions, attitudes, orientations, postures, habits and values conveyed to individuals by their cultural surround. That broad conceptualization suggests (a) that culture shapes groups of people, attuning them to sharing modes of construal and, hence, (b) that key systems of constructs are likely to be shared by groups embedded in social structure and involved in social processes. The sociological significance of this construction is disclosed in confrontations between groups who command social power and groups deprived of power. Each group commands a different habitus (the complex of dispositions and orientations, and so on) so they have different construals of reality. Those with access to power in different social, economic or cultural fields, tend collectively to anticipate ways to protect a system of construing that justifies their rights, while the less powerful and the powerless construe reality as a demand to withstand pressures. Because people are constantly anticipating the far as well as the near future, and experimenting to test those anticipations, meetings between differentiated groups constitute an ongoing series of contested experiments in which all those involved are seeking validation. With the help of the Fundamental Postulate, the 'habitus' can, therefore, be understood as the resultant of encounters between dynamic construing individuals and the equally dynamic constraints on their right to use social resources. The sociologist who works with the construct of habitus can, therefore, with the help of the Fundamental Postulate, understand how social process leaves its stamp on individuals.

The concept of 'habitus' specifies the various ways in which construals are manifested. For the psychologist, this reading of the confrontation between persons in culturally differentiated groups introduces an understanding of how the political is implicated in development and in education, as well as of how the person is caught up in history. Group chronicles record how apparently haphazard strings of incidents provide grist for the mills of anticipations; how outcomes record the successes and failures of experiments in context, and how evidence from validation or invalidation governs what is appraised as success and what anticipations are viable. Thus, insight into the workings of the dialectic between power in every domain and the habitus can be of aid not only in helping people to adjust, but also in empowering them.

Kelly's Ideas and Parsons' Structural Functionalism

The dominant paradigm in twentieth-century sociology was that of *structural functionalism* as developed by Talcott Parsons. The theory assumes that every society provides a structure that fulfils at least four functions: adaptation to the physical environment (economy), collective decision-making and action (polity), sharing symbols and values (culture), and transmitting patterns of behaviour from generation to generation (socialization/education). It also presupposes that people further these functions with their actions. Several central ideas in personal construct psychology fill significant gaps in Parsons' theory. Basically, the philosophical hypothesis of 'man the scientist' and three corollaries: the Organization Corollary, the Dichotomy Corollary and the Choice Corollary, breathe life into Parsons' formulation of the 'theory of action' that is designed to bridge the distance between society and the acting person or collective. In turn, the insights of structural functionalism enrich the corollaries with social meaning.

Organization

This is central to Parsons' analysis. The Organization Corollary states that: '*a person's constructs are organized into a construction system embracing ordinal relationships between constructs*'. Parsons' analysis describes the qualities of the social setting that actually oblige persons to develop an organized system of constructs. In the analytical model he compiled, reality is hierarchically organized in systems: the physical, the biological, the psychological, the social and the cultural. Each of the systems can be analysed separately, but also serves as 'environment' for the others. To explain that relationship, Parsons proposed the concept of 'emergence'—with each system emerging from the other because agents act systematically. Still, despite Parsons' insistence that action is necessarily systematic in a world of systems, his description of what comprises action remains static. Only by relating the Parsonian construction to Kelly's ideas about 'man the scientist' can we imagine how the actor–agent actually gets into the fray of living in a social system.

Man the Scientist

Kelly proposed that because of their nature, people act like scientists in everyday life. Parsons hypothesized a system of action operated by agents, whether individuals, groups or collectives. The model of the system of action asserts that in action energy is expended (as motivation) in order to achieve a goal by using appropriate normative means. Although Parsons' actor is a pre-Kellyian person who is prodded into action by a particular impetus, we can easily show the parallels. As in the laboratory, every action involves construing a situation (defining the problem), anticipating the next step and planning action (designing an experiment according to rule), acting (carrying out rule-governed intervention), and checking for validation (confronting findings with the initial hypothesis(es)). That is the dynamic image of agents that invoke the Parsonian 'system of action'. According to Parsons, agents are bound to confront existential dichotomies in which they make choices.

Dichotomies and Choices

In the Dichotomy Corollary, Kelly specifies that a person's '*construction system . . . is composed of a finite number of dichotomous constructs*' and, in the Choice Corollary, he asserts that a person chooses '*that alternative in a dichotomized construct through which he anticipates the greater possibility for extension and definition of his system*'.

According to Kelly, there is a 'reality' out there, but that reality awaits our construal and experimentation. What is often ignored, however, is that in his theorization of the person, Kelly implies not only that there are differences between individuals, but also that there may be different kinds of reality that change over time. Parsons' models provide an appropriate framework for understanding this supposition. The integration of Parsons with Kelly provides a social perspective on aspects of reality that impose organization and enable choices that are anchored in existential dichotomies.

The exercise of choice between dichotomies is central to Parsons' system of action. In his view, however, the very structure of society requires the constant exercise of choice. As he puts it, an actor has to find solutions for five superordinate dilemmas, which are inevitable in every action and in every society, even if the actor is not aware of them. In most cases, actors are guided by preverbal construing. As agents, actors are confronted with dichotomies and have to deal with issues of deciding: whether in an anticipated situation one should be guided by desire (affectivity) or affective-neutrality; whether one should attempt to realize private or collective interests; whether actions should be based on universalistic norms, or on the norms that govern the particular relations of actor and other; whether one should relate to the objects of one's action according to their potential accomplishments or according to a construal of each object's innate qualities. Finally, when acting, the agent solves the dilemma of 'scope of significance', that is, how specifically or how diffusely he or she wishes to be involved with the object. The dilemmas that confront the actor hint at the types of norms and values (the elements of the system of culture) that can diverge and show discrepancies when specific social contexts are construed.

Kelly's insight as to the nature of the person as he explains the Fundamental Postulate is an almost uncanny complement to Parsons' modelling of organization, dichotomization, and the necessity for choice as qualities of the real world. For application, Parsons' models of social functioning and of action can serve to fire the psychologist's imagination in regard to clients' stories. From the point of view of the psychologist, the set of superordinate constructs identified by Parsons provides a gateway to assessing the dimensions of subordinate construals and their relation to the actions generated. Thus, Parsons hypothesizes what it means to be governed by a cultural system. With the aid of his models, psychologists are supplied with parameters that shed light on the kinds of constructions a client is led to make in and through participation in a social system. This kind of analysis provides concrete meaning to Kelly's proviso that a person's 'culture' has to be taken into consideration whenever one tries to understand how another person views the world.

Kelly's Ideas and Garfinkel's Ethnomethodology

Garfinkel's contribution to the many paradigms of sociology, first systematized in *Studies in Ethnomethodology* (1967), elaborates on his emphatic declaration that people are not 'existential dopes'. Society is possible because people know what they are doing and, furthermore, adapt themselves to different events in assorted ways. The sociologist should be aware of the fact that persons in society are methodical. It is because they share methodologies that institutions such as the state and its politics, religion and its rituals, can be established and maintained. People know what methods are appropriate and meaningful for acting in familiar situations in each institutionalized framework. They identify similarities between events, understand what rules can be applied, and act within the available range of variations that all the members of the group grasp explicitly or implicitly. For members, the meanings attached to actions may be invisible, but that is because they are 'natural' and therefore rarely examined. In this type of sociological analysis, every group in an identifiable social location can be considered an *ethnie* that has its own, taken for granted, ways of living.

The approach of ethnomethodology is peculiarly congruent with the openness that Kelly preached and exemplified both in elaborating a psychological theory and in his work as adviser and therapist. For instance, both the Construction Corollary and the Fragmentation Corollary are pertinent to the type of world envisioned by the school of ethnomethodology.

Construction

In line with the Construction Corollary, individuals in this type of reality have to be understood as anticipating events *'through construing their replications'*. Ethnomethodologists agree that the methods people use in order to construct actions are not random. But they cannot account for why certain methods have taken hold. They lack the Kellyian insight that a capacity for anticipating repetitions of occurrences, and for recognizing them when they arise, is inborn. Nor do they have means for recognizing the validation that enforces people's methods of coping with situations identified as similar. Were replication the only criterion for construing situations and constructing actions, people might, however, still be relatively unaware of the potential for variety in construal and in action.

Fragmentation

This is where the Kellyian construct of fragmentation is placed in a normative perspective. According to the Fragmentation Corollary, *'a person may successively employ a variety of construction subsystems which are inferentially incompatible with each other'*. In the best scenario, fragmentation is an opportunity for formulating superordinate constructs that can accommodate the subsystems. If, however, that opportunity is not seized, fragmentation may be the key to severe psychological unease. Ethnomethodologists agree that people do not have to give up an old idea before considering a new one. In their view, we do not have to show with every action that we fit into an obviously systematic context. Every person who is a 'member' of a society—and that means *every person*—necessarily makes use of construction subsystems that may not be congruent without self-consciousness. This possibility is vital in a society that requires individuals to move in several social domains; people are flexible enough and smart enough to fit in with all of them. The capacity for fragmentation in the Kellyian sense is, therefore, actually a sign of one's ability to be a 'member', and that is a condition for survival. Like all other modes of construal (and in tune with the claims of ethnomethodology), fragmentation turns into a problem and people undergo invalidation only if and when domains are confused.

For the psychologist, the paradigm of ethnomethodology provides scaffolding for construing the authority of 'membership' in different circles with their diverse repertoires of what is to be taken for granted. Although construction systems that evolve through membership in different circles may be 'inferentially incompatible', they make sense in the life world of the actor. That 'sense' is the tool for unravelling the client's construals because it is possible to follow up the distinctions between the logic of life world know-how and the logic of cognition. By construing actions as applications of ethnomethods, the psychologist is alerted to the significance of differences between what is implicit in the client's milieu and what has to be spelled out. Thus, the grasp of society put forward by ethnomethodology opens an avenue for getting at the non-verbalized constructs that are embedded in habitual action. Through this insight, psychologists and clients, or subjects, are part of a collaborative process. The methods each uses have to be subjected to scrutiny for clarifying the construction of membership. When the paradigm of ethnomethodology is taken as a working description of the nature of society, negotiating meanings is understood to be inherent to the social structure.

Kelly's Ideas and Critical Theory

The basis for exploring the connections between Kelly's ideas and critical theory in sociology is the Modulation Corollary. *'The variation in a person's construction system is limited by the permeability of the constructs within whose range of convenience the variants lie.'*

The Modulation Corollary helps to solve difficulties explored in the paradigm of critical theory—a sociological paradigm elaborated by the Frankfurt School on the basis of the writings of Marx. Sociologists of this school study ideas and their stubborn reproduction in social structure. With the Modulation Corollary, Kelly indicates how it is possible for prevailing ideas to be reproduced by individuals even when overtly there are good reasons for effecting change (Kalekin-Fishman, 1993).

In critical theory, the aggregate of ideas prevalent in a society, the ideology, is part of the strategy for preserving social arrangements that benefit the few. This claim stems from the sociological construal of society as a class structure, with classes differentiated according to their locations in processes of production. Because thinking and feeling inevitably arise from material conditions, each class should have different conceptualizations of the nature of the world (Marx & Engels, 1970/1845–6). Under capitalism, there is generally a division between workers whose contribution to production is using their minds for thinking and planning (owners, highly placed administrators, engineers, for example) and workers whose contribution to production is in the main manual—carrying out instructions. The distinction between mental and manual labour is conceived as defining how people live and, therefore, what and how they think. Critical sociology assumes that the connection between the material context and the ideas people hold requires explanation.

The view of this school is that the owners of the means of production—whose interest it is to ensure continued control—frame ideas, beliefs and values that legitimate the status quo. These are conveyed in education, in the media, and through all kinds of cultural enterprises. Thus, the conglomeration of 'mental productions' that express the interests of the ruling classes become the ruling ideas; they are taken for granted as representing the true and the good in society. Perpetrated as concepts and beliefs that are 'natural' and 'logical', the ruling ideas become a multifaceted tool for concealment. There is no need to suppose that this is a conspiratorial plan in order to see that since they serve class interests they are likely to hide injustice and deprivation. According to the paradigm of critical sociology, the deprived classes can see through the veil of ideology if they discover the contradictions in systemic outcomes. But unless they take on some of the apparatus of personal construct psychology, sociologists have no gear for facilitating such discoveries.

The Modulation Corollary actually pinpoints the psychological effects of ideology in the sense of critical theory. Because the patterns of collective living that serve the governing interests are imposed on everyone, people are likely to have adopted constructs, even systems of constructs that are in principle impermeable. Constructs that limit criticism of the political system and constructs that restrict the identification of opportunities for resistance to coercion are probably most opaque. We must remember that the psychologist, like the client, is swayed by the 'ruling ideas'. Although every person is susceptible to the ruling ideology, at least in part, informed use of personal construct theory can shed light on how to let go of the fetters of ideology. The view that the least permeable constructs are likely to contribute to the preservation of the status quo in society can indicate to the psychologist what types of situated construals can pry open the limitations of ideology—the nexus of impermeable constructs.

If the psychologist discovers that the client construes society in class terms, he or she has a tool for exploring and tempering impermeability.

SUMMARY

Sociology, a discipline with multiple paradigms, is a realization of Kelly's philosophical ideal—constructive alternativism. The diversity shows that despite the disciplinary presumption that it makes sense to talk about society as an entity, there is no consensus about the shape and form of that entity, or about how it should or must be described. Hence, there is no definitive conclusion as to how people fit in. Because of this indecision, however, sociology provides a fund of resources for the psychologist who works within the framework of personal construct psychology.

This chapter has outlined four sociological paradigms and indicated initial possibilities of the promise they hold for extending the scope of personal construct theory. Similarly, personal construct theory—the Fundamental Postulate and the specific Corollaries—shows how an understanding of the Kellyian person can contribute to extending the scope of sociology, by clarifying ongoing relationships between societies and the people that comprise them. It is possible to show that other of Kelly's Corollaries relate to sociological paradigms such as rational choice theory, exchange theory, sociobiology and symbolic interaction. The expansion of Kelly's ideas proposed here enables all practitioners to open their thinking to the possibility that the influences of social reality on people's development throughout the life cycle cannot be interpreted unambiguously. Different schools of sociology propose alternative construals of the social and therefore hint at varied types of impact on individuals. Those who use ideas and methods of personal construct psychology to be creative are constantly challenged by diverse perspectives to revise and reconstrue the meanings attached to social relations.

CHAPTER 14

Cross-Cultural Construing

Jörn W. Scheer
University of Giessen, Germany

> Looking through glasses that are not your own can permanently affect your eyesight.
>
> (Kelly, 1962, p. 90)

COMMONALITY AND SOCIALITY

The psychology of personal constructs is primarily concerned with the ways persons, that is, individuals, find their ways through the hassles of life. Using their own personal constructs to anticipate events by construing the repetitions of earlier events, individuals 'make sense' of their lives and of the events they encounter. In principle, others are involved only as sources of validation or invalidation of the individual's personal constructs. Assumptions about similarity of construing ('commonality') and trying to understand others' construing ('sociality') are appropriate as soon as more than one person is involved.

The notion that groups of individuals may share their ways of construing is an extension of that idea. It makes sense to assume that people who grow up together or who live together construe in similar ways. That some family members may dissent does not necessarily mean they have other constructs: it may simply be that they locate themselves at the opposite pole of some constructs. People who work together may share certain constructs. Adrian Robertson elaborates on Kelly's notion of 'super-patterns' (see Chapter 34, pp. 339–348). People of the same religious denomination share certain constructs. The same may apply to residents of a country or a region.

CULTURES

Obviously there are different levels of sharing of construing. That can be as confusing as the use of the term 'culture', which is applied to a multitude of social

International Handbook of Personal Construct Psychology. Edited by F. Fransella.
© 2003 John Wiley & Sons, Ltd.

entities: youth culture, corporate culture, national culture, Islamic culture. It can be said that inasmuch as someone shares important ways of construing with a group of people, he or she is part of that culture.

It is easy to see that an individual can in effect belong to several cultures. In writing this, I am aware that I am writing as a psychologist, as an academic, as a (West) German, as a male person of retirement age, as a 'Westerner', to name just a few bio-psycho-social affiliations. In some ways I find myself construing like the majority of my various peers, in others I most certainly am a dissenter. That in itself is probably due to the specific combination of my affiliations. If I were living in a different country or at a different time, my constructions would probably be more like those of others, I would experience more commonality of construing. That has to be kept in mind when speaking of 'cross-cultural' construing. Not every member of a culture shares all the constructs seemingly characteristic of that culture.

The term 'culture' has a variety of meanings and is used on a variety of levels of abstraction, and the term 'cross-cultural' therefore may apply to a variety of settings. It is not necessary to try to be overly precise about that. Cross-cultural construing occurs whenever people belonging to different cultures meet. In general, the term is used to describe relationships between members of different national or ethnic entities.

WHEN CROSS-CULTURAL CONSTRUING OCCURS

Encounters between members of different cultures have occurred throughout the history of mankind. Travellers, explorers, traders, conquerors and anthropologists have had to 'make sense' of what they experience when meeting foreign peoples. The idea of 'construing others' constructions' was certainly not on their minds, but they still had to think about what 'the others' may have meant when they said and did something. For travellers this was necessary to be able to survive, for traders it served their interests, for ethnographers it was at the core of their business. Conquerors, on the other hand, did not necessarily have to care about others' constructions.

These days, much cross-cultural construing is required: of the common *tourist*, of professionals doing *business* in other countries of a globalized world, of *politicians* involved in international affairs, of *migrants* in need of survival in a new society; not the least, of *researchers* doing cross-cultural research. So far, all of these activities have been carried out without resorting to theoretical constructs, and it remains to be shown how those constructs can improve an understanding of these activities.

GEORGE KELLY'S VENTURE INTO CROSS-CULTURAL CONSTRUING

In 1960/61, George Kelly travelled to 37 countries in 12 months, with—among others—the aim of exploring '*Europe's matrix of decision*' (1962). In some ways, his journey can be compared to the expeditions of early explorers who set out to discover the ways other people make sense of their lives and who, like him, had to rely on locals as informers and translators. Kelly's informers were mostly psychologists, and he employed several strategies to elicit the information he was interested in, including group discussions with certain recurring questions as stimuli.

Among the dimensions of construing that he noted were *humanitarianism* vs. *opportunism*, *idealism* vs. *materialism*, or, more concrete, *German cars* vs. *American textbooks*. Some of these 'personal' constructs are of a more general, philosophical character, some of them bear a certain resemblance to stereotypes. Anticipating future developments on a larger scale was an important issue for Kelly. That is, of course, as hazardous as a weather forecast. Another aim of his was to inform his fellow Americans about their own impending choices. Cummins (2002) has revisited Kelly's report almost 40 years after the original journey with interesting insights on the nature of anticipations. Predictions about the future of the European countries are limited by the failure of anticipating certain other developments, such as the reduced importance of a national identity and the lessening of the influence of World War II. Perhaps the 'decision matrix' has too many components to allow an accurate prediction. Or, long-range predictions may always lie outside the range of convenience of any construing system!

Since Kelly's tour, the personal construct literature has not produced many examples of cross-cultural research, although it has been argued that personal construct concepts are well suited to such attempts (for example, McCoy, 1983). Davidson and Reser (1996) have connected the Kellyian approach to the distinction between 'etic' (intercultural or universal) and 'emic' (intracultural) research in anthropology.

THEORETICAL CONSTRUCTS RELEVANT TO CROSS-CULTURAL CONSTRUING

Naturally, the concepts of *sociality* and *commonality* are of prime importance in the cross-cultural context. Immersing in a foreign culture also requires the ability to *loosen* one's own construing, but also facilitates resorting to *tightening* when exposure to new environments poses a *threat* to the individual's core constructs. *Validation* and *invalidation* of one's construing probably occur more frequently and with more dramatic results in cross-cultural contexts, compared to the calm waters of everyday life within a given culture.

AIMS AND OBJECTIVES OF CROSS-CULTURAL EXPERIENCE

Travelling

Walker (2000, 2002b) has analysed the processes occurring in travelling from a personal construct perspective. Travellers can be considered as being continuously engaged in construing in the personal construct sense, looking for differences and similarities. 'Here in Australia they have roundabouts just like in England': *similarity* if observed by a British tourist; *contrast* from a German point of view. 'In our country we don't have flag-poles in our front gardens like the Americans do': *contrast* and it is clear that construing such as that may have implications such as 'we are less nationalistic'. What begins as mere observation leads to the attachment of meaning and from there to the confirmation of identity. Walker (2002b) has suggested that cross-cultural travelling may lead to an *extension* of a person's identity—including personal development—but that may be accompanied by *consolidation* of identity—possibly *constriction*. Such changes, however, may also be a painful experience.

Global Economics

In these days of global economic interrelationships, understanding others, in the literal sense, may be crucial. Devi Jankowicz (see Chapter 36, pp. 359–366) shows that this is not simply a matter of one-to-one translation of words and terms. Language represents the cultural experience of a group and may therefore transport idiosyncratic meanings. 'Language acts as a unifying force'. Commenting on the task of knowledge transfer from 'Western' economics to 'post-command' economics, Jankowicz stresses the necessity of 'negotiating common meanings'.

It should not, however, be overlooked that this does not necessarily happen in an atmosphere of trust and good-will—the credulous approach that Kelly emphasized, the 'working alliance' in a therapeutic relationship, or the innocent curiosity of the globe-trotting traveller. It is also about power and dominance, and the downside of 'transfer' can be takeover and submission. The story of the re-unification in Germany and how it is represented in the minds of the people, is enlightening. The considerable transfer of financial resources from the former West to the former East is construed by many West Germans as an act of generosity, while many East Germans feel humiliated by being seen as receivers of alms. After construing their Eastern 'brothers and sisters'—a preferred term in the 1950s and 1960s—as victims of oppression for many years, Westerners now seem to blame the Easterners as accomplices of the former regime. Language is also an instrument of exerting power, and this may happen even in the comparatively mild form common in scientific communication (Scheer, 1996b). Many East Germans now stick defiantly to the somewhat different usage of German that they have developed over the past half century.

Politics

Global economics is intimately related to international politics, which is historically older. Given the importance of understanding the meanings that 'the other side' attaches to events, it is surprising that personal construct psychology has not delved more into this field. Kelly's paper on 'Europe's matrix of decision' was not followed up for more than 30 years. Since then, Cummins (1996) has commented on the British construing of European affairs, Scheer (1996a) on the relationship between the two parts of Germany, and Stojnov discusses the relationship between the peoples in former Yugoslavia (see Chapter 18, pp. 191–198). It is to be hoped that Don Bannister's hitherto unpublished paper (see Chapter 17, pp. 181–189) will encourage personal construct scholars and practitioners to discover the 'political Kelly'. It may be particularly interesting to explore the notion of *choice* in this context: to what extent is it really a 'national identity' (like being a Serb) that determines the construal of self and also the construal of others? Cummins (2000) mentions his surprise when realizing how much of his own thinking along these lines is rooted in his (Irish) background. But he also quotes du Preez who wrote:

> We may construe a person's identity in terms of peripheral or even irrelevant constructs. That is we may simply misunderstand him. We may think that his nationality or his race is the key to his identity; whereas he attaches importance to his religion, the fact that he is a good musician, and his loyalty to his family.
> (Du Preez, 1979, p. 352)

Why does he or she do this? A study using the 'laddering' technique might be particularly helpful to explore aspects of cross-cultural construing such as these (see Chapter 10, pp. 105–121).

Again, cross-cultural construing may be considered irrelevant as long as power relationships prevail. The dominant culture can afford not to bother about 'shared meanings'.

Migration

The situation of migrants can be seen as a classical stage for the study of cross-cultural construing. Migrants of necessity 'attach meaning' to their new experience. Often differing interpretations of the same events, such as the behaviours of men and women towards one another, can lead to clashes of a serious nature—'she asked for it—the way she looked'. Since here, too, power is involved it is often not about negotiating shared meanings. It is rather about taking over others' constructions or forcefully maintaining one's own constructions. What Walker (2002b) has elaborated for travellers, applies to a much greater degree to migrants, because of the vital necessity to consolidate one's identity or system of core constructs. That may be a reason for the 'ghettoization' often observed with migrants once higher numbers arrive, such as Chinatown and Little Italy. It also leads to frequently reported tighter construing in migrants compared to fellow nationals who stayed at home. Many Turkish migrants in Germany keep to a much stricter regime with respect to religious matters as well as to family structure than they would back home. English residents abroad are often called 'Little Englanders'.

Cummins (2002) has described the changes in his identity after migrating from Ireland to England, using the dual constructs *safety* vs. *danger* and *legitimate* vs. *illegitimate*, as well as the construct poles *degradation of social role* vs. *advancement*, and *ascribed* vs. *attained*. That is also a good example of the usefulness of the *Choice Corollary*. Migrants are not necessarily bound by their position in society. McCoy (1983) has described the 'culture shock' experienced by a temporary migrant from Australia to Hong Kong, using repertory grids to document the changes in construing that occurred over a two-year period.

RESEARCH

Finally, the context of research into the lives of people living in foreign countries, in different cultures, is a prime example of the importance of adequate cross-cultural construing. The history of ethnography and anthropology abounds in misunderstandings due to the lack of ability to see the world with the eyes of the people under scrutiny (again the 'emic–etic' dilemma). This is in part a question of language. In hindsight it is not difficult to see that the language of a European country may not be the best tool to represent the constructs of the South Sea Island people, especially if natives of these islands use a rudimentary English or French to communicate their constructs to the explorer.

Methods of Research

As always, personal construct-related methods of research include semistructured exploration on the one hand and highly structured repertory grid techniques on the other. Different objectives require different techniques depending, for instance, on whether other people's construing of *their own* world is the object of investigation, or whether the *same* issue is under study with members of *different* cultures.

Kelly apparently used somewhat systematic but loosely employed interviewing or conversational techniques in his cross-cultural study tour. Others, such as Blowers and McCoy (1986), have used repertory grids in comparing responses to film sequences elicited from Australian and Hong Kong Chinese participants. Ross (1996) found a version of the pyramiding technique particularly useful when exploring attitudes of Australian desert Aborigines towards housing facilities, but also employed group grids with supplied constructs. Scheer and colleagues (1997) used repertory grids to compare constructs of elderly Germans and Australians about successful ageing. The elements included retrospective self-elements, such as 'me when I was a child, about 8 years of age', and anchor elements such as 'the happiest person I know'. Neimeyer and Fukuyama (1984), in an effort to enhance the effectiveness of counsellors dealing with members of ethnic minorities in the USA, developed the 'Cultural Attitudes Repertory Technique'. The aim was to assess the clients' and the counsellors' own cultural value systems by using members of different cultural groups as elements in the grid.

McCoy (1983) has argued that the flexibility and sensitivity of the repertory grid technique makes it particularly well suited to the needs of a value-free approach required in cross-cultural studies.

PROBLEMS AND LIMITATIONS OF A PERSONAL CONSTRUCT PERSPECTIVE

Conceptual Issues

At first glance, comparing, identifying similarities and making distinctions seems to be a fundamental cognitive, emotional and pragmatic activity, one of the basic principles in making sense of events. Therefore, personal construct *concepts* should be universally applicable across cultures even if the range of convenience of certain constructs appears limited. But *using* these principles does not necessarily mean employing them explicitly, let alone communicating about them. Hence difficulties may arise in eliciting personal constructs.

However, another important aspect of personal construct theory is the notion of an *individual* behaving like a personal scientist—acting, making choices, and experimenting. That notion is not shared universally. In some Asian cultures there exists the notion of a group ego which is seen as being superordinate to the individual. Some cultures are reported not to enhance the notion of an autonomous individual but an individual *in relation to*, for example, 'me as a nephew' when talking to or dealing with my uncle. The psychiatrist Wulff (1978) has observed such an understanding of self in Vietnam and related it to the notion of a 'group ego' described by Parin and Morgenthaler for the Dogon people in West Africa (Parin, 1967).

The multiplicity of relational selves could imply something like Mair's (1977) 'community of selves', but this issue has not yet been explored. Ross (1996) remarks that 'many cultures do not customarily follow the modes of discourse and inquiry necessary for the completion of a grid such as asking and answering questions and making direct comparisons' (p. 184). According to her, in Australian Aboriginal cultures it is considered impolite to ask direct questions. Many of her respondents were unable to verbalize comparisons although they could describe elements. Blowers (1995) notes in Chinese respondents a 'cultural imperative not to pry too deeply', and furthermore suspects that an 'individualist view of the world' as implied by a personal construct psychology approach 'could appear dangerously radical'. A personal construct enquirer (like a therapist or counsellor) needs not only to be able to *speak* the language of the interviewee but also to be aware of the importance of gaining some understanding of the specific *usage* prevalent in the interviewee's social or cultural group. Then it might be easier to use Kelly's metatheoretical approach to construe the others' behaviour as an experiment that tests out their hypotheses about the current situation or event.

Language

The question of language is, in my view as a non-native speaker of English, grossly underestimated. This refers not only to the specialist personal construct psychology language but also to the effect of a language on the ways its speakers construe.

Blowers (1995), as a resident of Hong Kong, points out that 'the translation of the Kellyian terminology'—like *construe, repertory, grid*—'presents major problems'. Scheer (1996b) has reported similar problems with translations into German. The term *Korollarium* is alien to anyone not versed in academic philosophy. For *grid* the dictionaries list *Rost* (grid-iron, as in barbecues), *Netz* (a fisherman's net, or figuratively a railway system or a power distribution system), and *Gitter* (lattice, fence, railing, some sort of enclosure), all of them with misleading connotations. Several of these words have been used in the German personal construct literature. The solution that I, and most authors, finally came up with is—*Grid*. Since Kelly's terms do not seem to be used in the same way in non-academic English there may also be an issue of scientific jargon as opposed to common usage.

Still, language barriers seem to be a major stumbling block for a more general proliferation of personal construct psychology ideas. In the non-English-speaking world, only in countries where personal construct psychology textbooks have been written in the respective language (Italy, Spain, Germany, Russia, China) has there been a noticeable if still limited adoption of personal construct ideas. That is even more so if we look beyond academic circles where competency in English is more common.

Furthermore, we do not know the extent to which properties of the language available to *express* constructions may themselves *affect* the ways we construe (see Chapter 36, pp. 359–366). In translating Kellyian terms into Polish, Jankowicz (2002) found that 'different languages encode, that is to say, arrange, or structure, or slice up experience differently, and in any language, a construct only exists because idiom or metaphor permit it'. Blowers has observed a 'strong cultural tendency for concrete construing' in Hong Kong Chinese students. Davidson and Reser (1996) report that in certain Australian Aboriginal languages there is no word for *compare* or *better*. Thus even in competent translation, construing systems may appear much simpler (more constricted, one-dimensional and so forth) than they really are.

Surprisingly, Kelly (1962) in his report does not mention issues of language. While he could probably rely on competent interpreters, this, to many native speakers of English, does not even seem to occur as a potential problem—understandably, for wherever they travel in the world there are always people who speak English (or try to).

Social Constraints

Although the choices that migrants are faced with have been mentioned, it must not be ignored that socioeconomic conditions, cultural traditions and historical ties in fact limit the range of choices for a person in a given social context. The assumption of an individual in a constant process of experimentation with respect to the options available in life, always the master of one's own fate, is probably in itself culturally biased.

POTENTIAL BENEFITS OF A PERSONAL CONSTRUCT APPROACH

In spite of the limitations discussed in the previous section, adopting a personal construct perspective may open up promising avenues into cross-cultural understanding. Openness to the constructions of others may free the traveller, migrant, or researcher from his or her preferred ways of construing and so liberate those individuals from the restrictions that are imposed. The habit of questioning one's own construing, and engaging in the exercise of reconstruing will certainly help to avoid misinterpretations.

The 'cargo cult' that certain people in New Guinea adopted in the early stages of contact with Europeans need not be ridiculed as 'primitive'. The unexplainable regular spotting of high-flying shiny objects 'made sense' in the spiritual construing of these people. Or, more seriously, what appears to 'Westerners' as nepotism or corruption in some African countries makes sense in a society without a state-supported social security system where survival traditionally depends on clan loyalty.

More generally, the notion that apparently contradictory constructs may be compatible on a higher hierarchical level of construing can be applied to many 'alien' events or behaviours. Above all, the intellectual discipline and rigour that are characteristic of personal construct theory as a system, in conjunction with the basic openness mentioned above, offer promising possibilities for the 'soft science' of cross-cultural endeavours.

ANGLO-CENTRISM HURDLES

In conclusion, it is my opinion that people involved in personal construct psychology should be encouraged to cross boundaries and borders, both in the figurative and the literal sense, and become more internationalist. To achieve this, it is probably necessary to overcome a certain Anglo-centrism that personal construct psychology seems to share with modern science in general. As demonstrated in the research of Ross, Davidson and Jankowicz, being creative in developing methods and concepts adapted to the different cultural environment of other peoples is essential.

But there is no need to reinvent the wheel altogether. A vast body of evidence has been collected by cross-cultural travellers, explorers and researchers over the course of centuries. It might be worthwhile to take a fresh look at this evidence, informed by a personal construct psychology perspective.

CHAPTER 15

Forensic Personal Construct Psychology: Assessing and Treating Offenders

James Horley
Augustana University College, Alberta, Canada

> Sometimes the punished person turns the tables on the punishing people . . . He moves towards establishing a core role for himself which includes the very behaviour which others have found threatening. Now he can be threatened, not by his evil ways . . . but by the prospect of losing his status as an 'evildoer'.
>
> (Kelly, 1955/1991, p. 506/Vol. 1, p. 373)

Forensic psychology is a subdiscipline of psychology concerned with applications of psychological principles and research to aspects of the justice system. It has flourished over the past two to three decades, although the origins of this field can be traced to at least the late nineteenth century (Bartol & Bartol, 1999). Its application has been felt in three areas of the justice system: rehabilitation of offenders, consultation of various forms with the police, and research and consultation on legal issues and processes. In spite of this being a young field, and the obvious need for further work in some areas, a significant body of work has already been produced. The focus of this chapter is on the assessment and treatment of sexual offenders.

Much of the clinical work with offenders to date has been informed, either explicitly or implicitly, by biomedical perspectives. Included here would be personality type-trait approaches (for example, Eysenck, 1977) that emphasize inborn, enduring characteristics that lead to criminal behaviour. This is unfortunate for a number of reasons. First, it leads to the paradoxical and disturbing situation of finding individuals criminally responsible for their actions, yet their actions are not seen as under their control. Learning theories, too, remove personal responsibility from the individual and shift it to the social and/or physical environments. Perhaps a more serious concern from a rehabilitative perspective is the lack of hope for change that results from a 'diagnosis' of paedophilia, antisocial personality disorder, and so

International Handbook of Personal Construct Psychology. Edited by F. Fransella.
© 2003 John Wiley & Sons, Ltd.

forth. The individual offender is left with some hope of a medical breakthrough that produces a 'magic pill' to address the problem, but the pill will probably only address the symptoms of the 'illness', rather than provide any real hope for a 'cure'.

That raises a related concern about the dominance of biomedical models, namely 'symptom management'. Rather than address underlying reasons for offensive acts, we are often content, perhaps because of the ease and power of modern psychiatric medication, to contain the aggressive or abusive expressions of offenders. Finally, alternative perspectives have not been seriously considered for the most part. Even when other approaches are presented (for example, Houston, 1998), they are often compromised by attempts to reconcile them with the biomedical perspective and, thus, they fail to outline and to document the actual and potential richness of the other perspectives. Obviously biomedical considerations, such as neural injury or disease and biochemical imbalances, should be examined in specific cases of offensive behaviour, but theoretical alternatives, such as personal construct theory, provide an important perspective in the assessment and treatment of the majority of offenders.

EXPERIENCE, LABELLING AND OFFENDING

In general terms, how might a personal construct account of offending appear? Needs (1988) has noted that, while Kelly had nothing to say directly about offending and forensic issues, his theory can be applied to the field both broadly and narrowly.

Freedom to choose a course of action based on personal experience, even if the act might be interpreted by the vast majority of observers as 'negative' or 'undesirable', is emphasized by personal construct theory. In his Choice Corollary, Kelly says a person chooses for himself that alternative in a dichotomized construct through which he anticipates the greater possibility for extension and/or definition of his construing system. What Kelly is concerned with are the psychological reasons, or motives, for particular acts. The importance of asking and examining responses to motivational questions for offenders has been accepted by many investigators in various disciplines but examined by few.

Extending our construing system is a major reason for selecting one act or behaviour rather than another. Kelly (1970) viewed all behaviour as experimental, or a tentative trial to observe whether an outcome was as predicted. Having sex with a young boy or killing a rival gang member could allow an individual, as unappealing or repulsive as it may seem to most people, to experience power or status through self-understanding as 'attractive' or 'tough'. The extension of an individual's construing system does not require any degree of social acceptability, although social demands undoubtedly shape an individual's likely construal of an act before, during and after the experience. *Defining* our construing system refers to more explicit and clear self-definition. The act of murder or rape could lead to a more refined sense of self. Whether the self-referent includes a 'negative' label such as 'killer' or 'pervert', or whether it would lead to a 'positive' label such as 'predator' or 'tough', will be a function of the actor's thinking at the time and the immediate social response he receives.

One difficult issue to consider is the question of limits on freedom, many of which are placed by lack of awareness and 'conditioning'. Certainly when Kelly uses the term 'choice' he is not suggesting that all individuals have access to all pertinent information before choosing a course of action. We are well aware of limitations on thought processes and 'stated' versus 'real' reasons for behaviour (see Nisbett & Wilson, 1977). We simply cannot know everything about ourselves and the world around us to state categorically and correctly why we choose one act over another. Also, once chosen, we must accept the consequences of an act which clearly limits freedom. An individual appears free, for whatever conscious or less than conscious reasons, to enact and to re-enact any behaviours, offensive ones included. Why would an individual choose the actions of a 'creepy pervert', or why would a person act in a manner that appears to be both self-injurious and injurious to others? The answer may ultimately be an individual one, namely, it depends on his or her own experience and past efforts to construe that personal experience. But it can also be a simple, shared one, namely, it depends on perceived construct extension and definition. Pain, whether through physical injury, humiliation or negative descriptors, can be self-confirming and hence very positive. Being physically injured and/or humiliated during what one construes as a sexual act can confirm self-identity as a sexual masochist. The pain, in effect, is pleasure for that individual. In the same way, a painful or negative label like 'heartless killer' or 'rape hound' can, when reinforced by the experience of homicide or sexual assault, provide reassurance through a more complete identity.

Kelly and other personal construct theorists say little about the origins of construing, especially as applied to oneself. The origins of self-referencing constructs, negative and otherwise, undoubtedly lie in how personal experience is construed. For instance, a child may desire to hurt a parent through shame, or possibly want to please friends in a particular deviant peer group. The origins of such construing may well be lost to everyone forever. It is probable that the social environment (such as family, peer groups) is responsible for the initial application of these descriptions (see Mead, 1934/1977). Often, offenders can remember one incident in which a parent or school-mate called them 'Sicko' or 'Bastard'. The acceptance of such labels may be instantaneous or very gradual, but their impact may be profound. Even well-intentioned professional labels, such as 'paranoid schizophrenic' or 'psychopath', can also lead to negative behaviour. Many offenders accept personal labels quite freely in an attempt to interpret their own bewildering and harmful acts. As Kelly put it: 'psychological symptoms may frequently be interpreted as the rationale by which one's chaotic experiences are given a measure of structure and meaning' (Kelly, 1955/1991, p. 366/Vol. 1, p. 272). Many of these self-referencing constructs, tentative and fuzzy though they may be, only appear to exacerbate the situation, making reoffending more likely. See Chapter 27 (pp. 275–282) for a discussion of the development of construing in the baby and young child.

SEXUAL OFFENDERS

As noted by many authors (for example, Quinsey, 1986), sexual offenders do not represent a homogeneous group psychologically, and even subgroups of sexual offenders, such as men who molest children, are very heterogeneous. Perhaps in part due to this important consideration ignored by early researchers and clinicians, there are no generally acceptable theories of sexual abuse. The field is, therefore, open to accounts of different types of sexual offenders provided by personal construct theory.

Child Molesters

Several writers (see Chin-Keung, 1988; Horley, 1999, 2000) have suggested that personal construct psychology can provide a theoretical and therapeutic basis for child sexual abuse. Following on from the early work of Marks and Sartorius (1967) and Frisbie and colleagues (1967), Horley and Quinsey (1994, 1995) have developed a ratings repertory grid to examine child molesters' attitudes or thoughts about themselves and others. Child molesters, relative to non-molesters, described themselves as submissive and sexually unattractive, while they described women as oppressive and unattractive. Examination of the child molester group alone revealed some intragroup differences. Molesters who had exclusively victimized girls had significantly more external appearance constructs, while offenders against young boys used more emotional and self-sufficiency terms to describe people. A subsequent study (Horley et al., 1997), using a revised ratings repertory grid, confirmed that molesters described themselves less positive sexually than did non-molesters. Women were seen by molesters more negatively in terms of sexual descriptors than by non-molesters although, somewhat paradoxically, molesters described women as more trusting and mature than non-molesters.

One point called into question by that research is the belief that child molesters offend simply because of low self-esteem (see Marshall, 1999; Marshall & Mazzucco, 1995). Horley and Quinsey (1995) and Horley and colleagues (1997) suggest that the situation may be more complex, in that child molesters may perceive themselves as inadequate sexually, or not very physically attractive, but they do not show low self-esteem in general.

Rapists and Other Sexual Offenders

There are a variety of other forms of sexual deviation, varying from 'nuisance' offences such as exhibitionism to very serious offences such as rape-murder. Relatively little work has been done from a personal construct perspective on men who assault adult females sexually. Shorts (1985) reported on a single rapist who, over the course of therapy in a forensic hospital, came to view himself as more like men who assault women. Rada (1978) argued that rapists suffer from what he terms the 'Madonna–Prostitute Complex', or a tendency to think in extreme terms of women as either extremely pure, and not to be touched, or extremely impure, and to be touched whenever desired. Carnahan (1988) investigated that hypothesis using a ratings repertory grid with incarcerated rapists, and found no overall support for the findings, although he did find that rapists viewed rape victims as 'less pure' than did incarcerated property offenders. Carnahan's sample included only rapists who had been sentenced to confinement of two years or less, and it is possible that a group of more serious or repeat offenders might show more extreme construal patterns. One problem with the limited work on rapists to date, however, is the tendency to view all rapists as having common constructions. In fact, Prentky and Knight (1991) have demonstrated that there are many different subtypes of rapists.

Men who exhibit their genitalia for sexual gratification, or exhibitionists, are very seldom studied despite very high offence rates (Mohr et al., 1964). Landfield and Epting (1987) reported on a single exhibitionist who, when completing a rep grid, had difficulty nominating acquaintances, especially women, for specific role titles. Whether this is a common circumstance of these individuals, and whether it is a precursor or effect of the problem, is unknown. One clinical treatment that Horley (1995) conducted with a repeat exhibitionist, only somewhat successfully, showed that this individual viewed himself as a 'pervert' who repeatedly offended in part to strike back at his family.

Certainly a number of more exotic forms of sexual deviance, such as frotteurism, have been examined, albeit infrequently, from a personal construct perspective. In the case of frotteurism, or the public rubbing against other individuals for sexual gratification, Horley (2001) presented a case study to support his argument that there is no need for a separate diagnostic category. Frotteurs may well be timid or would-be rapists.

VIOLENT OFFENDERS

Some first-time violent offenders, especially assaultive individuals, may act to validate essentially invalid predictions (Houston, 1998). Many repeat violent offenders, however, act in line with self-related constructs and views of others that involve aggressive or violent labels (Needs, 1988). Gang violence, in particular, may be the 'cement' by which individuals establish a group identity for themselves (see also Chapter 8 on anger, pp. 83–91).

Specific forms of violent offence have been examined by a number of investigators. Howells (1983) administered repertory grids to a number of violent offenders deemed to be 'mentally disordered' (see Houston, 1998; Winter, 1992). He found that repeat offenders, compared to first offenders, saw themselves in a more positive light despite, or perhaps because of, their lengthy criminal histories. Needs (1988), too, found that a repeatedly violent offender saw himself in a positive manner (for example, *wild* as opposed to *soft*). Landfield (1971), however, found evidence that some violent offenders do not construe violence positively. One violent individual saw many people as violent and unhappy, including himself, and lashed out impulsively to perceived offences of others. This individual was a severe alcoholic, however, and that may have had a significant impact on his construal of self and others. A case of an arsonist (Landfield, 1971) was similarly intriguing in that the arsonist had a very tight construct system with themes of religion and morality, and generally saw herself as a good and God-fearing person, but may well have shifted to the 'bad, Devilish' view when unable to keep to her very high standards. The arsonist of Fransella and Adams (1966), too, was a very religious man. His repertory grids showed that, in his view, he was not committing acts of arson but was punishing wrong-doers.

One problem with these and other studies of violent offenders is that they involve very different expressions of violence. If we accept that specific types of sexual offenders are heterogeneous, no doubt violent offenders cannot be considered a single group. More consideration of the specific nature of the violence, such as assault or homicide, is required in further research.

OFFENDER THERAPEUTIC ISSUES

Individual Psychotherapy

The principles of fixed-role therapy are now well established (see Chapter 23, pp. 237–245), but use of fixed-role therapy with offenders has not been examined in detail. In some ways, it is straightforward because they tend to relate well to 'conning', or a swindle using a 'confidence' tactic to gain a victim's trust. Adopting a benevolent role can be more difficult, but the ability to adopt new roles is well within many offenders' abilities.

One difficulty with fixed-role therapy for offenders in a prison setting, or even certain community-based forensic settings (for example, a half-way house), is the limitation set on trying out the new role. The social and physical environmental conditions of most prisons do not permit the range of experiences that allow for behavioural try-outs based on new ways of construing. Often, only poor substitutes are available for a client in a prison, such as talking to a female guard in an appropriate manner in place of asking a female for a date. In many cases, especially in maximum secure facilities, 'imaginary encounters', with substantial discussion of how the new person would respond or think, can be substituted.

It is important to consider the nature of the forensic setting when writing the sketches. Some sketches could result in a client's death if enacted in the wrong place, and some prisons are completely the wrong places for someone attempting to become more sensitive to others or concerned about a neighbour's well-being. The 'inmate code', or the unwritten yet prescribed set of acceptable behaviours for prison inmates, needs to be considered. This varies somewhat from facility to facility, but all offenders in any facility, even forensic hospitals, need to conform to this code. A prudent approach would be to go over the new sketch with the client in extreme detail about possible negative outcomes of implied behaviours from the sketch, expressing warnings wherever necessary. It might be necessary to send a sketch to the street upon release with a client accompanied by a warning not to attempt it while incarcerated. Feedback can then be provided via phone conversations, letters, or contacts through probation-parole officers or therapists.

One of the most common forms of individual therapy for offenders is cognitive restructuring. This form of individual therapy is useful in situations where fixed-role or enactment therapies are difficult to use or when clients object to enactment-based approaches. This can be viewed as an elaborative technique as described by Winter (1992). A client is invited to identify and to explore his own construing system by 'talking about yourself, your past, and how you think about things'. Clearly this may involve some relatively minor movement from one construct pole to another, but changing the use of a particular construct can be significant when it comes to, for instance, reconstruing oneself as *thoughtful* versus *thoughtless* and avoiding a rape.

Challenging accounts or understandings of one's life and actions are part of the process of cognitive restructuring but, because this is not a rationalistic therapy, there is no 'name-calling' or 'finger-pointing' with respect to a client's account of events. Use of guilt in the Kellyian sense, displacement from negative core roles (such as 'solid con'), can be an important tool in getting an offender to reconstrue himself and relations with others. The offender client must be allowed to express himself, with his views respected, and given hope for long-term change. This is important because respect and hope are experienced all too seldom in forensic settings.

GROUP THERAPY

Horley (1999) developed 'problem identification' as a general first step for offenders interested in some help with psychological problems. It is intended to provide a supportive environment for offenders to discuss their lives, personal difficulties and construct systems in order to receive feedback from therapist(s) and peers. As such, this process-oriented group becomes a first step rather than an end in itself. Clients, usually six to eight, are allowed to speak without fear of verbal assault, although questioning and 'challenge' is encouraged. Each group member is permitted to 'tell his story' through a detailed and coherent autobiographical account or simply recounting specific episodes that are construed as meaningful for some reason. The group composition that seems to work best is a homogenous one with respect to offence (such as all child molesters with offences involving male victims) and client background. One pitfall with this arrangement includes 'alliances' where individuals band together to support each other and to validate each others' deviant perspectives. While that is a real danger, challenges to all potential allies at the first sign of such a development can counter it.

'Relapse prevention' is a popular form of therapy, typically in group format, borrowed from the alcohol treatment area and used by various therapists, including those who work with sex offenders (see Laws, 1989). It is described as a cognitive-behavioural approach to help clients to recognize how and why problem behaviours occur and how to avoid repetition. A number of topics for discussion are presented that include the role of negative emotion in sexual offending, victim empathy, developing helping networks, and avoiding high-risk situations. Homework in the form of mock letters to victims and decision-making exercises is an aspect of the treatment. Relapse prevention from a personal construct perspective may not emphasize behaviour as such, or the didactic information to prevent re-offence, but allowing offenders to explore how their own constructions of the world can lead directly to inappropriate actions is important (for further discussion of relapse, see Chapter 20, pp. 211–222).

FINAL THOUGHTS

It appears that we have, or soon will have, a forensic personal construct psychology (see Horley, in press). Some gaps that remain reflect the problems with the area as a whole, for example, a preoccupation with male versus female offenders, and some are very particular to personal construct psychology, such as the use of repertory grids with offenders (Horley, 1996). Addressing these issues will be the task of all concerned with developing a viable alternative to a biomedical perspective to work with offenders and, indeed, advancing the field of forensic psychology in terms of methods and practice.

CHAPTER 16

Making Sense of Dependency

Beverly M. Walker

University of Wollongong, Australia

Now, may I invite you to look at psychology in a new way, more particularly at counseling in a new way, and especially at interpersonal dependency. This is not an attempt to proselyte. You may continue to be as loyal as ever you like to whatever you believe to be true of the psychotherapeutic process in general, and of dependency in particular. This is, instead, a proposal to explore the implications of a new viewpoint, even to the extent of experimenting with it actively.

Now, let me see if I can shake the kaleidoscope for you. Watch closely. See what happens.

(Kelly, 1966a)

Kelly makes an important distinction between the ways in which we depend on others. Not surprisingly, the kind of construing involved is central. This chapter will explore this distinction, outline an associated methodology and use case studies to demonstrate contrasting examples, locating this distinction within broader theoretical issues.

Patterns of Construing

In presenting a way of understanding our dependence on others, Kelly (1969g) feels it important to consider the overall pattern. Do we concentrate our dependencies, so that those we depend on are each expected to provide the satisfaction of all our needs? Or do we view our support network and needs in more differentiated ways, so that some resources meet some, while others satisfy different needs. The first of these patterns he terms *undispersed*, the second *dispersed*, dependency. He regards undispersed dependency as a less useful way of taking care of needs. Its problematic nature stems, not from a link with unhappiness, nor with pathology as traditionally defined, but rather the vulnerability of the person when change occurs.

International Handbook of Personal Construct Psychology. Edited by F. Fransella.
© 2003 John Wiley & Sons, Ltd.

To explore these patterns, Kelly presents an instrument he called the 'Situation Resources Test' (Kelly, 1955/1991, pp. 312–317/Vol. 1, pp. 233–237), now known as a 'Dependency' grid. The grid indicates the perceived relationship between possible resources the person can call upon and a sample of problem situations. Respondents select resources from their current and past networks. In the original version, they think of a time when a particular problem occurred and indicate with crosses for which problems they would have been able to go to each resource in turn. The participants are asked to make a decision *as if* the resource had been available when the problem happened. Walker et al. (1988) propose a statistical means of assessing dependency dispersion. That Dispersion of Dependency Index has now been applied in a variety of contexts (Walker, 1997), and a worked example can be found in Fransella, Bell and Bannister (in press). Kelly's method has been further adapted to create two forms of dependency grids, the original termed a 'Being Helped' grid, and an adapted version, showing whom the respondent helps with particular problems, called a 'Helping' grid.

The initially curious thing about these grids is that they do not appear to contain personal constructs. In contrast with a repertory grid, which looks at the relationships between elements and constructs (see Chapter 9, pp. 95–103), dependency grids explore the relationships between two sorts of elements: resources and problems. The construing is implicit in the grid, reflected in the patterns of crosses and blanks. Construct poles can be made explicit by asking respondents questions such as why they went to the particular people for each problem in turn, with this questioning supplemented by obtaining opposites as well as laddering.

In exploring the importance of dispersion of dependency Kelly takes a developmental perspective. He rejects the commonly held position that children are more dependent than adults, suggesting that in some senses the reverse is true. He proposes instead that the important feature of dependence in childhood is that it is concentrated, so that immediate family members meet all the young child's needs. As the child matures the pattern of depending becomes more differentiated, so that ultimately the mature adult is maintained within a dispersed dependency network, although some adults retain the relatively undispersed pattern. Increasing dispersion is closely tied to our developing capacities and willingness to understand how others view the world, what Kelly termed 'sociality', since we need to balance our demands on others with their preparedness to give.

In terms of the construing involved with increased dispersion of dependency, it is not just that more discriminations are made between resources, problems and needs, but the nature of the construing changes as well. Kelly considers that constructs could be distinguished in terms of the extent to which they can apply to new contexts and events. 'Permeable' is the term he gave to those that could, 'impermeable' to those that could not. The former is associated with increased dispersion, the latter with undispersed dependency.

Another way of differentiating construing is in terms of its relationships to other constructs. Pre-emptive construing makes sense of the element in one, and only one, way, so that, for example, mother is 'just the person who looks after me', and hence is not seen in any other way. By contrast, constellatory construing means that once one dimension is applied to an element, a whole complex of other construct poles also apply. This happens with stereotyping, so that, for example, once an individual's gender is known, they may be construed as having many other additional characteristics. However, propositional construing entails no implications for how the construing relates to other constructs, neither involving its isolation nor the enlisting of a constellation of others. Kelly associated propositionality with dispersed dependency.

One way of looking at Kelly's proposals about these different ways of construing is to see them as a developmental progression. Impermeable, pre-emptive and constellatory construing would tend to be more common in childhood and, with maturity, replaced increasingly by permeable and propositional construing. To understand why some forms of construing are preferable to others it is useful to look at how they are applied in practice. The examples that follow, illustrating differing dispersion, clarify this issue.

TYPES OF DEPENDENCY

An Example of Dispersed Dependency

Karen, aged 18, explained that her parents were divorced and she lived with her mother and sister, but did not get on with her parents. Her Being Helped grid is shown in Table 16.1.

In the interview based on the grid, her most widely applied construct was *close relationship–not close relationship*, a distinction verbalized by many people, though varying in meaning. For Karen closeness concerned talking in an involved way (not superficially) and being understood. That construct was linked to whether the problems were serious and involved or merely required superficial help.

She distinguished people who listen and try not to sway her, as opposed to people, like her parents, who simply tell her what to do. The former gave an honest opinion and cared about how she felt. The latter were more concerned with what she had done, not her feelings. Of her parents she said: 'We're really different in values, have completely different ideas. Lots of these problems have to do with my parents. They cause them.'

While she felt she gained her security from her grandparents, sister and boyfriend, she had reservations about the help that her grandparents could give her in some areas as they were a bit old fashioned. Further, they were the sort of people whom she did not like to worry.

People *who take your mind off it cheer you up, make you forget about problems*, such as her teacher, were the supports she required for certain situations, such as when she felt lonely and needed to be more cheerful. By contrast, for other problems she wanted to be persuaded to think about better things (as when she was discouraged about the future) and so she would go to level-headed people, like her cousin. They were perceived as *older people, more grown-up, people who are still coping in their future*. By this she meant that they were coping at ages that still lie ahead for her.

Thus, from Karen's Being Helped grid were elicited a variety of elaborated clusters of predominantly propositional constructs, linking groups of people with groups of situations. Furthermore underlying these intersections of people and problems were constructs to do with the kinds of help required, including superficial talk,

Table 16.1   Karen's Being Helped grid

Problems	Self	Mum	Dad	Nan	Pop	Sister	Boyfriend	Female friend	Boss	Minister	Neighbour	Doctor	Adviser	Teacher	Cousin
With vocation	X	X	X				X	X						X	X
With opposite sex	X	X	X	X	X	X	X	X						X	X
Were unlucky	X	X	X	X	X	X	X	X	X		X		X	X	X
With finances	X	X	X	X	X		X								X
With illness	X	X	X	X	X		X				X	X		X	X
Made serious mistake	X	X	X	X	X	X	X	X	X		X		X	X	X
With failure	X	X	X	X	X	X	X	X	X		X		X	X	X
Were lonely	X	X	X	X	X	X	X	X	X		X			X	X
Discouraged with future	X			X	X	X	X	X		X	X			X	X
Felt better off dead	X			X	X	X	X	X			X				X
Were misunderstood	X		X	X	X	X	X	X			X				X
Were angry	X		X	X	X	X	X	X			X		X	X	X
Hurt someone	X	X		X	X	X	X	X			X				X
Were ashamed	X	X	X	X	X	X	X	X			X				X
Were frightened	X			X	X	X	X								
Behaved childishly	X			X	X	X	X	X					X		X
Were jealous	X	X	X	X	X	X	X	X							
Were confused	X						X	X	X						
With parents	X			X	X	X	X	X			X		X	X	X
With sister	X	X	X	X	X	X	X	X			X		X	X	X
With boyfriend	X	X	X	X	X	X	X	X			X			X	X

having a yak, cheering her up, providing material assistance, helping her to forget about problems, persuading her to think more positively. Indeed, one cannot help but agree with her that, as far as her future is concerned, she will indeed cope effectively.

Examples of Undispersed Dependency

Kam's Grids

Kam's Being Helped grid (Table 16.2) is illustrative of an undispersed pattern of dependency. Kam was the same age as Karen and had come to Australia five years ago as a refugee from Vietnam. He had no difficulties in understanding the task, also completing a Helping grid which is not shown here.

Two major sets of constructs emerged from both grids. The first concerned the priest and counsellor, the professionals. These were people *who give advice in my interest* as opposed to *people who tell me what to do, irrespective of my likes*. Professionals know a lot, are smart, are objective and understand human behaviours while the others express opinions rather than facts. With regard to the helping grid, professionals can handle things on their own, whereas non-professionals must canvass others' opinions. It was to the professionals that Kam takes problems that were major.

The second set of personal constructs differentiated people relative to Kam's age. He found it easy to talk with older people about personal things, but not younger ones. Paralleling this for the helping grid, he felt that older people would not come to a younger person like him if they were puzzled or confused. Further there were friends, *who tell everything*, in contrast to *those who are either younger or older*.

What is evident about these overarching discriminations is that they were what Kelly termed 'constellatory construing'. Once you know people are either professional or not, younger or older, all sorts of things follow on. People are either professionals who understand facts about human behaviours and to whom one can go for advice, or they are non-professionals who express mere opinion; they are either older than he or they may be younger and, if so, the appropriate interaction is proscribed by this comparison. Compared to Karen, the rigidity of the construing is apparent. With regard to his best friend of the same age, Kam would go to him for the problems indicated, not for advice, but merely to let him know. When asked 'why?' he explained 'because I think I can do it myself or go to someone who knows better, the professionals'. Unlike Karen he did not feel he personally could cope with whatever occurred. There are problems that he had control over and those that were more major, that he could not control, but nevertheless could solve by seeking professional advice.

Allen's Grids

A great deal of biographical information about Allen emerged in the process of the construct elicitation interview. He was 33 years old, worked at the Water Board and had finally fulfilled his ambition to come to university. He described his family of

Table 16.2   Kam's Being Helped grid

Problems	Self	Mother	Father	Male friend	Priest	Counsellor	Teacher	Young friend F	Young friend M	Female friend
With vocation						X				
With opposite sex	X				X	X				
Were unlucky	X				X	X				
With finances		X	X		X	X				
With illness		X	X		X	X				
When gullible					X	X	X			
Made serious mistake	X					X				
With failure	X				X	X				
Were lonely	X	X	X	X	X	X				
Discouraged with future	X	X	X	X	X	X				
Felt better off dead					X	X				
Were misunderstood		X	X	X	X	X		X	X	X
Were angry					X	X				
Hurt someone	X				X	X				
Were ashamed					X	X				
Were frightened	X				X	X				
Behaved childishly					X	X				
Were jealous					X	X				
Were confused	X				X	X				
With parents					X	X				
With sister					X	X				

origin, his parents and two sisters, as 'very close'. He was divorced, had remarried three years previously and his current wife had two married brothers, whom he saw a lot of on weekends. He and his wife were very close, 'talk over everything with each other', but regrettably were unable to have children.

Beginning construct elicitation with the Helping grid, Allen had a great deal of difficulty in operating in an 'as if' mode. To questions of 'Why could these people rather than those people come to you for this problem?' his answer focused on the fact that they *had* come to him previously. He gave reasons for this behaviour that focused on specific biographical details of their life or his.

As soon as this pattern became apparent, that he had responded in terms of who *had* come to him for help, not who *could*, this was pointed out. He understood the distinction clearly but when given the opportunity to make modifications, was unable to do so. He could make few predictions apart from those based on previous specific instances of help seeking. Similarly, he responded to the Being Helped grid (Table 16.3) in terms of to whom he had gone in those situations. The exception occurred with his wife: 'we're very close. We discuss things and not let them build up', 'we discuss everything we do'. Allen appeared to be highly motivated to be interviewed about his grids, having taken time off work to do so, and having discussed his responses to the grids at length with his wife. He was trying to make sense of what he observed on completion of them, particularly his differing response to his family of origin compared to his in-laws.

His constructs were isolated, rarely integrated into clusters, unlike the previous examples. Occasional exceptions occurred. In elaborating his relationships within his family he stated some of the subordinate constructs such as: 'I am the eldest. I have gone to uni. I haven't lived close to the family, so I've always been the odd one out, and the family turn to me because of this.'

Considering the construing of both grids together, the major construct he used was *close–not close*. Close people were either *part of the family*, *people I grew up with*, *have known a long time* and/or *have shared the same experience*. Such construct poles would not readily apply to new acquaintances, what Kelly termed 'impermeable'. You can not, after all, have new people you grew up with. While you can gain new members of the family, it is clear from Allen's puzzlement about the difference in the way he treated his own family of origin compared to his wife's, that the latter had not become close from his perspective. However this was not totally the case since Rass, his male friend, had become 'like part of the family', though some problems were too personal for a new friend. Further, work and non-work problems, work and non-work relationships, were kept totally separate.

His construing about himself, and indeed problems themselves, seemed more elaborated than those about others. The theme of wanting to work things out himself was one he emphasized, describing himself as 'a bit of a loner'. He distinguished problems that were a personal challenge from those that were not, as well as problems he preferred to work out himself, as opposed to those that he would discuss with others. There were also the things you hide from others, such as when he was gullible or ashamed. Looking at the other's perspective was quite important as a theme about himself. If he got angry he would cool down quickly by seeing the other's viewpoint. 'If in a situation, I'd quickly look at their perspective. This gives my wife the poohs.'

Table 16.3 Allen's Being Helped grid

Problems	Self	Mum	Dad	Sister 1	Sister 2	Wife	Male friend	Boss	Neighbour M	Neighbour F	In-laws	Female friend	Friend—Rass
With vocation	X					X		X					
With opposite sex	X	X	X			X						X	
Were unlucky	X					X	X					X	
With finances	X					X	X						
With illness	X	X	X	X	X	X							
When gullible	X	X	X			X							
Made serious mistake	X	X	X			X		X					
With failure	X	X	X			X		X	X	X			
Were lonely	X	X	X			X			X	X			
Discouraged with future	X	X	X			X		X					
Were angry	X					X							
Hurt someone	X					X							
Were ashamed	X					X							
Were frightened	X					X	X	X					
Behaved childishly	X					X							
Were confused	X	X	X			X		X					
With parents	X			X		X							
With sisters	X	X	X			X							X
With spouse	X					X							

TYPES OF CONSTRUING AND DEPENDENCY

What are the implications of these highly contrasting examples of dependency dispersion? The problem with lack of dispersion of dependency is that it leaves the person vulnerable to change. Commonly this involves a few resources meeting the host of varied needs that we all have. If those resources die, move or become exasperated at the demands from the undispersed person and withdraw their availability, then the undispersed are left high and dry. They may desperately search for someone else to replace the missing helper(s), or may be unable to substitute someone else without substantial reconstrual.

Integral to these patterns of depending, Kelly argues, is the link with certain sorts of discriminations. Clearly the dispersed pattern is accompanied by a rich, varied, multifaceted construing system, as Karen's example demonstrates. By contrast Kam and Allen show a more restricted range of constructs about resources as well as problems. But it was not just the number and complexity of construing that differentiated the patterns. The *kinds* of constructs were also important.

A striking characteristic of Allen's construing was its impermeability, that is its inability to encompass new situations. Allen based his sense-making on what had already occurred, which is a limited basis for construing the novel. The people he regarded as close were largely either family or people whom he had grown up with, both categories that are resistant to inclusion of new resources. By contrast Kam had a less vulnerable system, with constellatory construing being the predominant emphasis. Professionals had a variety of characteristics that differentiated them from non-professionals, seemingly without exception. Further patterns of helping depended on the age of the helper or the helped, not on characteristics self-evidently relating to helping behaviour. Elsewhere I have given an example of a further type of construing that has been linked to undispersed dependency; pre-emptive construing (Walker, 1993), which involves viewing the element concerned unidimensionally, in one and only one way, so that mum may be viewed as 'just the person who looks after me'.

Contrast these ways of construing to those used by Karen. She used what Kelly called 'propositional' construing, one 'which carries no implications regarding the other realm memberships of its elements'. Karen's construing did not mean a whole cluster of constructs were invoked once one feature of the element was known (constellatory construing), nor was the way elements were viewed restricted to one perspective (pre-emption). The system Karen used was one that could apply to new resources or problems she met, unlike impermeable construing. It was a flexible, adaptable system that could accommodate new challenges and contexts.

Of course impermeability, pre-emption and constellatory construing are not just confined to dependency construing but could be linked to more general developmental processes. But a further useful way of looking at them is as examples of what we have called 'non-validation' (Walker et al., 2000).

TYPES OF CONSTRUING AND EXPERIMENTATION

Kelly's assumption is that people have the *potential* to become like scientists in that their ways of seeing the world, like the scientist's hypotheses, are successively tested out and revised or retained depending on the outcome of that experimentation (Walker, 1992). However, all of us at times do not put our construing to effective test, illustrating 'non-validation' (Walker, 2002a). A number of examples of non-validation are detailed. But the kinds of construing associated with undispersed dependency are further illustrations.

If we construe close people as *those we have grown up with*, an impermeable construction, then we never effectively test this out as we cannot become close to those with whom we did not grow up. This is very different from linking close people to *people who will listen* or *people who will not judge you*, since these are ways of behaving that one explores, tries people out on, conducts experiments with, in order to evaluate who does or does not fit the bill.

Analogously, if we associate a constellation of constructs with a characteristic of the person, such as their age, gender or race, then we have no need to test out the applicability of that constellation to any one individual. Further, frequently in such stereotyped thinking, the associated construing justifies avoiding the stereotyped individuals, thus bypassing any challenge to the view of those involved. Similarly, for example, if we can only talk with older people about our problems, then we never find out that a younger person might be as effective as a helper. The experiment is not conducted. Finally, with regard to pre-emption, if someone is 'nothing but' a particular characteristic, then it is only *that* aspect of behaviour that is of interest, and other features are ignored as the focus of experimentation.

SUMMARY

Kelly has pointed to an interesting distinction between extremes of patterns of dependence on others. Kelly presented his account developmentally, detailing ways of construing that are related to increasing dispersion. These include taking into account others' ways of making sense of things, as well as a greater differentiation between potential resources, problems and needs. Additionally there is the increasing reliance on the kinds of discriminations that can be applied to new eventualities, as well as tested out effectively to assess their continued viability. The practical implications of viewing dependency in this way are far-reaching.

CHAPTER 17

Personal Construct Theory and Politics and the Politics of Personal Construct Theory

Don Bannister

INTRODUCTION BY FAY FRANSELLA

Don Bannister did more than anyone else to make personal construct theory more widely known. He felt passionately about it. He saw it as a way of liberating the individual, something no other psychology has ever been able to do. Kelly, himself, did little to promote his own theory. He even is quoted as saying that if he found he was getting 'followers' he would write a new theory.

Don, himself, felt passionately about politics as well. He was politically very active at one period of his life.

Back in 1981, he gave a talk on personal construct psychology and politics in the first series of lectures given by the Centre for Personal Construct Psychology in London. This was never published, but Don had prepared it for publication and that is the version that follows. He starts with a comment about a conversation with George Kelly.

DON BANNISTER'S TALK

The last conversation I had with George Kelly was over a meal. It was a very bad chilli con carne in Columbus, Ohio. We were discussing broadly where we would like personal construct theory to go in an elaborative sense and I remember at the end of the meal George suddenly and finally opting for politics. That is where the meal ended so I never did get to find out whereabouts in politics construct theory is going. And, alas, George died before I went back to the States.

So, I've been kind of stuck with his bald announcement that that's where we

International Handbook of Personal Construct Psychology. Edited by F. Fransella.
© 2003 John Wiley & Sons, Ltd.

were going to and I've been trying to think if we went where would we go. So, tonight I'd just like to, in a fairly simple-minded way, try to imagine what the political implications of personal construct theory are and, conversely, to imagine what personal construct theory looks like if you view it politically.

There is a common and simplistic way of linking psychology to politics. It consists of subsuming one under the other and thereby denigrating whichever is subsumed. For example, from the point of view of psychoanalytic theory, radical political positions and political attacks on social authority are sometimes seen as manifestations of unresolved oedipal conflict with political authority structures representing 'father'. Conversely, radical political thinkers sometimes take the view that, say, psychoanalytic psychology or some allied theory is merely part of the ideology of bourgeois individualism and psychologists adhering to the theory are thereby cultural lick-spittles of the capitalist class. Both kinds of theorizing, political to psychological and psychological to political, have one thing in common. They are both forms of pre-emptive construing. If this political stance is an unresolved oedipal conflict then it is nothing but an unresolved oedipal conflict; if this form of psychological theorizing is part of bourgeois ideology then it is nothing but part of bourgeois ideology.

Clearly personal construct theory is opposed in a broad sense to pre-emptive construing. The whole idea of constructive alternativism is opposed to the notion of 'nothing but' ways of construing. If we take a Kellyian stance, then what we might try to do is to apply construct theory to politics and vice versa but to try and take both seriously. That is, to see what light is cast on either in a constructive manner rather than to use one to put down the other.

CONSTRUING POLITICS

The Meaning of 'Personal'

We can begin a psychological analysis of political construing by examining it in terms of Kelly's construct 'personal'. Kelly argues that ultimately knowledge, choice and experience are essentially personal and yet if we look at knowledge, choice and experience in political fields we may recognize that, in our time, politics has been to a considerable extent depersonalized. During the Nüremburg Trials Nazi war criminals offered as their prime defence the assertion that they could not be held personally responsible for their actions because they had been done on orders from the State. Granted, most of the Nazi war criminals were hanged so, in that sense, they were held personally responsible in a fairly emphatic way. But at the time the argument of personal irresponsibility was largely dismissed as a piece of special pleading by Nazi war criminals and not considered seriously as a common social stance. There is a sense in which very often we do not hold ourselves personally responsible for what governments, political movements, societies at large do. We regard society as a force outside us for which we are not responsible. True, we do see consequences as personal. If we recognize that if there is an atomic holocaust then we may personally die, if there is massive unemployment we may be personally unemployed, if a totalitarian society develops we may personally have to be servile. We are used to seeing the consequences of political developments as personal to us but less commonly do we see political developments as personal from us.

There are a number of constructs in common use which serve to depersonalize politics. For example, there is the construct of a 'politician'. This is an interesting construct because it implies that politics is the business of politicians, but to paraphrase someone it could be that politics is too important to be left to politicians. Certainly we may depersonalize politics by adhering to the notion of a special class or category of people who take care of political decisions and thereby we distance ourselves from those decisions.

The second and more subtle argument stems from the notion of the forces of history, historical determinism. In popular construing there is a folklore equivalent of the construct of 'historical determinism' as it is used in self-consciously intellectual circles. There is a background assumption that history marches on and there is nothing much to do about it except to suffer it, complain about it or witness it. If we took a more personal view we might suspect that when people say that this or that is happening because it is dictated by the forces of history, that it is happening because they want it to happen and that this is their way of making sure we think twice before opposing it. Certainly to blame particular people for what happens is in one sense simple-minded but in another sense it is the beginnings of a way of espousing personal responsibility rather than off-loading the responsibility onto the forces of history.

Most pervasively we have used the notion of complexity, the complexity of political and economic events, to try to distance them from us. Society as a whole and particularly the media encourage this kind of distancing. Television documentaries, newspaper articles, political speeches convey the impression that there is this vast array of complex events happening all over the world which constitutes 'politics' and that all that is demanded of the individual citizen is that they should take 'an intelligent interest' in them. In other words, they ought to watch the television programmes, read the newspaper articles and listen to the political speeches with voting at long intervals representing their only substantive contribution to these complex events. Thus political analysis is presented as essentially like weather forecasting. You should, as an intelligent layperson, be interested in the words of the weather forecaster, be grateful for his or her meteorological explanations of what is happening and what is likely to happen, but you should recognize of course that there is nothing you can do about the weather except perhaps personally to take cover. Thus your duty is fulfilled when you take your 'intelligent interest', but of course action, involvement, personal responsibility and personal reaction are not envisaged.

The Meaning of 'Construct System'

Political theorizing is a particular form of construing and we can examine the specific bipolarity of political constructs, consider their controlling functions and the way in which they govern our anticipations. A traditional bipolar superordinate is the conventional construct of *left* versus *right*. This has dominated political thinking in Western industrial countries and in much of the rest of the world for nearly a hundred and fifty years. We can question it by examining what the construct excludes as well as what it includes, what cannot be taken into consideration if the construction is given its conventional superordinate role.

In essence the left–right argument is broadly between those who favour control of the means of production, distribution and exchange by state managers, as contrasted with those who favour control of said means of production, distribution, exchange by private owners. Nowhere within the range of convenience of the construct is there adequate space for discussion of the possibilities of collective democratic control, direct workers' control, syndicalism or whatever. The construct polarizes political argument and action into two competing notions of control, both of which invest authority in a relatively distinct elite group, under which workers shall work. If we wished historically to check how far the construct has dominated our political thinking we may note the fact that the whole issue of democratic collectives of workers' control is not and has not been a major political issue in our time. There are a few anarcho-syndicalists, the occasional democratic collective, who write the odd pamphlet, but by and large it has not been a major issue and has certainly not been the axis around which political struggle has evolved.

It is argued in construct theory psychotherapy that one of the most difficult things to help a client to undertake is shift change as opposed to slot change. The difference is simply that in slot change the person rattles from one pole of the construct back to the other and then perhaps back to the first pole again. In shift change he or she actually changes to another construct, reviews the situation using an essentially different mode of construction. Clinical experience suggests that it is relatively easy to encourage slot change and incredibly difficult to achieve shift change.

Consider the kind of client who divides the world into angels and devils, usually sectioning it so that he or she is a devil and the rest of humankind are angels. Surprisingly little encouragement will often reverse the position so that he or she may come to the conclusion that he or she is an angel and the rest of the world are devils. Further work may reverse the position again so that he or she joins the devils and the rest of humankind shifts down to the angelic end of the construct. It may even be possible without too much effort to get the client to use the construct in the scalar mode and adopt some midway position as half angel half devil. The really difficult undertaking is to get the client to entertain the idea that the total construction is self-defeating, that it has too narrow a range of convenience, that it cannot be elaborated, that it does not generate rewarding experiments and so forth. This might well be a paradigm of political construing in that left–right and all stages between represent barren way-stations from pole to pole and what is needed is shift change rather than slot change.

The Meaning of 'System'

Talking of a personal construct *system* draws our attention to the fact that our constructs are integrated; but integration is never final or complete, we are constantly struggling to interrelate our many subsystems. This raises the question of how do we integrate our personal and political life? What are the common implications of constructs we use to make sense of 'politics' and the constructs we use to make sense of 'life'?

Let us consider, for example, a construction like *authority* versus *liberty*, a construction which deals with the issue of whether you favour hierarchical, disciplined, controlled forms of organization or whether you favour open-ended, more libertarian forms of organization. We may recognize such a construction as part of our way of viewing the world but we may also recognize that we often use it in a very partial way with a very restricted range of convenience. It is not unusual to come across the free-wheeling, libertarian, political democrat who is also tyrannically authoritarian within his or her family. It is not unusual to come across the political authoritarian who is easy-going and tolerant socially and in interpersonal relationships. It seems as if, in many cases, we do not extend and link up our political constructions to our constructions about family, personal relationships, social life and so forth. This, in turn, implies a restricted construction of what political action is about. If you have a narrow range of convenience of political construction you may accept that 'political' action is restricted to elections, to being a member of a political party, to being a member of a trade union, to taking part in local government; to a relatively restricted range of human activity. You may then have lost the opportunity of seeing the possibilities of political action in much wider terms. If you are truly a democrat, whatever that may mean to you, and if you have a very wide range of convenience for that construction then you will be a democrat within your family, you will be a democratic parent, a democratic family member. There is a fair chance then that your children will grow up thinking in a decentralist, libertarian, democratic way. You will, thereby (depending on the size of your family) have multiplied the number of people who take a democratic political stance by two, three, four, five or six or whatever. In other words, there is a possibility of quite a healthy continuity in political views if they have a vivid and living form of expression within the family.

Clearly it can go a good deal further than that. Given a wide range of convenience notion of *authoritarian–libertarian* then you may choose to be a libertarian within the institution within which you work in relation to the hierarchy of your profession, your industry or whatever. To this extent, your interaction at work may help to create the experience of democratic interplay within what is a central part of most people's lives, that is, their work.

Equally, everyone is socially a propagandist for political points of view, consciously or unconsciously. By propagandist I don't mean simply a hander-out of pamphlets. I mean that in the way you conduct yourself, in the kinds of things you say, the kind of things you act out, you represent a political philosophy and the view you represent is socially diffused by you. And this diffusion is powerful. It can be argued that forms of society are not simply created by forms of leadership. If we consider the example that anyone of my age tends to think of—Nazi Germany— then it is clear that Nazi Germany was not created simply by the acts of a limited number of Nazis. There is no way in which a small group of people can create a totalitarian state. What was necessary for the creation of that particular form of totalitarian society was that there exists a society which had the theme of authority in every part of it. In other words, the theme of authority in Germany prior to the Third Reich was deep and prevalent; it manifested itself in family life, in factories, in voluntary societies, it was elaborated in novels, films and newspapers, it was imminent in millions of personal conversations conducted every day. In other words, it needed the generation right through the society over many years and in the lives of many people of an authoritarian theme to make it possible for that theme to be structured finally into a totalitarian state.

This returns full circle to the argument that everything you do at work, in your family, socially, is politically significant. This is not pre-emptive construing. I am not arguing that your acts are nothing but political acts. I am saying that, among the many implications which they have, there are political implications. The values which you personally represent in your life are diffused into the structure of your society. There is no way in which the totality of a society can represent something which is alien to the kind of themes underlying the day to day life of the people in that society.

THE POLITICS OF PERSONAL CONSTRUCT PSYCHOLOGY

We could now turn round this elementary analysis of political theorizing from a psychological (specifically personal construct theory) point of view and examine personal construct theory as a political entity, as a piece of political theorizing to see what it implies.

Be it noted again that in arguing that all psychological theories can be politically evaluated the argument is not pre-emptive. It is not saying that a psychological theory is *nothing but* political propaganda. A psychological theory can be all sorts of things: it can be aesthetic, it can be a philosophy, it can sometimes be a religion, it can be a set of handy hints and tips for running your Christmas party, it can be all kinds of things, but among the other things it can be is it can be a political statement. Every psychological theory is a picture of humankind, it is a statement about what human beings are like and when you make a statement about what human beings are like you are thereby taking a stance towards human beings. Your picture of what they are like will very fundamentally affect your relationship with them, how you think they ought to be related to and how you think they ought or ought not to be controlled.

PSYCHOLOGICAL THEORIES AS SONGS OF SOCIAL SIGNIFICANCE

Many psychological theories seem to take a pessimistic view of humankind and thereby to have at best paternalistic and at worst despotic political themes running within them.

Looked at very simply (but not necessarily simple-mindedly) behaviourist theories seem to imply the inevitability of social control. If you believe that people behave in terms of reinforcement history then your belief raises the paradoxical question of who is going to control reinforcement so that they will be the 'right' reinforcements which will historically produce the 'right' behaviour. Reading *Walden II*, Skinner's novel portraying his ideal society, I can only conclude that somewhere there must be a group of political managers controlling this ideal society. Skinner says remarkably little in the novel about who they were and how they worked, but one cannot imagine that just by sheer accident all these reinforcement schedules were arranged neatly to produce such nice, white, cloak-wearing, Bach playing, decent ladies and gentlemen. Somewhere there must have been a group of social managers running the show to make sure that the reinforcements were not of the kind which produce a mutinous, uncontrollable, combative citizenry. Granted, we are in any case left with the puzzle of how the reinforcement history of the planners had brought them into such amiable, organized being but, at best, a token economy can only be seen as benevolent despotism, not as democracy.

Many psychological theories and mini-theories hinge on the notion of a genetically determined and fixed endowment in terms of personality and abilities. Given 'fixed endowment', there is a danger of a sequential logic that argues for a society which apportions differential status, differential powers to these fixed and differential endowments. Equally, you may well conclude that what is needed is control of genetics so that you can achieve the 'right' endowments. Certainly it is difficult to derive any kind of faith in a changing and elaborative society given the notion of unchanging, unelaboratable individuals. Even if we shift to psychoanalytic theorizing we are confronted with the notion of inevitable psychic original sin and from this may flow arguments that, just as we individually need some already analysed saint to free us of original psychic sin, then we need some social controllers with an equivalent function.

THE POLITICAL IMPLICATIONS OF PERSONAL CONSTRUCT THEORY

Personal construct theory is politically libertarian. The philosophical basis of the theory is constructive alternativism. This essentially denies the possibility of any indisputable or absolute truth. It denies that there are indisputable truths not only in psychology, but there are no religious, social or political indisputable truths either. This basic political value embedded in personal construct theory is not difficult to detect because Kelly took the unusual step of stating his philosophical assumptions in very clear terms. In fact, Kelly was setting up a philosophic doctrine, a doctrine about the nature of what we know and an epistemology as a basis for psychology. Constructive alternativism argues for an open society in which the pursuit of alternatives is central to the way in which we live. Political doctrines favouring authoritarian forms of social structure require the acceptance of indisputable truths, indisputable 'realities'. This is seen in its purest form in the theocratic state.

Personal construct theory is politically egalitarian. True, the concept of equality is one which takes on varying meanings in varying social theories. In some societies it seems to mean that we all have an equal opportunity to make money and in other societies it means that we have an equal responsibility to sacrifice ourselves to the State. Personal construct theory is politically egalitarian in a rather curious way in that it is based on the argument that a construct system sets its own validational terms. This means that construct systems are essentially different, not only in terms of how they work but what they are working for, what would represent the fulfilment of values. Once you accept that all construct systems are in this fundamental sense potentially different then it is difficult to argue that one is in any fundamental sense better than another.

Even 'standards of comparison' only have meaning within the context of particular construct systems. We can recognize this if we look at the judgmental boundaries of even widely accepted dimensions which are taken to imply *superiority* versus *inferiority*. Consider a dimension such as *verbally articulate* versus *verbally inarticulate*. This is a frequently used construct in our society. People rank each other in terms of their degree of verbal articulation. Furthermore, it is considered to be 'a good thing' to be verbally articulate. People are put in therapy groups if they are not and given better jobs if they are. As in the case of Shakespeare et al., immortality is awarded to the verbally articulate and pity to the verbally inarticulate. Yet if we examine the boundaries of the construction we can see that it has no unvarying link to value. Behaviour therapists are enthusiastic to treat muteness or poor verbal skills yet do not rush to treat monks of the Trappist order although they are manifestly silent. Why not? Perhaps because we recognize that construct systems contain within them their own validity. We accept that Trappist monks are not simply *verbally inarticulate*. They have chosen not to talk, they have taken a vow of silence, it is how they want to be. We *sometimes* recognize the internal validational quality of a construct system. At other times we singularly fail to recognize it. Current educational systems by and large set up the same goals, the same standards, the same targets and then process children and rank them according to how well they meet these standards. What the child is in business for, individually and personally, is not seen as a matter of importance. What is seen as important is how they are to be taught to race in particular races and how they will be judged as having run well or badly at the end of them. In contrast to this, if we accept that a construct system is ultimately its own judge and jury then we are taking a politically egalitarian stance.

Clearly I have gone back to old French Revolutionary slogans in choosing to link personal construct theory to liberty, to equality and finally to fraternity (granted these are ideals and that, as has often been pointed out, the French revolution was followed by Napoleon who replaced liberty, equality and fraternity with cavalry, artillery and infantry). Personal construct theory is politically fraternal, not because it explicitly sings a song of human brotherhood—it is in fact stylistically a cool theory. But it does propose that brotherly love is not simply a good thing or a nice thing, but it is necessary for survival. Personal construct theory argues that we elaborate ourselves through others, that our picture of what life is about is painted on a social canvas, that our personal image of ourselves is built up as a mosaic out of interplay with others. Kelly proposed this view in his essay 'Social Inheritance' (Kelly, 1979) twenty-five years before he formally elaborated personal construct theory. In this essay he argued that we not only evolve, elaborate and experiment through those who are immediately around us, 'significant others', but that we build ourselves through many people we have never met, many people long dead.

This seems obvious enough. The language you speak you did not invent, nor did the people you know invent it. It was invented by millions of people over hundreds of years and finally you have inherited it. That language is a tremendous part of your capacity to make sense out of the world. It is a gift given to you by many people long dead. The whole network of custom, legal formulation, economic structure, sense of history, artistic and folk metaphor and so forth are all presented to you by societies present and past. In that sense, your construct system is not your private, isolated invention, your desert island. It is essentially partly a fraternal gift to you and partly your fraternal gift to others.

CONCLUSION

One of the most encouraging developments in psychology over the past few decades has been a growing awareness that the pursuit of a value-free science is a myth. We increasingly recognize that science is a human endeavour and, like all human endeavours, it either values or devalues humankind. All human endeavours imply something for our vision of what being human is about. Historically, personal construct theory is part of that humanistic elaboration of psychology, part of an elaboration which has accepted that values are intrinsic to and not extraneous to psychology. Kelly's particular virtue is that he made his values very explicit. Because he made his philosophical stance and his human values explicit within his psychological theory, the political values of the theory are equally manifest. The *elaboration* of these values is a task which lies ahead of us, but their fundamental nature is clear.

CHAPTER 18

Moving Personal Construct Psychology to Politics: Understanding the Voices with which we Disagree

Dusan Stojnov

University of Belgrade, Serbia and Montenegro

CONSTRUING: KELLY'S INTELLECTUAL TESTAMENT

As Don Bannister says in the previous chapter, George Kelly suggested moving his theory into politics, but he did not leave concrete instructions on how he would go about that, although 'Europe's matrix of decision' (Kelly, 1962) is interpreted as a move in that direction. In the 1970s, when political psychology began to be recognized as an area of systematic study, Don Bannister shows not only that personal construct analysis can be successfully applied to political issues, but also construes psychology itself as an area being far from politically innocent.

Apart from Peter du Preez's pioneering analysis of political processes in South Africa in 1980, very few articles have appeared in response to Kelly's tempting invitation. However, several articles I have written over the last ten years (Stojnov, 1996a, 1996b, 1999) have been construed as examples of the application of personal construct psychology to politics. That was surprising since they were actually written in order to grasp some understanding of the very disturbing events occurring to my country, Yugoslavia. This chapter builds on that work and looks at just a few other ways in which Kelly's intellectual testament regarding political construing might be applied.

Several authors, recognized as experts in the field of political psychology, share many anxieties. Besides showing tensions while choosing one of the many psychological theories as a starting point, they also disagree on what the fundamentally important question should be. Some assert that political psychology has developed from the convergence of psychology and politics studying the effects that psychological processes have on political behaviour, as well as the psychological effects political structures have on individuals and groups (Stone, 1974). Others express doubts that the study and criticism of politics can be based on psychology at all (Brewster-Smith, 1977).

The diversity and discord of these views has helped me articulate Kelly's unrealized project in a manner that, it is to be hoped, avoids the tensions expressed above. 'Moving Personal Construct Psychology to Politics' can be construed as using Kelly's theoretical framework as an extremely convenient tool to understand, and make sense of, those events affecting the realm of life that we usually call 'psychological' by those events and decisions in the realm of life that we usually call 'political'. Expressed in an invitational mood, it is hoped that the approach is comfortable and promising enough for further elaborations. Events in the world offer reason enough to put as much of our efforts as we can into understanding what is going on.

A STUDY OF POLITICS USING THE PSYCHOLOGY OF PERSONAL CONSTRUCTS

Since this is not a classical review of work in a highly elaborated area, but is an anticipation of a promising extension of personal construct psychology to an important field, two points should be made clear. First, it aims to highlight those issues neglected in other approaches to political psychology. Second, the issues mentioned are the ones found relevant in my previous work, and are by no means presented as an exhaustive cover of *all* potential topics. This chapter will concentrate upon issues of the rationality of human conduct; alternatives of choice; and psychological transitions in a political context.

Human Conduct: Rational or Irrational?

A point achieving unquestionable and unequivocal accord in the area of political analysis is the condition of the human being as social and political—*zoon politikon*. Politics, as a significant component of human history, and political theory as a major perspective on it, make sense only on the assumption that politics is a highly *rational* effort trying to fulfil objective needs of society. But psychology is striving to make sense of human conduct that is too often not easily understood. It does so by constructing invisible mental entities accounting for behaviour that is visible. It deals primarily with subjective desires, wishes, fears and threats that are seen as *irrational* in the light of the biological heritage of human nature.

Kelly solved the problem between the claims of politics, striving to deal with the heights of human rationality, and of psychoanalysis, dealing with the poor capacity of humans to deal with supposed lower instincts coming from biology. Bannister described the latter view of the person as being in 'a dark cellar in which a maiden aunt and a sex-crazed monkey are locked in mortal combat, the affair being refereed by a rather nervous bank clerk' (Bannister, 1966a, p. 363). Instead of pre-empting humans mainly as biological organisms, Kelly offers his model of the person as a scientist. He suggests that every person might best be understood as a scientist in continuous efforts to predict and control the constant vicissitudes of life, instead of being treated merely as a perplexed subject of scientific scrutiny propelled by inexorable biological drives. The only remaining task is to account for so-called 'irrational' behaviour. Kelly puts it thus:

> The psychologist who attempts to understand human behaviour often finds it convenient to envision man's action in terms of what the man knows—or thinks he knows. When the device works it is said that the behaviour is *rational*. Strictly speaking, however, it is not the behaviour that is rational; it is the explanation that is rational. . . . When, on the other hand, the device fails and the psychologist tries in vain to see a logical relationship between what his friend knows and does, he is inclined to give up and say simply that the behaviour is *irrational*.
>
> (Kelly, 1977, p. 1)

The seemingly innocent question of 'what are we actually saying when we call certain behaviour irrational?' was posed. The answer Kelly provides is simply that psychologists call irrational those behaviours that they do not understand. That has far-reaching consequences. Construing all behaviour as an experiment in which certain hypotheses are being tested, he asserts that the term 'irrational' is being used mainly when we fail to subsume the inner coherence of someone's conduct. The logic of someone's behaviour does not necessarily have to be transparent to others. Thus, by calling certain behaviours 'irrational' one avoids the need for further explanation in the light of the meaning used. The integrity of the chosen system of explanations is saved, and the desires and wishes of individuals or groups expressed in such a way are discounted. The problem arises only if we construe psychology as a discipline trying to understand people and help *them*, not its own system of explanations.

In the context of political conflicts, people often behave in a so-called 'irrational' manner: they kill each other, sacrifice their compatriots, betray their country, lose their beloved ones, go willingly through long periods of starvation; sometimes even kill themselves. Whatever they do is frequently seen as 'good' from the viewpoint of the group to which they belong, and as 'bad' from the viewpoint of the outer, opposed group. Politicians either learn how to use this behaviour in the best possible interest for them, their party or country, or discount it as counter-productive. When psychologists say that certain behaviour is irrational, they also discount it saying that they do not understand the behaviour from the standpoint of their explaining system, and that they are not interested in understanding it from the point of a view of the person who is acting in such a manner. When politicians say that certain behaviour is irrational, they discount it on the ground of it being an illegitimate desire not to be counted in their bag of objective society needs. Whatever the differences between the two, the similarity lies in the discounting attitude towards behaviours labelled as 'irrational'.

Personal construct psychology challenges this fragile alliance and offers a somehow different solution. In the light of the model of person as scientist, every single act of behaviour of every human being can be seen as the rational effort to test certain important hypotheses. The person does not necessarily 'know' they are testing hypotheses. More often, this process runs tacitly, without appearing in

Figure 18.1   Implications of going to war for Serbs

Figure 18.2   Implications of going to war for Croats

consciousness. Recent analysis of conflict in former Yugoslavia (Stojnov, 1996b) shows that choosing war is as rational a choice as choosing between going to the cinema and going to the theatre.

From the point of view of Serbs (see Figure 18.1), the only alternative to going to war was being slaughtered by the institutions of the Croatian Government, which had already happened once in 1941. From the point of view of Croats (see Figure 18.2), the alternative to fighting and expelling Serbs from Croatia was losing the territory inhabited by Serbs, thus being fragmented, divided and dominated by the Serbs—which meant losing their way of being.

For both sides, going to war was a rationally anticipated decision to save their core national interests; whether it was a good or viable choice is a completely different question. Personal construct analysis is concerned with identifying anticipated implications of the choices from the perspective of a person who has to choose.

After investigating the superordinate implications of the construct *war* versus *peace* by the method of laddering, different alternatives emerge. *Choosing to be yourself* instead *losing your being* and *surviving* versus *being slaughtered* does not seem irrational any more. The old adage 'It is better to burst out than to fade away' should not be understood as a work of ancient biological drives check-mating the thin layer of juvenile human rationality. It implies that certain choices should be carefully investigated from the perspective of the person who is making them.

DO POLITICAL DECISIONS LEAVE US WITH A CHOICE?

Connected closely with the issue of rationality is the question of understanding the choices people make. The famous statement politicians frequently use 'I had no choice', seen in the light of personal construct psychology can be understood as a way of escaping responsibility for the choices they *do* make. Politicians always have a choice. So does anybody else, as Kelly says in his Choice Corollary. We are always free to choose between two alternatives, two poles of a dichotomous construct. Our psychological processes are based on construing similarities and differences; everything presented to us is in pairs of opposites. We choose one alternative, that which we construe as likely to lead to the greater extension and definition of our construing system, from the other alternative, which we construe as not likely to have these benefits. Unfortunately, we are too often fully convinced that the remaining alternative is the *only* remaining alternative. An abandoned lover considering suicide may be elaborating a choice between anticipated poles of a construct *endless pain and suffering* versus *the end of painful suffering*. Deciding to choose the latter not only seems fairly rational from the standpoint of this person, it also presents a more personally relevant choice from the remaining alternative. What this person does not have in the grasp of his alternatives, and what can be clearly seen from the outer perspective, is that suicide is only *one* of the many possible ways, not the *only* way to stop the suffering.

Constructs of identity are not always obvious. The issue of identity in personal construct terms is addressed by the notion of *core* constructs governing a person's processes by which we maintain our identity and existence, as opposed to *peripheral* constructs that can be changed without serious modification of core structures. Collective agents can, like persons, be defined in terms of peripheral or core construing. In that case, core constructs can be understood as:

> Images of the relation of members of the collective to others. . . . The test of the core construct is that the collective begins to disintegrate if the core construct is invalidated: morale declines after invalidation and must be restored to maintain the collective. (Du Preez, 1980, p. 124)

To understand someone's identity we have to construe his core constructs. Several things can go wrong in this attempt. We may construe a person's identity in terms of peripheral or even irrelevant constructs. That is, we may simply make an act of misunderstanding. We may think that his nationality or his race is the key to his collective identity, whereas he actually attaches importance to his religion, the fact that he is a good musician, and his loyalty to his family.

Some research results on Serbian national identity (Stojnov et al., 1997) unequivocally indicated that the Serbian people chose to consider belonging to Serbian nationality as a peripheral social issue. The analysis of their core constructs showed that this ostensively puzzling result revealed a choice, which can easily be interpreted as *both* deliberate and rational. It seemed that people were saying, 'If I have to be a Serb who is demonized in the eyes of the international community, or a fading victim in the eyes of my own nation, perhaps I can give up my national identity and avoid the pitfalls of being a Serb!' *Serbian demon and Serbian victim*, on the one side, versus *somebody who is not Serbian, and not a demon and not a victim*—which one would you prefer? That sort of construing seems much more acceptable for the generation which has stated constructs such as health, self-respect, love and acceptance as their collective core—their social identity. If the others pre-empt Serbs as killers, and if Serbs pre-empt themselves as victims, the strategy that appeared as the easiest to deal with the problem was to give up being Serbian. A nation that respects itself and its collective core must 'kill and survive', and not allow other ethnicities to impose their language, customs, totems, taboos and other things, which make life unpredictable and threatening. A nation wanting to get respect for its own conduct from a wider international community must adhere to imposed standards and not kill but live peacefully in a multi-ethnic community—which for Serbs (backed up by the happenings in their national history in the last couple of centuries) means to die out and fade away to the Kingdom of Heaven. Stated otherwise, 'die and become'.

TRANSITION: A ROAD TO HEAVEN IN POLITICS; A ROAD THROUGH HELL PSYCHOLOGICALLY

Politics and psychology do share an important similarity: they are both concerned with a process of change. They both consider change as something desirable, often called political progress or psychological development, and they are both afraid of its undesired effects—disorders—be it a political bloodshed or psychological disturbance. Important differences arise when desired change in one of these fields induces undesired effects in the other.

Political discourse is equipped with many terms describing current societal states: post-traditional, post-industrial, post-capitalist, and so forth. Transition in political terms refers mainly to periods in which an important aspect of State organization is being changed. However, the most recent use of that term applies to the specific process of change affecting mainly the countries of middle Europe 'turning back the clock of history' and changing their governmental structure from communist to capitalist.

However, there is one crucial difference between transitions in politics and psychology. The aim of politics is to change outer circumstances in order to produce desired effects. Capitalist means of production based on laws of economy are desirable because they will help people in these countries to produce higher annual income and have measurably more resources to fulfil their objective needs. The aim of psychological change, on the other hand, tends to produce change in meaning. In personal construct psychology, the desired change of meaning is called reconstruction. This means that what we call a change in the outer world is not reached by the change of the inherent properties of it, but in the change of meaning we ascribe to that world.

Sometimes, we find our construing system does a poor job of anticipating. We are not always good scientists. Instead of changing the world in order to fit our anticipations, we change our anticipations to fit the world. We may try using new constructs—not totally opposite but reasonably different from the old ones—and look at events afresh. If the change fits in terms of offering clearer and more predictive anticipations, the job is successfully done. Although it may appear that change in the realm of meaning is much easier compared to changing the world, the highly demanding work of psychotherapy has taught us not to trust appearances. In order to reach reconstruction, we often have to pass through a road to hell. The period in which we do this travelling is psychological transition.

The meaning Kelly gave to transitions is different from one given to the same term in politics. Kelly is concerned with the construing process in a period of change. Politicians have to work very hard to build a better society, but if they want their effort to be complete, they also have to produce equivalent minds to go with it. A system of anticipations well fitted to one political system does not necessarily have to fit in another. When political changes are put into effect, we may experience that our construing system, which has served us reasonably well in the past, fails to antici- pate new events with sufficient clarity (anxiety). We may realize a need to replace a part of it (fear) or start building it afresh (threat). The change can be so deep that it may affect our self-governing processes and make us feel different from what we think we ought to be (guilt). If we do not have enough psychological resources to afford a reconstruction, we may try to service our old construing system with exist- ing resources to make it do a better anticipative job (aggression), or avoid the change by means of rhetorical pirouettes claiming that everything else in the world save our construing does not work correctly (hostility). We can trap the world in a poor outlook that our construing system gives it.

People always choose that alternative through which they anticipate the greater possibility for extension or definition of their construing system. So do politicians. Unfortunately, political transitions aimed at the better life often induce a painful period of psychological transitions, dangerous enough to affect people's belief in a better future, their voting habits, or even threaten their lives. A personal construct approach to politics highlights the cost of political change in the realm of individ- ual lives. Recent research into the crisis in the former Yugoslavia (Stojnov, 1996a), exploring the effects of political change on psychological functioning of individuals, clearly showed that transition in political terms can become a way of life in psy- chological terms.

CONCLUSION

The change Kelly advocates is a reconstructive change. He was painfully aware how difficult that is to reach. People will do almost anything to resist it and to save their precious ways of construing the world. Politicians will discount all behaviour they do not understand by labelling it 'irrational'. They will claim that they have no choice but to do what they have already done—introducing *their* best solutions leading to the social welfare. Instead of being greeted by their voters, politicians are all too often opposed by the public whose voices helped them carry out the change. The public claims that changes voted for cannot be afforded. Politicians discount this claim as 'irrational', because it comes from people that do not come to want the things that can fulfil their objective needs. In return, a disappointed public discounts politicians as insincere, without any trace of genuine interest for social welfare, only trying to satisfy their greed. And this happens in all relevant areas referred to as political psychology—leadership, conflict, authoritarianism, power, political perse- cution, terrorism, power of minorities, to name but a few. Too many voices are silenced, and the tension remains.

Perhaps personal construct psychology can point to a way out from this too common misunderstanding. It starts by enhancing the process of understanding— understanding all those voices we disagree with (see also Chapter 36, pp. 359–366). This means understanding them from the point of view of those who are articulat- ing them. Construing them from their own perspective, as an alternative to our own. Measuring them with their own original yardstick, not with ours. Judging them at their own price, including all the genuine anxieties, threats and guilt, not our own affordances. Rallying all voices different from our own—and that takes some understanding.

Simply stated, the point is that one does not have to be like certain people in order to understand them, but we do have to understand how they see things in order to lead them. That sentence expresses the most important theme of what psychology of personal construct has to say in its numerous areas of application: We have to strive to understand the voices of all the people we deal with, even if we strongly disagree with them—political psychology notwithstanding.

Personal Change and Reconstruction

INTRODUCTION

This large section takes a quantum leap. It is about individuals rather than the person in relation to others. We are moving into the world of personal change, psychotherapy and counselling.

Because of the wealth of ideas and work to be covered, this section is divided into two parts. The first part is more theory-based while the second part has more to do with the process of psychotherapy and counselling and how that has evolved.

It is not surprising that there are eight chapters in this section, as the focus of Kelly's thinking is about change. We are forms of motion. But sometimes we get psychologically 'stuck' and cannot seem to move on. It happens to us all from time to time. Mostly we pull ourselves up and get going again. But there are times when we may feel the need to seek professional help in the form of psychotherapy or counselling. Of course, what is covered in this section is not altogether new. Many of the theoretical and practical ideas appear in other parts of the book, but each time they occur, the focus is on different aspects of the same ideas.

A THEORETICAL UNDERSTANDING OF THE RECONSTRUCTION PROCESS

David Winter describes the new constructs needed to 'diagnose' what is preventing a person getting on the move again. Kelly called these 'professional constructs'. It is important to know that Kelly was very much against the so-called 'medical model'. But he continued to use the word 'diagnosis' in order to simplify communication with others.

Fay Fransella emphasizes that theory leads to research which, in turn, can lead to a programme for psychological reconstruction. Kenneth Sewell illustrates how, in practice, theory and research can lead to a reconstruction programme by describing his own work with those suffering from Post-Traumatic Stress Disorder.

PERSONAL CONSTRUCT PSYCHOTHERAPY AND COUNSELLING

George Kelly starts off the second part of this section, as is only appropriate, by discussing why he thinks 'treatment' it not a good idea. We are back again to the 'medical model' issue. Kelly says it is not a good idea because people with psychological problems are not 'ill' in the medical sense. He even considered using the term *reconstruction* instead of therapy.

One of George Kelly's students, Franz Epting, tells how Kelly saw psychotherapy and counselling, calling it 'an audacious adventure'. Bob Neimeyer and Scott Baldwin write about ways in which personal construct psychotherapy has evolved into, for example, narrative psychotherapy. Larry Leitner and Jill Thomas then describe a particular development of personal construct psychology—called 'experiential personal construct psychotherapy'.

Finally, David Winter addresses that much-discussed issue that the only psychotherapy approaches that should be used with clients are those that have evidence to show they are 'successful'. He gives an overview of the evidence that personal construct psychotherapy and counselling should, indeed, be considered 'successful'.

CHAPTER 19

Psychological Disorder as Imbalance

David Winter

University of Hertfordshire and Barnet,
Enfield and Haringey Mental Health Trust, UK

> Gradually my clients taught me that a symptom was an issue one expresses through the act of being his present self, not a malignancy that fastens itself upon a man.
>
> (Kelly, 1969h, p. 19)

George Kelly viewed psychiatric diagnosis as 'all too frequently an attempt to cram a whole live struggling client into a . . . category' (1955/1991, p. 775/Vol. 2, p. 154). Such a system, exemplified by the internationally used *Diagnostic and Statistical Manual of Mental Disorders*, is often applied without allowing alternative constructions of the problems thus categorized. A client (the term preferred by Kelly to 'patient') may, for example, be construed as a schizophrenic and nothing but a schizophrenic. By contrast, Kelly adopted the approach of 'transitive diagnosis', using diagnostic dimensions focusing upon the avenues of movement open to the individual presenting with a psychological disorder rather than classifying this person in terms of disease entities and as suffering from a mental illness. An important aspect of that approach is that the dimensions, or diagnostic constructs, used are as applicable to the explanation of 'normal' as to that of 'abnormal' behaviour.

A disorder in Kelly's terms is 'any personal construction which is used repeatedly in spite of consistent invalidation'. That definition implies that disorders involve failure to complete the Experience Cycle, the process of experimentation which characterizes the 'optimally functioning' person (see Chapter 23, pp. 237–245). In this cycle, the person anticipates some event, invests himself or herself in this anticipation, actively encounters the event, assesses whether predictions have been confirmed, and revises the construct system accordingly. Neimeyer (1985b) suggests that the earlier in the cycle a blockage occurs, the more severe is the resulting disorder.

Although a disorder may be seen as some aspect of construing which appears to fail to achieve its purpose, it can be regarded—just like the constructions of non-

International Handbook of Personal Construct Psychology. Edited by F. Fransella.
© 2003 John Wiley & Sons, Ltd.

disordered people—as the individual's attempt to make the best sense of his or her world and to cope with or avoid invalidation. All of us, to this end, employ the strategies which Kelly describes in his diagnostic constructs: for example, tightening and loosening of construing; and constriction and dilation. Optimally, there is a cyclical and balanced interplay of contrasting strategies, but disorders tend to involve the almost exclusive use of a particular strategy. Recently, Walker (2002a) has taken a similar view in suggesting that disorders can be regarded as 'non-validation strategies' which are used repeatedly in most, or the core areas, of a person's life to allow avoidance of the risk of invalidation entailed in completion of the Experience Cycle.

Disorders may therefore be classified in terms of the strategies which most characterize them. Kelly made a start on producing such a classification system, but did not consider it practicable to produce a 'cookbook' of all the major disorders. This chapter attempts to provide a model of psychological disorder which, if not a cookbook, is a little more systematic than Kelly's.

STRATEGIES IN PSYCHOLOGICAL DISORDER

Loose Construing

Loosening is a stage in the Creativity Cycle in which constructions are vague and variable—as in dreaming. They will be tightened and tested if the cycle proceeds to that stage, but if not, those constructions will be very difficult to invalidate since they can accommodate virtually any event. Loosening may, therefore, serve to protect the individual from invalidation and the anxiety which may accompany that. However, it is likely ultimately to fail to increase the predictability of the individual's world, as indicated by the fact that the interruption in the loose construer's Experience Cycle occurs at its very first stage, the person being unable to formulate any coherent anticipations of events.

Kelly proposed that the client exhibiting extensive loose construing is likely to be diagnosed as schizophrenic. That proposition was examined by Bannister in a series of studies associating schizophrenic thought disorder with weak relationships between constructs and inconsistencies in the patterns of these relationships. Bannister's work led to his 'serial invalidation hypothesis' accounting for the origins of such thought disorders (see discussion in Chapter 20, pp. 211–222). Several subsequent studies are consistent with Bannister's findings and, while alternative explanations have been proposed for his results, none is entirely convincing (Winter, 1992).

Although all of us may loosen our construing to cope with invalidation, this strategy is likely only to be adopted throughout a person's construing system after alternatives (involving reconstruing and perhaps manifested in a disorder of thought content) have been attempted without success. The option of massive loosening is more likely to be adopted by some people than others: for example, those whose construct systems are already loosely structured may resist the structural collapse which could result from further loosening (Lawlor & Cochran, 1981). As Lorenzini and colleagues (1989) suggest, the age at which major invalidation occurs may also be a factor in determining the response to it. They consider that the person diagnosed as schizophrenic is likely to have suffered invalidation at an earlier age, when there is not yet much hierarchical organization in the construct system, than, for example, the person diagnosed as paranoid.

Gara and colleagues (1989) have demonstrated that a particular construct sub-system which is poorly elaborated in the person diagnosed as schizophrenic is that concerning the self. These authors contrast the schizophrenic person's predicament with the state of optimal functioning reflected in a hierarchical system in which the person has several identities, so that if one identity is invalidated another may be enacted. In the schizophrenic person, invalidation of the individual's identity may result in what the authors term 'not-me' experience and behaviour, and possibly the construction of a new identity based, for example, on delusions or being 'a patient'.

The adoption of a strategy of loose construing in response to invalidation may lead to the presentation of difficulties other than thought disorder, the nature of these perhaps depending upon the extent and persistence of the loosening. If, rather than persistent invalidation, the person experiences a single profound invalidation, for example of a view of the world as a safe place, his or her response may be a fragmentation of construing. As will be seen in Chapter 21 (pp. 223–231), this pattern has been observed in post-traumatic stress disorder.

Tight Construing

While some people remain in the loose construing phase of the Creativity Cycle, others fail to complete the cycle because they adopt the converse strategy of con-sistently construing tightly. Kelly (1955/1991, p. 849/Vol. 2, p. 205) describes them as developing a construing system with 'no loose fits which might let anxiety seep in' and, indeed, they may find themselves sheltered from anxiety if they were to live in an unchanging world. However, since the predictions derived from it are so precise, such a system is very vulnerable to invalidation by new events, and the effects of this may be far-reaching, reverberating from the invalidated construct to others related to it (Lawlor & Cochran, 1981). The threat posed by invalidation to the tight construer is such that he or she is likely to engage in hostility in Kelly's sense, that is to extort evidence to prove he or she was right all along. In terms of the Experi-ence Cycle, he or she fails to pass through the 'confirmation or disconfirmation of anticipation' phase.

The likely reason for very tight construing is that the individual's superordinate constructs are not sufficiently permeable to accommodate changing events. In Kelly's view, which has received some empirical support (Winter, 1992), this is the predicament of the person diagnosed as neurotic. Furthermore, in such people, tight construing has been found to be particularly characteristic of the subsystems of con-struing concerning the symptoms and the self, which is generally seen unfavourably and as different from other people.

Dilation

Another contrasting pair of strategies, which may be used in an imbalanced way in an attempt to avoid invalidation, are dilation and constriction. In the former, the person faced with incompatible constructions extends his or her perceptual field to try to reorganize his or her construing system at a more comprehensive level. In disorders involving dilation, 'the person's exploration has outrun his organization' (Kelly, 1955/1991, p. 846/Vol. 2, p. 203). Such a person may be diagnosed as 'paranoid' or 'manic'.

Constriction

The converse strategy to dilation is constriction, in which an individual attempts to minimize apparent incompatibilities in construing by drawing in the outer boundaries of the perceptual field. While possibly providing some temporary relief from anxiety, 'it may let issues accumulate which will eventually threaten a person with insurmountable anxiety' (Kelly, 1955/1991, p. 908/Vol. 2, p. 246), and its manifestations in psychological disorder may be observed in many people classified as neurotic or depressed. For example, agoraphobia is a clear behavioural manifestation of constriction of the person's world to, ultimately, his or her own home. Research indicates that it may allow the avoidance of anxiety associated with interpersonal conflict, an area in which the agoraphobic's construing tends to be at a low level of awareness (Winter, 1989). This research also suggests that the agoraphobic's interpersonal world may be constricted to only include his or her spouse, whose construing is similar to his or her own and who is likely, therefore, to be a constant source of validation.

While constriction may lead to more certain anticipations of a narrow range of events, a consistent use of this strategy is likely to preclude the extension of the system to encompass events other than these. The Experience Cycle of such an individual is interrupted at the 'encounter' phase.

Faulty Control

Another cycle which may be inadequately completed in disorder is the Circumspection–Pre-emption–Control Cycle. Indeed, Kelly says that 'all disorders of construction are disorders which involve faulty control' (1995/1991, p. 927/Vol. 2, p. 258). In some individuals, the circumspection phase of this cycle is very prolonged, and the process of experimentation consequently delayed. In others, this phase is foreshortened and the person behaves impulsively. Such impulsiveness may be an attempt to escape from uncertainty and consequent anxiety, or to return to a familiar old role and thus reduce guilt. However, if the individual is to carry out the evaluation of his or her actions which allows the possibility of constructive revision and completion of the Experience Cycle, a period of circumspection must follow his or her impulsive behaviour.

Covert Construing

Other strategies which may be adopted to avoid anxiety, and may be evident in disorder, involve covert construing, in which the person is not fully aware of all of his constructions. For example, one pole of a construct may be 'submerged', or relatively inaccessible. This may prevent the construct from being tested out, and therefore forestall the reconstruing that such experimentation might require. Another strategy involving a low level of awareness of construing is 'suspension', in which a construction is held in abeyance because it is incompatible with the person's current construing system and hence is threatening. For instance, in people suffering from agoraphobia such strategies may characterize their construing of interpersonal conflict.

A further type of covert construing, but in this case one that could not be regarded entirely accurately as a strategy, involves the use of preverbal constructs. These have no consistent verbal labels, generally because they were developed in infancy before the person had the use of words. Their expression in symptoms of a disorder may therefore take the form of, for example, bodily sensations rather than verbalized complaints of psychological problems.

CORRELATES OF PSYCHOLOGICAL DISORDER

The view of psychological disorder as involving a block in the process of experimentation suggests that a disorder may involve several potentially negative consequences for the individual.

Idiosyncratic Content of Construing

Kelly states that some disorders arise from the content of the person's construing system rather than the construing process itself. That suggests that his diagnostic dimensions are less relevant in such cases. As an example, he notes that a person who believes that punishment expunges guilt is likely to be self-punitive. However, for such a construction to be maintained the person must either be in a situation where it is validated by others, or strategies have to be employed to avoid invalidation or extort validation. In the former case, the individual cannot strictly be said to have a disorder in the sense of having a construction used repeatedly in the face of consistent invalidation. In the latter, the strategies reflected in Kelly's diagnostic dimensions may be of considerable relevance. Indeed they, and not the idiosyncratic construing itself, may be considered to represent the disorder.

Nevertheless, an idiosyncratic pattern of construing may arise as an initial response to consistent invalidation, the person changing the meaning of constructs in an attempt to avoid further invalidation. In other individuals, such as those diagnosed as depressed, idiosyncrasies of construing may be expressed in negative constructions of the self or change-inhibiting dilemmas (for example, 'if I am happy then I have to be insensitive'). Some of these dilemmas may be derived from experiences of people, such as parents, who served as 'prototypes' of the constructions concerned.

Difficulties in Role Relationships

Another likely consequence of the inadequate formulation and testing of constructions in disorders is difficulty in anticipating other people's construction processes, and hence in role relationships. For example, the person whose construing is very tightly organized may find it difficult to take another person's perspective (Adams-Webber, 1969), whereas the consistently loose construer may be unable to form any testable anticipations of the construing of others. A further possible basis for inaccuracy in construing the constructions of others, as Widom (1976) has observed in clients diagnosed as psychopathic, is the assumption that others share one's own idiosyncratic view of the world.

Undispersed and Undifferentiated Dependency

A further major dimension regarding the individual's approach to interpersonal relationships concerns the extent to which dependencies are dispersed across a range of people. Although dependency was not one of the principal axes of Kelly's diagnostic system, he did make it clear that optimal functioning involves a variety of dependency relationships of different types. By contrast, psychological disorder may be associated with either depending on only one person, or a limited number of people; or, on the other hand, turning to a very large number of people to satisfy every need. Beverly Walker has indicated that such patterns are related to pre-emptive and impermeable construing, and associated with vulnerability to invalidation (see Chapter 16, pp. 171–180).

'Negative' Emotions

The definition of negative emotions as those which 'follow unsuccessful' construing (McCoy, 1981, p. 97) suggests that such emotions are likely to be implicated to some degree in all disorders. Kelly describes, for example, disorders involving guilt, in which there is a sense of loss of role; and those involving anxiety, in which the person is faced with the confusion of finding his or her world unpredictable. He also describes disorders involving aggression and hostility, which McCoy regards as behaviours associated with emotions. In the former, the person may, for example, elaborate his or her position with little understanding of the construing of others and hence little regard for role relationships. In the latter, the person acts in such a way as to extort evidence for some construction, perhaps of the self as a failure or of other people as rejecting.

THE SYMPTOM

Rather than being manifestations of some disease process of which the person is a passive victim, Kelly considers symptoms to be 'urgent questions, behaviourally expressed, which had somehow lost the threads which lead either to answers or to better questions' (1969h, p. 19). They may be relatively direct expressions of the experience of invalidation, such as the anxiety associated with this. In other cases they may reflect aspects of the person's strategy for coping with invalidation, such as the thought disorder associated with a loosening strategy. However, they can always be considered to involve an element of choice, the choice of a particular symptom being grounded in aspects of the person's construing system and their validational experiences. For some individuals, an elaborated role of sufferer from a particular symptom may be available within their social context. For example, media portrayals of eating disorders may provide ready-made roles which can be adopted if no equally elaborated alternative role seems to be available, while involvement in a drug subculture may equally offer an attractive role of addict.

The validational influences on the development of a particular symptom may, however, be more subtle than this. For example, the individual from a family which predominantly communicates by means of physical illness may be expected to develop an elaborated subsystem of 'somatic' constructs, in contrast to the elaborated 'psychological' construct subsystem of the person whose family is characterized by open discussion of emotions. When faced with an experience of persistent invalidation, which is likely to be accompanied by a high level of arousal with both physiological and psychological components (Mancuso & Adams-Webber, 1982), these two individuals are likely to focus pre-emptively on different aspects of this experience and to present with somatic (such as headaches) or psychological (such as social anxiety) symptoms respectively. There is some research evidence for this view, and similarly for a relationship between the symptoms which individuals present and the extent to which they are predominantly concerned with the outside world or their inner worlds (Winter, 1992).

The possible basis for the presentation of psychosomatic symptoms is also considered by Kelly, in cases where the person's preverbal core and dependency constructs are likely to be involved. He argues that the involvement of the latter constructs explains why these symptoms may 'appear as if they were something which the client requires just as urgently as he requires sustenance and safety' (Kelly, 1955/1991, p. 868/Vol. 2, p. 218).

Whatever symptom the person presents, it can be considered to involve both gains and losses. The gains may include the provision of a degree of structure in an uncertain, anxiety-provoking world. For example, not only has it been found that people tend to use a large number of constructs with content relevant to their symptom but also that these constructs tend to be tightly interrelated. Kelly's notion of choice would suggest that for such individuals construal of the self as suffering from the symptom is preferable to not doing so because it carries greater possibilities for elaboration of the construct system. As Fransella (1970) has described, the person's symptom becomes their 'way of life'. However, they are then trapped in a vicious circle in which the role of a sufferer from the symptom concerned becomes ever more elaborated and there is no opportunity to develop an alternative, non-symptomatic role.

Symptoms may serve other purposes. For example, they may have the 'payoff' (Tschudi, 1977) of allowing the self to be construed in a favourable light in those cases where the symptom carries some positive implication for the individual, such as gentleness. Whatever their purpose, this view of symptoms as offering both gains and losses makes it unsurprising that often a person may both seek therapy and appear to resist the therapist's efforts to help (see Chapter 20, pp. 211–222).

AN ILLUSTRATION OF PERSONAL CONSTRUCT FORMULATIONS OF DISORDER: DELIBERATE SELF-HARM

Deliberate self-harm is on the increase. In the United Kingdom, approximately 150 000 people harm themselves every year, while around 3000 people kill themselves every day worldwide. The routes which have led to self harm for these individuals differ, but can be conceptualized using some of the notions presented above.

Kelly distinguishes between different types of suicidal acts. Suicide as a 'dedicated act' is 'designed to validate one's life, to extend its essential meaning rather than to terminate it'. This may be so, for instance, in the case of the suicide bomber in a cultural setting where such an act is construed as honourable and a passport to paradise. He differentiates suicide as a dedicated act from 'mere suicide'. This may occur in two circumstances, which he terms 'realism' and 'indeterminacy'. In the former case, which is often associated with very tight construing, 'the course of events seems so obvious that there is no point in waiting around for the outcome' (Kelly, 1961, p. 260). In the words of John, who marked his fiftieth birthday by taking fifty sleeping tablets, 'I can't see the point of being alive . . . No romance, the kids couldn't care two monkeys, my relatives don't see me any more'. Of relevance to such a fatalistic view of the world may be undispersed dependency. Consider, for example, individuals who focus all their dependencies on another person, who then dies, leaves them, or is seen as betraying their trust. For such individuals, their future only offers the certainty of isolation.

In contrast to suicides in conditions of 'realism' are those in conditions of perceived indeterminacy. In such cases, which are often associated with very loose construing, 'everything seems so unpredictable that the only definite thing one can do is to abandon the scene altogether' (Kelly, 1961, p. 260). One reason for the person's interpersonal world appearing very unpredictable, and consequent suicide, may be a difficulty in anticipating other people's construction processes. The suicidal act may be seen as the ultimate expression of a process of constriction, in which the person increases the predictability of his or her world by drawing in its boundaries, and this notion is particularly applicable to chaotic suicides.

Acts of self-harm may serve to reduce uncertainty, and the anxiety associated with this, even when not committed with suicidal intent. Thus, for some individuals self-harm may provide a way of life, perhaps not a very attractive one for most people but one which is at least familiar and may provide an island of structure and predictability in a sea of chaos. To quote Fred, whose history of self-harm involved swallowing not only tablets but also an impressive array of other objects, from razors to starter motors, 'I don't really want to stop. It doesn't harm me. It's just part of me, going to hospital and getting better.'

Two further processes of construing may be particularly relevant to suicidal gestures. One is foreshortening of the Circumspection–Pre-emption–Control Cycle, the person acting impulsively without taking account of all the issues involved. In Jim's case, when asked to explain his self-harm, he said that 'I was thinking about a person I worked with who cut himself and killed himself. I thought that if he can do it I can do it . . . I ran to the kitchen, grabbed a knife and started cutting myself.' Stefan and Linder (1985) also consider suicidal gestures to be hostile acts, in that they attempt to extort validation of some construction, for example that a partner is uncaring.

Formulation of an individual's self-harm in terms of the processes of construing underlying it provides a basis for selection of a therapeutic intervention. For example, the type of intervention used with the person whose self-harm occurs in the context of a fatalistic view of the world may be diametrically opposed to that used with the person with a world view characterized by indeterminacy. Winter and colleagues (2000) provide some evidence of the effectiveness of such a personal construct psychotherapy approach.

SUMMARY AND CONCLUSIONS

Faced with invalidation of constructions, the individual will generally attempt to reconstrue so as to increase the ability to anticipate future events. However, in a situation of consistent invalidation or when alternative constructions are unavailable, the person may cling to a particular construction regardless of evidence which appears to disconfirm it, and therefore exhibit a disorder. The disorder is likely to be reflected in the exclusive use of a particular strategy, as opposed to the cyclical interplay of strategies which characterizes optimal functioning. Diagnosis of disorders in terms of the strategies and processes of construing which characterize them allows the planning of a therapeutic approach for the individual client.

Although used in this chapter, the term 'disorder' is an unfortunate choice by Kelly since it carries mechanistic implications, is suggestive of a state rather than a process, and its dictionary definition includes such words as ailment and disease. Might imbalance be a more appropriate term?

CHAPTER 20

From Theory to Research to Change

Fay Fransella
University of Hertfordshire, UK

> Instead of being a problem of threatening proportions, requiring the utmost explanation and control to keep man out of trouble, behaviour presents itself as man's principal instrument of inquiry. Without it his questions are academic and he gets nowhere. When it is prescribed for him he runs around in dogmatic circles. But when he uses it boldly to ask questions, a flood of unexpected answers rises to tax his utmost capacity to understand.
>
> (Kelly, 1970, p. 260)

Bannister and Fransella (1986) argued that one of the prime effects of carrying out research within a specific theoretical framework is that the theory decides the questions that are to be asked; that it not only provides the research with a language and a methodology but should also indicate what issues are fundamental. The tie-up between a theory and the questions that one asks is obvious enough. Not only does theory generate issues for experimental investigation, it also provides ideas for designing ways in which individuals may be helped to reconstrue. In particular, work within the framework of the psychology of personal constructs does not see 'normal' and 'abnormal' as two psychologies, but as merely different ways of construing described in the same terms. The following examples illustrate the tie-up between theory, research and practice.

DISORDER OF THOUGHT PROCESSES

Bannister's Theory

It was Don Bannister's theorizing and research work on the nature of the type of disordered thought processes seen in those diagnosed as suffering from schizophrenia that alerted the academic world in the United Kingdom to George Kelly's theory and repertory grid method. Bannister argued that it was excessive loosening

International Handbook of Personal Construct Psychology. Edited by F. Fransella.
© 2003 John Wiley & Sons, Ltd.

of the thought process that produced language that is, in the experience of the listener, incomprehensible. In personal construct theory terms, one can ask whether it is a private language or just a very weak language. Many groups use subsystems of constructs that are incomprehensible to most of us. Mathematicians debating the deeper mysteries of their subject may be incomprehensible, but we would not judge them to be thought-disordered. We accept that they are probably saying something very meaningful and that it is we who lack the specialist construct subsystem to enable us to understand them. The shortcoming is ours not theirs. The same with painting. The loosely construed paintings of schizophrenic people used to be likened to the work of abstract artists. But it was pointed out that abstract artists differ in that they can tighten up their construing when it is time to go home and those with 'schizophrenia' cannot.

The Research Programme

Bannister's theory was tested in series of experiments using repertory grids (Bannister, 1960; Bannister et al., 1971; McPherson et al., 1973). They all found that thought-disordered schizophrenics do, indeed, suffer from a gross loosening of construing. That is, the mathematical relationships between the constructs were very low and the pattern of relationships between the constructs was unstable over time. In contrast, grids repeatedly given to other groups showed significantly closer relationships between constructs and the pattern of these relationships remained relatively consistent over time.

However, his early work with Phillida Salmon showed that such thought-disordered people are not equally perplexed by every aspect of the world in which they live. The greatest difference between them and other so-called 'normal' groups lay in the discrepancy between 'object' and 'people' construing. The thought-disordered group were only a little worse than 'normal' groups in their construing of objects, but they were vastly less structured and consistent in their construing on psychological dimensions. That suggested that schizophrenic thought disorder may not occur throughout their whole construing system, but may be particularly related to *interpersonal* construing (Bannister & Salmon, 1966).

Bannister argued that if it is interpersonal construing that has been specifically affected in thought disorder, then any theory about it being the result of brain disorder has to postulate an unlikely bug or 'schizococcus' that bites 'person-thinking' but not 'object-thinking' brain cells.

The Origins of Thought Process Disorder

Personal construct psychology places great stress on process and change. Thus, any research on thought disorder or any other problems, very rapidly forces the researcher to face the question of how do people come to have that problem. It is not enough to give an account of the condition as it stands.

Bannister's initial hypothesis about what causes thought disorder was that it is the ultimate result of the experience of *serial invalidation*. He argued that thought-disordered schizophrenics have been driven to loosen their construing *beyond the point* at which there are enough workable lines of implication between their constructs for them to re-tighten their system. By loosening our construing we place ourselves in the position of neither being right or wrong in our predictions. Loosening and tightening are not of themselves pathological reactions, but are normal reactions to varying validational fortunes.

To test his hypothesis Bannister conducted experiments in which so-called 'normal' people were 'serially invalidated' (Bannister, 1963, 1965). The experiments showed that successively telling people they were *right* did, indeed, cause them to tighten their construing. However, those who were successively told that they were wrong, did not loosen the interrelationships between their constructs immediately, but responded markedly with another strategy—they changed the *pattern* of inter-relationships. Thus, on one occasion a person might have a high positive correlation (say, 0.70) between *kind* and *sincere* then, on a later grid, these two constructs might be highly negatively correlated (say, −0.90). That wild swinging of the pattern of relationships between constructs seemed to be an initial and marked reaction to invalidation. However, in a final experiment it was shown that if only one cluster of constructs at a time, rather than a whole subsystem, was invalidated, then loosening did take place.

Bannister's ideas and research sparked a vast amount of activity among researchers, some producing results supporting his hypotheses, some against. Included in that research activity was the development of the standardized *Grid Test of Schizophrenic Thought Disorder* (Bannister & Fransella, 1967). The aim was to provide an aid to a reconstruction programme to help such people to become 'thought-ordered'. But it was destined to become only an aid to diagnosis.

The Resulting Therapy Research Programme

Although Bannister's research was an artificial and laboratory model of the process of serial invalidation, he felt that the experiments did suggest that thought-disordered people may have been wrong too often. That raised the question of how thought-disordered schizophrenics could again achieve 'ordered' thinking.

He suggested that a reduction of thought disorder might take place as a result of serial *validation* (having one's expectations confirmed). The programme he designed began with a very extensive search of each individual's construct system for dealing with people. The aim was to find some residual structure; some group of still semi-clustered constructs that would serve as a starting point for an elaboration of the whole system.

The thought-disordered schizophrenic people were encouraged to think about/relate to others and start having expectations about them. They were then encouraged to experiment with their environment in order that they could test out the implications of their construing. This research (Bannister et al., 1975) produced no startling 'cure' for thought disorder, but it did suggest that a 'journey back' may be possible, long and arduous though that journey would be.

THE CONSTRUING OF STUTTERING

As this is about my own theorizing and research, I will talk about it personally. Don Bannister's research in the 1960s made me realize that personal construct theory was a powerful way of trying to give meaning to the behaviour of some people that otherwise seemed incomprehensible. My particular interest in the mid-1960s was those who stutter. Why did they not stop doing something that obviously caused them so much unhappiness? There is no body of evidence to suggest that people stutter because of some brain malfunction. Like him, I turned to theory to provide an explanation for the continuance of stuttered speech in those who had been labelled 'a stutterer' from an early age.

A Personal Construct Theory of Stuttering

Kelly's model is of the *personal construer.* Those who stutter construe. They, like everyone else, have developed subsystems of constructs throughout their lives, through which to view the universe of events that confront them and enable them to predict and hence have some control over the course of these events.

Our personal construct systems make us both free and prisoners. We are free in that we can change our construing of events in the light of the results of our predictions. But we are trapped by that same construing system. We have choice, but we can only choose between the dichotomous constructs that make up our system; we cannot view the world along totally new construct dimensions at will. I was struck by Hinkle's (1965) rewording of the Choice Corollary:

> a person always chooses in that direction which he anticipates will increase the total meaning and significance of his life. Stated in the defensive form, a person chooses so as to avoid the anxiety of chaos and the despair of absolute certainty.
> (p. 21)

Eventually I came to theorize that *a person stutters because it is in this way that he or she can anticipate the greatest number of events: it is by behaving in this way that life is most meaningful to him or her.* Someone who stutters cannot change because none of us willingly walks the plank and so drops off into an unknown, unpredictable world. In the world of fluency there lie many unknown hazards for someone who stutters and a vastly decreased ability to predict these pitfalls.

People who stutter know all about being 'a stutterer'. They know the variety of ways in which a person is likely to react to their way of speaking, and know what their reactions will be to the listener's reactions. But they are unable to interpret the subtler forms of communication such as eye contacts, hand gestures and general body movements which usually accompany speaking for the fluent person. I argued that one of their problems is that they do not try to see the situation through the eyes of the listener. There is no role relationship as described in the Sociality Corollary. No attempt is made to see things through the listener's eyes, only an interpretation of the listener's behaviour.

The Resulting Therapy Research Programme

My reasons for carrying out this research were two-fold. One was purely theoretical, a wish to show that behaviour is directly linked to construing—as personal construct theory suggests. The other was to test whether personal construct theory could be of use in gaining insight into another human problem that is also very resistant to change. That, in turn, might lead to an approach to helping sufferers find a path to fluency. The research was not designed to test the efficacy of personal construct therapy.

In addition to basing the research on Hinkle's rewording of the Choice Corollary, my principal research tool was a modified form of his *Implications Grid*. There are no elements to be construed in the Impgrid, constructs are compared with constructs. My simplified modification of Hinkle's grid was to take one pole of a person's constructs at a time and ask that person to look at all their other constructs—laid out on the table before them. The question asked was, for example, 'if all you know about a person is that they are *thrifty,* are there any other characteristics among those on the table here that you would *expect* a *thrifty* person to be?'

Twenty people, who, starting in 1966, were successively referred to me for treatment of their stutter, completed two such *bipolar impgrids*—one with constructs elicited from 'me as a stutterer' and the other from 'me as a fluent speaker'. These were repeated at intervals during the therapy. On each of those occasions, measures were also taken of severity of stuttering and self-characterizations were written.

The precise prediction was that, as fluency increased, the implications of being a fluent speaker would increase—it would become a more meaningful way of being.

Reconstruing from Stuttering to Fluency

As with all forms of therapy, the method stems from the theory about the problem. If it is argued that people continue to stutter because that is the most meaningful way for them to behave, then the therapy will be directed to making fluency a more meaningful way to behave. Until that has increased meaning, the person who stutters will not experiment with being a fluent person. The same applies to anyone with a long-standing problem—to people who have a problem with weight, as is described later in this chapter, to those who smoke (Mair, 1970) or who drink to excess (Hoy, 1973). All ways of behaving that a person has adopted over many years becomes part of their 'self' construing. The problem such people have 'is not a symptom but a way of life' (Fransella, 1970).

The main therapeutic method used was what Kelly described as 'controlled elaboration'. That is described more fully in Chapter 23 (pp. 237–245). In this case, any occasion in which the client had experienced fluency was focused on. 'What did it feel like?' 'How did the other person react to your fluency?' But the crucial question was, 'Did you predict you would be fluent?' If the person said they did 'know' they would be fluent, they soon came to realize that it was they themselves who were responsible for the fluency and that it was not something that just 'came upon me'. It was their own construing that resulted in their response of stuttering or fluency.

At the end of the two-year programme, the results supported both my aims. Behaviour and construing were shown to be inseparable. The degree of increase in fluency was highly related to the number of implications people had for being a fluent speaker. The more meaningful a fluent speaker was being, the more fluent the person had become. Apart from that, there was also a decrease in meaningfulness of being a stutterer as fluency increased. Personal construct theory states that we do not have to give up one set of ideas before embarking on the elaboration of another. It is reasonable then to suppose that as one subsystem of construing becomes more meaningful and is seen to have increased predictive capacity, the other subsystem will eventually start to 'shrivel up'. Apart from that, it was shown that the personal construct theory of stuttering had led to a treatment programme that produced positive results.

Therapeutic Constraints

The very precise nature of my hypotheses meant that only work based on personal construct theory could be used to help the client reconstrue. But it seemed likely that using some speech modification technique would speed up the development of 'spontaneous fluency', and thus make reconstruing easier. Margaret Evesham and I (1985) investigated that hypothesis. One group of stutterers had fluency training in 'prolonged speech' and the other group had that training plus personal construct work. Measures were made of disfluencies and all forty-eight participants completed grids and self characterizations.

People in both groups experienced a decrease in their disfluencies, but the technique group showed more improvement. Although a seemingly disappointing result, it was of particular interest that the relapse rate for the personal construct group was significantly lower than for the technique group. That would, of course, be predicted from personal construct theory. Those in the personal construct group were actually changing how they saw themselves as a person. Once that happens, a person is less likely to go back to the beginning, although there may be sporadic relapses. Those who simply learn a technique for changing their behaviour, may or may not reconstrue themselves as a person.

Over the 30 years since that original research work, considerable use has been made of the personal construct approach by speech and language therapists in the United Kingdom (Stewart & Birdsall, 2001) but, as DiLollo and colleagues (2001) have pointed out, its application to the treatment of stuttering in the United States has been almost non-existent. These latter authors suggest that one of the reasons for that is the requirement of specialist training and the complexity of the assessment methods. While agreeing that some knowledge and experience of personal construct theory is necessary for any practitioner, the assessment methods are not a requirement of the reconstruction programme. I used the bipolar impgrids to test specific hypotheses and not as an integral part of the therapy.

DiLollo and colleagues recommend the use of *narrative therapy* (see Chapter 24, pp. 247–255). The framework outlined by White and Epston (1990) and cited by DiLollo and colleagues, is not far removed from that of the personal construct approach. For instance, they suggest that there is a need to talk about the relationship between the person and the problem; find out how the person is able to predict that they are about to stutter; and that there should be a focus on fluency.

A PROBLEM OF WEIGHT

Like stuttering, disorders of weight are notoriously resistant to change—particularly that described as anorexia nervosa, a potentially life-threatening disorder in which the extreme pursuit of thinness and avoidance of fatness dominates a person's life. Eric Button has spent many years trying to understand why these people, commonly young women, look as if they want to starve themselves to death (see Button, 1993, for full coverage of his work). His starting point was my work on stuttering.

His general hypothesis was that resistance to weight gain was related to the meaning of being a normal weight. The results from his first piece of research gave some support to that hypothesis and also showed that a greater degree of meaningfulness of being at a normal weight was associated with better weight maintenance following discharge from hospital. That is, relapse rates were lower.

A second study had one particularly striking finding, contrary to what one might expect. The young women construed 'me at my thinnest' in very negative terms compared to their ideal self. However, the picture was complex. For example, one person generally construed being normal weight as preferable to being thin, but in one crucial respect there was a snag. For her, being normal weight meant being *conspicuous*, which was the last thing she wanted, she would like to have been virtually invisible.

In addition to such findings about the *content* of their construing, later research demonstrated the importance of *structural* aspects of construing. These young women, compared with both healthy individuals and those suffering from bulimia nervosa (those who binge-eat, typically followed by vomiting), showed more limited and rigid forms of construing of people. Button's central theme now is that it is this limitation in how they construe people which leads them to take refuge in the more predictable and controllable world of just focusing on food, eating and weight.

Therapeutic Implications

Button now argues, in line with Fransella's approach, that therapeutic efforts should focus on developing 'person construing' rather than on weight. He comments that:

> Sadly, some thirty years after my original research, I am less optimistic about the possibilities of change in many of these individuals whose styles of construing can prove highly repetitive and resistant. My goal, however, is to help them find and be themselves in their own terms, in spite of their limitations and with or without their anorectic way of life. (Personal communication)

The above examples and many other psychological problems are characterized by the sufferers finding it very difficult to change and being subject to relapse. Why can we not become what we want to become? Why do people, who seem to be making good progress, in their own terms or those of others, suddenly stop that progress and sometimes even 'take a step backwards'?

RESISTING CHANGE?

Resistance to change for both psychoanalysts and cognitive-behaviour therapists involve some notion of failure on the part of the client. The personal construct practitioner strongly disagrees with that view. How can a client fail? If the client is seen as failing so must be the therapist, since they are struggling together on the same problem. If the client demonstrates that he or she is not seeing the problem as the therapist does, some reconstruing—on the part of the therapist—is required. As Kelly put it:

> The client who exasperates the therapist by his failure to deal with what the therapist wants him to, or by his refusal to see things the way the therapist so clearly sees them is not necessarily warding off the therapist as a person; more likely he is demonstrating the fact that his construct system does not subsume what the therapist thinks it should. (Kelly, 1955/1991, p. 1101/Vol. 2, p. 379)

The Choice Corollary leads us to think that the essence of living is to grow and develop, to extend and/or define our construing of the world—and therefore to change. Taking that view, clients are not *resisting* change, they are *choosing* not to change.

WHY CHOOSE NOT TO CHANGE?

Although this chapter focuses primarily on the process of reconstruction for those seeking professional help, it is important to remember that Kelly's ideas are relevant to us all, whether or not we have a serious problem with which we need help. We all experience times when we choose not to change. These times can be looked at in terms of structure of a person's construing system and also in terms of transitions.

When the Problem is Part of the Core Role

For many people, their complaint is part of their core role and the alternative way of being has some serious negative aspect to it. That applies to both those who stutter and those with anorexia nervosa already described.

But choosing not to change is not an uncommon experience. For instance, many current change programmes require people, say, middle managers, to become *caring managers* rather than *directive*. These managers will resist change if that change requires them to become something they, at a core level, think is not *them*. In one organization this resulted in an alarming number failing their assessment at the end of a lengthy change programme. Through individual interviews involving elicitation and laddering of personal constructs, it was found that to be *caring,* for some, was the equivalent of being a *bad manager,* quite unacceptable. Once a problem such as this has been put into words, it can be discussed. In this case, many of these middle managers said that they were prepared to 'give it a go'. The majority passed at the assessment centre the second time round. They always had the skills to pass, but their understanding of their role did not allow them to. It is important to state that their jobs were not at risk.

Tight versus Loose Construing

It is often found that those who had tight construing subsystems of themselves change less than those who construe their world more loosely, for example, Fransella (1972) with those who stutter, Button (1980) with those suffering from anorexia nervosa and Sheehan (1985) with those who are depressed. That is easy to understand. If we are fairly certain how things are, we may realize, at some level of awareness, that one or two seemingly simple changes could have serious reverberations throughout the system. We choose not to change.

When there is Nowhere to Go

People who have stuttered for as long as they can remember have no alternative but to value the *status quo*. To suddenly find themselves fluent would plunge them into a world in which they can predict very little when speaking with other adult people. They cannot change until being fluent is meaningful to them. It is the same for anyone who has behaved in a certain way for a very long time.

When the Alternative is an Ideal

For many of those with long-standing problems such as stuttering, obesity, alcoholism or smoking, the alternative to being a stutterer, obese, an alcoholic or a smoker is to be 'an ideal'. They cry 'if only'. 'If only I were not someone who stutters I would be a great orator.' 'If only I were not an alcoholic I would be a powerful businessman.' 'If only I were not obese I would be one of the most successful fashion models.' Most of us cannot live an ideal.

THE EXPERIENCE OF NOT WANTING TO CHANGE

Having looked at reasons why a person chooses not to change how they see themselves and their problem 'just like that', the experience of such choice can be looked at in terms of 'transitions'.

Threat

A major reason for maintaining the psychological status quo is the awareness that, if change takes place, it will result in a comprehensive change in one's core construing. Luke spelled it out like this:

> I have a confession to make. I sort of feel that in the past I should have taken a more active interest in getting rid of my stammer. . . . I feel I'm capable of thinking about the situation and trying to work out some new ideas—in general help you along as much as possible—I've been a bit on the lazy side. . . . I could easily sit down and think about my stammer, but when it came to the time, then I didn't feel like it and I think that this could well be the fact that probably somewhere, subconsciously, I didn't want to get rid of it because it was—you know—just this sort of thing. That there was something in the fluent world that I was afraid of.
>
> (Fransella, 1972, p. 195)

He had definitely become aware of the imminent possibility of comprehensive change in his core construing. He was correct in asking for more time to reconstrue.

Hostility

One of the most often experienced ways of making sure that no more change occurs is by being hostile. As Kelly points out, hostility is often construed by the therapist as 'resistance'.

> If the client is hostile he may, indeed, be making a whipping boy out of the therapist; but even this, we feel, is more profitably seen as an effort to retrieve some bad bets on which the client wagered more than he could afford. If the therapist has no more enlightened construction of what is going on than to insist that the client 'is being stubborn', it would seem that the therapist is hostile too.
>
> (Kelly, 1955/1991, p. 1101/Vol. 2, p. 379)

Clients are extremely creative in the ways they find to convince the therapist that there has really not been any improvement. Relapse can readily be seen as one hostile strategy. Just to complete the theoretical picture, Kelly suggests that, where there seems to be hostility, one should look for the guilt.

Guilt

That is felt when the client actually glimpses, for instance, that new 'fluent self' or that 'normal weight self'. They become aware that they have gone too far in their psychological change and, for however short a time, have been dislodged from that treasured core role.

It seems likely that some fairly radical core role reconstruing has to take place before a person is able to judge whether what was so desirable to begin with is really so desirable after all. What looked so wonderful when it was unelaborated and its implications unknown may look very threatening in the cold light of reconstrual. Evidence has to be extorted to show that, whatever change there is in the offing, it is unimportant. That hostility prevents the person having to face the *guilt* of not being the person they always thought they were. Kelly felt that *guilt* can be so serious that he said:

> Since guilt, as we have defined it, represents dislodgement from one's core role structure, we could scarcely expect guilt not to be related to 'physical' health.

Strictly within the psychological realm one might transpose the Biblical saying, 'The wages of sin is death' into 'The wages of guilt is death'. It is genuinely 'difficult to sustain life in the fact of guilt'. Some people do not even try.

(Kelly, 1955/1991, p. 909/Vol. 2, 246)

RELAPSE

Everything that has been said about choosing to resist change is relevant to our understanding of why people relapse. The speed of change is too fast. Reconstruing keeps sending shock waves up to those core role areas and signals imminent change in the system itself. Something has to be done about it. What better than to go back a few steps to where it may be more uncomfortable but at least it is home.

But personal construct theory leads one to view relapses during therapy as useful. They provide the person with a breathing space. Time to work out what all the change they have experienced actually means. What is useful and what is still too threatening to contemplate? As has been said before, such construing does not go on 'in one's head'. It takes place below the level of conscious awareness. Relapsing provides the client and therapist with much needed space to back-track and attach more words to the underlying construing that is causing painful threat or guilt.

THEORY AND MEASUREMENT OF RESISTANCE TO CHANGE

Denny Hinkle (1965) outlined a theory of personal construing that he called a 'theory of construct implications' and described how that theory led to an understanding of change in construing. To test his theory he described the 'hierarchical technique for eliciting the superordinate constructs of the preferred self hierarchy', which has subsequently been called laddering, created the 'implications grid' and also a way of measuring resistance to change. Basically, he was suggesting that the meaning of a personal construct is provided by that construct's relationship to other constructs. Thus, the meaning of each personal construct is to be found in the poles of those other constructs that it implies plus those that are implied by it. So each personal construct has a range of both superordinate and subordinate implications.

His theory of construct implications led to his arguing that the range of implication of a construct could be used as a measure of the meaningfulness of that construct. He set about testing a number of hypotheses in his research. He theorized that the relative resistance to change of personal constructs would be related to how superordinate they are for an individual:

> ... the relative resistance to slot change of personal constructs will be directly related to the superordinate range of implications of those constructs. This is based on the principle of maximizing the total implicativeness of the system and the notion that the anticipated degree of threat will be a direct function of the number of implications involved in the change. (Hinkle, 1965, p. 28)

Another hypothesis was that:

Constructs functioning at a higher level of superordination in a hierarchical context will show a greater relative resistance to slot change than constructs function at a low level. (Hinkle, 1965, p. 29)

Hinkle's research supported his hypotheses. He found also that the degree to which personal constructs are resistant to change is related to whether they are superordinate (laddered) constructs or are subordinate (elicited). The more superordinate personal constructs are, the more likely they are to resist any change.

Measuring Resistance to Change

His resistance to change grid is quite simple if somewhat laborious. Each personal construct, written on a card, is paired with all other constructs. The person is first asked to state which pole of each construct they would prefer to describe themselves, and these preferred poles are underlined. A form of questioning that has been found easy to use is: 'tomorrow morning you are going to wake up and find that you have changed on one of these two constructs. In this case, you will have changed from being *glamorous* to being *plain* or from being *thoughtful* to being *impetuous*. Which would you find it most difficult to change on?' The number of the construct on which the person indicates it would be most difficult to change is noted. The scoring is simply the sum for each construct on which it has been nominated as resisting the change. (See Fransella et al. (in press) for details.)

Another way of getting an indication of how resistant to change personal constructs are is simply to ask the person to rank their elicited and laddered personal constructs from most important to them to least important.

SUMMARY

Personal construct theory can lead to new ways of looking at old problems. Different people have taken different aspects of the theory as their starting point. Thus, for instance, Don Bannister focused on loosening of construing as the basis of his theory of the type of disordered thinking found in some of those diagnosed as suffering from schizophrenia, and I found it was the Choice Corollary that led me to a new way of thinking about the problem of stuttering. The resulting theories not only lend themselves to testing but also lead to new approaches to helping the sufferers.

That same theory can then be used to explain why some people find it so difficult to 'give up' their problem. If the person feels that change resulting from the therapy is too fast, he or she may well *choose* to stop changing or even to go back a few steps. The therapist may well see the former as resistance and the latter as relapse. But the reflexive nature of personal construct theory enables the therapist to look at his or her own construing to find out what is going on.

CHAPTER 21

An Approach to Post-Traumatic Stress

Kenneth W. Sewell
University of North Texas, USA

> If, then, we are to comprehend what [a man] knows, or what he wants to know, or what he thinks, or feels, or dreads or does, we must understand the system of contradictions within which his possibilities hold their shape and his choices—deliberate or impulsive—are made.
>
> (Kelly, 1969k, p. 115)

The essential feature of Kelly's theory from a post-traumatic stress point of view is found in his Fundamental Postulate. Our psychological processes are channelized by the ways in which we *anticipate* events. Anticipation is thus integrally linked with interpretation and understanding of experience. That emphasis makes personal construct theory particularly useful in conceptualizing and helping those who have experienced some trauma.

Although Kelly focused on the 'personal' side of construing, there is a recognition within personal construct psychology that humans construe in social contexts. Indeed, Kelly's concept of sociality as the role-relationship potential created by persons attempting to anticipate the constructions of others is central to understanding phenomena as diverse as schizophrenia, love and psychotherapy. With the present framework, both of these emphases are incorporated into the understanding of trauma by stipulating that traumatization, although individual in expression, is inherently social insofar as the trauma itself has social components. Furthermore, a traumatized person's attempts to improve symptomatically occur in social context.

UNDERSTANDING REACTIONS TO TRAUMA

More than a decade ago, a personal construct explanatory model of Post-Traumatic Stress Disorder (PTSD) was devised (Sewell & Cromwell, 1990). That model proposes that a person who encounters an extreme experience that cannot be construed in relation to their other life experiences often creates a fragmented trauma-related

International Handbook of Personal Construct Psychology. Edited by F. Fransella.

construct subsystem. Thus, a person with PTSD is predicted to be operating, at least sometimes, from within an outlook on life that might have been validated by his traumatic experience, but is not being validated by the rest of his life. Such fragmentation, along with other more esoteric aspects of the model, is said to account for the various symptoms and presentations of PTSD.

The personal construct PTSD model led to further refinements based upon a variety of research findings, for example with Vietnam combat veterans (Sewell et al., 1996; Sewell & Williams, 2001), disaster survivors (Sewell, 1996), sexual assault survivors (Moes & Sewell, 1994) and bereaved persons (Gamino et al., 1998). These particular research studies are not the focus here, but the lessons learned from more than a decade of research and from clinical application of the model are distilled and presented in what follows.

CURRENT CONSTRUCTIONS OF PTSD

Individuals who persist with PTSD seem to view their lives in extreme, negative and relatively unelaborated ways. That is, they tend to become 'stuck' in their construal of experiences around one or two core constructs (such as *good* versus *bad* or *in-control* versus *out-of-control*).

Although there are some difficult-to-assess individual differences in who develops symptoms following a trauma, these differences may have little importance in understanding recovery. It is possible to identify 'risk factors' for PTSD. However, even individuals at low risk can develop PTSD if traumatized at a high level. Perhaps more importantly, once a person develops PTSD, the original risk factors fail to predict the recovery pattern (Sewell, 1996). In other words, once a person has PTSD, it does little good for the treating clinician to focus on what might have made that person vulnerable to the trauma in the first place. The more appropriate therapeutic focal point is how the person is construing and trying to make sense of the traumatizing experience.

The re-adaptation process after developing a post-traumatic stress reaction appears dependent upon elaborating the traumatic experience such that it enters into more varied and hierarchically abstract relations with other life experiences. Elaboration of a trauma is likely to require both the development of new dimensions of meaning as well as some reorganization of how their current constructs relate to each other.

A central focus of this chapter is the important distinction of 'event' versus 'social' elaboration. When a person is traumatized, there is a disruption in at least two different and important areas of construing: event construction and person/social construction. When a person's construing of events is disrupted, the individual's sense of order in the world is disturbed. The result can be catastrophic anticipations and anxiety. When a person's social construing is disturbed, the result is an inability, sometimes leading to an unwillingness, to anticipate and thus effectively participate in social relationships. This impaired ability or unwillingness to relate to other people leads to a sense of social isolation that is independent of the anxiety created by event construal.

In considering what is disrupted in any one person—event construction or social construction—it is crucial to understand that it is almost always *both*. Within this framework, traumas are therefore seen as disrupting a person's construction of experience in both event and social domains. However, the disruption in one of these domains is likely to predominate at any given time in the experience of a person.

These changes in predomination of event versus social disruption imply differences in the optimal role of the therapist as the person recovers. When the disruption of event construing predominates, the therapist can collaborate with the client in combating symptoms, and designing novel behavioural experiments outside of therapy. On the other hand, when social construction disruption is predominating, therapy should be viewed as a controlled microcosm of the client's world in which he or she can be socially related. The therapist's optimal role becomes that of collaborative social problem-solver. In this role, the therapist must invalidate the negative social predictions but persist in valuing the client and offering the self as an available target, rather than retreating from attacks, as most others in the client's environment might. In reference to the client's life story, this role is that of a valued audience member—someone with whom the client *cares* to share her story.

BEST-LAID PLANS

In order to fully understand the invalidation a traumatized person experiences in the social and event domains, a 'planning' metaphor is offered based upon the convention of referring to one's main plan as 'Plan A' and the back-up plan as 'Plan B'. It is important to note that although all plans are forms of anticipation, not all anticipations are plans. Thus, this explanation uses the 'planning' concept in a truly metaphoric manner.

Plan A: How I anticipate the world will work and how I will be humanly connected within it. Plan A is the basis of my ongoing anticipation. In personal construct terms, Plan A is made up of my 'emergent' construct poles.

A non-traumatic example will be carried through the metaphor. As a prelude to the example, I must reluctantly admit that I was an American football player throughout my university years. Suppose that after a game I walk into the football locker room, anticipating a male environment, with lots of testosterone flying about, and with collegial relations. These anticipations are based upon the emergent constructs of *male*, *testosterone-oriented* and *collegial*.

The level of elaboration of Plan A will determine the likelihood that various happenings will be experienced as validating or invalidating. Trauma is invalidation to the extreme.

I walk out of the shower in the locker room, and there are women standing around with note pads and pencils. Plan A explodes into vapour.

Plan B: How the world must work and how I would fit into it if Plan A fails. Plan B consists of the implicit poles of Plan A constructions. Implicit poles of constructs are the tools with which invalidation is anticipated.

The level of elaboration (complexity, intricate contingencies, and so forth) of Plan B will determine the likelihood that trauma will result in sustained disruption. This is because trauma causes Plan B to *become* Plan A (the basis of ongoing anticipation). Once Plan B becomes Plan A, psychological energies must be devoted to making the world make sense (be predictable) from this new frame.

> If the implicit poles of my original constructions were *female* (as opposed to *male*), *femininely sexual* (as opposed to *testosterone-oriented*), and *adversarial* (as opposed to *collegial*), the Plan B that gets invoked might lead me to anticipate, even if only briefly, that the women were there to evaluate the bodies of the male athletes (myself included) in order to choose a sexual partner and/or report their findings to others outside the locker room.

Now where is Plan B? A new one must be developed. Due to the energy and attention required to try to make the original Plan B function as a Plan A, the development of a new Plan B can be difficult at best, and neglected at worst. That often leads to the paranoid stance that the new Plan A *must* hold; there simply is no choice. There is no perceived Plan B. That is an expression of a highly simplified (unelaborated) Plan B in which the implicit poles of all constructs are essentially the unitary anticipation that 'I will be out of control' or 'I will cease to exist'. That stance leaves the individual with both symptoms as well as vulnerability to continued invalidation.

> When I see that the women along with some men are interviewing the quarterback about the strategy that was being employed during a crucial part of the game, my new Plan A (old Plan B) is invalidated. If my new Plan B is composed of the single construct pole *I will be overwhelmed with confusion*, I am likely to have a psychological melt-down and run from the locker room naked and screaming. If, however, my new Plan B contains a complex set of contingent possibilities such as *newspaper reporter* (rather than *male* or *female*), *non-sexual* (rather than *masculinely* or *femininely sexual*) and *objective* (rather than *collegial* or *adversarial*), I might be able to get dressed and be only slightly offended that no one is interviewing *me*.

A non-traumatic example was chosen to aid in conceptualizing the Plan A/B metaphor without muddling the explanation with the human pain and suffering involved in the kinds of traumas our clients bring with them. Clearly, a soldier who has seen horrific acts, or a sexual assault survivor who now sees even the most trusted men as potential attackers, may have had the whole of Plan A ripped away in a matter of moments. Plan B cum Plan A—though filled with pain, anxiety and social disconnection—may be the only thread of sensibility in sight. A therapist must assist traumatized clients in elaborating alternative constructions, such that the invalidation experienced daily can be met with positive change rather than relapse. To achieve that end, a model of post-traumatic stress psychotherapy has been developed.

A PERSONAL CONSTRUCT INTEGRATIVE MODEL OF POST-TRAUMATIC STRESS PSYCHOTHERAPY

This model of psychotherapy integrates the descriptive model of post-traumatic stress disorder described above as well as lessons learned from research and clinical application to date. In addition to describing the elements of the process of reconstruction, there is a need to create a mindset or frame for construing a traumatized client from within this theoretical perspective. Toward that end, this section begins with a discussion of the concept of 'metaconstruction' and a metaphorical image of traumatization to exemplify the concept.

Metaconstruction

Metaconstruction is the construal of a construction process. One type of metaconstruction is Kelly's construct of sociality, in which a person construes the construction processes of another. But we also construe and reconstrue our own construction processes. Metaconstruction comprises the sense of self when an individual construes her or his own construction processes at present in relation to her or his own construction processes at various points in the past. That allows the person to build a sense of a future self. In other words, we construct/construe our future construction processes on the basis of past and present processes.

Metaconstruction is the overall process by which individuals constitute themselves, both psychologically and socially. As discussed above, traumas disrupt construing in both the social and the event domains, which affect the self-concept deriving from each type of disruption. Thus, a post-traumatic stress reaction represents a breach in the continuity of metaconstruction—a breach that implies disintegration of the self.

A Reflective Metaphor

Imagine sitting in a barber's chair with a mirror in front and behind. The images of front and back, front and back, front and back . . . repeat until they disappear into infinity. Think of the back image as representing the past, and the front image as representing the future. The chair itself (and your experience of it) is the present. A trauma results when the figure in the chair is different from the image in the back mirror. When this is the case, predicting what will appear on the front mirror from image to image seems mind-boggling at worst, and not conducive to self-definition at best. In this way, any dramatic 'change' can potentially be traumatic.

Thus, a trauma often initiates a construction of the present that seems too incongruous with the past to be seen as emerging from it. Consequently, the lack of continuity between metaconstrued present and past impairs the ability to make a coherent future metaconstruction.

Growth involves elaboration of the present and past metaconstructions of both events and relationships such that they are construed as continuously linked.

Then, the future can be metaconstructed in a non-fragmented, non-constricted fashion.

ELEMENTS OF RECONSTRUCTION

It must be borne in mind that the items discussed here as 'elements of reconstruction' are not to be understood as stages or phases. The elements are discussed in the order that they are likely to emerge in any one therapeutic relationship. For example, it is difficult to engage in effective 'trauma reliving' without first doing a substantial 'life review'. However, it is not the case that a client graduates from one element to the next, never to return to it. Cyclical repetitions of utilizing these elements should be anticipated and validated. The synopses of the elements of the reconstruing process and the case examples provided below are drawn from Sewell and Williams (2002)—see also Sewell (1997) and Sewell and Williams (2001).

Symptom Management

This element can be thought of as the negotiation of present metaconstruction, such as examining what it is like in the barber's chair. The over-riding goal of this reconstruction element is to gain the trust of the client by helping to alleviate some of the presenting distress. In addition to installing the therapist as an important social figure in the client's life, the relief of debilitating anxiety and/or social dysfunction also enables the therapist to 'recruit' the client's energies toward elaborating his experience, as opposed to simply surviving. Any relevant method can be employed in this reconstruction element to find a way to relieve some of the client's pain.

Case Example

Gary had clear memories of sexual abuse as a child but could express only vague complaints upon entering therapy. Early in therapy, Gary started to realize that he would over-eat to protect himself from painful introspection. He and the therapist began assertively distinguishing his emotions from the sensations of physical hunger and satiation. Several symptom management techniques such as scripted self-talk, 'feeling' journals and relaxation training were successfully employed to assist Gary with flashbacks, lack of sleep and anger outbursts. More importantly, however, Gary's successes in collaborating with the therapist to address his pain taught him the process of overt introspection. With this new skill and an important new social role relationship, Gary began his journey of reconstruing with an entrusted therapist.

Life Review

The evocation of past metaconstruction (exploring the rear view mirror) is accomplished via life review. This involves the client sharing her past metaconstruction with the therapist so that the therapist and client share the story of the life upon which the traumatic experience apparently intruded.

Case Example

Michelle was consumed with self-blame for getting in the car with the stranger who later assaulted her. When asked to describe her life before the assault, she reflected on the abandonment by her parents and her street-wise nature at a young age. Although she had become 'tough' as a way to survive her predicament, Michelle also remembered times of great vulnerability—particularly when someone showed signs of caring for her. Reconciling what for Michelle were experienced as opposite self-constructions (*street-smart and tough* versus *vulnerable and needy*) would prove to be a substantial task requisite to re-adjusting after the trauma. The life review helped to identify the elements of her past and the dimensions of her evaluation in need of reconstruction. Moreover, the process recapitulated the content; in other words, Michelle had to risk vulnerability in order to bring the therapist in as audience to her world.

Trauma Reliving

Specific trauma-related metaconstruction is evoked to bring the therapist *into* the trauma (examining how we got in this chair) and allow the experience to be reconstructed together. This element involves psychologically taking the therapist to and through the trauma. The prefix 're-' is never constrained to simple repetition; instead it is open to reformation/transformation. Thus, reliving does not mean 'living it then, the exact same way'; rather reliving requires that the client 'live it now, with my new resources, my new co-narrator, my new audience, toward a new resultant self'. It is in this focus of therapy that the therapist begins to leverage the valued co-narrator and audience status nurtured via symptom management and life review.

Case Example

Every time Tom would begin to approach the details of his traumatic Vietnam combat memories, he would find a reason not to delve deeply into them. He tried simultaneously to glean what he could from therapy, and to protect the therapist from the pain of his experience. In spite of this, Tom would grow frustrated at not being more fully understood by the therapist. Tom was repeatedly encouraged to take the therapist through the story: 'You'll be safe this time; I'll be there with you.' Tom and his therapist went behind enemy lines. Tom and his therapist stayed hidden as the enemy disembarked from a gun-boat and searched among the tall grass, eventually finding several of Tom's comrades. Tom and his therapist listened to the screaming of the soldiers until their screams were punctuated by gunfire. After the gun-boat drifted away, Tom and his therapist arose to find that his partners had been tied to trees and skinned alive before being shot. . . . Now Tom and his therapist could speak the same language. Reconstruction, though by no means an easy task, was now at least possible.

Constructive Bridging

Once the therapist and client are facing the abyss of the client's traumatic experience in a collaborative, joint manner, the therapist can begin juxtapositioning the client's various metaconstructive levels (sketching on the rear view mirror and on the chair . . . that were really sketches all along). The therapist helps the client to lay remembrances alongside introspection, introspection alongside reflection, reflection alongside the sociality with the therapist, and weave stories between these metaconstructive levels that cohere and communicate a viable sense of self. Bridging the temporal and social dimensions of understanding the self in relation to the trauma serves to build a new construct, that is, a new experience of the trauma.

Case Example

Darla was verbally and physically assaulted by a delivery man in her home. She blamed herself for letting the assailant into her home and for not stopping his behaviour. Initially, Darla's sense of her own survival efforts and the sequence in which the trauma occurred were confused and vague. After writing and talking about the trauma, then reading her own writing and processing her previous accounts of the trauma with the therapist, Darla remembered many ways that she had acted to protect herself. Darla was aided in providing links between seemingly inscrutable aspects of her experience: apparently meaningless behaviours on her part, the attack itself, and her survival being highly prized by a caring and empathic therapist. Thus, she was able to reconstrue herself as an active agent in ensuring her safety, rather than as an ineffective and powerless victim.

Intentional Future Metaconstruction

This reconstruction element involves the co-construction of a future for the client (sketching out several front mirrors and trying them on). Often, traumatized clients have no clear sense of the future. With others, the future is seen as presenting only more trauma. Extending the co-creative process of constructive bridging and intentional future metaconstruction involves composing possible future selves.

Case Example

Later in therapy, Gary felt that his depression had lifted and that he had resolved several traumatic incidents from his past, including the early sexual abuse. As termination of therapy was discussed, Gary became anxious and was unsure of a future that did not include the therapist. Gary and his therapist discussed a variety of conceivable challenges, victories and defeats. Then Gary would be asked to write and talk about how he might react to these situations; additional alternative reactions would then be explored in session. By co-constructing his future with the valued therapist, Gary came to see his therapist as an important internalized part of himself and of his future—even after the termination of therapy.

More Constructive Bridging

As intentional future metaconstruction is explored in therapy, new ground for constructive bridging becomes available. These iterative processes continue until the trauma is storied within the client's grand narrative as an important but integrated component of the overall story—one that has influenced but has not single-handedly determined the client's life.

CONCLUDING COMMENTS

Clearly, this presentation of a treatment model for post-traumatic stress lacks the technical precision of a treatment manual or a cognitive-behavioural regimen. As discussed under the 'Symptom Management' section above, there are places within this personal construct model of reconstruction for including such technical interventions. In describing this approach, I make the assumption that any professional psychotherapists reading this either can perform such technical interventions of their own accord or can access instructional resources to lead them through exposure/response prevention methods easily enough. In presenting the model here, I am concerned less with technical instruction and more with attempting to orient the therapist towards helping the 'whole' client. Technical interventions of the sort promulgated by manualized programmes tend to target the clients' *disorders* or *symptoms* as though they exist apart from the person and her or his identity. The theoretical framework presented here, and the broad technical conceptions outlined as 'Reconstruction Elements', are intended to centralize the client and her or his overall (social as well as symptom-based) functioning as the target of psychotherapy.

CHAPTER 22

Is Treatment a Good Idea?*

George A. Kelly

'Is treatment a good idea?' When one poses such a question to an audience like this—an audience dedicated to the mission of treating patients—he opens himself immediately to one of three charges: Perhaps he has nothing more to offer than the traditional answer and everyone hopes he will sit down as soon as he has said what he has to say. If not that, he must be a die-hard hereditarian who doesn't think crazy people can be helped and who is optimistic enough to think that his pessimism will be listened to. Or, perhaps, he is merely employing a speech-maker's sensational-ism in order to get folks to listen to what otherwise is going to be a very dull talk.

Now let me say at the outset that I do not want to be placed into any of these categories. What I have posed is an honest question that I believe is worth exam-ining carefully. Moreover, to show my good faith and make it clear that I am not merely dangling a question in front of you in order to make you keep your eyes open, let me say at the outset that my answer to this question is going to be 'No'. 'No, treatment is not a good idea.'

Now, will you examine, along with me, the notion of treatment itself—what it means—what it implies about the nature of man—and, in addition, some of the serious mistakes the idea of treatment has led us to make. I am inviting you to do this because I am convinced that a re-examination of the concept of treatment will have a salutary effect on what we all do as professional people.

First of all, I would like to say that, along with most of you, I still think it is good for people who are sick to get well. In addition, I still think there are things each of us can do to help them to get well. And I think some of those things are already being done here and there—not as often as they should be, perhaps, and maybe only in the out-of-the-way corners of hospitals and clinics, but still they are being done. Sometimes they are done by professional or administrative intent, and sometimes, you all would agree, in spite of it.

During the past century the notions of modern science have been extended to the realm of human behaviour. One of those notions is that everything that happens

---

*Address to a Conference on Treatment, 1958: US Veterans Administration Hospital, Sheridan, Wyoming.

International Handbook of Personal Construct Psychology. Edited by F. Fransella.
© 2003 John Wiley & Sons, Ltd.

can be explained in terms of what preceded it. More particularly, this means that if we know everything that is going on today we can put it together and tell exactly what will happen tomorrow. Of course, in the down-to-earth practical sense, it is impossible to know absolutely everything that is going on today. Besides, as some scientists have recently argued, even if today's events are known, their consequences can be predicted only probabilistically. But here I am not concerned with either of these two interesting reservations on scientific reasoning. What I am concerned about is the effect such reasoning has on the human enterprise, particularly when the human enterprise begins to involve itself with the alteration of human behaviour.

Most psychologists, when they try to think scientifically about human behaviour, boil it down to two notions—something that goes on independently of the person, usually outside his skin, and something he does which is attributable to that outside event. The former the psychologist calls a 'stimulus' and the latter—once he had invoked the notion of 'stimulus'—the psychologist has no choice but to call a 'response'.

This little solipsistic invention of 'stimulus and response' underlies the major portion of psychology's scientific efforts to figure out what people are up to. While these efforts have by no means proved futile, the reasoning upon which they are based forces a strong bias on what men try to do for each other. If a person's behaviour is faulty, change the stimulus—change the stimulus, for are not his responses attributable to events which preceded them? Once we start to think this way the net result is inevitably to focus our attention upon the treatment rather than upon the person who is in trouble, as if something inherent in the treatment itself carries the seeds that will sprout into behaviour.

Let us approach treatment from another angle. Suppose, instead of abstracting the constructs of 'stimulus' and 'response', we talk about persons in 'dynamic' terms. In psychiatric circles this is supposed to be good and if you are wise you will always be careful to use such language in the presence of properly educated people, unless you happen to be one of those poor benighted creatures known as a 'state hospital' psychiatrist. It has for some time been a matter of interest to me why it is that people who can afford to pay private fees always have 'dynamics', while those who can't have 'diagnoses'. I have observed also that the more fees you can afford to pay the more dynamics you are likely to have. But, then, this is not what I came here to talk about.

Dynamic interpretations explain human behaviour in terms of such notions as motives, needs, and incentives, or, if you have invested in the Freudian lexicon, in terms of such artistic inventions as oedipal strivings, hostility, libidinal cathexes, etc. While, as a model of human thought, this is more primitive than the stimulus–response—in fact, if the truth is to be known, even more primitive than Aristotelian thinking—it does provide certain advantages over its competitors. For example, the dynamic model envisions the determinants of human behaviour as residing within the person, a more helpful way of looking at the matter if you hope to see him accomplish anything.

Treatment, under the aegis of dynamic thinking, becomes a matter of uncovering psychological forces and mechanisms, of venting pent-up impulses, of supporting some self-critical evaluations and undermining others, and various other interventions in the turmoil of the person's psyche. But still, even under this system of thought, the determinants of behaviour, while now residing within the person, are abstracted from him as extra-personal entities and not altogether his own doings. Treatment continues to be undertaken as something imposed from without—something done to juggle the patient's dynamics. The person is still a 'patient' with all the inert passivity that that unfortunate term has implied throughout its long history.

May I approach my thesis from still another angle. Mankind has a long history of intolerance and brutality. Over the centuries this history has been unfolding itself alongside an equally impressive story of expanding humanitarianism. For a long time it has been firmly believed that when a person went off his rocker he should first be given loving admonishment, and if that did not work he should be punished good.

In the meantime, medical science had made great progress in treating illness. Naturally enough it occurred to some physicians like Pinel that it might be better to treat certain kinds of misbehaviour as if they were symptoms of illness rather than outcroppings of devilment. This way of thinking has led to the employment of far more humane methods of dealing with certain people. Incidentally, it has served to create an enormous paradox in our system of social thought; some people get solicitous treatment for their misbehaviour while others, judged to be ineligible, get punishment measured out to them. Thus we try to live under two quite different and quite incompatible psychological systems for explaining human behaviour and for deciding what we ought to do about misbehaviour.

Treatment, of course, seems to hold more promise than punishment. It seems more civilized to say that a person is acted upon by forces over which he has no control and that therefore the corrective measures must likewise be provided by an external agency. By this line of reasoning any person who finds that he has done something he should not, is constrained to start looking for someone who will treat him, and while he is waiting for the doctor to come he may apply a little first aid, such as figuring out how it happened that his mother—the witch—made him into the kind of a person he turned out to be. He won't get far with this on his own, of course, because it requires some pretty time-consuming rationalization, and some kind of treatment, at least in the big cities nowadays, is not likely to be long in arriving.

Now what has all this to do with the topic of this symposium: 'Therapeutic Roles in Patient Treatment'? As you have probably already guessed, I am for assigning the most important role to the patient himself—only, I would prefer not to call him a 'patient'. This means developing a kind of psychology that is not especially popular these days, a psychology that envisions human behaviour as something initiated by the person who does the behaving. As I see it, such a psychology would have to abandon such notions as 'stimulus' and 'response' as well as a lot of psychodynamic constructs that imply that the determinants of human behaviour are independent operants within the psyche. Personally, I would just plain throw them all out, but I would be willing to settle for a compromise if psychodynamic concepts were used differently.

Something else follows from this line of thought. From our present vantage point in the course of human thinking it now seems to be a historical misfortune that psychological problems were ever placed in the medical context of illness. The twenti-eth-century institution which has emerged as 'the hospital' is so conceived, orga-nized, and committed that it represents altogether too much that is unwholesome for the troubled mind. The societal features which enlightened mankind seeks to reform—a rigid class structure stratifying both for staff and patients, listlessness, futility, anonymity, loss of family and community relationships, irrational authori-tarianism, regimentation, economic helplessness, endless waiting to 'be treated' *for something to happen*[1] and passive conformity to 'treatment programs' *what the straw boss says is 'good for you'*[1] to mention only a few.

Most of what I have said thus far will seem negative and destructive. If treatment is such an inappropriate idea what then, one may well ask, are the roles that are to be played by those who want to help? Certainly one thing becomes clear about such roles: they are to be played out as person-in-relation-to-person roles rather than as specialist-in-relation-to-illness roles. The primary question to answer about a staff member is: what do disturbed persons do with him? His area and degree of com-petence, when the chips are down, are operationally defined not so much by his edu-cation and list of former job incumbencies as by the practical uses to which he is put by those who need his help.

Mankind's approaches to its psychological problems are in for some drastic revi-sion. The notion of treatment, derived as it is from our fumbling efforts to apply notions of scientific determinism to human troubles, misplaces the emphasis on the various external roles to be played. But restoration of the wholesome life is some-thing done by the person whose life it is. His, then, is the principal role, and any system of psychological thought which envisions other roles as more important than his will serve only to stagnate mankind's efforts and turn out, for somebody to take care of, a generation of helpless creatures who seek 'treatment' every time they slip up, rather than doing something about it themselves.

---

[1] Struck-out words were deleted by George Kelly and those in italics written in the document by hand in their place.

CHAPTER 23

An Audacious Adventure: Personal Construct Counselling and Psychotherapy

Franz R. Epting
University of Florida, USA

Marco Gemignani
University of Florida, USA

and

Malcolm C. Cross
City University, London, UK

Psychotherapy should make one feel that he has come alive.

(Kelly, 1980, p. 29)

The project of helping others to undertake profound changes in their lives is the central mission of personal construct psychology. It is undertaken within a very special relationship with someone who helps open up space for personal development and understanding. Perhaps the best way to view what has gone wrong is to envision the person as having become stuck or trapped. In the everyday course of events, one would be getting on with life and not need professional assistance. As a matter of course there would be an opening up of new possibilities for either expanding one's interests or refining existing projects or both. Something, however, has come up which has impeded growth, despirited or disoriented the person and has resulted in some degree of helplessness and hopelessness. In these circumstances, personal construct psychotherapy or counselling offers hope and helps the person to feel alive again. Feeling alive means much more than just getting out of the bog. It means getting on with the most creative aspects of what life might hold.

International Handbook of Personal Construct Psychology. Edited by F. Fransella.
© 2003 John Wiley & Sons, Ltd.

For the person in difficulty, the world has become solidified in such a way that there are no acceptable choices. There is at least boredom that often escalates to fear, dread or anxiety or the person escapes into fantasy. The central mission of the personal construct professional is to invite the person to see the world as pliable and as having the ability to offer up more possibilities than were seen on first inspection. For Kelly insists that one need not paint oneself into a corner. There are always choices and often choices that will offer relief and possibly an escape from some of the more dreadful aspects of the problem; if not escape, then more interesting corners in which to get stuck or choices that offer some level of human dignity while dealing with tragedy. It is often the case that the person has bought into some restricting social constructions of herself or her world so readily offered up by friends or injected into consciousness through the general social surround. She then takes these constructions to be real and sees no possibilities for viable change.[1] In order to explore just how soft this hard 'reality' might be, Kelly suggests casting our verbs in an invitational mood rather than in the usual indicative, conditional, subjunctive, or imperative moods, '. . . a verb could be cast in the form which would suggest to the listener that a certain novel interpretation of an object might be entertained' (see also Chapter 7, pp. 75–82). Such a restatement could leave 'both the speaker and the listener, not with a conclusion on their hands, but in a posture of expectancy' (1969d, p. 149). Following the lead of Hans Vaihinger (1924) in his philosophy of 'as if', Kelly is suggesting, in a pragmatic vein, that we abandon a slavish devotion to reality and start entertaining alternative constructions.

Cast in the invitational mood, the ultimate aim of personal construct psychotherapy is to enable the person to pursue full cycles of experience which consist of anticipation, investment, encounter, confirmation and disconfirmation, and terminate in constructive revision. By completing full cycles of experience a person is able to 'rise above what he thinks he knows and so often then to do better than he knows how' (Kelly, 1977, p. 11). In this way the person is able to transcend the obvious. In approaching any significant issue the person is invited to take an active stance in anticipating what might be possible. This is followed by an invitation to make a personal investment in what is anticipated; letting the anticipations matter in a personal way rather than remaining detached from them. The invitation is to go to a level of involvement where the person has to cope with circumstances on an embodied-primitive-emotional-preverbal level as well as in an articulate manner using words. Then is added the further invitation to truly encounter these life circumstances. That means making a commitment to be fully self-involved in the moment as well as affirmatively anticipate what self-implications these events might have; thereby entering into possibilities for self-alteration and/or situation redefinition. Then comes the courage to face the confirmation or disconfirmation of what has been intimately anticipated at the outset; recognizing the fact that disconfirmation might hold the more exciting possibilities for further growth. Finally there is the invitation to constructive revision whereby the person is asked to receive the full impact of the experience in full cycle and undertake profound life changes. In

---

[1] Gender balance, in personal pronouns, is attempted by using both forms, intermittently, throughout the chapter.

short, at the end of the cycle both the client and therapist are changed by the enterprise, for this is truly a reflexive approach to psychotherapy.

CONSIDERATION OF OTHER APPROACHES

Before presenting the structure and process of personal construct psychotherapy, it might be most helpful to locate personal construct psychology itself in relation to the major theoretical classifications of cognitive-behavioural, psychodynamic and humanistic theories.

Cognitive-Behavioural Therapies

On the surface of things, it might appear that personal construct theory and cognitive-behaviourism are very similar, both being cast on a conceptual-cognitive level. However, there are substantial differences between them. These are spelled out in Chapter 4 (pp. 41–49).

Psychodynamic Theories of Freud and Others

Comparing psychodynamic and personal construct theories, one does find common interest in the interior meaning of events. However, for the psychodynamic theorist, a person's words have to undergo a content-specific and theory-based unique interpretation in order to be understood. In contrast, the personal construct theorist views the nature of this unique interpretation as resting entirely with the client. While the psychodynamic approach relies on an essentially thermodynamic model, in which energy and instincts represent the basis of motivation, personal construct theorists do not rely on such deterministic explanations for understanding others. In personal construct theory, personal and social constructions replace the absolute and universal causes used in the psychodynamic approach. Personal construct theory also highlights the process of knowledge creation and optimal functioning in contrast to the psychodynamic approach that stresses psychopathology and universal conceptualizations of human behaviour formulated as a 'treatment'. As a consequence, in therapy the 'psychoanalyst must become a kind of crossword puzzle solver' (Warren, 1990, p. 454) while personal construct therapists and counsellors rely on how the client personally and socially construes the world.

Humanistic Psychotherapies

Here the picture shifts to seeing many more similarities than differences. Leitner and Epting (2001) have reviewed concepts such as levels of awareness, dignity, optimal functioning and so forth, showing that there are substantive similarities between the two positions. One important difference is that personal construct theory opposes the notion of an essential human nature and argues for the importance of invention over discovery in trying to discern the most telling aspects of a person (Butt et al., 1997a; Kelly, c. 1954). We are seen as constructing or inventing ourselves rather than finding our essential natures. For this reason personal construct psychology is very sceptical of the notion that there are human potentials patiently waiting to be discovered. Along the same lines, the notion of self-discovery or the idea of a true self is not espoused. In fact, personal construct theorists are always trying to get the concept of self out of the way. Self-consistency and being true to a real self are seen as the very things getting in the way of a person's trying out new ways of being and behaving. In terms of style, the personal construct therapist and counsellor are much more active than, for instance, a Rogerian would be (Raskin & Rogers, 1989). There are many more personal experiments to be run and direct lines of inquiry to be made into personal meanings than one would expect in a Rogerian approach.

THE THERAPEUTIC ENTERPRISE

In the normal course of events the therapeutic enterprise starts by focusing on the client's immediate concerns or problems. That does not mean that we want the client to stop voicing complaints and simply conform to existing conditions, nor does it mean that the problem is viewed in purely personal terms independent of the meanings the client has unwittingly accepted from the social surround. Instead the intention is for the client to come to the widest possible understanding of his or her situation in such a way that some change can take place in the direction of either undertaking personal change or mobilizing the courage needed to change social conditions or both.

Controlled Elaboration

Nevertheless, the place to start is in the present moment so that an elaboration of the complaint can take place. The aim of the elaboration is to enable the client to place the problems along a time-line, to be able to see them as temporary rather than permanent and then to see them as responsive to reconstruing, the passage of time and varying conditions.

That is all undertaken in what Kelly calls a *controlled elaboration* of the complaint and even leaves room for confrontation when carefully planned. The therapist or counsellor is responsible for bringing up obviously omitted topics and is also responsible for dealing with the client's possible anxious or angry reaction to them. The counsellor does not just toss out new material simply to see if the client will react strongly. Confrontation is undertaken only when the counsellor has a good idea, ahead of time, of how the client will construe the material. Throughout the therapy, the counsellor or therapist must engage in *differential predictions*. These are guide-posts marking danger areas which include notations on the counsellor's ability to predict what the client will say next in such a way that clearly differentiates the choices the client is making in developing the interview material.

All this planning in psychotherapy must be balanced with periods of spontaneity.

It is important for an effective therapist or counsellor to go beyond what he or she can precisely verbalize. It is a mistake to think of the personal construct therapist as someone who completely maps out and completely knows the personal constru-ing system of the client and then carefully says just the right (premeditated) thing. In Kelly's terms: 'The psychotherapist who dares not try anything he cannot verbally defend is likely to be sterile in a psychotherapeutic relationship' (Kelly, 1955/1991, p. 601/Vol. 2, p. 32). In addition, the effective therapist has the ability to be playful and creative and has the courage to be selectively self-disclosing (Epting, 1984; Epting & Suchman, 1999). See Chapter 10 (pp. 105–121) for an outline of some of the other skills that Kelly thought a personal construct psychotherapist and counsellor should have.

Transitive Diagnosis

Before any therapy is too far along, however, a *transitive diagnosis* is offered. The term 'diagnosis' might be better stated as a transitive understanding (Raskin & Epting, 1995). It is the planning stage of, and a mapping out of, the terrain using the professional constructs provided in personal construct theory. Personal construct diagnosis and these professional constructs are discussed more fully in Chapter 19 (pp. 201–209). Transitive diagnosis might also include notes to consider techniques borrowed from other theories. As Kelly (1980, p. 35) says, at the technique level:

> Personal construct psychotherapy does not limit itself to any pet psychothera-peutic technique. More than any other theory it calls for an orchestration of many techniques according to the therapist's awareness of the variety and nature of the psychological processes by which man works towards his ends.

After spending time elaborating the complaint using an accepting and sup-portive attitude, it is very important to move to the elaboration of the person or personal construing system. In fact, this is the central task of the psychotherapist. It gives a broader context for understanding the complaint in relation to other areas of the client's life. It also serves the purpose of broadening the therapeutic rela-tionship; a relationship made by a broadly defined problem-centred attitude in which the client and therapist are seen as co-investigators working on the client's issues. It takes the focus off the client and places it on to the task at hand. The focus is on finding a way for the client to move forward. It makes the client's issues the problem and not the client's way of being. It also reduces the dependency in the relationship and what others might call the transference. In fact, the personal con-struct approach to counselling and therapy sees transference as a potentially useful aspect of therapy and not something that gets in the way. Transference is the process whereby clients use their construing of how to handle another person and then transfers that, unchanged, to the therapist. One of the aims would be to help the client transfer only selected qualities and use them as tentative constructions. It gives clients a way of understanding themselves better.

Another way of elaborating the personal construct system is to use structured and partially structured psychological tests including the rep-test (see Chapter 9, pp. 95–103). Of equal importance is the use of self-elaboration procedures such as self-characterization where the person is asked to write out a description of himself as if a character in a play (see Chapters 11 and 38, pp. 123–131 and pp. 379–386). If that is too much for the client to manage, more structured questions might be used, such as 'Who are you?', 'What kind of person are you?', What kind of child were you?', or 'What kind of person do you expect to become?' Following that may be the elaboration of the *life-role* structure where the person starts to envisage changing over the years instead of in daily cycles. That may include what clients expect from therapy in conjunction with all this projected change.

At that point primary importance is given to invoking a progressive confrontation with alternatives in living where the client is asked 'What kind of action does this call for?', 'What could you have done?', 'What else could you have done?', and 'Having done that, what comes next?' Even further, a controlled elaboration by means of *prescribed activities* is often called for. In cognitive-behaviour therapy this is often called 'homework' but the emphasis in personal construct therapy is on exploring the meaning of the task rather than being concerned with its corrective nature as such. Clients are invited to engage in social, recreational or occupation activities to test out sets of understanding they are just beginning to grasp. 'Not all elaboration need be limited to verbalization in the therapy room. Some of the most important elaborations take place outside, and some of them are expressed only incidentally in words' (Kelly, 1955/1991, pp. 986–993/Vol. 2, pp. 299–304). After all, this approach to therapy is as much about action as it is about a verbalized way of knowing. It all might be extended further into play activities and creative production. In that way the person can begin to explore uncertain and vaguely grasped aspects of themselves and their world which cannot be explored in the more reality-based kinds of prescribed activities.

Tight and Loose Construing

One of the most important professional dimensions used in personal construct psychotherapy concerns the loosening versus the tightening of constructs. Much of the work in personal construct psychotherapy can be seen as helping clients to weave back and forth between loosening and tightening. Loose constructions are those notions of the world which vary in their meanings, whereas tight constructions are those which offer definite statements of structure and in which meaning can be clearly specified. Kelly describes creativity as a cycle involving the weaving back and forth between loose and tight constructs. That is a cycle that starts with loose conceptions which allow wonderful new insights. It is followed by a gradual tightening in such a way that some definite statement can be made or some act can be performed.

One of the most important areas for therapeutic gain, using this dimension, is the work done with the reporting of dreams. Dreams are the most loosened constructions that can be verbalized. The potential for gaining knowledge through loosening can offer insight into concealed reservoirs of experience. Of primary interest is the meaning which emerges out of loose construction as the dream is recalled. It is very important not to offer any type of interpretation in the early stages of reporting because a type of tightening may start to take place which could conceal the productive material contained in the loosened construction. Of special interest are *milepost dreams* which are ones that are profound in their implications. In these dreams the main themes of the client's life occur and should not be interpreted as they stand on their own. They offer the client the opportunity to grasp the monumental movement which is about to take place in therapy. Another special category of dream is the *preverbal dream*. These dreams are vague and filled with visual imagery, have little or no conversation, and are slow to unfold in the telling, seeming as much imagined as dreamt. Here the therapist is more active, helping the client to activate his or her creative imagination in order to allow some meaning to emerge either verbalized or as a felt sense.

Often the most intense and exciting aspect of personal construct counselling and therapy comes when client and therapist are ready to undertake techniques designed to invite the client to experiment with new ideas and new behaviours. It is the point when the client is ready to undertake constructive revision with all the profound implications this will involve. The constructs to be revised are often core constructs; ones on which the person's identity rests and ones on which the person relies to maintain life itself. In using interpretations as an aid in this process, it is important to remember that it is the therapist's role to suggest things but it is the client who really does the interpreting. The important task for the therapist is to gauge the client's readiness for constructive revision. Resistance to an interpretation is not seen as something used to thwart the therapist's design but rather is seen as either a protective reaction in the face of anxiety or an attempt to point to other important directions neglected thus far. When the client manifests anxiety and/or guilt when anticipating constructive revision, they are viewed as useful, not obstructive. Anxiety is the awareness that there is not yet sufficient structure provided in the interview for the client to take steps into the unknown. Therefore, the anxiety needs to be managed by the client through gaining more structure in order to ensure safety and make it possible to see the exciting aspects of anxiety in the face of new exploration. Guilt, on the other hand, is the awareness that core aspects of her identity have been shaken and work needs to be undertaken so that an emerging new identity can take place.

The central technique used for constructive revision is experimentation in which, initially, the therapist serves as the main validator of the new constructions. Experimentation may take the form of role playing in the therapy room. That can then be extended to new life-roles in relatively safe outside situations. Much careful preparation has to be undertaken before extensive outside experimentation begins. The client is given permission and is encouraged to enter into limited situations where something new will be expected of him. He is invited to set up specific expectations and to make both negative and positive predictions of what will happen to him. In addition, the client is invited to interpret the outlooks of others in the situation and to find evidence for his interpretation. If the client cannot manage it on his own, he is invited to act 'as if' he had the kind of support and encouragement that would give him the self-confidence needed to be in a given situation. Obstacles to this experimentation include both hostility and threat among other reactions. The hostile person tries to extort validation for his present system rather than experiment with it. This is because he feels backed into a corner; therefore additional time must be spent in making him feel comfortable before further experimentation can be undertaken. The threatened client, on the other hand, sees the experimentation as having far too many long-term implications and much time needs to be spent in trying to limit these implications as least long enough for him to actually get into the new situation.

Fixed Role Therapy

The final aspect of a therapeutic enterprise might be the use of fixed role therapy. If personal construct therapy is like rebuilding a ship under full sail one plank (construct) at a time—ripping up one or several planks at a time and slapping new ones in before too much water sinks the vessel—then fixed role therapy is like jumping ship for a brief period of time (Bannister, 1975). It is a way for the client to experience, briefly, being in the world in a different way. This is done not to 'fix' the person by having her adopt a new way of being, but to simply offer her an opportunity to experience herself and her world in a new way in order to demonstrate that change is possible and offer an opportunity to find out what new things might or might not fit (Epting & Nazario, 1987).

In the classical form, fixed role therapy begins by having the client write a brief characterization sketch describing herself. The therapist then prepares an enactment sketch based on the self-characterization and presents it to the client. Complete with a new name for the client, this sketch is a brief account of another person who is somewhat similar to the client but has one or two features that are quite different. The new features represent what the therapist thinks might be some growth opportunities for the client. After the presentation, the client and therapist modify it until the client is satisfied that enacting the new role is possible and even offers some fascination. Starting with role plays in the therapy room, the client is then invited to carry the new role out into the world. The amount of risk is calculated as each new outside situation is suggested and close contact is maintained with the therapist for support and reassurance. After about two weeks the experiment is ended and the client is invited to examine what has happened with an eye on selecting some aspects of the new role that she will start to make her own.

There have been many modifications of this procedure. It is most frequently used in a mini-fixed role form where the client is invited to take on just one new characteristic for a one- or two-day trial. In fact there might be several mini-fixed roles being carried out simultaneously. Brophy and Epting (1996) have even found good use of this procedure in a mentoring programme for a large corporation where the goal was to invite middle management executives to reinvent themselves.

IN A NUTSHELL

It is our hope that this chapter has provided the reader with something of the spirit of personal construct counselling and psychotherapy. We have tried to include most of the basic components of the therapy as outlined in Kelly's original work, but have taken the liberty of including some lines of thinking which have grown directly from the original formulation. Perhaps this chapter will serve as a reference point as readers consider the directions taken in related positions. Most of all it is our wish that the spirit of openness and sense of inquiry, so pervasive in the theory, comes across. Above all Kelly valued questions over conclusions. 'There is something exciting about a question, even one you have no reasonable expectation of answering. But a final conclusion, why that is like the stroke of doom: after it—nothing, just nothing at all!' (Kelly 1969l, p. 52).

CHAPTER 24

Personal Construct Psychotherapy and the Constructivist Horizon

Robert A. Neimeyer

University of Memphis, USA

and

Scott A. Baldwin

University of Memphis, USA

> Personal construct psychotherapy is a way of getting on with the human enterprise.
>
> (Kelly, 1969i, p. 221)

What is personal construct therapy, and how has it evolved across time? Franz Epting et al. have already addressed the first of these tandem questions in the preceding chapter, so we concern ourselves with the second question. Kelly continues the above quotation as follows:

> (psychotherapy) may embody and mobilize all of the techniques . . . that man has yet devised. Certainly there is no one psychotherapeutic technique and no one kind of interpersonal compatibility between psychotherapy and client. . . . Hence one may find a personal construct psychotherapist employing a huge variety of procedures—not helter skelter, but always as part of a plan for helping himself and his client get on with the job of human exploration and checking out the appropriateness of the constructions they have devised for placing upon the world around them. (1969i, pp. 221–222)

Considered closely, that original definition of psychotherapy emphasizes several features that are relevant to the evolution of personal construct therapy over the half-century of its development. Kelly viewed his therapy as simply an accelerated form of personal development; it has more to do with facilitating the essentially human 'effort after meaning' and experimenting with new social actions than with an arcane set of procedures for diagnosing and curing 'psychopathology'. Such therapy

International Handbook of Personal Construct Psychology. Edited by F. Fransella.

is technically eclectic, evolving to embrace all manner of techniques and procedures, whose variety is limited only by the imaginations of the therapist and client—and perhaps implicitly, by the historical and cultural framework that shapes and constrains their efforts. Despite this methodological openness, personal construct therapy maintains a certain level of conceptual consistency, carefully coordinating its change strategies in the light of a responsive reading of the client's unique efforts to engage life constructively.

This chapter discusses some of the ways in which contemporary personal construct therapists have extended Kelly's ideas to address a broader range of problems and generate an expanding repertory of interventions, while still exemplifying a recognizable therapeutic stance. We will therefore begin by considering the intellectual *zeitgeist* that has informed many of the developments in personal construct therapy, and note the major themes that define the stance of the therapist, before reviewing a representative sampling of recent developments in this clinical perspective.

THE CONSTRUCTIVIST HORIZON

In many respects, Kelly's vision of psychotherapy, although iconoclastic in the 1950s, proved to be a prophetic preface to the psychology of the next millennium. Sharpening existential themes in psychology that emphasized human agency and choice, Kelly nonetheless embedded the individual in a social world, emphasizing the identity-defining nature of *core roles* that the person constructs with reference to others. To a far greater extent than most psychologists of his day, Kelly offered an image of persons as authors of their own biographies, but in a way that acknowledged their anchoring in the social realm.

As psychotherapy grew beyond the psychoanalytic and behavioural orthodoxies that dominated the field in mid-century, other theorists began to elaborate similar constructivist ideas, sometimes consciously borrowing from Kelly, and sometimes appropriating these concepts from broader discourses. The result, by the early 1990s, was a loose confederation of constructivist psychotherapies joined by their resistance to more authoritative, objectivistic approaches that emphasized the therapist's power, and that viewed intervention as improving the client's 'reality contact' through challenging clients' 'irrational thinking' and training them in approved 'social skills' (Neimeyer, 1995). Instead, constructivist therapists focused on the way in which clients construct a model of self and world in the context of close attachment relationships (Guidano, 1991), articulate and symbolize their own internal complexity in experiential therapy (Greenberg et al., 1993), and maintain 'symptoms' that are coherent with their unconscious 'emotional truths' about life (Ecker & Hulley, 1996). Meanwhile, family therapy was being revolutionized by a wave of social constructionism, which focused on how problems are created and dispelled in the way they are formulated in language (Efran et al., 1990; see also Procter in Chapter 43.2, pp. 431–434). The result was a broad coalition of approaches sharing a 'family resemblance' with personal construct therapy, while moving the field in new directions (Neimeyer & Mahoney, 1995; Neimeyer & Raskin, 2000). (See also Chapter 4 on constructivism and constructionism, pp. 41–50.)

THE NARRATIVE APPROACH

One of these directions has been the *narrative trend*, the idea that human lives can be viewed as 'stories' that are formulated, told, and enacted on a social stage (Polkinghorne, 1988). In keeping with the postmodern Kellyian view that our identities are constructed rather than simply discovered, narrative theorists address the processes by which people can perform 'preferred' stories of who they are, or alternatively, live lives 'colonized' by a 'dominant narrative' that defines their identity only in terms of problems (White & Epston, 1990). Like the pre-emptive construing that Kelly cautioned could define someone as 'nothing but' a depressive, anorexic, borderline, or some other diagnostic category, dominant narratives can marginalize and obscure the person's resources and positive features.

Accordingly, narrative therapists draw attention to moments that clients resist the call of problem-saturated identities, and instead act in ways that are more self-nurturing and affirming of their relationships to others. Therapy then turns towards building an alternative story of who one is, by anchoring it in 'dependable strengths' the client has exemplified in the past (Forster, 1991), projecting the story into an anticipated future, and recruiting an audience of receptive others who will affirm the positive potentials being enacted in present relationships (Neimeyer, 2000; Neimeyer & Stewart, 2000).

As constructivist, social constructionist and narrative discourses have permeated the helping professions (see Chapter 4, pp. 41–49), personal construct theorists have found further inspiration in these trends, using them to extend their own distinctive contributions to clinical conceptualization and intervention. Before reviewing these developments, however, we will address a few remarks to the stance of contemporary personal construct therapists, insofar as it is in the context of the therapeutic relationship that clients are encouraged to articulate, test and revise those constructions on the basis of which they live.

THE STANCE OF THE THERAPIST

Perhaps one of the most unsatisfying aspects of many traditional psychological theories is that they do not provide a way to understand the theorizing of the theorist—most theories lack reflexivity (see Chapter 6, pp. 61–74, and Chapter 10, pp. 105–121). Dunnett and Miyaguchi (1993) point out: 'Like young children who forget to include themselves when counting the number of people in a room, psychologists have consistently failed to include themselves as humans to which psychological theories need to also apply' (p. 19). Kelly and subsequent constructivist theorists attempt to address this shortcoming in psychotherapy by providing an account of not only the client's behaviour, but also the therapist's, and stressing that a credulous, unassuming attitude on the part of the therapist is the foundation of any healthy therapeutic relationship. This credulous stance creates an accepting environment, in which clients need not feel defensive about their experience, but instead are free to 'try on' new constructs and meanings without the fear of judgement or rejection. With a clearer understanding of the problem at hand, the client and therapist can work together to develop potential solutions to the problem.

CLINICAL CONCEPTUALIZATIONS

Although personal construct theory has been applied to a vast range of clinical problems (see Chapter 19, pp. 201–209 and Chapter 20, pp. 211–222), we will concentrate on two—substance abuse and grief and loss—that convey some of the breadth
and novelty of this clinical perspective.

Substance Abuse

The ways in which reflexivity, a credulous approach, and creativity are manifested
in the clinical context can be illustrated by looking at how substance abuse problems are understood within a constructivist framework. According to many substance abuse experts, addiction is a disease. The disease process begins with one
drink of alcohol or one dose of heroin in a genetically vulnerable person, where-
upon the abuser progressively loses control, and experiences physical addiction,
social and occupational problems, medical complications and, in the worst case,
death.

In contrast to this traditional framework, constructivist theorists view substance
abuse not as the necessary consequence of a disease process, but as a method of
constructing or preserving meaning in a social environment (Burrell, 2002). For
example, consider the story that Burrell and Jaffe (1999) relate about Steve, a young
man struggling with cocaine addiction. Steve stated that his cocaine use was pointless and it led him to waste both time and money. Nevertheless, when viewed from
a constructivist point of view, his abuse was not pointless. For example, 'Steve
reported that when he wasn't focusing on cocaine, he usually thought about very
disturbing and experientially "overwhelming" aspects of his past and current life
(divorce, despair about the future, etc.). He felt like he was "living someone else's
life" and "lost"' (p. 53). Cocaine became a way for Steve to avoid the feelings of
being overwhelmed and lost—wasting money was preferable to facing these existential challenges.

If therapists view substance abuse problems in a constructivist light, a credulous
attitude to the client's problem and a creative implementation of interventions is
required. Addicts actively create meaning through the use of chemical substances,
meaning which is highly personal and often idiosyncratic. Moreover, when problems are deeply ingrained, maintaining them can become a purposeful activity that
protects the client's core identity—even if this identity is problematic (Klion &
Pfenninger, 1997). Because of the personal and identity-defining nature of the
problem, therapists must adopt a credulous attitude to discover its significance to
the client. In the case of substance abuse, pat interventions would stifle the exploration of the deep meanings of addiction. Suppose Steve had just been told that he
was an addict because he had an addictive disease and protocol interventions had
been used. Perhaps Steve would have reduced his cocaine use, but he might never
have confronted his existential problems, for they never would have even been considered. His addiction would have forever remained pointless and without meaning.
But the creative therapist could, together with the client, create highly personal solutions to the problem. One such intervention is the tendency of narrative therapists

to 'externalize' the problem, by regarding cocaine as an intruder into Steve's life, one that beguiles him into regarding the drug as a comforting friend, while insidiously destroying his sense of self and relationships with others. Once the effects of 'cocaine's behaviour' are clearly recognized, they can be resisted, and a less drug-saturated identity can be constructed and socially validated by others (Winslade & Smith, 1997).

Grief and Loss

In traditional psychological theories, mourning is understood as a process of 'letting go' of a loved one who has died, and grieving is depicted as a stage-like process of adapting to this harsh emotional reality. Prolonged signs of grief such as enduring sadness and longing are in this view considered symptoms to be medically managed or eliminated with the goal of fostering recovery, resolution or 'moving on'. In contrast, the overarching proposition animating constructivist work in this area is that *grieving is a process of reconstructing a world of meaning that has been challenged by loss* (Neimeyer, 2002b). Issues of meaning-making in the wake of loss had of course received some attention in earlier work on bereavement (Marris, 1974), but for the most part this had been a side note to a psychiatric preoccupation with acute symptomatology of grieving construed in largely pathological terms. But by the 1990s a new breed of grief researchers began to attend to the ruptured assumptive world of the bereaved person, the cognitive processes by which the bereaved cope with loss, and the post-traumatic growth displayed by many of those who suffer adversity. Likewise, scholars began to take a second look at time-worn assumptions about the need to 'withdraw emotional energy' from the one who had died, in order to 'reinvest' it elsewhere. Instead, thinkers were beginning to focus on the potentially sustaining continuing bonds the bereaved construct to the deceased, and the active processes by which they strive to 'relearn the world' in the wake of loss (Neimeyer, 2001a).

An initial constructivist contribution to this reorientation took place at the juncture of grief theory and personal construct theory, conceptualizing loss in terms of the traumatic assault on the survivor's world of meaning (Neimeyer & Stewart, 1996). The guiding metaphor in this work was the *self-narrative*, defined as the life story one both enacts and expresses that gives a sense of coherence to one's identity over time. In this view, traumatic loss disrupts the continuity of the narrative construction of self, dislodging the individual from a sense of who he or she is (Neimeyer, 2000). For example, the struggle to incorporate traumatic events within one's self-narrative can leave one with a fragmented sense of autobiographical continuity through time, much as a previously naïve conscript into the Vietnam War might survive horrific experiences of combat that his fellow infantrymen did not, only to find it impossible to build a bridge between the person he once was and the person he has become. Traumatic losses can introduce sharp experiential discrepancies into the survivor's self-narrative, while at the same time challenging the individual's capacity to include the traumatic events into the pre-existing construct system. Adaptations of repertory grid technique (see Chapter 9, pp. 95–103), which prompt the traumatized person to compare and contrast 'chapters' of her life (for example, 'me as a young mother', 'me as a widow') on important life themes (for example, *secure* versus '*at sea*') have proved illuminating both in grief counselling (Neimeyer et al., 2000) and in more formal research efforts.

Although grid technique can aid in the articulation of meaning systems disrupted by loss, broader narrative methods also can provide a valuable glimpse of how people accommodate death in their life stories. For example, Neimeyer and his colleagues[1] (Neimeyer, 2001b) invited hundreds of bereaved people to respond to probing questions regarding (a) the *sense* they had made of their loss experience, (b) any form of unexpected *benefit* or life lesson the experience had brought them, and (c) and progressive or regressive shifts they had noticed in their sense of personal *identity* in the wake of the loss. They found that bereavement is accompanied by a painful but profound growth for many people, who reported that the experience made them appreciate the brevity of life (19%), or left them more sensitive and open to others (15%). However, these positive forms of meaning reconstruction were by no means assured, as others emphasized how their losses left them sadder and more fearful (12%), or made it harder for them to be close to others (6%). Thus, attention to the meanings people place upon their bereavement experience, as opposed to a pre-emptive focus on presumably universal grief symptoms, highlights the remarkable individuality in how people respond to loss, in ways that leave some resilient, and others as candidates for psychotherapeutic help.

One of the strengths of a constructivist approach to loss is its encouragement of imaginative practices—biographical, interview-based, reflective, metaphoric, poetic and narrative—that help bereaved people take perspective on their losses and weave them into the fabric of their lives (Neimeyer, 2001b, 2002a). Some of these consist of straightforward adaptations of personal construct techniques, such as 'loss characterizations' that invite survivors to ponder in writing who they are 'in light of their loss,' through a modification of Kelly's self-characterization technique described in Chapters 11 (pp. 123–131) and 38 (pp. 379–386). Others involve creative exercises to foster greater reflexivity through writing about the 'life imprint' of the lost loved one on the bereaved person's own life or the videotaping of storytelling with a seriously ill family member prior to her or his death.

One unanticipated offshoot of this work has been the discovery by other clinicians and helping professionals that a constructivist and narrative approach provides a more coherent and useful framework for their best practices (for example, the creation of meaningful rituals; transformative procedures for restoring a sense of community in the wake of violation or loss) than did traditional theories (Neimeyer & Tschudi, 2002). Such reports are highly affirming as, in the words of an insightful participant in one recent meaning reconstruction workshop, 'we as bereavement professionals finally have a chance to put our practice into theory'.

---

[1] This work has been pursued over the last two years in conjunction with Adam Anderson, James Gillies and Scott Baldwin, who are currently studying the relationship between intensified grieving and such factors as the bereaved person's continuing bond to the deceased, and various narrative themes and processes in their accounts of loss.

PSYCHOTHERAPEUTIC FORMATS AND PROCEDURES

Apart from the interventions linked to particular presenting problems such as sub-stance abuse or traumatic loss, personal construct theorists have also devised a wide range of procedures that can be flexibly applied to a great range of clinical issues. To supplement coverage of individual and family therapy in other chapters, we will look at innovations in group work that trace their roots directly to personal con-struct theory.

Interpersonal Transaction Group

First introduced by Landfield (1979) as a means of exploring socialization pro-cesses in small groups, the Interpersonal Transaction or IT format has proved to be a flexible and powerful approach to brief therapy. The distinctive structure of IT groups is grounded in Kelly's Sociality Corollary, 'with its emphasis upon "constru-ing the construction processes of the other" as a prerequisite for enacting mean-ingful social roles' (Neimeyer, 1988, p. 181). IT groups use what are termed rotating dyads, in which group members engage in a series of one-on-one interactions with other group members to converse about topics agreed upon in advance as relevant to the group's problems (for example, 'ways people understand and misunderstand me', 'positive and negative things about getting close to others'). The intimate context of disclosure, in combination with the 'bipolar' phrasing of the discussion topics, encourages a permissive exploration of similarities and differences among group members. In this way, IT groups provide psychotherapists with a 'happy medium' between the sometimes threatening atmosphere of process-oriented groups and the rigid, impersonal style of psycho-educational groups. The primary aim of the IT group is in harmony with other constructivist therapies, 'since [the group] emphasizes the elaboration of a broader range of social construing without first having to invalidate the client's existing constructions' (Neimeyer, 1988, p. 182).

IT groups consist of six to twelve members and meet in a room large enough to allow for the rearranging of chairs for the dyads. The group members begin the session by discussing an assigned topic with each member of the group (rotating dyads) for about five minutes. Leaders are encouraged to set guidelines for these discussions, encouraging members to listen carefully to each other and allow their disclosures to evolve or deepen across their successive encounters. Following the dyadic phase, the members reconvene to discuss their experiences in the dyads, aided by the therapist's 'bridging questions' to help them integrate personal obser-vations into the plenary group format, for example: 'What did you learn that most surprised you?', 'Whose experience did you most identify with, and why?' The length of this phase varies from 15 minutes to one hour depending on the purpose of the group. Often the groups end in a ritual of integration, sharing food and drinks while members casually interact (Neimeyer, 1988).

Empirical studies of IT groups have suggested that they have beneficial effects, particularly for such clients as incest survivors, who have grappled with issues related to threat and betrayal in close relationships (Alexander et al., 1991). There are several potential reasons for the success of the IT group that relate to its distinctive format and structure. Because all group members participate equally in the dyads, there tends to be even group participation, high levels of group cohesion, and the development of heightened empathy for other group members. Participants experience themselves not simply as disturbed and distressed patients, but also as healthy, supportive listeners. The most important advantage of the IT group could lie in its adaptability, as therapists can 'tweak' the structure of the dyad interactions to address special problems (Neimeyer, 1988). For example, therapists can participate in the rotating dyads to provide more individual attention to needy group members, or gradually 'fade out' dyadic interactions in longer-term groups once high cohesion among members is attained (see Neimeyer, 1988, p. 188, for more suggestions).

Multiple Self-Awareness Groups

Like IT groups, Multiple Self-Awareness groups (Sewell et al., 1998) have a decidedly constructivist orientation and, perhaps, an even more postmodern flavour. The structure of the group revolves around its conception of the self. Most psychologists would conceptualize a healthy self 'as a dominant single entity in control of all aspects of psychological functioning' (Sewell et al., 1998, p. 60). The constructivist theorist, however, tends to take an alternative view, contending that identity is better conceptualized as a 'community of selves' (Mair, 1977) than as a fully coherent and essential 'I'. That is, various partial identities are organized as distinctive subsystems of constructs associated with different self-roles. This 'decentralized' view might seem strange or even pathological to some, but this is likely to be a reflection of how dominant is the accepted view of a unified self.

The aim of Multiple Self-Awareness groups is to provide a stage on which group members can explore the role of these multiple selves in their interpersonal relationships. After the group members have an understanding of the concept of multiple selves, time is spent eliciting each participant's different identity characteristics, such as shy or incompetent, and creating character names for each of these partial identities, such as Mr Wallflower or Little Man. The group members are then assigned to write 'autobiographies' for each of these characters. This writing exercise facilitates an understanding of the role each self has played or continues to play in the group members' lives. Next, the group leader helps to construct a scenario in which each member plays a role, perhaps a fictional joint outing on which they must all decide, or the allocation of responsibilities for running a make-believe business.

The catch is that each member must select one of his or her characters to take part in the collective enactment. This exercise provides a powerful method by which group members can understand the ways in which their selected role (that is, the character they play—Mr Wallflower) influences their interactions with others. Following this exercise, participants process the results, achieving greater clarity about the intrapersonal and interpersonal dynamics that shape their relational styles.

RETROSPECT AND PROSPECT

Working in a distinctively postmodern *zeitgeist*, present-day personal construct theorists have extended the boundaries of Kelly's original vision, while also drawing inspiration from other constructivist, social constructionist, and narrative perspectives that share some of its iconoclastic premises. In this brief chapter we have tried to suggest the vitality of this perspective by surveying some of the ongoing contributions of personal construct theorists to the conceptualization of human problems, as well as to their treatment.

CHAPTER 25

Experiential Personal Construct Psychotherapy

Larry Leitner
Miami University Oxford, Ohio, USA

and

Jill Thomas
Miami University Oxford, Ohio, USA

> Our constructions of our relations to the thinking and expectancies of certain other people reach down deeply into our vital processes. Through our construction of our roles we sustain even the most autonomous of life functions. These are indeed core role structures.
>
> (Kelly, 1955/1991, p. 909/Vol. 2, p. 246)

Experiential personal construct psychotherapy (Leitner, 1988) is based upon an elaboration of Kelly's Sociality Corollary. That corollary, more than any other, provides the basis of an extension of personal construct psychology into the profound joys and terrors of relationships, the central concern of experiential personal construct psychotherapy.

OVERVIEW OF THE SOCIALITY COROLLARY AND ROLE RELATIONSHIPS

Kelly considered the Sociality Corollary his most important theoretical statement, and here he introduced relationships in the most provocative of ways. As Stringer and Bannister (1979, p. xiv) say:

> But for Kelly, the person, which is all that his psychology deals with, was only constituted in relations with others; constructs were chiefly available through interactions with others and obtained their meaning in the context of that interaction.

International Handbook of Personal Construct Psychology. Edited by F. Fransella.
© 2003 John Wiley & Sons, Ltd.

In other words, one *is* because one is in relation to others. Human being, human meaning-making, cannot be understood apart from the profound world of inter-personal relations.

One of the implications of the Sociality Corollary is that people need profoundly intimate contact with others in order to live a life filled with richness and meaning (see Leitner, 1985, for an elaboration of this aspect of the corollary). These rela-tionships are based upon sharing core meanings with another, meanings so central to our lives that we may choose to die rather than give them up. Thus, in a ROLE relationship (a relationship based upon such sharing), you hold the central identity of another person in your hand. (We capitalize 'ROLE' in order to distinguish Kelly's more profound use of the term from the traditional sociological definition.) The choice to engage in such relationships and the affirmation of these most central aspects of one another creates a powerful sense of wonder, of awe (Leitner & Faidley, 1995). No wonder such relationships provide the foundations of life itself.

Sometimes, instead of affirming, one may invalidate the core of another's being. Leitner (1985) details how such disconfirmations can lead to a conglomeration of threat, fear, anxiety, hostility and guilt, which he termed 'terror'. Thus, ROLE rela-tionships may not only enrich but may also damage (even destroy) psychological life. Not surprisingly, then, people also choose to limit or avoid ROLE relationships, leading to the experience of safety yet the emptiness of an existence filled with strangers rather than unique, subjective, evolving, persons. Engaging clients in that human struggle between the richness yet terror of true intimacy versus the safety yet emptiness of isolation is the central aspect of experiential personal construct psychology.

RETREATING FROM ROLE RELATIONSHIPS

As a ROLE relationship is one in which two persons are intimately interconnected through the mutual construing of the process of the other, a retreat from such rela-tionships is defined in terms of the minimization or distortion of the essential com-ponents of them. A ROLE relationship is the construction of the very process of the aliveness of the other, involving a profound connection to, yet ultimate separa-tion from, the other. There are many ways in which these two aspects—connection and separation—are minimized and distorted as people retreat from the terrors and joys of ROLE relating. In any case, when we retreat from ROLE relationships, we numb ourselves to the interpersonal world, and others become more exclusively objects for our needs or means to our ends (Leitner, 1999b).

People can retreat from ROLE relationships through a denial of the connection inherent in them. The evolving, wondrous, awe-full subjectivity of the other is minimized or ignored. Sometimes this retreat manifests itself through physically distancing from the other (for example, breaking off relationships as soon as you know the other person is invested in you). At other times, that retreat occurs through a psychological distancing (for example, being 'too busy' to invest time and energy into the other). People can use sexuality, control, anger, humour or any of the other myriad forms of human interaction to limit connection with the other.

In all of these cases of retreat through denial of connection, the need to be separate, to protect oneself from injury by the other is paramount (Leitner, 1985).

People can also retreat by denying the fact that there are two *separate* persons connecting in a ROLE relationship. Here, one actually limits the potential for profound connection in the relationship by becoming fused, eliminating the sense of separateness, of the individuality of both parties. For such people, any indication that *you* are separate from, other than, *us* is experienced with great terror. I will be very threatened by the parts of me that are different from you. Often, this results in my ignoring or attempting to eradicate those aspects of my meaning system. Again, people can use all of the innumerable forms of human interaction to attempt to fuse with the other (Leitner et al., 2000).

RECOGNIZING RETREATS FROM ROLE RELATIONSHIPS

Both styles of retreating minimize the experience of co-creating a shared reality in a ROLE relationship. In the first style, I attempt to deny you the power to affirm or disconfirm my heart and soul, thus minimizing your presence by limiting my ability to be fully present. The second style attempts to give you all of the power to define you, me and us, thus discounting my presence and distorting yours. However, because we need to connect with and separate from a constantly evolving other, it often is difficult to recognize when someone is *excessively* retreating from ROLE relationships.

The first principle in recognizing excessive retreating is to use the client's experience of life. Is life rich, meaningful, filled with satisfaction and zest? Or is life basically empty, unemotional, meaningless? Can I say what I need to say to the others who are close to me or do I end up not being as open as I need to be? Do I truly feel like I understand the essence of the important others in my life? Do they believe that I really understand the central aspects of their being? Do I feel profoundly understood by these others? Do they believe they understand me in great depth? Trusting the client's experience around questions like these can be a profound indication of whether the client is excessively retreating from ROLE relationships.

In addition, our problems, like all experiences, can be seen as a communication from us, to us, about us (Leitner et al., 2000). If we have the courage to explore our problem credulously (that is, believing that it is telling us about an inner truth to our life), we often can see the ways that we are excessively retreating from ROLE relationships.

Most importantly, the client's struggles over ROLE relationships will be a part of the therapy relationship itself. The therapy relationship, then, can become a living laboratory (Leitner, in press) for exploring the ways the client (and the therapist) approach and retreat from ROLE relationships. The therapist, then, through interaction with the client, can come to understand the client's (and the therapist's) style of relating to others in intimate relationships and can develop hypotheses about the client's excessive retreating which can be either validated or invalidated by the client (Leitner & Guthrie, 1993). In some ways, the therapist's most important task is to safeguard the therapy relationship such that life-changing transformations might occur.

LEVELS OF AWARENESS

Psychological problems in experiential personal construct psychology are defined in terms of the retreat from the risks and joys of ROLE relationships. Related to this, it is important to note that there are aspects to our construction of experience that exist at different levels of awareness. We are well aware of some of our meanings and can readily experience life through them frequently. Other meanings exist at a lower level and can only be glimpsed when the right relational context is present. Many core constructs exist at a lower level of awareness because of the profound threats and invalidations experienced by the person (Leitner, 1999a). Many of these meanings are at our core and are crucial to our ability to engage in ROLE relating.

Core meanings are ones that are central to our psychological existence; they are not isolated, cognitive events. Rather, they exist at a deeper, more integrated level. As such they are experienced physiologically as well as psychologically. This is an elaboration of Kelly's view that preverbal construing is linked with psychosomatic problems. Experiential personal construct psychology therefore works extensively with the body as a means of accessing deeper levels of experience, which are ultimately tied to one's tendency to engage in or retreat from intimate relations. A critical aspect of life-changing therapy is to provide the relational context that helps raise the levels of awareness of these meanings. In so doing, the therapist may eventually help the client to reconstrue terrible injuries in ways that help to enrich relational life by negotiating a more meaningful balance between interpersonal engaging and retreating.

DIAGNOSING HUMAN MEANING-MAKING

In experiential personal construct psychotherapy, as in personal construct psychotherapy, a diagnosis is not a static label but rather suggests a means of helping the client continue to evolve and elaborate his or her system of meaning in such a way that enriches life. Kelly terms this a transitive diagnosis, as it is a transition for the client from the past and present to the future (see Chapter 19, pp. 201–209).

In experiential personal construct psychotherapy, a diagnosis can be made on three axes, pointing to ways in which people negotiate ROLE relationships, thus indicating ways of helping people change (Leitner et al., 2000). The first axis of diagnosis concerns developmental structural arrests, essentially a freezing of the construing process that occurs with trauma. During development, many important meanings about self, other and relationship are created, and if trauma occurs before certain meanings are created, a person may face serious difficulties throughout life.

The process of meaning-making involves not only the creation of meaning but action based on these meanings. The second axis of this diagnostic system describes problematic styles of action in relationships in terms of dependencies and distancing. While dependency in and of itself is not problematic, we are concerned with how one handles one's dependencies—either underdispersing, overdispersing or avoiding them (see Chapter 16, pp. 171–180). Psychologically or physically distancing is also an unhelpful way of interacting interpersonally.

The third axis of this diagnostic system deals with the experiential components of human meaning-making. Leitner and Pfenninger (1994) describe nine aspects of optimal functioning (discrimination, flexibility, creativity, responsibility, openness, commitment, courage, forgiveness and reverence), indicating not only struggles faced by many in relation to others, but also great strengths seen in those trying to negotiate the complicated and ambiguous interpersonal world. Overall, the goal of diagnosis in experiential personal construct psychotherapy is to discover both strengths and struggles in ROLE relationships that point to systems to help the client to find ways to enrich life with relational meaning.

THE THERAPY RELATIONSHIP

Experiential personal construct psychology involves the client in the human struggle over 'engaging in' versus 'retreating from' ROLE relationships in the lived encounter in the therapy room. It is the means through which the therapist helps the client to explore and identify struggles as well as to explore alternatives. As such, the relationship between the therapist and the client becomes the healing instrument. The therapist and the client each bring ways of approaching and retreating to this relationship, often manifesting themselves through the experience of transference and countertransference in therapy.

Transference and Countertransference

Experiential personal construct psychology elaborates on Kelly's classic views of transference and countertransference by seeing them in terms of the struggles over ROLE relationships described above. In essence, these experiences are communications about our excessively retreating from ROLE relationships due to previous relational wounds we have experienced. With transference, for example, the client is acting in the current relationship as if the (potential) wounds from previous relationships are real. In other words, rather than experiencing the therapist as a unique person, the client is assuming that the therapist is like people who have been injuring to the client in the past. In this manner, the client objectifies the therapist and retreats from the ROLE relationship. A major aspect of experiential personal construct psychology involves dealing with the transference material presented by the client. In general, therapists need to deal with more pervasive transference issues that could threaten the therapy relationship earlier and more aggressively than more circumscribed transference experiences or those that are less of a direct threat to the continuation of therapy.

Countertransference involves experiences in which the therapist is retreating from the intersubjective connection of the ROLE relationship. Similar to transference, countertransference is an objectification of the client as a way of dealing with previous wounds of the therapist. A major aspect of the role of the therapist is to monitor, recognize and utilize the countertransference and forms a major part of personal construct psychotherapy training. As a matter of fact, a major difference between the skilled and the unskilled therapist involves the skilled therapist's ability to recognize not only more subtle countertransferences but also to use the countertransference to further the work of therapy (Leitner, 1997).

Validation of Interventions

A therapist experiencing countertransference struggles is seeing the client in ways other than as a subjective process of construing and creating. Not surprisingly, interventions based upon countertransference struggles often miss the mark, as they do not accurately reflect the client's lived struggles in the world. Therapists can learn about their countertransference struggles by paying attention to the ways that clients tell them that they are accurate or inaccurate in their interventions. Experiential personal construct psychology relies on the client's experience to tell the therapist whether or not the intervention is on target (Leitner & Guthrie, 1993).

For Kelly, behaviour is an experiment—a way of asking questions of the world. The therapist's behaviour, then, is often the therapist's way of asking questions about the construing of the client. The client's response to the intervention is the validational material of therapy. Experiential personal construct psychology holds that the therapist's intervention is validated to the extent that the ROLE relationship with the client becomes deeper, new material is introduced into the therapy, and the client's problem decreases (Leitner & Guthrie, 1993). Of course, part of the art of therapy involves inferring validation or invalidation when the signals from the client are more 'mixed'. For example, the ROLE relationship deepens but the client's problem increases in severity.

The Timing of Interventions

Interventions can be invalidated because the therapist has fundamentally misunderstood the construing of the client. All too often, the therapist understands certain aspects of the client's construing but fails to grasp other, more fundamental aspects. In those situations, the therapist might be correct in the assessment of a part of the problem but wrong in the assessment of the client's present ability to tolerate dealing with that issue. Such problems in the timing of interventions are a central issue of working with countertransference within experiential personal construct psychology.

Many therapies have been damaged by interventions that were poorly timed. Therapists who too aggressively force certain issues into the conversation risk damaging their clients. On the other hand, clients often have much greater strength and courage than the therapist gives them credit for, and the therapist does a disservice by delaying introducing a topic when the client is able to deal with it. Typically, therapist anxiety is at the root of mistiming interventions. For example, some therapists feel the need to impress the client with how brilliant their insights are and intervene prematurely. These therapists lack faith that the client will construe them as they see themselves. Others do not have faith that their clients will arrive at the issue in their own time, an implicit vote of non-confidence in the person of the client. The anxiety behind missed interventions lies in the therapist not trusting that the client is strong, mature or courageous enough to wrestle with painful issues. Views of the client as too fragile, too weak, too frightened are implicitly disrespectful and disempowering. When interventions are crisp and well-timed, powerful things happen in the therapy. 'The therapy relationship deepens; the client feels more alive, connected, heard by the therapist; the client's dilemmas seem a bit more solvable' (Leitner, 2001, p. 109).

Optimal Therapeutic Distance

Optimal therapeutic distance, a blend of the experience of connection and separation inherent in a ROLE relationship, is experienced when the psychotherapy relationship is at its best. When optimally distant, I am close enough to my client's experience to feel the client's feelings inside of me and separate enough to recognize these feelings as my client's, not mine (Leitner, 1995). In other words, I am powerfully subsuming the client's process of meaning creation. In contrast, 'therapeutic' unity is experienced when the therapist is so close to the client that the client's experience is felt as the therapist's own. 'Therapeutic strangers' is the experience of being so distant that the therapist cannot feel with the client.

When optimally distant, the therapist can resonate deeply with the felt meanings of the client. Interventions are powerfully validated by the client as the therapist can say what needs to be said in the ways it needs to be said. In contrast, 'therapeutic' unity and 'therapeutic' strangers illustrate the experience of countertransference. Skilled therapists always monitor the connection with the client, quickly recognizing when they are not optimally distant. With that recognition comes exploration of why the therapist is not optimally distant, revealing important aspects of the client's struggles.

THE THERAPIST AS IMPROVISATIONAL ARTIST

Obviously, understanding another's process of construing is a challenging task. One has to use the content of constructs to infer the process of construing. Further complicating this task, most therapy involves the therapist using the client's words to infer the client's constructs. In other words, we are interpreting symbols as we engage another. Obviously, as the process of coming to understand another's process of construing is inexact and somewhat ambiguous in general, the process of deeply connecting with a client who may be completely petrified by intimacy challenges the therapist to be most creative (Leitner & Faidley, 1999). The therapist's use of symbolism, plus regressing in the service of the ROLE relationship, are two ways to attempt to connect with the client.

SYMBOLISM

Words are not constructs but are verbal labels that we think best capture the meaning of a construction; they are symbols of the underlying meaning rather than being the meaning itself. Kelly described symbols as a 'very useful' way to shape experience. He also defines communication as 'a matter of reproducing the symbolic element in hopes of eliciting a parallel construct in another person' (Kelly, 1955/1991, p. 140/Vol. 1, p. 98). The therapist needs to constantly remember that the client's words may not mean what the therapist thinks and should frequently check with the client to increase confidence that the therapy dyad is connecting (Faidley & Leitner, 2000).

Other meanings defy words, lying at a non-verbal level not describable in language. However, when the therapist creatively uses language to test an understanding of the client, the client may be able to grasp these words and begin to express the construction in word symbols. Still, other symbols simply cannot be grasped adequately by words, no matter how creative the therapist. There may be no words to capture the precise meaning for the person. In these cases, the therapist may need to create other ways to symbolize these meanings in order to communicate an understanding of them to the client. For example, the therapist may infer meanings through the client's facial expression, posture or body movement. Faidley and Leitner (2000) describe the technical principles behind dealing with symbols in the therapy relationship.

REGRESSION IN THE SERVICE OF THE ROLE RELATIONSHIP

Regression in the service of the ROLE relationship is another way of describing the artistry necessary for life—changing psychotherapy. When I regress in the service of the ROLE relationship, I lose conscious awareness of my being a separate individual. My client's world and experiences dominate my experiential field and my 'self' disappears. We call this 'regression' as there is a way that, at those moments, there is no sense of 'you' and 'me' as separate entities. However, it is not 'therapeutic' unity as my sense of separateness is still present, although it is outside of my awareness, in the background, much like my e-mail program while I work on a paper.

SUMMARY

This chapter has provided a brief overview of experiential personal construct psychotherapy, based on an elaboration of Kelly's Sociality Corollary. This therapy holds that deeply intimate interpersonal connections are the foundations of life itself and the fountain of awe and reverence. However, the nature of those intimate, rewarding connections requires risking injury to the most central aspects of our personhood, which can ultimately be terrifying. As such, in order to live a rich and meaningful life, one must risk terror to experience joy. It is a complicated and constant struggle for all who choose to engage in ROLE relating. Many, as an alternative, choose to retreat from these relationships, opting for safety but emptiness. Through the therapy relationship, co-created by the client and the therapist, experiential personal construct psychotherapy creatively and respectfully attempts to engage clients in the struggle between approaching and retreating and to help them to continue to negotiate the terrifying yet awe-full world of ROLE relationships.

CHAPTER 26

The Evidence Base for Personal Construct Psychotherapy

David Winter

University of Hertfordshire and *Barnet,*
Enfield and Hanrigey Mental Health Trust, UK

> It is quite possible and thoroughly reasonable for a personal construct approach to psychology to lend itself to the requirements of empirical science. Indeed, if the notion of science is taken seriously as refinement of the psychology of man, something like the psychology of personal constructs is a natural consequence. Moreover, such a notion extends from the experimental laboratory to that special kind of laboratory we call the therapy room.
>
> (Kelly, 1959a, p. 54)

Clinical practice is increasingly required to have a demonstrable evidence base, or to be 'empirically validated' by research findings. In the USA, systems of managed health care and insurance companies generally require evidence of the efficacy of a particular therapeutic approach before agreeing to fund it, and may prescribe what form, and how many sessions, of therapy a client should receive. Although in Europe clinicians are currently allowed a little more freedom than this (Strauss & Kachele, 1998), the same trends are apparent. For example, a review of policy on psychological therapies by the British Department of Health states that:

> ... it is unacceptable ... to continue to provide therapies which decline to subject themselves to research evaluation. Practitioners and researchers alike must accept the challenge of evidence-based practice, one result of which is that treatments which are shown to be ineffective are discontinued.
>
> (Parry & Richardson, 1996, p. 43)

The British Department of Health also commissioned a review of psychotherapy research findings, entitled *What Works for Whom?* (Roth & Fonagy, 1996), to assist health care purchasers to decide on the appropriate mix of therapies for their populations. It is of considerable concern that *What Works for Whom?* makes no

---

International Handbook of Personal Construct Psychology. Edited by F. Fransella.
© 2003 John Wiley & Sons, Ltd.

mention of personal construct psychotherapy, since its readers may conclude that this form of therapy works for no one and, if they are health care purchasers, that it should not be funded.

Despite such dangers, there has been some resistance by personal construct psychotherapists themselves to carrying out empirical research on their therapies because it has been viewed as incompatible with the constructivist and humanistic assumptions which underlie them (Bohart et al., 1998; Botella, 2000). Specifically, it has been suggested that such therapies will be 'empirically violated' by the apparent emphases of empirical research on knowable realities, treatment manuals, treatments targeted for specific disorders, and natural science methodology. While many constructivists have some sympathy with these arguments, it could be contended that failure to enter the arena of evidence-based practice and empirical validation in effect displays a refusal to present our therapeutic approach to health care purchasers, policy makers, and probably most potential clients, in terms which are likely to be understood by them (Winter, 2000). The result of this could be that personal construct psychotherapy will be faced with extinction and that clients will increasingly be denied access to therapeutic approaches such as this, which are not based on the mechanistic assumptions (that is, viewing people as operating like machines) of those therapies which have more readily embraced the notion of empirical validation.

THE EVIDENCE

Fortunately, however, not all personal construct psychotherapy researchers have eschewed empirical research, and as a result there is a growing evidence base for this form of therapy.

Personal Construct Theory

Kelly's theory has generated a considerable amount of research, much of it employing repertory grid technique (see Chapter 5, pp. 51–58). Some of the research findings, for instance, that superordinate constructs are more resistant to change than are subordinate constructs (Hinkle, 1965) and that invalidation may lead to particular changes in an individual's construing system (Lawlor & Cochran, 1981), are of clear relevance to, and provide indirect evidence for, the approach adopted by personal construct psychotherapists.

Personal Construct Formulations

A review of the extensive clinical research literature derived from the theory has been provided by Winter (1992). This includes evidence supporting the formulation of particular disorders in terms of certain features of the client's construing system. It therefore provides an empirical foundation for therapeutic approaches based on such formulations (see Chapter 19, pp. 201–209, for details). Also included in that review is evidence of changes in construing accompanying positive outcome in a wide range of different forms of therapy; of features of construing which predict response to particular therapies; and of aspects of construing related to the therapeutic process. For example, a particularly influential early study was Landfield's (1971) demonstration that the more similar the constructs used by client and therapist, but the less similar the structure of their construing systems, the more improvement the client experienced. Although many of these studies have investigated therapeutic approaches other than personal construct psychotherapy, their findings indicate the value of conceptualizing therapeutic process and outcome in personal construct terms.

The Personal Construct Psychotherapy Process

The literature contains numerous single case reports of personal construct psychotherapy (for example, Neimeyer & Neimeyer, 1987; Winter, 1992), but there are relatively few empirical studies of the therapeutic process in this form of therapy.

Individual Therapy

Viney (1994) provided some evidence of similarities between personal construct and client-centred therapy, which differed from rational-emotive therapy, in how therapists responded to expression of 'distressed emotion' by the client. In the former approaches, there was more therapist acknowledgement of the client's distress, tending to lead to further expressions of distress, whereas in the latter the client's negative emotions tended to be viewed as manifestations of irrationality. However, the conclusions that can be drawn from this study are limited by the fact that, in each therapeutic approach, transcripts of the sessions of only one therapist were examined.

A study involving a larger number of therapists was conducted by Winter and Watson (1999). They demonstrated that personal construct psychotherapy differs significantly from rationalist cognitive therapy in terms of various aspects of therapist and client behaviour in therapy sessions and therapist perceptions of the therapeutic relationship. Analysis of transcripts of therapy sessions indicated that personal construct psychotherapists used less directive responses, but more interpretation, confrontation and exploration, and showed less negative attitudes to clients, than cognitive therapists. On a questionnaire measure of conditions that facilitate therapeutic change, personal construct psychotherapists showed more positive feelings for their clients but were less likely to assume that they understood their clients' views of the world. In the therapy transcripts, their clients showed greater participation and more complex levels of 'processing' of their experiences. A more facilitative therapeutic process was observed in personal construct psychotherapy for those clients who construed less tightly and were more concerned with their inner worlds, while the reverse was true in cognitive therapy. Finally, leading exponents of the two forms of therapy, Fay Fransella and Windy Dryden, were able to differentiate between the transcripts of the therapies without knowledge of the group to which they belonged. This study is of importance, among other things, in demonstrating that descriptions of personal construct psychotherapy as a cognitive therapy are erroneous.

Group Therapy

There has also been some investigation of the process of personal construct group psychotherapy. Winter (1997) demonstrated that the interventions which personal construct psychotherapists anticipate that they would make in groups differ significantly from those of group analysts, making less reference to the therapist's view of the underlying meaning of group events. In a particular type of personal construct psychotherapy group, an interpersonal transaction group (see Chapter 24, pp. 247–255), Harter and Neimeyer (1995) found that incest survivors saw the groups as involving less conflict than did those attending 'process groups', which focused upon group interactions. Agoraphobic clients in personal construct interpersonal transaction groups have been found to perceive the group as characterized by greater smoothness, less avoidance, and more experiences of self-understanding than did clients receiving therapy offering just support in an interpersonal transaction group format (Winter et al., 1999).

Self-understanding has also been identified as a therapeutic factor, as have increased identification with others, acceptance, instillation of hope, and self-disclosure, by survivors of breast cancer attending personal construct psychotherapy groups (Lane & Viney, 2001b). In interpersonal transaction groups with adolescents, group members have been found to experience increasing levels of belonging to, and understanding and acceptance by, the group, as well as greater self-understanding and acceptance (Truneckova & Viney, 2001). Their group leaders evaluated the members as increasingly experiencing validation and understanding from, and trust by, others in the group; as questioning more their construing; as experimenting with new behaviours inside and outside the group; and as increasing self-validation and self-regard by a process of understanding similarities and differences between group members. Qualitative analysis of reports from some of these groups, conducted with school-based adolescents, identified four main themes of group sessions, concerned with trust, closeness to others, sexuality and power (Viney et al., 1997). Recent research with clients with a diagnosis of borderline personality disorder has also indicated that they perceive interpersonal transaction group sessions in a distinctive fashion, as compared to dialectical behaviour therapy group sessions, although the particular differences identified between the approaches are not entirely consistent with research on other client groups (Winter et al., 2002).

An Alternative to Empirical Validation

In considering the process and outcome of the experiential form of personal construct psychotherapy (see Chapter 25, pp. 257–264), Humphreys and colleagues (2001) adopt an interesting alternative approach to the demand for empirical validation. They argue that, since the essential ingredients of the process of this therapy have obtained previous empirical support, as components of forms of treatment which have been empirically validated, it can be claimed that experiential personal construct psychotherapy has already received empirical validation. The ingredients concerned include aspects of the therapeutic alliance and of the role relationship between therapist and client, the client being an active change agent, the need for empathy, and an emphasis on process rather than content. However, there is no empirical evidence to date that these ingredients do indeed characterize experiential personal construct psychotherapy, although studies such as that by Winter and Watson (1999) might provide some support for this argument.

Characteristics of Personal Construct Psychotherapists

Of some relevance to the process of personal construct psychotherapy is the question of whether practitioners of this form of therapy differ from those of other approaches. Winter and colleagues (2001) found that personal construct psychotherapists were more inner-directed and less rationalist (for example, tending not to accept that there is a knowable external reality) in their philosophical beliefs than were cognitive-behaviour therapists. They also differed in the latter respect from hypnotherapists and neuro-linguistic psychotherapists. In addition, there were differences in the content of the constructs used by therapists of different orientations in construing therapeutic approaches, with personal construct psychotherapists being particularly characterized by the use of constructs concerning personal meaning. The therapists in this study tended to differentiate cognitive-behaviour from humanistic therapies, and to place personal construct psychotherapy at the humanistic end of this dimension.

The Outcome of Personal Construct Psychotherapy

As in the literature on therapeutic process, there is a large number of single case studies of the outcome of personal construct psychotherapy. In addition, there is a growing body of group studies providing empirical evidence of therapeutic outcome. These have been reviewed by Winter (1992) and also by Viney (1998), who reports that the effect sizes (indices of degree of improvement) in studies of personal construct psychotherapy are comparable to those in studies of cognitive-behaviour therapy and psychodynamic psychotherapy. For ease of comparison with literature on other therapies, conventional psychiatric diagnostic categories will be used below in grouping these studies, although it should be noted that many personal construct psychotherapists would not employ such a classification, preferring to make a 'transitive diagnosis' with the constructs devised by Kelly for this purpose.

A few studies have examined the outcome of personal construct psychotherapy of clients within the spectrum of *neurotic disorders*. For example, Watson and Winter (1997), comparing personal construct, cognitive-behaviour and psychodynamic therapies in a British National Health Service setting, found significant improvement on several measures in personal construct psychotherapy, with a degree of improvement equivalent to that in cognitive-behaviour therapy. Also investigating a heterogeneous sample of psychiatric outpatients, Morris (1977) found in an uncontrolled study—that is, one which did not include a comparison group of, for example, untreated clients—that during personal construct group psychotherapy the repertory grids of five of the eight group members became similar to grids which their therapists considered to reflect an ideal outcome.

There has been some research on the outcome of personal construct psychotherapy with particular anxiety disorders. Two studies used therapies described as variants of Kelly's fixed-role therapy (see Chapter 23, pp. 237–245). Karst and Trexler (1970) found this to be somewhat more effective than rational-emotive therapy in the treatment of *public speaking anxiety,* and Lira and colleagues (1975) found that it was more effective with people who were *phobic of snakes* than exposure to a videotape of a model handling a snake, or one of a snake alone, or no treatment. Beail and Parker (1991), in another uncontrolled study, demonstrated reductions in *social anxiety* and *social phobia* during group fixed role therapy for clients presenting with these complaints. Winter and colleagues (1999) demonstrated greater improvement in *agoraphobic* clients during a treatment that combined personal construct psychotherapy in an interpersonal transaction group format and exposure to anxiety-provoking situations than while they were on the waiting list. However, the evidence that personal construct psychotherapy was any more effective than therapy offering support provided in a similar format was more equivocal.

In an uncontrolled study of individual personal construct psychotherapy for *depression,* Sheehan (1985) demonstrated reductions in clients' depression and in the negativity of their self-construing, coupled with an increase in their capacity to tolerate logical inconsistency in construing. While she also found the two former types of change in a previous study of pharmacological therapy for depression, the change on the measure of logical inconsistency was specific to personal construct psychotherapy. Also investigating the treatment of depression, Neimeyer and colleagues (1985) found greater improvement on measures of depressive symptoms, suicidal ideas and self-construing in clients receiving group cognitive therapy incorporating personal construct interventions than in clients on the waiting list. Winter and colleagues (2000) have also provided evidence of more positive outcomes on measures of depression and feelings of hopelessness, and on repertory grid measures of construing in clients presenting with *deliberate self-harm* who received a personal construct psychotherapy intervention than in those receiving 'normal clinical practice'.

An uncontrolled study of *people who stutter* by Fransella (1972) indicated significant improvement in their speech following individual personal construct psychotherapy, such improvement being highly correlated with increase in the meaningfulness to them of being a fluent speaker. In a subsequent study of a group treatment approach combining personal construct therapy and speech techniques, Evesham and Fransella (1985) found that while clients receiving this treatment showed less improvement at post-treatment assessment than those whose treatment only involved speech techniques, there was a predicted significantly lower relapse rate after eighteen months in the group containing the personal construct psychotherapy component (see Chapter 20, pp. 211–222).

In an uncontrolled study of an interpersonal transaction group (see Chapter 24, pp. 247–255) for clients with *eating disorders,* Button (1987) observed a decrease in

extreme views of the self and other people, an increase in self-esteem, and a reduction in perceived dissimilarity to others. Similar changes have been found by Coish
(1990) in therapy groups for bulimic clients which drew upon personal construct
theory. Group members also improved more than waiting list controls on measures
of bulimia, depression, self-esteem, assertiveness and body image (Wertheim et al.,
1988).

Bannister and colleagues (1975) compared their 'serial validation therapy' (see
Chapter 20, pp. 211–222), which attempted to validate *thought disordered schizophrenics'* predictions about their world, with a 'total push regime'. They report a
'not proven' verdict, although there were more within-group changes indicative of
improvement in the former condition.

Studying interpersonal transaction groups for *problem drinkers*, Landfield (1979)
found that only one of twenty clients was still drinking at six-month follow-up, and
that various positive changes were apparent in clients' grids, whereas there were no
significant changes in the grids of a control group of students who underwent a four-
session interpersonal transaction group experience.

Various studies have evaluated personal construct group therapy for disturbed
adolescents. Jackson (1992) found that adolescents attending a group focusing on
construing of the self and others made more significant gains on various measures
than did a control group; Viney and colleagues (1995a) reported similar gains in
social maturity in personal construct and psychodynamic groups for juvenile
offenders and non-offending adolescents, in contrast to adolescents receiving no
group work; and Truneckova and Viney (1997, 2001) provided indications that personal construct group work for adolescents with problems in an interpersonal transaction group format was associated with progressive attainment of the goals of
therapy, greater use of abstract and interpersonal constructs, and less disruptive
behaviour.

Viney and colleagues (1989) carried out a randomized-controlled trial of personal
construct psychotherapy for *elderly people* with psychological problems, finding evidence of reductions in anxiety, depression and indirectly expressed anger in the
treated group. This group also reported fewer physical symptoms after therapy than
did the control group but made more visits to health professionals, these decreas-
ing at follow-up (Viney, 1986). In a controlled study of a personal construct-oriented
group incorporating autobiographical writing for elderly people who had experienced losses, Botella and Feixas (1992–93) found evidence of reconstruction during
the group.

Several investigations of personal construct counselling and psychotherapy in the
general medical setting have been conducted by Viney and her colleagues. With
medical inpatients, they found evidence of differences in the effects of counselling
programmes that focused on different types of feelings (Viney et al., 1985d); greater
improvement on measures of negative emotions in the counselled group than in a
group having no counselling (Viney et al., 1985a); and quicker physical recovery
(Viney et al., 1985b) and lower health care costs (Viney et al., 1985c) in the former
group. Lane and Viney (2001a) have also demonstrated a greater decrease in
depression and anxiety, and a greater increase in hope, in *breast cancer survivors*
during personal construct group psychotherapy than in a waiting list control condition. Finally, Viney and colleagues (1995b), in an uncontrolled study, have provided

evidence of reduction in anxiety in *AIDS caregivers* following personal construct counselling. In another randomized controlled study of people with physical problems, in this case chronic musculo-skeletal pain, those who attended a personal construct group were found to have reconstructed some of their life patterns (Steen & Hauli, 2001). One year after the intervention they showed significant pain reduction, greater ability to cope with pain, and reduced health care consumption as compared to clients receiving 'treatment as usual' (Haugli et al., 2001).

Alexander and colleagues (1989) have found interpersonal transaction groups for *women who had been sexually abused as children* to be comparable to less structured 'process groups' in their effectiveness in reducing depression and alleviating distress, relative to change while on the waiting list for therapy. However, there was greater enhancement of social adjustment in the process groups.

CONCLUSIONS

There is a growing body of evidence indicating that:

- psychological disorders are characterized by particular features of construing;
- effective psychological therapy is associated with reconstruing;
- the process of personal construct psychotherapy is distinctive, and contrasts in practice with that in rationalist cognitive therapy;
- personal construct psychotherapy is effective, in an individual or group format, with a range of client groups;
- the degree of improvement in this form of therapy is similar to that in other therapies.

Personal construct practitioners are urged to continue to take up the challenge of evaluating their therapeutic and counselling practice. They might usefully adopt a 'methodological pluralism' in which the constructivist approach to research advocated by Botella (2000) is combined with the use of methods, such as standard outcome measures, which may be more meaningful to a wider audience. Among the priorities for further research should be studies of personal construct psychotherapy with larger sample sizes, and investigations of its outcome with couples, families and young children.

At the time of writing, a second edition of *What Works for Whom?* (Roth & Fonagy, 1996) is in preparation, and I have been asked to provide the authors with evidence for the effectiveness of personal construct psychotherapy. It is not known how that evidence will be evaluated. If the new edition has been published by the time that this volume goes to press, the reader may wish to find out whether personal construct psychotherapy has at last been 'officially' designated as a therapy that works for someone.

Development and Education

INTRODUCTION

Kelly wrote a long, angry, poem about education entitled: 'Nursery rhymes for older tots: to all you kettles from all us pots.' There are seventeen short verses, the last one of which says:

> Critics, teachers, kettles, pots,
> Boobies, bullies and bigots,
> Whilst flushing freedoms down the drain,
> Cry, '*Education* is to blame!'

The two parts of this section move to another aspect of change: how construing may develop in a child over time and then to how construing may develop—or not—as a result of organized education.

Development

It may seem strange to have a separate section on 'development' in a book on personal construct psychology because the whole psychology is about change. But, as Jim Mancuso shows, there are some changes that can be construed as fundamentally different from other changes. In his opinion, personal construct psychologists should look at the research people are doing in all branches of psychology. He does just that and interprets results to indicate that newborn infants, as well as foetuses, can be seen as construing.

Tom Ravenette recounts his approach and describes some of the ways he has developed to understand and help teachers and children with their problems. The child has not arrived, saying 'I have a problem', so whose problem is it? He also gives some details of methods he has developed during his lifetime of experience working with children.

Education

The second part of this section starts with a discussion of teacher–student relationships at university level in excerpts from an unpublished paper of George Kelly. It not only shows some of his radical views on teaching at that level and dissatisfactions with teaching expressed in his poem, but also give an insight into how he put his own theory to use.

Maureen Pope scans the world showing just how widespread is the use of personal construct psychology in the world of education and teacher training. She emphasizes the need for teachers to be aware that their professional lives are intimately related to their personal construing.

Phillida Salmon moves nearer home to focus on teaching in British schools. She discusses how personal construct psychology can make a difference to how children are taught in the classroom.

Martin Fromm's account of his work in Germany with university students shows how students may not learn what teachers think they are teaching. He continues the theme of exploration of what students learn by citing some of his own research work with German university students.

CHAPTER 27

Children's Development of Personal Constructs

James C. Mancuso
New York, USA

> ...the constructs, in turn, we have envisioned as avenues of movement which the person opens up for himself through the bewildering tangle of life's events.
>
> (Kelly, 1955/1991, p. 731/Vol. 2, p. 123)

As long ago as 1979, Salmon suggested that the use of personal construct psychology would provide a remedy for major shortcomings of then-prevailing theories of psychological development. She observed that prevalent theories made:

> no references ... to any mediation or agency on the part of the child. The cause–effect relationships [proposed] are of an essentially mechanical kind; ... put forward as though they have an absolute positive power, without any consideration of the symbolic significance they might have for children.
>
> (p. 222)

Though such formist and mechanist perspectives (see Pepper, 1942) continue to guide some developmental psychologists, many contemporary investigators assume that the personal construct systems of children must be regarded as a central strand in the processes affecting a child's development. Prominent investigators now routinely take into consideration and explore the meanings that events have for developing children. Theorists, having adopted constructivist orientations, comfortably work from the principle that alteration of a developing child's knowledge and the new behaviours that are associated with that knowledge are the product of the interaction of the stimuli provided by the events and the meanings a child imposes on those events.

International Handbook of Personal Construct Psychology. Edited by F. Fransella.
© 2003 John Wiley & Sons, Ltd.

CONSTRUING IN NEWBORN INFANTS

Does a Foetus Construe?

A psychologist who promotes personal construct psychology to frame propositions about knowledge development can expect to encounter the challenge, 'What meanings can a newborn impose on to an object or event? Isn't a newborn a "blank slate"?'

Dismissal of the blank slate metaphor gains support from work like that of DeCasper and Spence (1988), who have reported a study that indicates that a foetus can 'learn' during its last six weeks of gestation. They had 33 healthy pregnant women recite a poem out loud, each day, during the last six weeks of their pregnancy. The experimenters showed that if the newborn infants (average age about 56 hours) again heard the poem recited by their mothers, they would more vigorously suck on a nipple. DeCasper and Spence wrote:

> The conclusion implies that the fetuses had learned and remembered something about the acoustic cues which specified their particular target passage [. . . prosodic cues such as syllabic beat, the voice-onset-time of consonants, the harmonic structure of sustained vowel sounds and/or the temporal order of these sounds]. (p. 17)

Does a Newborn Infant Use Two-poled Judgement Constructs?

A personal construct psychologist would assume that in order to make the distinctions described by DeCasper and Spence, the foetuses, even while in the uterus, could make non-verbalized discriminations between certain events—they could construe. One can expect, then, that newborn infants can also build bipolar constructs that allow them to distinguish between some events that are similar compared with others that are different. A very young infant can use a combination of constructs to impose meaning onto a repeated stimulus pattern so that the pattern can be judged to be the same as, or different from, another stimulus pattern. One can assume that very young infants can elaborate that set of simple discriminations so that they can apply them in a learning situation requiring that they construe similar stimulus patterns. That is, infants form new, complex bipolar constructs that one could designate as superordinate bipolar constructs. Then, by use of such complex, elaborated constructs, the infant can make inferences about novel objects and events so that they can begin to anticipate the outcomes of their responses to those objects and events.[1]

---

[1] Theorists who have used classic cognitive theories might, at this point, discuss an infant's *category formation* and use. Personal construct psychologists work from propositions about a person's development of elaborated, complex, bipolar constructs. When a person construes an object by locating that object on one pole of a superordinate construct, that object, one could say, has been assigned to a personal category.

Visual Patterns Created

Results obtained by Pascalis and colleagues (1995) indicated that newborn infants (about seventy-eight hours after delivery) are able to use some kind of dimensions to compare visual patterns. The researchers arranged a situation in which an infant could choose to view either the face of that infant's mother or the face of a strange woman. They measured the amount of time that the newborn infant focused on each of the simultaneously presented faces, and found that an infant fixated on the face of the mother for considerably longer than they fixated on the face of the stranger.

In order to find out whether or not the infants used dimensions relevant to the specific facial features, or whether they used dimensions having to do with the overall configuration of the face, Pascalis and colleagues repeated the study, but this time they draped a light pink scarf around the facial outlines of the mother and of the stranger, so that the perimeters of the hair lines could not be seen by the infants. Under these conditions the infants did not react in ways that indicated that they could distinguish the face of their mothers from the face of strangers. One can conclude, then, that the infants could detect and use inputs construable by use of bipolar construct such *up/down*, and *left/right* to discriminate the two different faces on the basis of height and width.

Similar conclusions seem justified by the findings reported by Quinn and colleagues (2001). They studied older infants (average age 3.3 months) responding to stimuli that those children had not encountered in their day-to-day life. For example, they first showed the infants two similar silhouettes of cats, allowing the infants 15 seconds to view the images. The infants were then given two 10-second test trials during which they were presented with one image of a familiar silhouette and a second image of a cat with which they had not been familiarized. The researchers assumed that these older infants would use an information-gathering approach to the stimuli and would look at the novel stimulus for longer periods than they would look at the familiar stimulus. Their results affirmed their assumption.

In sum, the results of formal studies such as these can convince a personal construct psychologist that a healthy foetus, after five months of gestation, has already developed a neural system with which it can develop bipolar constructs. Further, newborn infants can quickly respond to variations in stimulus inputs by forming two-poled judgement scales (constructs) that they can use to construe objects and events. The psychological system that can result from the formation of constructs, then, is available to newborn infants, and they can take that rudimentary system into the myriad of contexts in which they will very rapidly develop more and more constructs that they can use to 'know' the events and objects that they will encounter.[2]

Can Infants Use Constructs to Form Constructions or Categories?

Quinn and colleagues (2001) also showed that young infants can use complex constructs so that they could discriminate between novel stimuli representing dogs and

---

[2] In this chapter, the term *know* signifies the successful locating of an object or event at one or another pole of a personal bipolar construct. In more common terms, one might speak of *assigning attributes* to an object or event.

novel stimuli representing cats. These infants first looked at a series of 12 silhou-ettes of cats, presented in pairs. A personal construct psychologist would assume that the infants had applied a set of subordinate constructs (for example, *wide/narrow, above/below*) as they viewed these pairs of cat silhouettes. The inves-tigators then presented the infants with a series of pairs of different stimuli. Instead of seeing two cat silhouettes, the infants saw a cat silhouette that they had not yet seen and the silhouette of a dog. The constructs that the infants had used to deter-mine the similarities of and differences between the paired cat stimuli, however, would not be applicable to construing the dog stimuli. The contrasting silhouettes would influence the infants to develop their complex *dog/cat* construct by using con-structs that would allow them to determine similarities and differences as they com-pared the dog silhouettes to the cat silhouettes.

As Quinn and colleagues had expected, the infants spent more time looking at a novel stimulus (the dog silhouette) than they spent looking at novel silhouettes that could be construed using the constructs that they had used to construe the cat sil-houettes. A personal construct psychologist would claim that the infants needed to study the dog silhouettes intently in order to invent and use constructs that allowed them to differentiate the visual patterns. Once the infants had subordinated that set of constructs to a complex, personal *dog/cat* construct, they could then locate any of the presented visual patterns at one or the other end of that construct—they could categorize the different visual patterns.

The evidence strongly suggests that young infants can develop categories based on locating simultaneously presented visual inputs on two-poled constructs such as *down/up* and *wide/narrow*. Can they develop and use superordinate constructs by which differences and similarities of sequentially presented auditory patterns may be discriminated? Parents who have undertaken to prompt their child to use rhyme to learn to read and spell, know that children can respond actively to instruction that allows them to recognize that the word *bat* can be transformed readily into the word *cat*.

Hayes and colleagues (2000) showed that infants (average age 10 months) can construe simple consonant–vowel–consonant combinations as rhymes; that is, as belonging to a useful category. They presented to the infants a series of conso-nant–vowel–consonant rhymes, such as *bad, dad, sad*, and so forth. Then the infants would hear a word (for example, *beg*) that could not be construed by use of the constructs that were used to construe the rhyming words. If, on hearing the word change, the infant turned his or her head towards a place where there would appear a moving, illuminated toy, the toy would appear. The behaviour of the infants clearly showed that they could detect the change to a non-rhyming word and that, on detecting that change, they would turn their heads towards the toy, expecting to see it become illuminated and active.

Labels and Construct Development

As Waxman (1998) cogently proposes, the infant who brings into its rich world of stimulation the ability to form and use complex constructs to construe objects and events is prepared to begin to use words (nouns such as *dog, cat, face*, and so on) to label categories. After that, the infant can use its ability to cross-compare examples of different categories to attach labels (adjectives such as *wide, black, striped,* and so on) to the bipolar constructs (dimensions) that allow him or her to invent the complex constructs that one uses to categorize. An infant who sees various faces of cats can efficiently learn, through using verbal labels, to use the constructs *plain/striped, pointed/rounded* (ears), *flat/curved,* and so forth to build the complex construct *dog/cat.* In turn, with infants who hear a word attached to a series of objects that can be construed by locating those objects at one end of a construct, their use of the word will allow them to elaborate that construct so that it can be used to construe and to anticipate other objects that can be taken as exemplars of that category. Infants who hear the word *apple* applied to a series of varied objects, can learn to locate those objects at the *apple* pole of a superordinating *ball/apple* construct and then can elaborate that construct in order to anticipate the outcome of actions on objects that can be located on the *apple* pole. An apple, which the infant had never seen before, can be construed by using that complex construct. An infant can infer that objects that can be assigned to the *apple* end of the construct can be cut into bits. An infant can infer that the apple bits can be assigned to the *edible* end of the subordinate construct *inedible/edible.*

CONSTRUCTING SELF-GUIDING ANTICIPATORY NARRATIVES

With the ability to categorize through the use of a system of personal constructs, a child then can use complex constructs to anticipate the outcomes of self-guiding anticipatory narratives. The categorizing child can then anticipate the outcomes of personal actions by inferring how he or she will be construed following his or her enactment of a particular behaviour. That is, by being able to locate an object (including self) on a particular complex construct, a child has the base for making inductive leaps (see Gelman, 1996) as he or she construes persons (including self as person [see Mancuso & Ceely, 1980]). Children can observe new acquaintances, construe them in terms of some of the set of bipolar constructs that they had used to construe persons during previous social encounters, and then determine the location of a new acquaintance at one or the other end of a superordinate construct. Once the child assigns a stranger to a position on a superordinate construct, the child can deduce that the person can be construed by use of other subordinate constructs. For example, Peter meets and engages in an interaction with Mr Muldoon; and on the basis of constructs applicable to the tone of the man's voice, his facial expression, his body movements, and so forth, Peter determines that Mr Muldoon can be located on the *gruff* end of a *gruff/kind* superordinate construct. Having thus placed Mr Muldoon in the *gruff* category, Peter will anticipate that Mr Muldoon will not welcome a child's effort to engage in extended conversation.

A major part of a person's actions can be seen as an exercise of the ability to deduce outcomes of self-guiding narratives by having cast the self as a protagonist who exemplifies a category. Children who can locate their selves at the *sad* pole of the superordinate construct *sad/happy,* can enact a set of behaviours based on their 'knowledge' of the attributes[3] of persons who fit into the *angry* or *sad* category (Mancuso & Sarbin, 1998). Those children will enact those behaviours on the basis of having deduced that they can fit themselves at the *sad* end of the *sad/happy* superordinate construct and then inferring the outcomes of the self-guiding narratives in which they will cast their selves as a protagonist.

To support this line of theorizing, Mancuso (1986) offered a description of the ways in which children develop and use the complex construct *random text/story*. On the basis of a series of published studies, he concluded that by the age of 5, the average child has acquired a system of 'story grammar' that he or she can use to build anticipatory narratives that will guide his or her self enactments. As the child assembles such anticipatory self narratives, he or she can then cast 'self' in the role of the principal actor who sets out to achieve the outcomes specified in the narrative. When the outcome specified in the self-guiding anticipatory narrative is matched by the actual outcome, then the child may conclude that the self-defining category (for example, *sad child*) that was used in the narrative may be taken to be 'true' (valid).

SOCIALITY AND SELF-GUIDING NARRATIVE

In order to anticipate successfully the outcomes of many self-guiding narratives, a child must be able to construe the construction processes of other persons involved in the narrative enactment. When Patricia enacts the role of a *sad* person she must be able to construe her Aunt Wilma's construction of a *sad* person in order to deduce whether or not Wilma will construe her as deserving of sympathy.

Selman (1976) concluded that the average child reaches the age range of 6–8 years before showing awareness that dialogue partners might have a perspective based on their own reasoning and that that perspective may or may not coincide with the constructions of the developing child. Advancing from this basic understanding of sociality, an (average) early adolescent child will then proceed to develop constructions that allow him or her to know that mutual perspective-taking does not always lead to the removal of a discrepancy, and that a social organization must then rely on agreement to use conventional constructions; that is, rules, so that the organization can function effectively.

When Patricia enacts a self-narrative in which she plays the role of an *angry* person, caregivers around her would undoubtedly fail to agree on the appropriateness of her self-construction. Her mother might, for example, say, 'In this house, no one gets her way by stamping her feet and screaming. We just don't do that!' In effect, this kind of reaction to Patricia's rule violation would give her an opportunity to check the validity of her construction of her self as *angry* person. Patricia incorrectly had anticipated that her construction *angry* person would have been validated by her mother. Her mother's response would signal that she had violated a rule. She had failed to act on the basis of a socially agreed upon construction of her self.

---

[3] Some commentators have discussed category formation as a process of 'discovering the attributes' of objects and events. In this chapter, I assume that a learner assigns attributes by observing an object or event and then locating that object or event on a personal, bipolar construct.

CO-CONSTRUING AND CAREGIVER DISCIPLINARY ACTION

Mancuso and his associates (see Mancuso & Lehrer, 1986) have discussed reactions to rule violation in terms of 'reprimanding'. They worked from the position that reprimand situations could evolve whenever someone invalidated another person's construction of an event. For example, Oscar might use the self-defining construction *owner* to construe his self as he takes possession of a toy being used by Warren. A caregiver's construction of Oscar would not match Oscar's self-defining construction. Thereupon, the caregiver's construction would have been invalidated by Oscar's action. That invalidation would prompt the caregiver to deliver a reprimand to Oscar.

An effective reprimander, having construed Oscar's construction processes, might then say, 'Oscar, the toys in this room are for everyone to use. Warren was using that toy; you will need to wait until he is finished so that you can have a turn. How would you feel if you were using that toy and I took it away from you?' Through that kind of relevant reprimand, the caregiver can prompt a transgressor to elaborate a validatable self-construction by elaborating that construction to subordinate constructs such as *inequitable/fair, inconsiderate/considerate, wrong/right,* and so forth.

Packer and Greco-Brooks (1999) describe other processes by which children are prompted to use socially agreed upon constructions. They describe a teacher introducing newly arrived children to the order of her classroom. 'In the mundane details of classroom life we can discern the active co-construction that is central to schooling' (p. 137). For example, the teacher, calling attention to a picture that all the children can see, introduces the rule, 'No running'. Then, by explicitly singling out a child who wishes to respond to the teacher's inducement to explain the reason for the rule, she has the opportunity to validate publicly the child's socially acceptable construction when the child declares that the rule exists 'Cause you don't want us to get hurt' (p. 140). The teacher, implicitly taking into account the children's ability to locate their selves on bipolar constructs, prompts the children to construe their selves as *orderly, respectful, polite,* and so forth. The teacher prompts each child to accept, particularly, the teacher's construction of that child's self as *compliant learner* or *competent learner.*

CONSTRUING CHILDREN WHO FAIL TO USE SOCIALLY VALID SELF-CONSTRUCTIONS

Many children who enter modern educational systems cannot build and enact self-categorizing constructions that match their teacher's construction of *self-directed learner* or *compliant learner.* If the child fails to respond to the teacher's effort to have him or her build a self-construction that the teacher can validate, the teacher must try to elaborate a complex construct that might prove useful for construing the child. In our era, a caregiver can access and use the construct *disordered/normal.* Profound consequences can follow from the caregiver's application of such constructions to such children. As Bannister (1983, p. 384) has observed:

Social judgments, direct or implied, can implant a fixed picture of self, particularly in those too young or too socially restricted to have developed any elaborated construing of their own nature and potential. Such implanted identities tend to be self-fulfilling truths in that their acceptance discourages the active exploration of alternatives (to construing self).

Mancuso and co-workers (2002) extended Bannister's view to discuss the construction *attention deficit/hyperactivity disorder* (AD/HD) as that construction is commonly used to construe children who fail to fit themselves into an acceptable *learner* category. In the 'common sense' such children fail to 'pay attention' to the specification of 'proper' role definitions. In an era in which prominent behaviour scientists have assiduously supported diagnostic narratives to explain unwanted behaviour, many psychologists have adapted the diagnostic narrative to explain what teachers readily construe as the transgressing child's inability to 'pay attention'. Using the *attention deficit* construction, those psychologists have construed inattention as a 'symptom' that allows one to construe a child by using the complex construct *disordered/normal*. In many cases the diagnostician who sets out to eliminate the 'cause' of the 'disorder' induces the child to ingest a chemical agent. When the outcome of the 'treatment' appears to concur with the anticipated outcome of the diagnostic narrative, the advocates of the AD/HD narrative affirm the validity of the *attention deficit* construction—as would any person enacting a self-guiding anticipatory narrative.

   Mancuso and colleagues have pointed out that the diagnosed child and his or her family can then adopt the view that the 'diagnosed' child can be construed as a person who is the victim of a 'disorder'. As a result, the child will consistently construe his or her 'self' in terms of a pathological object that is manipulated by external forces, and will fail to develop the ability to construct and apply to his or her self a socially acceptable construction of *competent* or *compliant learner.*

CONCLUSION

Developmental psychologists have provided a sound base of findings from which to consider the kinds of construing systems and psychological processes that children can take into a learning context. Such findings, inserted into a framework such as that provided by Kelly's personal construct psychology, can guide both the theorist and the practitioner to use procedures by which to prompt young people to develop flexible, open construct systems by which they can confront invalidations of their constructions and then proceed to develop more adequate constructions. Additionally, use of personal construct theory cautions practitioners about the consequences of prompting children to build constricting constructions, particularly when they are building self-defining constructions.

CHAPTER 28

Constructive Intervention when Children are Presented as Problems

Tom Ravenette

Meadway House, Epsom, UK

> . . . no psychologist, I think, is all that he might be until he has undertaken to join the child's most audacious venture beyond the frontiers of social conventions and to share its most unexpected outcomes.
>
> (Kelly, 1969h, p. 8)

The first part of this chapter is largely theoretical and the second part is pragmatic. The two are connected through their relevance to action. The context needs to be recognized as not academic, not research, not teaching, not therapeutic and not counselling. It is that of a school psychological service within which the task has been to intervene in schools when teachers have been sufficiently worried about children to seek outside help. More specifically such intervention will have been limited, probably, to one visit to a school with a follow-up some time later. It is a matter of some moment that Kelly was involved in a comparable task when operating a travelling service to schools some 20 years previously in Kansas and it will be seen that his observations arising from the experience have been a major influence behind the practice described in this chapter.

THEORY

In the practitioner's view the task is to make sense of the 'problems' as they are presented and to respond, if possible, in such a way as to 'make a difference'. Although personal construct theory works very effectively at the individual level there are two areas in which it is relatively weak. The first of these is concerned with interaction and communication and the second with child development.

Just as I was fortunate in coming across Kelly's theory, in like manner I acquired

International Handbook of Personal Construct Psychology. Edited by F. Fransella.
© 2003 John Wiley & Sons, Ltd.

The Pragmatics of Human Communication (Watzlawick et al., 1967). That text is directed specifically at human interaction and communication. Part of their message is that the human needs to 'seek for contexts and sequences in the stream of events'. The authors make a link with personal construct theory when they say:

> A similar concept is at the basis of Kelly's monumental 'Psychology of Personal Constructs' although (he) does not consider the question of levels and presents his theory almost exclusively in terms of intrapsychic, not interactional, psychology. (p. 263)

More importantly, their analysis of the communication process is highly relevant both for understanding the nature of, and the basis for, a teacher's complaint about a child. As the complaint arises from pupil–teacher interaction, it therefore has implications for action. Every communication has three components. The first is its 'content' which may be verbal or non-verbal, for example, tone of voice, a look, a movement. The second is a communication of 'how I see you' and 'how I see myself'—that is, an implicit statement of 'relationship'. This clearly will be a reflection, in personal construct terms, of 'self constructs'. The third is 'context', that is, the circumstances in which the interaction is taking place. At a very simple level the communication between teacher and pupil in terms of 'content' and 'relationship' needs to be appropriate to the 'context', that is, what is appropriate in the playground may be completely inappropriate in the classroom.

There are also three forms of response in relation to each or any of the three components. The first is simply to 'confirm', to validate. The second is to 'reject', to invalidate. The third is to 'disconfirm', to ignore, to act as though the statement did not exist.

Communication between individuals usually happens naturally, easily and harmoniously. By contrast, problem situations may well be tantamount to disordered communications, especially around the 'sense of self'. Perhaps the most disturbing instance is reflected in the statement: 'While rejection amounts to the message "You are wrong", disconfirmation says in effect "You do not exist"' (Watzlawick et al., 1967, p. 85). How much of a child's disturbing behaviour is an assertion that 'I *do* exist'?

The second alternative theoretical framework is that of Piaget who, through observation and experiment, developed an encompassing theoretical system of the individual from infancy to late adolescence. Kelly, by contrast, saw children through the eyes of his theory but gave little guidance on the actual interviewing of them. Flavell, however, in his *The Developmental Psychology of Jean Piaget* (1963) is able to forge a link:

> Every act of intelligence, however rudimentary and concrete, presupposes an interpretation of something in reality, that is an assimilation of that something to some kind of meaning in the subject's cognitive organization. To use a happy phrase of Kelly's (1955), to adapt intellectually to reality is to *construe* that reality, and to construe it in terms of some enduring *construct* within oneself. Piaget's epistemological position is essentially the same on this point, requiring only the substitution of *assimilate* for *construe* and *structure* or *organization* for *construct*. (Flavell, 1963, p. 48)

As the links between Kelly and Piaget have been comprehensively described elsewhere, such as in Mancuso and Hunter (1985a, 1985b) and Soffer (1993), I shall not elaborate further.

PRACTICE

Who has What Problem?

Kelly eventually recognized that the complaint about a child which led to a referral arose from the teacher's construction of the child's behaviour. Different teachers
may indeed vary in the extent to which they see the same child as a problem. It is
worth a thought that, on occasion, a child's 'problem behaviour' may be indeed a
solution, albeit inadequate, to some underlying issue in relation to that specific
teacher.

This needs to be taken forward. When a child presents 'difficulties' to a teacher
there may well be grumbles in the staff room and, perhaps, some invalidation of
the teacher's peripheral 'self-constructs'. By contrast, 'problems' which lead to
a referral may represent challenges to a teacher's 'professional core constructs'.
These latter problems can be seen as four-fold:

1. This child's behaviour/failings is a challenge to my professional understanding.
2. Whatever I do with this child makes no difference. My professional competence
   is at stake.
3. In my view this child has 'special needs' and it is not my job to deal with such
   children.
4. This child is a 'problem' but I have been able to cope. I don't want the next
   teacher to blame me for not referring.

The importance of this analysis lies in the fact that the referral of a child represents
double problems, problems separately to both teacher and child. An investigation
of the child should hopefully lead to some understanding of his or her putative
underlying problem and, sharing that with the teacher, should lead to an enlarge-
ment and simultaneous validation of the teacher's professional 'sense of self'.

The aim of an interview with the child is not specifically to investigate the validity of teacher's complaint since that is his or her construction of events. In fact the
first part of the intervention needs to be a preliminary discussion at the school in
order to find out what the complaint is all about. That means going beyond obvious
generalities to a more precise statement of the troubling happenings.

THE INTERVIEW

Language in the Interview

The myth of the two-faced Janus provides a suitable metaphor for the nature of
language. Language, at one and the same time points in contrasting directions. In
one it points to 'commonality', to commonly accepted or dictionary meanings. In
the other it points to 'individuality', to that which is personal and experientially
based. Whereas in ordinary discourse we can get by with an assumption of
'commonality', the acceptance of such an assumption between interviewer and
interviewee may lead to serious misunderstandings.

It is a part of the function of language in the interview to go beyond assumed 'commonalities' of meanings by seeking their 'individuality' aspects and this is done through the elaborative exploration of 'obvious' answers. In this way new 'commonalities' or shared meanings may be developed between interviewer and interviewee. This argument is reflected in the style and structure of the interview.

Structure

The first part of the interview with the child involves getting his or her view of 'what it is all about'. Children have not asked for an interview so why has he or she been taken out of class to see this strange person? They seldom know, hence 'your teacher is worried about you, do you know why'? 'I'm not learning', 'I don't behave myself', 'I don't get on with other children', 'I don't get on well with teacher' and so forth. It is useful then to say, 'I like to explore with children how they see themselves and their world. In that way they can sometimes then understand themselves better and in the outcome that can help teachers to understand them better too.'

The second part of the interview involves the exploration with the child of his or her ways of making sense of 'themselves and their circumstances'. Since this exploration needs to be methodical it involves using a range of interviewing techniques. It is important not to rely on words alone but also to use pictures and a child's drawings in order to elicit matters which are not so easily verbalized. This may then suggest underlying issues which make the child and the behaviour potentially more understandable.

The third part of the interview will be 'reconstructive'. It will attempt to create, out of the substance of the preceding part of the interview, alternative views of the 'child's sense of self and circumstances'. That can be communicated to the child, not as a prescription, but merely as a different way of seeing things, as an extension of potential awareness. Occasionally, in the light of this alternative view, a child may indeed be invited to experiment, for a limited time only, with some change of habitual behaviour.

A caution surrounds the use of the motivational 'Why?' When adults ask the question of a child it is usually perceived in a threatening or accusative way, implying that the child is somehow 'in the wrong' or 'ought to know'. And if the child says 'Don't know' is he or she then guilty of prevarication? The use of 'Why?', therefore, is usually ambiguous and is not necessarily motivational. How much less threatening it is to ask quite simply 'How come?' The interview with the child, however, is not the end of the matter. The teacher's problem, given shape by the 'complaint', will be considered later.

Once we are in the business of asking questions in the interview, my observations on the Janus nature of language require that we become circumspect in accepting answers at their face value. At the back of the interviewer's mind the following further elaborative explorations have been found helpful as ways for clarifying meanings and arriving at understanding.

1. *What, at the same time, is being denied.* This is in line with Kelly's bipolarity principle and is fertile in illuminating meaningfully the original statement,

in yielding more content and at the same time giving hints of underlying contrasts.

2. *What the statement further implies.* That gives some clue as to the underlying 'construct system' within which the original statement was given.
3. *The context within which the statement makes sense.* That follows from my earlier references to communication and interaction.
4. *The experiential grounds on which it is based.* 'How come?' will reveal something of the circumstances within which the statements were appropriate.
5. *The importance of the statement to the interviewee.* Whether or not it is important may reflect aspects of the child's attitude to the interview and interviewer. 'How come?' again is an invitation for elaborating the response.
6. *What's good and bad about what's 'good' and 'bad'?* That is an aphoristic version of Tschudi's (1977) 'ABC' model of questioning and invites a balanced evaluation of contrasting poles of a personal construct (Chapter 10, pp. 105–121).

A RANGE OF TECHNIQUES

As I see it, the purposes of all techniques in the interview are two-fold. The obvious purpose is the elicitation of information, of facts, of incidents and so forth, from and about the child. The more profound purpose, however, is to commit the child to seek for those answers which, within his or her own experiential reality, will be held at a lower level of awareness. The great power of the elaborative enquiry is to bring to light hidden aspects of that reality. In particular, together with the search for contrasts, it opens up the possibility to the child of an alternative 'sense of self', a 'self' whose behaviour might just cease to be a cause for concern. The techniques which I present below should be read in the light of these observations. They are just some of those methods that have proved effective in eliciting children's construing. With the first five techniques the elaborative questioning is along the lines described in the previous section.

Who are You?

This extended version of Bugental's (1964) technique asks for three responses to each of the questions: 'Who are you?', 'What sort of person would you say that you are?' and 'What sort of person would other persons say that you are?' (listing family members and others). A fully elaborated version is given in detail in Ravenette (1997, 1999).

How would you Describe . . . ?

Four persons, two of whom are friends, one who is admired and one who is disliked are specified. Again three responses are required. This is not necessarily 'construct eliciting' but, if the material is needed for subsequent use in a 'grid' procedure, contrasts may be sought.

The Trouble with Most Mothers (Fathers, Brothers and so Forth) Is?

Kelly (1955/1991, p. 994/Vol. 2, p. 303) cites this technique and acknowledges his debt to Mahrer who devised it.

Personal Troubles

This is a direct enquiry and not to be confused with 'A drawing and its opposite', which is described below. A sheet of paper is divided into six boxes and the child is asked to draw in five of them situations in which he or she would be troubled or upset. The child is then asked what is happening and his or her responses are amplified along the lines previously described. The sixth space is reserved for a contrasting situation which is similarly elaborated.

Perception of Troubles in Schools

The child is presented with eight drawings of situations which might occur in or around school and is invited to say what is happening in just three of them. These *were drawn* at my request by Arthur Jordan, then a trainee, to whom I acknowledge a debt. They have been used widely and are reproduced in *Educational Psychology Casework* (Beaver, 1996).

Family Interaction Matrix

This is a technique of a completely different order and can be used with a family of four members and upwards. The child is asked to say for each member of the family, which members he or she finds 'more easy' and 'less easy' to get on well with. The number chosen to fit each category of response is varied according to the size of the family but it is an essential feature of the design that, by implication, at least one member will be judged as neither 'more' nor 'less easy to get on with'. The matrix which arises from this procedure is then easily analysed in terms of family interactions. A worked example appears in Ravenette (1999, pp. 184–185).

Portrait Galley and Self-description Grid

We are indebted indeed to Kelly for grids, but the usual practice is to use them for looking outwards to the world of people or situations in order to arrive at a person's underlying construct system. With the self-description grid, however, the aim is somewhat different. Can the child, using a grid format, give an indication of how different people will see him, how they form clusters of validators and how he views himself. One version is given in Ravenette (1999, p. 192). The version here is less formal in style and format thereby increasing the boy's involvement in the whole process. Figure 28.1 shows an actual grid which was developed in an interview together with a verbal analysis of its linkages.

	intelligent			Polite	world agianst	Kind	
M	7	1	6	2	3	4	5
F	7	1	6	3	2	3	5
Br	6	7	1	2	3	5	4
Si	7	6	1	2	5	3	4
Bo	1	7	2	6	3	5	4
Te	7	1	4	2	6	3	5
S_1	7	1	6	2	5	3	4
R_2	1	7	2	5	3	6	4

Figure 28.1 R's completed repertory grid

The boy in question (R) was a 12-year-old attending daily at a residential school for 'disturbing' pupils. His life had been one of constant moves in and out of children's homes. The current 'cause for complaint' was that although he got on very well with staff, he manipulated the other pupils so that they bullied him. I do not report the whole interview but the analysis of the grid data will be seen to illuminate the matter.

As can be seen, oval shapes representing faces are drawn along the top of the grid. The child then fills them in to create portraits which illustrate the descriptive language given previously in the interview, writing the descriptions underneath each. In this example the first four attributes were provided by the boy, while the other three were hypothetical, derived from the interview, and inserted for their potential relevance. It is a matter of significance that in the outcome those three received 'neutral' rankings! Along the side of the grid are written the names of members of the family: mother (M), father (F), brother (Br), sister (Si), teachers (Te), boys (Bo) and Self (S_1). R_2 is when he is a 'cause for trouble'.

The instruction then is: 'If I were to ask your mother, which of these would she say was most like you, which would it be? Put a 1 under that face. And which would she say was least like you? Put a 7. Which now would she say was most like you? Put a 2. And least like you? Put a 6, and so forth. Use the same process for each person in turn. When the child has completed this for 'Self ', he or she is asked to repeat the process for that version of self when 'in trouble' ('R_2').

A McQuitty Cluster Analysis (Ravenette, 1968) indicates that, in the boy's eyes:

Parents, teachers and Self form a cluster agreeing that he is *Polite* and *Intelligent* and denying that he *Doesn't care* and is *Naughty*.

Brother and sister agree that he is *Polite* and *Naughty* and deny that he is *Intelligent* and *Doesn't care.*

Boys and R₂ agree that he is *Naughty* and *Doesn't care* and deny that he is *Intelligent, Kind* and *Polite.*

In the light of the description above, this analysis seems to confirm that R identifies himself with the adult world view of him. At the same time, however, arising from his behaviour with his peer group, he creates for himself, in their eyes, the antithesis of that adult view. His siblings partly share the parental and partly the peer group view of him.

A Drawing and its Opposite

This technique is written up fully in Ravenette (1997, 1999) and is important in contributing material for the third stage of the interview. It involves the drawing, in the centre of a sheet of paper, of a three-inch-long line, bent over at an angle of about 45 degrees for a further half inch. The child is then invited to turn the line into a picture (not just an object). When that is finished, and only then, the child is asked to draw a picture which is an opposite. To achieve that aim the child will have to re-examine the first picture, and attribute a meaning to it, in order to draw the second picture. It may then be possible to derive from the child's account of the two drawings the unverbalized expression of an underlying bipolar 'construct'. More importantly, however, since each pair of opposites is held together by some underlying theme, the elucidation of that theme may have important implications both for understanding and for change. As a final part of the interview with R (above), he produced the two drawings shown in Figure 28.2.

Just as the analysis of the self-description grid data called for comment, so do these drawings. When I asked R for a contrast to the first drawing he was puzzled and then said 'Ah, I've got it!' and drew a repeat of the first but without the car. He said that it represented looking at the other side of the road. I reminded him that the interview had been concerned with looking at opposites and tentatively offered the following hypothesis, based on the manifest presence–absence of the car and its potential relevance to his 'sense of self'. Unless R can be like a big limo, bright and able (from his 'self-description'), he is afraid he might be like nothing. Perhaps he needs to put something there (in the lower drawing) 'that can grow'. He then drew in the diminutive matchstick figure!

Mutual Story-telling

This technique is one way of implementing the reconstructive stage of the interview. It is derived from Gardner (1971) but is modified to fit in with a personal construct style of interview. The child is invited to choose one picture from a set for which he or she can make up a story. The pictures I use come from a set of 30 postcards of 'Naïve Paintings' (Magna Books, 1993). The interviewer's task is not to 'interpret' but to make up a story in exchange, one which will honour the child's story but will

Figure 28.2 R's elaboration of a line and its opposite

be an alternative, drawing also on salient themes from the preceding interview. Like all stories, it will be fictional but one in which the child is offered a different view of things. It can be ignored, accepted or used to generate yet other views. Truth and theoretical correctness are not at issue, just the possibility of alternatives. The technique calls on the interviewer's recollection of what has arisen in the interview and his or her imagination and creativity. The very writing down of the exchange story is a great help to the creative and imaginative process since it gives time to select an appropriate continuation of theme.

A RETURN TO THE BEGINNING

In my opening paragraphs I have said that the matters to be discussed arose within a context where teachers referred children who were presenting as 'problems' but that, following Kelly, it was possible to see that their 'problems' arose from their constructions of events. Although the child may indeed have problems they would probably be on a different dimension. The body of the text has been concerned with the practice of intervention, directed primarily at the child, but with the aim also of helping to resolve the teacher's dilemmas. The child may, indeed, change, arising from personal 'reconstructions' in the interview; nonetheless, completeness demands a return to teachers.

Essentially the issue is one of a resolution of the teacher's 'problem' signalled by the original referral. The approach may best be seen in two dimensions. On the one hand, because the referral is a reflection of 'interaction and communications' involving child and teacher, change may be looked for in any or all of the 'content', 'relationship' and 'context' aspects of the interchanges. Exceptionally, the last of these may well involve action under the rubric of 'Special needs'. On the other hand, action to bring about change may best be seen within a personal construct framework—that is, arising out of the teacher's 'construct system'.

Firstly, there needs to be illumination, thereby leading to a 'reconstruing' by the teacher of the child and the situation. Sharing the information arising from the interview with a child can achieve that. Two cases illustrate the effect of that strategy; in each case teacher (or head teacher, or head of year) action was taken in the light of the discussion following the interview. An infant school head teacher handled a child's incomprehensible backwardness by taking him into her own special reading group (changing the teaching context) and, importantly, inviting the mother to 'stand back' from the child's learning (changing the relationships). The boy quickly made progress. A 'head of year' teacher resolved the problems around a troublesome 13-year-old boy by asking him to look after a new admission, a boy described as 'wet', to the school (changing the relationships and 'sense of self'). That also proved effective. In each case the teacher was able to reshape the children's actions from his or her own resources. All I had done was to shed new light.

Secondly, there can be a deliberate experimenting. Despite an interview with a primary school boy, neither his teacher nor I could throw light on 'the complaint'. I asked her to stand back from the boy as much as possible for the next four weeks (change of role and relationship) when perhaps we might understand better. I agreed a time and a date to meet again. The teacher was waiting at the door and said 'There's no problem, I saw a different boy'. She had had a trainee teacher with her and, therefore, was able to stand back and observe. Did she see a 'different' boy or the same boy 'differently'? No matter, there had ceased to be a problem.

Thirdly, and more rarely, there can also be a profound exploration of a teacher's understanding. My interview with this particular primary school boy was unrewarding except for recognizing an attitude in the boy of 'don't get too near'. After sharing this with the teacher I took my courage in both hands and asked what, deep down, it was that made her a teacher (personal exploration). She said how hard that question was and then 'I suppose it is that I care'. She then saw that the problem in relation to the boy was her sense that he was invalidating a 'core' sense of herself. When I enquired some time later she said that the boy was no longer a problem, it was 'just a reading difficulty'.

EPILOGUE

In an earlier formulation of approaches to promoting change, I gave a fourth channel. The channel goes back into antiquity and is recognized in the various fables and stories associated with all religions. It is simply the telling of a story. In fact I described earlier the 'mutual story-telling' technique as a way of ending an interview with a child. Likewise, when I relate my interview to the teacher, I am also telling a story albeit an alternative to the one he or she has long been holding.

In following the same train of thought, has the writing of this chapter been yet a further example of telling a story?

CHAPTER 29

Teacher–Student Relations at University Level*

George A. Kelly

. . . But I believe this: that every individual has a right to choose the persons to whom he will relate himself. This means that, *by and large,* I think students have the right to choose their professors, to choose their universities, to choose the subjects in which they will do well and to choose the subjects in which they will do poorly. Now, the choices may not always be wise. Some of you are going to disagree with me on this. But I believe that one's education is his own responsibility, primarily; and you cannot have responsibility without, at the same time, risking authority. Thus, if a student is to be held responsible for his education, he then must have some authority for it, some right to choose it.

I think the student should exercise considerable initiative in determining what he should study, what he should not study, with whom he should study and with whom he will not study, and what he should think and what he shall choose not to think. What I am saying is this. That the patterns of student–professor relationships will have to be varied. And what I have been saying about students I think also can be said about professors.

Perhaps less so because professors are employed and they are supposed to be more flexible in dealing with different students. Let me put my main points under four headings. The task of the university professor who is meeting students coming to the university for the first time is to establish four new kinds of relationships. I think he wants to help the student to establish new kinds of relationship to knowledge itself. Second, new relationships to authority. Third, new relationship to truth itself. And last, new relationships to the students' own colleagues.

As for the new relationships to knowledge, this requires the university professor to do some shifting on his own. He takes the students in the autumn. He sees them in one kind of relationship to knowledge and he has to shift that relationship so that

---

*Excerpt from a previously unpublished lecture given at the Faculty of General Studies, University of Puerto Rico, 1958.

International Handbook of Personal Construct Psychology. Edited by F. Fransella.
© 2003 John Wiley & Sons, Ltd.

by the end of the year it's a somewhat different kind of relationship. It's a very subtle thing and a very important thing.

Perhaps I can put it this way. You have, in the Spanish language, I believe, a way of punctuating questions. You put the question mark upside down at the beginning of the question and then, just in case you forget that it is a question, you put it right side up at the end of the question. It strikes me that this is a very good thing because you warn a person in advance that it's going to be a question, and when you get through you remind him that it is a question. Now I think this is a good deal like what we need to do in university teaching. Perhaps I can put it figuratively this way. All statements in the classroom should start with this inverted question mark and conclude with a question mark. It means then, that while in high school there were declarative sentences ending with full stops and often with exclamation marks, in the university, nearly all of the sentences are implicitly sentences which start with a question mark, so there is the implied inflexion of the question mark in everything that is said. Now, this can be very distressing to students and it can be very distressing to professors, for to tell that everything you are saying ends with a question mark is sometimes to feel that you are saying nothing, that you are giving nothing firm. And sometimes your students embarrass you because of this and they hold up their hands and they say 'Don't you know anything?' And they'll trap you into putting exclamation marks after your remarks instead of question marks, because they get so disgusted with you and with your question marks!

I suppose another way of saying the same thing is that you teach students in the university how to ask questions whereas the high school has often tried to teach them how to give answers or to regurgitate answers, to throw them back out of their mouths. Now the task is to teach them how to ask questions. In lots of instances they ask very bad questions, questions which can't be answered. So, I think, often the problem of the university professor, in trying to establish new relationships to knowledge, not only is to teach the asking of questions but to teach people how to relinquish questions as badly posed, as poor issues, as poor dichotomies. We can set up these 'either–or' types of questions and get ourselves into a lot of difficulty.

There's another shift, and this is a hard one for many a professor to make. It is a shift from controlling students, from managing them, to challenging them. It is the shift in the role of the professor. In high school perhaps you try to control students; you try to get them to do the things they ought to do; you try to get them to wash behind their ears, or to use the dictionary, or to discover the encyclopaedia or to read a book that has not been assigned. You try to control them. But in the university the task becomes one of shifting from that over to challenging them, to making them so miserable with their present state of knowledge that out of sheer exasperation with you or with their own ignorance, or with something else, they go out and they find out something. So, the task is to stop controlling and to challenge instead. But sometimes when we attempt to challenge we only destroy. Sometimes our efforts to challenge really degenerate into a kind of negative hostile control; and this is of course a pitfall for us. We have to teach our students how to replace certainty with uncertainty. There's a line in the musical play 'The King and I' where it says that people fight most violently for the things they are not quite sure are so, but which they don't want to admit they are questioning. The things that you really feel comfortable about you don't usually get quite so violent over. But things which you feel you must believe even though you doubt, are the things we become unreasonable about. And so I think we have to teach students how to live with uncertainty.

Basically, this is a problem of taking people who come as students, and changing them into colleagues. Does this seem like a radical idea? In a way it is like saying: 'You come to me as students sitting in the classroom before me. I am up here on the pedestal. But I am here to destroy this relationship we have between us. And when we get through I want us to be sitting around a table, and I want you as my colleagues upon whom I can lean, who will support me, who will keep me from making mistakes and slap me down when I get out of line. This is the transition that I want to take place. And I am going to destroy your present attitude toward me as an authority, as an authoritative person.'

Now you see, this is a very difficult thing for a teacher to do. It means essentially that the teacher takes his own status and there, before the eyes of the students, he destroys himself as an authority, and he asks the students to come up and sit with him and to join him as a colleague.

Now this is humiliating. Sometimes I say that there's nothing more humiliating than being a university professor. If you don't want to be humiliated, then teach kindergarten. If you want to be an authority, if you want to be 'boss', then get way, way down the line; because the university professor destroys his own status by the very nature of his teaching. One way of thinking of it is this. We are teaching, we are interacting with the very people who a generation from now, or perhaps sooner, will be proving us wrong. These are the people who will be giving the lie to many of the things we are saying in the classroom. There they are, sitting around, looking at us. To be sure, now we have the advantage of them. But at some time that rascal back there, who is so dumb that he just can't get one of my points, at some time that fellow is going to write a book that will tear my writings all to pieces, and he'll destroy me. And I'm here to help him do it. These are the people who will undo what we are doing today. These are the people who will stand up before the world and prove us wrong.

It means also, I think, that we have to share our perplexities with students, if we are genuinely worried about something, if we are genuinely perplexed, if we have our own doubts, I think we have to transmit those doubts, admit them to our students. And I think in the long run they'll appreciate it. At least my students seem to. They take advantage of me at first. If I tell them I'm not sure about certain things, they do indeed take advantage of me! And there are a lot of things that I'm sceptical about. One of the sacred cows of psychology, for example, is this concept of learning. Every textbook in psychology has chapter after chapter on learning. As I read those chapters I get more and more disturbed, because it seems as if the verb 'to learn' has degenerated simply into the verb 'to become'. 'Learning' has become such a broad concept that I think it is nothing but a form of the verb 'to become', or 'to be'. And so I say to my students, 'I doubt if this concept of learning means anything. It just bothers me. I am perplexed about it.' So they set about to try to tell me what *learning* is. And they say 'Well, you should read this and this.'

And they bring in articles for me to read. My students are always bringing in things for me to read, to take care of my education. Most of them do it very gracefully. They say, 'Well, I know you've been very busy. I know it will take you some time to get this out of the library. So I've checked it out for you, and I've marked the places I thought you might like to read.' They're always doing that. I've got one student who brings in a paper-backed book, or something for me to read just every couple of weeks or so, and they are somewhat stacked up, I'm afraid, on the edge of my desk.

I am perplexed and I think it is all right for students to learn that professors are perplexed. And as they learn this they will discover that professors are not very good authorities. I think also we need to teach students not to teach. (I guess none of this is teaching, is it?) We need to invite students to share in our own efforts if we are trying to solve a problem, if we are doing a piece of research, if we are preparing a manuscript. I think it is very helpful to ask students to help work out the ideas; but I warn you it is also very painful.

Like many of you, I thought years ago that I wanted to write a book. Most of you, I suspect, are planning to write a book, or feel that you should write a book. Well, years ago, I came down with this disease, too; and I kept telling myself I was going to write a book. I would potter around with it and I wrote notes and tried writing chapters. And they were horrible things, So, finally, the years went by and I got older and older, and I got lazier. Then I began to be afraid I would never get this book written. So finally I took myself in hand and I said, 'I am going to get this book written, good, bad, or indifferent. I have to get it out of my system.' So I sat down and I really began writing it. I hated what I wrote, but I was going to write it anyway.

I did something else. I invited anybody who wanted, including my students, to come every Thursday evening to listen to me read what I had written during the week and to make comments on it. Now this was a very rugged experience. Sometimes we covered as much as one page of manuscript and sometimes we covered much more. But they forced me to rewrite. Some of them told me that what I had written made no sense at all. They couldn't understand it. Besides, I didn't really believe all that nonsense, they were sure. They enjoyed this and I have never had a stronger group of student come through a programme. Not all of them were students.

Some of my colleagues came too, to listen to this monstrosity of an author reading his own manuscript. Some time later, some of the students said, 'Do you know, when you were doing that' (this happened over a three-year period, by the way; it was a long torture for me), 'we would go out together afterwards, and sit around the table and say "Now do you think we hit him too hard tonight? Do you think maybe he'll quit writing?"' And some of them were worried for fear they may have hit me too hard and I might give up the project. So then they would come around to me individually and say 'Now, don't give up. Just because the rest have criticized. Come on, keep going, I'm on your side.' And then they would usually decide as a group that they would hit me again the next week, until it really looked as if I was going to go down. Then, they would pick me up. Now this really went on among my students. And while it was a painful experience, it turned out to be a very good learning experience for them. While nearly all of them have their PhDs now, as a group, they are very loyal to me and to this experience, and I feel I have colleagues to whom I can go for advice. There was a remarkable shift in the authority relationship there. . . .

It is unfortunate for a student to go through the university without sharing his professor's efforts. I think he needs to see his professor as one who is striving as a scholar, and it is just too bad that a student can't sit at the professor's elbow and the two of them together puzzle about the problem that the professor is interested in. We have, in our own Department of Psychology (in the clinical psychology area, where I teach) what we call 'seminars', and these seminars are not student centred, nor curriculum centred. They are deliberately professor centred. They are taught for the amusement of the professor, and we announce them this way. But they are this. They are invitations for the students, for any student who wants to come in and join the professor as he puzzles about problems that he is interested in. And it is not expected that the professor will try to teach them anything at all, but that only he will share his questions, share his quest with them. And students like this. They come in; the professor says, 'I am worried about this. I am trying to solve this. I am going to have a series of discussions on this topic. I invite you to come with me as I explore this area of the unknown that I am puzzling about. Come and join me.' And so he puzzles about it, thinks out loud, questions out loud, and they chime in and react to him. I think these are very important kinds of classes. They are different, you see. I think it is too bad for a student not to have a chance to join with a professor in this quest for knowledge.

My third new-relations topic is new relations to truth, new relations to truth itself. I separate this from new relations to knowledge, knowledge being more of a factual nature, truth being presumably something which is basic and general. How shall we say this? I think, first of all, it means something like this: that the university professor has to teach the student, or help the student to understand, that the truth that is capsulated in words, that is packaged in words or formulated in words, is only a partial truth, that the great truths have not yet been reduced to words. Thus, when you ask most young students how they would discover some truth that was not in the library, that had never been enunciated, never been said, had never been put into words, most of them are confused, and yet, this is the task of university education, I think—to go beyond mere words and to seek out truth which exists in the amorphous, unverbalized form.

One of the students recently asked me something like this. He asked whether a certain kind of a student organization would work. He was asking me to put in words the answer to his question, and I said, 'I don't know.' 'Where could I find out?,' he asked. I answered, 'I doubt if anyone knows whether this would work.' Then it seemed for the moment as if he was completely blocked. If truth had not yet been reduced to words, how can you find it? And I suggested that one of the ways we find truth is by experimentation, by trying things, by observing, by exploring, for there is the vast world of truth that does not exist in words, and yet is still open for exploration. And this I think is a real challenge to teaching to get youngsters to go after truth which is beyond words. Sometimes it means a formulation of programmes of inquiry, formulation of hypotheses, sometimes a formulation of experimentation, sometimes it means only going to where the truth may be, except that you don't know how you will find it. A very good research professor that I know once told me that if you don't know how to break open a problem, don't sit behind your desk and try to break it open. Go to where the problem is, you may not know for sure what the problem is, but go to its locus, get in the midst of it, and sit there in the midst of it, or act in the midst of it, and then maybe you will find a way to get hold of it.

One of the greatest examples of this kind of grasping of a very difficult problem is the problem faced by Binet, the psychiatrist and psychologist in Paris at the beginning of the twentieth century, known for the Binet intelligence testing. There had been efforts to measure intelligence after some manner or another for approximately a century before the twentieth. And most of them had fallen flat on their faces. In 1903, the city commissioners of Paris got worried about the tax problem and got worried about the question of the school budget, and whether they were educating a lot of youngsters who really didn't have the mental ability to be educated. . . . And so they appointed a commission of two men, Simon and Binet, to make a study, to find out whether funds were being used to educate youngsters who were worth educating. Simon, having been an army physician, no doubt decided that the proper approach was to give all the children a physical examination. In the army, every time you turn around, you get a physical examination. So, he got busy with that right away, and this left Binet with nothing to do. He wished he had thought of that first. But Simon got the jump on him and so he had to think of something different. He sat in his office and puzzled day after day. How do I get at this question of children's ability? And not knowing what else to do, finally he just put on his hat and went out and went to the school. He asked teachers if he could sit in the back of the classroom and he just sat in classroom after classroom. 'How do I do this?' he asked himself, 'Puzzling!'

He was going where the problem was. He talked to children. He couldn't get anywhere. He talked to teachers. He asked them if they could measure mental ability. 'Of course'—you know how teachers are. They all said they could. So he asked them how they did it. One of them said, 'Why yes, I give them problems in arithmetic because mathematics really tests the mind.'

Another said, 'I take an opportunity to feel their heads, to feel where the bumps are, and that's the way I tell.' Another said, 'I just get one good look at the light in their eyes; that's the way I tell.' He felt rather badly about this, but he still wanted to be with the problem. So he said to these teachers: 'Look. Can you spare some time on Saturdays, and come down to my office? I'll have some children there that you haven't seen before. If you don't mind I'll sit in the back of the office while you look at these children, interview them, do with them whatever you want to do with them. I'll see if I get any ideas from that.' So he watched teachers facing children for the first time, right in his office, and he took notes. And then the idea began to dawn on him. And it was out of this kind of immersion in the problem, going to where the problem was, that he developed his concept of intelligence. Of course, after we got it over in the United States we rode it into the ground. But his is an example of a kind of scholarship that breaks open problems that have not yet been cast in words. This is one of the great teaching responsibilities.

And finally, the task of the university professor is to help the students to establish new relations to their own colleagues. I think this is one of the most frequently overlooked functions of the university education. A number of years ago, twelve and a half years ago to be exact, I went to the Ohio State University to direct the clinical psychology programme. I got myself immersed in a little bit of administrative responsibility, from which I was able later to extricate myself, and I've been trying ever since to avoid administrative responsibility. But that is another matter. When I first went there, there were a great many students who wanted to become clinical psychologists. We started holding special seminars. I'm a great believer in doing your teaching in non-credit courses. I don't think it is possible to teach very much in a course that has credit, or where roll is taken. I think the best teaching is done where people don't have to come, and where there is no standard syllabus ... Anyway, in some of these special seminars, when I would mention statistics, for example, or a mathematical computation applied to human data, there would be a very dull silence around the room. They would look away, look at each other and murmur, 'Clinical psychologists must know statistical methods?' It was a very discouraging thing. And then I would talk about something else, or one of the other professors would talk about another topic. But always there would be a sort of a silence and a cringing away from these erudite topics.

The situation is different now. Rarely do we have to teach statistical concepts to the students. Why? They teach them to each other. Most of the teaching that goes on in our graduate programme is teaching that goes on from student to student. The first-year students go to the second- or third- or fourth-year students. All we, as professors, have to do is to present them with the new stuff, stuff that has just come out in the past two or three years. Students themselves mainly take responsibility for teaching each other the standard things. And it takes a great deal of the load off our shoulders. Moreover, I think they do a better job of it, because in the student–teacher relationship it gets pretty stiff and formal sometimes, especially if the teacher doesn't know it too well himself. So, I think one of the great tasks of the university is to create a kind of community in which a great deal of education goes on between students, to create a climate of interactive scholarship, so students know which other students to go to in order to get help on something. For if you depend upon education to take place in the classroom or in the library, or at home at the desk, you are missing one of the great resources of education. Think what happens after students go out. Then they will have to depend upon colleagues for educational resources. I think this is one of our tasks: to teach students how to use their own colleagues as instructors.

CHAPTER 30

Construing Teaching and Teacher Education Worldwide

Maureen Pope
University of Reading, UK

In the foreword to Kelly's chapter 'Social Inheritance', Bannister suggests that: 'the most significant aspect of this early essay is the argument running through it that education should be about personal meaning' (Kelly, 1979, p. 3). It is that emphasis on personal meaning that links Kelly to contemporary constructivist approaches in education. In particular, issues such as the 'perspective of the personal', his focus on relevance and responsibility within the teaching and learning process, his theoretical stance and his recognition and valuing of alternative perspectives, have all had an impact on education. Pope and Denicolo (2001) provide a comprehensive discussion of the ways in which his ideas have been used within education.

A GUIDING METAPHOR

The current vogue for constructivism within education has often failed to consider Kelly's pioneering spirit that enthused many personal construct psychologists to take his lead and explore the educational implications of his work. However, Bruner (1990, p. 163) acknowledged that Kelly's two volumes appearing in 1955, a year before the by-now-standard date for the 'opening of the cognitive revolution', was the first effort to construct a theory of personality from a theory of knowledge. Bruner recognized that Kelly was in the forefront of those concerned with how people make sense of their worlds. Since the 1980s many teacher educators and educational researchers have echoed this viewpoint. Clark (1986, p. 9) suggested that: 'the teacher of 1985 is a constructivist who continually builds, elaborates and tests his or her personal theory of the world . . . we have begun to move away from those . . . mechanical metaphors that guided our earlier work.'

International Handbook of Personal Construct Psychology. Edited by F. Fransella.
© 2003 John Wiley & Sons, Ltd.

Kelly's metaphor of person-as-scientist and, more recently, person-as-story-teller underpinning personal construct psychology have become guiding metaphors for many contemporary educationalists. The 'perspective of the personal' is central. It is explicit in his writings: 'we start with a person. Organisms, lower animals and societies can wait' (see Chapter 1 in this volume).

The importance of personal perspectives has been elaborated by Thomas and Harri-Augstein who argued that, if learning is to be an enriching experience, the meanings that emerge must be personally 'significant in some part of the person's life. The viability of these meanings depends on how richly the individual incorporates them into personal experience' (1985, p. xxiv). Thomas and Harri-Augstein encouraged learners, teachers, teacher trainers and managers in industry to recognize their potential through being able to become self-organized as learners. By *self-organization* they refer to a process by which learners are encouraged to reflect on their own learning process, often with the help of a facilitator. They have pointed out the limitations inherent in previous versions of learning theory that were predicated on experiments in the laboratory (see also Chapter 32, pp. 319–326).

They argue that construction of personal experience is prior. This process is essentially conversational. 'An awareness of this process demands an awareness of a meta-conversation about learning' (Thomas and Harri-Augstein, 1985, pp. 27–28). Their book shares with the reader the various technologies they have invented which can 'represent personal meaning in ways that enable reflection, review and effective transformation of the quality of human experience and performance'. Learning-to-learn becomes a central task for the learner and the facilitation of this meta-cognition, part of the role of the teacher.

Kelly recognized learning as a personal exploration and saw the teacher's role as helping to design and implement each child's own undertakings. 'To be a fully accredited participant in the experimental enterprise she must gain some sense of what is being seen through the child's eyes' (Kelly, 1970, p. 262). What is relevant to the person is of importance and, for education to be an effective encounter between the teacher and learner, it would be beneficial if each has some awareness of the other's personal constructs.

Bell and Gilbert supported this view in their book on teacher development. They suggested that:

> Kelly's great contribution to constructivism is his assertion that there are no predetermined limits on constructs in terms of the nature and range of their application. The limit to their creation is only set by the imagination of the individual concerned and by the constructs being continually tested. (1996, p. 46)

Constructivist educators, including teacher educators, pay attention to the learner's current ideas and how they change in addition to the structure and sequence of teaching 'received' knowledge.

THE TEACHER'S CHALLENGE

Kelly's theory of knowledge has implications for how the teacher helps the student to actively construe experiences. In viewing our constructions of reality as potentially open to reconstruction, Kelly's stance as a therapist *and* as an educator was to encourage clients/learners to articulate their world views and to recognize these world views as current hypotheses potentially open to invalidation. In this way he hoped the clients/learners would put themselves in the position of opening their minds to potential alternatives, which might serve their cause better. He saw his interest was in helping people to reconstrue their lives so that they need not be the victims of their pasts.

As a direct consequence of his Sociality Corollary, Kelly recognized that learning is a personal exploration and that the teacher must come to some understanding of the experiments, lines of enquiry and personal strategies used by the learner. He saw the teacher's role as helping:

> . . . to design and implement each child's own undertakings, as well as to assist in interpreting the outcomes and in devising more cogent behavioural inquiries. But usually she has to begin, as any apprentice begins, by implementing what others have designed; in this case, what her children have initiated.
>
> (Kelly, 1970, p. 262)

Implementing such advice within teacher education poses a challenge, particularly if governmental policies militate against it or such a view runs counter to the teacher's implicit theories of teaching and learning. Teacher educators may wish to encourage conceptual change in the way teaching and learning are promoted. They should remember that the goggles through which others view their worlds might not be easily altered. However, unless the learner's views are articulated, the teacher cannot devise a strategy whereby the learner's model can be put to the test. Kelly noted that change in construing will only take place if people experiment with their own way of seeing things, construe the implications of these experiments and see that it would result in an elaboration of their construing system.

For a personal construct educator, teaching should be based upon a rigorous consideration of alternative theories—those of the students and the teacher as well as 'received wisdom'. There should be a supportive climate for students as they try to articulate their construing by being encouraged to talk about their ideas. Talking about ideas and listening to the conflicting opinions of others and the putting of these ideas to the test is an approach to teaching which is consistent with Kelly's model of 'man the scientist'.

Finding ways to help learners articulate their construing is an important challenge for the teacher that also applies to those involved with teacher education. Within pre- and in-service professional development, teachers are being encouraged to rethink the metaphors they live by (Lakoff & Johnson, 1980). Kelly's guiding metaphor of man the scientist and his philosophy of constructive alternativism imply a view of knowledge and action which suggests that, if practices are to change, teachers need to examine some of 'their fundamental beliefs'. Teachers may find consideration of their current construing threatening, especially if they deduce that change is needed. Constructivist teacher educators see that as a challenge but one that provides potentially empowering experiences for the teacher and the learner. The following examples show that Kelly's challenge to teachers and teacher educators is global.

TEACHER DEVELOPMENT

In an early study of teacher development in Israel, Ben-Peretz (1984, p. 106) advocated participation in 'action research as a process of teacher development'. Curriculum planning exercises were seen as a useful vehicle for such an approach. In discussing her investigation of teacher thinking, Ben-Peretz suggested that assisting teachers to reflect on and become more aware of their construing patterns should be planned as part of a teacher's professional training and development. Denicolo and Pope (1990) agree that action research is potentially an emancipatory approach to staff development and point out a number of assumptions shared by personal construct psychologists and action researchers.

It has been assumed, in action research models, that learning and professional development are enhanced by reflection on and in practice. However, following Kelly's lead, Denicolo and Pope warn of the potential hostility and resistance to change of the individual whose core constructs may be threatened by the consideration of an alternative model which would require too much revision of their current ways of viewing their work. The teacher educator/action researcher needs to be aware of the extreme sensitivity of the reflective material that can be evoked. They must be prepared to give time and support during periods of deconstruction and reconstruction when an individual is confronted with an image or action that he or she may wish to change. That is a fundamental requirement within constructivist approaches to professional teacher education.

In the USA, Clark referred to the fact that, for many, the phrase 'professional development of teachers' contains 'a great deal of negative baggage: it implies a process done to teachers; that teachers need to be forced into developing; that teachers have deficits in knowledge and skills that can be fixed by training; and that teachers are pretty much alike' (1995, p. 124). Constructivist teacher education entails a process akin to the development of learners. The deficit model constrains development and pays insufficient attention to support mechanisms that may be needed during reappraisal.

Diamond, while in Australia, used a staff development approach based on fixed role therapy (see Chapter 23, pp. 237–245) and has conducted research on the constructs of pre- and in-service teachers regarding their role. He found that teachers would give up a viewpoint, even if it were an integral part of them, as long as they had become aware of the more personally meaningful implications of an alternative. As he said: 'if teachers can be helped to "open their eyes", they can see how to choose and fashion their own version of reality' (1985, p. 34). Later, Diamond moved to Canada where, at the time of writing, he continues to develop teacher education strategies based on personal construct psychology. In a subsequent book, Diamond commented that 'teacher education becomes a matter of travelling with different viewpoints and escaping being held prisoner by the fixity of any one perspective' (1991, p. 76). Kelly's voice is apparent here. In both of these works, Diamond provides illuminating examples of how he has worked as a teacher educator using repertory grids and fixed role therapy methods to encourage changes in teachers' construing.

In pre-service teacher education, the formal concepts presented on university and on college courses need to be transformed and assimilated into the particular frame of reference held by the student teacher. From the beginning student teachers, as learners, need to become aware of their implicit theories and continue to explore their developing assumptions, which underlie their teaching behaviour. Drawing extensively from my own work in pre-service education, Boei and his colleagues are concerned with the subjective theories of Dutch student teachers. They suggest that knowledge of these subjective theories would be useful within pre-service and in-service teacher training. Traditionally the task of teacher training in the Netherlands is seen as one of teaching students objective theories that can be put into practice. However, Boei and his colleagues propose that 'to be able to apply the taught objective theories, student teachers must convert them to their idiographic practice' (Boei et al., 1989, p. 175). They used repertory grids to investigate student teachers' construing about 'good' teaching. They first conducted open-ended interviews during which the student teacher's ideas were elicited. When deciding on the elements for the grids, they 'kept as true as possible to the formulations that were made by the student teachers' within the initial interviews (Boei et al., 1989, p. 179). The statements were reformulated in terms of teacher behaviour, for example 'the teacher pays attention to individual children'. In addition to 'teacher behaviour elements' the researchers provided two further elements, 'I as a teacher' and 'I as an ideal teacher'. They identified a number of common constructs used by student teachers. One interesting result was that the difference between 'I as a teacher' and 'I as an ideal teacher' was most marked in terms of the construct *professional activities inside class/school—professional activities outside class/school*. Boei and his colleagues suggest that in their opinion: 'this points to a rather narrow perception of the professional teaching role' (1989, p. 189). They advocated that outside activities should be considered within teacher training to avoid teaching being separated from its ethical, political and social dimensions.

Sendan (1995) saw learning to teach as a complex process of change in student teachers' personal theories during which they develop, test and reconstruct their own hypotheses about teaching. He followed Turkish student teachers throughout their three-year course. His study was concerned with the nature of, and changes in, student teachers' personal theories regarding teaching effectiveness throughout their initial teacher training. Sendan used grids and tape-recorded interviews with each participant. He then classified the various constructs elicited, deriving several categories. Sendan discussed the patterns of change in construing that he observed in his data. Between the first two occasions this was mostly in the area of teacher knowledge and characteristics. There was more focus on constructs concerned with lesson management between the second and third occasions and on lesson management and teacher/pupil relationship between the third and fourth occasion. Sendan (1995, p. 121) saw this as 'indicating a pattern of "deconstruction" of personal theories in the early years of training and "reconstruction" towards the end'.

How Student Teachers View Themselves

In the case studies, Sendan was able to focus on both the change in content and structure of each student teachers' construing. His experience of using the repertory grid technique confirmed his view that student teachers are capable of reflecting on their personal theories and training experiences when given the opportunity and a supportive environment. The student teachers' active involvement in the research process helped them to have a greater consciousness of their personal theories about teaching and their views of themselves as a teacher. This participation also helped them to reflect on various experiences during their period of training. As one student commented, 'I found it extremely useful to articulate my thoughts and feelings about teaching. I now feel more aware of who I am and who I would like to be' (Sendan, 1995, p. 229). Sendan and one of my doctoral students, Saka, have done much to develop a more constructivist approach within Turkish teacher education (Pope & Saka, 1997).

In the UK, Watts and Vaz drew on the work of Paolo Freire and Kelly because they both 'proposed forward-looking theories, the former at the level of the culture of the group and the latter at the psychological level of the individual' (Watts & Vaz, 1997, p. 334). Their research centred on the themes that emerged during conversations with primary teachers of science. These themes were those seen as emotionally significant for them. After the themes were identified they were re-presented to the teachers for further discussion. Watts and Vaz then designed what they referred to as a 'problematizing' programme for teachers' professional development, which drew on the elicited themes for its broad content. In the first session, Watts and Vaz presented the teachers with a number of questions related to recall of episodes of emotional experiences written on individual cards, and teachers were asked to write responses in a designated space. They were also given blank cards to provide any extra elements for discussion. Some cards prompted positive feelings and others prompted episodes associated with negative feelings.

The teachers were asked to select nine from their set of cards, which became the elements in a repertory grid interview. The second and third meetings were devoted to conversations with the teachers about their experience and their beliefs and assumptions about the teaching of science. These discussions began with a reflection on the analysed grid and, according to Watts and Vaz (1997, p. 336), a dialogue with a clearly 'problematizing' tone emerged. The repertory grids allowed the researchers to discuss very specific elements of the teachers' professional knowledge and experience while they were encouraged to justify their personal constructs. Reflection on the grids produced a rich source of generative themes. One example of the many themes which emerged during the course of the conversations concerned the teachers' need to exercise 'didactic restraint, to organize their classrooms for what became known as "hands-off teaching for hands-off learning"'. This theme reflected the teachers' dilemma of hoping to encourage pupils to find out about science for themselves while resisting telling children what to do and transmitting the 'received' view of science. The teachers in Watts and Vaz's study showed clear recognition of the importance of the child constructing their knowledge.

Mair (1989b, p. 5) invited personal construct psychologists to explore a story-telling metaphor and consider 'the stories that they live and that they tell'. Nelson (1993) was interested in teachers as story-tellers and personal meaning using the voice of practising teachers. Nelson sent letters to the entire teaching staff of one school district in the USA asking them to share their stories about meaningful moments in their teaching careers. Fifty-five teachers agreed to contribute stories, which they themselves audiotaped. Nelson, with the help of three independent readers, identified a number of themes from the transcribed tapes. She noted that, even though the stories were self-selected in response to an open invitation, the themes evoked revealed some commonality of perspectives and values. Using teachers' stories with teacher development programmes is a powerful means of helping teachers to reflect on the challenges and rewards of the teaching profession.

Apelgren (2001) also used a story-telling metaphor with Swedish teachers. She asked them to think back on their career in terms of a winding river in which each bend represented an experience that had influenced their direction. Each teacher was then asked to draw this river and write a few words about these critical incidents. The teaching stories that evolved as each teacher discussed the rivers, after they had spent a period alone drawing up their own river, were tape-recorded. The rivers became the agenda for an interview in which the teachers reflected on how they construed teaching.

Apelgren found qualitatively different ways of experiencing language teaching based on the participants' self-perception of the teacher's role and their personal theories of teaching. She identified four themes which, she suggested, were aligned with particular metaphors: *teaching as a mutual affair, teaching as guiding with an invisible hand, teaching as a social activity* and *teaching as being a captain of a ship*. Apelgren called her themes 'orientations' to imply potential fluidity in the teachers' construing. She was able to highlight the complexity of her participants' personal theories on teaching and their views on their own professional development. Apelgren noted that the opportunity to sit down and recollect past experiences with someone else listening was regarded as 'stimulating and satisfying'. As one participant commented:

> It also makes me 'clear my mind' and I have to decide what teaching is about, what goals I have and why I do certain things. Everyday life is so hectic so there is little time to evaluate what you do, what you have done and if you have achieved the goals you set up. (Apelgren, 2001, p. 327)

The expression 'clear my mind' indicates a possibility for the teacher to stop and move behind the actual practice, to reflect and reconstrue. Gaining a perspective means allowing the present to encounter the past, as well as realizing how the past influences teachers' thinking and guides future action. In my own work with teachers I have found similar reactions. One teacher, faced with issues surrounding the inclusion of disabled children within regular classrooms, commented on the importance of teachers confronting their own feelings:

> . . . think PCP could have a great impact in this area as teachers examine their own constructs towards students who have disabilities. If the teacher's perception of the disabled child is negative, then the mainstream experience would be a negative one for the child.

Helping pre- and in-service teachers to consider changing their current practice is not merely a technical process. As one of my teachers put it: 'It is not an easy task this process of being a "scientist" and the ways are very uncharted and at times uncertain. The process seems to require a great deal of emotional energy.'

CONCLUSIONS

Personal and professional change are inextricably linked. An implication of personal construct psychology is that teacher educators should take risks and adopt a reflective and enquiring stance as an example to their students. We must, from time to time, review how we are construing education and the extent to which we understand the position of others with whom we interact. This is a central message of Kelly's work for those striving for a more democratic educational process in schools and in universities and is one that many teacher educators throughout the world now advocate.

CHAPTER 31

A Psychology for Teachers

Phillida Salmon
Tadworth, Surrey, UK

For teachers working now in British schools at the beginning of the twenty-first century, the current educational *zeitgeist* carries little inspiration. Within a market model of education, teaching is viewed as no more than the simple delivery of a commodity: the pre-packaged bits of information that supposedly make up the school curriculum. The capacity of learners to absorb and reproduce this information in tests and examinations is the criterion of educational success. In today's society the function of the schooling system is to classify and grade its pupil intake. Through this grading young people will emerge with very different credentials: some with enhanced, others with diminished, life chances. Nor is it only pupils who are subject to classification within a hierarchy of competence. Even schools themselves must now compete with one another. Superior league tables boost pupil numbers; qualifying for specialist status brings extra money and more resources. The same competitive principle is also applied to teachers. Judgements of individual teachers as 'incompetent' or 'super' carry their own financial and career consequences.

This is a philosophy which reduces the complex processes of learning, teaching and knowing to the status of objects. Its picture of education is a picture of fixed and static entities which retain their identical character across the whole spectrum of widely different classrooms, of the huge variety of individual pupils and individual teachers. Processes in which everything is fluid and subject to varying personal meaning become simple products, predefined and easily measurable.

Current educational philosophy thus rests on a hierarchical model. All pupils are placed, through their various test performances, at some point on a scale of competence: a point which marks the fixed limits of their ability, a point beyond which they cannot go. On the assumption that learning ability is generalized and statistically distributed, young people become defined as good, average or poor learners, and learning is something that some people do well and other people do badly.

International Handbook of Personal Construct Psychology. Edited by F. Fransella.
© 2003 John Wiley & Sons, Ltd.

A PERSONAL CONSTRUCT THEORY ALTERNATIVE

In its vision of education, personal construct psychology stands in the greatest possible contrast to the current British philosophy. It is a psychology of processes, not products, of verbs rather than nouns. It sees learning, not as the reproduction of a ready-made information pack, but as the shifting of meanings within an essentially personal system of understandings. Teaching appears, in a Kellyian perspective, as the struggle to exchange understandings, to enlarge mutual comprehension between persons who may have widely different world views. 'Knowledge', far from being a standardized, externally defined entity, becomes something temporary and open to change. As Martin Fromm argues in the next chapter, the 'reality' status accorded to generally held assumptions cannot stand with a position which recognizes multiple realities, and the essentially provisional nature of what is known. Seen in this light, the school curriculum looks very different.

In a Kellyian perspective, a hierarchy of learning ability makes no sense. Learning, in this philosophy, is synonymous with living itself. As human beings we are all lifelong learners. While we differ hugely in what we come to know, each of us strives, in day-to-day encounters with our worlds, to understand the way things are. And for all of us, living cannot but entail experiencing what we did not anticipate. Wholly unexpected events, personal predicaments and dilemmas, the same mistake made yet again: these contingencies demand that we reflect in fundamental ways—rethink, if we can, some of our most basic assumptions. As Kelly himself vividly documented within psychotherapy, such change is seldom easy. Where our most basic sense of ourselves and our worlds seems to be at risk, we typically close ourselves off to the threat of reconstruing. Though there may be areas where new understandings seem viable, even exciting, there are others where change is strenuously resisted. Different circumstances elicit variable learning competence: we are all adept at some kinds of learning, deeply closed, even personally hostile, towards others.

If some ways of making sense seem congenial, while others appear threatening, this is because the material of learning is seldom neutral. As argued in the previous section, how we see things at any moment is a function of a whole system of intuitive meanings—meanings which sustain the personal projects that are our lives. Young people do not abandon their own personal projects when they enter the classroom. They bring with them their own worlds, and their personal identities within those worlds. It is in relation to that sense of themselves and their personal contexts that they hear their teachers. To a few perhaps, the material offered seems immediately interesting; it confirms the way they see things, and carries exciting possibilities for further exploration. But for others—probably many others—this classroom material may seem irrelevant, bypassing what they value, seemingly having nothing to do with them, even implicitly challenging their own deepest concerns.

Learning by Inquiry

Teachers themselves are generally all too well aware of the different personal, social and cultural worlds, the multiple realities sitting side by side at classroom desks.

Knowing the sense of irrelevance, even alienation, that the school curriculum can arouse, they strive to engage with pupils' personal meanings, to relate at least something of the curricular material to the urgent business of these young people's lives. The officially prescribed content to be presented in classroom work may seem to offer answers to questions that pupils seldom ask. Helping learners to achieve 'really useful knowledge' is no easy task: it stands a mile away from the facile depiction of teaching as a simple delivery of ready-made information packages.

As Kelly insisted, we all learn by asking questions. It is only by putting our uncertainties to the test—trying out the viability of our hunches, translating possibilities into actuality—that we discover something about the way things are. Of course the outcome of one enquiry typically leads to other uncertainties, and the need for further question-asking. The human quest, in Kellyian philosophy, is ongoing and lifelong. But no knowledge is ever achieved without active efforts to test out possibilities. Whereas the dominant model of learning in British schools accords pupils an essentially passive role, this philosophy demands an active participation from young people in the classroom.

A Kellyian vision of learning sees learners as necessarily being active and possessing initiative. Understandings cannot be reached through simple receptivity; pupils need to be active, argumentative, challenging. It is, as Michael Billig (1987) has tellingly shown, only through the to-and-fro of interpersonal debate that we become able to reason inwardly. Expressing personal ideas out loud, directly challenging another's opinion, playing devil's advocate: from these externalized modes come capacities to internalize—to argue with ourselves, to try out possibilities inwardly, to conduct an inner debate. This is what thinking essentially entails. And thinking, so fundamental to new understandings, can come about only in classrooms which allow space and encouragement for pupils to ask questions, and to follow up answers with further questions and challenges.

Because it allows the exploration of real questions and the active enquiries of young people, active communication between students, and between students and teachers achieves far greater dividends of understanding than the essentially short-term acquisition of unrelated facts that may result from simple teacher chalk and talk. But such methods are far from being an easy option. It is not just that in the present British educational context there are relentless pressures on teachers to produce good test results at every schooling stage. Beyond this, as Kelly was himself acutely aware, the thinking required in any new learning is difficult and often threatening.

New ways of seeing things cannot but throw a question mark over known and established ways—ways that may be buttressed by the confirmation and approval of important people. To take up the perspective entailed in what is offered, to speak in the terms, the language in which the curriculum is framed: this may seem a dangerous thing to try, a thing entailing risks to one's very identity. For 'knowledge' is never neutral; it carries the interests and concerns of particular sociocultural groupings. For school learners, the knowledge offered in their classrooms appears at first sight to 'belong' to the teachers who convey it. As such, it may seem attractive to some pupils for the very reasons that it seems alien to others.

But, as teachers often ably demonstrate, classroom knowledge is not immutable. When young people engage directly with their school curriculum, and bring their own personal issues and positions into relation with its ways of framing the world, there can be radical learning breakthroughs. And in the process whereby pupils come to enlarge their repertoires of personal meaning, the curricular material is itself altered. The understanding of English that follows from the sustained critical reflection, by themselves and their peers, on their own writings is something different from the understanding with which they began. In place of an impersonal, out-there curriculum are new meanings, personally created by those involved.

Learning Poses Risks

Real learning, learning that has genuinely personal implications, does not come easily. The psychotherapy clients described by Kelly do, like all serious learners, find their learning difficult and frustrating. Struggling to break out of long-established habits, familiar ways of reacting, they flounder in confusion and resistance, before, suddenly, other possibilities emerge. For this to happen, as Kelly insists, a safe, protected space is needed.

This is no less true of classroom learning. In a personal construct consulting room, clients have a place where any possible way of viewing things can be tested out without personal risk. In just the same way, young people need to be free to try out, provisionally, what it would mean to look at the world in a new kind of way. Classrooms are highly public places, with a potential, as pupils know all too well, for ridicule and humiliation. In trying out anything new, we are all apt to look clumsy and inept—to ourselves and to others who witness our performance. All this calls for a high degree of sensitivity on the part of teachers.

But there are other reasons, too, why the process of learning carries personal risks. Because any new construction has implications for other established meanings— ramifications within the whole construct system—new ways of looking at things have to be tried out first in a very tentative way. Learners needs to test out, without, as yet, commitment, what the new construction would mean for them—mean personally, that is. This is not just a matter, for instance, of working mathematically, setting out to learn the logarithmic system. It is, beyond that, a question of what it would mean to be the sort of person who does maths. Teachers need to act with delicacy, enabling their pupils to try out new material at a kind of distance, without demanding that they own it.

But what young people learn at school does not just concern curricular material. Schooling institutions do not exist in a vacuum, independent of the unequal society of which they are a part. Many teachers are committed, in their daily classroom work, to creating mutual understanding and respect. But in this they have to struggle against the racism, the sexism, heterosexism and 'injuries of class', which are endemic in the wider world in which they and their pupils live their lives. As members of this society with particular sociocultural identities, young people come, quickly and often painfully, to learn their place. Such learning is, of course, typically tacit and intuitive. It is arrived at through corridor and playground dealings, through classroom encounters, through attributions of success or failure. Even the hidden curriculum of school itself, where declared policies of equality may be contradicted by the differential treatment of its members, carries its own clear messages.

Superordinate constructs, those that stand most central to our sense of ourselves, are implicated in school learning. Most obviously, this applies to the personal identity that pupils come to acquire through their involvement, above all, with fellow-pupils. But the lessons of the classroom curriculum, if they are to be taken on personally by young people, also entail meanings which have superordinate ramifications. This makes school learning a highly complex business. What is defined in current educational philosophy as a simple act of transmission—the passing on of a predefined packet of information—appears in Kelly's philosophy as a process necessitating attention to whole networks of differentiated meaning-systems.

To take this philosophy seriously means a much larger concern than is usual with intuitive and unarticulated meanings. Without attention to such meanings, it is not possible to understand how learning occurs, and why, so often, it does not occur. For people concerned with the fundamental questions of education, Kelly's own work as a psychotherapist seems immediately relevant. Just as he strove to make explicit the intuitive levels of construing which held his clients where they were, so, to understand school learning, it is necessary to unearth, to bring into articulation, the underlying, inexplicit personal constructions of its learners. Just as Maureen Pope says in Chapter 30 in relation to teacher education, so it is in the classroom; what is as yet unverbalized personal meaning must become conscious and available to reflection.

EXPLORATION OF CONSTRUING

Until now, most explorations of personal construct systems have utilized some form or extension of Kelly's own method—the repertory grid technique (see Chapter 9, pp. 95–103). The advent of this method offered a huge breakthrough in an age where psychological assessment meant forcing 'subjects' onto a psychometric bed of Procrustes. In place of generalized, preset formats which flattened and deadened human realities, grids offered access to living material, to the very terms in which people experience and engage with their own personal worlds. It enabled the elicitation of hitherto unverbalized levels of construing, and revealed the complex intuitive ramifications entailed in making human sense.

The repertory grid technique has proved widely fruitful in a huge number of psychological explorations. Yet for some kinds of educational enquiry, rather different methods may be called for. Where learning is in question, the purpose is typically not just diagnostic—even diagnostic of change over time. Those who seek to explore the learner's construing do not generally want to stop at uncovering meanings that explain why learning is or is not happening, or even how the construing involved has changed since the last time. They want to go further than just understanding: they want a method which will underpin and facilitate learning itself.

Enquiries such as these are geared towards future educational progress. The aim is to alter the very parameters of learning: to set up a course of learning within the subject's own terms. This calls for something still more flexible than the grid format. It was to meet purposes such as these that the Salmon Line (Salmon, 1994) was developed. The name arises not merely from the egotism of its inventor, but also from its capacity to draw something lively from below the waterline. Its function, essentially, is to represent educational progression in the form of a single line: a line which allows the subject to define the personal, idiosyncratic meaning of such progression. This typically includes the curricular sphere itself, the meaning of progress within it, the evidence which would count as progress, and the kinds of experience which would enable such progress to happen. Just as importantly, it allows the identification of blocks towards positive movement.

I first used this technique many years ago in work with Hilary Claire (Salmon and Claire, 1984), in a London inner-city comprehensive school. Since the research project focused on collaborative modes of learning, we were interested in the commonality between teachers and pupils, in how they experienced the curriculum. We carried out the research with a Design and Technology teacher and his second-year class. This meant asking the teacher and each person in his class to use the line to represent this area of the curriculum. One end defined a very low level of ability in Design and Technology, the other end, the greatest possible ability. We asked the teacher to make marks along the line for each pupil in his class, according to the level of their current ability. Then we asked him why. What differentiated this pupil from that pupil, in terms of what they could and could not do? How had some individuals managed to be better than others? How far could less able pupils move up the line, and what would be needed to enable them to do so?

This way of using the line allowed this teacher's implicit theory of learning to be elicited: his sense of the curriculum, his way of evaluating progress, the expectations which guided his teaching. It also, of course, allowed us to compare his construing with that of his pupils. The group of young people who attended his classes were asked to use the line in a similar way. They marked their own positions on the line, and that of a few of their fellow pupils. We then asked them to explain their placements. Again, what could abler pupils do that less able ones could not; how had their competence come about; and what would need to happen for less able people to achieve the same level?

The outcomes of this inquiry showed a profound lack of commonality between this teacher and his pupils in how they construed the Design and Technology curriculum. On his side, the teacher saw his subject as entailing the development of designing capacity: a process in which pupils could work together to try out ideas, compare notes and challenge each other. For him, the curriculum encouraged personal creativeness, and was open to every pupil. In his perception, technical skills, and the quality of the particular article produced, were of secondary importance.

To the young people in his class, Design and Technology meant something very different. Almost universally they defined progression in the subject in terms of the quality of the object produced. They saw learning as developing from 'make-believe', practice objects, such as model bridges, to objects that were usable and 'for real', such as shelves. The finished quality of these artefacts was seen as paramount. This valuation stood in direct contrast to the teacher's priorities, which set imaginative power well above purely technical skills.

As their construing emerged from this technique, it became clear that for these pupils, the Design and Technology workshop was a kind of assembly plant in miniature. They did not see their work within it as creative, judging technical skills to be of paramount importance. In line with this perception, learning was seen as individualized, rather than involving collaboration with fellow pupils. And typically, both boys and girls saw competence as largely inborn, with female gender being an insuperable barrier.

This kind of material seems important, educationally. School learners read their own significance into what they are asked to do. They judge the progress of their work by their own criteria, and within their own, perhaps very different terms. To the extent that this happens, teacher and pupils are essentially bypassing each other. In this case, the teacher directly engaged with the lack of commonality which had emerged, making these major differences of perception the focus of class discussion. The findings of this exploration became part of the class curriculum. The wider ramifications of Design and Technology—its network of implicit connotations, its underlying significance—became the focus of group debate.

Defining a Goal

In another, unpublished study (Graham, 1986) the Salmon Line was adopted to help staff at an Intermediate Treatment centre to create individualized learning programmes for the young people who were to serve their sentences there. Each young person was invited to define one goal that they hoped to achieve during their year's stay. This might be anything, from learning to control their anger, to gaining greater literacy, or improved time-keeping, or staying off drugs. One end of the line was to stand for their present position: the opposite end, for the position hoped for at the year's end. The young person was then asked to make marks along the line which would represent meaningful transitions. What would be some small, personally manageable, step, from where they are now? What would they be able to do at that point that they could not yet quite do? And what kinds of opportunity could bring that about? And so on, fleshing out the possible steps towards the ultimate goal.

When the young people had expressed their own learning goals by this means, they each, together with Beverley Graham, the researcher, met the particular staff who would be guiding their learning programme throughout the year. Together, they discussed how the resources and facilities of the centre could be used to bring about the hoped-for learning, This always resulted in modifications and exensions to the line, defining new, mutually agreed points of transition, together with realistic learning opportunities which could be set up to achieve them. And as the year progressed, and the programme began to be implemented, other changes came to be made. The meaning of the goal itself, and the increments of learning which were to add up to its achievement, altered, for the young person and his team, as time went on. This was an attempt to plan genuinely personal kinds of learning—'really useful knowledge'—for a group for whom most institutionalized education typically carries heavily negative connotations.

More recently, the Salmon Line has proved fruitful in a project, carried out by the Language and Curriculum Access Service, Enfield (1996), which explored the way in which teachers of bilingual children construed educational progress. In this research, the line was used in a more limited way, to elicit factors associated with positive and negative kinds of change on their own part. For one teacher, for example, the starting point was defined by the pupil appearing isolated and withdrawn, while the end point—the hoped-for outcome—represented him as socially integrated and making progress. Meaningful transition points along the way were, in order: liaison between class teachers and the Language and Curriculum Access Service team, a home visit, the gathering of accurate information, opportunities to assess language learning, and the process being kept under review. Against these facilitating conditions, the equally important potential blocks to progress were, again in order: teachers seeing the pupil as 'a cause for concern', working on inaccurate information, making assumptions, negative attitudes, and feeling pressurized to come up with the answers. Teachers working in this way felt that it contributed to the process of developing new approaches to their work, and stressed the importance of noting both steps that moved things forward and those that were real or potential blockages to movement.

CONCLUSION

As the well-worn saying has it, there is nothing so practical as a good theory. In the field of education, personal construct theory has much to contribute to an understanding of the complex, difficult, rewarding process that is human learning. For teachers, at the front line of education, it is a psychology which sets the highest possible value on the potential of their work. And equally, through the Salmon Line and other techniques inspired by Kelly's psychology, this approach allows a very special kind of research: research which does justice to the human particularity of teachers and pupils, and the uniqueness of every classroom endeavour.

CHAPTER 32

Learning and Diagnosis of Learning Results

Martin Fromm

Universität Stuttgart, Germany

...We now have a statement of a fundamental postulate....in which the behaving person is credited with having some sense, (and) a learning theory in which learning is considered so universal that it appears in the postulate rather than as a special class of phenomena...

(Kelly 1955/1991, pp. 49–50/Vol. 1, p. 34)

A short description of different models of learning, including the personal construct approach, is followed by some possible consequences for teaching, and a new approach to the study of what students really learn is discussed.

MODELS OF LEARNING

Learning as Storage

The simplest model of learning is a storage model. Learning takes place when a person takes up information, stores it, and retrieves it at a later point in time. Learning of historical dates, prayers, words of a foreign language can all be described by the model. It applies if nothing more than a parrot-like reproduction of information is expected of the learner—because precise reproduction is vital and/or free use of information is to be prevented. The first is true, for example, for language learning; the second has always been the concern of those groups in society who want to keep things as they are. So there have been many attempts not only to control the access to information but also to limit the use of information for purposes which are regarded as correct and 'safe'.

The type of teaching that goes along with the storage model of learning is one of drumming things into pupils or, in a more sophisticated but nevertheless comparable way, adopting the method of the 'catechesis' which was used first in religious instruction, and still is. The method breaks down the information to be passed on

International Handbook of Personal Construct Psychology. Edited by F. Fransella.
© 2003 John Wiley & Sons, Ltd.

into small bits and creates an appropriate question for each bit of information. Teaching then means making pupils memorize the information bits along with the accompanying questions. Learning in that approach has been deemed to have taken place when the questions can reliably provoke the respective answers. Although such teaching uses a conversational style, no reasoning or higher cognitive activity on the part of the pupils is expected—indeed, the method is designed to prevent just that.

Learning as Processing

What is regarded as a problem and pitfall in the storage learning model is a positively valued characteristic of a learning model which regards learning as a process in which the person processes and digests information and puts it into contexts of personal relevance. Where the first model deals with reproduction the second one deals with production and creation.

It is this model of learning which most of the modern educational theorists now try to promote and establish. Obviously this is not a question of one or the other. Some drill and practice learning following the first model has to form a basis for more complex and individual processes. But many educationalists stress that individuals should be free and encouraged to go beyond pre-established paths of understanding and use of information. They also stress that this is not only an ethical but at the same time a very practical position. Because no one can know what people in a few years' time will need to know to solve the problems of the future, it is wise to support people in developing their full behavioural and cognitive potential and encourage them to decide for themselves. On the basis of the process model of learning, the teacher cannot 'make' pupils learn. The teacher can only provide information, tools and support (see also Chapter 31, pp. 311–318). Learning as individual processing of information and meaning-making has to be done by the pupils themselves. So the concept of teaching changes with the concept of learning from 'tamer' to 'facilitator'.

The Personal Construct Approach to Learning

Although not apparent at first glance, learning is a major topic in personal construct psychology. Like the second model, it treats the person as an active meaning-maker but in a more radical way. The assumption of that approach is that it is inevitable to regard people as meaning-makers if one is to understand human behaviour and internal processes. That is the reason why the great importance of learning in personal construct theory may not be apparent at first sight. In the more than 1200 pages of Kelly's main work there are no more than ten references to it. One of these passages, however, explains why the term 'learning' is hardly mentioned in his work: 'learning is not a special class of psychological processes; it is synonymous with any and all psychological processes' (Kelly, 1955/1991, p. 75/Vol. 1, p. 53). Writing about these processes, Kelly chooses the terms 'construct' and 'construing', where construing is the basic psychological activity. It is a discrimination a person makes between his or her experiences. When writing about the personal constructions of people, Kelly is in fact writing about the processes usually referred to as 'learning'.

When learning is viewed as construing, three aspects are of special importance in characterizing the personal construct approach. First is the idea that change is the norm. Learning, as construing, is an ongoing flow of countless discriminations between events of all kinds. Thus, for Kelly, the construing person is 'a form of motion', continuously changing/learning all the time. With these foundations, talking about psychological processes always means talking about learning processes too. His fundamental postulate and corollaries that describe how people develop their personal view of the world can also be used to describe and explain learning processes.

The second aspect of special importance is the activity of the person. As Kelly put it, people do not need to be pushed or pulled to learn. People in this view are not forced to deal with the ongoing events and experiences in their lives, they just cannot help doing it. The model of the person that Kelly proposes to characterize this readiness to explore the world is the person-as-scientist.

The third important aspect is that of individuality. The assumption is that while a person obviously has to follow conventional ways of construing experiences to a certain degree in order to communicate and interact with other people, his or her construing system as a whole will be composed and organized in a personal way.

On the basis of these assumptions, learning processes in general, and those which are organized institutionally in schools or universities in particular, can be described in the following way:

- When teachers try to initiate learning processes with students, they have to deal with people who are already engaged in attributing meaning to their experiences. Therefore, the learning items the teacher presents to his pupils have to compete with the events the pupils are already dealing with from the very start, as well as the ongoing flow of additional events.
- Pupils already possess strategies to deal with new experiences and make them meaningful. As a result, they deal with the teacher's learning items within the framework of the personal construct system they have already developed. This construct system is different for each individual.
- Furthermore, it is always possible to place the same (learning) item in numerous contexts and construe it in many different ways, because events 'hold no institutional loyalties'. The differences between teachers and pupils may involve the construing of items as separate units, the terms used to phrase such a unit, or the contexts of construction to which these units belong.

The focus of learning as personal construing is on making meaning. It is not just on *what* the students are supposed to learn (topics, items and so forth) but on *how* they learn it and how they make sense of information in a *personal* way.

One aspect of the assumptions above draws attention to the point that it seems naïve to expect that, at the end of a lesson, all pupils will have construed the items to be learned in the way, and only in the way, that has been proposed by the teacher. Because, if pupils' learning is seen as personal construing, the final results of the learning/construing process will depend on many individual features of the construction systems the pupils have developed. It is much more likely that pupils will also, or even instead, construe learning items in a way other than that expected. It can also be expected that they will do this in different ways according to their individual construing history.

THE EVALUATION OF THE RESULTS OF LEARNING

The reluctance in educational theorizing to acknowledge that not-intended learning outcomes, first, are normal and, second, may be even as valuable and important for the individual, is quite obvious. Educational reasoning is typically focused on what teachers want the pupils to learn and to be, and on the strategies to get them there. That focus is not surprising because that is what schools are for: to establish traditions and pass on accumulated knowledge and routines to the next generation so that the wheel does not have to be invented again and again. But that does not mean that not-intended outcomes can simply be ignored or treated as deviance: a motivational, disciplinary or learning problem, or the result of the 'hidden curriculum' and so forth.

Evaluation Based on the Storage Model of Learning

The preoccupation with planned outcomes becomes especially evident when, in the end, it comes down to testing and evaluating learning processes. In the storage model, learning is treated as a sequence of presentation, storage and retrieval and thus the efficiency of teaching and the quality of learning are evaluated by comparing input and output. Successful learning is characterized by a high correspondence between input of information and output, with some loss due to partial failure of proper recall after a certain period (see Figure 32.1). The important point is that this evaluation strategy is not only used with drill and practice concepts, but also with concepts which claim to be interested in the meaning-making activities of the pupils.

Evaluation Based on a Personal Construct Model of Learning

If, however, the individual strategies used by people in the making of meaning are taken into account, the relation of input and output is not just input minus a certain

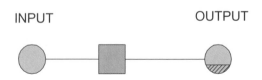

INPUT   OUTPUT

Figure 32.1   Learning as storage

INPUT   OUTPUT

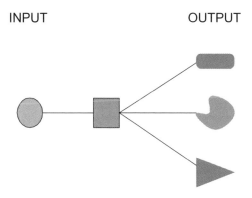

Figure 32.2   Learning as personal processing

INPUT   OUTPUT

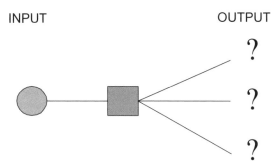

Figure 32.3   Learning as an open-ended process

loss. Individual constructions can change the input considerably when information is connected or broken down in several ways, put into different contexts and so forth. So, on the surface, the output may bear no similarity to the input at all and it may not disclose which input at what time contributed in which way to the present behaviour (see Figure 32.2).

Also, as long as we do not know the constructions which a person may find meaningful to apply to a certain learning item, the situation is actually more complex because we cannot even know where to search for learning results (see Figure 32.3).

The consequence is that an evaluation of learning processes must provide information not only about what students are supposed to learn but also about what students may have learned in addition or even instead. It has to be more open and methodologically sensitive to individual constructions than traditional methods of evaluation usually are. The following example shows how this specific view can lead to other research designs concerned with learning processes—when the focus is on the meaning-making activity of students and not just on what they know.

EXAMPLE: STUDENTS' PERSONAL CONSTRUCTIONS OF LEARNING ITEMS

Teaching in general can be seen as an attempt to change the students' ways of construing. They are provided with either new constructs or with new ways of using existing constructs. And usually tests and examinations concentrate on these latter constructs and the expected way to use them.

In contrast to this I decided not to ask just whether students learn what they are supposed to learn but also what they learned in addition, or even instead. To find out more about the construction process of the students, I was especially interested in the following stages of meaning-making where individual differences are likely to occur:

- One of the basic aspects of meaning-making/construing is the separation of events as meaningful entities—which Watzlawick calls the 'punctuation of the sequence of events' (1967). It is clear that in a seminar students are supposed to follow the official academic methods of determining what constitutes a professionally meaningful and relevant entity. But obviously they can do it in ways that differ from what the teacher expects. So the first question is: *Which learning items are distinguished by the students?*
- Once meaningful entities have been identified by the students, the next important decision is how to relate them to others—and so allocate a certain meaning to them. Again there are official expectations on how to proceed, as well as opportunities to add individually meaningful relations to the officially supported ones. So the second question is: *How are these learning items construed?*
- On a more superordinate level of meaning-making and organizing a construct system, there are more possibilities for individual variation—and for deviation from official expectations. So the third question is: *How are these constructs organized?*

To answer these questions, fifteen students of a seminar 'Concepts for the explanation of psychic disorders' were interviewed at the end of the semester. The interviews followed three steps:

1. *Elicitation/listing of learning items:* In this first step of the interview, the students were asked to write down all learning items of the seminar they could distinguish. The intention was to collect the learning items according to how the students saw and differentiated them in their own words.
2. *Association with/construction of learning items:* In the second phase of the interview, the learning items elicited were presented one after the other and the students were invited to associate other items/experiences with them.
3. *Construction of constructs:* In the last step of the interview, the students were asked to group the relations/associations they had named up to this point.

The first interesting finding was that the average number of learning items that the students discriminated was much lower than the number that could be discriminated from a professional point of view (for example, according to the programme of the seminar). This is worth mentioning because the interview could have been regarded as an examination. This was clearly not the case. The next important finding (step 1 above) was that the students not only *separated* the 'official' items in a personal way—used their personal punctuation of events—they also named *individually perceived* items (for instance, interaction in the seminar, appearance of other students ...); and they *expressed* them in their own words. So repeated attempts of a fellow student to impress the professor were mentioned as relevant incidents in the seminar, as well as a heated discussion concerning the question of whether to label someone, e.g. as mentally insane, is just a question of taste.

The relations between the learning items and other experiences (step 2 above) were even more personal and this was also true for the third step of the interview. The personal constructs which the students formulated in the interviews were neither connected to professional constructs mentioned during the seminar, but not dealt with in the literature, nor to other professional topics, such as those that could/should be known to the students from other seminars. Instead, professional construing of the students concentrated on a small section of what had been covered in the seminar. And that bit of professional construing was mainly repetition.

The overall impression was that the students tested the individual usefulness of the learning items. For example, they tried to explain past experiences (such as 'My naïve childlike constructions') on the basis of the information they received in the seminar. They compared case stories from the seminar with their personal situation ('Is the relationship with my mother a healthy one?'), questioned their own behaviour ('How do I present myself to be regarded as normal?', 'Reasons why I label someone as normal/disturbed'), or tried to gain some orientation for the future (such as 'Development of my professional self-concept').

If that seminar had been evaluated in a traditional way—by merely conceptualizing and measuring success as the relation of input and output—it would have been concluded that the participants of this seminar had learned nothing at all, or almost nothing. But the evaluation strategy used here clearly demonstrates that there is in fact much more to be said about the (personal) learning processes that took place in this seminar. The study provides some evidence that the topics of the seminar were important for the students mainly in terms of personal, not professional, development. It also illustrates potential threats to the psychic stability of the students if they leave the officially planned path of construing and try out personal ways of construing—a possibility that is usually ignored by professional curricula or by evaluation strategies of learning results.

While this study shows the possibility of underestimating the personal relevance of learning if a simple input–output model is used, the opposite can also be true if test results are prematurely regarded as indicators for a relevant personal processing of the information. A student once expressed it this way: 'Too much interest would result in too little work.' So much of what is taught is actually never tried out for personal relevance but just stored up to the date of the exam and cleared from memory soon afterwards—students learn 'how to give answers' but not 'how to ask questions' (see Chapter 1, pp. 3–20).

I found several disappointing examples of this kind in another study where academic progress between basic and advanced studies was to be checked in detail. In this case input–output relations were promising: the students correctly reproduced professional terms and explanations—but were completely unable to relate this to practical work and case stories.

On the whole, the above study illustrates that it is possible to get much more detailed information about the learning processes of students if learning is seen from a personal construct perspective and evaluated by methods that allow the subjects freedom to state their points of view. However, it is not possible to get simple answers to the question of what 'the' students learned in 'the' seminar, because, seen from a personal perspective, each of the students has attended a different seminar. The study presented here is only on a small scale. However, it shows that learning is a much more personal and individual process than is revealed by standard tests or evaluations of learning results—even if nothing more than storage of information is planned by the teacher. And this may also be true for other contexts like psychotherapy or organizational development. In these contexts, too, it is important not to confuse what is happening at a surface level with personal meaning and relevance for personal decisions and behaviour. Again, a personal construct approach to the evaluation of learning and change processes calls attention also to what is going on along with or even instead of what was planned by the teacher, the therapist or the manager.

CONCLUDING REMARKS

At present traditional teaching at schools and universities is undergoing dramatic changes due to computer-based learning, distance learning, and use of the World Wide Web. However, a basic shortcoming of many discussions concerned with these possibilities is apparent: the old storage model is still alive. All too often the supply of information is taken as a guarantee for significant learning. Seen from a personal construct view this is a question yet to be answered: How do people manage to process the overabundant input of information to make it personally meaningful knowledge?

Understanding Organizations

INTRODUCTION

There has been considerable development in the use of personal construct psychology within organizations. One hurdle that had to be overcome was the belief that Kelly's psychology was about individuals and not about large groups of individuals as in organizations. But, as is pointed out in the first chapter in this section, Kelly has, as the opposite of his Individuality Corollary, the Commonality Corollary. It is this corollary that enables useful work to be carried out in organizations.

The first chapter focuses on the usefulness of having a single theoretical model to work within. It means that, for instance, work carried out on the culture of the organization can be related to mentoring work with individuals within that organization. Adrian Robertson then explores the use of an idea Kelly described in 1932 when talking about groups. Robertson sees the 'superpattern' as a very useful construct to explain the difficulties organizations have in changing. He gives an example of how he used that idea within his own very large organization.

Nelarine Cornelius then takes up the issue of the difficulties organization have in changing and focuses on the personal construct ideas of 'transitions'. She gives examples of three organizations tackling change with varying degrees of success.

Devi Jankowicz talks about his work with Eastern European business people trying to help them to adopt business methods of the West. It is difficult to learn new business methods if words like 'manager' do not exist in your language. In the final chapter Sean Brophy gives a detailed account of working with one organization to help it to clarify its corporate values.

CHAPTER 33

The Power of a Good Theory

Sean Brophy
Dublin, Ireland

Fay Fransella
University of Hertfordshire, UK

and

Nick Reed
Petts Wood, Kent, UK

> Theories are the thinking of men who seek freedom amid swirling events.
> (Kelly, 1955/1991, p. 22/ Vol. 1, p. 16)

WHAT IS A THEORY?

Some choose to work within a theoretical framework—most often belonging to someone other than themselves—while others choose to rely on their own knowledge and experience. So, first, a few words on what is meant by the word 'theory'. A theory is a way of binding facts together so that they mean more than any individual fact itself. A theory consists of a formalized set of ideas which may ultimately explain much that was not even thought of at the time the theory was constructed. It is a place to go when in doubt. It informs future action. It is a framework within which certain deductions can be made and outcomes anticipated. A theory therefore needs to be as complex or as simple as its subject matter. Personal construct theory has to be as complex as we see ourselves as being. Theories are also, of course, expendable and designed to be tested to the limit. But as long as they continue to prove useful and fertile, they survive.

There is a certain resistance to theories within psychology. It is the belief of some that theories limit one's thinking; that they act like a pair of blinkers. But to those who work within the psychology of personal constructs, a theory is liberating and exciting. The theory allows one to be creative while, at the same time, setting limits on that creativity. It stops one going wild. The very flexibility of Kelly's

---

International Handbook of Personal Construct Psychology. Edited by F. Fransella.
© 2003 John Wiley & Sons, Ltd.

psychology has led to a wide range of interventions being conducted in the life of organizations.

One central premise must be stated from the outset. As with all other contexts in which this psychology is being found useful, *it is the construing of those people in the organization that matters and not that of experts or consultants.* That means that no ideas, hopes or fears are imposed. The only language of importance is that of the groups that make up the organization. In that way ideas and attitudes, which no one had guessed had existed, are given a chance to emerge.

WORK AT AN ORGANIZATIONAL LEVEL

Personal construct theory and repertory grid methods have been used to specify cultural and people/relationship issues within the organization. These studies have often been carried out to provide the baseline for designing and implementing change programmes. An important feature of this work is that the information yielded is couched in the language of the target groups and the data can be used to sign the way forward.

The theory and its underlying philosophy lead personal construct interventionists to carry out their work from the point of view that it is the person or client organization that has the answers to the issues confronting them. The approach provides the context within which those answers may be surfaced. No 'truths' are imposed on personnel. The only 'truths' are to be found within the organization itself.

There is one guiding principle that comes from personal construct theory. That is, one respects the integrity of the individuals with whom one works. In practice, that means that one never asks a person to change until one has at least a glimpse into that person's ways of viewing the world, and so has an idea of what that change might mean to them. That should apply as much to change programmes within organizations as it does in individual psychotherapy. However, when working with large groups of people, that principle must be violated. All that can be done is to ensure that one gains as much knowledge as possible about the current views of the target group before embarking on a programme that is asking them to change those views.

The Diagnostic Research Method

The Centre for Personal Construct Psychology in the United Kingdom played a role in developing ways of exploring the construing of groups within an organization (Fransella, 1988). The diagnostic research method it developed consists of linking personal construct qualitative interviewing methods with its quantitative tool—the repertory grid—to produce statistical data.

It has been said that this is 'nomothetic', focusing as it does on the construing of groups rather on the individual as Kelly envisioned. But Fransella argues that the approach is 'idiographic', in the sense that all the personal constructs are elicited from the group of people in question, and that the common constructs included in the final repertory grid have been derived from those individual interviews and not from work with thousands of workers and then imposed on participants. After all, the *Commonality Corollary* states that the more we share a given culture, the more our ways of construing will be similar. It is supposed that groups in organizations share such a culture.

The diagnostic research method was originally designed for the British Airways initiative *Putting People First* in the early 1980s. British Airways was concerned to find out what staff in various divisions of the company thought and felt about their work, the company, their passengers, their management and so forth. The results from twenty groups—ranging from different types of engineer to catering and information technology personnel—provided profiles of how people in the specified groups felt about the roles they were required to play, which could then inform the retraining programme. Hinkle's (1965) *resistance-to-change* grid was used to measure the relative importance of the constructs used in the grids (see Chapter 20, pp. 221–222).

A case study document of the Marketing Council (Galsworthy, 1997) describes the Centre's diagnostic research in some detail, and says of cabin crew:

> Sociability was identified as the dominant factor and that which caused the most problems. Staff would approach passengers in a friendly, social manner, but if the passenger for whatever reason did not respond in kind, they were classed as a 'bad' passenger and treated differently from then on.

The results clearly showed that cabin crew did not want to be like that. Instead they wanted to *meet the needs of individuals* and to *be professional*. Since that was how BA's Chairman and Chief Executive wanted them to be, the only retraining that was needed was for cabin crew to be given permission to behave as they felt right.

The report goes on to say that the Centre's research plus some market research on passenger attitudes 'set the direction for the first of British Airways' staff communication and motivation programmes, under the umbrella of "Putting the Customer First—if we don't, someone else will"'.

Apart from informing change programmes and identifying why some groups may resist change, the diagnostic research method can be used to study intergroup conflict, identify potential problems when two organizations merge, find out whether all levels of personnel agree on the meaning of a mission statement, and it can also help to address such difficult problems as bullying.

Bullying

Bullying has been described as endemic in British organizations whether in the public, private or voluntary sectors (Ishmael, 1999). However, the term 'bullying' is one of such imprecise meaning that carrying out research into the problem is often of little value. Standardized questionnaires, which either ask simply about 'bullying' or impose the researcher's construing of the meaning of 'bullying', can only provide limited and, possibly even misleading, data. Public, private and voluntary organizations all have different cultures. In addition, organizations in different sectors—industrial concerns, insurance companies, armed and public services, to name but a few—will all have their own 'definitions' of bullying. In a white collar office, the term 'bullying' may include something which is construed as innocent larking around in a Royal Marine Commando barracks.

Thus, the first task an organization committed to eradicating bullying has to address is how it is going to define 'bullying' behaviour, so that it identifies behaviours that are truly meaningful to those whom it concerns. If researchers impose their own definition, they are likely to get it wrong. One way of approaching the problem is to design a specially modified version of the diagnostic research method described above. The organization can then find out:

- the behaviours that people who work in the organization construe as 'bullying'
- the incidence of bullying in the organization
- who is bullying whom
- the effects of bullying behaviours on those who are bullied (for example, stress, anxiety, depression)
- the effect that bullying is likely to have on the organization (for example, in terms of absenteeism, low quality of work and staff turnover).

Further analysis of the repertory grid data can then be used to:

(a) inform the drafting of a detailed disciplinary code;
(b) inform the design of training programmes/workshops to reduce the incidence of bullying in the company;
(c) assist in the assessment of the financial costs of bullying behaviours to the organization, for example, in relation to reduced quality of work, absenteeism and staff turnover;
(d) enable the company to comply better with the various statutory provisions that exist in relation to bullying behaviours.

Knowledge Management

Knowledge management has proved to be of great interest to organizations in recent years and personal construct psychology offers both a theoretical and methodological approach (Reed, 2000). An early unpublished paper of Kelly's, entitled 'Knowledge: Discovery or Invention' (c. 1954), shows that knowledge and personal construct theory are intimately linked. He says:

> Man has a tendency to be mystified by his knowledge, even when it is his own. He is likely to think of it, not so much as a product of his own venturesome efforts, but as something that happens to him, like the wind and the rain. . . . It is terribly hard for most of us to be convinced that knowledge is something that we can and often do create for ourselves.

The aim of what has come to be called 'knowledge management' is to make explicit the knowledge that exists in an organization. In a sense, that is essentially what the personal construct diagnostic research method of focused interview and repertory grid administration and analysis does. Jankowicz (2001) has described this as the surfacing of tacit knowledge. Another way of eliciting or surfacing implicit knowledge is by the computer study of 'expert systems', as described in Chapter 12 (pp. 133–139).

ORGANIZATION STRUCTURE

Structure is an arrangement of roles used in organizations to focus power, responsibility and accountability. Usually when complaints are made about one or another structural feature, the underlying cause is a problem of power or lack of it. Personal construct psychology can be used to make explicit the construing of personnel about a problem inherent in a particular structure. That may be about inadequate decentralization of decision making, overly long lines of communication, inadequate personal discretion and autonomy. Moreover, when allied to a personal construct understanding of resistance to change in those centres of power under threat, the process of change can be rendered less painful and traumatic for those concerned (see Chapter 20, pp. 211–222, for a discussion of resistance to change).

WORKING WITH SPECIFIC GROUPS

Management Processes

Management processes such as meeting schedules, reporting formats and various policy guidelines for action can be rationalized. Personal construct research focusing on a range of management processes as elements in a repertory grid can highlight areas of dissatisfaction and malfunctioning. Feedback of the results of this research can lead to changes that allow organization members to function more effectively with their time more optimally focused on the core mission, such as service to clients as opposed to meeting internal bureaucratic needs that are often wasteful of effort.

Functional Processes

The possibilities here are many. The examples below offer a mere hint of the range of applications of personal construct psychology.

Planning

One possibility is to identify several planning scenarios as elements. For example, Enter Industry 'A', Exit Industry 'B', Take Over Business 'C', Merge With Business 'D' and so on. These can be construed by representative groups of different layers of management. Further, they can be rated in terms of the probability of their occurrence and attractiveness to the respondents. The results are a best guess of the future by the groups, allowing a planning team to pursue, from an evidential point of view, the hypothesis set out by the respondents.

Marketing

The construing of customers' needs for products and services and perceptions of those products currently on offer from an organization and its competitors can be elicited. Another use is for a group of product designers to construe their level of innovation as perceived by their major stakeholders—for instance, the sales personnel in an organization.

Customer Service

Customer service values espoused for a particular brand can be transformed into bipolar constructs in conversation with service personnel. They could then be asked to rate themselves as service providers 'now' and as they 'would like to be', say, in three months' time. Other elements rated could be 'my unit or department', 'my organization', 'how I think the customer sees me' and so on. The resultant analysis can form the basis for removal of factors that inhibit good service, training to provide good service and promotional programmes to highlight service features to customers.

Team Development

This can be based on generic aspects of intact groups. For example, Brophy (2002) has suggested that this can be based on the ideas of Schein (1985). Clear goals, roles and processes for dealing with the world outside the group and with relationships inside the group can be the focus. Initially each member of the group is asked to elaborate their understanding of their responsibilities and the expectations of critical stakeholders to their role. These statements are then tested in a plenary session with all team members to clarify understanding of and negotiation of changes to their responsibilities and expectations of each other. The facilitator can then elicit their construing of a range of elements consisting of the network of stakeholders external and internal to the group who are making demands on them, in terms of processes to deal with these demands. The resultant set of constructs can be arrayed on a repertory grid and rated by individuals on elements such as 'How I see my team now' and 'How I see my team in six months' time'. The ratings are pooled anonymously and displayed to allow for a group discussion. In the discussion the pattern of ratings can be examined on each construct in turn to search for the meaning behind the clustering or otherwise of ratings. Laddering and pyramiding questions (see Chapter 10, pp. 105–121) can be used to deepen their collective understanding of why the ratings are as they are and how they can be illustrated in terms of observable behaviours. The scope for, and desirability of, change on various constructs can be examined and ideas elicited for practical experimentation by individuals or through negotiation by stakeholders. A very early report on team building is that of Tony Armstrong and Colin Eden in 1979, in which they demonstrate the usefulness of using both implications and repertory grids (see Chapter 9, pp. 95–103, for repertory grids and Chapter 20, pp. 211–222, for implications grids).

Goal Setting

An example here would be to elicit a group's constructs of the demands made on them by a network of stakeholders by treating the group as an 'Open System' (Beckhard & Harris, 1977). Members are then invited to indicate how they are meeting those demands at present. That discussion is followed by a collective construing of trends likely to impact on the life of the group in such elements as economics, technology, politics, demography and the behaviour of consumers, competitors and new entrants into the group's markets. This analysis allows for a construing by the group of demands from stakeholders in, say, five years' time, followed by a debate on how to meet those demands. Options can be tested using some form of grid and their ranking in terms of effectiveness and viability using resistance-to-change grids. That final process allows the team to select goals and related action plans over the time period in question.

Training

An example could be training in leadership skills. One could take a generic list of the attributes of a good leader in the particular context of a business unit. Constructs elicited from these can be arrayed on a repertory grid. Clients on a training course rate themselves on a number of elements and the ratings are pooled anonymously to reveal a pattern for the group. Individuals can then see the degree to which they share experiences with their colleagues. Each client is then helped to find insights from the ratings and to consider actions whereby they could act on their own initiative through experimentation to reach the desired ratings over the time period agreed.

WORK WITH INDIVIDUALS

Coaching and Counselling

Coaching and counselling are at opposite ends of a spectrum of interventions with individuals in business contexts that might be described as 'Opportunistic' through coaching and 'Distress' through counselling.

Opportunistic Coaching

This is designed to improve their efficiency as managers. One way to do this is to help individuals to turn their desired management competencies, like 'Communicating well' into a series of dichotomous constructs in a repertory grid. They would be asked to rate themselves on two elements, 'Me in my job now' and 'Me in my job as I'd like to be, say, in six months' time'. Through a process of laddering and pyramiding coachees are helped to understand their own construing. They can then carry out experiments to test a desired view of themselves and are helped to reflect on the results.

Distress Coaching

An individual could, for example, be counselled to adapt to changes in his or her life, perhaps to help the individual to cope with the loss of a particular job through demotion or a failure to be promoted. In these contexts the counsellor helps the individual to reconstrue the events in question. The aim is to help clients to regain a sense of control and autonomy in their lives, through new interpretations, alternative perspectives and careful experimentation.

Improving Interpersonal Relationships

One example would be to meet two individuals who had a poor relationship separately, prior to a team-building exercise. That would allow them to express their feelings privately in the first instance. One could then elicit constructs to do with each client's expectations from the other and, reciprocally, their notion of what the other expects of him or her. These expectations are then converted into dichotomous constructs in conversation with each client to reveal what they wish to achieve and to avoid. The couple are then brought together against the background of ground rules for a fair process like, for example, separating the person from the problem, focusing on interests rather than positions and no monopolies on the truth or of being hurt (Fisher & Ury, 1991). The constructs based upon expectations of each other can then be checked with the two persons for clarity of understanding, and acceptance of the various terms can be negotiated. This can take up several sessions and the process can be helped by inviting the individuals to work on the relationship separate from the substantive issues that divide them. Fisher and Brown (1989) have evolved a series of principles for what they call an 'unconditionally constructive strategy' for collaboration. These principles can also be converted into dichotomous constructs by the participants to reveal what they want and what they wish to avoid. Further, they can be helped to consider the implications of adopting the principles and of accepting each other's expectations as valid within the relationship. Later sessions can be focused on reviewing their experiences.

Mentoring

The word 'mentoring' is a very abstract term which is used to describe a range of ways to help people in work and other settings. The most familiar concepts of the mentor are:

(a) the older, wiser person taking on the less experienced member of staff as a 'protégé', or

(b) the mentor as expert in a particular type of work, who tutors the novice such as the trainee psychotherapist and her supervisor, or

(c) the mentor who is a trainer, facilitating the training of an individual or group.

However, the concept of mentoring under which personal construct mentoring most usefully fits is the 'Developmental Alliance' (Hay, 1995). Hay describes such an alliance as:

> a relationship between equals in which one or more of those involved is enabled to: increase awareness, identify alternatives and initiate action (and) to develop themselves. (p. 3)

In personal construct terms, mentoring can be subsumed under such a concept as regards the *purpose* of the mentoring relationship. But the skills and methods used in personal construct mentoring can also be applied to the other types of mentoring.

Skills are those involved in any constructive intervention (see Chapter 10, pp. 105–121 for details). For instance, the mentor adopts a 'credulous attitude', he or she tries to see the world as the mentee sees it and accepts as 'true' what the person says. Often, the mentee will be asked to write a character sketch of herself in either her present role or in some other significant role that is relevant to her circumstances. She may to asked to complete a repertory grid, perhaps concerning her relationship with others in the organization. Very likely, the link between how she construes her situation will be explored in relation to her core personal values and beliefs using the technique of laddering—usually essential if a real understanding of the person is to be achieved. When appropriate, an action plan can be devised.

More concrete and precise ways of dealing with a situation can be established through the use of pyramiding (see Chapter 10, pp. 105–121). The end result is that the action plan and its implementation will relate precisely to that particular mentee based specifically on the information that she and her mentor have elicited using personal construct methods. The relationship and the product of the 'developmental alliance' will be truly personal in every sense.

SUMMARY

We believe that having a theory to work within is important. Its main importance when working within organizations lies in allowing the practitioner to relate understanding gained at different levels and in different contexts within the same frame of reference. There can be studies of culture, of selection, or of interdepartmental conflict, all of which are couched in the same language and use the same methods of enquiry. Under the direction of George O'Connor, the Irish Airports Authority set about applying a personal construct model to every aspect of its work that involves people. Apart from being seen as a valuable philosophy to permeate an organizational culture, a single theoretical model also provides a framework for creative thinking and action and offers a guiding hand to practice. Kelly puts it thus:

A theory may be considered as a way of binding together a multitude of facts so that one may comprehend them all at once. . . . But this is not all. A theory provides a basis for an active approach to life, not merely a comfortable armchair from which to contemplate its vicissitudes with detached complaisance. Mankind need not be a throng of stony-faced spectators witnessing the pageant of creation. Men can play active roles in the shaping of events.

(Kelly, 1955/1991, p. 18/Vol. 1, p. 13)

CHAPTER 34

Making Sense of the 'Group Mind'

Adrian Robertson

Admiralty Arch, London, UK

> But how can one spend his whole life, the one and only life that is given us, taking
> notes on things as they are, without once using his pencil to make a little sketch
> in the margin depicting things as they might be?
>
> (Kelly, 1978, p. 225)

Personal construct psychology offers a different way of looking at change in organizations from that often encountered in business books. Why? Because it is founded on comprehensive theory and method, yet seeks to encourage each person's creativity and emancipation as part of a broader social reform vision. For practitioners of change in organizations it offers an anchor framework and a springboard for harnessing other approaches. It also transcends the common basic error of making a false distinction between being practical rather than theoretical (Collins, 1998).[1]

PERSONAL CONSTRUCT PSYCHOLOGY: A DIFFERENT VOICE

Kelly proposes that we should look at humankind through the 'perspective of centuries rather than in the flicker of passing moments'. Not only that, but we should also take the view that *all people are scientists*.

The human story is a quest over numerous millennia 'to predict and control the course of events'. That suggests a longer-term view in trying to fathom and design a psychology of personal and social change. Kelly would have us consider that each person is trying to figure out how best to deal with the world as the future races towards him or her.

Kelly developed his ideas in the 1930s and 1940s when the whole enterprise of

---

[1] This text offers a well-argued critique of the lack of theory in management literature.

International Handbook of Personal Construct Psychology. Edited by F. Fransella.

psychology had a certain paucity of vision and imagination. He challenged psychologists to raise their sights and offer an alternative which sets out to uplift the human condition rather than be swept along in a tide of illusory 'scientific' progress. Kelly's criticism could be made for much that nowadays passes as 'change management' or 'organizational development', as a background hum of cynicism seems to be perpetuated rather than the generation of something that could appeal to the higher ethical and community-minded aspirations of a human person.

In Kelly's terms we would view all organizations from way back in time to the modern era as experiments in human progress. Kelly's philosophical starting point is not one of fixing fragments as we muddle along. He challenges us always to work from the big questions: Where are we in the evolution of organizations? What are organizations for—to cage in or liberate the human spirit? What alternatives can we imagine to the kinds of organizations we have now? Should we even care about these issues?

Personal construct psychology is a process of asking the most challenging and adventurous questions and to keep on asking them. This is not a pastime. It is essential to renew and refresh how we view things. It is our humanity—our capacity to free ourselves from the trap of only being able to look at situations in one way.[2]

DESIGNING CHANGE FOR SCIENTISTS

All people are scientists. That is a crucial point for any change practitioner to consider. All people have a wary eye on the future; everyone is trying to make the best guess they can about how things will really turn out, of what can be trusted, what is reliable and well-founded, as well as what is flaky, deceptive and downright hypocritical. Put more formally, each person is deeply immersed in a *psychology of anticipation*.

If everyone is a scientist, how do you deal with them? Kelly's first principle of learning is that if you think someone might have a problem you ask him or her what it is—they might even tell you! If you talk to them, and listen carefully, they might sense that you are a person who respects their scientific status. Moreover, as a scientist yourself, if you are seen as being open to changing your own way of looking at things, they might listen to you, and begin to reflect on their own theories about you. The alternative, sometimes encountered in organizational change and service delivery contexts, is to think *for* other people and do things *to* them. Kelly challenges us to be more generous with the idea of who may or may not be a scientist, and then get down to some practical ways of bringing about positive change.

SUPER-PATTERNS: PRACTICAL WORKING SKILLS

When people try to bring about change in organizations, they are sometimes not very clear or specific about what it is they are trying to change, and what new situ-

---

[2] The author would like to thank Denny Hinkle, one of Kelly's former students, for his memories and insights into Kelly's thinking about social reform.

ation they are trying to bring into being. That may be because there are few available constructs in the business literature to help get beyond vague notions such as 'culture change' or 'working with the soft issues'.

As early as 1930, Kelly addressed himself to issues of 'group mind' and came up with the idea of a 'super-pattern'. That turns out to be a particularly fruitful and strategic perspective which challenges us to be optimistic about the capacity even of lone individuals to be the instigators of significant social change in our workplaces and communities:

> The process of group behaviour is nothing but the behaviour of individual members, although the pattern may be super-individual. In this sense, then, we can say there is a group mind . . . But wait, we should be careful not to jump to conclusions. The group mind is not a separate organism, not a separate process, not a separate will, not a separate force from that of the individual. It is a super-pattern into which the individual sub-patterns fit. . . . The group mind is a situation into which individual tendencies are so combined as to make their effect violently felt by all. (Kelly, 1932)

It is important to link this idea with Kelly's philosophical proposition that personal change is always possible:

> We take the stand that there are always some alternative constructions available to choose among in dealing with the world. No one needs to paint himself into a corner; no one needs to be completely hemmed in by circumstances; no one needs to be the victim of his own biography.
>
> (Kelly 1955/1991, p. 15/Vol. 1, p. 11)

How do organizations become hemmed in by circumstances? How does each person contribute to the effects 'violently felt by all' in our organizations? In what way do we as individuals contribute to organizations becoming victims of their biographies? We may consider the extent to which underinvestment in British public services such as the railways, the Health Service, the school system, the police, social services, public transport and postal services has arisen because collectively we have painted our life-sustaining social systems into a corner?

A super-pattern is an operational way of getting a window on 'culture'. We can use empirical methods in the form of repertory grids to describe the personal constructs which make up the sub-patterns (see Chapter 9, pp. 95–103). In so doing, we can begin to see culture as a *structure of anticipations*—or predictions about how things will turn out. This is 'mission-critical' for organizational change practitioners because the only thing we can change about other people is their anticipations, their predictions, the outcomes on which they will wager.

HOW CAN WE SEE SUPER-PATTERNS?

How can we find compelling, persuasive and vivid ways of sketching, describing, caricaturing and representing a super-pattern, such that others can see it as well? In particular, how can we show that it has a repeating or replicating quality to it?

How can each individual steel themselves for the uncomfortable moment of seeing their own contribution to a troublesome super-pattern?

The change practitioner who walks through the revolving doors of an organization and encounters a sense of malaise about particular issues may well be on the scent of a troublesome super-pattern. There may have been attempts to change the 'group mind' which have bypassed the most perplexing questions, such as what actually is the super-pattern we are trying to change and how does each person take responsibility for their contribution to it? Such attempts can be called *meandering interventionism*. By working with the idea of super-patterns we can try to get beyond this. Within personal construct psychology it makes sense to talk about *constructive interventions*, and a *constructive interventionist* as a person who seeks to accelerate the capability of individuals and communities and work groups to enhance their experience of everyday living—to transform the super-patterns to which they contribute.

When it first becomes noticeable, a super-pattern is something felt intuitively rather than something that can be spelled out. Our job is to show it as clearly as possible, although in a way that includes, rather than excludes, the people who are involved in it. Super-patterns can be found in the stories people tell, and may be sketched out using flip-chart drawings of systems diagrams in the manner proposed by Senge and colleagues (1994). More formal and mathematically rigorous approaches are also possible, such as Forrester's (1993) work on population dynamics. It is also essential to look at the patterns of open or submerged contention. Mindell's (2000) work on conflict in social fields offers wise counsel about intervening in what may be violently polarized disagreements within super-patterns. Mindell's work supports observations by Collins (1998) that people who plan change in organizations often fail to take sufficient account of the contentious nature of organizational life, and may act with a naïve and false assumption that 'everyone will see the self-evident merits of our view'. What is needed, although often missing, are formal processes and group skills such as *dialogue* (see case study) for working productively with adversarial positions (see Bohm, 1996).

To some extent, seeing super-patterns involves opening our eyes to the unpleasant side of life, and asking if it is humanly possible to construct a better alternative. Psychologically troubling art or literature, such as Dali's warlike *Autumnal Cannibalism*, or Shakespeare's depiction of the self-perpetuating brutality of a military regime in his play, *Coriolanus*, may help to stimulate our super-pattern imagination.

FROM INTENTION TO METHOD

If we are trying to change people's thinking and feeling, it is important that we have a reputable method which is itself scientific, in the sense that its methods are transparent, yet it can modulate cycles of enquiry, creativity, personal experimentation in the real-time of living, and evaluation. Kelly went to great lengths to outline how this could happen in the area of personal change and development. Based on similar principles, Argyris and colleagues (1985) proposed *Action Science* as a way of formulating a more challenging, rigorous and intellectually enquiring approach to intervention in organizations.

When people at work are co-opted onto change programmes they sometimes find the experience threatening. This may well be because the 'change agents' are not treating people as scientists, reinforcing a psychology of anticipation that firmly entrenches itself in wariness and survival politics, even where something more 'wholesome' is proclaimed. This is exactly the kind of conundrum that Argyris has tried to point out in his theory of single- and double-loop learning.

Argyris has spent his career investigating why positive and constructive change at work is sometimes so difficult. He suggests that in our working lives many of us collude in highly skilful self-protection rackets of espousing socially desirable behavioural values, yet at the same time behave in ways that are disingenuous and covertly competitive. Argyris proposes that many of us are stuck in a behavioural loop which he calls Model I (see below).

Model I (*Theory-in-use*)	*Model II* (*Espoused theory*)
• Strive to be in unilateral control	• Access to valid information
• Seek to win at all times	• Free and informed choice
• Avoid expressing negative feelings	• Internal commitment
• Be rational—keep emotion out of it	

If we are stuck in this loop, then all our attempts at change and reform are destined to be mediocre because we disable ourselves from what Argyris calls double-loop learning. Double-loop learning is the capacity to change our consciousness and reorder our familiar constructs, although for Argyris, that can only take place in a climate of inquiry under-girded by democratic values, where group conversation is the medium for practice.

Single-loop learning traps are identifiable as super-patterns as Kelly defined the term. The root structure of such traps is a *psychological spiral* of anticipation built from the escalating interplay of personal constructs. If people's personal constructs, anticipations or mental models about change are broadly Model I, even though their espoused values are Model II, then change programmes are likely to stoke the embers of cynicism.

Argyris's ideas have a particular focus on management relationships in organizations (with peers or subordinates). They link with Kelly's super-pattern concept, because if Model I is widely followed as a style of reasoning (even if not consciously articulated) then the interventionist may be facing an organization with a preloaded *structure of anticipations*.

From the viewpoint of personal construct psychology, Argyris's distinction between espoused theory and theory-in-use does not tell us whether Model I and Model II are *superordinate* or *subordinate* constructs for any one individual. That is, perhaps, the most difficult challenge for the 'change practitioner', as it is essential to distinguish people's most important preferences from their more worldly pragmatisms. Only a process of careful investigative intervention will enable the interventionist to help individuals confront significant fragmentation between espoused values and theories-in-use, and how their own personal action might be sustaining the most problematic of super-patterns. These issues are illustrated in the following case study.

Addressing 'Real' Issues

Kelly believed that fragmentation between superordinate and subordinate constructs was not necessarily a bad thing. In his view, total consistency is 'an ideal that could not exist in reality' and a problem occurs only if the 'wagers one lays on the outcome of life cancel each other out' or do not 'add up'. A constructive interventionist is not in pursuit of perfection, yet where people are creating super-patterns which damage the capacity of organizations in critical ways, we must find ways to address the difficult human issues and not side-step them.

Within the investigative methods of both personal construct psychology and action science, we are trying to make explicit people's deepest values and consider how these can be lived and enacted in the real world. However, in our efforts to change a troubled super-pattern, we must first obtain the genuine consent of those we wish to co-opt. In the rush to reorder things in modern workplaces this essential requirement is easily overlooked. It may be why change initiatives at work are often experienced as coercive and fundamentally fail to engage individuals.

Change at work is a form of social change. As such, it will inevitably touch upon people's deepest values (or superordinate constructs). To work with this kind of sensitive psychological material we must be able to design and carry out interventions where such sensitive material is discussible. The alternative strategy, and common default approach is, in terms proposed by Argyris, to *bypass* them or render them *undiscussible*.

Kelly and Argyris are both concerned with creating laboratories for change—Kelly in the therapy room and Argyris in reflection and learning groups. In other words, real life is the practical laboratory for change, and there is a *conversational core* to initiatives which seeks to change people's thinking and feeling. The key skill is to design opportunities for people to talk openly and explore different ways of looking at things and alternative grounds for action. However, in practice doing this sort of thing in many organizations is extremely difficult.

To get beyond the impasse, it is necessary to foster *effective learning environments* at work, even in the most uptight organizations. This is a fragile, sensitive and at times unnerving process which requires personal courage and absolute respect for other people's rights and dignity if it is to have any chance of success.

It is also important to keep in mind our wider responsibilities to work as enquiring scientists, so there must also be a concern for understanding what will constitute effective evidence that our efforts are making a constructive difference. How do we know that change is occurring? How can we measure changes without producing meaningless data?

A CASE STUDY: ENGAGING WITH THE LIVED REALITY OF OTHERS

The author carried out the work described in this section in the consultancy wing of a large British public organization. It seeks to illustrate how the kind of ideas put forward in this chapter can influence troubled super-patterns through small-scale interventions which affirm the value of individuals and gently encourage people to share the challenges of creating something better. 'Big' projects and budgets are not always needed.

As indicated earlier, central to this case study is the assertion that constructive social change starts with group conversation of the kind suggested by David Bohm (as mentioned earlier). If we want to change people's thinking and feeling, to influence their scientific predictions, we need to create places and spaces where people can question their own impermeable or pre-emptive constructs, where they can speak personal truth without being a mouthpiece for rehearsed political positions or 'non-negotiables'.

The background to the work is that the consultancy had failed to recover its outstanding fees by a substantial sum. Difficulties were being experienced in getting some 20 divisional finance managers to produce timely and accurate forecast information. The financial regime was such that divisions inadvertently competed against each other to meet income targets, generating a management system that was fundamentally counter-collaborative. Many people were unhappy and disgruntled, there was much apportioning of blame, and little expectation that things could improve.

People in this system were operating with superordinate constructs (Argyris might say 'master programmes') which were combative and excessively self-protective. Three workshops were set up with the intention of improving collaboration by promoting open-hearted conversation about the key tensions of being a finance manager.

Early on in these workshops people were asked to write down in silence what they wanted to get out of them, and the kind of contributions they wanted other people to make. Silent exercises help people to concentrate and think about what is really important to them. Here are a few of the answers given by participants. They illustrate that people may have been experiencing some fragmentation between their superordinate and subordinate constructs, and desired much more enquiring and authentic communication than is permitted at work:

— 'By being personally open, encourage others to do likewise.'
— 'To be generous with my own listening.'
— 'Really listen to others.'
— 'Surfacing of real issues.'
— 'A willingness to appreciate the stance of others.'
— 'To share the burden of some of the tensions that finance seems to give rise to.'
— 'Help to create a sense of teamwork with finance.'

Each workshop progressed with phases of dialogue and synthesis. Some of the observations and issues that arose during the course of some exceptionally enquiring and reflective conversations were:

— 'There is a them and us culture in the way we handle finance, and it plays out in multiple layers—creating various "thems" and "usses".'
— 'We are not working together.'
— 'We play games.'
— 'Truth isn't justified, nor is honesty.'
— 'We need to work on building trust among ourselves.'

— 'We need to interrupt the trust/games playing cycle in forecasting.'
— 'We need to connect with each other better—build bridges and become tourists in each others' worlds.'

Shortly after these interventions there was a further request for a financial forecast. A full set of responses was collected within days. The Chief Executive of the consultancy commented that 'this is the first time this has happened in living memory'. Participants asked for more sessions, and improvements in the quality of internal finance and other management forums were reported to the author following these interventions.

The more general point here is that evidence in work of this nature may not present itself in forms that can immediately or easily be put on a spreadsheet. It may be simpler, as noted earlier, to invoke Kelly's first law of learning, which in this case, asked people to give oral testimony.

Super-patterns in Action

Each person in the finance system is contributing to a troublesome super-pattern, yet each can play a part in changing it. In the sessions some participants admitted to having deliberately avoided conversation with the finance director, and not responding to e-mail requests for information. As the workshops unfolded, people who had 'taken sides' became more human to each other, and began to develop some understanding of each other's dilemmas and difficulties. In Kelly's terms, they were more willing to see the world through the eyes of their colleagues. Such understanding can be scarce in work relationships, and that prevents people from working together to produce more fundamental solutions.

Taking the systems thinking model of Senge and colleagues (1994), the finance managers are creating an *addiction loop*. That is so, because people are committed to short-term coping strategies which sustain the system at a mediocre level of performance, although it perpetually teeters on the edge of collapse, as happened in this case. This is a classic case of single-loop learning, as no fundamental improvements are possible until the addiction system is modified. Moreover, the addiction system produces side effects such as low-trust relations, job stress and a sense that chronic issues will never be resolved (which further undermine the fundamental solution). A fundamental solution is possible where people can enquire collectively into their own patterns of behaviour, to stand behind their 'official selves' and reflect upon their own contribution to the prevailing super-pattern.

In situations like this, a process of enquiring and compassionate conversation is needed to bring about double-loop learning. A chance may be provided to become aware of the fragmentation between espoused values and covert practice, and for people to modify their anticipations of each other.

The Structure of Super-patterns

The underlying psychological structure of any super-pattern is a *spiral of anticipation*.

James anticipates what John will do. James also anticipates what John thinks he, James, will do. James further anticipates what John thinks he, James, will do. James further anticipates what John thinks he expects John will do. In addition, James anticipates what John thinks James expects John to predict that James will do. And so on! (Kelly 1955/1991, p. 94/Vol. 1, p. 66)

A spiral of anticipation is the repetition of a way of thinking and reasoning (Balnaves & Caputi, 2000). Single-loop learning is the repetition of a style of thinking and reasoning from which people stuck in the super-pattern it sustains feel they cannot free themselves. International politics is replete with super-patterns. In the absence of true dialogue people may take 'sides' and invent and perpetuate untested attributions and predictions about each other. By way of example, the following quotation has been attributed to Chou En Lai, adviser to Mao Tse Tung, in the 1970s:

I am sitting here surrounded by my advisers trying to figure out what they may be scheming against us in Moscow and in Washington. In Moscow, they are trying to figure out what Peking and Washington might be scheming against them. And they are doing the same in Washington. But perhaps in reality no one is scheming against anyone. (Cited in Mindell, 1989, p. 133)

As practitioners of change in organizations, rather than trying to figure out what others may be scheming against us, we would do better to employ Kelly's first law of learning, which is, as paraphrased before: if you think someone has a problem ask him, he may tell you what it is.

THE FUTURE OF ORGANIZATIONAL SUPER-PATTERNS

In her novel *Always Coming Home*, Ursula Le Guin (1985) suggests the idea of an 'archaeology of the future', where a distant future civilization critically examines the centuried progress of contemporary humankind. This seems like the kind of imaginative exercise Kelly would encourage, and could be quite revealing and fruitful if the key issue being evaluated is how humans changed and reformed organizational super-patterns over time. Key questions would be: How was power shared? Were differences between people celebrated or censored? Were individual humans treated with dignity or disdain by the prevailing super-patterns? What attempts were made to correct cruelty and suffering, such as that created by international labour supply economics?

How would it be if the future archaeologists discovered that after centuries of conflict humanity evolved super-patterns founded on the base principle that the origin of all compassionate and humane social change is to walk in the shoes of another? Could we imagine in our own lifetimes starting to build a civilization where creating boundless intimacy rather than cynicism between strangers became the first precept of each person's and each organization's foreign policy? Suppose we evolved practical ways of doing this for real in the United Nations, in peace talks between countries and between factions in organizations? How different would politics and international society be? How could we imagine daily life changing for individuals and communities the world over?

As Kelly suggests, if we only observe and do not innovate we are in trouble. It is easy to become a passive victim of the 'group mind' and believe we are stuck in situations that are both intractable and intimidating. Yet as many dictators, tyrants and supremacists have found to their cost, even the most brutally enforced super-pattern can become remarkably fragile when the normally quiescent citizen decides that enough is enough.

Our organizations are the very super-patterns we choose to live in, or design for others to live in—they are the products of our human civilization. The times we live in require people to make constructive interventions for greater mutual under-standing, compassion and sharing of the earth's resources. The place to start is with ourselves and the super-patterns of which we are a part.

CHAPTER 35

The Struggles of Organizational Transitions

Nelarine Cornelius
Brunel University, Middlesex, UK

> The old ways of looking at things are still so clear, so easily structured, so pal-
> pably available. A bit of confusion, a haunting situation not easily pictured in the
> new light, and click, everything might slip back into place in the old pattern!
> (Kelly, 1955/1991, p. 490/Vol. 1, p. 362)

In the previous chapter, Adrian Robertson provided a graphic case illustration of the 'rhetoric–reality' gap that was operating in his organization. He shows how that gap adversely affected a change programme that looked a sensible way to improve performance. Such 'rhetoric–reality' gaps are common in work-related problems.

Personal construct psychology is an extremely useful framework for making more visible what lies 'below the surface'. However, the challenge of accessing such theories-in-use really steps up a gear when change is attempted in areas which are more deeply personally sensitive to those involved. One such area is tackling work-place equality. The focus of other chapters in this section is very much on work groups. Here the emphasis is more on the total organization.

ADDRESSING WORKPLACE INEQUALITY

The most common approaches to tackling workplace inequality have been catego-rized according to their core principles, and the associated strategy and practices. However, in spite of the gains made by these traditional approaches, the breadth and depth of what is going on with regards to workplace inequality 'on the ground' is often weakly grasped by policy makers.

A classic example is illustrated in a report commissioned by the United Kingdom charity, The Runnymede Trust (Sanglin-Grant & Schneider, 2000). In the report on the policy and practices of Britain's 500 leading companies, the organizations believed that they were good employers. Indeed, against 'best practice' criteria, the

International Handbook of Personal Construct Psychology. Edited by F. Fransella.
© 2003 John Wiley & Sons, Ltd.

companies were *acting* in a fair manner. But the experience of employees was that the organization did not *feel* fair. One factor that is likely to contribute to this yawning gap is the limited information that these companies have gathered on how most effectively to engage with organizational *micro-processes*—the day-to-day factors that operate between individuals and groups 'on the ground'—that contribute both formally and informally to the *experience*. Indeed, equality management practice primarily promotes compliance rather than learning. The exception is some diversity management approaches, which are more concerned with culture change and organizational learning (see Thomas & Ely, 1996).

CHALLENGES TO TRADITIONAL VIEWS OF INEQUALITY

There are some important ideas that work well in practice as a means of understanding workplace inequality and also challenge more traditional thinking.

Equality of What?

First, it has to be decided exactly what the organization means by equality. The work of the developmental economist Amartya Sen (1992, 1999) and philosopher Martha Nussbaum (1999) have a different but related philosophical framework to most of the other approaches cited. Sen, in particular, is critical of many of the popular frames of understanding inequality. He argues that this is because they highlight some specific aspects while masking others and, potentially, allowing these other aspects to remain unchallenged (1992). Sen and Nussbaum have developed an alternative 'capabilities' approach. Their approach asserts that the answer to the question 'equality of what', is 'equality of capabilities', and that what is measured is the degree to which '*one is able to be or do what we have reason to value*'.

Put simply, basic or individual capabilities are the gifts and talents that individuals possess. It is in concert with factors such as education, legislation, policies, organizational culture and climate, and so on, that individual capabilities can be readily exercised. Crucially, the implications of Sen and Nussbaum's capabilities theory when applied to work organizations, is that attention should be paid to all 'levels': not just the individual, *or* the group, *or* the organization, *or* the organizational environment, but all of them. Working within one theoretical framework means all information can be cross-referred at all these levels, as discussed in Chapter 33 (pp. 329–338).

These levels are sometimes categorized as the micro-level (individual to group), meso-level (the whole organization) and the macro-level (the organization's external environment): by addressing all of these together, one would be adopting a meta-systemic approach (Gagnon & Cornelius, 2000; Cornelius, 2002; Clapp & Cornelius, 2002; Rattue & Cornelius, 2002). Sen and Nussbaum argue that as all of these levels are inextricably linked, it would be inappropriate to pick and choose what levels to pay attention to. Processes, systems, structures and events are interconnected, and attention to one level may lead to a lack of attention or indeed, resultant difficulties in another.

Non-decisions

Non-decisions are certain social choices, issues or aspects that, although present, remain largely hidden and, therefore, are never considered (Bachrach & Baratz, 1970). Often related examples include pollution control, parental child sexual abuse or universal suffrage: these issues have remained largely unconsidered for centuries. Non-decisions are present in all social groups, and work organizations are no exceptions, and they are likely to exist 'below the surface' of workplace inequality issues.

What do we 'Know'?

Frank Blackler (1995) has developed a typology of knowledge that captures the array of domains of knowing that operate within an organization; it has been drawn from a range of scientific and social science traditions.

- *Embrained Knowledge.* This depends upon conceptual skills and cognitive ability—Blackler argues that most models of organizational learning are based on this view of knowing.
- *Embodied Knowledge.* This is more action oriented and depends on physical presence, sentient and sensory information, physical cues and gestures.
- *Encultured Knowledge.* This is concerned with achieving shared understandings—these depend heavily on language, are socially constructed and open to negotiation.
- *Embedded Knowledge.* This lies in systematic routines. For example, economic behaviour relates to social and institutional arrangements, and is concerned with the significance of relationships and material resources, such as between technologies, roles, formal procedures and emergent routines.
- *Encoded Knowledge.* This is encoded in books, manuals, codes of practice and communication.

The kind of inequality knowledge captured by many of the organizations in the Runnymede Trust study was embedded and encoded: the above-the-surface knowledge that is more easily measured. The full Blackler typology would suggest that there are many gaps in knowing. Further, Blackler asserts that knowing is mediated, situated, provisional, pragmatic and contested—in other words, dynamic and changing.

Understanding the Characteristics of Transition

In practice, understanding why large-scale change succeeds or fails can be difficult, as there are a number of factors that might potentially interact and lead to the resultant outcomes.

In one area of large-scale change, that of strategic management, one of the most eminent researchers, Henry Mintzberg (1994), has argued strongly over the years that many accounts of strategic change are often unrepresentative of what actually happens in practice. Mintzberg suggests that the 'ideals' that writers create are too highly structured and overly rational: sanitized accounts of the messiness that really takes place. Such models of deliberate strategies do not reflect the emergent reality of what happens and crucially, such deliberate approaches fail to capture discontinuities that may signal important shifts away from current situations. For Mintzberg, the process of strategy is one of crafting, that reflects the 'below the surface' thinking in his ideas.

> The concept of strategy, as opposed to a planning one, focuses not so much on thinking and reason as on involvement, a feeling of intimacy and harmony with the materials at hand, developed through long experience and commitment. Strategies can form as well as be formulated, and companies can benefit from allowing their strategies to develop gradually through their action and experiences. Emerging strategy fosters learning as the strategy develops; purely deliberate strategy precludes learning once it has been formulated. Managers focusing on strategy need to consider a number of factors . . . It is crucial to detect emerging patterns and help them take shape; the manager should know when to change and when to continue. (Mintzberg, 1987, p. 66)

DIFFICULTIES IN THE EVALUATION OF CHANGE

It is not only the common prescriptions for change that fail to get below the surface; this also often applies to the evaluation of change. Take the example of the use of training programmes as a means of facilitating change. One of the most frequently used modes of assessment is the pre-test–post-test format. Put simply, the interventionist assesses what has changed as a result of the training. What is usually being measured with such tests is incremental change in what is assumed to be a stable domain, with constant intervals between measurement points. The change associated with this stable domain is referred to as *alpha change*.

Although such assessment may be sufficient for knowing whether trainees have learned to programme a video recorder, it is woefully inadequate for assessing most forms of training-facilitated change. Golnaz Sadri and Peggy Snyder (1995)[1] illustrate this with the example of a participant on a teller training course to improve customer sales, as part of an organization's strategic push to become more marketing- and customer-led. Before the training course, the participant is asked to rate what he thinks is his degree of assertiveness, measured on a scale of '0' for no assertiveness skills to '9' for expert assertiveness skills. He rates himself as '6'.

During the one-week training session, our participant is able to observe others in role-play sessions being more assertive than he is. As a result, he changes his view on what the points on the scale now mean: the scale has now been 'stretched' to take into account all that the participant has observed. Although he did not think of himself as very assertive before the training, he is clear that he is reasonably assertive now. But after the training, he still rates himself as '6'.

The interventionist might wrongly assume that the training has been ineffective.

---

[1] See also Vanderberg and Self's work (1993) on changing commitments to organizations by new entrants.

However, the yardstick by which our participant now measures himself has a new calibration, in other words, *beta change* has taken place, but this is not the change that our trainer is measuring: pre-test–post-test methods commonly measure alpha change only.

There are further subtleties. Imagine that the training also involved the use of video recording of our participant in role-playing exercises, which he can review and discuss. On reflection, what he had thought before the training was assertive behaviour is, in fact, aggression. Our participant redefines and reconceptualizes the construct of assertiveness, as not about aggression. In other words, a *gamma change* has taken place. The post-test score is still a '6'.

Change 'Burnout'

Robert Golembiewski (1986, 1995, 1997), the originator of the terms alpha, beta and gamma change, suggests that, in practice, the three are interlinked. An academic who specializes in organizational change, argues that accessing these below-the-surface beta and gamma changes bedevils not only training interventions but also many types of person-centred change from the micro- to the meta-systemic. Importantly, he argues that a consequence of seeing change at the alpha level only, while failing to capture beta and gamma changes, is 'change burnout'. That can result in a feeling of a lack of personal accomplishment and personal exhaustion for the interventionist, and depersonalization and pessimism for the target individual or groups of the intervention itself.

Kelly and Transition

Golembiewski (1986) has suggested that one of the challenges is evaluating below-the-surface beta and gamma changes, and that a potentially useful method might be the repertory grid (see Chapter 9, pp. 95–103, for a discussion of repertory grids). The repertory grid by the nature of its design, if skilfully used, is able to capture the changes in superordinate construing that by implication are at the heart of beta and gamma change. For example, a 'good' grid always contains an 'ideal' element, so that any beta or gamma change in the view of what it is to be assertive may be reflected in change in the character, and thus the construing, around the 'ideal'.

However, change and transition were key concerns to Kelly some 50 years before Golembiewski's work. Indeed, the final chapter in his Volume 1 is called 'Dimensions of transition'. The challenge of coping with transition is stated by Kelly in these words:

> Constructs enable a person to hear recurrent themes in the onrushing sound and fury of life. They remain relatively serene and secure while the events above which they rise rumble and churn in continuous turmoil. Yet constructs themselves undergo change. And it is in the transitions from theme to theme that most of life's puzzling problems arise.
> . . . If a person is to embrace the new in his organized system, he needs to have superordinate constructs which are permeable—that is, which admit new ele-

ments. Without such permeable superordinate constructs he is limited to a more or less footless shuffling of his old ideas.' (Kelly, 1955/1991, p. 486/Vol. 1, p. 359)

Charting New Routes

From a Kellyian point of view, although interventions have the potential to 'loosen up' construing, there is also the real likelihood of large amounts of energy—on the part of the interventionist, but particularly individuals or target groups—being expended. The result is running on the spot with no real movement forward: fundamentally, nothing really changes. Kelly also relates how specific processes either help or hinder transition. Diagnosis is clearly important. Kelly devotes a whole chapter to this and argues that:

> a diagnosis system, like a scientific theory, should be fertile as well as neat. . . . A good diagnostic system is a set of coordinate axes with respect to which it is possible to plot behaviour. It makes a great deal of difference, however, whether the axes are designed to catch our fellow men like a fly in a spider's web or are conceived as a series of streets and highways along which he can be encouraged to move in an orderly fashion. . . . The coordinate axes we set up should represent many different lines of movement which are open to him and not a labyrinth of one-way passages from which he can never escape.
>
> (Kelly, 1955/1991, p. 453/Vol. 1, pp. 335–336)

Therefore challenge for the organizational interventionist using a personal construct psychology approach is to map out the coordinate axes, the coordinates for the meta-system; that is a sufficient mirror of the way in which change is (or is not) occurring. It needs also to capture the interaction between 'hard' and 'soft' factors that are helping or hindering transition.

GETTING STUCK OR GETTING MOVING: CASE EXAMPLES OF TRANSITIONS

The three case examples presented here are illustrative of how workplace inequality may be tackled. The studies have been compiled over different time frames, from a minimum of three years to a maximum of five. In two of the organizations, the work is action research-based, and ongoing. The information that has been used to develop the cases includes interviews, questionnaires, jokes, gossip, repertory grid analysis, observation, action research and the analysis of organizational documents and public documents such as government reports and annual reports. All of these were data mined for constructs and structure.

The case illustrations are based on three large organizations: two United Kingdom police constabularies (A) and (C) and one private telecommunications company (B), all of which have been addressing the issue of workplace inequality. Clearly, the challenges and context of the three organizations are different. The interest here, however, is in how they went about things.

CASE SUMMARIES

Organization A: Stuck in the Past

Organization A has been addressing inequality and discrimination issues for over 20 years. Some progress has been made, but in spite of a number of interventions, major difficulties persist. Although the rhetoric changes, the degree of movement remains small. The main impetus for change has typically come from headquarters and central government, and the local divisions of the organization are very much evaluated against 'criteria' and 'rules' set by the former. There have been some strong-willed change champions, but in spite of the rhetoric of change, the reality of creating a critical mass and a 'shared view' has proved elusive. The views of those 'on the ground' are rarely sought explicitly or officially, but there is an awareness of their likely objections to equality action around, for example, reduced opportunities and unfair advantages to 'others'. There is limited likelihood of projecting 'self into the future', seen by Kelly as an important pre-condition for reconstruction. The organization's leadership and key personnel are *transition aspirant* but step change has not been achieved.

Broadly speaking, change is at the edges but not at the centre. It remains within the current and long-established paradigm. There is superficial change but the same structure.

This enables small improvements, but no step change in thinking or action. Drawing from Kelly's dimensions of transition, the organization has 'got stuck' through engagement primarily with *peripheral constructs*, *tightening of superordinate constructs*, and increasing levels of Kellyian *hostility* and *aggression*. Wellworn attitudes towards dealing with the public and minority groups in particular that have failed in the past, and will fail in the future, are clung to tenaciously. The talk in the canteen is about the good work that is done, and any attempts that are made to change this is just about undermining officers who only want to do their job in the way that they 'know' works best: the benefits of change that may accrue are just not seen or acknowledged. So, superordinate constructions are not rigorously challenged or subject to review and thus, reconstruction. The call for changes on the front line are just impositions from their superiors (who have forgotten what it is like at the sharp end) or the government (pen pushers who have no idea). It is *other people's* 'experiments' and 'laboratories', not theirs. So, in the face of such strong and resilient resistance to change, the end result of a wave of initiatives is tinkering at the edges of the real problem. Construing relating to addressing equality remains at a low level of cognitive awareness. Organization A is stuck, strongly resisting change, caught in a Kellyian 'more or less footless shuffling of old ideas'.

Organization B: Steady Progress

Organization B has systematically attempted to get to grips with equality issues over a period of about 18 years. Its sophistication in terms of the operational detail is far greater than for either Organization A or C. Clear vision and leadership at the top provided the initial impetus, but there were pushes forward on a number of fronts. A great deal of attention was paid to unearthing the 'below the surface' views, as well as putting into place a range of more 'equality friendly' policies and practices. The new paradigm sought was to some extent 'designed' but getting there has been by a process of 'strategic crafting' in order to continually improve the sophistication of outlook and develop on the basis of new insights and challenges. The transition has been made, but a process of continuous development towards new transitions continues.

Organization B has moved slowly but surely towards a new way of thinking, acting and feeling regarding inequality, and has arrived at and elaborated a new paradigm. Irrespective of the level of seniority or role, people are able to understand what they are striving towards and what needs to change to get there. In Kellyian terms, there are commonly held values about inequality issues: the *collective self* is present in visions of the future (*CPC Cycle* involving circumspection, pre-emption and control) and the development of new ideas (*Creativity Cycle*), both key cycles in reconstruing. There is sufficient flexibility for a range of approaches in addressing inequality to be incorporated, but values, superordinate constructs, enable people to make better, more consistent judgements about what might or might not work. Risk taking is seen as legitimate and there are what Kelly calls 'learning laboratories' within which experimentation can take place, such as new personnel procedures, decision-making structures, volunteer networks and initiatives with local communities. This enables the whole organization to move forward in a coherent, but not too rigid, manner. Organization B has found ways of ensuring that it refreshes its views of workplace equality, and is less susceptible to 'getting stuck'. The mechanism is largely a systematic, continuous improvement approach. There is new structure, and different construing.

Organization C: Rapid Movement

Organization C has made a concerted effort to 'step up a gear' from the equality approaches that it had, until six years ago, decided were sufficient. It should be noted that it is in the same line of business as Organization A—it is a police force—but has managed to find a route forward in a sector where this is often difficult. The impetus for change has been largely internal, and 'root and branch' changes in structure, policy and practice have been undertaken. Also, attention has been paid to revising ethical policy and core values. Senior managers created a clear vision and purpose, but the views of those 'on the ground' are critical influences on both the vision and operational issues. The coordination of effort has been substantial, and what has changed in particular is the attitude towards *risk* in relation to dealing with these issues. The organization has become more risk-tolerant in relation to inequality issues, which is important given the speed with which the organization is progressing and the likelihood of making mistakes.

The organization is driven by the start-up momentum, and is aiming to get as many quick wins in place as quickly as possible. The transition has been rapid. Although the organization has only a partial picture of the future possibilities, it is reflective enough to recognize what it has left behind and what continues to limit its advancement towards its desired future. Enhancing knowledge and learning through training, personnel practices and dialogue within the organization and with the community is regarded as core to the change process. Organization C has moved with extraordinary speed, on a 'fast track', towards a new paradigm. The necessary catalysts (radical thinking, management of fear of failure, new leadership) were, in part, happened upon by chance but were sufficient to draw the organization's attention to the limitations of its current *modus operandi*. Important changes regarding working practice and human resource policy and practices created shifts towards new construing.

Although the detail of the new paradigm is not as fully formed or understood as for Organization B (much of the construing is covert), it is *sufficient* to inform new ways of thinking, doing and feeling. The new paradigm acts as a rough template for placing clear blue water between the 'new' view and the old one: for projection into a different future. Aspects of the validation of the 'new' paradigm are more felt than reasoned, and the language with which to express the difference is emerging slowly. Changes appear to have taken place to *comprehensive constructs*, and construction shifts that involve CPC and Creativity Cycles and crucially, the CPC Cycle is foreshortened by not circumspecting all the options: which Kelly referred to as *impulsivity*. The process of change has been one of a desire to get below the surface rapidly and an emergent organizational environment that enables fast and continuous learning. New structure and new construing has occurred, but very quickly indeed.

CONCLUSIONS

New patterns and new paradigms are important outcomes of a step change, but the character of the transition between states also merits scrutiny, as it reveals something about the nature and detail of the reconstruction processes and therefore, why and how, for example, new patterns become established. However, it also allows for an assessment of whether an organization is merely at the stage of being 'transition aspirant', irrespective of the amount of time and effort poured into trying to create the shift.

Organizations B and C have both created the step change into new ways of seeing the world, a new paradigm, while A remains stuck in the groove of a long-established paradigm, and in the Kellyian 'labyrinth of one-way passages from which (they) can never escape'. Kelly's constructs of diagnosis and transition are vital parts of the armoury for those choosing to work with personal construct theory in organizations. The case illustrations highlight the power of the theory. Importantly, it is possible to demonstrate that by fitting personal construct theory into a more meta-systemic configuration than it usually is, it still retains the power to reveal things about change in difficult arenas such as workplace inequality that help us to understand success and failure in new ways.

CHAPTER 36

How can we Understand One Another if we don't Speak the same Language?

Devi Jankowicz
University of Luton, UK

> For any bold venture into human understanding leaves the wreckage of sacred ideas in its wake.
>
> (Kelly, 1996, p. 39)

TWO TRANSLATORS

More than ten years ago, a businessman trading into the post-command economies of Central and Eastern Europe described his experiences of those early days of radical transformation—the first few years which followed the dismantling of the Berlin Wall and the reintroduction of the market economy. Asked for his single most useful recommendation to anyone engaging in the same activity, his advice (McNeill, 1991) was simple but profound. The activity depends crucially on translation between English and the foreign language in question; and his suggestion was to use two translators rather than one, the purpose of the second translator being to check on the success of the first.

Apart from businessmen and managers, a second type of West European was operating in Central and Eastern Europe in those days. Academics were seeking to transmit ideas about the market economy to academics and managers in the post-command economies, as part of a vast programme of development efforts which continues to this day. As they went about their job of communicating ideas, techniques, and principles of capitalist enterprise and its management, neither academics nor business people appreciated the soundness of McNeill's advice. That is a reassessment which came later. At the time their material, apparently competently translated, was being met with incomprehension ranging from simple misunderstanding to sheer disbelief. Those reactions were usually masked, to varying degrees, with the conventional politeness which the host extends to a visitor.

International Handbook of Personal Construct Psychology. Edited by F. Fransella.
© 2003 John Wiley & Sons, Ltd.

It appears that there were two interrelated problems, the first to do with technique and the second with concepts and values. First, translators who should have known better were struggling with an unfamiliar vocabulary and providing crass and misleading translations—for instance, translating the word 'account' as 'record of financial holdings in a bank', where 'financial report' had been intended. The problem here (and actually, it was an infrequent one) is that the translator lacked the subject-matter experience to recognize, from context, the appropriate *dictionary equivalent* term, and hence failed to realize that financial reports rather than bank accounts were intended by the speaker.

The second problem was more profound and much more frequent. It had little to do with dictionary equivalence and familiarity or otherwise with subject matter or context, and everything to do with the structure of the languages involved. It appeared that there were no direct equivalents for many of the ideas, current in English-speaking capitalist economies, in the Central and Eastern European languages, because there had been no directly equivalent experiences in the countries concerned. To do business, to engage in management, had been to do something different than in the West, and the language reflected that. Rather than a matter of *dictionary* equivalence, the issue was one of '*construing* equivalence', to coin an adjectival term.

Tokens and Rules

Perhaps the Westerners should not have been as surprised as they were. After all, if one is to offer Western know-how, the assumption is that that particular form of know-how is absent in Central and Eastern Europe, so the concepts on offer will not map easily onto those that are in place. Language, as a medium of communication, is going to be problematic in translation. But the real surprise comes from the second, and some would say more profound, function of any language. As well as being a medium of *communication*, it is a medium of *representation*. It is a system of tokens and rules for encoding (representing, recording, reporting) experience in a particular culture. If the nature and range of experiences in that culture differs from another, so will the language. The vocabulary will be different, and so some words will be missing, and will not translate. The structure of the language, the rules by which phenomena are noticed and placed in relationship to each other, will also differ. Different cultures notice different things standing out as meaningful figures against the background of the phenomenal flow. Since meaning is a matter of associations and relationships between ideas, different cultures will give different meanings to events. Another way of saying this is that experience in one culture does not match experience in another. What are recognized as distinct, nameable events in one culture may be regarded differently, or even be unnoticed, in another. As a system which encodes those events, the language of each of the two cultures will therefore slice up the phenomenal flow differently. When one language is translated into another, there may be nothing that can be transferred. Meaning evaporates in translation.

No Word for Manager

There is no word for 'manager' in Polish (Jankowicz, 1994), or in the related Slavonic languages, because there was no activity quite like 'management' as the Western business person understands it. There are parallel terms and corresponding terms, but they correspond to the local reality and not to the reality of the West. There is 'Zarządca' (a noun linked to the verb 'Zarządzać', to rule or govern); there is 'Kierownik' (the corresponding verb is 'Kierować', to steer); and there is 'Dyrektor', which looks similar to 'Director' but is not confined to members of a Board. All of these terms overlap with part of the meaning of 'manager'; that is, they represent one or two of the associations to 'manager' without covering them all. The result is that none of the Polish words covers the manager's *role* as it exists in the market economy, and the new business culture emerging in Poland has had to invent a new word, 'Menedżer', to represent the role when it became known and enacted in the post-command economy.

'So what?' you might ask. The translator can surely work a little harder. Instead of establishing a single dictionary equivalence, he or she has to establish several, and regard the resulting blend of meanings as the meaning of 'manager' to a Pole. That is one way in which the meaning of a local usage can be appreciated by a foreigner. Unfortunately, establishing an extended dictionary equivalence in this way is not sufficient. Each of the Polish words carries different associations to the English word 'manage', and so they mean something different. In English, 'managing' associates with directing, organizing, administering, just about succeeding at something, handling, gaining control and using it, coping, bringing about consent. The two networks of associations, one English and one Polish, do not overlap, and the result is two rather different structures of meaning. This has practical consequences.

For example, in English, the way in which one engages in one or more of the activities associated with 'managing' is unspecified. The management style one might adopt is entirely open, and academics may spend time in researching the most appropriate style for the manager to adopt contingent on the situation. In contrast, for Polish managers 'ruling'/'governing' is something one does fairly authoritatively to someone who is, *de jure* or *de facto*, subordinate to one as a superior, and kept in that position thereby. 'Steering' is a matter of setting out a specific and single course and actively correcting the slightest deviation from it. There is no question of a variety of possible styles.

Indeed, there is a sense in which the concept of 'management style' does not exist, for there is just one way of being a manager. One does what one does directively as superior to subordinate, and that's that. Suddenly, the world of enterprise looks a little different. Without a concept of 'management style' Western notions of industrial participation do not transfer straightforwardly. The idea of varying one's approach to leadership depending on the experience and competence of a particular employee needs to be explained as something that is not, in fact, removed from effective management but is, in contrast, an intimate part of it. A variety of ways of conferring agency (representing, or delegating, or mandating, or contracting) become possible, and the conduct of business, directly or on behalf of someone else, takes on a different range of possible flavours. That is not to say that these options do not exist in the Polish culture. Rather, it is to say that they are structured differently with respect to each other. Their meanings differ—in other words, they are construed differently—because that particular part of experience has been partitioned differently by the language that represents it.

LANGUAGE AS A SYSTEM FOR REPRESENTING EXPERIENCE

Perhaps the most useful way of addressing these unfamiliar difficulties is to see them as an extreme form of the familiar; as international variants of local issues with which we are familiar within our own, single nation state. Kelly's Individuality Corollary, 'People differ from each other in their construction of events', is relevant within our own local culture. We are not carbon copies of each other because we develop different ways of making sense of events—and we develop different ways of making sense of events because our personal explanations of those events are systematically validated or invalidated in a particular way in the light of our personal experiences of those events.

We discover, among the ways in which we are similar to other people, that there are common words and grammatical rules with which to do the encoding, and we find ourselves sharing a common language with which to represent, and share, that varied experience. The language acts as a unifying force, which offers shared ways of making sense of experience. Localized discourses reflect localized subcultures within single organizations. One thinks of technical acronyms, 'war stories', ceremonies and symbols which give identity to those subunits while dividing them from each other (Young, 1989). Technical and professional argots reflect the shared meanings that are found to be useful forms of construing by people within one craft or profession as distinct from another, but within a single national culture (Wright, 1974).

When we generalize these processes across national boundaries, we see how the differing experiences of Western states and their Central and Eastern European counterparts led to different ways of construing. Different ways of recognizing and allocating meaning to business phenomena developed, together with different symbols and language rules in which to represent them. To the extent that people within a single culture encode experience similarly among themselves but differently from people across different cultures, their language will be different, and this will have practical consequences.

Varied Teaching Concepts

This poses problems when we seek to teach the Western way of management. Not only because the concept of management differs, but also because the concept of teaching varies! In Polish, Russian, and the related Slavonic languages, 'teaching' and 'learning' share a common root. 'Teaching' is '*Uczyć*' and 'learning' is '*Uczyć się*'. Now, '*Się*' is a reflexive term, which conjures up associations of learning as a relatively passive experience. It is as if, in English, we were to use the word 'is-taughtsing' instead of the word 'learning'. The teacher teaches; the learner 'is-taughtses', a term which carries associations of subordination, the main initiative in the endeavour lying with the teacher. And indeed, there is a Polish cultural preference for learning through *ex-Cathedra* professorial pronouncement. Writing an authoritative presentation of Western-style management education which emphasized the great importance of active learning methods in MBA programmes, the Polish authors (Sulejewicz et al., 1994), searching for an alternative to the word 'student' to apply to the mature, post-experience senior managers taking part, chose the word '*Słuchacz*', 'listener', rather than the equally valid Polish word 'Uczestnik', the dictionary equivalent of our English term 'participant'.

And so, an activity construed differently (management) is taught to people who construe the encounter by which this happens (teaching and learning) differently. It is obvious that we are no longer dealing solely with political differences, Marxist or capitalist, which have existed for a half-century, but with cultural, historical and institutional differences, as encoded by distinct languages, which have existed for a half-millennium!

Take that simple word 'capitalism'. Kelly (1962) gives an account of the varied meanings associated with the word 'capitalist' among Georgian speakers in the Caucasus. Historically, it was the local princeling who had the means to engage in trade and business activity; this, however, was also the person who, as absolute ruler, exercised *droits de seigneur* when a villager married, and had the right to decide on the amount, if any, of schooling which the villagers' children received. One can see how these associations, involving some rather fundamental values of life and existence, would have informed the meaning of 'capitalist' in Georgian culture over the centuries, while providing a background of meaning into which the communist stance towards capitalist economics might fit compatibly (but as recent froth on a centuries-old brew), resulting in a specifically Georgian variant of the command economy.

UNDERSTANDING THE OTHER PERSON'S EXPERIENCE

Understanding one another as the first step towards effective knowledge transfer about how a market economy should be run is only a little to do with a search for dictionary equivalence, and much more to do with similarity of construing at a much deeper, cultural level. But how might one arrive at this understanding? How can one do business effectively in a different culture, and how might we teach about the market economy with sufficient understanding of each other? Teaching and learning, however construed, are collaborative processes.

In suggesting we use one translator to check the success of another, McNeill was advocating an exercise in sociality. The role relationship of 'doing business across cultural boundaries' is enhanced to the extent that each participant is enabled to construe the other's construing. Using one's own constructs to characterize the other's constructs requires one to elicit, and then to understand, the other's constructs, as far as possible *using* the other person's constructs—the other's personal meanings for the terms in question—rather than one's own.

When translating, one can use general and specialist dictionaries (business and etymological dictionaries; dictionaries of popular usage and of terms with foreign origins) and, through translation and back-translation, get a good feeling for the web of associations which give a particular term its meaning. Jankowicz (1994) used dictionary techniques to show that the absence of an equivalent term for 'marketing' in Polish meant that local construing emphasizes operational issues relating to bargaining and selling, with the result that there was no concept of marketing as a strategic discipline. The meanings associated with 'accounting' were encoded in words of similar scope and cultural origin to the English terms and were thereby, for all practical purposes, similar to English. 'Training' carried associations which made the Western distinction between teaching strategy and learning strategy problematic.

One can go further than vocabulary, and utilize the grammar, metaphor and style of the language in question. Gutt (2000) lists a variety of stylistic clues to meaning (forms of semantic representation, syntactic and phonetic properties of utterances), and Jankowicz (1999) shows how metaphors (live and 'dead') and idiom add to vocabulary and grammar in encoding experience and hence establishing meaning.

Differing Terms

However, successful understanding also requires that one goes beyond the purely linguistic analysis and establishes the significance of the transaction from the other's point of view, establishing the other's personal goals, values and preferences, and the ways in which these are construed within that person's culture. It requires an appreciation that the other party may not simply be disagreeing with one's own way of construing the issue in question but, rather, choosing to think of it in entirely different terms.

For example, the Westerner might describe the meaning of 'managing', and of 'teaching', in terms of Western constructs such as:

'*Autocracy* versus *participation*'
'*Directiveness* versus *avoiding indifference*'
'*Ex-Cathedra teaching* versus *the development of a community of enquiry*'

The Western position would be identified with the right pole of each of these constructs and the Central/Eastern European position with the left pole of each. The person from Central/Eastern Europe might well respond that the constructs he or she prefers to use are entirely different:

'*Wise governance* versus *individualist anarchy and fragmentation*'
'*Specification of required actions* versus *underspecified inaction*'
'*Authoritative statement* versus *having little to offer*'

while identifying his or her own position with the left pole of each.

The process is usually bidirectional. Each participant seeks to establish the other's goals and intentions as a way of illuminating the utterance and capturing all the shades of meaning entailed. Much of that information will be shared, though some will remain private. Sometimes we have no intention of revealing our private values and objectives, and at others we would if we could but we do not, since we cannot quite put them into words ourselves! A construct is a choice among alternatives and independent of the medium in which it is might be expressed. It is possible to experience preferences by means of feelings, intuitions, and indeed unreflective actions— doing one thing rather than another. A construct is not the words in which it is expressed. It is a preference that entails a particular meaning.

It helps if we model this bidirectional exchange of meanings as a negotiative process. Since the point of the exchange is for each party to understand the other, the negotiation of meaning is collaborative. In other words, its purpose is to arrive at a outcome which pleases both parties at minimum costs in terms of concessions of time, effort, and personal or organizational privacy.

In this kind of collaboration, the two parties negotiate common meanings, checking one another's understanding of each other's private terms of understanding, choosing to reveal more, or less, of their personal goals, motives and values in doing so. Doing business across linguistic barriers involves experimentation as much as any other social transaction. One attempts an understanding of the other's position by inference from common observation, and then checks the accuracy of that understanding, by asking the other party directly (always the most informative way, since the reply will automatically be in the other's own terms), or by making inferences from behaviour as both parties engage in further action. Teaching across linguistic barriers is somewhat simpler, in the sense that one engages in an activity which both parties expect to be propositional from the outset, defining the meaning of terms explicitly. But teaching is just as complex in another sense, since there is a process to be discovered, examined and mutually reflected on, to the same extent as there is in a business transaction.

It is assumed throughout that both parties have the opportunity for reciprocity. For every transaction in which one person is the active agent, seeking to construe the other's construing, there can in principle be a corresponding transaction in which the other seeks to construe the first person's construing. If I am teaching you something about the market economy, checking how you are understanding me in the terms suggested by my understanding of your constructs, you may try to explore my constructs, as you seek to understand my material and the assumptions on which it is based.

Transferring Knowledge

In the Western mission to the post-command economies, that kind of reciprocity was rarely achieved. Much of the literature of the 1990s comments on the efforts made by the trainees to understand the trainers' constructs, and the frequent oblivion, on the part of the trainers, that there was a different way of construing the realm of discourse in question. Perhaps this is not surprising, People can engage in role relationships with one another without reciprocity. Kelly's account of sociality presents the leadership role, and the therapist–client role, as situations in which there is an imbalance; in which one person is more successful in understanding the other's construing, or indeed better equipped to do so.

The task of transferring knowledge about the market economy to the post-command economies was construed with that sort of imbalance built in at the outset. It is difficult to offer reciprocity when one takes part in a programme called 'The Know-How Fund', whose purpose is defined as a replacement of failed ideas which led to the collapse of the communist economies, engaging in the role of trainer with trainees whose cultures tend to define the teacher–learner role in a way that gives the trainer maximal authority, initiative and power!

Though the intention of each transfer programme was that it should be designed in collaboration with the Central and Eastern European participants, in the early stages the practical constraints of funding (all Western), time (a matter of weeks to design international programmes with budgets of over £300 000), and reporting (a preponderance of Westerners engaged in monitoring and evaluation) gave maximum initiative to the Western parties, and created a precedent for the later years.

And so a great opportunity for mutual meaning creation was missed. The new meanings which, undoubtedly, were required as replacements for the failings of the command economy were not negotiated on the basis of a reciprocity that would have taken local culture into account through an understanding of its language.

Rather than offering Western solutions to Central and Eastern European problems under the neo-liberal assumption that there is just one best way for a business to be run in a global economy, the opportunity might have been taken to discuss and debate versions which might be newly created, bearing the circumstances, values and history of the local culture in mind. To do that, a reciprocal attempt would be required to understand the ways in which the two languages represent experience. It did not occur. The adjustment of the foreign ideas to local circumstances in order to make them truly local, came later, after the event.

Perhaps there is something about international aid in times of catastrophic change which puts both participants into an expert–client relationship, eschewing mutual meaning creation. Knowledge transfer is limited to a good-willed one-way transmission of one party's meaning into a void. The local parties are left to make local sense of the transaction later when they have had time to draw breath.

CHAPTER 37

Clarifying Corporate Values: A Case Study

Sean Brophy
Dublin, Ireland

> Science is a system of anticipation: so are values.
> (Kelly, 1959, p. 6)

The subject of this case study was founded in the first decade of the twentieth century and operated as a family firm committed to a participative management style for 80 years. The third generation of the family decided to float part of the equity of the firm to provide capital for expansion and to bring in professional managers to operate the company. Tension between staff and management and within the Board of Directors soon revealed themselves. These tensions were the inevitable accompaniment of what Chandler (1977) calls the transition from 'family' or 'entrepreneurial capitalism' to 'managerial capitalism' wherein a shift in values takes place and the needs of the family gradually yield to the overarching need to provide an attractive return to capital.

A values task force was established by the Board and in conjunction with the shareholders' values and ethics committee, recommended the use of a personal construct psychology facilitator to clarify the shared values of Board, Management and Staff.

THE PROCESS

After an initial briefing, the facilitator proposed the following process. The objective of the facilitator was to maximize the scope for involvement of important constituencies within the organization in working through the implications of the changed context in which they found themselves and in the search for an agreed set of values to guide them in the future.

(a) Workshops with various staff groups, the senior management and Board members to elicit their values and their assessment of the company's adherence to them.

International Handbook of Personal Construct Psychology. Edited by F. Fransella.
© 2003 John Wiley & Sons, Ltd.

(b) A search for commonality across the groups.
(c) The drafting of a Values' Statement, and a communications' programme to establish the response to it by the three core groups, Staff, Management and Directors.

THE WORKSHOPS

At each workshop the facilitator first sought the groups' understanding of what they meant by 'values'. The responses invariably included words like 'honesty', 'trust', 'doing the right thing' and so on. The facilitator then gave a short introduction to personal construct theory with the emphasis on the person as scientist. Values were described as wagers on the future. George Kelly contrasted the scientists' testing of the truth with that of the moralist and concluded that the difference lay in the time lapse between prediction and ultimate verification. He goes on:

> Values differ from other forms of belief mainly in the dimension of time lapse, the lapse between anticipation and realisation. Science looks for verification to appear as soon as possible; in the cases of values one waits. The scientist is prepared to change his anticipation in the light of tomorrow's outcomes. But values are likely to get changed only when people forget what they were wagering on. While no outcomes ever quite provides a final verification of the anticipations laid for it, we are placed in the position of having to accept in the case of values, conclusions which are much further in advance of their ultimate evidence.'
>
> (Kelly, 1959b, p. 6)

So, values are like a wager. The facilitator moved to get each group to reveal the contexts in which these 'wagers' took place. The firm has been described as an 'open system' (Beckhard & Harris, 1977, p. 58). From this perspective the firm is viewed as having a set of stakeholders, the support of each one being necessary for the firm's survival.

Initially, the stakeholders were identified by the group and usually included the following: customers, suppliers, staff, shareholders, local community, environment and world community.

Each group was asked, 'What must the company do to ensure the long-term support of this particular stakeholder?' They were effectively being asked what they were wagering on, that is, what 'value' they held in relation to this element. The answer provided the preferred pole of a construct. Another question elicited the opposite of this statement. In this way, a number of constructs (or values) were revealed. The facilitator tested the understanding of the group by asking 'Why?' questions to ladder these constructs up to a superordinate to do with *survival* as opposed to *out of business*. Also, he asked 'How?' questions to pyramid downwards to search for examples of particular values in practice (see Chapter 10, pp. 105–121).

When the group had agreed the wording of about 12 values the facilitator listed them and invited the group to write them onto a repertory grid form. The grid in Figure 37.1 is an example of the values of one employee group's values (Task Force). Each group was then asked to rate this grid on a seven-point scale on three elements: (a) 'The company now', (b) 'The minimum standard tolerable' and (c) 'The company as I expect it to be in five years' time'.

Pole		Scale							Contrast	Rank
		1	2	3	4	5	6	7		
1	Respond to the needs of our Customers and Suppliers								Ignoring the needs of our Customers and Suppliers	2
2	Treat people with dignity								Don't recognize their value as a person	1
3	Encourage personal growth								Discourage growth, stagnant	8
4	Treat people fairly								Exploit people for personal gain	3
5	Pay people = or > what could earn elsewhere								Pay people as little as possible and still keep them	9
6	Caring about providing a person's ability to have a job								Not caring	5
7	Holistic approach to meeting employees' work-related needs								Ignores relevant work-related needs	10
8	Attract and give a fair return to investors who share our values								Give as little as have to, to whoever	7
9	Provide an honest flow of good information								Keep them in the dark	5
10	Be a good corporate citizen in the communities in which we operate								Indifferent to the communities and their environment	11
11	Endow future generations with an understanding of the best knowledge we have								Not thinking about them	12
12	Commit to grow and adapt								Stay the way we are	4

Key: ↓ = Average scores
●– – – – ● = Range of scores for 'My company now'
◆———◆ = Range of scores for 'The minimum standard'
◀·············▶ = Range of scores for 'How I expect my company to be in 5 years' time'

Figure 37.1 Sample repertory grid rated by one employee group

The individual ratings were pooled on to three overhead transparencies and the aggregate raw data displayed for the group to appraise and react to. These ratings are represented in the grid as a range of ratings and the average for the group. Finally, to check the relative importance of the constructs, the group was asked to complete a Hinkle's Resistance to Change Grid (Hinkle, 1965). The pooled results were shown as a ranking on the right-hand side of the grid (see Chapter 20, pp. 211–222).

The data yielded a comprehensive picture of the group's construing of the three elements. Comments below are confined to the three most important and three least important constructs in the grid.

The most important construct for this group, No. 2, was *Treat people with dignity*. Here the group saw the company as being quite good on average, with some persons demurring from this viewpoint. Minimum standards were not being adhered to and the situation, on average, was seen as likely to remain the same in five years' time, though some individuals saw it deteriorating.

On the second most important construct, No. 1, the company was seen, moderately, to *Respond to the needs of our customers and suppliers*, though not quite as well as it should. The situation was expected to improve slightly over five years.

The third most important construct, No. 4, *Treat people fairly*, was rated down, indicating some personal anguish. Minimum standards were not being adhered to, though the situation was expected to improve somewhat over five years, but not up to minimum standards.

All told, the data in the grid reveals a picture of some anxiety in the sense that people could not anticipate reaching minimum standards on some important constructs over the next five years. Further, they displayed fear in the sense that their cherished order of priority was going to have to give way to a greater emphasis by management on the right of investors to a fair return, via short-term dividends (construct 8) over the staff's need to have a commitment to develop the company over the long term (construct 12). For people who had worked under a paternalistic regime, characteristic of family capitalism, where dividends are often reinvested in a firm, the transition was mildly threatening. The tension in the values is apparent when we compare the employees' ranking of stakeholders with those of the management team as set out in Table 37.1.

Here we see that there is agreement on the core constructs to do with treating people with dignity (construct 2) and in responding to the needs of customers and suppliers (construct 1). Where the groups parted company, it is interesting that the managers were more concerned with paying people the same as or more than they could get elsewhere than the employees (construct 5). It was as if the employees' security needs (construct 5) were deemed to be subordinate to their needs for growth and a meaningful quality of work life (construct 3). The managers gave joint fourth ranking to the notion of treating people fairly, and the creation of opportu-

Table 37.1 Employees' ranking of importance of constructs compared with that of managers

No.	Stakeholder expectation	Employees' ranking	Managers' ranking
2.	Treat people with dignity	1	1
1.	Respond to the needs of customers/suppliers	2	2
4.	Treat people fairly	3	4
12.	Committed to grow and adapt	4	8
9.	Provide an honest flow of good information	5	11
6.	Caring about a person's ability to have a job	6	4
8.	Attract and give a fair return to investors	7	4
3.	Encourage personal growth	8	7
5.	Staff (fair pay)	9	3
7.	Staff (work related needs)	10	10
10.	Be a good corporate citizen	11	12
11.	Endow future generations	12	9

nities for staff to have a job with a fair return to shareholders. The staff had ranked the shareholders (construct 8) lower down, at 7th place. Herein lay the point of greatest tension with the managers.

A simple reading of the data suggested that the managers were trading off the involvement of staff as innovators and participants in the life of the firm to focus on a better return for shareholders. They were of a mind to satisfy the staff with fair pay and an ethos where a person's dignity was respected. The clash of values was around the employees' freedom to participate in the running of the firm, a tradition that had been built up over decades. Freedom to participate depended on communication, providing an honest flow of good information (construct 9), which was ranked 5th by the employees but ranked 11th by the management. However, the average rating by this staff group on this construct indicated very little change from a moderately good position being anticipated over the next five years.

At each workshop with a particular group, the results of preceding groups were shared to facilitate understanding between groups, culminating in a session with the Board of Directors six months after the commencement of the process. The Board committed itself to reiterating the values of the enterprise in three ways:

1. An elucidation of the basic assumptions underpinning the values.
2. A statement of the values themselves.
3. A formula by which the values would be embedded in the enterprise.

DRAFTING THE CORPORATION'S CODES

The facilitator and the Board Sub-Committee, together with the Human Resources Director, collaborated to draft the following basic premises on which the values were based.

The Values of the Corporation

Most would agree that the value dimension of ethics and morality is an essential characteristic of human existence. Since moral issues transcend economic issues, the starting point for our values is the basic moral premise of respect for the dignity and worth of the human person as an end, and not as a means. We ought to deal with each person in a truthful, honest and just way.

Our greatest dependence is upon our customers. The basic economic rationale for our business is to create value through serving their needs.

Our greatest resource is our employees who create the wealth within our enterprise. Their greatness stems from their strength of character, self-esteem and genius.

We are responsible to the communities in which we work and operate. The decisions we make should be reached in a context that allows the common good to be discovered.

We are responsible to future generations to be wise and careful stewards of their heritage and to provide an endowment of shared values carefully fostered and adapted as our enterprise evolves.

Our final responsibility is towards our investors as trustees of their assets. We ought to make fair profits. We ought to be adaptable, to experiment with new ideas, carry out research, engage in innovative programmes and pay for our mistakes. We ought to invest wisely to grow our enterprise in a planned and orderly way. We ought to create reserves for adverse times. We ought to provide our investors with necessary information to help them to understand and be involved with the enterprise and share in our corporate pride. When we operate according to these values our investors ought to realize a fair return on their investment with security.

The purpose of a business enterprise is to meet society's human and material needs by providing goods and services as efficiently as possible. All business is concerned with human relationships, not only with those who work in the enterprise but also those who provide the financial resources, those who buy its products and services and the wider public whose lives are affected by the business activity.

In a business enterprise the values in use represent the application of knowledge in perspective, i.e. knowledge that these values will lead to a fulfilment of the organization's purpose in the long run. Values therefore cannot be validated immediately, one has to accept conclusions in advance of their ultimate evidence. Immediately this creates the problem of individual world views and competing predictions of what can ensue from which value. It is essential therefore, that any statement of values is rooted in a key assumption concerning the nature of human nature as outlined in the opening paragraph of the Draft Code. This will act as an anchor to restrain competing interpretations of the Corporation's values from diverging too far.

Having underpinned the values with a statement of fundamental assumptions, the Values Task Force, with the facilitator and Human Resources Director, went on to draft the following Values Statement entitled 'The Corporation's Commitment to Value'.

The Corporation's Commitment to Value

We the employees and the shareholders believe that the inherent dignity and worth of the individual are the bedrock of the Corporation's commitment to values. All the other values we cherish flow from and are dependent on this belief.

We freely choose to form partnerships with other stakeholders in mutual pursuit of our common good. Our relationships as stakeholders in the Corporation have significantly deeper meaning than any purely financial transaction.

Our greatest resource is our employees. We place a high value on the continuing development of our participative management system. We expect competent leadership at all levels to foster employee strengths. We are committed to using authority in an affirming way, as a service to those being led and to modelling our values in action. We commit ourselves to creating trust and openness of communication in an ethical workplace. We commit ourselves to providing the Corporation's employees with fair compensation, with job security and with a physically safe environment.

We recognize the reality and truth of each unique person. The well-being of the corporation and our commitment to the individual both require that each employee, and every stakeholder, have the opportunity to grow and to develop our human capabilities within our relationship to the Corporation. We hold ourselves as individuals, accountable for our values and our actions.

We have a responsibility to be stewards of our resources, the physical environment, our immediate and our global communities, as well as our families. We are committed to dealing ethically and honestly with our stakeholders and with the larger community.

We have both financial and ethical responsibilities to our investors as trustees of their assets and as guardians of these shared values. We are committed to giving them both a fair return on investment and the necessary information to help them understand our goals and share our corporate pride.

We are responsible to future generations of stakeholders. We will provide a legacy of shared values that we carefully foster and adapt as our enterprise evolves, and an inheritance of a viable and profitable Corporation.

We are, therefore, committed to making decisions with a long-term perspective. We commit to research products and processes, to adapt to the changing markets and world, to experiment with new ideas in the social structure and management system of the Corporation, to create reserves to carry us during adverse economic times or the necessary failures of risk-taking. We commit ourselves as a partnership of stakeholders, customer, employees, investors, suppliers, communities, to the planned growth which marks a living and successful system.

FINALIZING THE DRAFT CODE OF VALUES AND EMBEDDING THEM IN USE

The facilitator was satisfied that the Draft Code, summarized above, represented a true synthesis of the views of the people who attended the various workshops. It was desirable that those participants had an opportunity to give the Values Task Force their observations on the Draft Code before it was finalised with the management team and Board. A process of consultation was designed and implemented by the Values Task Force members themselves.

The Corporation's Employees Council also reviewed the draft code of values. In the event not much modification was required to the code itself. Some questions regarding the sequence of values arose. A few people found the prospect of living up to these values a little daunting and sought a dilution of the language. The facilitator advised the Task Force to resist these attempts and encourage those concerned to rise to the challenge and experience personal growth in the process.

IMPLEMENTING AND SUSTAINING THE CODE OF VALUES IN PRACTICE

Values are an integral part of the culture of the Corporation. Culture basically serves two purposes for an organization, to integrate people, that is, to cooperate, to be productive, to grow as individuals, and help them to adapt to the world outsides—that is, to respond to customers and so forth. Thus, these values represented the organization's knowledge, or prediction, that their use will serve these two fundamental purposes. To do this, the values had to be reflected in the norms of behaviour and sustained by the customs, practices and institutions within the firm. New people joining the firm (recruits or because of acquisitions) would have to be socialized into adopting these values through appropriate induction, behaviour modelling and reinforcement.

In the final analysis, organizations protect the integrity of their culture by disengaging people who flagrantly violate their values. Thus, the process of implementing values had to be eclectic and ongoing. A useful way to address this issue was to consider a number of 'levers' for applying pressure to have the values used. Those could include, *inter alia:*

1. ***Induction and orientation process***
   — A written history of the firm, an explanation of the Values Statement, and a code of conduct based on the values provided to all new employees.
2. ***Personnel policies***
   The following have criteria related to the values:
   — Promotion, appraisal, equity, grievance process, benefits.
3. ***Reinforcement***
   — Creation of 'Heroes', through history, anecdotes, stories, newsletters, awards, rites, ceremonies, competitions.
   — Use of slogans, symbols, language in speeches, promotional material directed at various interest groups, official reports.
4. ***Technology/structure***
   — Work designed to maximize the scope for self-determination.
   — Appropriate decentralization.
5. ***Management style***
   — Behaviour modelling of the values through visible observance by management of the code of conduct appended to the values statement, especially when responding to critical incidents like a breach of values in a case where a staff member is being disciplined or an issue of job redundancy.
6. ***Training***
   — Values awareness training to refresh and renew the living out of the values.
   — Self-development to promote personal growth.
   — Training in personal construing of self and others to facilitate mutual respect and understanding.
   — Management effectiveness training, based on practices derived from values.
   — Quality management training to affirm the company's commitment to value.
7. ***Information and decision processes***
   — Information used to foster a sense of participation and inclusion in the running of the company.
   — Quality and Customer Service Information Systems.
   — Application of values during strategic planning and goal-setting processes.
8. ***Values audit***
   — Benchmark study of perceptions of values in use.
   — Regular, e.g. annual/biennial, audit to evaluate change occurrence or required.

These initiatives spanned a range of norms within the firm, yet, creative people inside the organization could add to them. Culture is merely a root metaphor for the organization itself. Values are the deepest discussible aspect of culture, therefore, every aspect of the organization is ultimately connectable to its values and can be used for initiatives to promote their use.

'MEANING' FROM VALUES STATEMENT

The test of a Values Statement is to ask the question 'Why?' one or more times after each value. The answers from individuals should converge rapidly onto the fundamental superordinate assumptions regarding the nature of human beings, of reality and truth, of morality and of cooperative pursuit of the common good. Similarly, the question 'How?' after each value should reveal the many possibilities for action which reflect the reality of the various individuals who subscribe to them (see pyramiding in Chapter 10, pp. 105–121 in this volume). This process of questioning reveals the Values Statement as a dynamic, living document at once rooted in firm assumptions and also capable of being construed, manifest (and monitored) in explicit language, behaviour and institutions.

OUTCOME

The facilitator reframed his role in the process from being catalyst, leaving the internal Values Task Force to complete the draft Values Statement. It was approved by the Board of Directors three months later. Finally, the Values Statement was shared with all employees in small groups where discussion on its working out was encouraged. The dilemmas around participation and providing a fair shareholder return were discussed and people were helped to come to terms with new realities.

The collective struggle to create a Values Statement was in itself an indication of the authenticity of these values. With the sharing with staff of the Board approved statement, 'The Corporation's Commitment to Value', this chapter was closed and the Corporation moved into the next phase, living the values and monitoring progress.

Personal construct psychology was useful as a theoretical framework in this intervention in several ways. First, its use engendered a great empathy between the facilitator and the various groups he interacted with. That had the effect of legitimizing and engendering trust in the authenticity of the process and confidence in the direction that the facilitator was charting for the organization. Further, the hierarchical character of construing systems inherent in personal construct theory made it easy to transfer this concept to the elucidation and embedding of values at the three levels of the organization's culture, assumptions, values and code of conduct, as set out in Schein (1985).

Philosophical and Religious Influences on the Thinking of George Kelly

INTRODUCTION

Gabrielle Chiari and Maria Laura Nuzzo discussed Kelly's philosophy of *constructive alternativism* in Chapter 4. They described how it was opposed to the prevalent science of the time—for which Kelly coined the words *accumulative fragmentalism.* That term is a good example of Kelly's love of writing with 'tongue in cheek'. But the point is a serious one as it highlights the radical nature of his philosophy of *constructive alternativism* which has been a major influence on the development of the current approach to science under the names of *constructivism* and *constructionism.*

Kelly explained that all psychological theories have an underlying philosophical base, but these are rarely spelled out. This section looks in depth at the influences on Kelly's thinking coming from philosophy. Trevor Butt shows the extent to which phenomenology may well have played a part in the formulation of Kelly's ideas and Bill Warren discusses the influence of Dewey's pragmatism. Dewey's philosophy was also related to religion. That is of interest because it is known that Kelly was a religious man. His father had been a Presbyterian minister, he went to a Quaker school and then to a Quaker university. He knew his Bible backwards, living as he did in the so-called 'Bible Belt' of the United States of America. Did Kelly become particularly interested in Dewey because of Dewey's ideas on religion? Bill Warren addresses this question as well.

CHAPTER 38

The Phenomenological Context of Personal Construct Psychology

Trevor Butt
University of Huddersfield, UK

> From a phenomenological point of view, the client—like the proverbial cus-
> tomer—is always right.
>
> (Kelly, 1955/1991, p. 322/Vol. 1, p. 241).

When Kelly published *The Psychology of Personal Constructs* in 1955, he issued a challenge to the positivist behaviourism that had dominated American psychology for the previous 40 years. It was, in fact, the 'contrast pole' to personal construct psychology, with its faith that psychologists could understand human action in terms of simple responses to environmental stimuli. Following the natural sciences, it promoted a strict separation between the subjective and the objective, in an attempt to discover lawful relations between the person and the environment.

Behaviourism, in its turn, had displaced pragmatism, the approach of William James, George Mead and John Dewey. Kelly wrote in the pragmatist tradition, and was especially impressed with the ideas of Dewey, 'whose philosophy and psychology can be read between many of the lines of the psychology of personal constructs' (1955/1991, p. 154/Vol. 1, p. 108). Pragmatism was based on a rejection of the dualisms that psychology had inherited from Descartes. For the pragmatists, the taken-for-granted separations of theory from practice, mind from body and subject from object all impeded our understanding of the person. Bill Warren writes in the next chapter about the influence of Dewey and pragmatism on Kelly's thinking.

Phenomenology was a European philosophy that was a parallel development to American pragmatism. It will be argued that personal construct psychology may fruitfully be seen as a phenomenological approach to the person and that its methods for investigating the experience of individuals mirror and indeed extend phenomenology's reach. It will also be contended that personal construct psychology is enriched by the insights of other phenomenologists, in particular, those of Merleau-Ponty (1962/1945).

PHENOMENOLOGY

Phenomenology is one of several currents of philosophical thought that dates back to the beginning of the twentieth century. It is usually seen as beginning with Edmond Husserl. Building on the descriptive psychology of Brentano, Husserl advocated a psychology that studied phenomena—the world as it appears to us. Traditionally, philosophy and psychology have attempted to separate events in the world from our perception of them. Kant referred to the former as *noumena* and the latter as *phenomena*. In Kelly's terms, there is a real world of events, and a multiplicity of constructions that can be placed on it and through which we interpret it. Phenomenology's focus is purely on phenomena, on the world as it appears, because that is all we can ever know. In this sense it is a prototype of a psychology of personal constructs.

Merleau-Ponty (1962/1945), one of Husserl's students, was particularly critical of psychology's adoption of a natural sciences agenda. Like Kelly, he was writing at a time when behaviourism was the dominant psychology. His contention was that psychology had become the prisoner of 'objective thought'—a way of thinking that separates subject from object, and attempts to define the features in the real world that cause behaviour (see Hammond et al., 1991, for an in-depth coverage). His contention was that objective thought did not do justice to the 'lived world', the world of our experience. It maintains a clear separation of subject and object, and proposes that the world consists of separate objects whose dimensions and properties can ultimately be known and measured. Because these objects exist independently of each other, external, that is, causal relations exist between them. Objective thought has been validated in the natural sciences, where it has so often given us a purchase on the world that has enabled us to master aspects of it. But unfortunately, the lived world is messier than this; everything in it is ambiguous, and objective thought simply does not represent our experience. For example, when psychologists have studied emotions, they have sometimes attempted to account for the complex mix of our feelings by proposing a number of primary emotions that can be mixed together, like primary colours, to produce any number of secondary emotions. But we often feel two supposedly opposite emotions at the same time—love and irritation, joy and sadness. When this happens, one emotion does not cancel out the other; we do not end up with one diluting the other. If only life were so simple!

As Kelly frequently observed, psychological entities like thought, emotion and behaviour are not separate from each other. Psychologists have usually separated the person's processes into these different faculties, but we know that our experience cannot be split up in this way. Therefore, 'internal relations' apply, where one feature of the lived world cannot be specified without implying the others. When I wave enthusiastically at a friend, it is not *because* of a feeling of warmth and friendliness, and my feelings are not *caused* by a cognitive construction of friend/enemy along which the person is placed. Friendliness *is* the whole configuration. In a similar way, internal relations apply between the person and their world. We simply cannot talk about what the world is really like. Every description comes from a particular perspective, and we cannot put all perspectives together to arrive at a God's eye view. It is because of this grounding of perspective as belonging to embodied subjects that Merleau-Ponty, along with others who followed Husserl, have been termed 'existential phenomenologists'. Because we are in internal relationships with the world, we cannot separate the subjective from the objective; there is no clear separation between what we project and what is 'really there'. As Warren (1992) affirms, it is useful to talk of 'subjecting' and 'objecting' as processes, but it is a mistake to imagine that we can ever separate ourselves entirely from our own perspective.

PERSONAL CONSTRUCT PSYCHOLOGY AND PHENOMENOLOGY

Kelly's main project was to develop practices that would help to bring about personal change. In typical pragmatic fashion, he argued that the value of a theory is not its truth-value, but its utility—its ability to give us a hold on the world. He was clear that the predominant psychology of his day—behaviourism—did not match up well to this test. It held that the way a person thinks, feels and acts is determined by what happens to them. In complete contrast, Kelly insisted that people are not the victims of their pasts. His Fundamental Postulate speaks of the *person's processes* (rather than an 'internal substance' that thinks, feels and acts), their *channelizing* (not what causes them) and *anticipation* (not reaction). These emphases are mirrored in phenomenologists' accounts of the person. Phenomenology looks at what people do, rejects causal explanations for their action and tries to understand them in terms of their interpretation of events. Here we can see the same principles behind both pragmatic and phenomenological thought.

Yet Kelly himself dismissed phenomenology as a subjective view of the person that he found unacceptable:

> This view keeps all the turmoil within the man and offers him neither the challenge of external threats nor the comfort of resources beyond himself . . . phenomenological man cannot share his subjective plight, for even his most beloved companion is a manikin fabricated out of his own moods.
>
> (Kelly, 1969h, p. 24)

So, Kelly saw 'phenomenological man' as one imprisoned in his subjective world, disconnected from the reality of other people. However, phenomenology, as we have seen, is concerned with the study of *phenomena*—the way things appear to us. As such, it focuses on personal meaning and construing. So what was the basis for Kelly's view? Both from the context of his comments, and discussion with those who knew him, it seems that his understanding of phenomenology came from a knowledge of those American personality theories that imported a particular version of phenomenology. Indeed, many contemporary texts on personality theory still use 'phenomenology' to refer only to the work of Rogers and Maslow. However, in laying out the basis of his theory, Kelly commented:

> ... We believe it is possible to combine certain features of the neophenomeno-
> logical approaches with more conventional methodology. We cannot, of course,
> crawl into another person's skin and peer out at the world through his eyes. We
> can, however, start by making inferences based primarily upon what we see him
> doing, rather than upon what we have seen other people doing.
>
> (Kelly, 1955/1991, p. 42/Vol. 1, p. 29)

And this linkage has been underlined by some contemporary construct theorists. Warren (1998, p. 41), for example, claims that Kelly's position falls most comfortably into the tradition of phenomenology. So perhaps in coining the term 'neophenomenology' Kelly wanted to distance himself from the psychology of Rogers and Maslow, while at the same time recognizing the phenomenological nature of personal construct psychology. In fact, Kelly's interpretation of phenomenology as a private and subjective psychology is commonplace among psychologists. In order to deal with this misconception, it will be necessary to look more closely at the mind/body dualism, noting the convergence between pragmatism and phenomenology.

The Mind/Body Dualism

Kelly's mentor, John Dewey, saw the mind/body dualism as the main problem in modern times:

> The question of integration of the mind/body in action is the most practical of
> all questions we can ask in our civilisation. Until this integration is effected in
> the only place where it can be carried out, in action itself, we shall continue to
> live in a society in which a soulless and heartless materialism is compensated for
> by a soulful but futile idealism and spiritualism. (Dewey, 1931, p. 299)

This separation of mind and body became, if anything, more of a problem 70 years later. In the wake of computer models of the mind, the dominance of behaviourism has been replaced by that of cognitive psychology (see Chapter 2, pp. 21–31, and also Chapter 4, pp. 41–49).

The pragmatic Kelly had very little to say about the self, confining himself to observing that the self is a construction in which some events are seen as belonging to 'self' and 'not other' poles. For Kelly, the subject of psychology is not a substance, but a process. Phenomenology too is concerned with this process, and like Kelly, does not reify the self. It is concerned with the correlation between what is perceived and the way it is perceived, and not between what is perceived and the person who perceives it. Its focus, therefore, is on the interaction between person and world, not on what is going on in the world or what is going on inside the person. Merleau-Ponty puts this nicely: 'Truth does not inhabit the "inner man", or more accurately, there is no inner man, man is in the world, and only in the world does he know himself' (1962/1945, p. xi). From this point of view, consciousness is not an inner state, a mind inside a body that we get at through introspection. It is a relation to things, the *way* something is perceived. Merleau-Ponty talks about the person as an embodied subject, emphasizing that we do not have minds inside bodies, rather the mind is a way of talking about an aspect of our bodies—how we have developed the power to reflect on what we are doing.

Kelly emphasizes this when he argues that there does not exist a psychological realm, only processes that can be construed psychologically: 'We do not conceive the substance of psychology to be itself psychological—or physiological or sociological, or to be pre-empted by any system' (1955/1991, p. 48/Vol. 1, p. 33). Both Mead and Merleau-Ponty considered consciousness to be an emergent property of humankind, one that has developed with language and our ability to conduct inner dialogues in thinking. After all, all animals, including humans, relate intentionally to their environment, whether or not they can think and talk about it. When Merleau-Ponty argued that we only know ourselves in the world, he meant that before we are conscious of our intentions, we are already immersed in a flow of interactions in the physical and social world. We find ourselves already engaged, and might or might not reflect on this state of affairs. Of course we can deliberate before we act, but this is the exception rather than the rule. Indeed it is a common experience that self-consciousness often interferes with smooth action. Normally, our pre-reflective engagement does not require any reflection. This is mirrored in Kelly's assertion that the person is 'a form of motion'. It is best to think of the person as a process rather than a substance, always engaged in action, always doing something, however it may look to an observer. Constructs are not internal cognitive entities that cause emotions and behaviour:

> A construct owes no special allegiance to the intellect, as against the will or the emotions. In fact, we do not find it either necessary or desirable to make that classic trichotomous division of mental life. (Kelly, 1969b, p. 87)

Interactive Thinking

The model of the person as a form of motion, in which action, emotion and thought are intertwined, is a pragmatic parallel of what Merleau-Ponty called 'internal relation'. That reading of personal construct theory sees construing as a process that does not originate in reflective thought, but in interaction with the social and physical world. As Kelly insists, the most important constructs may have no clear-cut symbolism. Indeed, our most vital constructs may be pre-verbal. And emphasizing construing as a process moves us away from a search for 'constructs' inside the person.

Kelly was very aware of the traps set for us by language. One that concerns us here is that when we talk of constructs rather than construing, it is all too easy to imagine cognitive entities inside the person that we can discover. Self-characterization, the elicitation of personal constructs, repertory grids, laddering (see Chapter 10, pp. 105–121)—all are extraordinarily useful methods for helping the person to spell out their engagement with the world. The techniques give a person the tools to reflect on and make sense of the way in which things appear to them. They tell of the stance we adopt: the characteristic intentional approach we take up. But they do not uncover internal cognitions that have caused the person to act and feel as they do. Psychological reconstruction is not just cognitive reconstruction. In Kelly's day, the problem was to free psychology from the unre-constructed behaviourism that dominated it. Now it is to prevent the cognitive rev-olution from re-establishing and underlining a mind/body dualism that impoverishes our understanding of people.

PERSONAL CONSTRUCT PSYCHOLOGY AND PHENOMENOLOGICAL INVESTIGATION

Phenomenologists claim that the more we look, the more we can see: that the world will reveal more of its complexity if only we can free ourselves from our presuppositions and pre-emptive construing. The principle of constructive alterna-tivism underlines this point, and the personal construct methods referred to above are excellent examples of techniques that achieve what Ihde (1986) calls 'phenom-enological seeing'. One technique, the analysis of self-characterization sketches, will be considered later in order to demonstrate how personal construct methodology extends the reach of phenomenology.

The dualism in traditional psychology separates the object and subject and always resolves into an overemphasis on one or the other. This is the old debate between realists and idealists. Realists suggest it is events in the world that cause our per-ceptions through the sense organs of the body. Idealists point to illusion and ambiguity and claim that perception is more of a projection of the subject. For phenomenologists, this is a pointless and uninteresting debate. It is enough to focus on phenomena, the world as it appears to us. Like Kelly, they eschew causal expla-nation; the impact of the world and the force of projection. Instead they focus on the relationship between things and the way they are perceived. The phenomeno-logical account of perception is not causal but relational. As in Gestalt Psychology, the world is conceived as multifaceted, lending itself to various perceptions and con-structions, some of which are afforded more readily than others. There may not be an infinite number of constructions that events will bear, and some are more obvious to us than are others, but certainly there are many more interpretations possible than those that present themselves immediately.

Standing Back

The problem is how to reveal the richness of the world of appearances, just how to stand back from our 'sedimented' natural attitude to achieve the openness of phenomenological perception. Husserl has suggested a number of steps to help to achieve this. Firstly, analysts attempt to bracket off their preconceptions in under-standing phenomena. Secondly, phenomena are described, but causal explanation is avoided. Finally, no assumptions about relative importance of phenomena are made. Ihde (1986) demonstrates phenomenological methods with reference to ambiguous figures like the Necker cube, which is used in so many introductory psy-chology texts on perception. He shows how this figure is open to many more inter-pretations than the two normally indicated. Using the device of simple stories, he guides the reader towards seeing new inversions of the cube. In the social sciences, there are a number of ways of analysing interview material in order to bring out the possible meanings in the text that might not be immediately apparent to the interviewer. Moustakas (1994) notes the common qualities of these phenomenological approaches. The researcher uses qualitative designs that focus on wholeness of experience, in a search for meanings rather than explanation. In these first-person accounts, the data of experience are primary, and the researcher does everything possible to capture the construction of the person. Knowing how easy it is for the researcher to interpret the other's account in terms of his or her own constructions, there is an emphasis on reflexivity, where researchers are always conscious of their own perspective.

We can see this process at work in all personal construct methods. In the analysis of self-characterization sketches, Kelly (1955/1991, pp. 319–360/Vol. 1, pp. 239–267) lays out ways in which the protocol is not 'scored, but brought into focus'. He was writing at a time when clinical psychology was dominated by psychometrics, in which psychologists scored tests to discover underlying pathologies and personality dimensions in order to explain behaviour. It is important to appreciate the radical and phenomenological nature of his thinking. His proposition was simple but revolutionary: we have to make sense of a person's conduct in terms of their idiosyncratic system of personal constructs. To do that, psychologists must adopt a 'credulous approach', in which they are open to the client's world view, suspending disbelief and their own preconceptions in an attempt to understand the client's perspective. Kelly emphasizes that in the quotation at the start of this chapter. In the self-characterization sketch exercise (see also Chapter 11, pp. 123–131) the clients are invited to describe themselves in their own words, and inevitably, within their own framework of meaning—their system of personal constructs. They are asked to write a description of themselves in the third person, from the point of view of someone that knows them intimately and sympathetically. Kelly recommended various ways in which this sketch should then be considered, illustrating his approach with reference to a client he calls Ronald Barrett. He emphasizes throughout that the aim of the analysis is phenomenological:

> Strictly, within his personal world, matters *are* as they *are now seen*. Since, first of all, it is Ronald whom we wish to understand, rather than the world which is external to Ronald, we study *the way Ronald sees that world*.
> (Kelly, 1955/1991, p. 359/Vol. 1, p. 267; emphases in the original)

Kelly suggests various ways in which the psychologist can try to adopt what he terms the credulous approach (what phenomenologists term 'phenomenological seeing'). The analysis of the sketch involves careful reading and re-reading, paying particular attention to its structure: the sequence, organization and context of the self-description. The whole text may be read several times as though different parts of it are of central importance. In order to avoid imposing one's own meaning on the protocol, alternative emphases and inflections in reading each sentence and paragraph should be tried. For example, the following passage should be read seven times, each time stressing a different line:

> On the whole,
> he tries to impress people,

especially his elders,
with his knowledge,
poise,
and sincerity.

Kelly points out that we cannot assume that the client is always able or willing to express themselves, and the psychologist's job is to arrive not at conclusions, but hypotheses that can later be discussed with the client. Here we see Kelly anticipating the cooperative inquiry that qualitative researchers recommend today. The aim of the self-characterization sketch is not a frozen psychometric slice through a client's life, but the beginning of a phenomenological inquiry, an opening into a life-world, a person's way of experiencing things.

CONCLUDING REMARKS

This chapter has underlined some of the ways in which personal construct psychology can be seen as a member of the phenomenological family. Both its emphasis on the person's meaning-making and its ways of investigating this process bear the hallmarks of a phenomenological approach. Kelly's thinking is embedded in the pragmatist tradition that, like phenomenology, rejects the dualistic thinking of orthodox psychology. Personal construct psychology's methods have supplied powerful ways of helping people spell out the way the world appears to them. The importance of reflexivity and cooperative inquiry were recognized in personal construct theory very early in its career. Now that psychology has at last recognized the value of qualitative research, a number of phenomenological approaches to the person are being advocated (Smith et al., 1995; Willig, 2001). Yet there has been little appreciation of the potential contribution of personal construct psychology's rich methodology in understanding the life-world. When that growing community of psychologists who draw on phenomenological methods recognize the phenomenological nature of personal construct psychology, its powerful methodology will become increasingly available to those carrying out qualitative research.

CHAPTER 39

Pragmatism and Religion: Dewey's Twin Influences?

Bill Warren

University of Newcastle, Australia

To the extent that psychology fails to touch the intimate life of man it makes the same mistake that was made in Eden, a mistake compounded by the religionists who make all those legalistic and punitive interpretations of what happened there.

(Kelly, 1969c, p. 212)

Kelly fully acknowledged the influence of John Dewey's philosophy on his thinking, implying the significance, for him, of the philosophy with which Dewey is commonly associated—pragmatism. In its turn, pragmatism had an impact on philosophy of religion, and Dewey (1934), like James (1982) before him, wrote specifically on religion from that perspective. As Kelly certainly appears to have been a committed Christian (Fransella, 1995), the question thus arises: Does personal construct theory derive whatever religious dimension it has, significantly from the pragmatist perspective on religion in general and Dewey's ideas on religion in particular? This chapter explores this question.

JOHN DEWEY, PRAGMATISM AND RELIGION

Pragmatism, in its original usage, signified the view that meaning, understanding, knowledge—generally, our 'grasp' of the world—lay in the practical significance of an idea or concept. The major theorists of this perspective, William James, C.S. Peirce and John Dewey settled on different concepts to describe their own particular perspectives: Peirce took the term *pragmaticism*, leaving *pragmatism* to James, while Dewey was to use the term *instrumentalism*. Dewey's instrumentalism was:

an attempt to constitute a precise logical theory of concepts, of judgments and inferences in their various forms, by considering primarily how thought functions in the experimental determinations of future consequences. (1968, p. 26)

International Handbook of Personal Construct Psychology. Edited by F. Fransella.
© 2003 John Wiley & Sons, Ltd.

Ideas, formed from sense impressions of the world, functioned as 'instruments' with which we operate in and on the world.

That there are specific connections between pragmatism, particularly Dewey's elaboration of it, and personal construct theory, need not rely merely on the fact that Kelly says so. Dewey's own observations resonate with such connections as, for example, in the last quotation, and also in the account wherein he notes the recognition of the mind as something which 'tests the meanings of behaviour' (1966, p. 323).

Again, Morrish could as well be describing a core notion of personal construct psychology when he summarizes Dewey's instrumentalism as holding that:

> knowledge was always a 'means' and each individual uses it for the purpose of adapting himself to new problems, new situations and new involvements . . . to find personal solutions to his daily problems. (Morrish, 1967, p. 110)

Just as Dewey would say that ideas functioned as instruments, personal construct psychology would take this view further in stressing a similar, though more active, 'intentional' role for *constructs*.

The influence of pragmatism on personal construct psychology should now be taken as read, and this does not pose a problem for the link to phenomenology that is persistently highlighted (Warren, 1985, 1998; Butt, 1996; see also Trevor Butt's discussion in the previous chapter). This is because phenomenology and pragmatism share core elements and the general theme of an active mind fully engaged in a life-world that provides the ground for meaning-making that is itself a given for human existence. None of the historical developments in relation to pragmatism generate difficulties for personal construct psychology which from the beginning was seen as a social psychology (Jones, 1971), and a theory of social action (Butt, 1996).

What is less clear and worthy of enquiry, however, is the significance of pragmatism's perspective on religion. More particularly, Dewey's views on religion are of interest given that it was specifically Dewey's philosophy with which personal construct psychology is saturated. Dewey's ideas on religion are scattered throughout his writing and developed over time, but they find a more focused expression in his more or less final position *A Common Faith* (Dewey, 1934).

The first part of *A Common Faith* argues a distinction between *religion, a religion*, and *the religious*. Dewey argues that the core concepts of the definition of religion (for example, unseen powers, the manner of expressing obedience and reverence, and the moral imperatives that issue from particular beliefs) are conceived in such a multitude of incompatible ways that we cannot talk intelligently of religion *per se*, but only of *this* or *that* religion.

A Religious Outlook

Dewey's more general purpose was to distinguish a religious outlook or attitude from any particular, doctrinal religion. He suggests that religions prevent the religious quality of experience from coming to consciousness and finding a form of expression that is consistent with the modern intellectual and moral conditions of life. In elaborating this, Dewey argues that this last perspective can be found in our quest to know and understand, in that faith 'in the continued disclosing of truth through directed cooperative human endeavor [which] is more religious in quality than any faith in a completed revelation' (1934, p. 26). The religious attitude is one facet of a general attitude that is 'displayed equally in art, science, and good citizenship' (p. 23). The 'unseen power' of the dictionary definition is read as the notion of people living in accord with an *ideal*. Anything we do on behalf of an ideal outcome, particularly when we do this against obstacles and dangers, particularly the danger of threatening our current convictions, is religious in quality (p. 27).

Further, just as Dewey argues that the *aesthetic* is potentially an element of every experience, so also is the religious. In this regard, Miedema draws out the analogy with Dewey's discussion of the aesthetic. Dewey had criticized what he called 'muse-ologization', the locking up of art and artistic experience in special institutions and thus removing the understanding of the aesthetic as an inherent aspect of all experience. Thus, too, with 'the "museologization" of the religious in religions' (Miedema, 1995, p. 71).

Dewey goes on to argue how new methods of enquiry had supplanted the notion of revelation and faith, methods which emphasize a particular mode of access to truth: 'the road of patient, cooperative inquiry operating by means of observation, experiment, record and controlled reflection' (Dewey, 1934, p. 32). Even so-called 'mystical experience' will yield to this enquiry.

He goes on to contrast the 'method of intelligence' that is characteristic of science with the appeal to authority and doctrine that is characteristic of religions. The former is open and public, the latter limited and private. Nor is it adequate to claim 'symbolic' or 'metaphorical' meaning for stories in religion, for there is symbol and metaphor in science. The symbols and metaphors of a religion soon become, in practice, intimately connected to the notion of 'truth', whereas the metaphors, the 'ideal types' of scientific enquiry, are discarded when they no longer assist understanding.

Dewey offers a view of 'the religious' that sees it as integral to all human experiencing, and as impacting the person's whole life in the sense of generating basic and lasting changes. As Miedema (1995) has it, drawing on Joas (1993) who is part of a revival of interest in Dewey's philosophy of religion, Dewey's position 'can adequately be described as an empirical philosophy about the constitution and the roles of ideals in human action' (p. 68). Dewey's position originated in the philosophy of the German philosopher G.W.F. Hegel, and developed over time and partly from Dewey's own personal experiences of the harsh realities of life (both personal and social). In terms of recent scholarship on Dewey (Rockefeller, 1991; Joas, 1993; Miedema, 1995), which emphasizes that Dewey's philosophy of religion remained significantly Hegelian throughout its development (especially Rockefeller, 1991), it is interesting to recall my earlier discussions of Hegel's ideas on Christianity (Warren, 1993, 1998) which were considered useful to understanding religion in personal construct psychology.

PERSONAL CONSTRUCT PSYCHOLOGY, DEWEY, AND RELIGION

The foregoing discussion of Dewey's philosophy and religion resonates with core elements of personal construct psychology. A psychology grounded in an ongoing process of making sense of the world, and which bases that on a creative and imaginative approach to life, harmonizes well with Dewey's concept of the religious. Some specific points of contact draw out this harmony.

We might first note how Dewey's religious position has centred on an idea of a person striving towards an ideal, and a key notion of his later thought, particularly in relation to education, was that of *growth*. When we form our ideal and have to make judgements concerning it—for example, about what it is right or wrong to do in a particualar circumstance—the principal question is what choice is more likely to 'expand, invigorate, harmonize, and in general organize the self?' (Rockefeller, 1991, p. 200). That observation has clear affinity with Kelly's Choice Corollary, the view that human beings are continually attempting to elaborate their construing systems, attempting to enhance and broaden their understanding. Further, there is another connection here between Dewey's thought in relation to education and Kelly's (1969l) observation that 'psychotherapy' could just as easily be called 'learning', as long as that term is meant to convey an activity which helps a person get on with their life (p. 64). Dewey's notion of growth, in which his whole philosophy of religion and of education was grounded, stressed the idea of a continuous *process* rather than a state at which one arrives: 'The end of human life is not to attain some static ideal state and stop growing. The end of living is to be found in a way of living' (Rockefeller, 1991, p. 426).

The most directly relevant discussion Kelly has of religion is his *Sin and Psychotherapy* (Kelly, 1969c), where he does not compare or contrast, nor criticize religions, and from this source alone one could not judge on his own commitment. He discusses core ideas of Christianity such the Garden of Eden story in the Bible, and other stories, and Jesus is considered as much a good and wise man as the son of God. There is more a *familiarity with* the Bible as any tone of *commitment to* it. Again, he focuses on the four major world religions in terms of their social-moral aspects rather than their truth claims. He writes of the different religions without favouring any particular one and suggests that guilt may arise (not *will* arise) from an 'interpretation of the outlook of a divine Being' (p. 179); that is not *the* divine Being. He notes also how, when one settles for ready-made answers to the quest that Kelly believes the Garden of Eden story illustrates—that is, the intention of humankind to take on the responsibility of gaining knowledge of good and evil— the quest is negated. The loss of interest in this quest is quite understandable when it is recognized that:

> most systems for dealing with good and evil are designed to circumvent the necessity for coming to grips with the problem. Why struggle . . . when this culture, or that religion, will provide you with a thumb-indexed set of answers.
>
> (Kelly, 1969c, p. 183)

Equally, the most powerful mechanism for cutting short the individual's search is 'excommunication', which brings about 'individual conformity and [cuts] short man's personal quest for distinguishing good from evil' (p. 185). This, Kelly argues, was not the intention of Jesus's teaching in the story of those who have no sin casting the first stone; which is taken as encouraging constructive revision. He draws attention to what Jesus did once the would-be stoners had departed, that is, he advises the woman to 'make something out of the experience so as not to repeat it'; she was left alone to continue to think about the difference between good and evil (p. 188). Rue Cromwell cites an exchange of letters with George Kelly on the issue of good versus evil in Chapter 42 (pp. 415–423).

Organized Religion

Kelly had already considered the place of organized religion in his discussion of the wider field in which an individual lives and how this needs to be taken into account when considering the personal constructions of any particular individual (1955/1991, pp. 702–703/Vol. 2, pp. 102–103). Thus among such institutions as schools and recreational resources, he talks of the significance of religious organizations. He notes, too, that many religious taboos are not strictly spiritual in nature but are 'as thoroughly "materialistic" as anything one can imagine', with a significant stress on organizational control and official authority (1955/1991, pp. 702–703/Vol. 2, pp. 102–103). In general, Kelly considers organized religion as but one of various social impacts on the individual, it is not singled out as specially important.

Another matter concerns Dewey's location of religion as something that is emergent from the conditions of life of a people. He emphasizes the social origins of religion and rejects the idea that religion is inherently a matter of belief in the supernatural and particular ceremonies and rites designed to effect communication with that realm. Dewey harmonizes religion as a natural feature of all societies with the developing emphasis on reason, intelligence and enquiry that are the essence of *pragmatism*. Thus, too, Dewey de-emphasizes core notions of Christianity such as belief in God as a specific 'Being', in a supernatural realm of existence, in original sin, in atonement for sin by a specific 'penance'. Superstitions have scant chance of surviving in the face of the legacy of scientific and democratic revolutions. However, the shared experiences of people that generate those superstitions in earlier historical periods will give way to new expressions in social life and be absorbed into a 'moral background'. Here they will be understood as a set of ideas to be discussed and argued, rather than taken as truth, therein supporting the operation of that religious spirit which he saw as consistent with the pursuits of science (Rockefeller, 1991, p. 264).

Again, in Kelly's idea of humankind not being limited by circumstances but striving to see them differently, there is consistency with Dewey's (1934) insistence that when the religious is operating in one's life one is actively engaged in life. The religious attitude finds people opposed to 'a mere Stoical resolution to endure unperturbed throughout the buffetings of fortune' (p. 16). For Kelly the universe does not map out our lives, is not inexorable unless we choose to construe it that way. Thus we might so choose and adopt the doctrines of a convenient religion; but he makes no judgement as to the truth claims of any particular choice in this direction, and he allows with similar absence of critical judgement, that one might construe one's way *out* of such position. Indeed, Kelly (1969j) suggests that this refusal to allow circumstances to dictate to us and to seek to know the world more fully, is seen in the Biblical story of Adam and the Garden of Eden, where 'Man made a fateful decision. He chose to live his life by understanding, rather than obedience' (p. 207).

Related to this last point is the importance of imagination for Dewey, because imagination was vital to that harmonizing of the self which, for him, was the ideal to which humankind strives. Dewey distinguishes imagination which 'supervenes' and that which 'intervenes'. The first involves merely specific, special and partial activities of life or activity. The second, that which intervenes, interpenetrates 'all the elements of our being'. Unless imagination 'intervenes' it will not generate that creative movement which is the 'firm basis for ideal constructions in society, religion, and art' (Dewey, 1934, p. 18). Kelly had made observations in relation to creativity that echo Dewey's discussion here. He notes that Fixed Role Therapy (see Chapter 23, pp. 237–245) involves essentially a process of creativity, and distinguishes between a backward-looking perspective focusing on one's past, and a 'rebirth' which focuses on the future; urged, he suggests, in the teachings of Jesus. He argues that those teachings stressed 'repentance' as a 'rethinking process rather than as an expiation process' (Kelly, 1955/1991, p. 381/Vol. 1, p. 282).

Creative thinking originates in 'preposterous thinking', though, to be effective, this must be progressively tightened in hypothesis formulation and testing. The loosened construction that sets the stage for creative thinking releases 'facts, long taken as self-evident, from their rigid conceptual moorings' (1995/1991, p. 1031/Vol. 2, p. 330). Further, and creating significant difficulty for a religious position that is rooted in texts and teachings of the past, is his contention that what is said of the creative process applies equally to the way hypotheses are formed in scientific reasoning; that is, as *predictions* designed to 'embrace the future rather than to embalm the past' (Kelly, 1955/1991, p. 381/Vol. 1, p. 282). More generally, it is the 'bigger picture', as focused by Dewey in relation to religion, that Kelly urges us to see *all* human beings as aspiring towards.

There is also a clear echo of Dewey in Kelly's observation concerning the manner in which the Reformation attacked the limiting effect of the institutionalization of the religious, and the 'concretistic classification of certain men as priests' (Kelly, 1955/1991, p. 4/Vol. 1, p. 4). Likewise, Kelly criticizes classification and categorization in psychology in a fashion which recalls Dewey's concept of 'museologization'. In each case there is the same 'hardening of the categories' (Kelly, 1969e, p. 294) which will retard enquiry just as, for Dewey, it restricts the operation of the religious in human life.

Natural Sinfulness

In relation to sin, Dewey rejected the appeal to some sort of 'natural sinfulness' in human beings in explaining the inhuman things we do to each other, saying it was akin to appealing to demons in explaining bodily illness. Rather, he argued we will locate the causes of oppression and cruelty in social conditions under which human beings are asked to live. An appeal to supernatural redemption as the only way forward from sin, and the acceptance that human beings are naturally corrupt, were notions that could be subjected to the critical intelligence that he championed. But, whatever the methodological difficulties, it needed to be acknowledged that human beings had an equal tendency towards justice, kindness and struggle against oppression that was as much a liberation as was 'divine forgiveness'. Individual 'sinfulness' had always to be put in a context, and that context was the social. Thus, for Dewey, the destructive behaviour of individuals could be significantly overcome 'by changing the social environment, including the schools', the chief problem being not a corrupt will but 'ignorance, a lack of social planning, and the absence of a strong moral faith in intelligence' (Rockefeller, 1991, p. 484). Kelly (1969c) identifies sin as a personal experience but, like Dewey, proceeds to locate that experience in a social matrix, one that generates *guilt*. Guilt arises when one finds oneself acting inconsistently with one's role, and a role arises only in the context of the expectations of others. In the social context, outcomes and consequences, rather than God's interests, are at issue. Thus, too, what counts as 'sin' is relative: 'what we shall come to realize as sinful a thousand years from now may bear no resemblance to the evils that preachers talk about today' (Kelly, 1969j, p. 210).

We might also look to the tone of Kelly's discussions of religion in the context of Dewey's (1934) concluding comment. That is, we must look for the ideals which drive specific religious outlooks and expression in our interaction with other people, and in a shared understanding of the values that we express in that interaction. The 'common faith' to which he refers is a striving towards an ideal of understanding and a harmonizing of the self that transcends particular sects, classes, or races. One specific section of Kelly's discussion of organized religion conveys this similarity of tone well. In considering the various influences on personal constructs, Kelly (1955/1991, p. 702/Vol. 2, p. 102) suggests that one of numerous sources will be any religious organizations or mores to which the individual has been exposed. He refers here to 'religious sects and denominations', and considers their impact to extend beyond the strictly 'spiritual' domain to an impact on one's interpersonal and social life. There is no special place or special significance for organized religion, it is discussed matter-of-factly and as continuous with other dimensions of the formation of constructs. Thus can Al Landfield report to Fransella (1995, p. 22), and from his own personal experience, that Kelly's religion was not dogma.

CONCLUSION

We have developed a modest degree of circumstantial evidence relating to the question of whether Kelly's implicit religious perspective might be illuminated by reference to Dewey's manifest position. While not decisive, the evidence is tenable, and suggests a positive answer to the question posed at the outset. In a sense, such an answer is not surprising in that Dewey's philosophy that is acknowledged to be lying between the lines of personal construct psychology, embraces Dewey's philosophy of religion; just as his philosophy of education is highly compatible with personal construct psychology (Novak, 1983; Warren, 1998).

Kelly stressed that personal construct psychology has the same limited range of convenience as other theories and it is equally not surprising that he does not discuss religion any more than he discusses education or politics. Indeed, in relation to religion he notes specifically that in his discussion of sin he was not offering a definition that would satisfy formal ethics or theology, merely a psychological discussion. Yet, just as it is possible to develop more fully both the links with other philosophical perspectives that he merely mentions, and 'latencies' within the theory (phenomenology, for example) so it is possible to align Dewey's philosophy of religion with that theory.

Like Dewey, Kelly appears to have naturalized and socialized religion. He does not appear to have so clearly or explicitly delineated *religion, a religion* and *the religious*, but the general tone of his discussion any time he does refer to religion is highly compatible with Dewey's ideas. Kelly appears to accept the deepening of understanding that a religious metaphor might provoke, that one individual might voice a cry for the whole of mankind and that the metaphor of the Garden of Eden links all humankind in a deeper quest. Dewey concluded his discussion by emphasizing that the religious attitude that underpins all experiencing is not confined to one sect, race or class but implicit in a common faith of all humankind.

Whatever the final resolution of the question of religion in personal construct psychology and the true origin of or significant influences on Kelly's views, from the present discussion there is strong circumstantial evidence to implicate Dewey. Indeed, Fransella's (1995) discussion of Cromwell's and Landfield's views on the matter of religion in personal construct psychology could equally well apply to Dewey. Cromwell indicates that Kelly saw science and religion as two ways of stretching out and making sense of the universe, and Landfield notes that Kelly saw the mainspring of life as a creative search in which Kelly respected both science and religion. So, too, for Dewey.

Whatever the final resolution, personal construct psychology offers an expanding rather than a degenerating approach for a contemporary consideration of the role of religion in human life. That consideration appears well informed and itself well elaborated by Dewey's philosophy of religion.

Living with Personal Construct Psychology: Personal Accounts

INTRODUCTION

George Kelly's theory is, above all else, a theory about the individual: how we all go about the business of trying to make the most sense of our world. We gain control over ourselves and our worlds by laying bets on the outcomes of our actions that are based on our present construing of the situation. The crux of the matter is that we never know whether our present construing is relatively correct until we have behaved. Our behaviour is, indeed, to borrow the words of Einstein, a question we put to nature.

In this section we have three leading thinkers who have contributed greatly to personal construct psychology. Dorothy Rowe tells of her early years in Australia and of how Kelly's ideas have been a major influence not only in her work but also in how she has lived her life. Her many books, especially those on depression, have all been influenced by personal construct ideas.

Miller Mair talks in a more reflective way. He tells how Kelly's writing played a central role in his development as a psychologist; and how he came to develop the idea of 'community of selves' and the use of metaphor. He then moves into self-exploration about psychology being a psychology of questions and what differences that would make from a psychology of answers. He asks himself such questions as how would a profound psychology of understanding and misunderstanding be different from a psychology of knowledge production, and what issues would arise if we paid more attention to psychological searching rather than re-searching?

Rue Cromwell was a student of George Kelly. As well as giving some very intriguing insights into the experience of being one of his students, he shows how Kelly's thinking has influenced his wide-ranging research projects.

CHAPTER 40

Personal Construct Psychology and Me

Dorothy Rowe

Middlesex University, London, UK

I have been a personal construct psychologist from my earliest childhood in Australia, though many years passed before I discovered that I could describe myself in this way. I always knew that each of us has our own individual way of seeing things and that we can choose how we interpret events. As a small child I soon discovered that, if I were to survive in the family into which I had been born, I had to watch people and be aware of what they could do. I realized that, if I could understand why people did what they did, I could protect myself more effectively from their actions.

Although I look back on my childhood without any pleasure I must acknowledge that my parents gave me one great gift. This was that they were incapable of presenting to me one consistent view of the world. They could not agree on the rules which should govern my conduct, while their attitudes to life were diametrically opposed. Pity the poor child whose parents are in league with one another to present their child with one consistent, unarguable view of the world. That unfortunate child soon comes to believe that whenever he sees some aspect of the world differently from his parents he is wrong, or even wicked. Such a belief diminishes his self-confidence and prevents him from understanding himself and other people except in terms of being good or bad or mad.

My mother and my sister undermined my self-confidence by constantly criticizing me and by telling me that I was lying whenever I made an observation which ran counter to what they wished was actually the case. However, being criticized teaches a child how to be critical, and so I became intensely critical of their points of view. In contrast, I valued my father's perspective on life. He was, though he did not know it, a personal construct psychologist.

My father had good reason to see the world in bleak, unhappy terms. He valued education, but he had had to leave school when he was 11 to work as a delivery boy, driving a horse and cart alone through the bush to deliver groceries to outlying farms and hamlets. His beloved father died in a mining accident when my father was 16. There was no compensation from the mine owners, and my grandmother had to struggle to bring up six children. My father developed into a fine sportsman, but his years in the Australian Army in France in the First World War ended those ambitions. His wartime experiences made him keenly interested in politics and economics, and the Great Depression of the 1930s showed him the utter wickedness of an unregulated capitalist system. However, he knew that, while we control very little of what happens in the world, we always have a choice about how we interpret what happens. He knew that our interpretations were theories about what was going on, not mirrors of real events, and that these theories needed to be checked and, where necessary, modified. He saw that, if we choose to interpret in negative ways, we will ensure that we will be unhappy. Choose positive ways of interpreting, and life, though difficult, will bring joy and happiness.

Why my father married a woman who was determined to prove his philosophy wrong I do not know. My aunt, his sister, told me that he had met my mother not long after he returned from the war and had instantly fallen in love with her. Perhaps he believed that he could make her happy. By the time I was born he knew that he had set himself an impossible task.

My mother was never wrong. She never had any reason to revise an opinion or to say that she was sorry. Anyone who did not share her views was not only wrong but bad. She disapproved of the universe. People were not to be trusted, and everything always turned out badly. She looked to no one as an authority. She always knew that she was right.

Thus I was introduced early to the concepts of relative and absolute truth, and I learned to fear those who claim to be in possession of absolute truth. My mother insisted that I attended the Presbyterian Church, though she herself did not attend. I listened to the sermons with an increasingly well-honed scepticism about all claims to be in possession of absolute truth.

However, I was also learning that there is a way of thinking where truth, relative or absolute, is irrelevant. My sister is six years older than I am. She insists she remembers little of her childhood, so I can only guess at what led her to see every event in terms of one simple dimension. This was, 'Of use to me: of no use to me.' Anything my sister deemed to be of no use to her vanished from her sight. When I was of use to her I existed in her sight. When I was of no use to her I ceased to exist. No wonder fear of annihilation as a person plays such a big part in my theory of meaning!

Thus in my home there were three very different ways of interpreting events to which I added a fourth. I could see how these different ways of interpreting produced different ways of behaving. My father had a host of friends and was interested in everything. My mother allowed no visitors into our home except for three or four close family members. She read little and she tried to prevent me from reading anything other than my school books. My father tried to be happy, and often was, while my mother was determined to be miserable. My father rarely got angry, while my mother and sister were frequently consumed by rage, sometimes violent rage, at the failure of the universe to conform to their wishes.

MEANING OF PSYCHOLOGY

So there I was, a personal construct psychologist but not knowing that I was. I did not even hear the word 'psychologist' until I was 14 and my friend Betty wanted to inscribe a verse containing the word 'psychologist' in her boyfriend's autograph album. Betty wanted to know how to spell the word and, under the pretext of looking up the spelling, I got out my dictionary and looked up its meaning. I did not encounter this word again until I entered university in 1948 and added a psychology course to my English and history majors.

The lecturers at Sydney University were devoted to taking the infinitely rich subjects of English and history and rendering them stale, flat and unprofitable, so I stayed with the marginally more interesting subject of psychology. Unfortunately, all the psychology I studied bore no relation to real life. We were taught that human beings operated in three separate modes—cognition, volition and emotion. This way of thinking is still very prevalent with many psychologists believing that cognition and emotion are two separate modes of behaving when in fact both are ways of creating meaning. To respond to a situation with anger is to interpret that situation, just as responding to a situation with 'this is unacceptable' is an interpretation.

In my second year at university we studied nonsense syllables and proved beyond all doubt that that which is meaningful is remembered more easily than that which is not. We moved on to factor analysis where we were required to believe that the factors considered to be revealed by clusters of test scores really existed as parts of a human being. I was amazed to discover that respected psychologists actually believed that we each had inside a lump of intelligence called 'g' surrounded by lots of 's's, that is, smaller lumps of different kinds of intelligence. They also believed in the reality of personality factors garnered from personality tests. The existence of all these factors meant that we each resembled a bottle packed with boiled sweets of different sizes and colours. None of these psychologists would speculate about how these boiled sweets interacted to produce behaviour. However, they so wanted psychology to be accepted as a science that everything they did was presented 'scientifically', that is, in psychological jargon and in the passive voice so that the fact that a real person carried out the research was completely hidden. I thought all of this was complete rubbish so when I left university I abandoned psychology, taught for a while, married and had a child.

At home with my baby I read novels and history. When I went back to teaching I was invited to train as an educational psychologist, or, as it was called in New South Wales, a school counsellor. In training we spent much time on intelligence tests, which we then inflicted on every school-age child, but some of what we studied did relate to real human beings. Most importantly we were told to take account of the child's point of view. One of our lecturers gave us some advice which I have found to be invariably true. It was, 'the presenting problem is never the real problem'. Behind the meanings that a person presents to the world lie other, more important meanings.

However, mythical factors remained popular now that the work of Hans Eysenck was becoming known in Australia. This so infuriated me that years later I could not believe my own findings in laddering people; I found that at the top of each person's ladder was not, as I had expected, some totally individual, ultimate construct, but just one of two constructs which relate to how the person experienced his sense of existence and saw the threat of annihilation as a person. These two constructs can be expressed in an a infinite variety of ways, but the meanings contained therein were either that the person experienced his sense of existence in terms of relationship to others with the accompanying fear of complete abandonment and rejection, or the person experienced his existence in terms of a sense of order, achievement, clarity and control with the accompanying fear of total chaos. It was very hard for me to admit that Hans Eysenck was right, that people do divide into two groups, extraverts and introverts. However, I saw this difference, not as relating to traits of extraversion and introversion, but to the reasons or meanings which determine what a person chooses to do (Rowe, 1989).

REAL LIVES

As a school counsellor working in primary and secondary schools covering a large part of Sydney I had no office but kept my files and test materials in the boot of my car. I talked to children and parents in classrooms, school playgrounds and their own homes. I saw them in their own environment, and so I learned a great deal more about these people than I would have learned had I interviewed them in a proper professional office. What I saw was not the operation of factors or traits producing automatic responses but individuals acting as agents in their own lives, trying to make sense of their lives, making decisions and trying to maintain a sense of self-worth in a world full of dangers and difficulties.

When I was asked to change my job to one which came with the grand title of Specialist Counsellor to Emotionally Disturbed Children, I realized that I needed to know much more than I did. Sydney University ran many evening courses, including a Diploma in Clinical Psychology. This course had one strand concerned with intellectual assessment particularly of people suffering brain damage, and another strand concerned with personality assessment. Factors played little part in this course, which was mainly psychoanalytic. I spent many happy hours reading Otto Fenichel's *Psychoanalytic Theory of Neurosis*. Not for a minute did I think that we are each inhabited by an id, an ego and a superego with a great unconscious sloshing about underneath, but I did think—and still do—that psychoanalysis was a powerful theory of meaning. From the work which I did with the Rorschach and the Thematic Apperception Test, I learned a great deal about how individuals structure meaning and project this meaning onto the world around them.

My work as a counsellor involved a great deal of writing. There was a file for each child which had to be kept up-to-date and which read like a story in progress. Reports had to be written, and each of these was an individual case study. Such material should have been the subject of research, but all research in psychology then was nomothetic, despite the fact that the results of studies of very large groups of people could not be applied to individuals. When I went to the University of New South Wales to do a masters degree I learned that Monty Shapiro at the Institute of Psychiatry in London was developing a research technique which could be applied to individual case studies. I wrote to him for advice and we corresponded regularly. One night I came home late and waiting for me was one of his letters. In this he had added, perhaps as an afterthought, 'Why don't you come to England? There's lots of work for psychologists here.'

This suggestion shocked me. I could not possibly go to England. I had no money. My marriage had ended and my young son and I lived from one pay cheque to the next. My dreams that night were very disturbing, but I awoke the next morning with my mind made up. I would cash in my superannuation and long-service leave and that money would pay our fares to England.

Thus it was that in February 1968 I began work at Whitely Wood Clinic in Sheffield. This clinic was part of the Department of Psychiatry at Sheffield University where Alec Jenner had recently been appointed as professor. Alec brought with him a large research grant with which he proposed to discover the metabolic basis of mood change. He suggested to me that I should join his research team and take as my research topic 'Psychological Aspects of People with Regular Mood Change'. No such people actually existed, but I did not know that then.

REPERTORY GRIDS

My immediate problem was to find some way of measuring change. In those days psychological tests were reliable, that is, they were constructed with the express purpose of giving the same result in repeat testing. However, at the Department of Psychology at Sheffield University I heard a lecture by Pat Rabbit where he mentioned repertory grids, and Peter Clark, a close friend of Don Bannister, told me that there was going to be a summer school at York University on Personal Construct Psychology and that I should attend.

I left that summer school with feelings of both peace and excitement. Peace because I had at long last encountered psychologists who wanted to study real people and not some kind of fictitious person constructed from some psychological theory. Excitement because personal construct psychology and the repertory grid offered a wealth of methods to use and material to study. No sooner was I back in my office than I was constructing grids suited to the individuals I was talking with and relevant to each person's predicament. I analysed these grids using a simple method of correlation which Don Bannister had devised.

I sent one of my grid studies to Eliot Slater, editor of the *British Journal of Psychiatry*. He wrote back to tell me that there was a psychologist at the Institute of Psychiatry, Patrick Slater, who had a computer program for the analysis of such grids. I should contact Patrick and then resubmit my paper.

In those years the *British Journal of Psychiatry* was devoted solely to physiological research and large-scale studies which compared the effects of different drugs. The reason Eliot Slater accepted my first paper and others that followed was not because of the genius of my work but because Patrick was his brother. I did not complain because, not only was it a thrill to have something published, but because Patrick gave me enormous help by constantly telling me that my work was worth while. He did not expect me to understand the inner workings of his software but to be able to read the results and make sense of them.

Actually the grids I was doing told me little more than what was already apparent in the conversations I had with my patients, but the grids changed my status in the eyes of the consultants at the clinic. Alec Jenner's weekly case conference was a major professional event and was always well attended. Its aim was to arrive at a consensus on the diagnosis and treatment (drugs and electro-convulsive therapy) of the patient presented. There was little room for psychological speculation. If I said something about, say, what Mrs Smith had told me in one of our conversations I would be ignored or told to shut up. However, if I arrived carrying a great slab of computer paper to which I appeared to refer as I spoke about principle component analysis and loadings on factors I was listened to in respectful silence. If it came out of a computer it must be true.

Being one of the first psychologists to work in a completely new field is very advantageous. Whatever the merits of my PhD thesis it was certainly original. My thesis and papers did not have to be weighed down by a long list of references to Jones et al., or anyone else. There was no authority looming over me, limiting my range of inquiry and the originality of my hypotheses. Moreover, my study of psychoanalysis stood me in good stead in interpreting my grids because the groupings of elements and constructs often revealed the functioning of projection and the mechanisms of defence, while the grids which used 'self' and 'ideal self' in the elements often related directly to what Freud had described as the operations of the superego.

THREE GROUPS

As the personal construct psychology movement grew it was interesting to see how different psychologists responded to the freedom that personal construct psychology gave them. Gradually they sorted themselves into three groups which I came to think of as the 'gridders', the Kellyians, and the mavericks.

Among psychologists there have always been some who feel safer with numbers than with people, and grids certainly generated lots of numbers. The use of grids coincided with the growth in computers, and soon there was fierce competition among the gridders over whose computer analysis was the best. By then I had given up using grids because, no matter how original they were and how cleverly analysed, most grids dealt only with surface constructs when what is important is what lies beneath the surface constructs, the reasons for the reasons. Laddering is a powerful technique, so powerful that it has to be used with care and discretion. At the top of each person's ladder the constructs are concerned with survival as a person, and bringing that out into the open can cause the person to feel very vulnerable.

The Kellyians devoted themselves to understanding and extending the work of George Kelly. I always claim, probably unjustly, that every article and chapter by a Kellyian begins with 'As George Kelly said' or carries an epigraph by Kelly. I had read *The Psychology of Personal Constructs* in 1968 and I knew that Kelly was right, but his use of postulates was, for me, very close to the psychology of the 1930s and 1940s and I could not go back to the pseudo-scientific methods of that time.

So I became one of the mavericks, what I like to think of as a very distinguished group. We each go our own way. Whenever we meet at conferences we beam at one another and compliment one another on our wisdom and perspicacity. We have even been known, on rare occasions, to read one another's books.

All this is in keeping with the basic democracy of personal construct theory which is inherent in its understanding that each of us cannot help but have our own way of seeing things. As a result, personal construct psychology cannot produce a leader who will set the agenda and tell his disciples what to do. There can be no Freud or

Jung or Aaron Beck. Without an authoritarian and authoritative leader personal construct psychology cannot become a powerful movement determining the course of academic psychology. It is the Liberal Party of psychology. As a result, undergraduates are lectured on cognitive therapy, not personal construct psychology, unless there is a personal construct psychologist on the staff. Even then, such psychologists, surrounded by colleagues devoted to 'objectivity' and terrified of 'subjectivity', can have a very difficult time.

Some personal construct psychologists, wanting to be accepted by academic colleagues, try to achieve this by using the old, pseudo-scientific method of writing only in jargon and in the passive voice. This is such a pity because doing this drives away non-psychologists. Even worse, such psychologists fail to recognize the considerable body of evidence which shows that any psychologist (or psychiatrist) who has to resort to jargon has nothing original to say. We are not like nuclear physicists who have to create words in order to describe phenomena which lie outside human experience. We are writing about human experience, and in English—an extremely flexible language with an enormous vocabulary. Jargon in psychology is unnecessary.

AN ACCEPTED WAY OF THINKING

I often feel that many personal construct psychologists do not appreciate how important their theory is and how, in many fields, it has become the accepted way of thinking and is used by many different people who would not recognize the term 'personal construct theory'.

For instance, my son Edward never considered following in my footsteps since, in his experience, all psychologists were mad, but in his work in public relations in the motor industry he uses personal construct theory. Nowadays every model of car is excellently designed and is efficient, attractive and reliable. People buying a car choose a particular model according to price and whether that model fits their image of themselves. In the vast motor industry all marketing, advertising and public relations operate on the premise that what determines our behaviour is not what happens to us but how we interpret what happens to us.

In the football industry the word is 'psychology'. This relates both to how a player sees himself and the opposition, and how the team manager seeks to manipulate how the opposition see themselves and the manager's team. Currently all the Premiership teams are equally able, and so it is expected that the Premiership will be won, not on skill, but on 'psychology'.

The Peace Agreement in Northern Ireland could never have been arrived at had not George Mitchell persuaded the leaders of both sides to attempt to understand how their long-time enemy saw themselves and their world. Research on chronic pain has now established that the degree of pain which a person feels relates not so much to the site and degree of the injury as to how the person interprets the pain he feels. Geneticists repeatedly point out that genes cannot be the determinants of complex behaviour, and that what determines complex behaviour is how an individual interprets the potentiality which the gene provides.

I could give many more examples, but suffice it to say that over the past 15 years there has been a sea change in the number of people who understand why they do what they do. I would not claim that we personal construct psychologists have effected all these changes, but we should take pride in being part of a change comparable to the change in ideas that occurred in ancient Athens—a change that made famous and influential, not just the ideas of Socrates and Plato, but those of Epictetus. We should never underestimate the importance of personal construct psychology.

CHAPTER 41

A Psychology of Questions

Miller Mair

Glasgow, Scotland

I first read George Kelly's *The Psychology of Personal Constructs* when I was a clinical psychology trainee, many years ago. Since then I've danced with his ideas, and my ideas about his intentions, many times.

Like so many others, I was first attracted to his most concrete offering, the repertory grid. While it seemed like the psychological tests we were familiar with, it was quite liberatingly 'empty'. This was not a measuring of how much of a predetermined 'psychological stuff' a person contained. It was an invitation at quite a different level of abstraction. It offered a way of attending to the person's ways of making sense of their world.

That was such a revelation in those days. A completely different kind of psychological sophistication was being made available to us. My enthusiasm for this approach lasted quite some time, but I came to feel that this formal procedure was limited too. It seemed to me to be too cumbersome and unfocused. It would provide a huge amount of data, but very little of it seemed to be informative. You could pick and choose bits that seemed to make sense, rather than being able to trust much of it as evidence. The approach came to seem like a great, simple-minded giant, unable to string two words together. That is to say, there was no language, no syntax, no grammar. You ended with only statistical rather than linguistic connections.

His emphasis on the 'personal' was very welcome to me. What this led to was a much greater willingness to trust *my own concerns*, rather than those offered by others. This led me to a greater awareness of the 'meta level' of understanding in his psychology. He was placing his psychology 'above' the level of the individual and giving form to the kinds of issues which affect everyone, regardless of their specific content or context.

This meant that 'going away from' Kelly was part of the deal. His was not to be an approach which determined the boundaries of my concerns. My concerns were primary, and in following them I could find considerable help in the 'prosthetic' constructions he offered for those undertaking their own psychological journeys.

I was drawn to explore metaphor in relation to construing; the fundamental place of conversation in relation to Kelly's concerns with meaning and role relationships;

International Handbook of Personal Construct Psychology. Edited by F. Fransella.
© 2003 John Wiley & Sons, Ltd.

the multiple nature of ourselves as 'communities of selves', a way of giving more life to Kelly's notion of 'construct systems', as well as his idea of 'fragmentation' in construct systems; the profound importance of a 'personal' perspective on 'coming to know', as including the 'impersonal', rather than being replaced by it; and the centrality of 'feeling' as a mode of knowing, given form through imaginative participation in the here and now.

From here I found myself drawn away from direct attention to Kelly's writing for a time, often coming back again to find fuller understanding of what I'd been exploring in aspects of his writing that I hadn't appreciated before. Thus I followed threads of inquiry concerning the importance of rhetoric and poetic diction in giving shape to communication and understanding, welcoming the ambiguities of language rather than seeking simplicity in the seeming clarity of numbers. In doing so, I became more aware of the rhetorical sophistication in Kelly's ways of offering and shaping ideas.

I began to recognize the very different challenges we face when we realize that we must always 'inquire *in* conversation', rather than as isolated blobs of being set over against a separate world. Involved in this is a very different strategy of psychological and psychotherapeutic inquiry which involves us in 'standing under' (in order to understand) rather than 'standing over' (in order to master and control). It was a surprise to find that Kelly seemed to have been concerned with just these kinds of distinctions, though in different terms.

I also became interested in the relationships between 'quest' and 'questions'. A quest is a journey or search which involves head, heart and the whole being, rather than the intellect only. The whole person is engaged and challenged, just as Kelly said could be the case in his kind of psychology. In all of this I came to sense that Kelly was engaged in the creation of a new kind of discipline in which religious/spiritual searching and scientific inquiry into psychological life are in living relationship with each other, rather than poles apart.

NEW POSSIBILITIES

The invitation to write this chapter has given me a chance to play, to reflect on some things past and glance towards possible futures. What is presented here is not an argument, tightly structured towards a clear conclusion, but a gentle loosening of the earth in anticipation of another season of planting and the hope of new growth to come.

One of the things I find inspiring about Kelly's approach is his emphasis on becoming able to *imagine* new possibilities, and then working towards realizing these in practical ways. He speaks of how the practice of creativity involves cycles of engagement with 'loosening' and 'tightening'. In the 'loosening' phases, the person is trying to break out of the familiar ways in which they think, feel and act in relation to some topic. In the 'tightening' phases, the person is trying to clarify, sharpen, act on and put to the test of experience some of the changed notions which may be emerging for them. I want to use something of this approach in what follows.

One way of trying to allow new ideas to emerge is to undertake a writing exercise (sometimes called 'flow writing'), where you set yourself the task of writing continuously on a topic, for a short time, without taking your pen from the page or without stopping to think what you are typing. You have just to keep going and let whatever comes arrive 'loosely' on the page, without criticism or selection. If any of what you write seems worth taking further, you can use your critical judgements to 'tighten' your argument or sharpen your conceptions at a later stage.

In thinking about this chapter I followed something like this pattern. I started by feeling for an aspect of Kelly's ideas which attracted my present interest, and then set myself the task of typing continuously for 30 minutes or so. In what follows I've chosen a few of these 'flow writing' pieces to present here. In each case I start by indicating the aspect of Kelly's work, or my concern, which is the focus for my writing task. After each piece, I try to put some of the issues raised in a wider or clearer context, in the hope that this will make my meanderings more intelligible.

In each case I then pose a question which seems to me to merit further exploration in relation to personal construct psychology and associated ideas.

REFLECTIONS AND QUESTIONS

24 January 2002

I wanted to begin by attending to one of the hints in Kelly's writing which I find most tantalizingly inviting, his idea that we may need a *psychology of questions* rather than, or as well as, *a psychology of answers*. This is what I wrote:

> I am a question which is struggling to know itself. I am a question searching for ways to give itself form. I am not all of a piece, already in place, at peace with myself and the world. I am an intensely squirming and unsettling clutch of questions, seeking for articulation.
>
> Until that becomes possible, I am in question. My very being is in question. I do not just ask questions about things out there and set over against my comfortable life. The moving structure of my life is the question, the family of questions, that it is my responsibility to confront.
>
> My life is an often uncomfortable journey of inquiry, a searching to see and say, a quest for understandings of myself/my world which are other than I yet know. Psychological inquiry is not, for me, a professional activity which I undertake in office hours and then leave behind when I return home. Psychological inquiry is what my life is about. It is a 'calling' or a 'need' or a 'journey' which involves who I am as well as what I do.
>
> Only superficial questions are easy to ask. Questions which put you in question have to be lived with, travelled with, wrestled with, cared for and coaxed into being. They will be loved and hated. They lead you through places of delight as well as dread. They can be more demanding than any companion, more engaging than any friend. They can be endlessly frustrating and skippingly releasing when, little by little, they partially resolve.

Kelly offers the idea that we are, in a sense, asking questions in everything we do. We are asking something of the world, of ourselves, of other people, even when we may not be clear that we are doing so. He suggests that we are always stepping into the unknown and are always giving some shape to what is to come by our ways of 'asking', which may be disguised as statements, demands or assertions.

What my reflection suggests is something more than this. We are not just question *askers*, we ourselves can be seen as *embodied* questions. We may take years to clarify for ourselves and others what we are asking with our whole lives. This is a level of questioning which needs much more consideration than has yet been undertaken.

How would a psychology of questions be different from a psychology of answers, and what issues would become important that are hidden or ignored at the present time?

26 January 2002

I was still wondering about questions, but taking this further to think about 'psychological inquiry' more widely. I believe that Kelly was outlining a different approach to psychological inquiry from what was available at the time.

> Psychological inquiry is not as easy and straightforward as it is often made to seem. How our questions are twisted into the shapes of our own needs makes it a more uncertain affair than the introductory texts make it appear. In fact, as far as I've been able to find in all my years as a psychologist, no one has written of how it is for me.
>
> There is no blueprint for the personal searching that any of us may have to do. We each have to find our own way. We each have to walk into being on our own path.
>
> Much is written about psychological research, as presently conceived. Almost nothing seems to be written about the kind of personal searching we may have to do if we are to engage with the questions we cannot yet ask.
>
> In the way psychological inquiry is written about, it seems mostly to be something which is relatively routine. You have to learn the well-worn footpaths and be sure you keep to them. If you wander off into the surrounding bushes of personal concerns, you are likely to take too long, get lost, be confronted with issues that are outside the tramlines of familiar ways. Any such deviation is dangerous, not to be attempted till you have learned and practised the 'right' way of doing things, and with any luck (our profession seems to say), by then you will be too old, too tired, or too timid to attempt anything which is not structured by what is already known.
>
> Each of us is coiled into the hidden forms of questions which may eventually be articulated and engaged with in the world of self and others. Each of us is a special case, seeking to arise from the inarticulate marshland of the as yet unimagined. There are miles to go before we can lay some of our troubling concerns to sleep. These, our problems, are our 'stores and treasures'. They are where our power is, where the energy of our lives is a compressed spring of our still-to-be-realized possibilities.
>
> We start in the dark and struggle towards the light. We imagine we are in the clear and find that the invisibly obvious hides what we need to see.

Kelly seems to be questioning the very nature of personal inquiry rather than just presenting another set of methods to follow. Although there are very many books on 'research methods' and 'experimental design', these present claims to official knowledge about 'how to do it'. They do not explore how people actually, in all their diversity, do go about the business of making sense and new sense in their lives.

They say a lot about what is to 'count' as official psychological research, but say almost nothing about how people actually go about the business of *searching* for meaning and understanding in the first place.

What issues would arise if we were to pay as much attention to psychological searching as we currently do to psychological re-search?

5 February 2002

What attracted me to Kelly's kind of psychological thinking? What place does one's sense of 'beauty' or 'rightness' have in the search for truth and understanding? This was what I wrote:

Let me try to be truthful. I both hate and love psychology. The hating comes first, but is more superficial. The loving is a deeper river which flows through a larger landscape of human understanding and misunderstanding than we mostly imagine.

I can remember sitting with Don Bannister, at many talks by distinguished psychologists at many meetings of the British Psychological Society, and really hating almost everything I heard. In those days, both of us hated so much of what most mainstream psychology was about, but Don was struck by how I would hate even some of the things he felt quite charitably towards.

My hatred was aesthetic. It was to do with beauty. I found almost everything in 'scientific' psychology to be ugly, hard edged, angular, uncomfortable, unconvincing. So much of what I was taught in my first psychology degree was unbelievably obtuse. Grown men were trying to build a psychology of human life on the unlikely foundations of Hull's peculiar equations or Skinner's sadly trapped but frantically active pigeons. In those days it seemed quite natural for the brightest and best to believe that the way to move towards greater human knowledge was by means of rats and pigeons.

I'd had glimpses of psychological beauty before meeting Kelly in his writings. It hadn't all been ugliness. Rex Knight, the Professor of Psychology at Aberdeen University, was a man with a beautiful mind. He was also a barrister by training and had a lucidly delightful way of speaking his mind too. He taught us about anthropology and industrial relations, Freudian psychology and post-Freudian developments. More than any of the content, I loved the way he spoke to us of all these exotic places, so very different from the rats and pigeons, statistics and experimental design, computer development and psychophysiology that were all around.

But a more elaborated psychological beauty opened out before me as I sat, that summer of 1960, in the glassed-in verandah outside the clinical psychology students' common room at the Maudsley Hospital, London. I was reading volumes one and two of *The Psychology of Personal Constructs*, all thousand plus pages of them in their faded blue covers and oddly old-fashioned type setting. The books themselves, as objects of desire, were not attractive. What was in them was a revelation I'd been preparing for, without really knowing what that might mean.

What was beautiful? It was, and is, really hard to say. I was startled by being offered a perspective, a view in psychology, as if from a high place from which everything else I'd been taught seemed concrete, particular, awkwardly fragmented. Rather than telling me what people were like, how I was to colour in their bits and pieces, Kelly took me off the edge of a high cliff in the hang glider of his words. I realized I was a creature of the air as well as the earth. I could learn to fly as well as walk lovingly on the ground.

My ways of going about making sense of the world mattered too. For the very first time, I was given something of myself as a treasure to explore. I was not taken away from myself and told by others what was so and how it was to be dealt with in personally deadening ways. I was a talking partner with others and my world. We were in it together, actively on about the business of making sense of our lives even without the constricting professional constructs of a paid elite.

In the very opening movement, a marvellous idea came soaring in, high above my cluttered bric-a-brac of beliefs and failures to believe, 'everything can be other than we imagine it to be', everything can be seen in other ways, told in other stories, opened towards other worlds. Not that we are easily set free in this kind of way, but with sufficient imagination (wonderful word), courage (necessary word) and determination (a working word) we can take steps towards what previously we have not known. We can bring into being new places for the mind.

It has taken me forty years to gain some fuller understanding of what flew into my heart and mind in those early days. I knew that I had been touched and moved, but a lot of work was involved in coming to understand a little more of what was only felt in the white joy of a coming home to a place I'd not visited before.

As part of my work as a psychologist, I've been practising psychotherapy for many years. If I'd had doubts about the importance of one's sense of 'beauty' or 'rightness' before then, these years of experience have certainly removed them. But I have to say that, from the beginning of my engagement in psychology, I felt a need for a discipline which appealed to me aesthetically as well as practically.

Kelly is concerned with imaginative and courageous exploration, seeking to reach into what is not yet known or understood. Like so many creative scientists before him, he recognized that we move forward by hint and feel. When we are searching for threads of further understanding, we do not have 'evidence' or 'proof' at our disposal. We are in the dark and have to rely on what feels right, on what satisfies some silent sense of line and form. In this, Kelly is a psychological poet, imagining new places for the mind to move, as an essential aspect of the kind of *scientist* he sought to encourage.

What freedoms and fun could be released if psychological inquiry were to draw forth the imaginative poet or artist in us, as part of our becoming creative, adventurous scientists?

15 February 2002

When psychology was created as a formal discipline, just over one hundred years ago, those involved seemed to make a big thing of disowning their disciplinary ancestors and trying to separate themselves from their deep, dark roots in history and culture. My next reflection was on this theme:

Just like plants, we need a root system to nourish our lives. We need a root system to keep our psychological work alive.

This is also the case for any psychology. So much of psychology is dry and impoverished because of a hundred years of living with minimal roots. Psychology, in many of its forms, turned away from its deep roots in philosophy, religion, art and literature. It wanted to prove that it was a man (yes, mostly man) in its own right and could stand tall in the world it defined for itself. Leaving father and mother, uncles and aunts, cousins and long-term friends, it locked itself in its own neon-lit laboratories. What emerged was distinctive but lifeless. It will always be so when we deny our roots.

The same progression is true of individuals becoming psychologists. So many courses make it very clear to them from the first moment that being a Psychologist with a capital P is not about understanding yourself better or doing the other things that the wider public might suppose (like reading people's minds, or knowing how to live a better life or bring up happy children). It is about 'Science' with a capital 'S', even when the most successful scientists are happy to go around in shirt sleeves and open-neck shirts, with only a casually small 's' above the door.

And with Personal Construct Psychology it should be the same. George Kelly clearly valued his roots. They show up in his texts.

He was inspired by a life-long involvement in and commitment to the teachings of Christ. He loved the humanist adventure of living by understandings that had never before been risked. He had a considerable respect for philosophy, especially the get up and go philosophy of John Dewey, and the imaginative springboard of Vaihinger's 'As If'. He was familiar with the ancient discipline of Rhetoric, having taught it for many years. He had a deep knowledge of mathematics and engineering, building and design. He enjoyed verse and poetry and offered us a variety of amusing ditties to lighten the tone of more serious things.

But this is not how it seems to be with some who have followed the path Kelly offered. Many papers and books take up residence in this new language and in the concepts he offered as though these could live on their own without the sustaining root system of a personal and cultural history. To draw on your own life concerns and the life and understandings of your time is not to be bound by these, but to both show something of where you are coming from and something of who you are. If this is not done, your own prejudices, and the blindnesses of your place and time are likely to make your work a caricature of your times rather than pose questions that open new doors.

Kelly's psychology will thrive when it is lived into and from the life you lead. Don't abandon the wonderful gifts of your common language for the limited, but valuable, meaningfulness of his. Elaborate your understandings in your common tongue, bringing the rich treasures of your roots to feed the flowers of understanding which may come from marrying old with new.

Over the past years, many psychologists have been acknowledging and coming to respect their personal and cultural roots again. Issues of consciousness and art, religion and spirituality can again be found within the discipline, even though many of the more strictly scientistic may huff and puff. I believe it is necessary for those who seek to explore and elaborate further psychological understandings to be open to any and all aspects of human life and history. Those who are concerned with psychological life may need the inspiration of ideas which may be more fully developed in other disciplines than their own. Thus we may find inspiration for our psychological work in ecology or theology, astronomy or literary theory, rhetoric or economics.

How do we prepare ourselves to be open to new possibilities? How do we preclude or shut ourselves off from possible sources of inspiration? How do we prevent our-

selves from noticing what people in other disciplines or contexts may already know?

Central to Kelly's psychology is the idea of 'anticipation' or making ourselves ready for the future. 'Anticipation' means to 'prepare for, preclude or prevent'. His fundamental postulate can thus be expressed in a slightly different way to propose: 'A person's processes are psychologically channelized by the ways in which he/she prepares for, precludes or prevents event(s).'

8 March 2002

I am wondering how the kind of psychology Kelly was developing could be relevant to major issues in the world we live in. The news is full of human conflicts which seem so painfully difficult to resolve.

> This world we are living in is riddled with misunderstanding, fear, anger, prejudice, greed and the desire to dominate others. There are huge abuses of so many kinds all around (and through us).
> In Northern Ireland, as well as Palestine and Israel, there is a terrible history of loss and abuse of rights, fear of what others will do and hatred for what has been done. Understanding between individuals and communities is limited. Only a tiny percentage of adolescents in Belfast have ever had a meaningful conversation with youngsters of a similar age but in the other 'religious' camp. How are the Israelis and Palestinians, the Americans and the Arabs, the Chinese and the Tibetans to move towards understanding of each other, respect for each other, care for each other, rather than stay entrenched in their positions of fear and violence?
> Learning to live together in understanding seems to be very difficult for us. There is no doubt that we are in danger. September 11th 2001 made that more clear than ever. We are practised at solving our problems by war and physical domination, putting in prison, torturing and eradicating. Ethnic cleansing is not a new invention. It is a favoured method for solving human problems.
> What is obvious is that we need to give far more attention to the issues involved in understanding and misunderstanding than we do now. We have to attend much more to what is involved for individuals and groups in seeking greater understanding of each other, what dangers they are undertaking and what abuses may be entailed.

Kelly spoke of us being on a 'long, long quest for understanding' and the kind of psychology he was reaching for seems to have more to do with human understanding than with the accumulation of bits of information or chunks of knowledge. He was concerned with how we can make sense of the sense-making of others, and with the demands this can place on us, with the ways in which we can be tested at every level of our being if we are to reach beyond what is safe and familiar. This seems to be the kind of psychological journey which we need to become more able to undertake in many more aspects of our lives together.

How would a profound psychology of understanding and misunderstanding be different from a psychology of knowledge production?

As you can see, this is a 'loose weave' presentation. It is not rounded off and tied up into a neat bundle. Arms and legs are hanging out, not yet adding up to a complete being.

I am reaching towards some understanding of a different kind of psychology which will be contributed to by participants in many disciplines, in many different contexts. Kelly's is likely to be an important voice here, but there are many others too. We live in a time of ever-increasing speed, rushing towards achievement and destruction on so many fronts. Old ideas of 'science' as the way to solve most of our human problems are no longer as believable as they were, as we have created the means of destroying our fragile world many times over. Older ideas of 'religion' as the route to salvation are mired in trouble too, as living questions are strangled, again and again, by tribal rivalries, fear and anger at those who hold different views. Old assumptions that the world will always be there for us to use and abuse can no longer be relied upon as our ravaging of the earth, its many fruitful environments and sustaining atmosphere, proceed at an increasingly alarming speed.

In this situation we need a different kind of psychological discipline which asks profound questions like 'What is going on?', 'What are we up to?', 'How are we arrayed in relation to the major issues that confront us?'. George Kelly's hopes for a 'psychology of questions' may point in a helpful direction.

CHAPTER 42

Kelly's Influence on Research and Career

Rue L. Cromwell

Lawrence, Kansas, USA

I came to Ohio State University after having studied with Jacob R. Kantor at Indiana University. Kelly had published in the journal Kantor edited, and they held some common views. This was 1950 and Kelly's personal construct theory was something yet to come. Indeed I knew nothing of Kelly's thinking or of the person himself. As a new graduate student my 'entry discussions' necessarily focused upon Kantor. That changed. Before it did, however, we enjoyed discussing the many pitfalls of dualism and reductionism in psychology and in science. We also discussed the semanticists' emphasis upon constructionistic (circular) error, the name of a thing causes the thing to exist; the map causes the territory. Kelly sometimes noted that I made Kantor more clear for him, and we both agreed that Kantor's early writings were not always clear. Although mindful of these philosophic issues Kelly did not belabour them as he stepped up his theory writing. He had other fish to fry. Most of all, I became aware that I was dealing with another awesome person.

Only from these early circumstances can I begin to describe the influence Kelly had on me and on my research career. The influence was more than just the psychology of personal constructs as a personality theory. He was attempting to teach me, and all of humankind, how to dance.

CONSTRUCTIVE ALTERNATIVISM

Kelly helped to orient me to the possibilities of the future rather than just detecting the philosophical and logical flaws of the past. Constructive alternativism is the view that any event may be described not with *one* true and absolute construction, not with a fixed range of alternative constructs, but instead with *any* number of arbitrary alternatives. Moreover, the goal in science (and in person) is not just to pare down these alternatives to the *one* that is final and true (see Chapter 4, pp. 41–49). Instead, alternative views may well be required to anticipate and reliably predict

International Handbook of Personal Construct Psychology. Edited by F. Fransella.
© 2003 John Wiley & Sons, Ltd.

different kinds of subsequent events. What would be a valid and useful construction to link one experience with outcome might not be valid and practically useful for portending another. Those alternatives that fail to be validated become discarded or disregarded. Our job, as scientists, is to discard one and another option until we find what works best. Then we fully expect that we, or some other scientist, will do it again! That is the ongoing game—the excitement—the job we have that makes science fun.

PROVISIONAL COMMITMENT AND PROVISIONAL DOUBT

As might be imagined, constructive alternativism is not an absolute prerequisite for the advancement of knowledge. When a scientist concludes that he has 'discovered' the final, true, or absolute answer to a question, he and his like-thinkers come to view their theory and supporting evidence as reality itself. They may even feel that they, as scientists, have closed out the area so that little is left to do. Dislodging one's own reality is not easy. It is even painful for the scientist who has worked hard, has made contributions, and is thereby highly committed to *his* reality. When invalidation of a crucial proposition finally occurs, some pretend, at least for a time, that it did not happen. Others display resistance. Hostility and retaliation may follow. If the invalidation is sustained, accommodation and reformulation occur. 'Truth' occurs again, but truth and reality are not what they once were. But, thank goodness, 'truth' has been found! Right? The scientists aggregate themselves around a new-found reality. The absolutist thinker is the one who feels the greatest jolt in this cycle of events. For the constructivist scientist disconfirmations are not so staggering. They are more smoothly accommodated as part of the game we play.

Kelly followed Kantor and Rotter in moving me towards this constructivist view. Sometimes I felt more constructivist than they were. Yet, full agreement existed for one notion: 'Observation that follows the construct, whether confirming or disconfirming, tells the tale.'

Kelly heaped this view of 'provisional commitment and provisional doubt' upon both himself and us. He repeatedly told us that he would stand behind our clinical decisions and actions. Regardless of their outcome he would support our right to take them. This, he said, would be true both in instances where he disagreed ahead of time and when impromptu decisions were made that were not discussed with him. It would be true in instances that led to failure or disaster in outcome. He wanted us to abandon the idea that his was the hovering final authority or that his was 'the manual'. His concerns were not only of the anxious beginning clinician but also of knowledge. He explained that if we did not take advantage of this freedom, knowledge could not easily advance. Knowledge can advance when new ideas are invented (Kelly, c.1954) and when extant ideas are disconfirmed.

Sometimes others become incredulous when I become excited about one of my own research hypotheses being disconfirmed. Is this a subtle defence concealing my 'underlying sense of failure?' I do not believe so. Beyond doubt I acquired this attitude from Kelly. Sometimes in our group meetings a student challenged or invalidated one of his ideas. Kelly would recount the preceding to affirm his understanding and then attempt to subsume this other way of thinking into his own.

His eyebrows would rise; his smile would redden and broaden. He would deliver credit to the contributor generously. To the extent that he viewed the reconstruction as important he would walk away from the meeting as if he had consumed the gourmet meal to exceed all gourmet meals.

Accordingly Kelly held disdain for people who identified their egos with their theories; they were not doing science but instead were becoming only promotional advocates. These aspects of Kelly's teaching have been telling through a half century. For one's own ideas to reach a status to merit formal disconfirmation is perhaps 'as good as it gets' in the game we play. Ask Ptolemy. Ask Newton. Ask Einstein. For those who believe that their ideas are truths to live forever, they and their disciples need only wait.

MY PERSONAL CONTACT WITH DR KELLY

In the couple of years following our 'Kantor discussions', my contacts with Kelly were not always happy ones. He supervised my master's thesis and enjoyed the fact that I derived testable hypotheses from Freud's psychoanalysis. This was at a time when many critics maintained that no concept in Freud's theory was testable. I showed that people indeed warded off from memory that which was deemed unpleasant. The order of recall of names of acquaintances was related not only to recency, frequency, and intimacy of contact but also, independently, to a pleasure ranking. In addition to these powerful predictors of sequence of recall, a construct-grouping by each participant of his acquaintances fell just short of reliable prediction. Kelly liked the research interaction with me but he could not tolerate my poor writing. His 'sink or swim' attitude made my life miserable. I fled to others for skill development. On the other hand, after many thesis rewritings, he liked my research results. Also he liked the statistical formula I had to derive in order to test the personal construct-grouping hypothesis. To my surprise I received a formal letter encouraging me to publish both accomplishments. I did not comply but, years later, I reported the empirical work (Cromwell, 1956).

I was also a member of the group who met one evening a week to listen to and critique Kelly's manuscripts. His major time commitment to the chapter manuscripts appeared to begin in 1951, and were completed in 1954. Early on, he called it role theory, not personal construct theory. Although I had to drop out when I was commuting daily to a VA internship, I well recall the intensity of attacks we levelled at him (see Fransella, 1995, for more details). He would often leave the meetings with head bowed but return the very next week with a completely rewritten manuscript. In spite of our blunt attacks (sometimes more in retaliation for barriers and pitfalls we had encountered in the graduate programme) he unceasingly gave verbal and 'eyeball' credit to the ideas and changes we had contributed. On some nights with certain chapters we sincerely felt he 'did not have it all together'. Yet we never failed to marvel at his one-week rebounds. We told him so. As young graduate students we were all impressed and honoured when we could see where our own comments made their way into the revised page. I confess that we became identified and our own egos were at stake in the books' eventual outcome.

After Kelly's volumes were published I discovered an error in his procedures for 'manual factor analysis' of the 'rep grid' matrix. I rewrote this complete section on 'Factoring the Rep Test' (Cromwell, 1961). I did it in a stepwise form that was both user-friendly and correct in the rotation method. Mostly I wanted to 'reply' to the brutal treatment I had received earlier with my master's thesis writing. When I presented my work to him and explained his error, not only did he approve of what I had done but also he asked permission to have copies mimeographed for his students and for those who wrote for information.

My major contact with Kelly came when I was named Clinic Coordinator and Assistant Instructor in charge of intake of new cases into the Ohio State Psychological Clinic. During this period I had almost daily contact and was privileged to sit in on his clinical supervisory sessions with other graduate students. I, of course, had the initial acquaintance with all the cases. It was also during this time that I sat over coffee and had long discussions with him. They usually occurred while we were waiting for the graduate students to return from seeing their clients. We discussed finer points in his theory. In particular he enjoyed dealing impromptu with implications it had for topics that sprang up that day. This was highly stimulating and it entailed the loosening and tightening in thinking one would expect. In spite of this privileged contact, sometimes I have felt out of synchrony with those who learned Kelly's theory solely by the book. I lack the formal precision that comes with that tighter approach.

One day in our chat I deduced a hypothesis that individuals, if permitted to use the two poles from their own personal constructs as a rating scale, would rate with greater extremity from midpoint than when they were using constructs of standard usage or elicited from others. As Kelly heard my offering he immediately reached for a clean sheet of paper. He portrayed my hypothesis to me in terms of angular difference between one's own personal construct axis and the axis of a standardized rating scale as it is retained by that person. The angular distance would be 90° if the person could not understand or construe the standard rating scale at all. By dropping a perpendicular from each pole of the standard rating scale axis down to the plane of the personal construct, he explained to me geometrically how the ratings of standard or non-personal constructs would be drawn more closely to the midpoint. Beyond the usual joy we shared from playing with ideas, Kelly said simply that this was a 'must do' study. Although my remaining graduate school time was already committed, I did the study with Don Caldwell (Cromwell & Caldwell, 1962) during my first year on faculty at Peabody College. I utilized a controlled design with a three-dimensional mixed analysis of variance that I knew Kelly would find new and interesting. As usual, he was generous in his recognition. As he made a world tour I began receiving reprint requests that tracked his itinerary.

My research career, moving on from Kelly and others at Ohio State, has been a peripatetic journey. He made it clear to me that to restrict my research to personal construct theory would not be a Kellyian thing to do. It was perhaps advice I did not need. I have made the rounds of inquiry in mental retardation; attention deficit with hyperactivity; classification and treatment outcome with emotionally disturbed children; stress factors, management and survival from acute myocardial infarction; attentional, perceptual, cognitive and genetic factors in schizophrenia; conceptual (rep grid) structure of those with history of trauma or abuse, and many other areas. While these areas of interest may seem diverse, the Kelly influence has been clear.

Never hold back from reaching for the farthest hypothesis. Don't scuttle creativity by staying within the mainstream and contemplating only the 'safe hypotheses'. Make the hypothesis a brittle one. Make the data snap it or sustain it. Ask nomothetic questions only after idiographic questions have been pursued to the limit. Ask questions within controlled research design. Strive as a mentor to credit generously the work and new ideas of others. Learn to think within and extrapolate from a single theory rather than sink one's ideas into the intuitive and eclectic hash. Nevertheless, never fear to go beyond a given theory when a more convincing theory can be formulated. Move within and reach beyond.

TRYING TO OUT-KELLY KELLY

After I received my doctorate and left Ohio State University, I continued to correspond with Kelly. As any young person seeking approval I informed him of my publications and grants. He sent me his writings. Since our correspondence continued over many years I, of course, had tried at times to 'corner' or 'outwit' him in the application of his own theory. An example of this occurred when he sent me a draft of his 'Sin and Psychotherapy' (1969c). I was excited about this paper, lost it immediately along a trail of loans from colleague to colleague, and was now writing for another copy. In this letter I said that he might be violating his own tenet of constructive alternativism in favour of an absolute or unalterable construction of *good* versus *evil*. In the spirit and anticipation of competitive dialogue I documented my arguments as best I could. His response to my challenge is of interest:

> It is true that there are many events with which man has dealt in terms of good vs. evil. I would still give it a very wide range of convenience, though I should add that one needs to be prepared continually to revise his judgment about particular events. Thus, while I agree with you that we need to continue to look for more complex and adequate ways of construing these events, I'm inclined to believe that we should retain the construct of good vs. evil as a superordinate construct—just as scientists retain truth vs. falsehood as an important superordinate construct governing their lives.
>
> In implying that we should continue the use of the good vs. evil construct, I don't think I am departing from the position of the psychology of personal constructs. Good vs. evil is still a construct invented by man. What I am saying is simply that I still think it is a useful construct, even though we have to keep it under continual revision. It is the construct of good vs. evil which I would advocate retaining during the foreseeable future, not the absolutistic labels that have been traditionally placed upon particular events. Let's continue to use the construct as a superordinate value in our lives but let's also elaborate and re-examine what falls under it. (G.A. Kelly, personal communication, 21 June 1962)

Near the end (although I did not realize it at the time) he concluded that he lacked the energy to be a researcher. Instead he expressed relief that he had resolved only to be a teacher. I was shocked. That he had not published research extensively in his career was something I already knew. He indeed had been a teacher, a theorist, a mentor, and an assertive advocate and supervisor of research. During the near time following his comment I concluded that declining health and energy probably led to his comment. One day a letter was returned to me with the information of his death.

TRYING TO GO BEYOND KELLY

In the previous section, 'Trying to out-Kelly Kelly', I assumed that, whatever idea was to be considered, the original Kelly assumptions prevailed. Kelly, in the inclusive sense, would still be Kelly. On the other hand, with the phrase 'Trying to go beyond Kelly' I ask different questions: Are there events to anticipate that require additional or revised assumptions? If such changes are made, can the revised theory then do a better job in anticipating these events? If indeed better, is the improvement in anticipatory range, precision, or both?

To ask these questions of Kelly's personal construct theory is not unlike what is always asked when theories change. Should Ptolemy's geocentrism be abandoned? Should certain tenets of Newton's theory of mechanics of physical objects be changed? The questions I pose are orderly. Yet when such questions are asked, the reactions of serious thinkers usually vary. Some would claim that the original theory accounts for all and it is not profitably to be altered. Some would say, 'Throw the rascal out, and let's start again with a new theory.' Above this range of opinion will finally emerge the empirical evidence that some reformulation allows better precision or range in prediction, or does not allow it.

What then is to be changed? And how, thereby, will prediction be improved? It is here that one can only dream and speculate. If one cannot engage in possibilities whose outcomes remain in doubt, then the effort is likely flawed at the start. Again I have not said anything new. In the prior examples, Copernicus and Einstein had to take their respective steps without knowing for sure that a heliocentric theory or a relativity theory would stand the test of time. As for personal construct theory it would seem in its interest that it evolve rather than be fixed in time and history. Whether the sprig I briefly nurture here eventually affirms its vitality remains to be seen.

In Kelly's opening pages he adopted from William James a view of the circumstance of humankind: 'Each man contemplates in his own personal way the stream of events upon which he finds himself so swiftly borne' (Kelly, 1955/1991, p. 3/Vol. 1, p. 3). To envision a person becoming a construer (coming to existence), the stream is undifferentiated. There is no up, down, right or left. There is no 'space' or 'external world' with which peremptorily to place these up–down directions. There is no time, with a reference point to mark what occurred before, during or after. There is no self within which somewhere, somehow, the construing starts. There is no non-self. To me Kelly chose the ideal starting point for a theory of person. As William James said, the individual must do his own packaging and ticketing. As I would say, each person must invent time and must invent space. From all of that he must invent what is self and what is non-self. From this infrastructure—each individual's own creative product—a manifold structure proceeds in each of us.

Already the need to organize, retain and apply constructs to predict one's own destiny in situations both new and old can be seen. Access within a few hundred milliseconds is not uncommon. Kelly and others later addressed the matter of subordinate–superordinate relations (hierarchy). Recently, from the contributions of Kelly (1955/1991), Bell (1996), Sewell (Chapter 21, pp. 223–231) and others I have been led to conclude that at least two important modes of superordination (hierarchy building) occurs. A complete presentation of this formulation will be available in the book I am preparing entitled *Being Human*. From these modes of superordination come not one but numerous variations of structure.

One kind of hierarchy building starts and stops with the identification of grouping of bilateral association among construct pairs. Very simply, if two constructs, *honest–dishonest* and *sincere–insincere*, are bilaterally associated, it makes no difference which dimension implies the other. It is like 2 + 4 and 4 + 2. Within a hierarchy the opposite poles retain their identity, so *dishonesty–honesty* and *insincerity–sincerity* have the same information as their opposites. It is a symmetric relationship. Each construct retains its bipolarity. Hierarchy benefits a generalization within the groups of bipolar pairings such as those these two constructs illustrate.

The other important kind of hierarchy arises from how the attributes of honest and sincere overlap when applied to a group of elements (people). If the overlap is sufficient, then hierarchical relationship will already be implicit in the matrix itself. No extra step of cognitive processing is needed. Moreover, a hierarchical arrangement is also implicit among the elements (people) that are construed in the matrix. However, the hierarchies are relatively unipolar (asymmetric). That is, when dishonesty and insincerity are considered (a reversal of construct poles), an entirely different hierarchy will emerge. The hierarchical relation of dishonesty–insincerity will be different from that of honesty–sincerity. Although the latter hierarchy including dishonesty and insincerity will be more obscure, it allows people to have meanings more greatly submerged. If a politician were to advocate 'family values', the hierarchical structure of what is 'not family values' will be more easily hidden to awareness, sometimes even to the politician himself. The symmetry and bipolarity are lost, but something else is gained.

Nothing in Kelly's 1955 exposition accounts for or portends these two separate modes of hierarchy. As Bell (1996) has suggested, a revision or addition in the Kelly structure of postulate and corollaries appears timely.

The difference between the symmetric and asymmetric hierarchical modes may be tedious to distinguish, but their implications are not. If validated as useful, the symmetric/asymmetric distinction would put Kelly's personal construct theory in a different place.

Returning to the onset of a person's construing, symmetric organization allows the invention of space and spatial dimensions. One can construe a given directional movement equally as well as its reverse. A map or picture may be perused without requirement of a given sequential procedure. Three-dimensional objects in space can likewise be perused.

An asymmetric organization allows the invention of time. If construct pairings move from X to Y, they cannot move from Y to X. As Hawking (1988) quoted Groucho Marx: 'Time flies like an arrow. Fruit flies like a banana.' In other words, the asymmetric is geared to understanding temporal relations and unidirectional sequences. Time is that component extracted from undifferentiated experience that does not subsume stoppages or reversals. Both Einstein and the newborn infant's construing exemplify the relativity that exists with our respective constructs of time and space.

As modern man evolved his language, he may have had symmetric construct organization first. The symmetric route is more clearly associated with forms of the verb 'to be' and with adjectival or adverbial modifications. For example, 'Me Rue', 'Wyn run fast', 'Beth is smart', 'Boy is inside the house', and so on. Such symmetric linkages permit associative, mosaic, configural or contextual descriptors for memory. Correlations become the highly convenient way to describe the magnitude of association between construct pairs.

On the other hand, the asymmetric organization can include hierarchical abstract thinking, stepwise goal-directed thought and behaviour. A future terminal point (a validating event, goal achievement, successful escape and harm avoidance) can be conceived. Transitive sentences with action verbs and objects are now possible. For example, 'The boy hit the ball into the street.' Such asymmetry allows temporal sequence, antecedent–consequent linkages, and potential cause–effect statements. The ball did not hit the boy. That possibility is excluded in asymmetric construct pairings.

That portion of mathematics that deals with counting and equations is symmetric. The portion that requires linear or sequential operations is asymmetric.

Symmetric organization allows field dependence. That is, the background affects how the central figure is construed. In this way the contextual and spatial processing of art, fabric, and other percepts are captured in a symmetric gestalt. Symmetric organization also allows a person to construe the blissful sense of 'now', a state of awareness that is detached from past or future controlling anchor points for its validation. The validation is within the experience mosaic itself.

Asymmetric organization more easily accommodates antecedent–consequent relationships and cause–effect statements. It allows a conceptual linkage to the past and to the future. The human features of guilt, responsibility, sustained effort over time towards a terminal point can be more easily subsumed in an asymmetric pairing.

The Garden of Eden myth has arisen in many isolated cultures around the world. It focuses upon the loss of a blissful state of 'now' wherein time has no meaning. Banishment from the Garden of Eden entails the assumption of responsibility, guilt and shame. Such worldwide mythic forms may derive from a period of prehistory where the construct organization was primarily symmetric. Then the acquisition of a more dominant asymmetric organization may have been passed down in the cultural heritage in such mythic forms.

The emergence of symmetric organization in prehistory would, of course, be reflected in cave pictures and designs in tools handles and other objects. The emergence of asymmetric organization would be reflected by evidence of planning or foresight. The manufacture of tools in one season and venue to be used solely in another season and venue would indicate a foresight or planning beyond the symmetry of 'here and now'.

The right cortical hemisphere of the human brain is reported to have relative advantage for thoughts and action involving space, contextual processing and the emotions of depression and fear. Field dependence is also a characteristic especially of contextual processing in this hemisphere. The left hemisphere of the human brain is reported to have an advantage for abstract thinking towards solution, symbol manipulation, assertive decision, and expressive speech, field independence, goal-oriented or harm avoidance sequences of thinking or action—a fully advantaged transitive language, and sometimes the loci of pleasure or euphoria. Although specialization is often dependent upon handedness, and in all cases appears only relative, it would nevertheless appear that the right hemisphere is the sponsor of more activities that require symmetric construct linkages. In contrast, the left hemisphere appears to sponsor many activities that require asymmetric construct pairings.

Psychological trauma has been found in studies by Sewell (Chapter 21, pp. 223–231) to result in a lack of elaboration in hierarchical organization, also more instances of 'bottom-class isolates'. There are constructs of elements that *do not* enter into hierarchical relationships with other constructs. The offender, perpetrator or trauma-giving agent, the critical combat event, and the constructs descriptive of the traumatic event are often found as bottom-class isolates. In this sense they have only a symmetric relationship to members within an individual's hierarchy. The various features of dissociation that help define post-traumatic stress disorder and dissociative identity disorder appear to have bottom-class symmetry. Thus, a tentative argument can be offered that all of these psychological trauma manifestations may have the common result of transformation from asymmetric and symmetric relationships upon the event of the trauma.

If only some of the preceding kinds of predictions can be validated, then Kelly's personal construct theory would rise to a different level of utility. Yet, to me, only one modification of corollary or postulate appears necessary to enable these new kinds of predictions.

FINAL COMMENT

As I recount these memories about the influence of George A. Kelly upon my research career, I am reminded that Kelly would give pleasant approval to attempts either to utilize or to extend his ideas, be they eventually valid or invalid. As I have learned from him, a good theory is one that sparks 'brittle' research hypotheses and thereby evolves itself out of existence quickly. A poor theory produces neither hypotheses nor modifications of itself. Its propositions remain static and thereby may obscure more productive ideas that follow from other premises.

Reaching Out

INTRODUCTION

One of the problems that soon emerged in creating this volume was that there was just too much material to cover. In the end, it was decided to try to cover those areas in which a considerable amount of work has been reported by several personal construct psychologists.

However, to ensure that as many areas as possible are covered, the first chapter in this section, Chapter 43, is divided into five parts, each part contributed by a different author who is an expert in that field. No doubt more than one of these authors thinks that he or she should have been given more space, but. . . . Perhaps that will be the case when the second edition of this book is written.

Jacqui Costigan (Chapter 43.1) tragically died before her contribution on nursing was completed, and Julie Ellis and Julie Watkinson, both nurses, kindly agreed to complete it. A great deal of work has been carried out in the nursing field within the framework of personal construct psychology, much of it influenced by the work and teaching of Jacqui Costigan.

Harry Procter, in Chapter 43.2, writes on family therapy. That is a rapidly developing field in which his thinking is central. In Chapter 43.3 John Porter gives a personal account of how he introduced Kelly's ideas into the Metropolitan Police in London. He illustrates nicely some of the difficulties that may be experienced when trying to persuade those in organizations to give personal construct psychology a try. David Savage, in Chapter 43.4, relates how Kelly's ideas can be of use in sports psychology. As he says, there is a growing awareness that the relationship between the sports 'client' and the sports psychologist is of vital importance and that a personal construct framework is a viable alternative to existing models. Jack Adams-Webber (Chapter 43.5) then calls upon his great experience to tell about work on artificial intelligence. Those interested in this development may find Chapter 12 (pp. 133–141), by Mildred Shaw and Brian Gaines on Expert Systems, of value.

The last chapter in this volume moves into the future and even into fantasy perhaps. Fay Fransella describes how musicians, literary critics and even historians are finding the ideas in personal construct psychology of use. There is even the idea that physicists might find Kelly's theory useful in their efforts to understand the dimension of time.

She then moves on to a description and discussion of Kelly's Alternative Fundamental Postulate. Perhaps, he says, it is actually that life itself construes. With body–mind thinking thrown out of the window, we can start to take Kelly's idea of the person being a construing system seriously. Psychoneuroimmunology sees the immune system as a construing process; plant biologists are saying that plant life 'construes'. And then there was Gaia. The Earth is a construing system. Perhaps George Kelly would have smiled one of his twinkling smiles at that idea.

Nursing

Jacqui Costigan
Late of La Trobe University, Bendigo, Australia

Julie M. Ellis
La Trobe University, Bendigo, Australia

and

Julie Watkinson
Flinders University, Adelaide, Australia

INTRODUCTION

Personal construct psychology provides a framework to guide holistic nursing, nursing education, nursing research and identification of nurses' constructs of themselves, other nurses and other health professionals. Nurse converts to this psychology have shown enthusiasm about the 'goodness of fit' of the approach and its methods with their clinical and research interests, and its potential for a humanistic approach (Costigan, 1985). Personal construct psychology has been recognized as valuable in any situation where the world of the client or patient needs to be explored in order to relate to them in a meaningful way.

However, to date, the range of personal construct applications by nurses to patients and their families, in relation to understanding their constructs of health and illness, diagnosis and treatment, has not been extensive. Obstacles include the lack of attention to this theory in nursing curricula, the nature of nursing work, and difficulties for clinical nurses in collecting data from ill patients.

Still, the usefulness of the personal construct approach has been demonstrated in a variety of aspects of the professional practice of nurses. The majority of nursing research papers using personal construct psychology have been focused on phenomena related to the *nursing role*. Research in this category includes research on *caring*, perceptions of self and others, professional identity, changing role perceptions, experiences in different roles and constructions of *the effective nurse*. There has also been some emphasis on *clinical issues*, often with an overlap between the

International Handbook of Personal Construct Psychology. Edited by F. Fransella.
© 2003 John Wiley & Sons, Ltd.

two. Clinical research has been used in *different fields of nursing*: mental health, drug and alcohol and aged care nursing, as well as nurses' constructions of patients, including the notion of the good or bad patient.

CONSTRUCTIONS OF CARING

While mainstream nursing literature is not replete with constructivist ideas and applications, Morrison and Burnard (1997) included the personal construct approach in research on the nursing role and on interpersonal aspects of nursing practice. Across two studies into nurses' perceptions of *caring* and the *interpersonally skilled nurse,* their findings were consistent in that the most frequently elicited constructs were personal qualities, rather than skills. This held implications for change to nursing curricula that, until then, were primarily based on skill development.

Dyson (1996) developed *themes* from the constructs elicited on caring: consideration and sensitivity, giving of self, work style, motivation, communication and meeting needs, knowledge and learning, individual approach, honesty and sincerity.

Ellis (1992, 1999) investigated ways in which nurses construed *self as a carer* in the context of caring for *older people* living in a nursing home. Personality characteristics (*kind* versus *unkind*, *giving* versus *selfish*, *considerate* versus *inconsiderate*) were more frequently used than constructs describing physical caring activities (*meeting needs* versus *frustrated*, *communicative* versus *reserved*). Personal construct theory notions of developing anticipations, validation and changing anticipations proved to be fruitful in understanding nurses' practice with elderly residents (Ellis, 1997).

In an investigation of nurses' professional identity Ellis-Scheer (2000) showed that, for most of the participants, '*caring*' was indeed an important theme among the constructs but it did not dominate their professional identity. Moreover, students and expert nurses were not homogeneous groups with respect to their professional identity. The majority of the student group did not yet have a clearly defined professional identity. In the expert nurses, two forms of professional identities prevailed: a patient-oriented one and an achievement-oriented one. A rather unsettling result, however, was that one third of the expert nurses were experiencing a conflict about their professional identity that may eventually cause them to leave the profession. This study differed from the majority of studies in that it analysed complex *construction systems of individuals* rather than simply categorizing collections of constructs compiled together from groups of respondents.

NURSES IN DIFFERENT WORKING ENVIRONMENTS

Since the professional role of nurses may vary according to the specific working environment (such as general hospital care, psychiatry, or community care), differences between groups of nurses in construing have been the focus of a number of studies.

Wilson and Retsas (1997) compared the personal constructs that three groups of nurses used to characterize effective nursing within their area of practice. They found that knowledge, technical skills and achievement orientation characterized effective *critical care nurses*, whereas being compassionate, empathetic, ethical and having an holistic approach were valued characteristics of *gerontology nurses*. Nurses in *general acute care* settings showed some similarity to both groups. March and McPherson (1996), also investigating the concept of 'the effective nurse', found that caring and good communication were the most important construct themes.

When comparing the role construct systems of *psychiatric nurses*, *general nurses* and *social workers*, Rawlinson (1995) found far more variation *within groups* than between them.

Nurses' constructions of their experiences as *intensive care nurses*—using situations as elements—were investigated by Laubach and colleagues (1996), and nurses' constructions of nursing expertise in *accident and emergency nursing* was the focus of the study by Edwards (1998).

NURSING EDUCATION

Some studies used personal construct theory and repertory grid techniques explicitly in both course design and educational research. Watts (1988) studied the effects of shared learning experiences on the attitudes of first-year psychiatric and general nursing students to patients and their nursing care. 'Before and after' repertory grids, together with reflection on and discussion of the findings, have been used as both research and learning tools in studies involving a midwives' refresher course (Diamond & Thompson, 1985) and nursing students' perceptions of their psychiatric practicum (Melrose & Shapiro, 1999).

The majority of studies concerned with nursing training investigated the development of their professional identity, often comparing student and 'expert' nurses (with many years of work experience). According to Heyman and colleagues (1983) nurses' *identification with the medical role* increased as a result of nursing training. They suggested that this is a move of psychological closeness to the role as a caring, supporting, health professional. Howkins and Ewens (1997) investigated the *changing role perceptions* of community nursing students. The majority of the nurses in the study, both when starting and finishing their course, identified 'Self' in a cluster with 'Self as a Community Nurse'. Apparently, these nurses had anticipated themselves as community nurses even before their education in this field of nursing commenced. Crispin (1990) found that both pertinent *events* occurring in the lives of student nurses (such as clinical placements) and *nursing lecturers' constructions* of nursing, influence the student's constructions of nursing. Feelings experienced by *new graduates* were examined by White (1996) who found that these nurses felt connected to the role, satisfied with the role, pressured by the work, and concerned about their skill level and effectiveness. They also had feelings of threat to self in the role as a clinical nurse.

NURSES AND PATIENTS

With nursing being a profession that implies intensive interaction with other, often 'difficult' people, nurses' construing of patients has been an important focus of research.

Some patients are viewed by nurses *less positively* than others (Barnes, 1990). The ideal patients were happy and satisfied and the nurses enjoyed caring for them. The nurses found the 'worst' patients (either overweight or underweight, difficult to feed, fussy or messy) stressful and frustrating to care for. The strategies used by nurses caring for *patients in pain* were focusing on the long-term outcomes for patients rather than on the immediate pain, enabling them to become emotionally distant from the patient and thus helping the patient deal with the pain more effectively. Similar findings were reported by Nagy (1992).

Pollock (1986) used repertory grid elicitation with nurses, patients *and families* as a *basis for collaborative care planning* for patients in the mental health system. Costigan and colleagues (1987) used a personal construct approach to raise student nurses' awareness of *pejorative attitudes towards people who had attempted suicide*. Ellis (1996) identified student nurses' negative and fearful *construing of old age* that appeared to be linked particularly to childhood experiences. This work highlighted the need for nurse educators to provide opportunity for exploration of alternative constructions or ways that student nurses view the aged, in order to avoid harmful consequences of stereotyping on elderly recipients of their care.

Clinton and colleagues (1995) studied *constructions of stress and coping* by nurses who worked in dementia units. The main stressors for these nurses were residents' behaviours, the work they had to undertake and the lack of time in which to do it all. Both adaptive (such as using social supports) and maladaptive (such as withdrawing and being hard towards residents) strategies were used in equal amounts by the nurses.

In the drug and alcohol nursing field, Watkinson (2001) studied *perceptions regarding mood-altering drugs in middle-aged women*, a group with a high incidence of prescribed psychotropic medication use, applying a *constructive alternativism perspective* rather than the traditional conceptualization based on a cost–benefit analysis.

CONCLUDING REMARKS

Despite this body of work, the challenge remains for personal construct psychology to be more effectively integrated into nursing curricula and for nurses to become more aware of the potential benefits of its application to patient care.

One of the reasons for the present situation is probably that the foci of research seem to be rather accidental and not inspired by a systematic research strategy. Furthermore, often the sole connection to personal construct psychology appears to be the application of repertory grids as research tools. Only a few studies use a personal construct *theory* approach. From a methodological point of view, the dominant strategy of data analysis seems to be the analysis of construct content, based on accumulations of constructs collected from groups of respondents. The specific strength of the personal construct approach, the analysis of complex constructions of human individuals, has, as yet, rarely been explored.

Family Therapy

Harry Procter

Child & Family Therapeutic Services, Bridgwater, UK

Personal construct psychology is ideally suited to making sense of the family and in guiding family therapists in their work. Families may be negotiating their circumstances in a developing and creative way, but when they become bogged down and problems arise, the personal construct approach offers effective help.

Family intervention has broad application—for example, to mental health, disabilities and illness, child protection, marital problems and forensic work. It is applicable across the lifespan from childhood to working with older adults. It may be the therapy of choice in working with *people who are unwilling to speak or have difficulty with communication,* for example those in catatonic states (Procter, 1985b) or with autism (Procter, 2000, 2001).

Personal construct psychology provides a model of the way the family operates (Procter, 1981, 1996). We can see members of families (and other ongoing groups) as Kellyian *scientists* making sense of their lives, and in particular each other, through their personal sets of constructs. Families evolve ways of viewing the world (family construct systems) in which the members hold both shared and idiosyncratic constructs. Each family has a set of constructs which, for example, define gender and generational roles. For example in a family, stepfather might be seen as the *soft one* and mother *strict.* There may be agreement or conflict about how things are seen. Contrasts may be made within the family (he is *soft* compared to her *strictness*) or with an outside figure (he is *soft* compared to grandfather, who is *firm*). The family is an important vehicle through which constructs and values in the wider culture and society, for example about gender roles, are transmitted to the new generation.

Differences in *power* among members may be seen as which member's way of construing things tends to prevail. Some construing may be thereby *suppressed* but continues to exist covertly in an individual or coalition of individual members. The children develop and learn from the way the rest of the family carve up reality but are likely soon to begin to challenge this construing, for example in adolescence.

Problems may exist in an individual member associated with the structure or the content of the way they are construing, as described in other chapters of this hand-

International Handbook of Personal Construct Psychology. Edited by F. Fransella.
© 2003 John Wiley & Sons, Ltd.

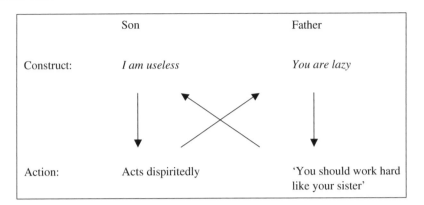

Figure 43.2.1   'Bow-tie' diagram of construing between father and son.

book. However, the family construct approach also emphasizes how problems may be maintained within the interaction patterns among family members. For example, a poor self-concept associated with depression in a young person may be maintained by the father, whose view the young person respects, but who is critical and compares his son unfavourably to his successful older sister. Figure 43.2.1 depicts this pattern between the two of them in the *bow-tie diagram,* so called because of its shape (Procter, 1987). The action resulting from each construct tends to validate the other's construct in a self-maintaining loop or circularity. How other members of the family view this state of affairs and link to this will be crucial. For instance, the mother may support the father or her son, she may help them with their predicament or distance herself, each possible position having very different implications. The task of the person working with the family is firstly to discover how the family members are making sense of their situation. *Constructive alternativism,* Kelly's basic philosophy, may be explained to the family at the outset, helping them to see different views among them as a *resource.* Families typically rarely have had the opportunity to sit down with someone who will respect all the views held and begin to help them to negotiate some new ways forward. As in individual work, the way they see things is *accepted* in a credulous way, the art here being to do this *simultaneously* with a group of people who may differ sharply.

The therapist listens carefully to what members are saying, understanding the main 'positions' that people take towards issues and noting particular constructs that crop up and the distinctions that they use. Helping each member to spell out their view, and what 'evidence' they use to validate their judgements, begins to help the others listening to get a richer understanding of the person. Often, in families, conflicts rage as members on each side are drawing on different validational evidence to back up the 'rightness' of their view. Parents may be emphasizing the *danger* in their adolescent daughter's escapades. She sees them as *over-intrusive* and *treating her as a much younger girl.* The therapist helps the members to look at the *same episodes* and explore agreements and differences of view. They are encouraged to *put themselves in the shoes* of the other. The therapist may say to the daughter, 'What do you think a mother should do if she is worried about her daughter?'

The mother may be asked what her experience was when she was the same age as her daughter. The constructs that people are using have often been carried over from earlier experiences, which are then brought into the discussion. The daughter may not have heard about the story of her mother's adolescence or have strong opinions about how different conditions apply to the two situations.

Techniques may be drawn from personal construct psychotherapy or, for example, Ravenette's approaches with children (Chapter 28, pp. 283–294) or from the various schools of family therapy. Personal construct psychology provides an overarching framework for making sense of what one is doing in therapy, which can then be shared with the family. The personal construct family therapist generally prefers to honour the family's way of construing things rather than imposing his or her own views on the situation. A family situation or genogram constitutes a veritable Rorschach inkblot when it comes to people making elaborate assumptions about what may be happening. We have all grown up in some sort of family or equivalent group and tend to assume what it is like, for example, to be a *middle child* or a *woman who has been cheated on.* Personal construct psychology disciplines us to check: '*Whose* construct are we talking about here?' We *elicit* constructs rather than *supply* them. Of course, if someone is having difficulty expressing themselves or finding a word, we might gingerly suggest a word, but always check with the person that it does justice to their own intended meaning. The therapist may gently begin to invite new ways of construing through questioning and clarifying inconsistencies or alternative views. The therapist is free to share his or her own experiences and ideas with the family, of course, if it is thought that the family can use them. Therapists in any context need always to be aware of their own power in pronouncing what they think is the case.

Many different approaches may be used, the key being to fit the approach to the particular family and the members within it. Kelly provides an ethos of playful and creative therapeutic work in which one is encouraged to be *experimental.* Being playful and humorous is invaluable in family work in encouraging new ways of looking at things and countering the often scary or painful emotion that the family has been experiencing. The family session should as far as possible be a pleasure to attend, especially for young people, with a focus on what interests them and fires their enthusiasm. This helps to put the problematic aspects of life more in perspective, however serious the difficulties may be. This all becomes much more possible given the personal construct axiom that problems, like everything else, lie in the 'eye of the beholder'.

One family therapy technique that fits well with personal construct psychology is the *reflecting team* (Andersen, 1987). An observing team join the family after a while and talk with each other in the family's and therapist's presence about what they have been hearing. They attempt to mirror what the family members are experiencing and to bring the information together in a new and compassionate framework. The team members become a living embodiment of *constructive alternativism* as each of them naturally construes the situation in a unique way. The reflection provides a rich fund of ideas and feelings on which family members are free to draw for inspiration. After the team has reflected, the therapist asks each member for their reactions about what they have heard, allowing the team to revise and elaborate their views.

As Kelly said of individuals, *the family is a form of motion*, and very often the family will return to the next session with some new ideas, or with something having gone slightly better for them.

Repertory grids may be used as part of the therapeutic process and also to evaluate process and outcome in family therapy (Procter, 1985a). A less time-consuming approach involves *qualitative grids* (Procter, 2002) where, for example, the family members write down on a large piece of paper how each sees all the others in the squares of the grid. The names of the members are assigned to the left-hand edge of the grid (as *perceivers*) and the same set of names along the top (how they are *perceived*). Young children may use drawings rather than words. The method helps family members to reflect on the fact that their views are in fact constructions and not objective reality. Given at the beginning and end of therapy, it provides an informal measure of change. It is particularly useful for children with autism who have a natural difficulty with *sociality* or 'theory of mind' (Procter, 2001) and who find it easier to understand communication presented in *visual form* rather than relying so much on words.

The personal construct approach to working with families, developed in the 1970s, predated other similar theoretical trends that have since become popular in the family therapy field such as *Constructivism* and *Social Constructionism*. These have seldom given Kelly's original writings sufficient acknowledgement and there has been a tendency to 'reinvent the wheel'. They do not have the detailed elaborate theory that personal construct psychology provides—for example, about constructs, construct systems, construing, bipolarity and emotions. The personal construct approach still has the advantage over these often much looser tendencies in providing a systematic psychology with a large research literature together with a long tradition of specific techniques for making sense of human experience, as presented in this handbook. More can be found about the specific applications of personal construct psychology to families in Dallos (1991) and Feixas (1995) as well as this author's various writings referred to above. The implications of the approach applied to the topic of *anger* will be found in Procter and Dallos (in press).

The Metropolitan Police, London: A Personal Account

John Porter

Interactions Ltd, Co. Wicklow, Ireland

In about 1983 personal construct psychology crept into the Metropolitan Police (the Met) quite unnoticed. Let me explain. In 1981–82 serious civil disorder broke out in London and in many other cities of England. These outbreaks were thought to be associated with social deprivation, racial disadvantage, and discrimination and endemic racist behaviours and attitudes among police officers. Of course, since racial prejudice was both a disciplinary and criminal offence, it was doubly difficult to investigate since the rules of justice and evidence precluded any 'factual' or direct approach. No officer could be required to incriminate himself and any investigating officer was likewise required to report any instance of which he had evidence. Once *evidence* was established no further inquiry as to *underlying* reasons was permitted under the Judges Rules. Thus those rules, designed to protect the innocent, created and continue to maintain an environment in which true understanding of the causes of injustice is inhibited.

An oblique approach to the problem was required. Various suggestions appeared in the national press among which was the contention that psychometric or personality testing would enable the detection of racially prejudiced officers (whether already in service or at selection stage). A policy decision was taken at the top level in Scotland Yard. As an officer in the Met at that time, I was asked to set up a 'Psychometric Testing Unit' within the Met's Training School.

If I had known any personal construct psychology at the time, I would have understood better the reception on my arrival. I presented myself in anticipation of the warm welcome and directions to my new office. Had I known about commonality of construing at this point, I might have wondered if anybody had understood

International Handbook of Personal Construct Psychology. Edited by F. Fransella.

(a) what I was supposed to do, and (b) what the personal advantage for them was.

Having got over the 'I didn't ask for you', and 'Where am I going to put you?', stages of the welcome, I just about managed to mumble that the Commissioner and Margaret Thatcher wanted the work done. From the office window a huddle of portacabin huts could be seen crouched under the shadow of the main Kings Cross railway line. 'You might find some space in there,' it was suggested. 'Make a plan and draw up a budget.' Problem solved!

So the 'problem' trudged across the field to the huts where he found a commune of enlightened, intelligent people. One or two kindly folk welcomed me and I eventually found an unoccupied section of carpet in a corridor between offices. This was my new home.

I 'stole' a chair and a desk, made a plan and drew up a budget. Now plans and budgets are things that *can* be construed, so before long a thriving 'Unit' of about five people was established.

We embarked on a programme of testing. At the end of 12 months' work and many hundreds of tests, we found that the Force had successfully recruited people with a psychological/personality profile that mirrored . . . the general population! Everybody was randomly normal.

During the time that this work was in progress my colleagues and I embarked on a personal construct psychology course run by the Centre for Personal Construct Psychology in London. After struggling hard with the notions of self-made reality, which contrasted sharply with divine and government-made law, we soon realized that here was a non-judgemental tool which might just give some insights to the 'realities' experienced by officers going about their everyday duties. Perhaps comparisons could be drawn between the 'real' world as seen by different police officers and members of racial minorities and the majority white population.

A study making such a comparison showed that officers who had taken part in race awareness training were more likely to be prejudiced. That rather perverse finding is easy to understand using personal construct theory. Race awareness training elaborated and made officers aware of the different perspectives and lifestyle of recent and first-generation Afro-Caribbean and Asian immigrants. Hence, the construing systems of officers were elaborated with respect to the cultural *differences* (individuality) rather than commonalities between peoples. Officers were thus better equipped by this training to pre-judge the outcomes of encounters with members of racial minorities. During any such encounter episode the officer would of course treat the member of the public as different—thus heightening alienation and laying the ground for increased aggression (actively trying to find out more about each other), and hostility (in the personal construct sense) by denying that here was another bloke just like me. In the context of the race-relations programmes, these findings did not achieve political favour since management did not have the necessary construing to understand them.

However, new avenues for the application of personal construct psychology were opening and these produced rapid and spontaneous change among those who were involved.

During the time of our investigations into racial prejudice, a small number of incidents occurred in which people were shot by armed police officers. Soon the spotlight was on the selection and training processes. A major part of our work was soon devoted to the world of strategic firearms use. Personal construct psychology was used as a diagnostic tool in the following areas:

- Diagnosis of personal qualities required in officers to carry guns in high-risk situations.
- Design of a multi-activity selection centre where officer qualities were assessed on specific behavioural and attitudinal constructs. Success in subsequent training rose from a pass rate of 20% to over 90%, bringing about significant cost and manpower savings as well as selection of a more reliable set of officers.
- Identification of key personal role constructs during stages of operational incidents leading to more realistic and focused training so that officers could better construe the environment, suffer less anxiety and concentrate on operational matters.
- Workshops on stress-coping mechanisms and post-event trauma management, introduction of support rather than straight disciplinary procedures following incidents.

The Research Unit soon became a centre for officers wanting to find out more about themselves and their roles within their jobs. Quite often workshops took place at weekends with officers attending in their own time (sometimes bringing family members). These workshops were mini-personal construct psychology courses with officers learning about eliciting techniques, laddering and pyramiding.

Personal construct psychology sold itself and was soon in even greater demand as the inadequacies of conventional questionnaires, selection, appraisal and management systems became more evident. At the height of activity of the Unit, work was underway in all of the following areas (in addition to the racial prejudice and firearms areas):

- Interviewing techniques
- Training and learning course design and methods
- Management of personnel in high-risk undercover situations
- Annual appraisal/assessment
- Promotion
- Selection
- Stress management

For two years little information was published from our Unit. We had failed to validate the official line that personality and other psychological tests (that is, conventional psychometric instruments) could solve problems of selection, training and behavioural prediction. The recognition of the success and impact of personal construct psychology occurred on a very significant day. It was time to present the results of our work to the Commissioner and his senior staff. As I presented the failure of our attempted validation of conventional psychometric tests compared with the achievements of a personal construct psychology approach, the Commissioner stopped me. 'Are you telling me I was wrong, Mr Porter, (for saying that personality tests would solve the problem)?' The room stiffened. Even more so when

I replied, 'Yes Sir.' 'Thank you,' said Sir Kenneth, smiling. The room relaxed. Personal construct psychology survived.

Since that time much work has been carried out within the personal construct framework in many police forces. Nelarine Cornelius provides two such examples in Chapter 35 (pp. 349–357).

A Sporting Use of Personal Construct Psychology

David Savage

University College of Chester, UK

Sport and exercise is a relatively new field of applied psychology and as such it is still vigorously growing and changing. Recent developments in the field mean that now is a good time for sports and exercise psychologists to consider the use of personal construct theory in their work. It is relevant to what they are trying to do. It can meaningfully inform their professional practice and extend their research options.

Historically, the focus was almost entirely on athletes and the psychological issues relating to their performance and well-being. But recently the focus of interest has widened to encompass issues of professional practice. What psychologists do, how they do it and the theories that guide them are all part of the new focus (e.g. Anderson, 2001). There is a growing awareness that alternative theoretical perspectives need to be explored and traditional approaches to research extended in accordance with the new emphasis of the field. Personal construct psychology is relevant to each of these developments and worthy of inclusion in the growing plurality of sport and exercise psychology. For example, the primary influence on the working partnership between psychologist and client is the guiding theory adopted by the psychologist and the core principles and assumptions that it makes about that partnership.

Change the guiding theory and the working partnership will change accordingly. It has been observed that sport and exercise psychologists have too often implicitly adopted the principle of 'working on' rather than 'working with' the client. This leads to an excessive assumption of psychologist as 'expert' in what the athlete should do and athlete as 'novice'. The principle of 'working with' the athlete leads to some redressing of that balance. A greater emphasis is placed on the psychologist and athlete exploring issues from the athlete's perspective. The expertise of the psychologist now shifts towards being expert at uncovering the athlete's perspective, which is totally congruent with a personal construct way of working with a

International Handbook of Personal Construct Psychology. Edited by F. Fransella.
© 2003 John Wiley & Sons, Ltd.

client. Sports psychologists now choose to approach their athlete in the way that counsellors approach their client.

As an example of the value in uncovering a client's meaning of events, consider how individuals construe exercise (or training). The personal construct *having obligations* at one pole and *can choose* at the other, can be used to appraise an event and give it meaning. One person, for example, who construes an event as having *no specific obligations* might also construe it as *free time* and as *an opportunity*, while another construes it as *wasting time* and *a loss of opportunity*. As the number and type of constructs used by individuals increases, so too do the possible meanings of events. Each person would behave in accordance with his or her personal construction of the event. This individuality of behavioural choice is emphasized as the example is developed further. A person who construes *no obligations* as meaning *free time* and *an opportunity* may, in addition, construe engaging in exercise either as an *exhausting* and *unpleasant* experience or as a *healthy* and *pleasant* one. In the former instance they would be unlikely to choose to exercise. They would choose an alternative activity such as watching television or eating chocolates as that would bring about a more meaningful experience for them. In the latter instance, exercising is construed in a way that gives rise to positive anticipations and the probability that the person would choose to do it.

An implication of the above example is that to move a person from choosing not to exercise to choosing to do so requires a change in the meaning that events have for them. That would occur, for instance, in relation to the reluctant exerciser who is advised to exercise for health reasons and be the joint venture of the psychologist and athlete. Such a venture would involve facilitating athletes' awareness of, reflection on, and alternatives to their personal meaning of events. These are central tasks for the personal construct sports psychologist. The personal meaning of events may typically be explored through eliciting constructs, repertory grids and/or narrative accounts. They can be a powerful means of promoting change in an athlete since the athlete is often unaware of how specific actions come to be chosen and thus can have difficulty in changing them. Meaning needs to be systematically elicited and explored.

A more active intervention on the part of the psychologist could be required for change to occur. Introduction and elaboration of a new construct, such as *long-term benefits* versus *short-term benefits*, may be needed before choosing to exercise becomes a very meaningful option to take.

PERFORMANCE PROFILING

The most established use of a personal construct-based technique in sport psychology is Performance Profiling (Butler, 1996). It is a form of repertory grid that enables a coach or psychologist to uncover an athlete's (or a group of athletes) meaning of their performance. Using their own constructs, a comparison of performance influences can be assessed by comparing 'as I am now' and how the athlete would 'ideally like to be' when performing. That enables areas of the athlete's strengths and weaknesses in relation to performing to be identified and experiences to eliminate the gap devised. The coach may indeed, with this athlete-centred information, be able to spot where new ways to construe performance could be introduced that would be of value to the athlete's development. In one personal athletic consultation, performance profiling was used to enable an athlete to reflect on her sports technique. That, combined with reflection on how the coach viewed 'good' technique, enabled the athlete to become aware of why she was frequently in disagreement and conflict with the coach at training.

A case study with an athlete who had been injured showed both research and intervention uses of personal construct psychology (Savage, 2000). Information was first collected through multiple interview techniques and sessions, and that produced extensive and detailed information which needed to be organized and interpreted. For this purpose, a repertory grid was used which enabled the phases of injury, and what each meant to the client, to be mapped using the client's own constructs. The more abstract representation then enabled the specific information contained in the narrative accounts to be organized without the imposition of the researcher's construing.

BOTH THERAPY AND RESEARCH

As well as richly informing the researcher about the meaning of injury for the athlete, the process gave the athlete a deep insight into the meaning the injury experience held for him. He found that to be therapeutic. The barrier between research and intervention can be blurred and this will often be the case in the future development of sport and exercise psychology. In personal construct work research and practice are often very close together. This theory has relevance in both of these domains whether the focus is on the athlete or the psychologist working with the athlete.

Artificial Intelligence

Jack Adams-Webber

Brock University, Canada

The hybrid field of artificial intelligence (AI) is still an 'open' intellectual frontier which psychologists, together with computer scientists, anthropologists, cognitive biologists, linguists, physicists and philosophers, among others, can explore on a more or less equal footing (Adams-Webber, 1993). All participants in AI research agree that it is potentially useful to construe at least some facets of cognition as involving computation. Computational models of thought processes can be characterized abstractly as based on formal rules that are independent of context. Some advocates of AI adopt a strictly computational approach to understanding all human cognition. Their ultimate goal is to design an abstract machine whose linguistic behaviour is equivalent to that of humans (e.g. Turing, 1950). That objective presupposes that the conceptual bases of all of our linguistic behaviour are amenable to formalization. Others subscribe to the more modest agenda of using computational procedures to model only some aspects of human cognition, for example, 'expertise' in chess or medical diagnosis (see Chapter 12, pp. 133–139).

Proponents of both approaches have developed simulation programs which are models of human cognitive processes in the form of computer software. Such models are essentially theories. The main idea is that the linguistic behaviour of the program should closely approximate that of humans (Simon, 1995). The detailed internal functions of the model are viewed as a potential theoretical explanation of the corresponding human performance when the input–output behaviour of the computer running the program closely resembles that of humans. These computational models can be specified fully in mathematical terms and are unprecedented in the field of psychology with respect to their level of precision and internal consistency.

Kelly's Range Corollary applies to an important problem in the theory of knowledge which has extensive implications throughout the field of AI. That is, the *frame problem* (also called the 'temporal projection problem'). As formulated by Fodor, this is essentially 'the problem of putting a "frame" around a set of beliefs that may need to be revised in the light of specific newly available information' (1983, pp. 112–113). Perhaps the most interesting facet of the frame problem from a psycho-

International Handbook of Personal Construct Psychology. Edited by F. Fransella.
© 2003 John Wiley & Sons, Ltd.

logical perspective is that humans, in contrast to computer programs, rarely suffer from it. As the Dreyfuses note,

> when faced with real world situations, humans need not list in advance all possible relevant features plus rules for determining under what circumstances each feature may become actually relevant, and rules for when these rules are relevant, and so forth. (1986, p. 88)

For example, before picking up the coffee mug on my desk, I do not usually pause to consider whether this action will change its colour, or the location of the desk in my office, or bring down the current government of Canada, or dislodge the earth from its orbit. If designers of computational models of cognition could explain how humans routinely solve the frame problem in their everyday lives they could possibly incorporate formal rules into their models that are consistent with our common-sense intuitions about relevance.

From a Kellyian point of view, the basic issue underlying the frame problem can be understood as essentially one of 'range of convenience' (Adams-Webber, 1989; Ford, 1989). Kelly's Range Corollary stipulates that 'a construct is convenient for the anticipation of a finite range of events only'. It follows that any construct, or by extension, any system or subsystem of interrelated constructs, has a limited range of convenience, which comprises 'all those things to which the user would find its application useful'. According to Kelly, any particular construct may have a somewhat different range of convenience for each person who uses it, or even for the same individual on separate occasions.

A particular construct seldom, if ever, stands alone in our experience. It is typically deployed together with one or more other related constructs in establishing a specific 'context of meaning' for anticipating events. Essentially, in interpreting any event, we categorize it in terms of one or more constructs; and then by reviewing our personal networks of related constructs, we often can derive some predictive inferences or 'hypotheses' about future events. Indeed, this is precisely the operational definition of 'temporal projection' that is entailed in Kelly's Fundamental Postulate: 'A person's processes are psychologically channelized by the ways in which he (or she) anticipates events.'

By definition, only events within the *range of relevance* of a hypothesis can constitute either confirming or disconfirming evidence for that hypothesis (von Wright, 1966). Adams-Webber (1992) has demonstrated that the range of convenience of any construct must necessarily delimit the range of relevance of all possible anticipations (hypotheses) based on that particular construct. In short, Kelly's Range Corollary is an *a priori* formal principle which serves the important logical function of restricting the range of relevance of all empirical hypotheses. It necessarily imposes boundary conditions on the scope ('frame') of a cognitive system, either human or artificial, because the range of relevance of any hypothesis or set of hypotheses is automatically constrained by the ranges of convenience of the constructs used in its formulation.

The Range Corollary also entails the possibility of differentiation of function, not only among constructs, but also systems and subsystems of interrelated constructs in terms of their combined ranges of convenience (Adams-Webber, 1996a). By extension, the more functionally differentiated any system or subsystem of constructs, the wider the potential range of relevance ('frame') of hypotheses that can be derived within that system. Kelly's (1969h) 'minimax principle' implies that an ideal cognitive system, either human or artificial, would allow the maximum number of differential predictions concerning future events with the minimal number of constructs.

CHAPTER 44

New Avenues to Explore and Questions to Ask

Fay Fransella

University of Hertfordshire, UK

> To construe is to invent, pure and simple. As far as discovery is concerned, all that one ever discovers is whether or not the predictions, to which his inventions have led him, actually pan out.
>
> (Kelly, 1959b, p. 9)

In Chapter 43.1–43.5 five authors have given their accounts of the development of their work in areas not so far covered in this volume. Here we can look at some other applications of personal construct psychology in very diverse areas that have still to become well established. One point to be noted is that by no means are all these areas being explored by psychologists. For instance, here we have musicians, literary critics and historians describing the advantages of using a personal construct framework for their work.

THE WORLD OF MUSIC

One of the few accounts of Kelly's ideas being applied to the world of music comes from Kelly himself in his description of the Construction Corollary. Every time we hear a piece of music with which we are familiar, it may have changed key, changed rhythm or volume, but we still recognize the melody. Construing is about prediction and anticipation and a piece of music can only be recognized by our being able to predict those notes that are about to follow.

An early study by Davies (1976) provides a fascinating account of how brass and string players in a orchestra construed each other. For instance, string players saw brass players, among other things, as less intelligent, liking the limelight and as being the clowns of the orchestra. Brass players saw string players as like a flock of sheep, oversensitive and seeming to think they were 'God's gift to music'. Eric Button (1988) talks about his own experience as someone who always wanted to study music and how our construing processes relate to our understanding of music. He

International Handbook of Personal Construct Psychology. Edited by F. Fransella.
© 2003 John Wiley & Sons, Ltd.

points out that music is all about movement—'music is always going somewhere'. He also talks of its predictability. As he says, we would soon get bored if our music were entirely predictable. Catherine Butler has spent many years working with music students. Among other things, she has isolated some of the factors that may lead to music students failing during their studies. She found that those failing suffered both internal and external stresses. For instance, their parents tended not to play instruments or sing, they saw their peers as competitors, as well as having high levels of performance anxiety. Successful students, on the other hand, only experienced one kind of stress. They had good self-esteem and enjoyed the excitement of performing, seeing it as a challenge to be met (Butler, 1995). Ben-Peretz and Kalekin-Fishman (1988) discuss how the construing of music might be related to sociocultural constructs. Blowers and Bacon-Shone (1994) looked at methods for detecting perceptual differences in jazz. All these authors give us a glimpse at how easily personal construct theory can be used to gain a greater understanding of why, for many people, music is an essential part of life. There is enough interest in the construing of music to suggest that this could burst into life at any time.

LITERARY CRITICISM

John Lee is a literary critic who has made a study of the difficulties literary critics have had over the years in dealing with what he terms 'interiority'. They have a problem construing the inner nature of a literary character. Lee has looked at this issue in his book *Shakespeare's 'Hamlet' and the Controversies of Self* (2000). He says (2002) that his work started in response to the influential movement within recent literary criticism that sees individuals, whether in plays or in life, being little more than the products of their cultures. Such a movement, to those outside literary criticism, may well look rather out-of-date, particularly if one has constructivist sympathies. However, within literary criticism it proved very successful, in part because the modern vocabulary of 'interiority' tended not to exist before 1650, but more importantly because previous critics had themselves talked in very vague terms about how the inner worlds of dramatic characters are constituted.

When the relative importance of Shakespeare was being debated in the late seventeenth and eighteenth centuries, his promoters and detractors both chose his ability (for the detractors an inability) to create lifelike 'characters' as their proof. The promoters won out, and Shakespeare was installed as the national poet, but this was as much a theatrical and political victory as an argumentative one. Few critics talked convincingly about what it was in Shakespeare's *dramatis personae* that gave them lifelike personalities. Later attempts, often reliant on Freud, talked about this lifelikeness coming from the 'gaps' between—for example, what 'characters' said and what they did. The psychological depth of the character was then seen to be the measure of the complexity of contradictory elements that the critic needed to bridge. Such depth was easy to portray as a critics' fiction, and this was exactly the point of attack chosen by some recent literary critics; they allege that what Hamlet possessed was not a series of meaningful gaps, but rather, simple absences or, as one critic put it: 'At the centre of Hamlet, in the interior of his mystery, there is, in short, nothing.'

Lee makes a very interesting case for the importance of using personal construct psychology as a framework for literary critics to use for understanding the characters in literature. He says: 'Kelly's approach—in its humanist and constructivist aspects—lends itself to an account of the literally literary aspects of personality and of change' (Lee, 2000, p. 175).

In a sense, one might say that Kelly was, himself, something of a literary critic. He talks at length towards the end of his second volume about Hamlet in relation to the CPC (decision-making) and the Creativity Cycle. He sees these cycles as different in that the CPC Cycle involves the personal commitment to action at the end of the cycle, whereas no such personal commitment is involved in the Creativity Cycle.

Kelly then discusses the cycles that Hamlet was involved with in his soliloquy: 'To be or not to be?' In Kelly's view, Hamlet was involved in both cycles during that soliloquy, neither of which he was able to complete. First there is loose construing about his relationships with men and women:

> ... vaguely conscientious with respect to his father, vaguely incestuous with respect to his mother, and vaguely illusive with respect to Ophelia. His creative mind had contrived the notion of having a play presented which would dramatize, in some way involving his uncle, what he is not quite able to put into explicit terms. (Kelly, 1955/1991, p. 1061/Vol. 2, p. 351)

Having been through this loosening phase of the Creativity Cycle, Hamlet moves to the CPC Cycle. His words: 'To be or not to be' have pre-empted the issue. He has decided that this is the crux of the matter. He must now make the decision. 'He must fling himself to the one side of this slot or to the other; he must live or die—it is as simple as that.' But it does not end there and he moves into the Creativity Cycle again and then the CPC Cycle once more—and so on. Lee states that:

> Kelly's approach ... gives to man a radical degree of agency. One can free oneself from old constructs and enslave oneself to new constructs again and again. This is the process seen being repeatedly attempted in the soliloquies. ... At the same time, he gives us reasons why literature should create so powerfully and so well the effect of personality; since literature may be, like personality, an argued, philosophical representation of the world. (Lee, 2000, p. 183)

In fact, Kelly makes his admiration for Shakespeare's writings clear in his acknowledgements in Volume 1. He says '... and, of course, that distinguished and insightful colleague of all personal-construct theorists, Mr. William Shakespeare' (1955/1991, p. xii/Vol. 1, p. xiii).

CONSTRUING HISTORICAL DECISIONS

Why were great decisions of history made the way they were? Historians badly want to know, but they are balked by lack of evidence and denial of access to the long-dead players.

It is not possible for a historian to elicit from documents the personal constructs of, say, past policy-makers in the way a personal construct psychologist can from direct contact with the living. However, it has proved extremely useful to approach the problem from a Kellyian perspective. According to David Gillard (2002), we can assume that foreign policy consists of the construing by a small number of identifiable individuals of the behaviour of their counterparts in other states. This they do through identifying their opponents' personal constructs and trying to change or reinforce them by a wide choice of methods, which can range from intimate discussion to total war.

The challenge to the historian lies in the number of policy-holders involved in the voluminous but patchy records of their attempts to modify the construing of their own colleagues before a policy could be agreed and implemented. Gillard's forthcoming book analyses these data during the six months after the Munich crisis. His data come from tracing, on a day-to-day basis, the changes in thinking of a handful of individual policy-makers, in this case key British Cabinet ministers, Foreign Office officials and Service chiefs.

Historically, he finds this. Neville Chamberlain, the British Prime Minister's announcement in 1939 that if Germany attacked Poland, Britain would go to Poland's aid has always been a matter for controversy. Obviously it did Poland no good, as Hitler swiftly overran that nation, and it landed Britain in a war for which its armed forces were not yet ready. Britain had just reneged on a guarantee over Czechoslovakia, so why did Chamberlain expect Hitler to believe in a new guarantee a few weeks later?

A small group of some 20 people in Britain were the policy-makers construing the international situation at the time, and in a position to determine peace or war. Central to their task was the need to interpret the behaviour of Hitler, to anticipate what his moves might be, and to decide the means to deter him from threatening the security of Britain or its allies.

By diplomacy and propaganda those policy-makers relied on their own construing of Hitler's personal constructs in their bid to change them—and those of his subjects. Hitler, of course, was doing the same kind of thing. Both sides got it wrong.

It is Gillard's view that of all the possible approaches to the problems of international history, the theory of personal constructs comes closest to being scientific. He is about to finish a book on the whole subject with the proposed title of *Why Guarantee Poland?*

A PROBLEM OF 'TIME'

Time

Kelly's whole theory is permeated with references to and the importance of the dimension of time. In his 'Brief introduction to personal construct theory' at the beginning of this volume he states: '... the meaning of an event—that is to say, the meaning we ascribe to it—is anchored in its antecedents and its consequents. Thus meaning displays itself to us mainly in the dimension of time' (p. 4). In his first chapter in Volume 1, he says:

> Man ultimately seeks to anticipate real events.... Anticipation is not merely carried on for its own sake; it is carried on so that future reality may be better

represented. It is the future which tantalizes (us), not the past. . . . Always (we) reach out to the future through the window of the present.

(Kelly, 1955/1991, p. 49/Vol. 1, 34)

With this knowledge of the importance Kelly put upon the dimension of time, it was most interesting to view a British Broadcasting Corporation programme televised in 1999 in which two physicists discussed 'The flow of time'. They said that physics has a problem because it cannot account for the passage of time. They concluded that ultimately this sense of temporal flow must be attributed to poorly understood features of human perception. They agreed that 'human consciousness probably has the secret as to how and why we think of time as going by'. Did Kelly understand this dilemma in physics in the early 1950s, or before? Did he see that it was psychology that would be able to solve the problem of physics? Did he wonder what new questions would arise if physics and psychology were to work together? He says:

If man, as the psychologist is to see him, exists primarily in the dimensions of time and only secondarily in the dimensions of space, then the terms which we erect for understanding him ought to take primary account of this view. If we want to know why man does what he does, then the terms of our whys should extend themselves in time rather than in space; they should be events rather than things in the present. He stands firmly astride the chasm that separates the two universes. He, and only he, can bring them into harmony with each other.

(Kelly, 1969b, p. 86)

AN ALTERNATIVE FUNDAMENTAL POSTULATE

'There's no use trying,' said Alice: 'one can't believe impossible things.' 'I dare say you haven't had much practice,' said the Queen . . . 'Why sometimes, I've believed as many as six impossible things before breakfast.'

(Lewis Carroll, 1865, *Alice in Wonderland*)

We now enter the realm of loose construing if not fantasy. As this is a trail I have been following for many years, I shall finish this book by recounting my personal pursuit of the answer to the question 'Where does construing start?'

In the first chapter in this book, Kelly says his theory is about 'the person' and that 'organisms, lower animals, and societies can wait'. But for how much longer? Throughout this book, authors have provided support for Kelly's adamant conviction that the distinction between mind and body is not useful. We are a construing process, a form of motion. In his 1955 volumes Kelly suggests that the idea of non-verbal constructs may, indeed, embrace such things as digestive or glandular secretions.

In 1966, I went to the United States of America on a lecture tour and talked with George Kelly and his students at Brandeis University. He gave me copies of many of his unpublished papers, some of which were published later. Browsing through those, I came across his *Alternative* Fundamental Postulate. His 1955 Fundamental Postulate states that: *A person's processes are psychologically channelized by the ways in which he anticipates events.* His *Alternative*, biological Fundamental Postulate states that: *It is the nature of life to be channelized by the ways events are antic-ipated* (Kelly, 1980, p. 29). He goes on to say: 'This is a more venturesome postulate than the one from which the psychology of personal constructs was launched. But from it may spring some additional ideas about the whole of psychology.' Like the Queen in *Alice in Wonderland*, Kelly liked to think the impossible and then see where that might lead. So, as an exercise in loose construing, where might the idea lead that it is the nature of life or living matter to be channelized by the ways in which events are anticipated? Kelly argued against our talking across disciplines, such as physiological psychology, but it would seem here that the study of such inter-actions may be necessary. He did, after all, say: 'The notion of construing . . . may even be used within borderland areas of the realm of physiology' (Kelly, 1955/1991, p. 51/Vol. 1, p. 36).

There are two words in that Alternative Postulate which need exploring. One is the absence of the word 'processes'. Defining the word in his 1955 Postulate he says:

> Instead of postulating an inert substance, a step which would inevitably lead to the necessity for establishing . . . the existence of some sort of mental energy, the subject of psychology is assumed at the outset to be a process. . . . For our pur-poses, the person is not an object which is temporarily in a moving state but is himself a form of motion. (Kelly, 1955/1991, p. 48/Vol. 1, p. 33)

Since that is his view of living matter, there is no need for the word 'processes' in his Alternative Fundamental Postulate. The other word in both postulates is 'chan-nelized'. He defines this for the first postulate as:

> We conceive a person's processes as operating through a network of pathways rather than as fluttering about in a vast emptiness. The network is flexible and is frequently modified, but it is structured and it both facilitates and restricts a person's range of action. (Kelly, 1955/1991, p. 49/Vol. 1, p. 34)

If the word 'person's' is removed, we have a Fundamental Postulate that can be applied well beyond the human being.

I was personally very taken with that idea, and for years in various talks and the occasional paper, I slipped in the problem of deciding when construing starts. I would argue that there is no problem about the foetus construing. So, what about the sperm? If construing is all about predicting and then behaving in relation to those predictions, why not think about plants predicting where the best nutriments may be and then 'behaving' by sending their roots in that direction. I suggested that perhaps one has to go back as far as living matter to find where construing starts. Perhaps it is living matter itself that is in the anticipation business. I cannot say that psychologists got wildly excited by that idea! But in the past few years, things seem to be changing.

Psychoneuroimmunology

One link in the chain of events I followed in relation to Kelly's Alternative Funda-mental Postulate was attending a British Psychological Society branch scientific meeting in Cornwall in November 2001. I attended in spite of its user-unfriendly title of 'psychoneuroimmunology'. Not really my sort of thing, I thought. How wrong I was! Here I heard psychologists all saying that there is no boundary between mind and body—that there is empirical research to show that they are totally interconnected. Here I heard Marianne Morris talk about the use of guided imagery with patients with cancer or who are HIV positive. Of course, personal construct psychologists have considered the problem of cancer before now (for example, Nuzzo & Chiari, 2001, and Kenny, 1987). But here were people providing neuroscientific research evidence of the bidirectional connection between the physical and the psychological. John Gruzelier demonstrated how the immune function can be enhanced by self-hypnosis. The research that excited me the most was that of Marcel Ebrecht showing how cells of the immune system 'deal with' damage to the skin. He had a slide showing a 'killer cell' and described how that cell 'hangs on' to something until it can 'see' a way to go to the aid of that damaged skin. Would Kelly see this as construing? *It is the nature* of the immune system *to be channelized by the ways events are anticipated.*

The Construing of Plants

Well, at long last I do not feel I have to 'slip in' the idea about plants construing. Professor Trewavas at the Institute of Cell and Molecular Biology, University of Edinburgh, is one of the world's leading researchers into the sensory abilities of plants. He says:

> The problem is that plants don't move and that leads to the supposition that movement is essential to intelligence—and thus the word of contempt—vegetable. However, if one replaces growth for *movement* then intelligent behaviour there is. . . . The best known example of assessment and decision making comes from Cuscuta—a parasitical plant. This plant touches a potential host and is able to assess whether it is worth parasitising many days before it gains nutriments from the host. Also the investment in resources to produce parasitical structures is directly related to the resources the parasite will eventually achieve many days later. (Personal communication, 2002; see also Trewavas, 1999)

There was an article entitled 'Not just a pretty face' in the magazine *New Scientist* on 27 July, 2002, all about Trewavas's ideas. The problem people have is that he uses the word 'intelligence' for the behaviour of plants, and Trewavas is reported as saying that he uses it because it starts controversy, which will be 'all the better for our understanding'. Perhaps 'construe' would be a more acceptable word. After all: *It is the nature* of plants *to be channelized by the ways events are anticipated.*

A SELF-REGULATING EARTH

I do not expect many people care too much about being able to 'understand' the behaviour of plants, but there is more to Kelly's *Alternative Fundamental Postulate* than that. Soon after reading that plants may be seen to construe, I came across

James Lovelock's autobiography *Homage to Gaia* (2000). Here an eminent chemist-cum-medical doctor-cum-biologist explains how he devised the theory he called Gaia (Greek goddess of the earth). The earth is a self-regulating system—just like the human being. In effect, Lovelock sees the surface of the earth as being more like a living organism than a machine. It maintains conditions in which life can exist.

Lovelock used the growth of daisies as an example of what he was talking about. It goes something like this. We know the sun is increasing in heat over the centuries, but the Earth does not heat up accordingly. His 'Daisy World' is an earth covered with daisies orbiting a star. When the star was young it was cool and dark daisies covered the Earth and made it warmer by absorbing sunlight. As the star warmed up and got older, lighter daisies flourished and they reflected the star's heat and so cooled the earth down. It was an example that got him into a lot of trouble in the scientific world. But he and his colleagues have produced much evidence to support his theory.

Mary Midgley, a philosopher, calls Gaia 'the next big idea'. Like Kelly, she says that it is Cartesian dualism that has held back our thinking. 'Our moral, psychological and political ideas have all been armed against holism' (2001, p. 11).

Very fanciful, but is it more so that the 'behaviour' of the parasite plant? I, personally, believe that Kelly would be intrigued to know how others are seeing plants, the immune system and even the earth itself as 'construing' entities. Lovelock considers that there should be much more 'biodiversity' in science. That is, too much of science is divided into compartments such as biology, geology, chemistry and so forth. He says we need to combine biology with environmental sciences to be able to deal with the interaction he and others see as so important. That is what Kelly seems to be suggesting with his Alternative Fundamental Postulate. Dualism disappears completely, we are a construing system. One other point arises from Lovelock's ideas. If we were to conclude that there was something in his theory that is, indeed, relevant to construing, then perhaps we have a theory which would subsume personal construct theory itself. After all: *It is the nature of the earth to be channelized by the ways events are anticipated.*

AND SO, WHAT NOW?

A last quotation from George A. Kelly:

> ... what we know as the body of science, (is) in itself, an amazing display.
>
> But this is not the most exciting part of the story that history has to tell us. ... Infinitely more exciting is what potentiality these audacious feats suggest is locked up in the unrealized future of man. While the man of yesterday was developing a physicalistic science that tested itself by experiments and its ability to predict their outcomes, he was, without intending to do so, stating the basic postulates of a psychology for the man of tomorrow. Slowly he demonstrated not merely that events could be predicted, but, what was vastly more important, that he was a predictor. It was not only that hypotheses could be generated, experiments controlled, anticipations checked against realizations, and theories revised, but that he—man—was a hypothesizer, an experimenter, an anticipator, a critical observer, and an artful composer of new systems of thought. What he did, physically, portrayed what he was, psychologically. (Kelly, 1980, p. 23)

Theoretical Definitions

Kelly starts his Volume 2, which gives psychotherapy as an example of his theory 'at work', with definitions of his theoretical terms. After the Fundamental Postulate, which is 'the basic assumption upon which all else hinges', he details the eleven corollaries that elaborate it. He says: 'These, also, are assumptive in nature, and they lay the groundwork for most of what follows' (Kelly, 1955/1991, pp. 561–565/Vol. 2, pp. 4–8).

FUNDAMENTAL POSTULATE AND COROLLARIES

Fundamental Postulate: A person's processes are psychologically channelized by the ways in which he anticipates events.

Construction Corollary: A person anticipates events by construing their replications.

Individuality Corollary: Persons differ from each other in their constructions of events.

Organization Corollary: Each person characteristically evolves for his convenience in anticipating events, a construction system embracing ordinal relationships between constructs.

Dichotomy Corollary: A person's construction system is composed of a finite number of dichotomous constructs.

Choice Corollary: A person chooses for himself that alternative in a dichotomized construct through which he anticipates the greater possibility for extension and definition of his system.

Range Corollary: A construct is convenient for the anticipation of a finite range of events only.

Experience Corollary: A person's construction system varies as he successively construes the replication of events.

Modulation Corollary: The variation in a person's construction system is limited by the permeability of the constructs within whose ranges of convenience the variants lie.

Fragmentation Corollary: A person may successively employ a variety of construction subsystems which are inferentially incompatible with each other.

Commonality Corollary: To the extent that one person employs a construction of experience which is similar to that employed by another, his processes are psychologically similar to those of the other person (altered according to Kelly's footnote in Chapter 1 of this volume).

Sociality Corollary: To the extent that one person construes the construction processes of another he may play a role in a social process involving the other person.

FORMAL ASPECTS OF CONSTRUCTS

Range of Convenience: A construct's range of convenience comprises all those things to which the user would find its application useful.

Focus of Convenience: A construct's focus of convenience comprises those particular things to which the user would find its application maximally useful. These are the elements upon which the construct is likely to have been formed originally.

Elements: The things or events which are abstracted by a person's use of a construct are called elements. In some systems these are called objects.

Context: The context of a construct comprises those elements among which the user ordinarily discriminates by means of the construct. It is somewhat more restricted than the range of convenience, since it refers to the circumstances in which the construct emerges for practical use, and not necessarily to all the circumstances in which a person might eventually use the construct. It is somewhat more extensive than the focus of convenience, since the construct may often appear in circumstances where its application is not optimal.

Pole: Each construct discriminates between two poles, one at each end of its dichotomy. The elements abstracted are like each other at each pole with respect to the construct and are unlike the elements at the other pole.

Contrast: The relationship between the two poles of a construct is one of contrast.

Likeness End: When referring specifically to elements at one pole of a construct, one may use the term 'likeness end' to designate that pole.

Contrast End: When referring specifically to elements at one pole of a construct, one may use the term 'contrast end' to designate the opposite pole.

Emergence: The emergent pole of a construct is that one which embraces most of the immediately perceived context.

Implicitness: The implicit pole of a construct is that one which embraces contrasting context. It contrasts with the emergent pole. Frequently the person has no available symbol or name for it; it is symbolized only implicitly by the emergent term.

Symbol: An element in the context of a construct which represents not only itself but also the construct by which it is abstracted by the user is called the construct's symbol.

Permeability: A construct is permeable if it admits newly perceived elements to its context. It is impermeable if it rejects elements on the basis of their newness.

CONSTRUCTS CLASSIFIED ACCORDING TO THE NATURE OF THEIR CONTROL OVER THEIR ELEMENTS

Pre-emptive Construct: A construct which pre-empts its elements for membership in its own realm exclusively is called a pre-emptive construct. This is the 'nothing but' type of construction. 'If this is a torpedo it is nothing but a torpedo.'

Constellatory Construct: A construct which fixes the other realm memberships of its elements is called a constellatory construct. This is stereotyped thinking.

Propositional Construct: A construct which carries no implications regarding the other realm memberships of its elements is a propositional construct. This is uncontaminated construction.

GENERAL DIAGNOSTIC CONSTRUCTS

Preverbal Construct: A preverbal construct is one which continues to be used, even though it has no consistent word symbol. It may or may not have been devised before the client had command of speech symbolism.

Submergence: The submerged pole of a construct is the one which is less available for application to events.

Suspension: A suspended element is one which is omitted from the context of a construct as a result of revision of the client's construct system.

Level of Cognitive Awareness: The level of cognitive awareness ranges from high to low. A high-level construct is one which is readily expressed in socially effective symbols; whose alternatives are both readily accessible; which falls well within the range of convenience of the client's major constructions; and which is not suspended by its superordinating constructs.

Dilation: This occurs when a person broadens his or her perceptual field in order to reorganize it on a more comprehensive level. It does not, in itself, include the comprehensive reconstruction of those elements.

Constriction: Constriction occurs when a person narrows his or her perceptual field in order to minimize apparent incompatibilities.

Comprehensive Constructs: These are constructs that subsume a wide variety of events.

Incidental Constructs: These are constructs that subsume a narrow variety of events.

Superordinate Constructs: These are constructs that include others as one or more of the elements in their context.

Subordinate Constructs: These are constructs that are included as elements in the context of others.

Regnant Constructs: These are kinds of superordinate construct which assign each of their elements to a category on an all-or-none basis, as in classical logic. They tend to be non-abstractive.

Core Constructs: These are constructs that govern a person's maintenance processes.

Peripheral Constructs: These are constructs that can be altered without serious modification of the core structure.

Tight Constructs: These are constructs that lead to unvarying predictions.

Loose Constructs: These are constructs that lead to varying predictions, but retain their identity.

CONSTRUCTS RELATING TO TRANSITION

Threat: This is the awareness of an imminent comprehensive change in one's core structures.

Fear: This is the awareness of an imminent incidental change in one's core structures.

Anxiety: This is the awareness that the events with which one is confronted lie mostly outside the range of convenience of one's construct system.

Guilt: This is the awareness of dislodgement of the self from one's core role structure.

Aggressiveness: This is the active elaboration of one's perceptual field.

Hostility: This is the continued effort to extort validational evidence in favour of a type of social prediction which has already been recognized as a failure.

C–P–C Cycle: This cycle is a sequence of construction involving, in succession, circumspection, pre-emption, and control, and leading to a choice precipitating the person into a particular situation. (Later, Kelly suggested that 'control' be changed to 'choice'.)

Impulsivity: This is a characteristic foreshortening of the C–P–C Cycle.

Creativity Cycle: This is a cycle which starts with loosened construction and terminates with tightened and validated construction.

Some Basic Books on Personal Construct Psychology

General

Don Bannister and Fay Fransella (in production as an electronic book) *Inquiring Man* (3rd edn). London: Routledge.

Michael Bender (2003) *Explorations in Dementia: Theoretical and Research Studies into the Experience of Remediable and Enduring Cognitive Losses.* London: Jessica Kingsley Publishers.

Vivien Burr and Trevor Butt (1992) *Invitation to Personal Construct Psychology*. London: Whurr Publications (also in Chinese).

Peggy Dalton and Gavin Dunnett (1992) *A Psychology for Living*. Chichester: John Wiley & Sons.

Fay Fransella (1995) *George Kelly*. London: Sage Publications (also in Chinese).

Fay Fransella, Richard Bell and Don Bannister (in press). *A Manual for Repertory Grid Technique* (2nd edn). Chichester: John Wiley & Sons.

George A. Kelly (1955/1991) *The Psychology of Personal Constructs*, Volumes 1 and 2. London: Routledge.

Robert A. Neimeyer and Greg J. Neimeyer (Eds) *Advances in Personal Construct Psychology: New Directions and Perspectives*, Volume 5. New York: Praeger.

Dorothy Rowe (2002) *Friends and Enemies*. London: Harper Collins.

Bill Warren (1998) *Philosophical Dimensions of Personal Construct Psychology*. London: Routledge.

Counselling, Psychotherapy and Clinical Practice

Geoffrey Blowers and Kieron O'Connor (1996) *Personal Construct Psychology in the Clinical Context*. Ottawa: University of Ottawa Press.

Fay Fransella and Peggy Dalton (2000) *Personal Construct Counselling in Action* (2nd edn). London: Sage Publications.

Robert A. Neimeyer (Ed.) (2001) *Meaning Reconstruction and the Experience of Loss*. Washington, DC: American Psychological Association.

Robert A. Neimeyer (2002) *Lessons of Loss: A Guide to Coping* (2nd edn). New York: Brunner Routledge.

Robert A. Neimeyer and Jonathan Raskin (Eds) (2000) *Constructions of Disorder: Meaning-Making Frameworks for Psychotherapy*. Washington, DC: American Psychological Association.

Jonathan Raskin and Sara Bridges (Eds) (2002) *Studies in Meaning: Exploring Constructivist Psychology*. New York: Pace University Press.

Dorothy Rowe (2002) *Beyond Fear* (2nd edn). London: Harper Collins.

Dorothy Rowe (2003) *Depression: The Way Out of Your Prison* (3rd edn). London: Routledge.

Linda Viney (1996) *Personal Construct Therapy: A Handbook*. Norwood: Ablex Publishing Corporation.

David Winter (1992) *Personal Construct Psychology in Clinical Practice*. London: Routledge.

Working with Children

Richard Butler and David Green (1998) *The Child Within: The Exploration of Personal Construct Theory with Young People*. Oxford: Butterworth-Heinemann.

Tom Ravenette (1999) *Personal Construct Theory in Educational Psychology: A Practitioner's View*. London: Whurr Publications.

Culture and Society

Jim Horley (Ed.) (in press) *Personal Construct Perspectives on Forensic Psychology*. London: Brunner-Routledge.

Julia Houston (1998) *Making Sense with Offenders: Personal Constructs, Therapy and Change*. Chichester: John Wiley & Sons.

Devorah Kalekin-Fishman and Beverly Walker (1996) *The Construction of Group Realities: Culture, Society and Personal Construct Theory*. Malabar: Krieger.

Education

Pamela Denicolo and Maureen Pope (2001) *Transformative Professional Practice: Personal Construct Approaches to Education and Research*. London: Whurr Publications.

Maureen Pope and Pamela Denicolo (2001) *Transformative Education: Personal Construct Approaches to Practice and Research*. London: Whurr Publications.

The Family

Rudi Dallos (1994) *Family Belief Systems, Therapy and Change*. Milton Keynes: Open University Press.

Repertory Grids

Fay Fransella, Richard Bell and Don Bannister (in press) *A Manual for Repertory Grid Technique* (2nd edn). Chichester: John Wiley & Sons.

Devi Jankowicz (in press) *The Easy Guide to Repertory Grids*. Chichester: John Wiley & Sons.

There is also the *Journal of Constructivist Psychology*, published quarterly, and available from Taylor & Francis on e-mail: *online@tandfpa.com*.

SOME COURSES

Distance Learning

This is a six-modular programme on personal construct psychology and its method offered by The Centre for Personal Construct Psychology in the UK. The first two modules are combined into an Intermediate certificated course. These two modules provide a secure grounding in the basics of personal construct theory, its philosophy, its methods of assessment and some interpersonal skills. As far as possible, practical work focuses on the context within which the student works.

The grounding achieved in the first two modules is built upon in Advanced distance learning modules III, IV, V and VI. Each module covers four calendar months. The Advanced course includes monthly seminars, normally held in London. Special arrangements are made for those unable to attend the London seminars on a regular basis.

The personal work focuses on the individual needs of each participant, e.g. research work, work in organizations, clinical work or work with children.

A Diploma in the Applications of PCP in a specific area is offered by the Centre for Personal Construct Psychology, UK.

Full details of all modules from:

Professor Fay Fransella, The Sail Loft, Mulberry Quay, Falmouth TR11 3HD, UK
Tel: 01326 314 871; Fax: 01326 212 085; E-mail: *Ffransella@aol.com*

Training in Personal Construct Psychotherapy and Counselling

This is offered by *PCP Education and Training Limited*. Information can be obtained from Peggy Dalton, e-mail: *daltonpcp@talk21.com*.

Computer Programs and Websites

Supplied by **Richard Bell**

Sewell and colleagues (1992) have reviewed computer software for the elicitation and analysis of repertory grids available at the time. While the review is important for historical reasons, some of the programs continue to be available, such as OMNIGRID (Sewell et al., 1991) or FLEXIGRID (Tschudi, 1993). In general, computer programs are distributed by individuals and information about them is found on websites. At the present time the most up-to-date website is *http://www.pcp-net.de/info/index.html*. Intending users should monitor these sites as new programs are constantly being developed. Unless programs are described as 'freeware' there is a cost associated with obtaining them. Intending users should contact the source of the software to ascertain the current cost.

GRID ELICITATION SOFTWARE

REPGRID [see *http://repgrid.com/repgrid/*] provides grid elicitation procedures for Mac users, while FLEXIGRID [e-mail: *Finn.Tschudi@psykologi.uio.no*] or EnquireWithin [see *http://www.EnquireWithin.co.nz/*] provide elicitation procedures for PC machines. All of these programs also provide for the analysis of repertory grid data. There are usually two phases in the elicitation program. The first establishes the format of the elicitation, the second conducts the elicitation procedure. Freeware programs are available but are usually less sophisticated. There are some older programs written in the interpreter-Basic language, such as OMNIGRID or GPACK (Bell, 1987) which both elicit and analyse grids but require the presence of the interpreter program, while other elicitation-only freeware *are compiled basic programs* such as NEWGRID and RUNGRID (Bell, 2000b, 2000c) that do not require such support. These all need to be run under DOS which can be run from Windows. There is one web-based elicitation program, WEBGRID II (found at *http://repgrid.com/WebGrid/*) which is a simplified version of REPGRID, which also allows for both elicitation and analysis.

Grid Analysis Software

In addition to those mentioned above, there are a number of PC programs that can be used to analyse repertory grids. Unless otherwise stated, these run in a Windows environment.

- IDIOGRID [*http://www.idiogrid.com/*] contains a variant of Slater's original INGRID and a number of other univariate and bivariate statistics and measures.

- WINGRID [*http://homepages.ihug.co.nz/%7Eincome/tutor.htm*] is another variant of INGRID oriented to organizational use.
- GRIDLAB [*http://www.charite.de/psychosomatik/pages/forschung/groups/gridlab/index.html*] is a simple version of INGRID.
- GRIDCOR [*http://www.terapiacognitiva.net/record/gridcor.htm*] provides a correspondence analysis approach, a clustering representation, and some standard grid indices.
- GRIDSTAT (Bell, 1998) and GRIDSCAL (Bell, 1999) are freeware DOS programs: the former contains all of the major forms of analyses for a single grid, while the latter allows the analysis of multiple grids [see *http://www.pcp-net.de/info/index.html*].

References

Adams-Webber, J.R. (1969) Cognitive complexity and sociality. *British Journal of Social and Clinical Psychology*, **8**, 211–216.

Adams-Webber, J.R. (1970) Elicited versus provided constructs in repertory grid technique: a review. *British Journal of Medical Psychology*, **43**, 349–354.

Adams-Webber, J.R. (1979) *Personal Construct Theory: Concepts and Applications*. New York: John Wiley & Sons.

Adams-Webber, J.R. (1985) Self-other contrast and the development of personal constructs. *Canadian Journal of Behavioural Science*, **17**, 303–314.

Adams-Webber, J.R. (1989) Kelly's pragmatic constructivism. *Canadian Psychology*, **30**, 190–193.

Adams-Webber, J.R. (1990) Some fundamental asymmetries in the structure of personal constructs. In G.J. Neimeyer & R.A. Neimeyer (Eds) *Advances in Personal Construct Psychology*. Greenwich, CT: JAI Press.

Adams-Webber, J.R. (1992) Construct asymmetry and the range of relevance of personal anticipations. *European Journal of Social Psychology*, **22**, 465–481.

Adams-Webber, J.R. (1993) The robot's designer's dilemma. *American Journal of Psychology*, **106**, 300–303.

Adams-Webber, J.R. (1996a) Personal construct theory. In R. Corsini & A.J. Auerbach (Eds) *Encyclopedia of Psychology*. New York: John Wiley & Sons.

Adams-Webber, J.R. (1996b) Cognitive complexity. In R. Corsini & A.J. Auerbach (Eds) *Encyclopedia of Psychology*. New York: John Wiley & Sons.

Adams-Webber, J.R. (1997a) Positive-negative asymmetry in the evaluation of familiar versus unfamiliar persons and objects. *Journal of Constructivist Psychology*, **10**, 139–152.

Adams-Webber, J.R. (1997b) Self-reflexion in evaluating others. *American Journal of Psychology*, **119**, 527–541.

Adams-Webber, J.R. (1998) Differentiation and sociality in terms of elicited and provided constructs. *Psychological Science*, **9**, 499–501.

Adams-Webber, J.R. (2001a) Prototypicality of self and evaluating others in terms of 'fuzzy' constructs. *Journal of Constructivist Psychology*, **14**, 315–324.

Adams-Webber, J.R. (2001b) Cognitive complexity and role relationships. *Journal of Constructivist Psychology*, **14**, 43–50.

Adams-Webber, J.R. (in press) Cognitive complexity and evaluating self. *Journal of Constructivist Psychology*.

Adams-Webber, J.R. & Rodney, Y. (1983) Relational aspects of temporary changes in construing self and others. *Canadian Journal of Behavioural Science*, **15**, 52–59.

Alexander, P.C., Neimeyer, R.A. & Follette, V.M. (1991) Group therapy for women sexually abused as children: a controlled study and investigation of individual differences. *Journal of Interpersonal Violence*, **6**, 219–231.

Alexander, P.C., Neimeyer, R.A., Follette, V.M., Moore, M.K. & Harter, S. (1989) A comparison of group treatments of women sexually abused as children. *Journal of Consulting and Clinical Psychology*, **57**, 479–483.

Alford, J., Cairney, C., Higgs, R., Honsowetz, M., Huynh, V., Jines, A., Keates, D. & Skelton, C. (2000) Real rewards from artificial intelligence. *InTech*, 52–55.

Andersen, T. (1987) The reflecting team. *Family Process*, **26**, 415–428.

Anderson, J.R. (1983) *The Architecture of Cognition*. Cambridge, MA: Harvard University Press.

Anderson, M.B. (Ed.) (2001) *Doing Sport Psychology*. Champaign, IL: Human Kinetics.

Apelgren, B.M. (2001) *Foreign Language Teachers' Voices: Personal Theories and Experiences of Change in Teaching English as a Foreign Language in Sweden*. Gothenburg: University of Gothenburg Press.

Applebee, A.N. (1975) Developmental change in consensus of construing. *British Journal of Psychology*, **66**, 473–480.

Applegate, J.L. (1990) Constructs and communication: a pragmatic integration. In G.J. Neimeyer & R.A. Neimeyer (Eds) *Advances in Personal Construct Psychology*, Volume 1. Greenwich, CT: JAI Press.

Applegate, J.L., Kline, S.L. & Delia, J.G. (1991) Alternative measures of cognitive complexity as predictors of communication performance. *International Journal of Personal Construct Psychology*, **4**, 193–213.

Argyris, C., Puttnam D. & McClain Smith, D. (1985) *Action Science*. San Francisco: Jossey-Bass.

Armstrong, T. & Eden, C. (1979) An exploration of occupational role: an exercise in team building. *Personnel Review*, **8**, 20–23.

Bachrach, P. & Baratz, M. (1970) *Power and Poverty*. New York: Oxford University Press.

Bakan, D. (1966) *On Method: Toward a Reconstruction of Psychological Investigation*. Washington, DC: Jossey-Bass.

Balnaves, M. & Caputi, P. (2000) A theory of social action: why personal construct psychology needs a superpattern corollary. *Journal of Constructivist Psychology*, **13**, 117–134.

Bannister, D. (1960) Conceptual structure in thought-disordered schizophrenics. *Journal of Mental Science*, **106**, 1230–1249.

Bannister, D. (1962) Personal construct theory. *Acta Psychologica*, **20**, 104–120.

Bannister, D. (1963) The genesis of schizophrenic thought disorder: a serial invalidation hypothesis. *British Journal of Psychiatry*, **109**, 680–686.

Bannister, D. (1965) The genesis of schizophrenic thought disorder: re-test of the serial invalidation hypothesis. *British Journal of Psychiatry*, **111**, 377–382.

Bannister, D. (1966a) A new theory of personality. In B. Foss (Ed.) *New Horizons in Psychology*. Harmondsworth: Penguin.

Bannister, D. (1966b) Psychology as an exercise in paradox. *Bulletin of the British Psychological Society*, **19**, 21–26.

Bannister, D. (1968) The myth of physiological psychology. *Bulletin of the British Psychological Society*, **21**, 229–231.

Bannister, D. (1975) Personal construct theory psychotherapy. In D. Bannister (Ed.) *Issues and Approaches in the Psychological Therapies*. London: John Wiley & Sons.

Bannister, D. (1983) Self in personal construct theory. In J.R. Adams-Webber & J.C. Mancuso (Eds) *Applications of Personal Construct Theory*. Toronto: Academic Press.

Bannister, D. (1985) Foreword in N. Beail (Ed.) *Repertory Grid Technique and Personal Constructs: Applications in Clinical and Education Settings*. Cambridge, MA: Brookline Books.

Bannister, D., Adams-Webber, J.R., Penn, W.I. & Radley, P.L. (1975) Reversing the process of thought disorder: a serial validation experiment. *British Journal of Social and Clinical Psychology*, **14**, 169–180.

Bannister, D. & Agnew, J. (1977) The child's construing of self. In J.K. Cole & A.W. Landfield (Eds) *1976 Nebraska Symposium on Motivation*. Lincoln: University of Nebraska Press.

Bannister, D. & Fransella, F. (1967) *Grid Test of Schizophrenic Thought Disorder*. Barnstaple: Psychological Test Publications.

Bannister, D. & Fransella, F. (1986) *Inquiring Man* (3rd edition). London: Routledge.

Bannister, D., Fransella, F. & Agnew, J. (1971) Characteristics and validity of the Grid Test of Thought Disorder. *British Journal of Social and Clinical Psychology*, **10**, 144–151.

Bannister, D. & Mair, J.M.M. (1968) *The Evaluation of Personal Constructs*. London: Academic Press.

Bannister, D. & Salmon, P. (1966) Schizophrenic thought disorder: specific or diffuse? *British Journal of Medical Psychology*, **39**, 215–219.

Barfield, O. (1988) *Saving the Appearances: Study in Idolatry* (2nd edition). Middletown, CT: Wesleyan University Press.

Barnes, K.E. (1990) An examination of nurses' feelings about patients with specific feeding needs. *Journal of Advanced Nursing*, **15**, 703–711.

Bartol, C.R. & Bartol, A.M. (1999) History of forensic psychology. In A. Hess & I.B. Weiner (Eds) *The Handbook of Forensic Psychology*. New York: John Wiley & Sons.

Bauman, S. (1973) *Sociology as Praxis*. London: Routledge.

Beail, N. & Parker, C. (1991) Group fixed role therapy: a clinical application. *International Journal of Personal Construct Psychology*, **4**, 85–96.

Beaver, R. (1996) *Educational Psychology Casework*. London: Jessica Kingsley Publications.

Beck, A.T. (1976) *Cognitive Therapy and the Emotional Disorders*. New York: International Universities Press.

Beck, C.J. (1993) *Nothing Special: Living Zen*. San Francisco: Harper & Row.

Beckhard, R. & Harris, R. (1977) *Organisation Transitions: Managing Complex Change*. Reading, MA: Addison-Wesley.

Bell, B. & Gilbert, J. (1996) *Teacher Development: A Model from Science Education*. London: Falmer Press.

Bell, R.C. (1987) *G_PACK: A computer program for the elicitation and analysis of repertory grids*. Unpublished report, Department of Psychology, University of Wollongong, Australia.

Bell, R.C. (1988) Theory-appropriate analysis of repertory grid data. *International Journal of Personal Construct Psychology*, **1**, 101–118.

Bell, R.C. (1990a) Analytic issues in the use of the repertory grid technique. In G.J. Neimeyer & R.A. Neimeyer (Eds) *Advances in Personal Construct Psychology*, Volume 1. New York: JAI Press.

Bell, R.C. (1990b) Repertory grids as mental tests: implications of test theories for grids. *International Journal of Personal Construct Psychology*, **3**, 91–103.

Bell, R.C. (1994) *Using SPSS to Analyse Repertory Grid Data*. Unpublished report, School of Behavioural Science, University of Melbourne, Australia.

Bell, R.C. (1996) How can personal construct theory explain disorders of perception and cognition? In B. Walker, J. Costigan, L. Viney & R. Warren (Eds) *Personal Construct Theory: A Psychology for the Future*. Sydney: Australian Psychological Society.

Bell, R.C. (1998) *GRIDSTAT: A Program for Analysing the Data of a Repertory Grid*. [Computer software] Melbourne: Author.

Bell, R.C. (1999) *GRIDSCAL: A Program for Analysing the Data of Multiple Repertory Grids*. [Computer software] Melbourne: Author.

Bell, R.C. (2000a) On testing the commonality of constructs in supplied grids. *Journal of Constructivist Psychology*, **13**, 303–311.

Bell, R.C. (2000b) *NEWGRID: A Program for Setting Up the Data Collection of Repertory Grids*. [Computer software] Melbourne: Author.

Bell, R.C. (2000c) *RUNGRID: A Program for the Collection of Repertory Grid Data*. [Computer software] Melbourne: Author.

Bell, R.C. (2000d) Why do statistics with repertory grids? In J. Scheer (Ed.) *The Person in Society: Challenges to a Constructivist Theory*. Giessen, Germany: Psychosozial-Verlag.

Bell, R.C. (2001) Some new measures of the dispersion of dependency in a situation-resource grid. *Journal of Constructivist Psychology*, **14**, 303–311.

Bell, R.C. & Keen, T.R. (1981) A statistical aid for the grid administrator. In M.L.G. Shaw (Ed.) *Recent Advances in Personal Construct Technology*. London: Academic Press.

Bell, R.C., Vince, J. & Costigan, J. (2002) Which vary more in repertory grid data: constructs or elements? *Journal of Constructivist Psychology*, **15**, 305–312.

Benjafield, J.G. (1996) *A History of Psychology*. Boston: Allyn & Bacon.

Ben-Peretz, M. (1984) Kelly's theory of personal constructs as a paradigm for investigating teacher thinking. In R. Halkes & J.K. Olson (Eds) *Teacher Thinking: A New Perspective on Persisting Problems in Education*. Lisse: Swets & Zeitlinger.

Ben-Peretz, M. & Kalekin-Fishman, D. (1988) Applying PCP to constructs related to music. In F. Fransella & L. Thomas (Eds) *Experimenting with Personal Construct Psychology*. London: Routledge.

Berger, P.L. & Luckmann, T. (1966) *The Social Construction of Reality: A Treatise in the Sociology of Knowledge.* Garden City, NY: Doubleday.

Bieri, J. (1955) Cognitive complexity–simplicity and predictive behavior. *Journal of Abnormal and Social Psychology*, **51**, 263–286.

Billig, M. (1987) *Arguing and Thinking: a Rhetorical Approach to Social Psychology.* Cambridge: Cambridge University Press.

Bivens, A.J., Neimeyer, R.A., Kirchberg, T.M. & Moore, M.K. (1994) Death concern and religious belief among gays and bisexuals of variable proximity to AIDS. *Omega*, **30**, 105–120.

Blackler, F. (1995) Knowledge, work and organisations: an overview and interpretation. *Organisational Studies*, **16**, 1021–1046.

Blowers, G. (1995) Notes from afar: Kelly in Hong Kong and China. *NAPCN News* (May), pp. 1–3.

Blowers, G.H. & Bacon-Shone, J. (1994) On detecting the differences in jazz: a reassessment of comparative methods of measuring perceptual veridicality. *Empirical Studies of the Arts*, **12**, 41–58.

Blowers, G. & McCoy, M.M. (1986) Perceiving cinematic episodes: a cross-cultural repertory grid study of a narrative film segment. *International Journal of Psychology*, **21**, 317–332.

Boei, F., Corporaal, A. & Wim, H. (1989) Describing teacher cognitions with the rep grid. In J. Lowyck & C.M. Clark (Eds) *Teacher Thinking and Professional Action.* Leuven: Leuven University Press.

Bohart, A.C., OHara, M. & Leitner, L.M. (1998) Empirically violated treatments: disenfranchisement of humanistic and other psychotherapies. *Psychotherapy Research*, **8**, 141–157.

Bohm, D. (1996) *On Dialogue.* London: Routledge.

Bonarius, J.C.J. (1965) Research in the personal construct theory of George A. Kelly: role construct repertory test and basic theory. In B.A. Maher (Ed.) *Progress in Experimental Personality Research*, Volume 2. New York: Academic Press.

Bonarius, H. (1977) The interaction model of communication. In J.K. Cole & A.W. Landfield (Eds) *1976 Nebraska Symposium on Motivation.* Lincoln: University of Nebraska Press.

Boose, J.H. (1984) Personal construct theory and the transfer of human expertise. In *Proceedings AAAI-84.* California: American Association for Artificial Intelligence, pp. 27–33.

Boose, J.H. (1986) *Expertise Transfer for Expert Systems.* Amsterdam: Elsevier.

Botella, L. (2000) Personal construct psychology, constructivism, and psychotherapy research. In J.W. Scheer (Ed.) *The Person in Society: Challenges to a Constructivist Theory.* Giessen, Germany: Psychosozial-Verlag.

Botella, L. & Feixas, G. (1992–1993) The autobiographical group: a tool for the reconstruction of past life experience with the aged. *International Journal of Aging and Human Development*, **36**, 303–319.

Bourdieu, P. (1977) *Outline of a Theory of Practice.* Cambridge, UK: Cambridge University Press.

Bourland, D.D. & Johnston, P.D. (1991) *To Be or Not: An E-prime Anthology.* San Francisco: International Society for General Semantics.

Brewster-Smith, M. (1977) Metapsychology, politics and human needs. In R. Fitzgerald (Ed.) *Human Needs and Politics.* Oxford: Pergamon Press.

Bright, J.C. (1985) *A pack of lies.* Unpublished dissertation. London: Centre for Personal Construct Psychology, UK.

Brophy, S. (2002) *Organisation development interventions using PCP.* Paper read at the 6th Conference of the European Personal Construct Association, Florence, Italy.

Brophy, S. & Epting, F.R. (1996) Mentoring employees: a role for personal construct psychology. In B.M. Walker, J. Costigan, L.L. Viney & B. Warren (Eds) *Personal Construct Theory: Psychology for the Future.* Carlton, South Victoria: The Australian Psychological Society.

Brown, R.W. (1958) Is a boulder sweet or sour? *Contemporary Psychology*, **3**, 113–115.

Bruner, J.S. (1956) A cognitive theory of personality. *Contemporary Psychology*, **1**, 355–358.

Bruner, J.S. (1986) *Actual Minds, Possible Worlds.* Cambridge, MA: Harvard University Press.

Bruner, J.S. (1990) *Acts of Meaning*. Cambridge, MA: Harvard University Press.

Bugental, J.F.T. (1964) Investigations into the self-concept: instructions for the Who-Are-You method. *Psychological Reports*, **15**, 634–650.

Burleson, B.R., Applegate, J.L. & Delia, J.G. (1991) On validly assessing the validity of the Role Category Questionnaire. *Communication Reports*, **4**, 113–119.

Burrell, M.J. (2002) Deconstructing and reconstructing substance use and 'addictions'. In R.A. Neimeyer & G.J. Neimeyer (Eds) *Advances in Personal Construct Psychology*, Volume 5. New York: Praeger.

Burrell, M.J. & Jaffe, A.J. (1999) Personal meaning, drug use, and addiction: an evolutionary constructivist perspective. *Journal of Constructivist Psychology*, **12**, 41–63.

Butler, C. (1995) Investigating the effects of stress on the success and failure of music conservatory students. In *Medical Problems of Performing Artists*. Philadelphia, PA: Hanley & Belfus.

Butler, R.J. (1996) *Performance Profiling*. National Coaching Foundation. Leeds, England: Coachwise.

Butler, R.J. (2001) *The Self Image Profiles: Manual*. London: The Psychological Corporation.

Butler, R.J. & Green, D. (1998) *The Child Within: The Exploration of Personal Construct Theory with Young People*. Oxford: Butterworth-Heinemann.

Butt, T. (1995) Ordinal relationships between constructs. *Journal of Constructivist Psychology*, **8**, 227–836.

Butt, T. (1996) PCP: cognitive or social psychology. In J.W. Scheer & A. Catina (Eds) *Empirical Constructivism in Europe: The Personal Construct Approach*. Geissen: Psychosozial-Verlag.

Butt, T., Burr, V. & Epting, F.R. (1997a) Core construing: self-discovery or self-invention? In G.J. Neimeyer & R.A. Neimeyer (Eds) *Advances in Personal Construct Psychology*, Volume 4. Greenwich, CT: JAI Press.

Butt, T., Burr, V. & Bell, R. (1997b) Fragmentation and the sense of self. *Constructivism in the Human Sciences*, **2**, 12–29.

Button, E.J. (1980) *Construing and clinical outcome in anorexia nervosa*. Unpublished PhD thesis, University of London.

Button, E.J. (1987) Construing people or weight? An eating disorders group. In R.A. and G.J. Neimeyer (Eds) *Personal Construct Therapy Casebook*. New York: Springer.

Button, E.J. (1988) Music and personal constructs. In F. Fransella & L. Thomas (Eds) *Experimenting with Personal Construct Psychology*. London: Routledge.

Button, E.J. (1993) *Eating Disorders: Personal Construct Therapy and Change*. Chichester, UK: John Wiley & Sons.

Caputi, P., Breiger, R. & Pattison, P. (1990) Analyzing implications grids using hierarchical models. *International Journal of Personal Construct Psychology*, **3**, 77–90.

Caputi, P. & Keynes, N. (2001) A note on the stability of structural measures based on repertory grids. *Journal of Constructivist Psychology*, **14**, 51–55.

Caputi, P. & Reddy, P. (1999) A comparison of triadic and dyadic methods of personal construct elicitation. *Journal of Constructivist Psychology*, **12**, 253–264.

Carnahan, T.E. (1988) *Rapists' perceptions of women: A repertory grid study*. Unpublished BA (honours) thesis, Guelph: University of Guelph.

Carr, J. & Townes, B. (1975) Interpersonal discrimination as a function of age and psychopathology. *Child Psychiatry and Human Development*, **5**, 209–215.

Chandler, A.D. Jr (1977) *The Visible Hand: The Managerial Revolution in American Business*. Cambridge, MA: Harvard University Press.

Chiari, G. (2000) Personal construct theory and the constructivist family: a friendship to cultivate, a marriage not to celebrate. In J.W. Scheer (Ed.) *The Person in Society: Challenges to a Constructivist Theory*. Giessen, Germany: Psychosozial-Verlag.

Chiari, G., Mancini, F., Nicolo, F. & Nuzzo, M.L. (1990) Hierarchical organization of personal construct systems in terms of the range of convenience. *International Journal of Personal Construct Psychology*, **3**, 281–311.

Chiari, G. & Nuzzo, M.L. (1996a) Personal construct theory within psychological constructivism: precursor or avant-garde? In B.M. Walker, J. Costigan, L.L. Viney & B. Warren

(Eds) *Personal Construct Theory: a Psychology for the Future*. Sydney: The Australian Psychological Society.

Chiari, G. & Nuzzo, M.L. (1996b) Psychological constructivisms: a metatheoretical differentiation. *Journal of Constructivist Psychology*, **9**, 163–184.

Chin-Keung, L. (1988) PCT interpretation of sexual involvement with children. In F. Fransella & L. Thomas (Eds) *Experimenting with Personal Construct Psychology*. London: Routledge.

Clancey, W.J. (1989) Viewing knowledge bases as qualitative models. *IEEE Expert*, **4**, 9–23.

Clapp, R. & Cornelius, N. (2002) *New views on equality action in organisations*. Paper read at the 6th Congress of the European Personal Construct Association, Florence, Italy.

Clark, C.M. (1986) Ten years of conceptual development in research on teacher thinking. In M. Ben-Peretz, R. Bromme & R. Halkes (Eds) *Advances in Research on Teacher Thinking*. Lisse, Netherlands: Swets & Zeitlinger.

Clark, C.M. (1995) *Thoughtful Teaching*. London: Cassell.

Clinton, M., Moyle, W., Weir, D. & Edwards, H. (1995) Perceptions of stressors and reported coping strategies in nurses caring for residents with Alzheimer's disease in a dementia unit. *Australian and New Zealand Journal of Mental Health Nursing*, **4**, 5–13.

Coish, B.J. (1990) *A personal construct theory of bulimia*. Unpublished PhD thesis, La Trobe University, Australia.

Collins, D. (1998) *Organizational Change: Sociological Perspectives*. London: Routledge.

Cornelius, N. (Ed.) (2002) *Building Workplace Equality: Ethics, Diversity and Inclusion*. London: Thomson.

Cortazzi, D. & Root, S. (1975) *Illuminative Incident Analysis*. London: McGraw-Hill.

Costigan, J. (1985) Personal construct psychology: a theoretical and methodological framework for nursing research. *The Australian Journal of Advanced Nursing*, **2**, 15–23.

Costigan, J., Closs, B. & Eustace, P. (2000) Laddering: theoretical and methodological contingencies—some order and a little chaos. In J.W. Scheer (Ed.) *The Person in Society: Challenges to a Constructivist Theory*. Giessen, Germany: Psychosozial-Verlag.

Costigan, J., Humphrey, J. & Murphy, C. (1987) Attempted suicide: a personal construct psychology exploration. *The Australian Journal of Advanced Nursing*, **4**, 39–50.

Crispin, W.M. (1990) *The personal myths, mysteries and metaphors of student nurses as they adapt to the educational process*. Paper presented at the 4th National Nursing Education Conference, Melbourne.

Crockett, W.H. (1982) The organization of construct systems. In J.C. Mancuso & J. Adams-Webber (Eds) *The Construing Person*. New York: Praeger.

Cromwell, R.L. (1961) *Factoring the Rep Test*. Unpublished manuscript.

Cromwell, R.L. & Caldwell, D.F. (1962) A comparison of ratings based on personal constructs of self and others. *Journal of Clinical Psychology*, **18**, 43–46.

Cummins, P. (1996) Britain after the Chunnel. In J.W. Scheer & A. Catina (Eds) *Empirical Constructivism in Europe*. Giessen, Germany: Psychosozial-Verlag.

Cummins, P. (2000) Snakes in Ireland (Europe's matrix of decision revisited). In J.W. Scheer (Ed.) *The Person In Society: Challenges to a Constructivist Theory*. Giessen, Germany: Psychosozial-Verlag.

Cummins, P. (2002) 'Wo kommst Du her?'—Die Bedeutung des verorteten Selbst. In J.W. Scheer (Ed.) *Identität in der Gesellschaft*. Giessen, Germany: Psychosozial-Verlag, (English version: Where are you from?—The importance of the located self. http://www.pcp-net.de/papers/cummins02.pdf).

Dallos, R. (1991) *Family Belief Systems, Therapy and Change: A Constructional Approach*. Milton Keynes: Open University Press.

Davidson, G. & Reser, J. (1996) Construing and constructs: personal and cultural? In B.M. Walker, J. Costigan, L.L. Viney & B. Warren (Eds) *Personal Construct Theory: A Psychology for the Future*. Australian Psychological Society Imprint Book.

Davies, J. (1976) Orchestral discord. *New Society*, 8 January, pp. 46–47.

DeCasper, A.J. & Spence, M.J. (1988) Prenatal maternal speech influences newborns' perception of speech sounds. In S. Chess, A. Thomas & M. Hertzig (Eds) *Annual Progress in Child Psychiatry and Child Development*. New York: Brunner/Mazel.

Delia, J.G., Gonyea, A. & Crockett, W.H. (1971) The effects of subject generated and normative constructs upon the formation of impressions. *British Journal of Social and Clinical Psychology*, **10**, 301–305.

Dempsey, D.J. & Neimeyer, R.A. (1995) Organization of personal knowledge: convergent validation of implications grids and repertory grids as measures of system structure. *Journal of Constructivist Psychology*, **8**, 251–261.

Denicolo, P.M. & Pope, M.L. (1990) Adults learning–teacher thinking. In C. Day, M.L. Pope & P.M. Denicolo (Eds) *Insight into Teachers' Thinking and Practice*. London: Falmer Press.

Denicolo, P.M. & Pope, M.L. (2001) *Transformative Professional Practice: Personal Construct Approaches to Education and Research*. London: Whurr Publishers.

Dewey, J. (1931) *Philosophy and Civilization*. New York: Minton, Balch & Co.

Dewey, J. (1934) *A Common Faith*. New Haven: Yale University Press.

Dewey, J. (1968) The development of American pragmatism. In his *Philosophy and Civilization*. Gloucester, MA: Peter Smith. Original work published 1932.

Dewey, J. (1966) *Democracy and Education*. New York: Free Press. Original work published 1916.

Diamond, C.P.T. (1985) Fixed role treatment: enacting alternative scenarios. *Australian Journal of Education*, **29**, 161–173.

Diamond, C.P.T. (1991) *Teacher Education as Transformation*. Milton Keynes: Open University Press.

Diamond, P. & Thompson, M. (1985) Using personal construct theory to assess a midwives' refresher course. *The Australian Journal of Advanced Nursing*, **2**, 24–35.

DiLollo, A., Neimeyer, R.A. & Manning, W.H. (2001) A personal construct psychology view of relapse: indications for a narrative therapy component to stuttering treatment. *Journal of Fluency Disorders*, **26**, 1–24.

Dilthey, W. (1924) Die Natur erklären wir, das Seelenleben verstehen wir. In *Gesammelte Schriften, Vol. V: Die geistige Welt. Einleitung in die Philosophie des Lebens. 1: Abhandlungen zur Grundlegung der Geisteswissenschaften*. Leipzig.

Dreyfus, H.L. & Dreyfus, S.E. (1986) *Mind Over Machine: The Power of Human Intuition and Expertise in the Era of the Computer*. New York: Free Press.

Du Preez, P. (1979) Politics and identity in South Africa. In P. Stringer & D. Bannister (Eds) *Constructs of Sociality and Individuality*. London: Academic Press.

Du Preez, P. (1980) *Social Psychology of Politics*. Oxford: Basil Blackwell.

Duck, S.W. (1973) *Personal Relationships and Personal Constructs*. New York: John Wiley & Sons.

Duck, S.W. & Spencer, C. (1972) Personal constructs and friendship formation. *Journal of Personality and Social Psychology*, **23**, 40–45.

Dunn, W.N., Cahill, A.G., Dukes, M.J. & Ginsberg, A. (1986) The policy grid: a cognitive methodology for assessing policy dynamics. In W.N. Dunn (Ed.) *Policy Analysis: Perspectives, Concepts, and Methods*. New York: JAI Press.

Dunnett, N.G.M. & Miyaguchi, R. (1993) Reflexivity in theory and practice. In L.M. Leitner & N.G.M. Dunnett (Eds) *Critical Issues in Personal Construct Psychotherapy*. Malabar, FL: Krieger.

Durkheim, E. (1964/1895) *Rules of Sociological Method*. New York: Free Press.

Dyson, J. (1996) Nurses' conceptualizations of caring attitudes and behaviours. *Journal of Advanced Nursing*, **23**, 1263–1269.

Ecker, B. & Hulley, L. (1996) *Depth-Oriented Brief Therapy*. San Francisco: Jossey Bass.

Edwards, B. (1998) A & E nurses' constructs on the nature of nursing expertise: a repertory grid technique. *Accident and Emergency Nursing*, **6**, 18–23.

Efran, J.S., Lukens, M.D. & Lukens, R.J. (1990) *Language, Structure, and Change*. New York: Norton.

Ellis, J. (1992) *A personal construct approach to perceptions of care: The registered nurse and the elderly nursing home resident*. Unpublished masters dissertation.

Ellis, J. (1996) He was big and old and frightening: nursing students constructs' of older people. In B.M. Walker, J. Costigan, L.L. Viney & W. Warren (Eds) *Personal Construct Theory: A Psychology for the Future*. Melbourne: Australian Psychological Society.

Ellis, J. (1997) Nurses' anticipations of caring for elderly patients. In P.M. Denicolo & M.L. Pope (Eds) *Sharing Understanding and Practice*. Farnborough: EPCA Publications.

Ellis, J. (1999) Nursing care of older people: a personal construct theory perspective. *Journal of Advanced Nursing*, **29**, 160–168.

Ellis-Scheer, J. (2000) *The professional identity of nurses: An empirical investigation of personal constructions using the repertory grid technique*. Unpublished doctoral dissertation.

Epting, F.R. (1984) *Personal Construct Counseling and Psychotherapy*. Chichester: John Wiley & Sons.

Epting, F.R. & Nazario, A.Jr. (1987) Designing a fixed role therapy: issues, techniques, and modifications. In R.A. Neimeyer & G.J. Neimeyer (Eds) *Personal Construct Therapy Casebook*. New York: Springer.

Epting, F.R., Prichard, S., Wiggins, S.C., Leonard, J.A. & Beagle, J.W. (1992) Assessment of the first factor and related measures of construct differentiation. *International Journal of Personal Construct Psychology*, **5**, 77–94.

Epting, F.R., Probert, J.S. & Pittman, S.D. (1993) Alternative strategies for construct elicitation: experimenting with experience. *International Journal of Personal Construct Psychology*, **6**, 79–98.

Epting, F.R. & Suchman, D.I. (1999) The therapist's use of self and personal experience. In A.C. Richards & T. Schumrum (Eds) *Invitations to Dialogue: The Legacy of Sidney M. Jourard*. Dubuque, IA: Kendall/Hunt.

Evesham, M. & Fransella, F. (1985) Stuttering relapse: the effects of a combined speech and psychological reconstruction program. *British Journal of Disorders of Communication*, **20**, 237–248.

Eysenck, H.J. (1977) *Crime and Personality* (2nd edition). London: Routledge.

Faidley, A.J. & Leitner, L.M. (2000) The poetry of our lives: symbolism in experiential personal construct psychotherapy. In J.W. Scheer (Ed.) *The Person in Society: Challenges to a Constructivist Theory*. Giessen, Germany: Psychosozial-Verlag.

Feigenbaum, E.A. (1980) Knowledge engineering: the applied side of artificial intelligence. STAN-CS-80–812, Department of Computer Science, Stanford University.

Feigenbaum, E.A., Buchanan, B.G. & Lederberg, J. (1971) On generality and problem solving: a case study using the DENDRAL program. In D. Michie (Eds) *Machine Intelligence 6*. Edinburgh: Edinburgh University Press.

Feixas, G. (1995) Personal constructs in systemic practice. In R.A. Neimeyer & M. Mahoney (Eds) *Constructivism in Psychotherapy*. Washington, DC: American Psychological Association.

Feixas, G., Geldschläger, H. & Neimeyer, R.A. (2002) Content analysis of personal constructs. *Journal of Constructivist Psychology*, **15**, 1–9.

Feixas, G., Moliner, J.L., Montes, J.N., Mari, M.T. & Neimeyer, R.A. (1992) The stability of structural measures derived from repertory grids. *International Journal of Personal Construct Psychology*, **5**, 25–39.

Fenichel, O. (1963) *Psychoanalytic Theory of Neurosis*. London: Routledge.

Feyerabend, P. (1984) Science as art. *Art and Text*, **12–13**, 16–48.

Fisher & Brown (1989) *Getting Together: Building a Relationship That Gets to Yes*. London: Business Books.

Fisher, R. & Ury, W. (1991) *Getting to Yes: Negotiating Agreement Without Giving In* (2nd edition). London: Penguin.

Flavell, J.H. (1963) *The Developmental Psychology of Jean Piaget*. Princeton: Van Nostrand.

Fleck, J. (1982) Development and establishment in artificial intelligence. In N. Elias, H. Martins & R. Whitley (Eds) *Scientific Establishments and Hierarchies*. Holland: D. Reidel.

Fodor, J. (1983) *The Modularity of Mind*. Cambridge, MA: MIT Press.

Ford, K.M. (1989) A constructivist view of the frame problem in artificial intelligence. *Canadian Psychology*, **30**, 188–190.

Ford, K.M., Bradshaw, J.M., Adams-Webber, J.R. & Agnew, N.M. (1993) Knowledge acquisition as a constructive modeling activity. *International Journal of Intelligent Systems*, **8**, 9–32.

Forrester J. (1993) Systems Dynamics and the lessons of 35 years. In K.B. De Greene (Ed.) *A Systems-Based Approach to Policymaking*. Boston: Kluwer Academic Publishers.

Forster, J.R. (1991) Facilitating positive changes in self-constructions. *International Journal of Personal Construct Psychology*, **4**, 281–292.

Fransella, F. (1970) Stuttering, not a symptom but a way of life. *British Journal of Communication Disorders*, **5**, 22.

Fransella, F. (1972) *Personal Change and Reconstruction*. London: Academic Press.

Fransella, F. (1981) Nature babbling to herself. In H. Bonarius, R. Holland & S. Rosenburg (Eds) *Personal Construct Psychology: Recent Advances in Theory and Practice*. London: Macmillan.

Fransella, F. (1983) What sort of scientist is the person-as-scientist? In J.R. Adams-Webber & J.C. Mancuso (Eds) *Applications of Personal Construct Theory*. Ontario: Academic Press.

Fransella, F. (1988) The ideographic research unit of the Centre for Personal Construct Psychology. In F. Fransella & L. Thomas (Eds) *Experimenting with Personal Construct Psychology*. London: Routledge.

Fransella, F. (1995) *George Kelly*. London: Sage Publications.

Fransella, F. (2000) George Kelly and mathematics. In J.W. Scheer (Ed.) *The Person in Society: Challenges to a Constructivist Theory*. Giessen, Germany: Psychosozial-Verlag.

Fransella, F. & Adams, B. (1966) An illustration of the use of repertory grid technique in a clinical setting. *British Journal of Social and Clinical Psychology*, **5**, 51–62.

Fransella, F. & Bannister, D. (1967) A validation of repertory grid technique as a measure of political construing. *Acta Psychologica*, **26**, 97–106.

Fransella, F. & Bannister, D. (1977) *A Manual for Repertory Grid Technique*. London: Academic Press.

Fransella, F., Bell, R. & Bannister, D. (in press) *A Manual for Repertory and Technique* (2nd edn). Chichester: John Wiley & Sons, Ltd.

Frisbie, L., Vanasek, F. & Dingman, H. (1967) The self and the ideal self: methodological study of pedophiles. *Psychological Reports*, **20**, 699–706.

Gagnon, S. & Cornelius, N. (2000) Re-examining workplace inequality: the capabilities approach. *Human Resource Management Journal*, **10**, 68–87.

Gaines, B.R. & Shaw, M.L.G. (1980) New directions in the analysis and interactive elicitation of personal construct systems. *International Journal Man–Machine Studies*, **13**, 81–116.

Gaines, B.R. & Shaw, M.L.G. (1993) Basing knowledge acquisition tools in personal construct psychology. *Knowledge Engineering Review*, **8**, 49–85.

Gaines, B.R. & Shaw, M.L.G. (1997) Knowledge acquisition, modeling and inference through the World Wide Web. *International Journal of Human–Computer Studies*, **46**, 729–759.

Galsworthy, P. (1997) Pan-company marketing at British Airways 1983–1994. *Marketing Council Case Study*.

Gamino, L.A., Sewell, K.W., Easterling, L.W. & Stirman, L. (1998) Scott & White grief study: an empirical test of predictors of intensified mourning. *Death Studies*, **22**, 333–355.

Gara, M.A. (1982) Back to basics in personality study—the individual's own organization of experience: the individuality corollary. In J.C. Mancuso & J.R. Adams-Webber (Eds) *The Construing Person*. New York: Praeger.

Gara, M.A., Rosenberg, S. & Mueller, D.R. (1989) Perception of self and others in schizophrenia. *International Journal of Personal Construct Psychology*, **2**, 253–270.

Gardner, R.A. (1971) *The Mutual-Story-Telling Technique*. New York: Science House.

Garfinkel, H. (1967) *Studies in Ethnomethodology*. Englewood Cliffs, NJ: Prentice-Hall.

Gelman, S.A. (1996) Concepts and theories. In R. Gelman & T.K. Au (Eds) *Handbook of Perception and Cognition*, Volume 13. *Perceptual and Cognitive*. San Diego: Academic Press.

Gergen, K.J. (1985) The social constructionist movement in modern psychology. *American Psychologist*, **40**, 266–275.

Gergen, K.J. & Davis, K. (Eds) (1985) *The Social Construction of the Person.* New York: Springer.

Gergen, K.J. & Kaye, J. (1992) Beyond narrative in the negotiation of therapeutic meaning. In S. McNamee & K.J. Gergen (Eds) *Therapy as Social Construction.* London: Sage Publications.

Giles, P.G. & Rychlak, J.F. (1965) The validity of the role construct repertory test as a measure of sexual identification. *Journal of Projective Techniques,* **27**, 7–11.

Gillard, D. (2002) Personal communication.

Golembiewski, R.T. (1986) Contours in social change: elemental graphics and a surrogate variable for gamma change. *Academy of Management Review,* **11**, 550–567.

Golembiewski, R.T. (1995) *Managing Diversity in Organizations.* Tuscaloosa, AL: University of Alabama Press.

Golembiewski, R.T. (1997) Flight plan acknowledged: but definite restrictions apply; and more direct routes may exist. *Academy of Management Review,* **22**, 16–19.

Graham, B. (1986) *Creating learning programmes in intermediate treatment centres.* Unpublished MSc dissertation, London Institute of Education.

Greenberg, L., Elliott, R. & Rice, L. (1993) *Facilitating Emotional Change.* New York: Guilford.

Guidano, V.F. (1991) *The Self in Process.* New York: Guilford Press.

Gutt, E.A. (2000) *Translation and Relevance: Cognition and Context.* Manchester: St Jerome.

Hagans, C.L., Neimeyer, G.J. & Goodholm, C.R. (2000) The effect of elicitation methods on personal construct differentiation and valence. *Journal of Constructivist Psychology,* **13**, 155–173.

Hammond, M., Howarth, J. & Keat, R. (1991) *Understanding Phenomenology.* Oxford: Blackwell.

Harter, S.L. & Neimeyer, R.A. (1995) Long-term effects of child sexual abuse: toward a constructivist theory of trauma and its treatment. In R.A. Neimeyer & G.J. Neimeyer (Eds) *Advances in Personal Construct Psychology,* Volume 3. Greenwich, CT: JAI Press.

Harter, S., Neimeyer, R.A. & Alexander, P.C. (1989) Personal construction of family relationships. *International Journal of Personal Construct Psychology,* **2**, 123–142.

Hartmann, A. (1992) Element comparisons in repertory grid technique: results and consequences of a Monte Carlo study. *International Journal of Personal Construct Psychology,* **5**, 41–56.

Haugli, L., Steen, E., Nygard, R. & Finset, A. (2001) Learning to have less pain—is it possible? A one-year follow-up study of the effects of a personal construct group learning programme on patients with chronic musculoskeletal pain. *Patient Education and Counseling,* **45**, 111–118.

Hay, J. (1995) *Transformational Mentoring.* Maidenhead: McGraw-Hill.

Hayes, R.A., Slater, A. & Brown, E. (2000) Infants' ability to categorize on the basis of rhyme. *Cognitive Development,* **15**, 405–419.

Hayes-Roth, F. (1984) The industrialization of knowledge engineering. In W. Reitman (Ed.) *Artificial Intelligence Applications for Business.* Norwood, NJ: Ablex.

Hayes-Roth, F., Waterman, D.A. & Lenat, D.B. (1983) *Building Expert Systems.* Reading, MA: Addison-Wesley.

Heyman, R., Shaw, M.P. & Harding, J. (1983) A personal construct theory approach to the socialization of nursing trainees in two British general hospitals. *Journal of Advanced Nursing,* **8**, 59–67.

Higgins, E.T., King, G.A. & Mavin, G.H. (1982) Individual construct accessibility and subjective impressions and recall. *Journal of Personality and Social Psychology,* **43**, 35–47.

Hinkle, D.N. (1965) *The change of personal constructs from the viewpoint of a theory of implications.* Unpublished PhD thesis, Columbus, OH: Ohio State University.

Hinkle, D.N. (1970) The game of personal constructs. In D. Bannister (Ed.) *Perspectives in Personal Construct Theory.* London: Academic Press.

Hirst, W. (1988) *The Making of Cognitive Science.* Cambridge, UK: Cambridge University Press.

Horley, J. (1988) Cognitions of child sexual abusers. *Journal of Sex Research*, **25**, 542–545.

Horley, J. (1995) Cognitive-behavior therapy with an incarcerated exhibitionist. *International Journal of Offender Therapy and Comparative Criminology*, **39**, 335–339.

Horley, J. (1996) Content stability in the repertory grid: an examination using a forensic sample. *International Journal of Offender Therapy and Comparative Criminology*, **40**, 26–31.

Horley, J. (1999) *Psychotherapy with sexual offenders: PCT-based individual and group approaches*. Paper presented at the 13th International Congress on Personal Construct Psychology, Berlin, Germany.

Horley, J. (2000) Cognitions supportive of child molestation. *Aggression and Violent Behavior*, **5**, 551–564.

Horley, J. (2001) Frotteurism: a term in search of an underlying disorder? *Journal of Sexual Aggression*, **7**, 51–55.

Horley, J. (Ed.) (in press) *Personal Construct Perspectives on Forensic Psychology*. London: Brunner-Routledge.

Horley, J. & Quinsey, V.L. (1994) Assessing the cognitions of child molesters: use of the semantic differential with incarcerated offenders. *Journal of Sex Research*, **31**, 187–195.

Horley, J. & Quinsey, V.L. (1995) Child molesters' construal of themselves, other adults, and children. *Journal of Constructivist Psychology*, **8**, 193–211.

Horley, J., Quinsey, V.L. & Jones, S. (1997) Incarcerated child molesters' perceptions of themselves and others. *Sexual Abuse: A Journal of Research and Treatment*, **9**, 43–55.

Houston, J. (1998) *Making Sense with Offenders: Personal Constructs, Therapy and Change*. Chichester: John Wiley & Sons.

Howells, K. (1983) Social construing and violent behaviour in mentally abnormal offenders. In J.W. Hinton (Ed.) *Dangerousness: Problems of Assessment and Prediction*. London: Allen & Unwin.

Howkins, E. & Ewens, A. (1997) Community nurses' perceptions of self in role. In P. Denicolo & M. Pope (Eds) *Sharing Understanding and Practice*. Farnborough: EPCA Publications.

Hoy, R.M. (1973) The meaning of alcoholism for alcoholics: a repertory grid study. *British Journal of Social and Clinical Psychology*, **12**, 98–99.

Humphreys, C.L., Dutile, R. & Leitner, L. (2001) *Empirical support for experiential personal construct therapy: A common 'factor analysis'*. Paper presented at the 14th International Congress of Personal Construct Psychology, Wollongong, Australia.

Ihde, D. (1986) *Experimental Phenomenology*. Albany: SUNY Press.

Ishmael, A. (1999) *Harassment: Bullying and Violence at Work*. London: The Industrial Society.

Jackson, D.N. & Paunonen, S.V. (1981) Personality structure and assessment. *Annual Review of Psychology*, **31**, 503–551.

Jackson, S. (1992) A PCT therapy group for adolescents. In P. Maitland and D. Brennan (Eds) *Personal Construct Theory Deviancy and Social Work*. London: Inner London Probation Service/Centre for Personal Construct Psychology.

James, W. (1982) *The Varieties of Religious Experience*. Glasgow: William Collins. Original work published 1902.

James, W. (1884) Essay 'What is an Emotion?' See W. James (1890) The emotions. In *The Principles of Psychology*, Volume 2. New York: Dover Publications.

Jameson, F. (1991) *Postmodernism, or the Cultural Logic of Late Capitalism*. Durham, NC: Duke University Press.

Jankowicz, A.D. (1994) The new journey to Jerusalem: mission and meaning in the managerial crusade to Eastern Europe. *Organization Studies*, **15**, 479–507.

Jankowicz, A.D. (1999) Planting a paradigm in Central Europe: do we graft, or must we breed the rootstock anew? *Management Learning*, **30**, 281–299.

Jankowicz, A.D. (2001) Why does subjectivity make us nervous? Making the tacit explicit. *Journal of Intellectual Capital*, **2**, 61–73.

Jankowicz, D. (2002) *Cross-cultural knowledge transfer: translation as a mutual negotiation of disparate meanings*. Paper presented at the 6th Conference of the European Personal Construct Association, Florence: 26 March, 2002.

Joas, H. (1993) *Pragmatism and Social Theory*. Chicago: The University of Chicago Press.

Jones, H. (1992) Biography in management and organisation development. *Management Education and Development*, **23**, 199–200.

Jones, H. (1993) The core process interview. *EPCA Newsletter*, **2**, 19–20.

Jones, H.G. (1971) In search of an ideographic psychology. *Bulletin of the British Psychological Society*, **24**, 279–290.

Jones, R.E. (1961) Identification in terms of personal constructs: reconciling a paradox in theory. *Journal of Consulting Psychology*, **25**, 276.

Kalekin-Fishman, D. (1993) The two faces of hostility: the implications of personal construct theory for understanding alienation. *International Journal of Personal Construct Psychology*, **6**, 27–40.

Kalekin-Fishman, D. & Walker, B. (Eds) (1996) *The Construction of Group Realities: Culture, Society and Personal Construct Psychology*. Malabar, FL: Krieger.

Karst, T.O. & Trexler, L.D. (1970) Initial study using fixed role and rational-emotive therapy in treating speaking anxiety. *Journal of Consulting and Clinical Psychology*, **34**, 360–366.

Keen, T.R. & Bell, R.C. (1981) One thing leads to another: a new approach to elicitation in the Repertory Grid Technique. In M.L.G. Shaw (Ed.) *Recent Advances in Personal Construct Technology*. London: Academic Press.

Kelly, G.A. (1924) The sincere motive *The Messenger of Peace*. Indiana: Peace Association of Friends of America. Copy in Fransella PCP Collection, University of Hertfordshire, UK.

Kelly, G.A. (1932) *Understandable psychology*. Unpublished manuscript, Chapter 20. Copy in Fransella PCP Collection, University of Hertfordshire, UK.

Kelly, G.A. (c. 1954) *Knowledge: discovery or invention?* Unpublished manuscript. Copy in Fransella PCP Collection, University of Hertfordshire, UK.

Kelly, G.A. (1955/1991) *The Psychology of Personal Constructs*. Volumes 1 and 2. First published by Norton, 1955, then by Routledge in collaboration with the Centre for Personal Construct Psychology, 1991.

Kelly, G.A. (1959a) *The function of interpretation*. Unpublished manuscripts of three talks. Falmouth: Fransella.

Kelly, G.A. (1959b) *Values, Knowledge and Social Control*. Symposium of the American Psychological Association, Cincinnati (1989) Falmouth: Fransella.

Kelly, G.A. (1961) Theory and therapy in suicide: the personal construct point of view. In M. Farberow & E. Shneidman (Eds) *The Cry for Help*. New York: McGraw-Hill.

Kelly, G.A. (1962) Europe's matrix of decision. In R.M. Jones (Ed.) *Nebraska Symposium on Motivation*. University of Nebraska Press, Lincoln, Nebraska. Reprinted in D. Kalekin-Fishman & B.M. Walker (Eds) (1996) *The Construction of Group Realities*. Malabar, FL: Krieger.

Kelly, G.A. (1963) Aldous: the personable computer. In Tomkins, S.S. & Messick, S. (Eds) *Computer Simulation of Personality*. New York: John Wiley & Sons.

Kelly, G.A. (1966a) *Experimental dependency*. Unpublished unfinished manuscript, Brandeis University. Copy of manuscript in Fransella PCP Collection, University of Hertfordshire, UK.

Kelly, G.A. (1966b) Unpublished audio-taped interview with Fay Fransella.

Kelly, G.A. (1969a) Humanistic methodology in psychological research. In B. Maher (Ed.) *Clinical Psychology and Personality: The Selected Papers of George Kelly*. New York: John Wiley & Sons.

Kelly, G.A. (1969b) Man's construction of his alternatives. In B. Maher (Ed.) *Clinical Pschology and Personality: The Selected Papers of George Kelly*. New York: John Wiley & Sons.

Kelly, G.A. (1969c) Sin and psychotherapy. In B. Maher (Ed.) *Clinical Psychology and Personality: The Selected Papers of George Kelly*. New York: John Wiley & Sons.

Kelly, G.A. (1969d) The language of hypothesis: man's psychological instrument. In B. Maher (Ed.) *Clinical Psychology and Personality: The Selected Papers of George Kelly*. New York: John Wiley & Sons.

Kelly, G.A. (1969e) The role of classification in personality theory. In B. Maher (Ed.) *Clinical Psychology and Personality: The Selected Papers of George Kelly*. New York: John Wiley & Sons.

Kelly, G.A. (1969f) A mathematical approach to psychology. In B. Maher (Ed.) *Clinical Psychology and Personality: The Selected Papers of George Kelly*. New York: John Wiley & Sons.

Kelly, G.A. (1969g) In whom confide: on whom depend for what? In B. Maher (Ed.) *Clinical Psychology and Personality: The Selected Papers of George Kelly*. New York: John Wiley & Sons.

Kelly, G.A. (1969h) Ontological acceleration. In B. Maher (Ed.) *Clinical Psychology and Personality: The Selected Papers of George Kelly*. New York: John Wiley & Sons.

Kelly, G.A. (1969i) The psychotherapeutic relationship. In B. Maher (Ed.) *Clinical Psychology and Personality: The Selected Papers of George Kelly*. New York: John Wiley & Sons.

Kelly, G.A. (1969j) Psychotherapy and the nature of man. In B. Maher (Ed.) *Clinical Psychology and Personality: The Selected Papers of George Kelly*. New York: John Wiley & Sons.

Kelly, G.A. (1969k) The strategy of psychological research. In B. Maher (Ed.) *Clinical Psychology and Personality: The Selected Papers of George Kelly*. New York: John Wiley & Sons.

Kelly, G.A. (1969l) The autobiography of a theory. In B. Maher, *Clinical Psychology and Personality: The Selected Papers of George Kelly*. New York: John Wiley & Sons.

Kelly, G.A. (1969m) Hostility. In B. Maher (Ed.) *Clinical Psychology and Personality: The Selected Papers of George Kelly*. New York: John Wiley & Sons.

Kelly, G.A. (1970) Behaviour as an experiment. In D. Bannister (Ed.) *Perspectives in Personal Construct Theory*. London: Academic Press.

Kelly, G.A. (1977) The psychology of the unknown. In D. Bannister (Ed.) *New Perspectives in Personal Construct Theory*. London: Academic Press.

Kelly, G.A. (1978) Confusion and the clock. In F. Fransella (Ed.) *Personal Construct Psychology 1977*. London: Academic Press.

Kelly, G.A. (1979) Social inheritance. In P. Stringer & D. Bannister (Eds) *Constructs of Sociality in Individuality*. London: Academic Press.

Kelly, G.A. (1980) A psychology of the optimal man. In A.W. Landfield & L.M. Leitner (Eds) *Personal Construct Psychology: Psychotherapy and Personality*. New York: John Wiley & Sons.

Kelly, G.A. (1996) Europe's matrix of decision. In D. Kalekin-Fishman & B. Walker (Eds) *The Construction of Group Realities: Culture, Society and Personal Construct Psychology*. Malabar, FL: Krieger.

Kelly, G.A. with Warnock, G.W. (1935) *Inductive trigonometry*. Unpublished book manuscript.

Kennedy, P. & Llewelyn, S. (2001) Does the future belong to the scientist practitioner? *The Psychologist*, **14**, 74–78.

Kenny, V. (1987) Family somatics: a personal construct approach to cancer. In R.A. Neimeyer & G.J. Neimeyer (Eds) *Personal Construct Therapy Casebook*. New York: Springer.

Kim, J. (1993) *Supervenience and Mind: Selected Philosophical Essays*. Cambridge: Cambridge University Press.

Kirchberg, T.M., Neimeyer, R.A. & James, R.K. (1998) Beginning counselors' death concerns and empathic responses to client situations involving death and grief. *Death Studies*, **22**, 99–120.

Kirsch, H. & Jordan, J. (2000) Emotions and personal constructs. In J.W. Scheer (Ed.) *The Person in Society: Challenges to a Constructivist Theory*. Giessen, Germany: Psychosozial-Verlag.

Klion, R.E. & Pfenninger, D.T. (1997) Personal construct psychotherapy of addictions. *Journal of Substance Abuse Treatment*, **14**, 37–43.

Korzybski, A. (1933) *Science and Sanity: An Introduction to Non-Aristotelian Systems and General Semantics*. Lancaster, PA: Science Press.

Krieger, S.R., Epting, F.R. & Leitner, L.M. (1974) Personal constructs, threat, and attitudes toward death. *Omega*, **5**, 299–310.

Kroonenberg, P.M. (1985) Three-mode principal components: analysis of semantic differential data: the case of a triple personality. *Applied Psychological Measurement*, **9**, 83–94.

Krosnick, J.A. (1999) Survey research. *Annual Review of Psychology*, **50**, 537–567.

Kuhn, T.S. (1962) *The Structure of Scientific Revolutions*. Chicago: University of Chicago Press.

Lakoff, G. & Johnson, M. (1980) *Metaphors We Live By*. Chicago: University of Chicago Press.

Landfield, A.W. (1971) *Personal Construct Systems in Psychotherapy*. Chicago: Rand-McNally.

Landfield, A.W. (1977) Interpretive man: the enlarged self-image. In J.K. Cole & A.W. Landfield (Eds) *Nebraska Symposium on Motivation 1976: Personal Construct Psychology*. Lincoln, NE: University of Nebraska Press.

Landfield, A.W. (1979) Exploring socialisation through the Interpersonal Transaction Group. In P. Stringer & D. Bannister (Eds) *Constructs of Sociality and Individuality*. London: Academic Press.

Landfield, A.W. & Cannell, J.E. (1988) Ways of assessing functionally independent construction, meaningfulness, and construction in hierarchy. In J.C. Mancuso & M.L.G. Shaw (Eds) *Cognition and Personal Structure: Computer Access and Analysis*. New York: Praeger.

Landfield, A.W. & Epting, F.R. (1987) *Personal Construct Psychology: Clinical and Personality Assessment*. New York: Human Sciences Press.

Landfield, A.W. & Schmittdiel, C. (1983) The interpersonal transaction group: evolving measurements in the pursuit of theory. In J. Adams-Webber & J. Mancuso (Eds) *Applications of Personal Construct Psychology*. Toronto: Academic Press.

Lane, L.G. & Viney, L.L. (2001a) *When the unreal becomes real: an evaluation of personal construct group psychotherapy with survivors of breast cancer*. Paper presented at the 14th International Congress of Personal Construct Psychology, Wollongong, Australia.

Lane, L.G. & Viney, L.L. (2001b) *Role relationships and the restoration of coherence in the stories of women diagnosed with breast cancer: a group intervention*. Paper presented at the 14th International Congress of Personal Construct Psychology, Wollongong, Australia.

Language and Curriculum Access Service (1996) *Concerns About Progress*. London Borough of Enfield: LCAS.

Laubach, W., Brown, C.E. & Lenard, J.M. (1996) Nurses and physicians evaluate their intensive care experiences. *Heart and Lung: The Journal of Acute and Critical Care*, **25**, 475–482.

Lawlor, M. & Cochran, L. (1981) Does invalidation produce loose construing? *British Journal of Medical Psychology*, **54**, 41–50.

Laws, D.R. (Ed.) (1989) *Relapse Prevention with Sex Offenders*. New York: Guilford Press.

Le Guin, U. (1985) *Always Coming Home*. New York: Harper & Row.

Leach, C. (1981) Direct analysis of a repertory grid. In M.L.G. Shaw (Ed.) *Recent Advances in Personal Construct Technology*. London: Academic Press.

Leach, C., Freshwater, K., Aldridge, J. & Sunderland, J. (2001) Analysis of repertory grids in clinical practice. *British Journal of Clinical Psychology*, **40**, 225–248.

Lee, J. (2000) *Shakespeare's 'Hamlet' and the Controversies of Self*. Oxford: Oxford University Press.

Lee, J. (2002) Personal communication.

Lefebvre, V.L., Lefebvre, V.D. & Adams-Webber, J. (1986) Modeling an experiment on construing self and others. *Journal of Mathematical Psychology*, **30**, 317–330.

Leitner, L.M. (1985) The terrors of cognition: on the experiential validity of personal construct theory. In D. Bannister (Ed.) *Issues and Approaches in Personal Construct Theory*. London: Academic Press.

Leitner, L.M. (1988) Terror, risk, and reverence: experiential personal construct psychotherapy. *International Journal of Personal Construct Psychology*, **1**, 261–272.

Leitner, L.M. (1995) Optimal therapeutic distance: a therapist's experience of personal construct psychotherapy. In R. Neimeyer & M. Mahoney (Eds) *Constructivism in Psychotherapy*. Washington, DC: American Psychological Association.

Leitner, L.M. (1997) *Transference and countertransference in experiential personal construct psychotherapy*. Paper presented at the 12th International Congress on Personal Construct Psychology, Seattle, WA.

Leitner, L.M. (1999a) Levels of awareness in experiential personal construct psychotherapy. *Journal of Constructivist Psychology*, **12**, 239–252.

Leitner, L.M. (1999b) Terror, numbness, panic, and awe: Experiential personal constructivism and panic. In E.M. Stern & R.B. Marchesani (Eds) *Awe and Trembling: Psychotherapy of Unusual States*. Binghamton, NY: Haworth. Also in *The Psychotherapy Patient*, **11**, 157–170.

Leitner, L.M. (1999c) *Recent developments in experiential personal construct psychotherapy*. Plenary address: 13th International Congress on Personal Construct Psychology, Berlin, Germany.

Leitner, L.M. (2001) Experiential personal construct therapeutic artistry: the therapy relationship and the timing of interventions. *The Humanistic Psychologist*, **29**, 109.

Leitner, L.M. (in press) Therapeutic artistry: evoking experiential and relational truths. *International Journal of Personal Construct Psychology*.

Leitner, L.M. & Epting, F.R. (2001) Constructivist approaches to therapy. In K.J. Schneider, J.F.T. Bugental & J.F. Pierson (Eds) *The Handbook of Humanistic Psychology: Leading Edges in Theory, Research, and Practice*. Thousand Oaks, CA: Sage Publications.

Leitner, L.M. & Faidley, A.J. (1995) The awful, aweful nature of ROLE relationships. In G. Neimeyer & R.A. Neimeyer (Eds) *Advances in Personal Construct Psychology*, Volume 3. Greenwich, CT: JAI Press.

Leitner, L.M. & Faidley, A.J. (1999) Creativity in experiential personal construct psychotherapy. *Journal of Constructivist Psychology*, **12**, 273–286.

Leitner, L.M., Faidley, A.J. & Celentana, M.A. (2000) Diagnosing human meaning making: an experiential constructivist approach. In R.A. Neimeyer & J.D. Raskin (Eds) *Construction of Disorders: Meaning Making Frameworks for Psychotherapy*. Washington, DC: American Psychological Association.

Leitner, L.M. & Guthrie, A.F. (1993) Validation of therapist interventions in psychotherapy: clarity, ambiguity, and subjectivity. *International Journal of Personal Construct Psychology*, **6**, 281–294.

Leitner, L.M. & Pfenninger, D.T. (1994) Sociality and optimal functioning. *Journal of Constructivist Psychology*, **7**, 119–135.

Lemon, N. & Warren, N. (1974) Salience, centrality and self-relevance of traits in construing others. *British Journal of Social and Clinical Psychology*, **30**, 317–324.

Levy, L.H. & Dugan, R.D. (1956) Personal constructs and predictive behaviour. *Journal of Consulting Psychology*, **53**, 54–58.

Lewicka, M., Czapinski, J. & Peeters, G. (1992) Positive-negative asymmetry or when the heart needs a reason. *European Journal of Social Psychology*, **22**, 425–434.

Lighthill, J. (1973) Artificial intelligence: a general survey. In *Artificial Intelligence: A Paper Symposium*. UK: Science Research Council.

Lira, F.T., Nay, W.R., McCullough, J.P. & Etkin, W. (1975) Relative effects of modeling and role playing in the treatment of avoidance behaviors. *Journal of Consulting and Clinical Psychology*, **43**, 608–618.

Llewelyn, S. & Dunnett, G. (1987) The use of personal construct theory in groups. In R.A. Neimeyer & G.J. Neimeyer (Eds) *Personal Construct Theory Casebook*. New York: Springer.

Lohaus, A. (1986) Standardizations in methods of data collection; adverse effects on reliability? *Australian Psychologist*, **21**, 241–251.

Lorenzini, R., Sassaroli, S. & Rocchi, M.T. (1989) Schizophrenia and paranoia as solutions to predictive failure. *International Journal of Personal Construct Psychology*, **2**, 417–432.

Lovelock, J. (2000) *Homage to Gaia: The Life of an Independent Scientist*. Oxford: Oxford University Press.

Mackay, D. (1975) *Clinical Psychology: Theory and Therapy*. London: Methuen.

Mackay, N. (1992) Identification, reflection, and correlation: problems in the bases of repertory grid measures. *International Journal of Personal Construct Psychology*, **5**, 57–75.

Magna Books (1993) *Naïve Painting. Book of 30 Postcards.* Wigston: Magna Books.

Mahoney, M.J. (1988) Constructive metatheory: I. Basic features and historical foundations. *International Journal of Personal Construct Psychology*, **1**, 1–35.

Mair, J.M.M. (1970) Psychological problems and cigarette smoking. *Journal of Psychosomatic Research*, **14**, 277–283.

Mair, J.M.M. (1972) Personal communication.

Mair, M. (1977) The community of self. In D. Bannister (Ed.) *New Perspectives in Personal Construct Theory.* London: Academic Press.

Mair, M. (1985) The long quest to know. In F. Epting & A.W. Landfield (Eds) *Anticipating Personal Construct Theory.* Lincoln, NE: University of Nebraska Press.

Mair, M. (1988) Psychology as story telling. *International Journal of Personal Construct Psychology*, **1**, 125–137.

Mair, M. (1989a) *Between Psychology and Psychotherapy: A Poetics of Experience.* London: Routledge.

Mair, M. (1989b) Kelly, Bannister, and a story-telling psychology. *International Journal of Personal Construct Psychology*, **2**, 1–14.

Makhlouf-Norris, F. & Jones, H.G. (1971) Conceptual distance indices as measures of alienation in obsessional neurosis. *Psychological Medicine*, **1**, 381–387.

Mancuso, J.C. (1986) The acquisition and use of narrative grammar structure. In T.R. Sarbin (Ed.) *Narrative Psychology: The Storied Nature of Human Conduct.* New York: Praeger.

Mancuso, J.C. & Adams-Webber, J.R. (1982) Anticipation as a constructive process: the fundamental postulate. In J.C. Mancuso & J.R. Adams-Webber (Eds) *The Construing Person.* New York: Praeger.

Mancuso, J.C. & Ceely, S.G. (1980) The self as memory processing. *Cognitive Therapy and Research*, **4**, 1–25.

Mancuso, J.C. & Hunter, K.V. (1985a) Constructivist assumptions in the person theories of G.A. Kelly and Jean Piaget *http://www.capital.net/mancusolpiagkely.html.*

Mancuso, J.C. & Hunter, K.V. (1985b) Assunti construttivisti nelli teorie di G.A. Kelly e J. Piaget. In F. Mancini & A. Semerari (Eds) *La Psychologia dei Construtti Personali: Saggi Sulla Teoria di G.A. Kelly.* Milano: Franco Angeli Libri.

Mancuso, J.C. & Lehrer, R. (1986) Cognitive processes during reactions to rule violation. In R. Ashmore & D. Brodzinsky (Eds) *Thinking About the Family: Views of Parents and Children.* Hillsdale, NJ: Lawrence Erlbaum Associates.

Mancuso, J.C. & Sarbin, T.R. (1998) The narrative construction of emotional life: developmental aspects. In M.F. Mascolo & S. Griffin (Eds) *What Develops in Emotional Development?* New York: Plenum Press.

Mancuso, J.C., Yelich, G. & Sarbin, T.R. (2002) The narrative construction of AD/HD: a diagnostic fable. In G. Neimeyer & R.A. Neimeyer (Eds) *Advances in Personal Construct Psychology: Perspectives and Directions.* New York: Praeger.

March, P.L. & McPherson, A. (1996) The important attributes of a nurse from the perspective of qualified and student nurses. *Journal of Advanced Nursing*, **24**, 810–816.

Marks, I.M. & Sartorius, N.H. (1967) A contribution to the measurement of sexual attitude. *Journal of Nervous and Mental Disease*, **145**, 441–451.

Marris, P. (1974) *Loss and Change.* London: Routledge.

Marshall, W.L. (1999) Diagnosing and treating sexual offenders. In A. Hess & I.B. Weiner (Eds) *The Handbook Of Forensic Psychology.* New York: John Wiley & Sons.

Marshall, W.L. & Mazzucco, A. (1995) Self-esteem and parental attachments of child molesters. *Sexual Abuse: A Journal of Research and Treatment*, **7**, 279–285.

Marx, K. & Engels, F. (1970/1845–6) *The German Ideology.* New York: International Publishers.

Mascolo, M.F., Craig-Bray, L. & Neimeyer, R.A. (1997) The construction of meaning and action in development and psychotherapy: an epigenetic systems approach. In G.J. Neimeyer & R.A. Neimeyer (Eds) *Advances in Personal Construct Psychology*, Volume 4. Greenwich, CN: JAI Press.

Maturana, H.R. & Varela, F.J. (1980) *Autopoiesis and Cognition: The Realization of the Living.* Boston: Reidel. Original works published 1970–1973.

Maturana, H.R. & Varela, F.J. (1987) *The Tree of Knowledge: The Biological Roots of Human Understanding*. Boston and London: New Science Library. Original work published 1984.

McCarthy, J., Minsky, M.L., Rochester, N. & Shannon, C.E. (1955) *A Proposal for the Dartmouth Summer Research Project on Artificial Intelligence*. Dartmouth College. *http://www-formal.stanford.edu/jmc/history/dartmouth/dartmouth.html*.

McCoy, M.M. (1977) A reconstruction of emotion. In D. Bannister (Ed.) *New Perspectives in Personal Construct Theory*. London: Academic Press.

McCoy, M.M. (1981) Positive and negative emotion: a personal interpretation. In H. Bonarius, R. Holland & S. Rosenberg (Eds) *Personal Construct Psychology: Recent Advances in Theory and Practice*. London: Macmillan.

McCoy, M.M. (1983) Personal construct theory and methodology in intercultural research. In J. Adams-Webber & J.C. Mancuso (Eds) *Applications of Personal Construct Theory*. Toronto: Academic Press.

McDonagh, D. (1987) The implication potential of personal constructs in relation to their subjective importance and order of elicitation. *Social Behavior and Personality*, **15**, 81–86.

McFayden, M. & Foulds, G.A. (1972) Comparison of provided and elicited grid content in the grid test of schizophrenic thought disorder. *British Journal of Psychiatry*, **121**, 53–57.

McNeill, I. (1991) The reality of doing business in Poland. *The Intelligent Enterprise*, **1**, 9–16.

McPherson, F.M., Blackburn, I.M., Draffan, J.W. & McFadyan, M. (1973) A further study of the Grid Test of Thought Disorder. *British Journal of Social and Clinical Psychology*, **12**, 420–427.

McWilliams, S.A. (1988) On becoming a personal anarchist. In F. Fransella & L. Thomas (Eds) *Experimenting with Personal Construct Psychology*. London: Routledge.

McWilliams, S.A. (1993) Construct no idols. *International Journal of Personal Construct Psychology*, **6**, 269–280.

McWilliams, S.A. (1996). Accepting the invitational. In B.E. Walker, J. Costigan, L.L. Viney & W. Warren (Eds) *Personal Construct Theory: A Psychology for the Future*. Melbourne: Australian Psychological Society.

McWilliams, S.A. (2000) Core constructs and ordinary mind Zen. In J.W. Scheer (Ed.) *The Person in Society: Challenge to a Constructivist Theory*. Giessen, Germany: Psychosozial-Verlag.

Mead, G.H. (1934/1977) Self. In A. Strauss (Ed.) *George Herbert Mead: On Social Psychology*. Chicago: University of Chicago Press. Originally published 1934.

Melrose, S. & Shapiro, B. (1999) Students' perceptions of their psychiatric mental health clinical nursing experience: a personal construct theory exploration. *Journal of Advanced Nursing*, **30**, 1451–1458.

Mendoza, O. (1985) The exchange grid. In N. Beail (Ed.) *Repertory Grid Technique and Personal Constructs: Applications in Clinical and Educational Settings*. London: Croom Helm.

Merleau-Ponty, M. (1962/1945) *Phenomenology of Perception*. London: Routledge.

Metzler, A.E. (1996) *Personal Construct Clearinghouse*. Bethlehem, PA: Lehigh University.

Michie, D. (Ed.) (1979) *Expert Systems in the Micro Electronic Age*. Edinburgh: Edinburgh University Press.

Midgley, M. (2001) *Gaia: The Next Big Idea*. London: Demos.

Miedema, S. (1995) The beyond in the midst: the relevance of Dewey's philosophy of religion for education. In J. Garrison (Ed.) *The New Scholarship on Dewey*. Dordrecht: Kluwer Academic Publishers.

Milgram, S. (1974) *Obedience to Authority*. London: Tavistock Publications.

Mindell, A. (1989) *The Year I: Global Process Work*. Harmondsworth: Penguin Books.

Mindell, A. (2000) *The Leader as Martial Artist: Techniques and Strategies for Resolving Conflict and Creating Community*. San Francisco: Harper.

Mintzberg, H. (1987) Crafting strategy. *Harvard Business Review*, **65**, 66–76.

Mintzberg, H. (1994) Re-thinking strategic planning. Part 1: pitfalls and fallacies. *Long Range Planning*, **27**, 12–22.

Mischel, W. (1980). George Kelly's appreciation of psychology: a personal tribute. In M.J. Mahoney (Ed.) *Psychotherapy Process: Current Issues and Future Directions*. New York: Plenum Press.

Mitsos, S.B. (1958) Representative elements in the role construct technique. *Journal of Consulting Psychology*, **22**, 311–313.

Moes, A.J. & Sewell, K.W. (1994) *Post Traumatic Stress Disorder: a symposium on constructivist findings of combat, disaster, and rape survivors. III. Repertory grid and rape trauma.* Presented at the 6th North American Conference on Personal Construct Psychology, Indianapolis, IN.

Mohr, J.W., Turner, R.E. & Jerry, M.B. (1964) *Pedophilia and Exhibitionism*. Toronto: University of Toronto Press.

Morris, J.B. (1975) Personal communication.

Morris, J.B. (1977) Appendix I. The prediction and measurement of change in a psychotherapy group using the repertory grid. In F. Fransella & D. Bannister (Eds) *A Manual for Repertory Grid Technique*. London: Academic Press.

Morrish, I. (1967) *Disciplines of Education*. London: Allen & Unwin.

Morrison, P. & Burnard, P. (1997) *Caring and Communicating*. Basingstoke & London: Macmillan.

Moustakas, C. (1994) *Phenomenological Research Methods*. London: Sage Pubications.

Nagy, S. (1992) *Nurses' constructions of pain*. Paper presented at the 6th Australian Personal Construct Psychology Conference, Sydney.

Needs, A. (1988) Psychological investigation of offending behaviour. In F. Fransella & L. Thomas (Eds) *Experimenting with Personal Construct Psychology*. London: Routledge & Kegan Paul.

Neff, G. (1996) Developmental trends and gender differences in construing self and parents. *Journal of Constructivist Psychology*, **9**, 225–232.

Neimeyer, G.J. (1984) Cognitive complexity and marital satisfaction. *Journal of Social and Clinical Psychology*, **2**, 258–263.

Neimeyer, G.J. (1993) *Constructivist Assessment: A Casebook*. Newbury Park, CA: Sage Publications.

Neimeyer, G.J. (2002) Towards reflexive scrutiny in repertory grid methodology. *Journal of Constructivist Psychology*, **15**, 89–94.

Neimeyer, G.J. & Fukuyama, M. (1984) Exploring the content and structure of cross-cultural attitudes. *Counselor Education and Supervision*, **23**, 214–224.

Neimeyer, G.J. & Hagans, C.L. (2002) More madness in our method? The effects of repertory grid variation on construct differentiation. *Journal of Constructivist Psychology*, **15**, 139–160.

Neimeyer, G.J. & Hudson J.E. (1985) Couples' constructs: personal systems in marital satisfaction. In D. Bannister (Ed.) *Issues and Approaches in Personal Construct Theory*. London: Academic Press.

Neimeyer, R.A. (1985a) Problems and prospects in personal construct theory. In D. Bannister (Ed.) *Issues and Approaches in Personal Construct Theory* (pp. 143–171). London: Academic Press.

Neimeyer, R.A. (1985b) Personal constructs in clinical practice. In P.C. Kendall (Ed.) *Advances in Cognitive Behavioral Research and Therapy*. San Diego, CA: Academic Press.

Neimeyer, R.A. (1985c) *The Development of Personal Construct Psychology*. Lincoln: University of Nebraska Press.

Neimeyer, R.A. (1988) Clinical guidelines for conducting Interpersonal Transaction groups. *International Journal of Personal Construct Psychology*, **1**, 181–190.

Neimeyer, R.A. (1993) Constructivist approaches to the measurement of meaning. In G.J. Neimeyer (Ed.) *Constructivist Assessment: A Casebook*. London: Sage Publications.

Neimeyer, R.A. (1994) The Threat Index and related methods. In R.A. Neimeyer (Ed.) *Death Anxiety Handbook*. New York: Taylor & Francis.

Neimeyer, R.A. (1995) Constructivist psychotherapies: features, foundations, and future directions. In R.A. Neimeyer & M.J. Mahoney (Eds) *Constructivism in Psychotherapy*. Washington, DC: American Psychological Association.

Neimeyer, R.A. (2000) Narrative disruptions in the construction of self. In R.A. Neimeyer & J.D. Raskin (Ed.) *Constructions of Disorder: Meaning Making Frameworks for Psychotherapy*. Washington, DC: American Psychological Association.

Neimeyer, R.A. (Ed.) (2001a) *Meaning Reconstruction and the Experience of Loss*. Washington, DC: American Psychological Association.

Neimeyer, R.A. (2001b) Reauthoring life narratives: grief therapy as meaning reconstruction. *Israel Journal of Psychiatry*, **38**, 171–183.

Neimeyer, R.A. (2002a) *Lessons of Loss: A Guide to Coping* (2nd edition). New York: Brunner-Routledge.

Neimeyer, R.A. (2002b) Deconstructing 9/11: a constructivist perspective. *The Humanistic Psychologist*, **30**, 293–305.

Neimeyer, R.A., Anderson, A. & Stockton, L. (2001) Snakes versus ladders: a validation of laddering as a technique as a measure of hierarchical structure. *Journal of Constructivist Psychology*, **14**, 85–106.

Neimeyer, R.A., Brooks, D.L. & Baker, K.D. (1996) Personal epistemologies and personal relationships. In D. Kalekin-Fishman & B.M. Walker (Eds) *The Construction of Group Realities: Culture, Society and Personal Construct Psychology*. Malabar, FL: Krieger.

Neimeyer, R.A. & Chapman, K.M. (1980) Self/ideal discrepancy and fear of death: the test of an existential hypothesis. *Omega*, **11**, 233–240.

Neimeyer, R.A. & Dingemans, P. (1980) Death orientation in the suicide intervention worker. *Omega*, **11**, 15–23.

Neimeyer, R.A., Heath, A.E. & Strauss, J. (1985) Personal reconstruction during group cognitive therapy for depression. In F. Epting & A.W. Landfield (Eds) *Anticipating Personal Construct Psychology*. Lincoln, NE: University of Nebraska Press.

Neimeyer, R.A. & Jackson, T.T. (1997) George A. Kelly and the development of personal construct theory. In W. Bringmann, H. Lück, R. Miller & C. Early (Eds) *A Pictorial History of Psychology*. Carol Stream, IL: Quintessence.

Neimeyer, R.A., Keesee, N.J. & Fortner, B.V. (2000) Loss and meaning reconstruction: propositions and procedures. In R. Malkinson, S. Rubin & E. Wiztum (Eds) *Traumatic and Non-Traumatic Loss and Bereavement*. Madison, CT: Psychosocial Press.

Neimeyer, R.A. & Mahoney, M.J. (Eds) (1995) *Constructivism in Psychotherapy*. Washington, DC: American Psychological Association.

Neimeyer, R.A. & Mitchell, K.A. (1988) Similarity and attraction: a longitudinal study. *Journal of Social and Personal Relationships*, **5**, 131–148.

Neimeyer, R.A. & Neimeyer, G.J. (1983) Structural similarity in the acquaintance process. *Journal of Social and Clinical Psychology*, **1**, 146–154.

Neimeyer, R.A. & Neimeyer, G.J. (Eds) (1987) *Personal Construct Therapy Casebook*. New York: Springer.

Neimeyer, R.A., Neimeyer, G.J. & Landfield, A.W. (1983) Conceptual differentiation, integration and empathic prediction. *Journal of Personality*, **51**, 185–191.

Neimeyer, R.A. & Raskin, J.D. (Eds) (2000) *Constructions of Disorder: Meaning-Making Frameworks for Psychotherapy*. Washington, DC: American Psychological Association.

Neimeyer, R.A. & Stewart, A.E. (1996) Trauma, healing, and the narrative emplotment of loss. *Families in Society*, **77**, 360–375.

Neimeyer, R.A. & Stewart, A.E. (2000) Constructivist and narrative psychotherapies. In C.R. Snyder & R.E. Ingram (Eds) *Handbook of Psychological Change*. New York: John Wiley & Sons.

Neimeyer, R.A. & Tschudi, F. (2002) Community and coherence: Narrative contributions to a psychology of conflict and loss. In G. Fireman, T. McVay & O. Flanagan (Eds) *Narrative and Consciousness: Literature, Psychology, and the Brain*. New York: Oxford.

Neisser, U. (1967) *Cognitive Psychology*. Englewood Cliffs: Prentice-Hall.

Nelson, M.H. (1993) Teachers' stories: an analysis of the themes. In C. Day, J. Calderhead & P.M. Denicolo (Eds) *Research on Teacher Thinking: Understanding Professional Development*. London: Falmer Press.

Nisbett, R.E. & Wilson, T.D. (1977) Telling more than we can know: verbal reports on mental processes. *Psychological Review*, **84**, 231–259.

Norris, H. & Makhlouf-Norris, F. (1976) The measurement of self identity. In P. Slater (Ed.) *The Measurement of Intrapersonal Space by Grid Technique*, Volume 1. *Explorations of Intrapersonal Space*. London: John Wiley & Sons.

Novak, R.M. (1983) Personal construct theory and other perceptual pedagogies. In J.R. Adams-Weber & J.C. Mancuso (Eds) *Applications of Personal Construct Psychology*. New York: Academic Press.

Nussbaum, M. (1999) Women and equality: the capabilities approach. *International Labour Review*, **138**, 227–245.

Nuzzo, M.L. & Chiari, G. (2001) *The personal construction of cancer: A constructivist framework for exploring malignancies*. Paper read at the 7th International Congress on Personal Construct Psychology, Memphis, TN.

Osborne, R. & Gilbert, J. (1980) A technique for exploring students' views of the world. *Physics Education*, **15**, 376–379.

Packer, M. & Greco-Brooks, D. (1999) School as a site for the production of persons. *Journal of Constructivist Psychology*, **12**, 133–151.

Parin, P. (1967) Considérations psychanalytiques sur le moi de groupe. *Psychopathologie Africaine*, **3**, 195–206.

Parry, G. & Richardson, A. (1996) *NHS Psychotherapy Services in England: Review of Strategic Policy*. London: NHS Executive.

Parsons, T. (1949/1937) *The Structure of Social Action*, Volume 2. New York: Free Press.

Parsons, T. (1966) *Societies*. Englewood Cliffs, NJ: Prentice-Hall.

Pascalis, O., de Schonen, S., Morton, J., Deruelle, C. & Fabre-Grenet, M. (1995) Mother's face recognition by neonates: a replication and an extension. *Infant Behavior and Development*, **18**, 79–85.

Peck, D. & Whitlow, D.D. (1975) *Approaches to Personality Theory*. London: Methuen.

Pepper, S.C. (1942) *World Hypotheses: A Study of Evidence*. Berkeley: University of California Press.

Pervin, L.A. & John, O.P. (2001) *Personality: Theory and Research*. New York: John Wiley & Sons.

Piaget, J. (1971) *Biology and Knowledge: An Essay on the Relations Between Organic Regulations and Cognitive Processes*. Chicago: The University of Chicago Press. Original work published 1967.

Pierce, D.L., Sewell, K.W. & Cromwell, R.L. (1992) Schizophrenia and depression. In G.J. Neimeyer & R.A. Neimeyer (Eds) *Advances in Personal Construct Psychology*, Volume 2. Greenwich, CT: JAI Press.

Polanyi, M. (1958) *Personal Knowledge*. London: Routledge & Kegan Paul.

Polkinghorne, D.E. (1988) *Narrative Knowing and Human Sciences*. Albany, NY: State University of New York.

Pollock, L. (1986) An introduction to the use of repertory grid technique as a research method and clinical tool for psychiatric nurses. *Journal of Advanced Nursing*, **11**, 439–445.

Pope, M.L. & Denicolo, P.M. (1986) Intuitive theories—a researcher's dilemma: some methodological implications. *British Educational Research Journal*, **12**, 153–165.

Pope, M.L. & Denicolo, P.M. (2001) *Transformative Education: Personal Construct Approaches to Practice and Research*. London: Whurr Publications.

Pope, M.L. & Saka, R. (1997) The learning of English as a foreign language: a personal constructivist approach. In P.M. Denicolo & M.L. Pope (Eds) *Sharing Understanding and Practice*. Farnborough: EPCA Publications.

Popper, K.R. (1959) *The Logic of Scientific Discovery*. London: Hutchinson.

Prentky, R.A. & Knight, R.A. (1991) Identifying critical dimensions for discriminating among rapists. *Journal of Consulting and Clinical Psychology*, **59**, 643–661.

Procter, H.G. (1981) Family construct psychology: an approach to understanding and treating families. In S. Walrond-Skinner (Ed.) *Developments in Family Therapy*. London: Routledge.

Procter, H.G. (1985a) Repertory grids in family therapy and research. In N. Beail (Ed.) *Repertory Grid Technique and Personal Constructs: Applications in Clinical and Educational Settings*. Beckenham: Croom Helm.

Procter, H.G. (1985b) A construct approach to family therapy and systems intervention. In E. Button (Ed.) *Personal Construct Theory and Mental Health*. Beckenham: Croom Helm.

Procter, H.G. (1987) Change in the family construct system. In G.J. Neimeyer and R.A. Neimeyer (Eds) *Personal Construct Therapy Casebook*. New York: Springer.

Procter, H.G. (1996) The family construct system. In D. Kalekin-Fishman & B. Walker (Eds) *The Construction of Group Realities: Culture, Society and Personal Construct Psychology*. Malabar, FL: Krieger.

Procter, H.G. (2000) Autism and family therapy: a personal construct approach. In S. Powell (Ed.) *Helping Children with Autism to Learn*. London: David Fulton.

Procter, H.G. (2001) Personal construct psychology and autism. *Journal of Constructivist Psychology*, **14**, 107–126.

Procter, H.G. (2002) Constructs of individuals and relationships. *Context*, **59**, 11–12.

Procter, H.G. & Dallos, R. (in press) Making me angry—the constructions of anger. In P. Cummins (Ed.) *Working with Anger: A Constructivist Approach*. Whurr publications.

Quinn, P.C., Eimas. P.D. & Tarr, M.J. (2001) Perceptual categorization of cat and dog silhouettes by 3- to 4-month old infants. *Journal of Experimental Child Psychology*, **79**, 78–94.

Quinsey, V.L. (1986) Men who have sex with children. In D.N. Weisstub (Ed.) *Law and Mental Health: International Perspectives*. New York: Pergamon Press.

Rada, R.T. (1978) *Clinical Aspects of the Rapist*. New York: Grune & Stratton.

Raskin, J.D. & Epting, F.R. (1995) Constructivism and psychotherapy: transitive diagnosis as humanistic assessment. *Methods: A Journal for Human Science* (Annual Edition), pp. 3–27.

Raskin, N.J. & Rogers, C.R. (1989) Person-centered therapy. In R. Corsini & C. Wedding (Eds) *Current Psychotherapies* (4th edition). Ithaca, IL: F.E. Peacock.

Rattue, R. & Cornelius, N. (2002) The emotional labour of police work. *Soundings: Journal of Politics and Culture*, **20**, 190–201.

Ravenette, A.T. (1968) *Three methods of grid analysis*. Unpublished manuscript.

Ravenette, A.T. (1997) Open letter to the psychologists in training at Southampton University. In G. Daniel (Ed.) *Tom Ravenette: Personal Construct Theory and the Practice of an Educational Psychologist*. Farnborough: EPCA Publications.

Ravenette, A.T. (1999) *Personal Construct Theory in Educational Psychology: A Practitioner's View*. London: Whurr Publications.

Rawlinson, J. (1995) Some reflections on the use of repertory grid technique in studies of nurses and social workers. *Journal of Advanced Nursing*, **21**, 334–339.

Reed, N.B. (2000) *Personal construct psychology and knowledge management in organisations*. Unpublished dissertation, Centre for Personal Construct Psychology, UK.

Ritzer, G. (2001) *Explorations in Social Theory*. London: Sage Publications.

Rockefeller, S.C. (1991) *John Dewey: Religious Faith and Democratic Humanism*. New York: Columbia University Press.

Rogers, C.R. (1956) Intellectualized psychotherapy. *Contemporary Psychology*, **1**, 335–358.

Ross, H. (1996) Construing across cultures: aboriginal Australians construe their housing and histories. In D. Kalekin-Fishman & B.M. Walker (Eds) *The Construction of Group Realities: Culture, Society and Personal Construct Psychology*. Malabar, FL: Krieger.

Roth, A. & Fonagy, P. (1996) *What Works for Whom? A Critical Review of Psychotherapy Research*. New York: Guilford.

Rowe, D. (1989) *The Successful Self*. London: Harper Collins.

Rychlak, J.F. (1973) *Introduction to Personality and Psychotherapy: A Theory-Construction Approach*. Boston: Houghton Mifflin.

Ryle, A. & Lunghi, M. (1970) The dyad grid: a modification of repertory grid technique. *British Journal of Psychiatry*, **117**, 323–327.

Ryle, A. & Lunghi, M. (1972) Parental and sex-role identification of students measured with a repertory grid technique. *British Journal of Social and Clinical Psychology*, **11**, 149–161.

Sadri, G. & Snyder, P.J. (1995) Methodological issues in assessing training effectiveness. *Journal of Managerial Psychology*, **10**, 30–32.

Salmon, P. (1979) Children as social beings: a Kellyan view. In P. Stringer & D. Bannister (Eds) *Constructs of Sociality and Individuality*. New York: Academic Press.

Salmon, P. (1994) *Grids are all very well, but. . . .* Newsletter, European Personal Construct Association.

Salmon, P. & Claire, H. (1984) *Classroom Collaboration*. London: Routledge & Kegan Paul.

Sanglin-Grant, S. & Schneider, R. (2000) *Moving On Up? Racial Equality and the Corporate Agenda*. London: Runnymede Trust.

Savage, D.J. (2000) Telling the story finding the plot. In J. Fisher & N. Cornelius (Eds) *Challenging the Boundaries: A PCP Perspective for the New Millennium*. Lostock Hall, UK: EPCA Publications.

Schafer, R. (1980) Narration in the psychoanalytic dialogue. *Critical Inquiry*, **7**, 29–53.

Scheer, J.W. (1996a) After the Wall—construct systems in united Germany. In J.W. Scheer & A. Catina (Eds) *Empirical Constructivism in Europe*. Giessen, Germany: Psychosozial-Verlag.

Scheer, J.W. (1996b) 'Congress language', personal constructs, and constructive internationalism. In B.M. Walker, J. Costigan, L.L. Viney & B. Warren (Eds) *Personal Construct Theory: A Psychology for the Future*. Australian Psychological Society.

Scheer, J.W. (Ed.) (2000) *The Person in Society: Challenges to a Constructivist Theory*. Giessen, Germany: Psychosozial-Verlag.

Scheer, J.W., Ellis-Scheer, J.M. & Hundertmark, K. (1997) *Construing life satisfaction in old age: A binational study*. Paper presented at the 12th International Congress on Personal Construct Psychology Seattle, WA, USA.

Schein, E.H. (1985) *Organisational Culture and Leadership*. San Francisco: Jossey-Bass.

Schoeneich, F. & Klapp, B.F. (1998) Standardization of interelement distances in repertory grid technique and its consequences for psychological interpretation of self-identity plots: an empirical study. *Journal of Constructivist Psychology*, **11**, 49–58.

Selman, R.L. (1976) Social cognitive understanding: a guide to educational and clinical practice. In T. Lickona (Ed.) *Morality: A Handbook of Moral Development and Behavior*. New York: Holt, Rinehart & Winston.

Sen, A. (1992) *Inequality Re-examined*. Cambridge, MA: Harvard University Press.

Sen, A. (1999) *Development as Freedom*. Oxford: Oxford University Press.

Sendan, F.C. (1995) *Patterns of development in EFL student teachers' personal theories: A constructivist approach*. Unpublished PhD thesis, University of Reading, UK.

Senge P., Kleiner, A., Roberts, C., Ross, R. & Smith, B. (1994) *The Fifth Discipline Fieldbook*. London: Nicholas Brealey.

Sewell, K.W. (1996) Constructional risk factors for a post-traumatic stress response following a mass murder. *Journal of Constructivist Psychology*, **9**, 97–107.

Sewell, K.W. (1997) Post-traumatic stress: towards a constructivist model of psychotherapy. In R.A. Neimeyer & G.J. Neimeyer (Eds) *Advances in Personal Construct Psychology*, Volume 4. Greenwich, CT: JAI Press.

Sewell, K.W., Adams-Webber, J., Mitterer, J. & Cromwell, R.L. (1992) Computerized repertory grids: review of the literature. *International Journal of Personal Construct Psychology*, **5**, 1–23.

Sewell, K.W., Baldwin, C.L. & Moes, A.J. (1998) The multiple self awareness group. *Journal of Constructivist Psychology*, **11**, 59–78.

Sewell, K.W. & Cromwell, R.L. (1990) *A personal constructs model of Post-Traumatic Stress Disorder*. Presented at the North American Personal Construct Psychology Conference, San Antonio, Texas.

Sewell, K.W., Cromwell, R.L., Farrell-Higgins, J., Palmer, R., Ohlde, C. & Patterson, T.W. (1996) Hierarchical elaboration in the conceptual structures of Vietnam combat veterans. *Journal of Constructivist Psychology*, **9**, 79–96.

Sewell, K.W., Mitterer, J., Adams-Webber, J. & Cromwell, R. (1991) OMNIGRID-PC: A new development in computerized repertory grids. *International Journal of Personal Construct Psychology*, **4**, 175–192.

Sewell, K.W. & Williams, A.M. (2001) Construing stress: a constructivist therapeutic approach to posttraumatic stress reactions. In R.A. Neimeyer (Ed.) *Meaning

Reconstruction and the Experience of Loss. Washington, DC: American Psychological Association.

Sewell, K.W. & Williams, A.M. (2002) Broken narratives: trauma, metaconstructive gaps, and the audience of psychotherapy. *Journal of Constructivist Psychology*, **15**, 205–218.

Sharkins, B.S. (1993) Anger and gender: theory, research and implications. *Journal of Counselling and Development*, **71**, 386–389.

Shaw, M.L.G. (1980) *On Becoming a Personal Scientist: Interactive Computer Elicitation of Personal Models of The World*. London: Academic Press.

Shaw, M.L.G. & Gaines, B.R. (1981) Recent advances in the analysis of a repertory grid. *British Journal of Medical Psychology*, **54**, 307–318.

Shaw, M.L.G. & Gaines, B.R. (1983) A computer aid to knowledge engineering. In *Proceedings of British Computer Society Conference on Expert Systems*. Cambridge: British Computer Society.

Shaw, M.L. & McKnight, C. (1981) *Think Again*. Englewood Cliffs, NJ: Prentice-Hall.

Shaw, M.L. & Thomas, L.F. (1978) FOCUS on education: an interactive computer system for the development and analysis of repertory grids. *International Journal of Man–Machine Studies*, **10**, 139–173.

Sheehan, M.J. (1985) A personal construct study of depression. *British Journal of Medical Psychology*, **58**, 119–128.

Shortliffe, E.H. (1976) *Computer-Based Medical Consultations: MYCIN*. New York: Elsevier.

Shorts, I.D. (1985) Treatment of a sex offender in a maximum security forensic hospital: detecting changes in personality and interpersonal construing. *International Journal of Offender Therapy and Comparative Criminology*, **29**, 237–250.

Simon, H.A. (1995) The information-processing theory of mind. *American Psychologist*, **50**, 507–508.

Skinner, B.F. (1948) *Walden Two*. New York: Macmillan.

Slater, P. (1964) *The Principal Components of a Repertory Grid*. London: Vincent Andrew.

Slater, P. (1976) *The Measurement of Intrapersonal Space by Grid Technique*, Volume 1. *Explorations of Intrapersonal Space*. London: John Wiley & Sons.

Slater, P. (1977) *The Measurement of Intrapersonal Space by Grid Technique*, Volume 2. *Dimensions of Intrapersonal Space*. London: John Wiley & Sons.

Smith, J., Harré, R. & van Langenhove, L. (1995) *Rethinking Methods in Psychology*. London: Sage Publications.

Soffer, J. (1993) Jean Piaget and George Kelly: towards a stronger constructivism. *International Journal of Personal Construct Psychology*, **6**, 59–77.

Soldz, S. & Soldz, E. (1989) A difficulty with the functionally independent construction measure of cognitive differentiation. *International Journal of Personal Construct Psychology*, **2**, 315–322.

Space, L. & Cromwell, R.L. (1980) Personal constructs among depressed patients. *Journal of Nervous and Mental Diseases*, **168**, 150–158.

Spence, D. (1982) *Narrative Truth and Historical Truth*. New York: Norton.

Steen, E. & Hauli, L. (2001) From pain to self awareness: a qualitative analysis of the significance of group participation for persons with chronic musculoskolotal pain. *Patient Education and Counseling*, **42**, 35–46.

Stefan, C. & Linder, H.B. (1985) Suicide, an experience of chaos or of fatalism: perspectives from personal construct theory. In D. Bannister (Ed.) *Issues and Approaches in Personal Construct Theory*. London: Academic Press.

Stewart, T. & Birdsall, M. (2001) A review of the contribution of personal construct psychology to stammering therapy. *Journal of Constructivist Psychology*, **14**, 215–226.

Stojnov, D. (1996a) A personal construction of war in Yugoslavia: transition as a way of life. In D. Kalekin-Fishman & B. Walker (Eds) *The Construction of Group Realities: Culture, Society and Personal Construct Psychology*. Malabar, FL: Krieger.

Stojnov, D. (1996b) After 40 years of peace—war in the heart of Europe. In J. Scheer & A. Catina (Eds) *Empirical Constructivism in Europe*. Giessen, Germany: Psychosozial-Verlag.

Stojnov, D. (1999) Construing personality of political leaders in Serbia and Macedonia. In J. Fisher & D. Savage (Eds) *Beyond Experimentation into Meaning*. Farnborough: EPCA Publications.

Stojnov, D., Knezevic, M. & Gojic, A. (1997) To be or not to be a Serb: construction of national identity amongst Yugoslav students. In P. Denicolo & M. Pope (Eds) *Sharing Understanding and Practice*. Farnborough: EPCA Publications.

Stone, W.F. (1974) *The Psychology of Politics*. New York: Free Press.

Strachan, A. & Jones, D. (1982) Changes in identification during adolescence: a personal construct theory approach. *Journal of Personality Assessment*, **46**, 529–535.

Strauss, B.M. & Kachele, H. (1998) The writing on the wall: comments on the current discussion about empirically validated treatments in Germany. *Psychotherapy Research*, **8**, 158–170.

Stringer, P. & Bannister, D. (Eds) (1979) *Constructs of Sociality and Individuality*. London: Academic Press.

Sulejewicz, A. (Ed.) (1994) MBA, czyli Jak Kształcić Menedżerów (The MBA, or How to Develop Managers). Warsaw: Fundusz Współpracy (The Cooperation Fund).

Thomas, D.A. & Ely, R.J. (1996) Making differences matter: a new paradigm for managing diversity. *Harvard Business Review*, 79–80.

Thomas, L.F. & Harri-Augstein, S. (1985) *Self Organised Learning: Foundations of a Conversational Science of Psychology*. London: Routledge & Kegan Paul.

Trewavas, A. (1999) How plants learn. *Proceedings of the National Academy of Science, U.S.A.*, **96**, 4216–4218.

Truneckova, D. & Viney, L.L. (1997) *Assessing the effectiveness of personal construct group work with problematic adolescents*. Paper presented at the 12th International Congress of Personal Construct Psychology, Seattle, WA, USA.

Truneckova, D. & Viney, L.L. (2001) *Can personal construct group work be an effective intervention with troubled adolescents?* Paper presented at the 14th International Congress of Personal Construct Psychology, Wollongong, Australia.

Tschudi, F. (1977) Loaded and honest questions: a construct theory view of symptoms and therapy. In D. Bannister (Ed.) *New Perspectives in Personal Construct Theory*. London: Academic Press.

Tschudi, F. (1993) *Manual FLEXIGRID 5.21*. Oslo: Tschudi System Sales.

Turing, A.M. (1950) Computing machinery and intelligence. *Mind*, **59**, 433–460. Unpublished B.A. (honours) thesis, Guelph: University of Guelph.

Vaihinger, H. (1924) *The Philosophy of 'as if': A System of the Theoretical, Practical and Religious Fictions of Mankind* (C.K. Ogden, Trans.). London: Routledge & Kegan Paul.

Vanderberg, R.J. & Self, R.M. (1993) Assessing newcomers' changing commitments to the organization during the first 6 months of work. *Journal of Applied Psychology*, **78**, 557–569.

Viney, L. (1983) *Images of Illness*. Malabar, FL: Krieger.

Viney, L.L. (1986) *The Development and Evaluation of Short Term Psychotherapy Programs for the Elderly: Report to the Australian Institute of Health*. Unpublished MS, University of Wollongong, Australia.

Viney, L.L. (1993) Listening to what my clients and I say: content analysis categories and scales. In G.J. Neimeyer (Ed.) *Constructivist Assessment: A Casebook*. London: Sage Publications.

Viney, L.L. (1994) Sequences of emotional distress expressed by clients and acknowledged by therapists: are they associated more with some therapists than others? *British Journal of Clinical Psychology*, **33**, 469–481.

Viney, L.L. (1998) Should we use personal construct therapy? A paradigm for outcomes evaluation. *Psychotherapy*, **35**, 366–380.

Viney, L.L., Benjamin, Y.N. & Preston, C. (1989) An evaluation of personal construct therapy for the elderly. *British Journal of Medical Psychology*, **62**, 35–41.

Viney, L.L., Clarke, A.M., Bunn, T.A. & Benjamin, Y.N. (1985a) Crisis intervention counseling: An evaluation of long-term and short-term effects. *Journal of Counseling Psychology*, **32**, 29–39.

Viney, L.L., Clarke, A.M., Bunn, T.A. & Benjamin, Y.N. (1985b) The effect of a hospital-based counseling service on the physical recovery of surgical and medical patients. *General Hospital Psychiatry*, **7**, 294–301.

Viney, L.L., Clarke, A.M., Bunn, T.A. & Teoh, H.Y. (1985c) Crisis intervention counseling in a general hospital: development and multi-faceted evaluation of a health service. *Australian Studies in Health Care Administration*, **5**.

Viney, L.L., Clarke, A.M., Bunn, T.A. & Benjamin, Y.N. (1985d) An evaluation of three crisis intervention programs for general hospital patients. *British Journal of Medical Psychology*, **58**, 75–86.

Viney, L.L., Henry, R.M. & Campbell, J. (1995a) *An evaluation of personal construct and psychodynamic group work with centre-based juvenile offenders and school-based adolescents.* Paper presented at the 11th International Congress of Personal Construct Psychology, Barcelona, Spain.

Viney, L.L., Rudd, M.G., Grenyer, B.F.S. & Tych, A.M. (1995c) *Content Analysis Scales of Psychosocial Maturity (CASPM) Scoring Manual.* Wollongong: University of Wollongong.

Viney, L.L., Truneckova, D., Weekes, P. & Oades, L. (1997) Personal construct group work with school-based adolescents: reduction of risk-taking. *Journal of Constructivist Psychology*, **10**, 167–186.

Viney, L.L., Walker, B. & Crooks, L. (1995b) Anxiety in community-based AIDS caregivers before and after counseling. *Journal of Clinical Psychology*, **51**, 274–279.

von Glasersfeld, E. (1982) An interpretation of Piaget's constructivism. *Revue Internationale de Philosophie*, **36**, 612–635.

von Glasersfeld, E. (1984) An introduction to radical constructivism. In P. Watzlawick (Ed.) *The Invented Reality*. New York: Norton.

von Wright, G.H. (1966) The paradoxes of confirmation. In J. Hintikaa & P. Suppes (Eds) *Aspects of Inductive Logic*. Amsterdam: North Holland.

Walker, B.M. (1992) Values and Kelly's theory: becoming a good scientist. *International Journal of Personal Construct Psychology*, **5**, 257–266.

Walker, B.M. (1993) Looking for a 'whole Mama': personal construct theory and dependency. In L.M. Leitner & N.G.M. Dunnett (Eds) *Critical Issues in Personal Construct Therapy*. Malabar, FL: Krieger.

Walker, B.M. (1997) Shaking the kaleidoscope: dispersion of dependency and its relationships. In G. Neimeyer & R.A. Neimeyer (Eds) *Advances in Personal Construct Psychology*, Volume 4. Greenwich, CN: JAI Press.

Walker, B.M. (2000) Travelling: We don't call it travelling; we call it living. In J.W. Scheer (Ed.) *The Person in Society: Challenges to a Constructivist Theory*. Giessen, Germany: Psychosozial-Verlag.

Walker, B.M. (2002a) Nonvalidation vs. (in)validation: implications for theory and practice. In J.D. Raskin & S.K. Bridges (Eds) *Studies in Meaning: Exploring Constructivist Psychology*. New York: Pace University.

Walker, B.M. (2002b) Identität und Reisen. In J.W. Scheer (Ed.) *Identität in der Gesellschaft*. Giessen, Germany: Psychosozial-Verlag (English version: 'Identity and travelling,' *http://www.pcp-net.de/papers/walker02.pdf*).

Walker, B.M., Oades, L.G., Caputi, P., Stevens, C.D. & Crittenden, N. (2000) Going beyond the scientist metaphor: from validation to experience cycles. In J.W. Scheer (Ed.) *The Person in Society: Challenges to a Constructivist Theory*. Giessen, Germany: Psychosozial-Verlag.

Walker, B.M., Ramsay, F.L. & Bell, R.C. (1988) Dispersed and undispersed dependency. *International Journal of Personal Construct Psychology*, **1**, 63–80.

Warren, W. (1985) Personal construct psychology and contemporary philosophy: an examination of alignments. In D. Bannister (Ed.) *Issues and Approaches in Personal Construct Theory*. London: Academic Press.

Warren, B. (1990) Psychoanalysis and personal construct theory: an exploration. *Journal of Psychology*, **124**, 449–464.

Warren, W. (1992) Subjecting and objecting in personal construct psychology. In A. Thomson

& P. Cummins (Eds) *European Perspectives in Personal Construct Psychology*. Lincoln, UK: ECPA Press.

Warren, W.G. (1993) The problem of religion for constructivist psychology. *Journal of Psychology*, **127**, 481–488.

Warren, W. (1998) *Philosophical Dimensions of Personal Construct Psychology*. London: Routledge.

Watkinson, J. (2001) *Painting by numbers*. Abstracts of the 14th International Personal Construct Psychology Conference. *Australian Journal of Psychology*, **53**, *2001 Supplement: Combined Abstracts of 2001 Australian Patterns, Conferences*, W. Noble (Ed.), p. 107.

Watson, S. & Winter, D. (1997) *A comparative process and outcome study of personal construct, cognitive and psychodynamic therapies in a British National Health Service setting*. Paper presented at the 12th International Congress of Personal Construct Psychology, Seattle, WA, USA.

Watts, M. (1988) *Shared Learning*. London: Scutari Press.

Watts, M. & Vaz, A. (1997) Freire meets Vaz: using constructs to generate themes in education. In P.M. Denicolo & M.L. Pope (Eds) *Sharing, Understanding and Practice*. Farnborough: EPCA Publications.

Watzlawick, P., Beavin, J. & Jackson, D. (1967) *The Pragmatics of Human Communication: A Study of Interactional Patterns, Pathologies and Paradoxes*. New York: Norton.

Waxman, S.R. (1998) Linking object categorization and naming: early expectations and the shaping role of language. In D. Medin (Ed.) *The Psychology of Learning and Motivation*, Volume 38. New York: Academic Press.

Wertheim, E.H., Weiss, K.R. & Coish, B.J. (1988) Evaluation of a structured group therapy program for bulimics. In S. Abraham & D. Llewellyn-Jones (Eds) *Eating Disorders and Disordered Eating*. Melbourne: Astor.

White, A. (1996) A theoretical framework created from a repertory grid analysis of graduate nurses in relation to the feelings they experience in clinical practice. *Journal of Advanced Nursing*, **24**, 144–150.

White, M. & Epston, D. (1990) *Narrative Means to Therapeutic Ends*. New York: Norton.

Widom, C.S. (1976) Interpersonal and personal construct systems in psychopaths. *Journal of Consulting and Clinical Psychology*, **44**, 614–623.

Williams, E. (1971) The effect of varying the elements in the Bannister–Fransella grid test of schizophrenic thought disorder. *British Journal of Psychiatry*, **119**, 207–212.

Willig, C. (2001) *Qualitative Research in Psychology: Adventures in Theory and Method*. Buckingham: Open University Press.

Wilson, J. & Retsas, A. (1997) Personal constructs of nursing practice: a comparative analysis of three groups of Australian nurses. *International Journal of Nursing Studies*, **34**, 63–71.

Winslade, J. & Smith, L. (1997) Countering alcoholic narratives. In G. Monk, J. Winslade, J. Crockett & E. Epston (Eds) *Narrative Therapy in Practice*. San Francisco: Jossey-Bass.

Winter, D.A. (1989) An alternative construction of agoraphobia. In K. Gournay (Ed.) *Agoraphobia: Current Perspectives on Theory and Treatment*. London: Routledge.

Winter, D.A. (1992) *Personal Construct Psychology in Clinical Practice: Theory, Research and Applications*. London: Routledge.

Winter, D. (1997) Personal construct theory perspectives on group psychotherapy. In P. Denicolo & M. Pope (Eds) *Sharing Understanding and Practice*. Farnborough: EPCA Publications.

Winter, D. (2000) Can personal construct theory succeed in competition with other therapies? In J.W. Scheer (Ed.) *The Person in Society: Challenges to a Constructivist Theory*. Giessen, Germany: Psychosozial-Verlag.

Winter, D., Bhandari, S., Metcalfe, C., Riley, T., Sireling, L., Watson, S. & Lutwyche, G. (2000) Deliberate and undeliberated self-harm: theoretical basis and evaluation of a personal construct psychotherapy intervention. In J.W. Scheer (Ed.) *The Person in Society: Challenges to a Constructivist Theory*. Giessen, Germany: Psychosozial-Verlag.

Winter, D., Gournay, K. & Metcalfe, C. (1999) An investigation of the effectiveness of a personal construct psychotherapy intervention. In J.M. Fisher & D.J. Savage (Eds) *Beyond Experimentation into Meaning*. Farnborough: EPCA Publications.

Winter, D., Tschudi, F. & Gilbert, N. (2001) *Psychotherapists' theoretical orientations as elaborative choices: a study of personal styles, epistemological preferences, and construing*. Paper presented at the 14th International Congress of Personal Construct Psychology, Wollongong, Australia.

Winter, D.A. & Watson, S. (1999) Personal construct psychotherapy and the cognitive therapies: different in theory but can they be differentiated in practice? *Journal of Constructivist Psychology*, **12**, 1–22.

Winter, D., Watson, S., Gillman-Smith, I., Gilbert, N. & Acton, T. (2002) *Border crossing*. Paper presented at the 5th Conference of European Personal Construct Association, Florence, Italy.

Wittgenstein, L. (1953) *Philosophical Investigations*. Oxford: Blackwell.

Wright, P. (1974) *The Language of British Industry*. London: Macmillan.

Wulff, E. (1978) Grundfragen der transkulturellen Psychiatrie (Fundamental Issues of Trans-Cultural Psychiatry). In E. Wulff (Ed.) *Ethnopsychiatrie*. Wiesbaden: Akademische Verlagsgesellschaft.

Young, E. (1989) On the naming of the rose: interests and multiple meanings as elements of organizational culture. *Organization Studies*, **10**, 187–206.

Zalot, G. (1977) Cognitive complexity and the perception of neighbours. *Social Behavior and Personality*, **5**, 281–283.

Index

Index compiled by Indexing Specialists (UK) Ltd